Technology Integration for Meaningful Classroom Use

A Standards-Based Approach

Katherine S. Cennamo

Virginia Polytechnic Institute and State University

John D. Ross

Edvantia

Peggy A. Ertmer

Purdue University

WADSWORTH
CENGAGE Learning™

Australia • Brazil • Japan • Korea • Mexico • Singapore • Spain • United Kingdom • United States

Technology Integration for Meaningful Classroom Use: A Standards-Based Approach
Katherine S. Cennamo, John D. Ross, and Peggy A. Ertmer

Acquisitions Editor: Christopher Shortt

Development Editor: Tangelique Williams

Assistant Editor: Caitlin Cox

Editorial Assistant: Linda Stewart

Media Editor: Ashley Cronin

Marketing Manager: Kara Kindstrom

Marketing Assistant: Ting Jian Yap

Marketing Communications Manager: Martha Pfeiffer

Project Manager, Editorial Production: Tanya Nigh

Creative Director: Rob Hugel

Art Director: Maria Epes

Print Buyer: Paula Vang

Permissions Editor: Mardell Glinski Schultz

Production Service: Newgen North America

Text Designer: Diane Beasley

Photo Researcher: PrePress

Managing Editor: Jay Harward

Cover Designer: Lee Anne Dollison

Compositor: Newgen

For product information and technology assistance, contact us at
**Cengage Learning Customer & Sales Support,
1-800-354-9706.**
For permission to use material from this text or product,
submit all requests online at **www.cengage.com/permissions.**
Further permissions questions can be e-mailed to
permissionrequest@cengage.com.

Library of Congress Control Number: 2008937400

ISBN-13: 978-0-495-09047-2
ISBN-10: 0-495-09047-6

Wadsworth
10 Davis Drive
Belmont, CA 94002-3098
USA

Cengage Learning is a leading provider of customized learning solutions with office locations around the globe, including Singapore, the United Kingdom, Australia, Mexico, Brazil, and Japan. Locate your local office at **www.cengage.com/international.**

Cengage Learning products are represented in Canada by Nelson Education, Ltd.

To learn more about Wadsworth, visit **www.cengage.com/wadsworth**

Purchase any of our products at your local college store or at our preferred online store **www.ichapters.com**

Printed in the United States of America
1 2 3 4 5 6 7 12 11 10 09

To my digital natives, Alice and Elliott, for all you have taught me

– Katherine Cennamo

With thanks to the many teachers I have worked and taught with. A special thanks to the two principals who not only put up with my requests for more technology but actually encouraged them: Larry Meche, former principal, Clute Middle School in Brazosport I.S.D., Texas; and Dr. Barry Beers, former principal, York High School in Yorktown, Virginia.

– John Ross

In gratitude to all of the inspirational teachers I have known and worked with

– Peggy Ertmer

Brief Contents

Contents

CHAPTER 3

Supporting Student Creativity with Technology   47

CHAPTER 4

Digital Tools That Support Learning   75

CHAPTER 5

Developing Technology-Enriched Learning Environments and Experiences   107

CHAPTER 11
Diversity and Cultural Understanding   265

CHAPTER 12
Professional Growth and Leadership   287

PART II   TECHNOLOGY INTEGRATION IN PRACTICE   311

Preface

Our goal in writing this book is to help students of education develop the skills they need to successfully integrate technology throughout their professional practice. As we enter the 21st century, we assume that the majority of education students have a basic set of computer skills, developed primarily from routine use at home and school. We assume that they are able to start a computer, navigate the workspace, create and save files, and access the Internet for personal use. They may be familiar with the many social networking tools available on the web; online communications through e-mail, chat, instant messaging, and other means; and ubiquitous software applications, such as word processing, presentation software, and audio- and image-editing tools. What we have found in our own practice and what has been confirmed by our colleagues in the teacher preparation field, is that although most prospective teachers have these basic technology skills, they are typically unfamiliar with how to use technologies to support the unique requirements of teaching and learning.

Even when students enter our courses with basic computer skills, they face unique challenges to technology integration. Technologies change at lightning speed, making it difficult to keep up-to-date. In addition, these rapid changes are coupled with evolving state and national standards that require teachers to demonstrate competencies in specific technology skills and to teach in ways that ensure their students master specific content-area standards. So rather than focusing on a specific body of computer or technology content that will quickly become outdated, we empower students to be self-directed learners in order to successfully navigate the constantly changing environment of technology integration. We provide a standards-based approach to developing, modeling, and teaching the skills and knowledge necessary for integrating technology in teaching and learning throughout one's career. And please note that although our emphasis is on helping teachers develop an adaptive set of technology integration skills as they progress through their careers, the companion website provides links to tutorials in common software applications for learners who lack these basic skills.

Organization

The textbook is divided into two parts. In Part I, we introduce future teachers to the 2008 National Educational Technology Standards for Teachers (NETS-T) and the National Educational Technology Standards for Students (NETS-S) developed by the International Society for Technology in Education (ISTE). We discuss both their historical significance and current relevance to today's teachers and students. The NETS-T (both the 1998 and 2008 versions) serve as a road map for inspired teaching and learning and are credited with creating a target of excellence relating to technology use by teachers. While the earlier set of NETS-T defined what teachers needed to know and be able to do with technology, the 2008 NETS-T are designed to inspire teachers to be creative, innovative digital-age leaders; this textbook helps students translate those ideals and visions into practical learning experiences and assessments.

Using the principles of self-directed learning as its foundation, Part I of the text is designed to help future teachers learn to evaluate and reflect on professional practice to make informed decisions regarding the use of technology in support of student learning. They learn to self-assess what they currently know about the technology or learning requirement at hand, determine what they need to know, access resources to help them address their instructional challenges, evaluate the validity of those resources in terms of what they know and what they need to know, and evaluate the extent to which they met their learning needs. As they expand their knowledge through the use of additional resources, education students will learn to monitor the effectiveness of their learning and problem-solving strategies. In other words, we "teach them how to fish," rather than simply giving them "fish."

In Part II of the text, we provide examples of technology integration in practice. That is, content area experts (faculty in social studies, language arts, and so forth) serve as guest authors for the chapters that describe how technology applies within the specific content areas of English language arts, foreign language, math, science, social studies, health/physical education, visual arts, music, and working with English language learners. These discussions are guided by the national standards that apply to each content domain. In addition, many states have adopted technology standards that are adapted from ISTE's NETS for Students (NETS-S). In Part II of this book, each guest author addresses ways that technology can be used to create authentic learning experiences to meet both content areas and technology standards. Sample lesson plans illustrate these ideas in action.

Like most textbooks, we help students develop content knowledge in the area of technology integration within education, but experts in a domain possess more than content knowledge. They possess heuristic strategies or "tricks of the trade," control strategies that help them solve problems, and learning strategies that guide their knowledge construction. Several organizational and pedagogical features, some briefly described below, are used to develop these additional forms of knowledge and build self-directed learning strategies.

Features

The following organizational and pedagogical features appear consistently throughout the book:

- *ISTE standards*: Each chapter begins with a list of the 2008 ISTE NETS-T addressed in that chapter.
- *GAME plan self-directed learning activities*: Through the use of self-directed learning activities, we model control strategies that guide the development of students' problem-solving skills. This feature incorporates an easy-to-remember acronym called the GAME Plan.
- *Tools for use*: Extensive examples and "tools for use" features include models for technology integration, checklists, job aids, and other tips to provide learners with heuristic knowledge to guide their technology integration practice.
- *Stories from practice*: Case studies, anecdotes, and interviews with practicing teachers are used to place the content within the context of real classrooms. These stories from practicing teachers illustrate their learning trajectories from novice to expert, model their problem-solving strategies, and include tips and "tricks of the trade."
- *Apply to practice*: Throughout the chapters, activities are embedded that ask students to apply their knowledge to practical problems, investigate the topics in more depth, reflect on their practice, or share their developing knowledge with other members of their learning community.
- *Your portfolio*: At the end of each chapter, suggestions for portfolio-based artifacts are provided so students can demonstrate and document their progress toward attaining the ISTE standards addressed in the chapter.

In addition to these standard chapter features, several other features are provided to enhance student learning. Each chapter concludes with a summary of the chapter content and a list of references. The back matter includes an appendix that provides instruction in lesson planning, a glossary of terms, and an index.

Ancillaries

A variety of ancillary resources provide support materials and references for both students and instructors.

Support materials for students

1. A companion website that provides:

   - Links to relevant websites that serve as educational resources or examples and illustrations of concepts and content found in the book, many of which are identified in each chapter.
   - Links to tutorials for common software applications to help students develop basic technology skills or to learn new applications, when necessary.
   - An annotated list of common educational software and hardware, including websites that contain or feature pedagogical resources.
   - Interactive versions of the Apply to Practice and GAME Plan activities featured in the textbook.
   - Supplemental information such as checklists, job aids, and other tools.

2. A premium website that provides the materials listed above, as well as:

   - Videos of real teachers in their own classrooms that illustrate different pedagogies, technologies, and other resources. The classroom videos are supplemented with teacher interviews.

To access the premium website, go to www.cengage.com/login to register the access code packaged with this text or to purchase access.

Materials for instructors

1. An Instructor's Guide, available in a print version upon request.
2. An instructor's website that provides:

   - Video viewing guides that contain guiding questions to support classroom discussion or independent student work for each chapter.
   - Lecture presentation files in Microsoft PowerPoint® for each of the main chapters that include a list of the relevant NETS-T, chapter objectives, major points, and suggested activities.
   - An electronic copy of the instructor's guide for downloading.

3. WebTutor™ Toolbox for WebCT™ or Blackboard® that provides:

   - Access to all the content of this text's rich book companion website from within an instructor's course management system. Robust communication tools—such as course calendar, asynchronous discussion, real-time chat, a whiteboard, and an integrated e-mail system—make it easy for students to stay connected to the course.

Given the frequency with which technology changes, the ancillary websites will provide a means for delivering the latest up-to-date supplemental content.

Acknowledgments

Throughout this journey we have benefited from the support, advice, and encouragement from a number of individuals including Phyllis Newbill, who provided invaluable assistance in tracking down images, securing permissions, and formatting the manuscript; Joni Gardner and Laurene Johnson, who reviewed portions of the manuscript and provided helpful suggestions; Ross Perkins, Jamie Little, and Miriam Larson, who field-tested various versions of the manuscript in their classes; Anita Deck, Desiree Bradley, and Joy Runyan, who helped develop or review lesson plans in some of the content chapters. And for tolerating our absences throughout the many evenings, weekends, and holidays that we spent working on this book, we offer a heartfelt thanks to Arthur, Elliott, and Alice Cennamo; Jeff Mann; and Dave, Mark, Emilie, Laura, and Scott Ertmer.

We would like to thank all the authors who contributed to various portions of this text: John Burton, Sheila Carter-Tod, Gilbert Cuevas, Peter Doolittle, Shelli Fowler, Adam Friedman, Brian Giza, Glenna Gustafson, Lee Hannah, Richard Hartshorne, David Hicks, Mark Hofer, Greg Kessler, James Krouscas, Nancy Lampert, John Lee, Melissa Lisanti, Tammy McGraw, Christine Meloni, Ken Potter, Kerry Redican, Judy Reinhartz, Jill Robbins, Kathy Swan, and Craig Tacla.

We would also like to gratefully acknowledge our editors: Dan Alpert, who started us on this journey; Chris Shortt, who helped us complete it; and Tangelique Williams, who served as a bridge between the two.

And finally, we would like to express our appreciation to numerous reviewers who provided us with insights and suggestions throughout the development of this text, including:

Mara Murray, *Geneva College*

David Stoloff, *Eastern Connecticut State*

Katie Kinney, *University of North Alabama*

Jason Underwood, *Northern Illinois University*

Aimee Greene, *University of North Carolina, Wilmington*

Tris Ottolino, *Northern Illinois University*

Allen Grant, *Louisiana State University*

Shuyan Wang, *University of Southern Mississippi*

Judith Bennett, *Sam Houston State University*

William Martin, *Chicago State University*

Shannon Scanlon, *Henry Ford Community College*

Bernadette Kelley, *Florida A&M University*

Thomas Drazdowski, *King's College*

Wendy Marshall, *Armstrong Atlantic State University*

Mary Holmes, *Ferris State University*

Yuzhu Teng, *College of St. Rose*

Theresa Cullen, *University of Oklahoma*

Liz Osika, *Chicago State University*

Jennifer Lamkins, *California State University, Long Beach*

Mark Raffler, *Western Michigan University*

Simon Akindes, *University of Wisconsin, Parkside*

Teresa Blodgett, *Texas Tech University*

Margie Massey, *Colorado State University, Pueblo*

Leaunda Hemphill, *Western Illinois University*

Amity Currie, *Marist College*

Patricia McGee, *University of Texas, San Antonio*

John Meyer, *Governors State University*

A. Owusu-Ansah, *Spalding University*

David Goldschmidt, *College of St Rose*

Elizabeth Langran, *Fairfield University*

Jan Ray, *West Texas A&M University*

Catherine Tannahill, *Eastern Connecticut University*

Heng-Yu Ku, *University of Northern Colorado*

Christine Peters, *California University of Pennsylvania*

David Stoloff, *Eastern Connecticut State University*

Cheri Toledo, *Illinois State University*

Chenfeng Zhang, *Marygrove College*

Pam Nicolle, *Louisiana State University*

Lih-Ching Chen Wang, *Cleveland State University*

Anthony Owusu-Ansah, *Spalding University*

Kendall Hartley, *University of Nevada*

Devon Duhaney, *State University of New York, New Paltz*

Cheryl Ward, *University of Akron*

Manual Barrera, *Metro State University*

Carolyn Donelan, *University of South Carolina*

Beverly Ray, *Idaho State University*

Gladys Arome, *Barry University*

Ken Haar, *Westfield State College*

Michael McDonald, *Nebraska Wesleyan University*

Hayley Mayall, *University of Texas, San Antonio*

John Wells, *Virginia Western University*

John Dellegrotto, *Temple University*

David Stoloff, *Eastern Connecticut State University*

Beverly Bohn, *Park University*

Nancy Maloy, *University of West Florida*

About the Authors

Katherine S. Cennamo is a former elementary school teacher and current Professor of Instructional Design and Technology at Virginia Tech. She has a bachelor's degree in elementary education from Virginia Tech, a master's degree in educational media from the University of Arizona, and a Ph.D. in instructional technology from the University of Texas at Austin. Throughout her career, Cennamo's work has focused on the application of learning theories to the design of technology-based instructional materials. Through numerous funded projects, publications, presentations, instructional materials, and teaching activities, she has disseminated knowledge of instructional strategies based on established theories of learning. She has also explored the nature of instructional design practice so that scholars and designers alike better understand their work, and she has applied this knowledge in helping to prepare future instructional design professionals. Cennamo has synthesized much of this work in her textbook, *Real World Instructional Design,* co-authored with Debby Kalk. Currently, her research and service activities focus on developing and sustaining a classroom culture that fosters critical and creative thinking skills in K–12 and higher education environments.

John D. Ross spent the first ten years of his career as a classroom teacher. He taught instrumental music in middle and high school prior to receiving his Ph.D. in instructional design and technology from Virginia Tech in 1999, where his dissertation focused on investigating and promoting self-regulation in a hypermedia environment. His current work finds him collaborating with educators at every level as a senior Research and Development Specialist for Edvantia, Inc., an educational non-profit R&D laboratory. At Edvantia, he has helped develop numerous print, multimedia, and web products that support educators from the school house to the state house, including launching an online professional development environment, ePD@Edvantia, from which more than 8,000 educators across the Southeast have enrolled in one or more courses on topics related to literacy, instructional technology, and school leadership. He is a frequent presenter and trainer in areas related to educational technology, including technology leadership, planning for technology, total cost of ownership, and Universal Design for Learning. New technologies bring new opportunities, and Ross hopes to keep working with teachers as they harness these new technologies in their classrooms.

Peggy A. Ertmer is a Professor in the Department of Curriculum and Instruction at Purdue University. Peg completed her Ph.D. at Purdue, specializing in educational technology and instructional design. Prior to becoming a faculty member at Purdue, she was an elementary and special education teacher in K–12 schools. Dr. Ertmer's scholarship focuses on the impact that student-centered instructional approaches and strategies have on learning. She actively mentors both students and peers, including pre- and in-service teachers, in the use of case-based and problem-based learning (PBL) pedagogy, technology tools, and self-regulated learning skills. She is particularly interested in studying the impact of case-based instruction on higher-order thinking skills; the effectiveness of student-centered, problem-based learning approaches to technology integration; and strategies for facilitating higher-order thinking and self-regulated learning in online learning environments. Dr. Ertmer has published scholarly works in premier national and international journals, has co-edited three editions of the *ID CaseBook: Case Studies in Instructional Design,* and is the founding editor of a new journal, the *Interdisciplinary Journal of Problem-Based Learning,* published by Purdue University Press.

SW Productions/Photodisc/Getty Images

INTRODUCTION

O ur goal in writing this book is to help you learn the skills you need to be able to successfully integrate technology throughout your professional practice. More specifically, this book was written to help you meet the National Educational Technology Standards for Teachers (NETS-T), published by the International Society for Technology in Education (ISTE). Four premises provide the foundation for our approach:

1. You are a lifelong learner. This is best summed up by the proverb, "Give a man a fish and you feed him for one day. Teach a man to fish and you feed him for a lifetime." Based on this premise, we have included strategies to support your continued learning, even after this text is completed.
2. Technology provides a *tool* for solving problems—in your case instructional problems—as opposed to *being* a problem as in, "How can I use technology in my class?"
3. It's more important *how* you use technology than *if* you use it. This might sound strange, especially in a technology textbook, but we believe that the decisions you make about how and when to use technology are based on what you know and believe about good teaching. Although we describe many different uses of technology in this text, we believe that "best practice" is more readily achieved when technology is used to support an authentic learner-centered curriculum.
4. Multiple technologies, including computers, are a natural part of your lives. Most of you have grown up with computer technologies. Some of you have encountered more technologies and some less, but all of you

have had access to numerous, and often very powerful, technologies for much of your lives, whether in your schools, homes, jobs, colleges, or other locations. You will be the first generation to innately use such powerful technologies for teaching and learning and are poised to use them in ways we have not yet dreamed of.

Effective teaching for the 21st century requires that you possess more than content knowledge of math, social studies, Spanish, or whatever your discipline may be; it also requires pedagogical knowledge (i.e., knowledge of how to teach), pedagogical content knowledge (i.e., knowledge of how to teach specific content), and technological knowledge. You'll learn specific content and pedagogical knowledge related to your discipline in other courses throughout your college career. In this book, we focus on the intersection of pedagogical knowledge and technological knowledge. As we address this intersection, we'll introduce you to ways that technologies can be used to provide your students with meaningful learning experiences—and ways that technologies can support you in this process.

This book is organized around the ISTE NETS-T, but above all, it is intended to help you identify the learning goals you have for yourself and your future students. Furthermore, it is designed to help you decide which technologies provide the best tools to reach those goals. In Chapter 1, we introduce the ISTE standards around which Part I of this book is organized. In Chapter 2, we introduce you to our self-directed learning model used throughout this book. Remember, one of our guiding premises is to develop self-directed learners who are able to successfully navigate the constantly changing environment of technology integration. Chapters 3 through 12 directly address the ISTE standards for technology proficiency for teachers. In these chapters, you will learn to use technology in support of effective teaching and learning.

1

Technology Integration: A Standards-Based Approach

ISTE Standards addressed in this chapter

This chapter introduces the technology standards of the International Society for Technology in Education (ISTE), on which this book is based. We introduce both the National Educational Technology Standards for Teachers (NETS-T) and the National Educational Technology Standards for Students (NETS-S), developed by ISTE in 1998 and 2000, respectively, and revised in 2007 and 2008. These standards are placed in the context of the historical uses of technology in education. We address the value of standards for ensuring consistency in the quality of instructional experiences for all students. The chapter concludes with scenarios of how the application of ISTE standards affects the role of the teacher, the role of the student, the resources used, and the instructional activities that occur within the classroom.

I magine yourself teaching a lesson to a classroom of students. Exactly what would you do to convey the necessary information? Would you use technology? If so, what technologies and why? If not, why not? If you are like many college students, computers, cell phones, and other digital tools are interfaces to your life. You communicate there. You think there. You create there. You take care of the day-to-day events of your life there. You are entertained, informed, stimulated, and soothed. Technology provides a window into your world. But have you thought about how you will integrate technology into your teaching practice?

Outcomes

In this chapter, you will

- Reflect on the history of technology integration in relation to your teaching practice.
- Identify the technology standards that will guide your professional development.
- Begin development of a portfolio in which you will document your developing competencies in applicable technology standards for teachers.

Pre-mechanical   Mechanical   Electrical   Digital

Figure 1.1
Information and communication technologies: Pre-mechanical era, mechanical era, electronic era, and digital era.

Technologies in Teaching and Learning

Technologies have been part of teaching and learning for centuries. As the types of technologies have changed over the years, so, too, has their importance to the teaching and learning process. For example, consider two functions of technology, communication and information storage, and how they have evolved from pre-mechanical to mechanical to electronic and then to digital forms (see Figure 1.1). By improving existing technologies and developing new technologies, information and communication technologies have become more accessible to the general public while offering increased speed and greater quality at the same time. Can you imagine your life without cell phones, the Internet, and other digital tools that help you communicate with your friends and family?

If you were a teacher when very simple communication and information storage tools were available—in a time we refer to as the pre-mechanical era—you would have had to depend on real objects and face-to-face communication with your students to describe the past, explain the present, and encourage thinking about the future. The accessibility of pre-mechanical forms of information and communications technologies (such as quill, ink, and paper) and their products (such as legal proclamations and religious documents) was quite limited—often reserved for wealthy members of society. Neither the technologies nor their products were used extensively in educational settings.

As technologies moved into the mechanical phase through the creation and use of the printing press, it became possible to produce greater quantities of the products in a form that would have allowed teachers to retrieve and use information over an extended period of time. Storing and communicating information became much easier —for teachers, students, and the general public. Reliance on face-to-face communication lessened as books were printed and became more plentiful and accessible to wider audiences. Books were the new information technologies!

As information technologies entered the electronic age, accessibility increased even further. The widespread use of the phonograph, radio, and television increased opportunities for communication. You may not believe it, but when these technologies were first introduced they all were predicted to be valuable teaching tools. The development of audio and video recorders meant that information captured by these tools could be preserved on tape and then made available to the public and, of course, to educators.

As technologies entered the digital phase, additional communication tools were developed. Word processors, digital cameras, e-mail, cellular phones, and a continuing array of information and communication tools have been, and will continue to be, developed. Also, because of the ease with which digital information can be duplicated and transferred to other locations, high-powered storage and retrieval systems and software have become common in places you might not consider—like your car, television, and refrigerator. These technologies have powerful implications for education. For example, you might already access your textbooks through online databases or websites, or listen to entire books as audio files on your MP3 player.

The impact of technological improvements and innovations on education obviously goes well beyond the areas of **information and communications technologies**, now commonly referred to as **ICT**. Later chapters will present numerous ways in which modern technologies can affect your professional practice including providing lifelong learning opportunities for you and your students, promoting creativity and innovation, assessing students' instructional needs, evaluating their performances, encouraging the equitable use of existing resources, as well as facilitating your own professional growth and leadership through the effective use of digital tools and resources. We will discuss the many results you may expect to achieve using digital tools in your classroom and increase your awareness of the knowledge, abilities, skills, resources, and environments required for you to use them successfully. Specifically, we'll focus on the use of computers and related digital technologies in support of teaching and learning in educational environments.

Computer Technology in Education

It is customary when discussing computers in education to begin with a history of computers and to break this history into a relatively small number of meaningful phases. This history typically goes back to well-known predecessors of modern computers such as the automated loom, Babbage's Difference Engine, or the abacus. Although accounts of these early predecessors are often quite engaging, they may not seem very relevant to current computer users. For most of you who will be reading this text, the practical history that counts is largely within your own lifetime. It begins with the first commercially successful "microcomputer," the Apple II introduced in 1977, and gets serious with the first IBM PC in 1981 followed by the first Macintosh in 1984. Many of the early major players in the microcomputer arena such as Atari, Altair, Texas Instruments, and Tandy (see Figure 1.2) no longer produce computers.

Phase One—Computer as Object of Study (1977–1982)

In its short history, the computer has become more powerful, flexible, and easy to use. As it has done so, educators have struggled to understand its role in the classroom. At first, the computer itself was an object of study because computers were

rudybaby/Fotolia

Figure 1.2
Early computers became commercially successful in the late 1970s and early 1980s.

```
10 INPUT "What is your name?"; N$
20 PRINT "Hello "; N$
30 REM
40 INPUT "Do you use technology? Y/N"; A$
50 IF (A$ = "Y") THEN GOTO 70
60 IF (A$ = "N") THEN GOTO 80
70 PRINT "Good for you!";
80 PRINT "You should!";
90 PRINT "Goodbye";
100 END
```

Figure 1.3
In the 1980s, being technologically literate meant writing in BASIC.

supposed to be the wave of the future—everyone would need to know how to use them. The computer's entry into the mainstream classroom in the 1980s prompted the creation of new curricula and standards in an effort to help students become "**computer literate**." If you had been in school in the 1980s, you might have taken a computer class in which you learned about the history of computers, finding out that they used to be so big that they filled an entire room or series of rooms. You would have learned about now-antiquated punch cards and tape drives. Your studies also may have focused on learning the parts and functions of a computer rather than how to use it as a tool for learning. The yet-to-be-developed World Wide Web would not have been mentioned as you worked on stand-alone machines, and you probably would have created rudimentary programs using computer languages such as BASIC (see Figure 1.3). Being computer literate meant that you understood computer history, computer architecture and terminology, basic software applications, and programming. Being **technologically literate** is still important today, but the exact meaning of this term (as well as others such as technology proficiency and information literacy) continues to evolve, primarily because technology itself evolves.

Drawing on the earlier lessons of large-scale, mainframe computers, early instructional software was often created by computer scientists, engineers, mathematicians, and other scientists. Educators or instructional designers were seldom, if ever, involved even though the goal was to design software that could teach. As you might expect, given that the early machines were not very powerful and the software creators were seldom educators, much of the software from this era was not terribly memorable. The idea of designing programs to teach, of course, has survived and matured. Now such programs are usually developed by teams of educators, instructional designers, graphic designers, as well as programmers, and are tested on real students throughout the stages of development.

Phase Two—Computer as Programming Tool (1983–1990)

The second phase of computers in education was initiated largely in response to the development of the computer language Logo, which was based on an earlier computer programming language called Lisp (see Figure 1.4). Lisp was a complex programming language originally designed to handle mathematical notation and was used in early artificial intelligence programming. In an attempt to make aspects of Lisp more applicable to education, Wally Furzier and Seymour Papert developed Logo. Using the Logo programming language, users solved geometric problems by moving a robot-like "turtle" around the floor, and later, by moving a computer-generated "turtle" icon across the computer screen. Also during this period, the notion of "hypertext" was advanced by Ted Nelson. Hypertext allowed users to follow links to related information just like you follow hyperlinks on the web. Hypertext quickly blossomed into "hypermedia," in which buttons, images, and other objects

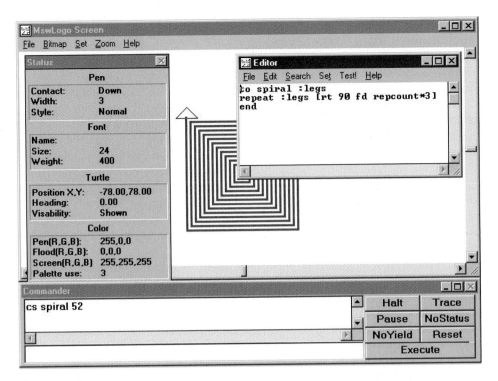

Figure 1.4

The early programming language Logo helped make programming applicable to education.

Source: http://www.softronix.com/logoex.html. Courtesy of Softronix.

could contain hyperlinks. One of the early multimedia programs, HyperCard, came bundled with the software that was included on Macintosh computers. With the subsequent release of SuperCard (also on the Mac) and Toolbook (on the PC), hypermedia began to flourish. Hypermedia, of course, is still used today, and is most often experienced on websites that contain multiple media and hyperlinks to remote resources.

These two advancements—1) the potential of using programming to teach general problem-solving skills, and 2) hypermedia's potential to "open up" learning software to provide greater control to learners to create unique paths through the content —heralded the use of the computer as a device to develop higher-level thinking skills. We now know that teaching programming languages to increase general problem-solving skills isn't any more effective than the notion, prevalent at the end of the 19th century, that teaching Greek would "discipline the mind." We also know that open-ended hyperspace that allows students to "find their own paths" through content often leads to no cohesive path at all. Just think about how often you have followed interesting links while using the Internet, only to realize that you had (unfortunately) spent way too much time, lost track of what you were doing, and not completed what you really needed to accomplish—it *is* called "surfing" after all.

It took educators a while to shift from learning *about* technology to learning *with* technology, while simultaneously trying to keep up with the many changes in technology. As computers moved from cumbersome DOS-based systems to easier graphics-based interfaces with the introduction of the Macintosh and then Windows operating systems in the mid-80s, the emphasis gradually shifted from learning programming languages to learning how to use new **productivity applications** such as word processors, spreadsheets, and databases. Both teachers and students began to use presentation software and were able to create colorful displays that helped to organize instruction or demonstrate learning. However, materials created with productivity tools, especially presentation software, were also sometimes confusing, especially when they incorporated features such as sounds, graphics, and animations at the expense of sound teaching strategies.

Phase Three—Computer as Communication Device and Resource Tool (1991–1996)

The third phase of computer use in education focused on using the computer as a classroom communication device and as a tool to access resources. This movement was grounded in projects funded by the Advanced Research Project Agency Network (ARPANET). The ARPANET was an early computer network that initially linked scientists and engineers, permitting communication and providing a shared space for collaboration. The size of this early network grew from six connected nodes in the early 1970s to a hodgepodge of several hundred connections by 1983 when a single standard for transmitting digital information across the network, TCP/IP (which stands for Transmission Control Protocol and Internet Protocol), was adopted. TCP/IP (and subsequent standards such as Simple Mail Transfer Protocol, or SMTP) opened up this early "hodgepodge" to almost anyone with a computer. This early network was a critical step toward creating the Internet that has become part of all of our lives.

The subsequent explosion of networked resources made information *and* misinformation widely available; anyone with a computer could "publish" research, opinion, pornography, or news. The potential for connecting students to each other and to the global community was unleashed. Initially, there was a widespread belief that placing technology in the schools would make a difference in the way teachers taught and students learned in this new, networked society. Thus, "one computer for every five students" became a national goal (e.g., President's Panel on Educational Technology, 1997); cash-strapped school systems rushed to get computers and networking infrastructure in place (see Figure 1.5). This ultimately led to the question of how to effectively integrate these technologies into the classroom.

Phase Four—Computer as Learning and Social Tool (1997–current)

Widespread access to the Internet and the growth of web-based information forced a paradigm shift in terms of what technology proficiency looked like and might become. The term **information literacy** became popular and was even a focus of the second national educational technology plan (U.S. Department of Education, 2000). This shift toward finding, analyzing, creating, and sharing information

Roxanne McMillen/Fotolia

Figure 1.5
Networked classroom computers in the "Computer Center."

encouraged educators to consider how technology tools could be used to support learning rather than requiring students to learn basic skills for tools that would become outdated within their school careers. An emphasis on basic technology skills has not disappeared altogether from the nation's schools, but many states and national organizations now take a broader view of technology proficiency.

In just the past few years, web-based applications have evolved to the point where it is very easy for web users, including teachers and students, to move from being passive consumers of information to creators of information, in a range of media formats. Social-networking tools, sometimes referred to as Web 2.0 tools, allow you and your students to quickly post text, images, videos, and other media, which other users can then comment on or add to. You can even bookmark information on the web and share those sites with friends and colleagues, a process sometimes called social bookmarking. Allowing users to shape and mold online content became prevalent with online merchants, like Amazon.com, which allowed users to comment on and rate products purchased in their store. This also allowed the merchants to make recommendations to their users based on their preferences and shopping history. More recent examples of this new form of socially generated content include the popular MySpace and Facebook networking sites; Wikipedia, the online, user-created encyclopedia; YouTube and the subsequent education-specific Teacher-Tube video repositories; Flickr, for sharing photos; and any number of weblogs—or blogs—created by journalists, teachers, and even students. You no longer need to know how to program for the web in order to post a daily journal or create your own online reference with text, graphics, video, and other media. Like most innovative technologies, these new tools are struggling to establish a firm foothold in educational settings. It is important to consider whether and how these tools can effectively support student learning.

Defining Technology Literacy

On a national level, several organizations have attempted to create current definitions of technology literacy or technology proficiency. Most recent definitions reflect the view that many information, communication, and productivity skills will remain constant while the tools we use to demonstrate them will change. In their description of ICT literacy, the Partnership for 21st Century Skills (2004, 2007) promotes the notion that to be competitive in this new millennium, K-12 students must develop a core of foundational skills (listed in Table 1.1). However, in the 21st century, these skills are often learned with and facilitated by the use of ICT tools such as e-mail, the Internet, and productivity software. It is critical that students be prepared

Table 1.1	21st-Century Skills
Learning and Innovation Skills	Creativity and Innovation Skills
	Critical-Thinking and Problem-Solving Skills
	Communication and Collaboration Skills
Information, Media, and Technology Skills	Information Literacy
	Media Literacy
	ICT (Information and Communications Technology) Literacy
Life and Career Skills	Flexibility & Adaptability
	Initiative & Self-Direction
	Social & Cross-Cultural Skills
	Productivity & Accountability
	Leadership & Responsibility

Source: Partnership for 21st Century Skills. (2007). Framework for 21st Century Learning. www.21stcenturyskills.org. Reprinted by permission.

APPLY TO PRACTICE

Defining Technology Literacy

Over time, many organizations have attempted to define computer literacy, information literacy, and technology literacy.

1. Find definitions for any of these terms from public and private national organizations, your college or university, or other sources. Capture a few of the definitions you find and determine whether you agree with them and, if so, to what degree.
2. Log on to a site that covers computer history, proficiency, or literacy. You can find examples of these resources on the textbook's companion website. How do these different sources address computer, information, and technology literacy?
3. Discuss your findings with a group of peers. Would you consider yourself to be technologically literate? Based on which definition? What consensus can you reach in your group?

WEB LINK

Visit the textbook's companion website for examples of websites related to computer history, proficiency, and literacy.

to not only use common technologies but also to continually upgrade their technology skills to include the new tools that take their place—just as you may have had to adapt from writing letters, to sending e-mail, to text-messaging. According to the Partnership, students demonstrate ICT literacy when they use appropriate 21st-century tools to develop and demonstrate learning skills. This is right in line with our current conceptions of technology proficiency as being able to function in a technology-supported, information-based economy that requires continual adjustments in the way we seek and use information, communicate with each other, and solve complex problems.

This focus on technology integration reflects the fourth and most current phase in the movement toward the use of digital technologies (computers, software, the Internet, etc.) as integral parts of the teaching/learning environment. No longer is the goal simply to place technology in the classroom. Rather, the goal is for these tools to become as important to the "work" of teaching and learning as power tools are to the work of building a house. For optimal technology integration to occur in your future classroom, you need to be able to

1. identify *which* technologies are needed to support your curricular goals and objectives;
2. specify *how* the tools will be used to help your students meet and demonstrate those goals;
3. *select* and *use* appropriate technologies to address needs, solve problems, and resolve issues related to your own professional practice and growth; and
4. *enable* your students to use appropriate technologies in all phases of the learning process including exploration, analysis, and production.

The current goal of technology integration in education is the inclusion of relevant technologies as integral and natural contributors to the entire educational process. Review Table 1.2 to consider how the role of computers in education has changed since Apple introduced its first desktop in 1977.

Summary of Technology Integration in Teaching and Learning

So what have we, as educators, learned as we moved through the various phases and stages of technology integration in education? We now know that replacing the teacher with technology will not work. Instead, we know that the role of the teacher has changed over time as teachers have benefited (maybe even just recently) from having powerful tools and ample resources available to support their teaching. New technologies make it easier to incorporate new learning theories and pedagogies such as active learning, knowledge construction, cooperative learning, and guided

Table 1.2	Computers in Education Timeline
First Phase—The computer as an object of study	
1977 Apple II is introduced	First microcomputer brings computing from the scientific, mathematical domain to home, school, and work settings.
1981 IBM releases the first PC	IBM releases DOS-based computers and coins the term PC, or Personal Computer, the new concept in computer technology.
1982	The computer is named *Time* magazine's "Person of the Year," the individual who has had the greatest impact on world events during the year.
Educational software introduced	Drill-and-practice educational software programs predominate.
Educational emphasis	Computer literacy: learning *about* technology
Second Phase—The computer as programming tool	
1983 Logo Programming Language	Logo programming gains acceptance in education in an attempt to address higher-order thinking and problem-solving skills in students.
TCP/IP, SMTP, FTP, HTTP	Standardized communications language, TCP/IP, enables communication between computers via network—the Internet for the "common man" is born.
1984 Macintosh	Apple's Macintosh introduces the terms "desktop" and "icon" into everyday language and ushers in more variety in educational software.
1987 Hypertext	Hypermedia becomes readily accessible with the distribution of HyperCard software on Macintosh computers.
1990 Multimedia boom	Multimedia PCs are developed; simulation software and gaming grow in popularity and complexity; educational databases and other types of digital media are available on CD-ROMs.
Educational emphasis	Learning programming languages and using "programmed instruction" such as drill-and-practice software.
Third Phase—The computer as a communication device and resource tool	
1991 WWW is born 1993 Mosaic released	The release of Mosaic, a browser with a graphical user interface (GUI), changes the look of Internet communications. "Surfing the web" becomes commonplace.
1993 White House goes online	President Clinton's administration develops www.whitehouse.gov. This heralds a new frontier in website development, with an abundance of educational sites for children.
1995	Microsoft releases the Windows 95 operating system. "Toy Story" is released, the first feature-length movie that is entirely computer generated.
1996 First Ed Tech Plan First national "Net Day"	The first national educational technology plan is developed. Volunteers help wire local schools for Internet access and local area network (LAN) infrastructure.
Educational emphasis	Information literacy: learning *with* computers. National education goals emphasize the acquisition of computer hardware and the development of network infrastructure.
Digital Explosion	Technology tools grow at an exponential rate and become faster, smaller, and more powerful. Digital music, pictures, audio, video—the applications of this new wave of technology—are virtually limitless.
Fourth Phase—The computer as learning and social tool	
Web 2.0	Teachers and students move from being consumers to becoming creators of online content using wikis, blogs, and other social networking tools.
Educational emphasis	ICT literacy: foundational information, communication, and productivity skills will remain similar while tools will continue to change. Technology as a tool for solving educational problems.

discovery in our classrooms. Notions such as "teachers as facilitators" or "students as active learners" can be implemented with the assistance of new technologies. Technology tools allow access to expanded resources and have the capacity to free students and teachers from mundane tasks so that they can focus on activities that promote greater collaboration, more in-depth study, and critical thinking skills. Now, educational software programmers and developers build their products based on well-founded learning theories and pedagogies. Of course, some software may be consistent with your style and goals as a teacher but others may not be. As you seek to integrate technologies in your future classroom, you must find the technologies that best support your curriculum, your teaching style, and your students.

Technology Standards

Along with the trend toward technology integration, the standards movement in education also heavily influences the use of technologies within education. Prior to 1983 there was little national discussion of standards in education. In 1983 the report titled *A Nation at Risk* (National Commission of Excellence in Education, 1983) was published and, in the eyes of many, the modern standards movement began. Among other things, this report included two goals directly related to academic achievement. One goal indicated that students in grades 4, 8, and 12 would demonstrate competency in English, mathematics, science, history, and geography by the year 2000. The other goal stated that U.S. students would be first in the world in science and math achievement by 2000. In an effort to determine the criteria for compliance with these goals, minimum standards were needed in many content domains where few, if any, had existed previously. And so, beginning in 1983, and continuing through 1999, efforts were undertaken by the national professional organizations in all the major content areas (English, mathematics, science, etc.) to create a set of curricular standards for their specific disciplines.

The development of technology standards started just a little later. In 1998, the International Society for Technology in Education, an organization whose mission is to provide "leadership and service to improve teaching, learning, and school leadership by advancing the effective use of technology in PK–12 and teacher education" (ISTE, 2008b), released a set of technology standards for students, the National Educational Technology Standards for Students (NETS-S). Since then, ISTE has developed multiple sets of technology standards, including the National Educational Technology Standards for Teachers (NETS-T) and for Administrators (NETS-A).

The original ISTE NETS were released in a "refreshed" version for students in 2007 and for teachers in 2008. Building on the original standards, the new standards reflect the change in emphasis from computer skills to 21st-century skills. The chapters in this book address the most recent standards for teachers, in other words, the ISTE NETS-T (see Figure 1.6); however, you will also learn about the NETS for Students in Chapter 7 as you learn to assess students' attainment of content area and technology standards (see Figure 1.7).

The Value of Standards

Today's teachers have dealt with standards for much, if not all, of their professional lives. As a student, you have probably faced academic standards from kindergarten through your current status as a college or university student. You probably had to meet minimum performance standards related to grades and test scores before you were admitted to your college or university. Further, you are likely to encounter multiple standards as you prepare for and ultimately become a member of the teaching profession. Your academic program of study has to comply with standards established by one or more accrediting agencies. When you become a practicing teacher there will be curricular standards, employee performance standards, and student performance standards. In general, standards refer to a degree or level of requirement,

The ISTE National Educational Technology Standards (NETS•T) and Performance Indicators for Teachers (2008)

Effective teachers model and apply the National Educational Technology Standards for Students (NETS•S) as they design, implement, and assess learning experiences to engage students and improve learning; enrich professional practice; and provide positive models for students, colleagues, and the community. All teachers should meet the following standards and performance indicators. Teachers:

1. Facilitate and Inspire Student Learning and Creativity

Teachers use their knowledge of subject matter, teaching and learning, and technology to facilitate experiences that advance student learning, creativity, and innovation in both face-to-face and virtual environments. Teachers:

   a. promote, support, and model creative and innovative thinking and inventiveness
   b. engage students in exploring real-world issues and solving authentic problems using digital tools and resources
   c. promote student reflection using collaborative tools to reveal and clarify students' conceptual understanding and thinking, planning, and creative processes
   d. model collaborative knowledge construction by engaging in learning with students, colleagues, and others in face-to-face and virtual environments

2. Design and Develop Digital-Age Learning Experiences and Assessments

Teachers design, develop, and evaluate authentic learning experiences and assessments incorporating contemporary tools and resources to maximize content learning in context and to develop the knowledge, skills, and attitudes identified in the NETS•S. Teachers:

   a. design or adapt relevant learning experiences that incorporate digital tools and resources to promote student learning and creativity
   b. develop technology-enriched learning environments that enable all students to pursue their individual curiosities and become active participants in setting their own educational goals, managing their own learning, and assessing their own progress
   c. customize and personalize learning activities to address students' diverse learning styles, working strategies, and abilities using digital tools and resources
   d. provide students with multiple and varied formative and summative assessments aligned with content and technology standards and use resulting data to inform learning and teaching

3. Model Digital-Age Work and Learning

Teachers exhibit knowledge, skills, and work processes representative of an innovative professional in a global and digital society. Teachers:

   a. demonstrate fluency in technology systems and the transfer of current knowledge to new technologies and situations
   b. collaborate with students, peers, parents, and community members using digital tools and resources to support student success and innovation
   c. communicate relevant information and ideas effectively to students, parents, and peers using a variety of digital-age media and formats
   d. model and facilitate effective use of current and emerging digital tools to locate, analyze, evaluate, and use information resources to support research and learning

4. Promote and Model Digital Citizenship and Responsibility

Teachers understand local and global societal issues and responsibilities in an evolving digital culture and exhibit legal and ethical behavior in their professional practices. Teachers:

   a. advocate, model, and teach safe, legal, and ethical use of digital information and technology, including respect for copyright, intellectual property, and the appropriate documentation of sources
   b. address the diverse needs of all learners by using learner-centered strategies and providing equitable access to appropriate digital tools and resources
   c. promote and model digital etiquette and responsible social interactions related to the use of technology and information
   d. develop and model cultural understanding and global awareness by engaging with colleagues and students of other cultures using digital-age communication and collaboration tools

5. Engage in Professional Growth and Leadership

Teachers continuously improve their professional practice, model life-long learning, and exhibit leadership in their school and professional community by promoting and demonstrating the effective use of digital tools and resources. Teachers:

   a. participate in local and global learning communities to explore creative applications of technology to improve student learning
   b. exhibit leadership by demonstrating a vision of technology infusion, participating in shared decision making and community building, and developing the leadership and technology skills of others
   c. evaluate and reflect on current research and professional practice on a regular basis to make effective use of existing and emerging digital tools and resources in support of student learning
   d. contribute to the effectiveness, vitality, and self-renewal of the teaching profession and of their school and community

Figure 1.6
ISTE NETS-T.
Source: National Educational Technology Standards for Teachers, Second Edition. Copyright © 2008, ISTE (International Society for Technology in Education), www.iste.org. All rights reserved.

excellence, or attainment expected of an individual or organization. Obviously there are many different standards. But what are standards, who creates them, and why are they important?

In simple terms, standards are **criteria**. Criteria define what is expected, such as the content you are expected to teach. These expectations can relate to the performance of individuals (teachers and students), organizations (schools and districts), programs, groups, or a host of other issues. In your case, you will be most concerned

National Educational Technology Standards for Students: The Next Generation

"What students should know and be able to do to learn effectively and live productively in an increasingly digital world . . ."

1. Creativity and Innovation
Students demonstrate creative thinking, construct knowledge, and develop innovative products and processes using technology. Students:
  a. apply existing knowledge to generate new ideas, products, or processes.
  b. create original works as a means of personal or group expression.
  c. use models and simulations to explore complex systems and issues.
  d. identify trends and forecast possibilities.

2. Communication and Collaboration
Students use digital media and environments to communicate and work collaboratively, including at a distance, to support individual learning and contribute to the learning of others. Students:
  a. interact, collaborate, and publish with peers, experts or others employing a variety of digital environments and media.
  b. communicate information and ideas effectively to multiple audiences using a variety of media and formats.
  c. develop cultural understanding and global awareness by engaging with learners of other cultures.
  d. contribute to project teams to produce original works or solve problems.

3. Research and Information Fluency
Students apply digital tools to gather, evaluate, and use information. Students:
  a. plan strategies to guide inquiry.
  b. locate, organize, analyze, evaluate, synthesize, and ethically use information from a variety of sources and media.
  c. evaluate and select information sources and digital tools based on the appropriateness to specific tasks.
  d. process data and report results.

4. Critical Thinking, Problem-Solving & Decision-Making
Students use critical thinking skills to plan and conduct research, manage projects, solve problems and make informed decisions using appropriate digital tools and resources. Students:
  a. identify and define authentic problems and significant questions for investigation.
  b. plan and manage activities to develop a solution or complete a project.
  c. collect and analyze data to identify solutions and/or make informed decisions.
  d. use multiple processes and diverse perspectives to explore alternative solutions.

5. Digital Citizenship
Students understand human, cultural, and societal issues related to technology and practice legal and ethical behavior. Students:
  a. advocate and practice safe, legal, and responsible use of information and technology.
  b. exhibit a positive attitude toward using technology that supports collaboration, learning, and productivity.
  c. demonstrate personal responsibility for lifelong learning.
  d. exhibit leadership for digital citizenship.

6. Technology Operations and Concepts
Students demonstrate a sound understanding of technology concepts, systems and operations. Students:
  a. understand and use technology systems.
  b. select and use applications effectively and productively.
  c. troubleshoot systems and applications

Figure 1.7
ISTE NETS-S.
Source: National Educational Technology Standards for Students, Second Edition. Copyright © 2007, ISTE (International Society for Technology in Education), www.iste.org. All rights reserved.

with meeting standards that relate to how well you address the requirements of your curriculum, how well your students perform, and—specific to this textbook—how well you integrate technology into your teaching. However, it is not enough to look only at criteria when discussing standards.

What distinguish standards from other types of expectations are the additional factors of **compliance** and **consequences**. Compliance refers to who is subject to the standards and on what basis. Compliance with some standards is voluntary. In such cases, the standards serve as recommendations with little or no consequence if they are not met. In other cases, compliance with standards is mandatory and you or your school will be expected to meet those standards.

In most states, you will be expected to demonstrate compliance with a set of technology standards for teachers, and in many cases those will be the ISTE NETS-T. Compliance with ISTE standards is voluntary. Although ISTE has no power to enforce compliance with its technology standards, these standards have taken on a mandatory quality in many areas because most states and some districts have adopted, adapted, or aligned their technology standards with them as policy or accreditation requirements for teachers. A few states and organizations have developed their own sets of technology standards and several of these reference the ISTE NETS-T without adopting them outright. The technology standards you encounter may be established by local, state, national, or international agencies and organizations. But as we've said before, the ISTE standards have become the most widely adopted technology standards in schools.

Standards typically have consequences associated with compliance or noncompliance. These consequences indicate what happens if you do or don't meet the expectations. For example, the National Council for Accreditation of Teacher Education (NCATE) requires that teacher preparation programs prepare preservice teachers to meet certain standards for integrating technology within their programs of study in order to obtain national accreditation. NCATE has adopted the computing and technology competencies created by the International Society for Technology in Education (ISTE) in 2001. In addition, many states have adapted or adopted the ISTE computing and technology standards for teacher certification or licensure.

In some states, you will be required to demonstrate how you meet or exceed technology standards, whether by being observed by an administrator or other teacher, documenting your proficiency in a portfolio, or perhaps even passing a test. Being compliant can help you get a job or obtain benefits once you are employed. Some benefits might include attaining tenure, earning monetary rewards associated with reaching higher levels on your career ladder, or even having the opportunity to teach different courses or work with different students. Failure to comply also has consequences, ranging from mandatory remedial instruction to delays in pay raises to limited employment opportunities.

So, there are three factors to consider with respect to any standard: criteria, compliance, and consequences. But don't worry—the intent of this book is to help you document your mastery of the required technology standards for teachers. ISTE (2003) suggests several methods to document your proficiency of technology standards (e.g., self-assessment instruments, classroom observations, performance tasks, and portfolio preparation). In this book, each chapter concludes with an opportunity to effectively document what you have learned in a portfolio. You may find other ways to document your skills and knowledge, but this book provides you with suggestions for creating and maintaining this common tool. In fact, your school or state may have a portfolio assessment system to which you are required to contribute. If not, in Chapter 2, you will learn about developing your own portfolio using common productivity tools such as word processors, web development software, and so forth.

WEB LINK

Visit ISTE's website at www.iste.org for a list of states that have adopted or modified ISTE's technology standards.

The information presented so far provides a glimpse of the roles of government and professional organizations in the development of standards. However, except for their ability to address legislative and political requirements, not much has been said about the importance of standards. Although many reasons can be advanced for the development of standards, the main reasons include (McREL, 2004):

- Standards provide a common set of expectations.
- Standards clarify expectations.
- Standards raise expectations.

So, technology standards, such as those from ISTE, provide a common set of *expectations* across states and localities. Moreover, they *clarify* the level of technological proficiency expected of teachers. Finally, they *raise expectations* by creating an awareness of what can be accomplished. When standards work as intended, they help us achieve first-rate quality—in services, products, and teaching. Throughout this book the ISTE standards are used to provide a common set of expectations, as

APPLY TO PRACTICE

Technology Standards

1. Identify the technology standards that your state expects teachers to meet.
2. How do they align with the ISTE NETS-T used in this book?

well as to clarify and raise the expectations regarding the skills you should obtain while developing competency in technology integration within the classroom.

New Learning Experiences

One intent of the ISTE standards is to enable teachers to create new learning experiences that capitalize on our understanding of how people learn and the technological tools available to support teaching and learning. Drawing from ISTE's intention, new learning experiences are ones in which teachers and students work together to address the requirements of the curriculum while still taking into account individual student needs, interests, and preferences. New information is readily linked to students' prior knowledge. Students are also given some degree of choice in terms of the ways they receive and process information and demonstrate their learning. Teaching methods rely on activities that encourage high levels of thinking and creativity, and that allow students to collaborate and communicate—both with other students and teachers—as well as experts outside of the classroom. Students are encouraged to solve problems drawn from real-world situations (e.g., "How can we improve our city so that everyone benefits?" "Why should kids care about the price of gas?"), within the context of one specific content area (social studies, mathematics) or across content areas. This type of authentic problem-based learning requires students to identify and describe the problem, relate it to prior knowledge, form hypotheses to solve the problem, select strategies to test their hypotheses, and monitor and evaluate how well their strategies worked in solving the problem. Supporting teaching and learning in this type of authentic environment are technologies (Internet resources, databases, spreadsheets, presentation software) that allow students to work as professionals in an information-based world, that support them across varied levels of need, and that are used to build and demonstrate both content and technology proficiencies.

The type of learning experiences you create in your classroom will influence the types of technologies that you and your students use (see Figure 1.8). It will also affect *how* you and your students use these technologies. For example, if teachers use presentation software to project to a screen what they used to write on the chalkboard,

Bonnie Jacobs/iStockphoto.com

Figure 1.8
Technology can help teachers develop new learning environments and experiences.

simply adding computer technology doesn't change their approach to one that is more powerful. What's most important is *how* the technology is used. For example, a more learner-centered approach may involve a group of students using this same presentation software to create a slide show that includes pictures of artifacts or charts and graphs that summarize research they have completed. While the same technology is being used in both classrooms, the *way* it is being used is quite different. Ultimately, the decision regarding how to use technology in the classroom will be yours to make.

Profiles of Technology Integration

In order to create new kinds of learning experiences, effective technology integration requires more than simply introducing computers and related technologies into the classroom. To **integrate** means to combine two or more things to make a whole; when we integrate technologies into instruction, we make them an integral part of the teaching and learning process. **Technology integration** requires changes to many instructional components including 1) what resources are used, 2) what roles the teacher performs, 3) what roles students play, as well as 4) the nature of the instructional activities (Dwyer, Ringstaff, & Sandholtz, 1991). The scenarios that follow illustrate each aspect of effective integration in greater detail.

Use of Technology Resources

The classroom scenarios below demonstrate different types of integration practices. As you read them, think about the *resources* available and how the teachers actually used them. How well are they matched to the instruction? What role do technology-based resources play?

- Wallace McManus is introducing the scientific method to his fifth grade class. He has used his computer to create a worksheet for his students that identifies steps in the process, including formulating and testing hypotheses. Learning stations are set up around the room where students find containers of water, several dry and wet ingredients, a heating element, and some ice. Wallace plans to have the students propose hypotheses about how the different materials will react to each other and at different temperatures. The students will write down observations in their lab notebooks as they walk around the room and later record their responses on their worksheets. Wallace knows this is a good lab for students to experience, although inevitably some of them tend to be kind of messy while completing the various activities.

- Cindy García-Stamos is planning a science lab for her fifth grade students. She and her students have downloaded a map and satellite images from a website of the area surrounding their school. She's asked her students to propose a hypothesis of the potential effects of the proposed building of a four-lane highway on the natural inhabitants of the grass, forest, and wetland areas near their school. She and her students collected soil and water samples during a recent field trip to key areas marked on their maps. They also took digital photos of the animals and plants in the areas they visited. The class will use several different probes to gather data from the samples and will track changes when new elements from the road development are added. Students are working in teams representing various stakeholder groups, including developers and business people in the community, local residents, and administrators at the school. They will use Internet resources in addition to their other data in order to develop multimedia presentations to share with the rest of their class. Presentations will propose at least one hypothesis about the highway development project and will use the data students have collected and analyzed to support or refute that hypothesis. Cindy hopes to put copies of the presentations on her class website as well.

The Teacher's Role

The scenarios below illustrate different approaches to facilitating instruction. What roles do *teachers* play in these classrooms? Do they lead instruction or do they enable students to engage in higher-order skills through collaborative problem solving? Does technology use replicate traditional seat-based activities or does it support diverse learning styles and preferences in unique settings?

- Principal Novella Mayberry is observing an American history lesson on the economic and political forces that led to The Great Depression. She and the teacher she is observing, Lynette Haines, have been friends and colleagues for a good part of their careers. Lynette's students are always well behaved and quiet as they furiously scribble down notes during her presentation. Novella notes that her friend is using presentation software to support her lectures and is fairly sure that the information is based on the lecture notes she's been using for years. There's little interaction between Lynette and her students, or among the students themselves. When Lynette asks the students questions, they usually answer by nodding their heads. The class comes to a close as Lynette gives the next reading assignment and distributes a worksheet she has photocopied to the students.

- The noise level in Shanika Wallace's fifth grade class is pretty high as her students are scattered around the room in pairs and small groups while they work on a local history project. It's good noise, though, thinks Shanika as students are busy sharing ideas, asking each other questions, and working out solutions. Shanika and her students began this multi-day lesson by developing a rubric that would be used to assess the quality of both the content and the design of the project. This time, Shanika allowed the students to create their own teams of up to four students to work on different aspects of the project. Some students are editing short movies of interviews conducted with their parents and other relatives using the digital video camera, while others are taking digital pictures or scanning artifacts to help document how their community has changed over time. All students are required to respond to prompts that Shanika posts on the class blog every day. This enables Shanika to review their progress and identify any misconceptions, by the class or an individual, that require attention. When they're done with this unit, the movies, pictures, and documents will be housed on her class web page, and both the students and Shanika will assess the work with the rubric, using completed copies posted in each student's online portfolio.

Nature of Instruction

As you read the two classroom scenarios below, focus on the *nature of the instruction* described in each. Do students encounter well-structured problems? Are assessments norm-based or do they allow for reflective responses and accommodate a variety of learning preferences? Is technology central to the instruction?

- Steven Tucker is head of the math department at Central High School and is proud of how much he has taught himself about computers and technology. He was one of the first teachers in his school to use presentation software and quickly taught himself how to use the many animations, sounds, and slide backgrounds to spice up his lectures. He has typed all of his lecture notes, for each of the three different classes he teaches each year, in separate word-processing documents and has organized them in chronological sequence in his folder on the school's file server. He has also typed all of his worksheets and has created folders for the students in each of his classes. He feels that teaching has gotten easier, since he can easily pull up his lecture notes, show the corresponding presentation to his class, and have them access their homework assignments from the file server. They just print them out and turn them in. No more illegible student handwriting to decipher. He has even started using scannable test forms for his tests and that is saving him even more time.

- The students in Brenda Williams' geometry class are putting the final touches on a semester-long project that has required them to really think about how math is used in daily life. The goal of the project was to design a new park and fitness center for the neighborhood. Students used the Internet to find suitable lots in the area and then used GPS (global positioning system) devices to measure the irregularly shaped lots. The students then created scale drawings of the lots and determined the areas of all major sections using geometry software. The students' drawings had to include all of the key features for the proposed facility, including parking, an area for water runoff, and access and features for persons with disabilities. The students estimated building costs using one of the online calculators that Brenda found for them and linked from her class website. They then created a spreadsheet outlining those costs. Brenda divided her classes into teams of two or three students and each team is preparing to present their ideas to the rest of the class over the last two days of the semester. The class will rate each group's solution based on criteria such as cost, feasibility, and creativity.

The Students' Role

As you read the two scenarios below, think about how the *students* are engaged in the instruction. On whom is the learning focused? How are the students engaged (see Figure 1.9)? How are individual differences supported and nurtured? How does technology support and motivate student activities?

- Amy Ferrell's cell phone startles her and she jerks up in her seat. She keeps forgetting to turn the ringer off when she gets to school and it's now ringing deep insider her backpack. She fumbles to find the phone in the darkened class while only her best friend Laurie notices and gives her a smirking grin. Amy and Laurie are in English and are watching a movie version of *West Side Story*, which has taken several class periods. She and her classmates poke fun at the costumes, the funny language, and all the singing and dancing, but at least she understands this language better than when they read *Romeo and Juliet*. She knows she's supposed to learn and respect the works of Shakespeare, but it was hard reading. Some of the students were picked to read some of the scenes in class, like that famous balcony scene that had those lines she didn't realize were from Shakespeare—"wherefore art thou?" and "a rose by any other name"—but she didn't want to read the stilted language in class and didn't volunteer. At least her teacher has let the class choose between watching this movie or a production of the real play. She turns off her phone and settles back down into her seat to watch the movie.

- Butch Simmons had never really been interested in English and hadn't looked forward to studying *Hamlet*, but his teacher, Mr. Fordham, made it interesting. They still had to read the play, which could be slow going at times, but Mr. Fordham had made it more interesting by explaining the social and political influences surrounding the play and using news websites to demonstrate how some of these same issues exist today. Of course, some of the drama kids wanted to act out scenes from the play, which Mr. Fordham let them do, but he videotaped the scenes and had the students write reflections about their own performances, which they posted on a class website in a section called "The Virtual Globe" after the famous theater. Some students had selected famous scenes, like Hamlet's soliloquy and had "translated" it into more modern speech—including a version Butch thought was really interesting that used some current slang. Another group of students had shown the same scene from three different movie versions of the play and had led a discussion about the decisions actors, directors, and other people like costume

Figure 1.9
Students engaged in technology-integrated learning experience.

and set designers make in developing the mood and character of their performances. Butch was surprised to find out that Shakespeare's work had been so influenced by the current events of his time and how some of those same issues were still prevalent in the world. In the past, it had just seemed old and hard to understand.

Stages in Technology Integration

A number of researchers have documented the developmental stages that teachers go through as they move from novice technology users to those capable of using technologies to create new learning experiences for meaningful learning. One of the most commonly used continuums was proposed by researchers from the Apple Classrooms of Tomorrow™ (ACOT™) (Dwyer et al., 1991). Between 1985 and 1998, Apple Computer collaborated with public schools, universities, and research agencies to investigate teachers' attitudes, practices, and integration behaviors when using technology. Early reports from this project identified a five-stage continuum of technology integration: entry, adoption, adaptation, appropriation, and invention. Although this study was conducted quite a few years ago, these stages can still be observed in teachers today and provide a useful way to frame the discussion on the evolution of technology integration within the classroom. Another helpful aspect of this early research is the identification of four essential components for effective technology integration described above: the resources used, the role of the teacher, the nature of the instructional activities, and the role of the student.

The new ISTE NETS-T are accompanied by a four-stage continuum that describes how teachers demonstrate each standard and sub-standard: beginning, developing, proficient, and transformative. Following are generalized descriptions of these four stages using the lens of the four essential components identified in the ACOT™ research. Notice how the actions of the teacher and students change as we move through the stages, as well as how resources are used and activities are structured. However, be aware that teachers and activities may exhibit characteristics across stages. As you read the descriptions of the four stages, think about where your former teachers and colleagues might fall on the continuum.

Characteristics of the Beginning Phase

- Teachers select and use technologies and other *resources* that support student learning experiences, but classroom instruction may still depend heavily on chalkboards, textbooks, workbooks, and worksheets to support lecture, recitation, and seatwork.
- *Teachers* research and discuss strategies students can use to promote knowledge construction and demonstrate creativity. They monitor safe, ethical, legal, and healthy use of technology and information resources.
- Teachers design *instructional activities* by using or modifying existing learning resources to collect information and create student products. Teachers select and use formative and summative assessments to inform teaching and learning.
- *Students* use technology tools to research and collect information and to plan and manage their learning.

Characteristics of the Developing Phase

- Teachers plan, manage, and facilitate student understanding of technologies and other *resources* best suited to support specific learning experiences.
- *Teachers* facilitate and guide students as they employ strategies to construct knowledge and promote creative thought; they model safe, ethical, legal, and healthy use of technology and information resources and help students address threats to security of technologies, data, and information.
- Teachers adapt or create *instructional activities* that allow students to collect and report information through a variety of products and formats. Teachers develop and conduct formative and summative assessments to inform teaching and learning.
- *Students* use technology tools to collect information, synthesize, and create new information in student projects guided by their teachers. They explore issues of individual interest related to their learning.

Characteristics of the Proficient Phase

- Teachers demonstrate and model effective use of a variety of existing and emerging technology-based *resources* to encourage students to engage in a range of learning experiences.
- *Teachers* model creativity and knowledge construction and enable students to demonstrative creativity and innovation. Teachers advocate for and effectively instruct students in the safe, ethical, legal, and healthy use of technology and information resources including emerging policies and practices related to issues such as security, intellectual property, and personal rights.
- Teachers design and customize *instructional activities* in response to students' learning styles, preferences, and abilities, so that students develop questions, propose solutions, and elicit feedback on their learning. Teachers provide students with various opportunities to demonstrate skills and knowledge to adapt future teaching and learning opportunities.
- *Students* use technology in support of collecting and synthesizing information, developing and demonstrating critical thinking, and solving authentic problems through the creation of projects they propose. Students use technology to plan, manage, and reflect on their own learning.

Characteristics of the Transformative Phase

- Teachers engage with students to explore and determine appropriate uses of existing and emerging technology-based *resources* so that students may effectively plan, manage, and evaluate their learning experiences.
- *Teachers* collaborate with and involve students as lead learners to engage in activities to promote creativity and innovation and explore complex issues.

APPLY TO PRACTICE

Stages of Technology Integration

1. Examine the video-based examples of teachers using technology that are available on the textbook's companion website that accompanies this book or make arrangements to observe in a classroom.
2. Use the rubric provided by ISTE to assess teachers' uses of technology across the four common components of instruction (resources, teacher role, lesson activities, and student role). Remember, teachers and activities may not fall neatly within one stage but may exhibit many characteristics across stages. Teachers also may vary in where they fall on the continuum on a day-to-day basis, depending on the topic to be taught, the time available for teaching, and a variety of other factors.

They engage students in becoming active participants in the safe, ethical, legal, and healthy use of technology and information resources by encouraging them to establish policies and procedures for its use and determining methods to address its misuse.

- Teachers collaborate with students to identify and develop personalized *instructional activities* that allow students to formulate, evaluate, and test hypotheses to address complex problems that address real-world local and global issues with their teachers, other students, and outside experts and share their information for real-world application. Teachers engage students in the development and analysis of various opportunities to demonstrate skills and knowledge to orient future teaching and learning opportunities toward areas necessary for greatest student success.
- *Students* collaborate and communicate with their teachers, other students, and experts to select and use technology tools that align with learning preferences, styles, and content requirements in order to address real-world, complex problems with multiple answers or solutions. Students routinely monitor, evaluate, and adjust their own learning strategies and thinking.

If you suspect you're at one of the early stages in technology integration, don't worry! An analysis conducted for the U.S. Office of Technology revealed that it takes time to perfect the skills necessary to effectively integrate technology in the classroom (Mehlinger, 1997). If you are currently using this textbook as part of a typical college course, you may expect to reach one of the higher stages by the end of the course, even if you entered the course without prior knowledge of how to use computers in the classroom. If you are taking this course early in your college career and continue to use your skills throughout your education courses, you can expect to be comfortably situated in the "Proficient" stage, as described by ISTE, by the time you graduate. Wouldn't it be wonderful if you were at that stage as you entered the classroom? And

APPLY TO PRACTICE

Technology in Education

1. Reflect on your own experiences using technology for learning. What technologies were used when you were a student? How were they used?
2. How were technology-related skills taught to you as a student? What was emphasized?
3. What skills and knowledge do you already possess to help you meet the challenges of effectively integrating technology into instruction? How did you learn those skills?
4. Discuss your experiences with your peers. Do you have similar experiences? What differences exist?

with more experience, we're confident that you will be one of those dynamic teachers who functions on a day-to-day basis in the transformative phase.

Chapter Summary

In this chapter we reviewed the history of technology integration within education. You were introduced to the ISTE NETS-T and encouraged to identify the technology standards that you will be expected to meet throughout your professional preparation and practice. You were introduced to stages of technology integration and asked to consider how different classroom practices (use of resources, role of teacher and students, and nature of instruction) change as one moves through the stages.

Throughout this book, you will consider how you will integrate technology into your own teaching. You'll think about how students will interact with technologies, the resources you will provide, the instructional activities you will use, and the role you will assume as a teacher in a technology-rich classroom. A guiding premise of this book is to help you develop as a self-directed learner who is able to successfully navigate the constantly changing environment of technology integration. In order to become and remain a creative, innovative teacher, you will need to continue to learn about new and emerging technologies throughout your career. So before we turn our attention to specific technology standards, in the next chapter, we focus on techniques to plan, monitor, and evaluate your own knowledge construction.

As a beginning teacher you will face multiple challenges—every teacher does. But as part of the first generation of teachers to enter the teaching profession already comfortable with computers, you are probably more prepared than we were, as beginning teachers. We believe that you are ready to go to the next stage of technology integration within education: using technology as a natural part of the learning process, for both you and your students. Our goal is to help you develop innovative pedagogies in order to reach the goals you have set for yourself and your students.

YOUR PORTFOLIO

Identify the technology standards that you are expected to meet throughout your professional preparation and practice.

References

Dwyer, D. C., Ringstaff, C., & Sandholtz, J. H. (1991). Changes in teachers' beliefs and practices in technology-rich classrooms. *Educational Leadership*, 48(8), 45–52.

International Society for Technology in Education (ISTE). (2003). *National educational technology standards for teachers: Resources for assessment*. Eugene, OR: Author.

International Society for Technology in Education (ISTE). (2007). *National educational technology standards for students*. Eugene, OR: Author.

International Society for Technology in Education (ISTE). (2008a). *National educational technology standards for teachers*. Eugene, OR: Author.

International Society for Technology in Education (ISTE). (2008b). *About ISTE*. Eugene, OR: Author. Retrieved August 28, 2008, from http://www.iste.org/AM/Template.cfm?Section=About_ISTE

Mehlinger, H. D. (1997). The next step. *Electronic School Online*. Alexandria, VA: National School Board Association. Retrieved March 16, 2006, from www.electronic-school.com/0697f2.html

Mid-continent Research for Education and Learning (McREL). (2004). Content knowledge (4th ed.). Retrieved July 28, 2005, from http://www.mcrel.org/standards-benchmarks/docs/purpose.asp

National Commission on Excellence in Education. (1983). *A nation at risk: The imperative for educational reform*. Washington, DC: Government Printing Office.

Partnership for 21st Century Skills. (2004). *Learning for the 21st Century: A report and MILE guide for the 21st century*. Washington, DC: Author.

Partnership for 21st Century Skills. (2007). *Framework for 21st Century learning*. Washington, DC: Author.

President's Panel on Educational Technology. (1997). *Report to the President on the use of technology to strengthen K–12 education in the United States*. Washington, DC: U.S. Government Printing Office.

U.S. Department of Education. (2000). *E-learning: Putting a world-class education at the fingertips of all children*. Washington, DC: Author.

Brand X Pictures/Jupiter Images

ISTE Standards addressed in this chapter

The ISTE standards emphasize the need for self-directed learning by both teachers and students. In this chapter, we introduce a model of self-directed learning (the GAME plan) that we use throughout this book as a prompt to remind you to actively plan, monitor, and evaluate your learning progress. We encourage you to self-assess your current competencies in the skills required by NETS-T and NETS-S and introduce you to critical reflection as a means of monitoring your learning. Finally, you are encouraged to develop a portfolio in order to evaluate your progress in meeting NETS-T.

Self-Directed Lifelong Learning

Outcomes

In this chapter, you will
- Identify the components of self-directed learning.
- Self-assess your current proficiency in the skills outlined in the ISTE NETS-S.
- Begin development of a portfolio in which you will document your developing competencies in applicable technology standards for teachers.

Think back to the first time you used technology. Undoubtedly, a wide variety of technologies were in use from the very moment you were born. You probably began to watch television very early in your life. Perhaps you played computer games before you even entered school. You probably began to type your papers on a word processor many years ago, perhaps even in elementary school. What about the first time you searched the web? Consider the first time you communicated with a friend via e-mail or sent an instant message on a computer, phone, or other device. It's likely that your initial experiences with technology were somewhat different from your experiences today. And we can assure you, your experiences today are quite different from the experiences you will have in the future.

This book is based on the premise that learning to teach generally, and to teach with technology specifically, are lifelong journeys. As a lifelong learner, much of your learning will be self-directed. That is, you will be responsible for locating learning opportunities and completing tasks to meet your own learning goals. So before we begin to discuss the specifics of NETS-T, in this chapter, we introduce you to a self-directed learning model that we'll use throughout this book. You'll have the opportunity to think about what you know about integrating technology into the classroom, as well as what you still need to know. We also introduce portfolios as a means of documenting your learning and professional growth. At the end of this process, you should have a plan for learning about the integration of technology throughout your professional career.

Self-Directed Learning

Gibbons (2002) defined **self-directed learning** (SDL) as "any increase in knowledge, skill, accomplishment, or personal development that an individual selects and brings about by his or her own efforts using any method in any circumstance at any time" (p. 2). The teacher highlighted in the previous *Stories from Practice* engaged in self-directed learning when he taught himself how to record his grades using a spreadsheet program and when he participated in online discussions about classroom issues with other teachers across the country. You are self-directed anytime you learn a new skill (for example, how to use a digital video camera) or pursue more information

STORIES FROM PRACTICE

Continual Learning

When I first went to college to become a teacher, I rarely saw a computer the entire four years I was there. My high school had only one computer—a TRS-80—which arrived during my senior year and only the very best math students were allowed to use it, at which times they'd usually write little programs in BASIC that ran their names across the screen or something else as equally silly. In college, one of my roommates purchased a Commodore-64 that had an external tape drive, but we used it mostly for playing games. I was never asked to use a computer in my classes and none of my education courses even covered the topic. It wasn't until working on my Master's Degree in Education that my advisor prompted me to investigate the two computers reserved for graduate students and suggested I use one for writing my thesis. Locked in a former closet were two new computers. One was a DOS-based machine that required a huge manual and a tiring array of key combinations I could barely remember just to apply formatting for different fonts, sizes, bold, italics, and the like. The other was one of the new Macintosh computers. The icons and menus were simple and intuitive. I was hooked.

That little Macintosh computer changed the way I worked and had a big impact on my use of computers in my classroom. I ended up writing my thesis about the growing field of educational software and used that information to help me find and evaluate software, beginning with drill-and-practice software in the early days up until now with the advanced web applications I develop and use to train other educators. Once in my classroom, I quickly learned how to put all my grades in a spreadsheet and created an inventory program for all the books and materials I was required to keep up with. Most of the time I'd experiment by working through the horribly written print manuals that came with the software, with their frequent mistakes and confusing language. Those manuals were definitely not written by teachers!

As I progressed through my career, the computers and software that I used became more sophisticated. I was excited to move from the rudimentary word-processing program on my computer to page layout software that I used to create newsletters to send home to parents. I created a monthly calendar that many parents said they kept

on their refrigerators. The day I got my first e-mail account, I think my professional life shifted. I had to use a text-based e-mail program, very different from the helpful e-mail programs available now, and I would spend hours sending and receiving very short, text-only messages to other teachers across the country and probably around the globe. That experience prompted me to buy a computer for home. I participated in some early bulletin boards for teachers where we'd "talk" about techniques we used in class and how we overcame particular problems.

I now provide teachers with online learning opportunities that are far more advanced than my early bulletin board days. Currently, I get a lot of my information through eZines and some helpful websites, and I try to attend at least one educational technology conference and one off-site training event each year. I know technology is going to keep evolving and I don't want to know or understand it all. Instead, I focus my own professional growth on figuring out what technology is out there to help me do my job faster, smarter, and better.

Source: John Ross

Figure 2.1
Self-directed teachers use online resources to increase their knowledge and learn new skills.

about an intriguing topic, sparked by something you read or heard (for example, how to create a profile on FaceBook or MySpace). As a future teacher you will be directing much of your own learning, so it is important that you think about the learning process and how you work best within this process (see Figure 2.1). Learners who "think about thinking" and apply strategies to regulate and oversee their learning are often referred to as **metacognitive** learners. To support you in this lifelong learning process, many of the activities in this book require you to be self-directed.

Self-directed, metacognitive learners engage in three key processes: planning, monitoring, and evaluating their learning activities (see, for example, Ertmer & Newby, 1996; Zimmerman, 1990; Zimmerman, Bonner, & Kovach, 1996). During the planning stage, you, as a learner, determine your individual learning goals. You identify what you already know about the task at hand and develop a plan of attack, otherwise known as a learning strategy. You determine what is required by the learning task, plan your study time and, if possible, arrange for the best learning conditions. During the monitoring stage, you take action to implement your plan, and, as you engage in the learning task, reflect on whether you are making sufficient progress toward your goals. You determine whether the strategies you have chosen are working to accomplish the learning task effectively and efficiently. During the evaluating stage, you reflect on how well you have met your goals and determine whether you should modify your strategies for future learning tasks.

The GAME Plan

We have translated the recommendations for self-directed learning into the following four steps, which we call the **GAME** plan:

1. Set **G**oals
2. Take **A**ction to meet those goals
3. **M**onitor progress toward achieving goals and
4. **E**valuate whether the goals were achieved and **E**xtend your learning to new situations.

Throughout this book, we'll use the GAME plan to guide your self-directed learning activities (see Figure 2.2). The GAME plan requires you to think about and take steps to direct your learning process, specifically while learning about technology and how to integrate it into the curriculum. The GAME plan enables you to customize

Goals	Action	Monitor	Evaluate and Extend
• What do I want to know or be able to do? • What do I already know about the topic? • How will I know if I have been successful?	• What information do I need to meet my goal? • How can I find the information I need? • What resources are needed? • What learning strategy will I use?	• Am I finding the information I need? • What patterns are emerging from the information sources? • Do I need to modify my action plan?	• Have I met my learning goals? If not, should I modify my goals or my learning strategies? • What will I do differently in the future?

Figure 2.2
The GAME plan.

your approach to learning tasks, to develop relevant skills that are important to you, and prepares you for lifelong learning.

Set Goals

During the first phase in the GAME plan, you set goals for learning. In order to stay up-to-date with current and emerging technologies for teaching and learning, you will need to constantly assess your technology integration skills in order to identify the new knowledge and skills you need. For example, you may want to know more about how you might use blogs in your classroom. First, you identify what you already know about the topic in order to identify what you need to learn. To select your goals and strategy, you need to answer questions such as:

- What do I want to know or be able to do?
- What do I already know about the topic?
- How will I know I have been successful?

Take Action

After you've identified your learning goals, you need to take action to meet those goals. So, if you want to learn more about the educational applications of blogs, you could take a class. You could ask others. You could research information online or in books. You might even ask your students. All of these approaches are valid and have a place in your lifelong learning journey. Before you take action, you need to determine the answers to the following questions:

- What information do I need to meet my goal?
- What learning strategy will I use?
- What resources are needed?

Of course, after you determine what information is needed to meet your goal, you'll search for and locate the needed information, using the resources you identified. And you'll also implement the learning strategies you've selected.

Monitor

As you take action to achieve your learning goals, you'll need to *monitor* whether you are making sufficient progress toward your goals and reflect on whether the strategies you have chosen are working. Are you learning enough about how to use blogs in the classroom? What about your time commitment? Are you making progress quick enough, or do you need to search for better resources to help you reach your goal? Is the topic too big or too complex? Consider questions such as:

- Am I finding the information I need?
- What patterns are emerging from the information sources?
- Do I need to modify my action plan?

Evaluate and Extend

During the *evaluate* stage in self-directed learning, you'll determine whether you met your goal and reflect on whether your approach worked or whether you should modify your strategies for the future. As you evaluate your learning progress, the most important question is whether you were successful in meeting your goals. For example, did you learn enough about blogs to apply your new knowledge to your classroom activities? How can you *extend* what you learned from this experience to your future learning efforts? Seek answers to questions such as:

- Have I met my learning goals?
- If not, should I modify my goals or my learning strategies?
- What will I do differently in the future?

The GAME Plan for Learning about Technology: An Example

We've mentioned the constantly changing landscape of computer technologies, but let's explore those ideas further in order to demonstrate the GAME plan technique that we'll use throughout this book. Imagine that your task is to evaluate a new technology for use in your classroom. This actually is something many teachers do on a routine basis. If you were asked to do this, how would you go about tackling this task? For the purpose of this example, let's say you selected a global positioning system (GPS) as a technology of interest to you.

The first step in the GAME plan is to set Goals. At this stage, you'll identify what you need to know as specifically as possible. Imagine that you are a second grade teacher. You've heard that some teachers are exploring the use of global positioning systems in education. You wonder whether this is something you should think about for your classroom. You'll also recall what you know about GPS already, based on your experience with the one in your car. You have some idea of the capabilities and limitations of a GPS but probably have a few questions related to your classroom needs: How have they been used in classrooms? How can they enhance student learning? Would they be appropriate for second graders? Questions such as these help you focus your goals. You want to learn more about global positioning systems, but your information needs would be quite different from those of a high school teacher or an engineer exploring the same topic. So you need to set subgoals (or objectives) for your information search. Your subgoals may be to

- determine how the capabilities of a GPS can be used in instruction
- determine how a GPS can enhance learning for second grade students
- identify the limitations of using these systems within the classroom

Next, you'll take Action. You might ask colleagues about their uses of GPS at your school, at a professional conference, or by e-mail or telephone. You might search the web for information on educational uses of this technology, using a variety of search tools (see Figure 2.3). You may use search terms such as "global positioning systems lesson plans second grade." Although the web is a convenient source of information, you might include other approaches such as talking to knowledgeable experts via e-mail, phone, or face-to-face; reading books; or visiting a store with GPS units. The best way to locate relevant information is to use a combination of search methods.

As you collect information, you'll Monitor your learning. In all likelihood, you'll find a wide variety of information. You'll probably find information from organizations that are selling this technology and from schools and universities, government and professional organizations, and private individuals with an interest in the technology. Often, if you're searching the web, you'll find excerpts from conversations that took place on message boards and in user groups. You're even likely to come across a few teacher blogs or lesson plans that describe how other teachers have used GPS systems. Some of the information may be highly technical, other information may be applicable in vary narrow situations, and some of it is probably of

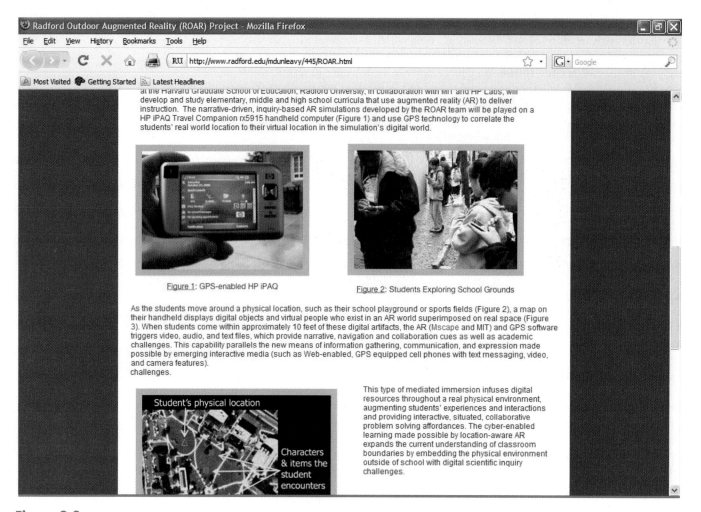

Figure 2.3
Information on educational uses of GPS technologies is readily available on the web.
Source: Image courtesy of Matt Dunleavy, Radford Outdoor Augmented Reality (ROAR) project http://www.radford.edu/mdunleavy/445/ROAR.html

questionable value. Each of these groups and individuals has their own particular slant on the technology.

As you review the information you found, you'll ask yourself, "Is my plan working? Am I finding the information I need?" In order to determine whether your action plan is successful, you might classify your information into that which addresses each of your subgoals: 1) how the capabilities of a GPS can be used in instruction, 2) how a GPS might enhance learning for second grade students, and 3) limitations of using these systems within the classroom. From this, you'll determine whether you need to modify your action plan.

As you evaluate your learning, you will determine if you have successfully found the answer to your questions about the use of a GPS in your classroom. In other words, you will evaluate whether or not you have achieved your specific learning goals. If not, consider whether you need to modify your goals or your learning strategy. If your learning strategy has consisted of searching the web, perhaps you need to broaden your information sources to include colleagues and regional experts such as your science curriculum coordinator. Or if you have focused on second-grade students in terms of your learning goals, perhaps you need to expand your focus to encompass educational uses of GPS across multiple grade levels. If your learning strategy has been successful, think about how you can extend the results of your learning to some future task. Have you learned something that will help you use a

APPLY TO PRACTICE

The GAME Plan

1. Practice using the GAME plan to guide your self-directed learning about a specific technology of interest.
   - **Set Goals**: Select a current or emerging technology of interest to you. Set specific goals for learning about this topic.
   - **Take Action**: Although there are many ways to gain information to meet your learning goals, for this activity, search the web for information on your technology of interest. If needed, see the tutorial on the textbook's companion website on *How to search the web*.
   - **Monitor Your Learning**: As you collect information, consider whether you are gaining the knowledge you need to meet your learning goals. Do you need to modify your learning strategy?
   - **Evaluate and Extend Your Learning**: Have you met your learning goals? What have you learned about what the technology can and cannot do? If your learning strategies were unsuccessful, what will you do differently in the future? If your strategies were successful, what have you learned that will be helpful in the future?
2. Discuss your experiences with a group of peers, either online or in class. How were your experiences similar to theirs? How were they different?

GPS in your classroom? Have you found a good source of information about current and emerging technologies that may be useful to you in the future?

Summary of the GAME Plan for Self-Directed Learning

As you set goals, take action, monitor your learning, and evaluate your progress, you take control of your own learning process. As a self-directed lifelong learner, you'll be able to respond to the rapid and continuous technological changes that inevitably will occur during your professional career, keep your skills up-to-date, and better meet the needs of your students today and in the future. Let's examine each of the steps in more detail.

Self-Assess Technology Skills and Set Goals

Learning, in general, and about technology specifically, is an ongoing process. In Chapter 1 you were asked to identify the technology standards that you are expected to meet as a teacher in your state and to begin to think about how you would incorporate technologies in your own teaching. As with any self-directed learning, updating your knowledge and skills begins with assessing your learning needs in order to identify your learning goals. You need to determine what you know and what you need to know before determining how you'll get there. To begin the process, reflect on your current technology skills, using the ISTE standards around which this book is organized (see Figure 1.6 in Chapter 1).

The student standards (NETS-S) also can serve as a starting point for you to assess your own technology skills. After all, you will be responsible for modeling the behaviors included in the student standards. Luckily, there is a lot of overlap between NETS for Teachers (NETS-T), around which this book is organized, and the NETS for Students (NETS-S). Therefore, as you are considering ways that you can meet the required teacher standards, you can simultaneously consider ways to help your students meet the required student standards.

As you may have noticed in Figure 1.7, the student standards are written in fairly general terms. Fortunately, ISTE has developed student technology profiles that provide examples of the types of activities students should be able to do to demonstrate

Table 2.1	Student Performance Profiles	
Grades (Ages)	Performance Profiles	NETS-S
PK-2 (4-8)	Illustrate and communicate original ideas and stories using digital tools and media-rich resources.	1, 2
PK-2 (4-8)	Identify, research, and collect data on an environmental issue using digital resources and propose a developmentally appropriate solution.	1, 3, 4
PK-2 (4-8)	Engage in learning activities with learners from multiple cultures through e-mail and other electronic means.	2, 6
PK-2 (4-8)	In a collaborative work group, use a variety of technologies to produce a digital presentation or product in a curriculum area.	1, 2, 6
PK-2 (4-8)	Find and evaluate information related to a current or historical person or event using digital resources.	3
PK-2 (4-8)	Use simulations and graphical organizers to explore and depict patterns of growth such as the life cycles of plants and animals.	1, 3, 4
PK-2 (4-8)	Demonstrate the safe and cooperative use of technology.	5
PK-2 (4-8)	Independently apply digital tools and resources to address a variety of tasks and problems.	4, 6
PK-2 (4-8)	Communicate about technology using developmentally appropriate and accurate terminology.	6
PK-2 (4-8)	Demonstrate the ability to navigate in virtual environments such as electronic books, simulation software, and websites.	6
3-5 (8-11)	Produce a media-rich digital story about a significant local event based on first-person interviews.	1, 2, 3, 4
3-5 (8-11)	Use digital-imaging technology to modify or create works of art for use in a digital presentation.	1, 2, 6
3-5 (8-11)	Recognize bias in digital resources while researching an environmental issue with guidance from the teacher.	3, 4
3-5 (8-11)	Select and apply digital tools to collect, organize, and analyze data to evaluate theories or test hypotheses.	3, 4, 6
3-5 (8-11)	Identify and investigate a global issue and generate possible solutions using digital tools and resources.	3, 4
3-5 (8-11)	Conduct science experiments using digital instruments and measuring devices.	4, 6
3-5 (8-11)	Conceptualize, guide, and manage individual or group learning projects using digital planning tools with teacher support.	4, 6
3-5 (8-11)	Practice injury prevention by applying a variety of ergonomic strategies when using technology.	5
3-5 (8-11)	Debate the effect of existing and emerging technologies on individuals, society, and the global community.	5, 6
3-5 (8-11)	Apply previous knowledge of digital technology operations to analyze and solve current hardware and software problems.	4, 6
6-8 (11-14)	Describe and illustrate a content-related concept or process using a model, simulation, or concept-mapping software.	1, 2
6-8 (11-14)	Create original animations or videos documenting school, community, or local events.	1, 2, 6
6-8 (11-14)	Gather data, examine patterns, and apply information for decision making using digital tools and resources.	1, 4
6-8 (11-14)	Participate in a cooperative learning project in an online learning community.	2
6-8 (11-14)	Evaluate digital resources to determine the credibility of the author and publisher and the timeliness and accuracy of the content.	3
6-8 (11-14)	Employ data-collection technology such as probes, handheld devices, and geographic mapping systems to gather, view, analyze, and report results for content-related problems.	3, 4, 6
6-8 (11-14)	Select and use the appropriate tools and digital resources to accomplish a variety of tasks and to solve problems.	3, 4, 6
6-8 (11-14)	Use collaborative electronic authoring tools to explore common curriculum content from multicultural perspectives with other learners.	2, 3, 4, 5
6-8 (11-14)	Integrate a variety of file types to create and illustrate a document or presentation.	1, 6
6-8 (11-14)	Independently develop and apply strategies for identifying and solving routine hardware and software problems.	4, 6
9-12 (14-18)	Design, develop, and test a digital learning game to demonstrate knowledge and skills related to curriculum content.	1, 4
9-12 (14-18)	Create and publish an online art gallery with examples and commentary that demonstrate an understanding of different historical periods, cultures, and countries.	1, 2
9-12 (14-18)	Select digital tools or resources to use for a real-world task and justify the selection base on their efficiency and effectiveness.	3, 6
9-12 (14-18)	Employ curriculum-specific simulations to practice critical-thinking processes.	1, 4
9-12 (14-18)	Identify a complex global issue, develop a systematic plan of investigation, and present innovative sustainable solutions.	1, 2, 3, 4

Grades (Ages)	Performance Profiles	NETS-S
9-12 (14-18)	Analyze the capabilities and limitations of current and emerging technology resources and assess their potential to address personal, social, lifelong learning, and career needs.	4, 5, 6
9-12 (14-18)	Design a website that meets accessibility requirements.	1, 5
9-12 (14-18)	Model legal and ethical behaviors when using information and technology by properly selecting, acquiring, and citing resources.	3, 5
9-12 (14-18)	Create media-rich presentations for other students on the appropriate and ethical use of digital tools and resources.	1, 5
9-12 (14-18)	Configure and troubleshoot hardware, software, and network systems to optimize their use for learning and productivity.	4, 6

Source: Profiles for Technology (ICT) Literate Students. Retrieved November 20, 2007, from http://www.iste.org/inhouse/nets/cnets/students/pdf/ NETS-S_Student_Profiles.PDF. Copyright © 2007, ISTE (International Society for Technology in Education), www.iste.org. All rights reserved.

APPLY TO PRACTICE

Assessing Your Skills

1. Select an appropriate technology assessment tool from the textbook's companion website.
2. Perform a self-assessment.
3. Identify and discuss gaps between what you know and what you should know.

competency in the required standards. A total of 40 profiles have been provided by ISTE. You will notice that the 40 profiles/competencies listed in Table 2.1 align with one or more of the six categories of student standards, listed in Figure 1.7. ISTE readily admits that these profiles simply represent examples of the types of activities students should learn how to do, rather than a "comprehensive curriculum, or even a minimally adequate one" (ISTE, 2007, p. 1.) Nonetheless, they do provide us with an idea of the types of activities that ISTE considers appropriate for demonstrating mastery of their most recent set of technology standards for students.

Examine the performance profiles listed in Table 2.1. Which of these skills do you already have? What do you still need to learn? If you feel confident in performing these tasks on your own, do you need to learn more about how to apply these skills to your teaching or how to develop these skills in your future students? Identify one or more learning goals that will enhance your ability to effectively integrate technologies within your teaching and learning. In the long run, if you are going to model all of these competencies successfully, you need to identify what you already know and what you still have to learn.

 WEB LINK

See the textbook's companion website for a list of self-assessment tools you can use to identify

Develop an Action Plan

Think for a while about the technology-related skills you already have. You can probably conduct research through searching the web, write papers using a word processor, and perform many other tasks using a computer. Think about how you developed those skills. Did you take a class? Did you learn from observation? Did you read a book or complete a tutorial? Did you ask questions of an expert or figure things out on your own? A careful consideration of your responses to these questions will tell you a lot about how you, personally, learn to use and apply technology. And this knowledge can help you learn about technology more easily in the future.

After reflecting on your preferred methods for learning technology-related skills, consider how you will take action to learn more. On one hand, you can attend formal university classes. In fact, you are probably enrolled in such a class right now. On the other hand, you can pursue informal learning opportunities by reading books, completing tutorials, asking others, or searching the web to find answers to your personal questions. In today's Internet-connected world, tried-and-true teaching strategies are available for you to access online. In other words, you can actually *use* technology to *learn more about* technology. As you well know, the Internet opens up a huge range of opportunities that you may not have locally. You can download lesson plans, or if you develop a lesson that works well, you can post it for others to download. "Teacher stores" and bookstores are at your fingertips. You'll find educational journals and magazines; subscription e-newsletters and eZines can deliver useful tips and new ideas to your desktop. And of course, you have access to a wealth of background resources and readings. You can find reference materials and others to talk with anytime, anywhere, with the click of a button. Now, this is not to suggest that you shouldn't also participate in local professional development opportunities; by all means, you should participate in the various opportunities available to you.

If you've never explored the many online resources available for teachers, you may want to begin by exploring the sites you locate during the Apply to Practice activity or using the resources listed on the textbook's companion website. If your learning goals include learning new software applications, you can use the GAME plan to facilitate your learning or explore the tutorial links on the companion website. As you review the online resources online, think about which of these tools could assist you in meeting your learning goals.

WEB LINK

Visit the textbook's companion website for a list of online tutorials from a number of hardware and software developers.

THE GAME PLAN

Learning New Software

Set Goals

Identify a piece of software that you would like to learn to use. Or perhaps you would like to learn to use a software program with which you are somewhat familiar to perform tasks that are new to you. For example, you may know how to use presentation software to support your lectures, but you want your students to use it to create interactive books.

Monitor

How well is the action you've selected helping you meet your goals? If you've selected an instructional manual, does it present things clearly and at an appropriate pace? Do workshops or other interactive settings meet your goals? Are you learning useful information or just reviewing skills you already know? Should you take a different action?

Take Action

Determine steps you can take to meet your goal within a reasonable timeline. You can explore an online tutorial or read an instructional manual. Perhaps there is someone you know who has advanced skills with the software and can show you how to use it. Your school or library may even sponsor mini-workshops on the software.

Evaluate and Extend

How effective were your actions in meeting your goals? What did you learn that you can incorporate into your practice? What do you think you still need to learn? Would you take different actions when learning a new software application in the future?

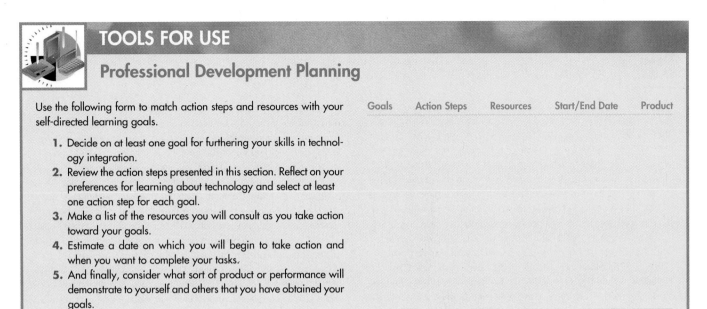

TOOLS FOR USE

Professional Development Planning

Use the following form to match action steps and resources with your self-directed learning goals.

1. Decide on at least one goal for furthering your skills in technology integration.
2. Review the action steps presented in this section. Reflect on your preferences for learning about technology and select at least one action step for each goal.
3. Make a list of the resources you will consult as you take action toward your goals.
4. Estimate a date on which you will begin to take action and when you want to complete your tasks.
5. And finally, consider what sort of product or performance will demonstrate to yourself and others that you have obtained your goals.

Goals	Action Steps	Resources	Start/End Date	Product

Monitoring and Evaluating Your Professional Growth

As in any self-directed learning activity, you need to set goals for your own professional growth, take action, then monitor and evaluate your progress toward obtaining your goals. In terms of technology use, you'll set goals based on your current skills and your vision of how you would like to integrate technology within your professional practice. You'll develop an action plan for achieving those goals. As you develop your plan for continued learning, consider how you will monitor and evaluate your progress toward meeting the goals of your plan. How will you know whether the resources you identified are helping you meet your goals? What product or performance might be needed to demonstrate to yourself and others that you have obtained your learning goals? Both self-monitoring and self-evaluation are considered essential components of self-directed learning.

The ability to monitor and evaluate your personal and professional decisions is enhanced through reflection both "in action" and "on action" (Schön, 1983). In reflecting "in action," you'll continually think about and modify your current behaviors based on the thought processes that occur simultaneously with the action. This relates to the monitor component in the GAME Plan. When reflecting "on action" you'll look back on what you did and think about what happened, why it happened, how the experience relates to other experiences, and how it should influence future behaviors—the evaluation component. As a reflective learner, you will think about what has been effective in the past, but also continually monitor and evaluate what is effective for you now.

You can use several techniques to facilitate your own reflective practice. On one hand, the simple act of keeping a journal can support reflection. Examining case studies, or teacher stories, such as those that appear in this text, also provide an opportunity for reflective thinking. Key to effective reflection is the ability to go beyond a simple description of what happened to consider why it happened, how it is connected to other events, and what adjustments should be made to subsequent actions based on this understanding. In Chapter 12, you'll learn a systematic form of reflective practice known as action research, also referred to as teacher research or teacher inquiry. Action research appears to be a particularly effective way to monitor and evaluate classroom innovations, such as new technology uses. But for now, let's turn our attention to another common method used to evaluate and reflect on professional practice: the portfolio.

TOOLS FOR USE

Practicing Reflection

You are now aware that a major focus of this book is to help you become self-directed, lifelong learners. Self-directed learning implies that you take it upon yourself to become your own teacher, that you take the initiative to determine your goals for learning, implement strategies to meet those goals, and monitor your own learning. A key method of monitoring your learning is through the process of self-reflection. You may use self-reflection informally in different settings, such as when you are studying, taking a test, or checking your work on a project. Reflections in a portfolio are more formal.

If you've never written a reflection on your own work, you may find it takes some time to develop the skill. Some experts (Hatton & Smith, 1995; Moon, 2001) note that there are different levels of reflection. When you first start writing reflections, you may find that they are more descriptive than reflective. A descriptive account may be a list of events that happened during a class or lesson. For example, a description of a class may include the following statement: "I used a PowerPoint presentation that included short segments from popular movies to accompany my demonstration of animation techniques."

It's important to be able to describe what has occurred, but reflection goes deeper. Reflection begins when you start to think about the events you have described. You start to analyze some of the events and may try to determine how you behaved, felt, or thought during those events. A reflective statement on the demonstration of animation techniques might include the following statement: "I thought I was really well prepared but I discovered that I had way too many slides for my 15-minute presentation. I guess I just had not planned for the time it would take to actually show the movies in addition to making my speech. Because of this, I had to rush through the end. I fear I did not make a very good impression!"

Of course, reflections can go much deeper. As you become more comfortable with writing reflections, you may be able to step back a bit and consider others' points of view. You may express your emotions or feelings, as well, and consider how those influenced the situation. In what some call **critical reflection**, you try to understand these different perspectives and use that understanding to set goals for your future behavior or learning. Continuing with the animation techniques example, consider the level of reflection in the following, "I certainly learned something though! I was probably a little too confident—I didn't actually practice the timing of the program, just ran through it to make sure all the slides loaded correctly and that the content was correct. Since I rushed through the demonstration, the class got a little confused and I had to spend a lot of time answering questions. Boy, in the future, I'll make sure I practice my presentation—out loud—and time myself. I did enjoy the process of developing the presentation though. It was a lot of fun to find snippets from popular movies to demonstrate the animation techniques I talked about."

Writing deeper reflections takes time and practice. As you craft reflections for your portfolio (whether in written, audio, or video format), keep in mind a few pointers:

- Write in first person.
- Read your reflections out loud, to yourself or a friend, to determine whether they are clear and express the level of reflection you desire.
- If the reflection is primarily for someone else, focus on describing the artifact and explain why it is there.
- If the reflection is primarily for you, focus on crafting a critical reflection that helps you take further steps in your professional growth.

Documenting Growth and Competency through Portfolios

Portfolios have been used to document student progress for years. Perhaps you or your teachers maintained a portfolio documenting your learning as you progressed through elementary school. You may have attended one of the many schools that utilized writing portfolios. Or perhaps you prepared an art portfolio in high school. From these experiences, you know that a portfolio is an organized collection of artifacts that are compiled for a specific purpose. In many cases, portfolios are used to demonstrate your skills and knowledge to others. Teachers have long used portfolios to document their skills and growth—from their initial teacher preparation programs through their teaching careers. Since portfolios can be used to document progress over time, they provide a means to reflect on, facilitate, and document your individual learning.

Educators describe the uses of portfolios in many different ways. For the purposes of this book, consider the following three categories of portfolio use:

- *demonstrate* compliance with specific requirements so that others can *assess* your skills, as in a portfolio that you would create to document your attainment of course goals/state standards or to obtain teacher certification or licensure (referred to as assessment portfolios).

- *present* and possibly market your skills to others, as in a portfolio that you would use to showcase your skills during your job search process (referred to as employment portfolios).
- *reflect* on your current skills and future learning needs to guide your individual learning and professional development (referred to as professional development portfolios).

The popularity of **assessment portfolios** is due largely to the belief that they represent an authentic form of assessing student learning. Chapter 7 includes information on how you can use portfolios to assess your students; here we focus on how your own skills might be assessed or evaluated. Assessment portfolios can differ in the amount of control you have in selecting and arranging the artifacts within them. Often, you may be required to include specific artifacts in order to demonstrate how you meet particular objectives or standards for assessment. Typically, such portfolios are evaluated using predetermined rubrics. In some cases, you may build your portfolio as you engage in the tasks of a curriculum. Individual artifacts may be evaluated as they are developed as part of regular class work. In other cases, you may have the freedom to select artifacts that you believe demonstrate your best work. In this case, you are responsible for documenting how you think a particular artifact demonstrates mastery of a standard or course objective. For example, combining artifacts of early work with well-polished examples is one way you can illustrate growth over time.

Employment portfolios showcase achievement in relation to a desired position or profession. Typically, you have complete control over the look and feel of this type of portfolio as well as the artifacts included. An employment portfolio should represent you well, demonstrating who you are at this particular point in time. The goal is to showcase your skills. As you develop an employment portfolio, think about your audience and try to create a persuasive document that reflects how you are best suited for the position for which you are applying.

Whereas the employment portfolio is developed for future employers and the assessment portfolio is developed for your teachers, the **professional development portfolio** is for you. One of the most rewarding uses of the portfolio is as a tool for individual learning and professional development. It provides a place for you to collect and reflect on artifacts that document your professional growth over time from a very personal point of view. You may even use it to identify areas for future learning and then document your progress toward those learning goals. These portfolios provide you with a place to celebrate your uniqueness while focusing on lifelong, self-directed learning. In all likelihood, the other portfolios will represent a subset of your professional development portfolio.

At the end of each chapter in this book, you will notice a "Your portfolio" box, where you will be asked to create artifacts that document your progress toward meeting the standards outlined in ISTE NETS-T. This assessment portfolio can be used to demonstrate your developing competencies in technology integration within the classroom and demonstrate to prospective employers how you meet the ISTE NETS-T. Your portfolio can enhance your professional development and showcase your skills to future employers as well.

Portfolio Development Tools

A major consideration in the selection of digital portfolio development tools should be the ease with which you can reuse the artifacts in a different context. When preparing an *assessment* portfolio, as you are in this book, you need to assemble a collection of documents and artifacts that demonstrate the achievement of specific standards or objectives. Often, the required items are mandated by someone else. Frequently, the format and organization are prescribed as well. When preparing an *employment* portfolio, you should select items that showcase your skills and present you in the best possible light. There, too, you may want to demonstrate how the

THE GAME PLAN

Portfolio Examples

In this book, you are encouraged to develop a portfolio to demonstrate your mastery of the ISTE NETS-T by completing the "Your Portfolio" activities at the end of each chapter.

Set Goals

Determine the type of portfolio that best meets your current goals. Whether you are demonstrating mastery of required competencies, documenting your own personal and professional development, or entering the teaching field at the beginning of your career, there are many examples to support your specific purposes.

Take Action

Find examples of employment, assessment, and professional development portfolios. Ask your friends or teachers if they have examples.

There are also several excellent portfolio resources available on the web.

Monitor

Are you finding examples of each type? Which examples best match your goal? Do you need to locate additional examples before you create a portfolio for your own use?

Evaluate and Extend

Classify the examples that you find as assessment, employment, professional development, or "other" portfolios. What are some distinguishing characteristics of each type? What characteristics or strategies do you think you might adopt or adapt for your own use? Discuss your conclusions with your peers to determine how you might generate a portfolio to meet your goal.

---

artifacts in your portfolio demonstrate your mastery of standards, such as the ISTE NETS-T. When preparing a *professional development* portfolio, you compile artifacts for your own learning and reflective practice, so these types of portfolios are never really completed. By far, the best approach is to create a professional development portfolio as a tool for lifelong learning and then to use a selected subset of that information, as needed, for assessment and employment portfolios.

Although there are several forms of portfolio development software, no specialized software is needed. Just about any software application that can link pages (or artifacts) can be used. The pages can be as simple as a series of word-processed documents that link to other artifacts. Tools that have been used to develop portfolios include:

- Presentation software
- Word processors
- Spreadsheet software
- Multimedia software
- WYSIWYG or HTML generators
- Weblog (blogging) software
- Content management systems
- Commercial portfolio development products
- Proprietary portfolio products, often developed by colleges or universities
- Open source tools

This textbook's companion website includes examples of portfolios created with some of these tools. It also links to step-by-step instructions to develop your own portfolio using a variety of common web development and productivity software tools.

You should use caution when selecting tools to create artifacts for your portfolio as well as the actual portfolio development tools to ensure that you can continue to access and use your portfolio over time. For example, some of us who have been teaching for a while may have old files saved on floppy disks, yet no longer have

WEB LINK

Dr. Helen Barrett has developed electronic portfolios using a wide variety of common tools. Visit the textbook's companion website for links to further information about Dr. Barrett's work with electronic portfolios and for examples of portfolios created with common software applications.

access to a computer with a floppy drive. This type of problem occurs routinely as software companies discontinue applications or new hardware and software standards are developed. As you select among potential development tools, you may want to consider the following factors:

- *Your skills.* We encourage you to increase your skills but it's important to select a tool that can help you create your portfolio without being so hard you spend all your time learning how to use it.
- *Ease with which you can cross-reference artifacts.* It should be easy to create and edit links among the items in your portfolio and to provide for simple navigation to all areas within your portfolio.
- *Ability to integrate information from a variety of formats.* Make sure all exhibits of your work (e.g., audio, video, images, documents in various formats) can be displayed easily with appropriate fidelity.
- *Access to the tool throughout your career.* Specialized portfolio development software isn't the best tool choice if you won't have access to it after you graduate. If your college or university does use such a system, consider how the artifacts in your portfolio can be presented in an alternative method, whether on a web page or in a series of linked documents.
- *Ability to display portfolio contents in ways that will be useful for multiple purposes and audiences.* Consider the many uses you may have for your portfolio: You may want to post an employment portfolio on the web for potential employers to view and also to create a print version to put in a notebook to take to interviews.
- *Ease of updating.* For a portfolio to be useful over time it must be dynamic. Select a tool that permits you to update pages quickly, again focusing on presenting your accomplishments to the intended audience rather than manipulating a complex tool.
- *Need for confidentiality.* If you want to keep any of the materials private, perhaps your personal reflections or sensitive information about students with whom you work, you may need to use a program that allows password protection of selected content, especially if you choose to post your portfolio on the web.

Steps in Portfolio Development

No matter what type of portfolio you develop, there are several steps in the process (see Figure 2.4). You need to:

1. Define your purpose, audience, distribution medium, and development tool.
2. Design your portfolio organization and layout.
3. Develop the portfolio.
4. Deliver it to its intended audience.

Define

During the initial phase of portfolio development, you need to define the purpose and audience for your portfolio, as these factors will influence the content and the look of the finished product. The audience for an assessment portfolio consists of the evaluators of the product. When in college, this most likely will be your professors; when in the workplace, it may be a district or school technology coordinator charged with documenting your competency on standards mandated by the state or school district. You may be the only audience for a professional development portfolio, or you may decide to share it with colleagues in order to stimulate conversations around specific professional development issues. Most professional development portfolios don't need a lot of "bells and whistles." And finally, your future employers are the logical audience for your employment portfolio, so you want this type of portfolio to be as polished as possible.

Portfolio Development

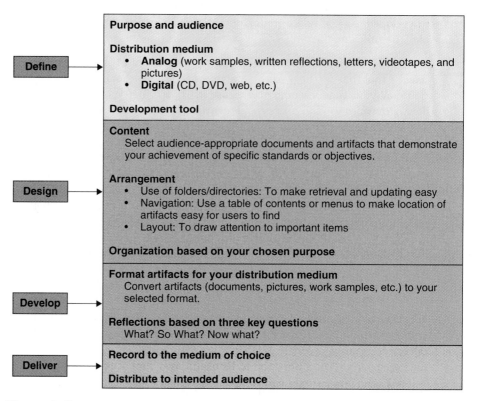

Figure 2.4
Steps in portfolio development.

Next, you need to decide on a distribution medium and corresponding development tool. Do you want to distribute your portfolio on CDs, post it on the web, create a notebook, or have the option of sharing any of these formats? Should you create it using a word processor, web development software, a database program, presentation software, or one of the other options mentioned above? In the previous section, we discussed several factors that you may need to consider as you make your decision.

Design

Once you have determined your audience, purpose, distribution medium, and development tool, you can select audience-appropriate artifacts and design the overall organization of your portfolio. In designing your portfolio, think about what you want to include and why you want to include it. Do you want to include video clips of your teaching? Interviews with your supervising teacher or students? Examples of student work? Lesson plans? As you identify the items that you want to include, plan for those items you may want to include in the future as well. This may mean designating space or a placeholder for items yet to be developed. At a minimum, portfolios consist of a collection of work samples. They may include paper items, videos, pictures, and projects.

Once you decide what you want to include in the portfolio, you need to decide on the best way to organize the materials. In terms of grouping and sequencing material, consider your purpose and audience. A chronological order of materials may be best if you're trying to demonstrate growth, or you may be required to organize your artifacts based on a rubric or checklist. If you are trying to demonstrate that you have met

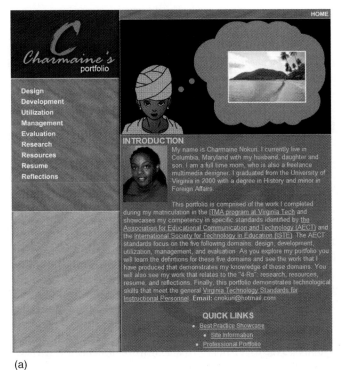

(a)   (b)

Figure 2.5
Examples of different portfolio designs.
Sources: Courtesy Charmaine Nokuri; http://edavenue.homestead.com/main1.html

certain standards, such as the ISTE NETS-T, you may group artifacts by each major standard, sometimes linking to, or replicating, artifacts that cover more than one standard.

Use common protocols for the medium you have selected to help people understand what is in your portfolio and how they can find it (see Figure 2.5). For example, books use tables of content and indices to help organize information. In a paper-based notebook, you may want to use dividers or tabs to organize your artifacts into sections that clearly identify the material within. Web pages and multimedia tools use navigation bars, buttons, and links. A consistent series of menus or links on every screen/page of your portfolio can help users understand where they are, what they are seeing, and how to navigate to the next section they'd like to review. Concept-mapping or flowcharting software can prove useful as you plan the organization of your portfolio. Like video and multimedia developers, you may want to create a storyboard of your proposed organization first. Depending on the size and scope of your portfolio, you may just need to create a list or outline. As you develop your organizing plan, consider the following factors:

- *How will you store and find the materials you need to create the portfolio?* Keep in mind that you will have to locate, retrieve, and update many of the items in your portfolio. Consider the use of folders or subdirectories on your computer to help you organize this process, and back up your work often.
- *How will the audience navigate through the artifacts?* The use of one or more menu pages may help someone viewing your portfolio easily locate sections of particular interest. It is better to use multiple pages with fewer topics per page than to confuse your audience by attempting to fit everything into a small number of pages.
- *How will you direct the audience's attention to important items within a page?* You want the audience to have a clear picture of what you are attempting to

convey. Consistent page layouts will help others locate items within a page, while formatting features can be used to direct attention to specific items on a page.

- *How will you tell your complete story?* A portfolio is often more than just a collection of artifacts. For many, reflections are an essential part of a portfolio that helps your audience understand what you selected and why. It is easier to collect your artifacts as they are being made, but if you plan to include reflective pieces, plan for them in your design so they can be added easily.

Develop

When the artifacts have been collected and the layout planned, it's time to actually develop the portfolio. If you're creating a digital portfolio, non-digital artifacts need to be converted to a digital format. This can involve photographing 3-dimensional items with a digital camera or scanning 2-dimensional objects (see Figure 2.6). Audio and video clips may need to be imported into your computer or digitized. Although it may sound like a lot of work to compile a portfolio, it can be rewarding to collect your work in one place.

You can also simplify the process by collecting artifacts as they are generated and later selecting the most appropriate ones for inclusion in your portfolio. For example, if you receive a positive letter or e-mail from a teacher or colleague, save a copy in a designated portfolio file or directory and later determine how it can be included. The same goes for pictures or videos you may collect that capture you working with students or examples of lesson plans or assignments you complete in your courses. You're not creating a scrapbook of every little detail of your life, so if you can save artifacts in one place as they are created, you can then select the best at a later date.

Typically, portfolios include reflective comments about how each piece fits into the larger framework of your learning progress. Professional development portfolios often include reflections related to three key questions: What? So what? and Now

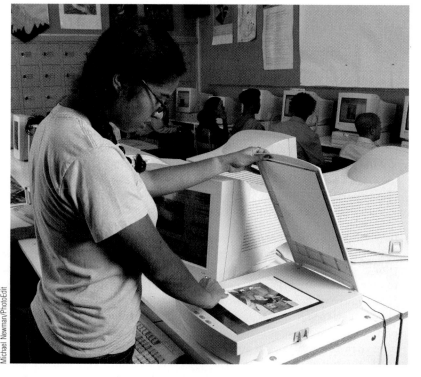

Figure 2.6
Converting paper-based artifacts to digital format.

what? (Kottkamp, 1990). "What" refers to the item selected for inclusion in the portfolio. "So what" refers to your rationale for selecting the artifact. In other words, why did you include the artifact? What does it mean to you and your personal growth? And when you consider "Now what," you'll reflect on your artifacts with the intent of looking ahead and setting new goals for future learning and professional development. You may want to include a more polished version of your reflections and learning goals in your assessment and employment portfolios as well. For example when preparing an assessment portfolio, consider how each item illustrates your achievement of the necessary standards or objectives. When preparing an employment portfolio, describe how each item illustrates specific skills.

Once the artifacts have been assembled, they can be organized and linked as needed. For example, one artifact may be used to demonstrate several competencies. Also, be sure to link your personal reflections on the artifacts.

Deliver

When you're creating an employment or assessment portfolio, you will need to present it to its intended audience. Digital portfolios can be distributed via the web, CDs, DVDs, or other storage media. Artifacts from the portfolios can even be printed and distributed in a notebook or collected in folders, which can be helpful in job interviews or other settings in which you don't have ready access to a computer.

Summary of Portfolio Development

As you go through this book, we suggest that you develop your own digital portfolio of artifacts to demonstrate your technology knowledge, skills, and attitudes. You will find that digital portfolios have several advantages over conventional paper-based portfolios. These advantages include:

- Easy to control as all artifacts can be conveniently located in one digital space
- Easy to cross-reference and link items
- Easy to repurpose the content to meet an alternative goal, for example to use artifacts collected for professional development for an employment or assessment portfolio
- Less bulky and take up less physical storage space than conventional collections
- Easy to distribute to individuals who want to view your work

WEB LINK

You can find and download a Portfolio Template on the textbook's companion website.

Chapter Summary

In this chapter, we introduced the idea of self-directed learning and asked you to reflect on how you learned to use technology tools in the past in order to identify methods that may work for you in the future. You explored the basic technology skills you and your students must have and completed a self-assessment of your current skills and knowledge. We asked you to think about how you have learned to use technology in the past in order to discover ways that you might best learn about it in the future. Finally, we introduced the use of portfolios as a means of supporting your personal growth over time and encouraged you to create your own digital portfolio.

In the next chapter, we turn our attention to ways that you can use your knowledge of teaching, learning, and technology to facilitate meaningful experiences for your students. Although you probably have known many excellent teachers, you may have few role models in the area of technology integration. As you lead the way and break new ground in the world of technology integration, self-directed learning will be essential. You and your peers have the opportunity to be the leaders in these efforts!

YOUR PORTFOLIO

1. Investigate whether your school or state has a portfolio system that you are required to contribute to for assessment purposes. If not, create the four key components of your portfolio:

   - *Define* your purpose, audience, and content.
   - *Design* your layout and organization. Don't forget to plan for future additions. You may want to organize your portfolio around the ISTE NETS-T addressed in this book.
   - *Develop* your portfolio template. Add the items that you developed in this chapter. Don't forget about the materials you'll add in the future.
   - Keep in mind the format in which you will ultimately *deliver* your portfolio as you plan and develop your materials.

   You may also want to use the Portfolio Template included on the textbook's companion website as a guide

2. Create a "technology resume." Use the skills and knowledge addressed in the ISTE performance profiles listed in this chapter as a starting point. Include

   - A list of the skills and knowledge you already possess to help you meet the challenges of effectively integrating technology into instruction
   - A list of the specific experiences that have contributed to your current knowledge in technology. This may include formal or informal professional development experiences.

3. Reflect on how you have learned about technology in the past and how those prior experiences will influence your learning in the future.

4. Locate a self-assessment instrument and use it to assess your ability to achieve the NETS-T standards or the technology standards required by your state or school district. Include the name of the instrument and the results of the assessment in your portfolio.

5. Develop a professional development action plan that includes:

   - One or more goal statements that resulted from your self-assessment or technology integration plans
   - An action plan that describes the steps you plan to take to meet your goals, the resources you will need, and how you anticipate using the resources to help you meet your goals
   - A projected timeline

References

Ertmer, P. A., & Newby, T. J. (1996). The expert learner: Strategic, self-regulated, and reflective. *Instructional Science*, 24, 1–24.

Gibbons, M. (2002). *The self-directed learning handbook*. San Francisco: Jossey Bass.

Hatton, N., & Smith, D. (1995). Reflection in teacher education—towards definition and implementation. *Teaching and Teacher Education*, 11(1), 33–49.

International Society for Technology in Education (ISTE). (2007). *Profiles for technology (ICT) literate students*. Eugene, OR: Author. Retrieved November 20, 2007, from http://www.iste.org/inhouse/nets/cnets/students/pdf/NETS-S_Student_Profiles.PDF

Kottkamp, R. (1990). Means for facilitating reflection. *Education and Urban Society*, 22, 182–203.

Moon, J. (2001). *Reflection in higher education learning. PDP working paper 4*. Generic centre. Retrieved April 12, 2006, from http://www.heacademy.ac.uk/resources/detail/ id72_Reflection_in_Higher_Education_Learning

Schön, D. A. (1983). *The reflective practitioner: How professionals think in action*. London: Temple Smith.

Zimmerman, B. J. (1990). Self-regulated learning and academic achievement: An overview. *Educational Psychologist*, 25(1), 3–17.

Zimmerman, B. J., Bonner, S., & Kovach, R. (1996). *Developing self-regulated learners: Beyond achievement to self-efficacy*. Washington, DC: American Psychological Association.

Jacek Chabraszewski/istockphoto.com

Supporting Student Creativity with Technology

Over the last few decades, as technology has become more prevalent in our everyday lives, both educators and business and industry leaders have increasingly stressed the importance of developing students' creative and critical thinking skills. As a nation, we want our students to be good thinkers, and we want our schools to teach thinking. One reason for this relatively new emphasis may be that new technologies have allowed computers to do the kinds of work that are readily automated (i.e., require little thinking), which then allows people to move into those jobs that computers *can't* do readily (i.e., require the ability to make subtle decisions and solve complex problems). A second reason is that, due to the rapid pace at which technologies are changing, the work place is also changing quickly. This puts a premium on teaching students *how* to learn as opposed to teaching specific skills that will be obsolete by the time they enter the workforce.

ISTE Standards addressed in this chapter

NETS-T 1. Facilitate and Inspire Student Learning and Creativity

Teachers use their knowledge of subject matter, teaching and learning, and technology to facilitate experiences that advance student learning, creativity, and innovation in both face-to-face and virtual environments. Teachers:

a. promote, support, and model creative and innovative thinking and inventiveness

b. engage students in exploring real-world issues and solving authentic problems using digital tools and resources

Note: Standards 1.c and 1.d are addressed in Chapter 4.

Outcomes

In this chapter, you will

- Develop and support students' creative thinking skills.
- Incorporate aspects of authentic instruction to promote creative and innovative thinking.
- Identify technologies that support the incorporation of real-world issues and authentic problems in learning experiences.
- Incorporate aspects of directed instruction to supplement instruction in response to student needs.
- Facilitate creative and innovative thinking within a context of meeting content standards.

NETS-T Standard 1 requires that "Teachers use their knowledge of subject matter, teaching and learning, and technology to facilitate experiences that advance student learning, creativity, and innovation in both face-to-face and virtual environments." In doing so, teachers "promote, support, and model creative and innovative thinking and inventiveness," "engage students in exploring real-world issues and solving authentic problems using digital tools and resources," "promote student reflection using collaborative tools to reveal and clarify students' conceptual understanding and thinking, planning, and creative processes," and "model collaborative knowledge construction by engaging in learning with students, colleagues, and others in face-to-face and virtual environments." In this chapter, we'll begin our discussion of Standard 1 by focusing on ways to promote creative thinking through authentic learning experiences. We'll conclude our discussion of Standard 1 in the next chapter.

Creative Thinking

If you were asked to define creative thinking, how would you do it? Most of you would probably use the words "original" or "unique." You might also refer to the word "innovative," or being able to "think outside the box." Most people would agree

---

STORIES FROM PRACTICE

Using Technology in a Learner-Centered Classroom

Marissa and Tonya both teach 6th grade language arts in a small, rural middle school with a one-to-one laptop initiative. That means that every student and every teacher in the school has access to a wireless laptop computer throughout the school day. When the laptop program began about five years ago, no one knew exactly how to use the technology to support meaningful teaching and learning. Lots of time was spent learning the various tool applications (e.g., word processing, presentation software, etc.) that were now available 24/7. Marissa and Tonya were no different. They would allow their students to type their papers and other assignments, and found many ways to use the tools themselves, but their classrooms still remained fairly teacher-centered. However, about two years into the laptop program, the school district received a large federal grant that enabled them to expand the laptop program to include the entire middle school and high school. And this time, the proposed program was not just about the computer; this time the program was situated within the context of a problem-based learning (PBL) pedagogy. That is, the technology was heralded as a

tool to enable authentic instruction in the form of problem-based learning. Marissa and Tonya attended special classes offered by the local university and participated in many, many after-school workshops to learn about PBL and how to implement it in their classrooms.

To get started, Marissa and Tonya attempted one multi-disciplinary unit their first year, converting a previous unit on the rainforest to one that used a more authentic approach. Instead of telling students why we need the rainforest and asking them to remember a list of reasons found in their readings, they allowed the students to explore different reasons on their own by anchoring the unit in the question, "Why should we care about the rainforest?" Students began by individually rank ordering a list of eight "belief" statements and then coming to consensus with fellow group members on their top two beliefs (e.g., "The tropical rain forest is home to many rare animals and plants. Destroying tropical rain forests could make these species extinct." "The tropical rain forest is home to different peoples. No one has the right to destroy these peoples' homes and

ways of life."). This initial activity quickly engaged students in a variety of important issues related to rainforest deforestation and gave them reasons to search for additional evidence to support their beliefs. Students searched the Internet, library books, and other available classroom resources (CD-ROMs and videos) to find information that could support their beliefs, converted the information to charts and graphs using spreadsheets, and then made presentations using presentation software to their classmates to convince them of the importance of their reasons for saving the rainforest.

According to Marissa and Tonya, students showed more interest and engagement in this unit than in previous years and were very vocal in their enthusiasm for the *way* the unit was run. They liked making choices, working in groups, and using technology to make persuasive presentations. And best of all, they seemed to really engage with the content, becoming quite passionate about what they could do to save the rainforest.

Source: Adapted from Simons, K. D., & Ertmer, P. A. (2005/2006).

that creative thinkers are able to generate a large number of original ideas. But there's more involved than just generating ideas. Creative thinkers also are able to determine which of those ideas are the best ones to use. How do they decide this? Typically, creative thinkers rely on a combination of: 1) their knowledge of the content domain, 2) heuristic knowledge or "tricks of the trade," (i.e., rules of thumb), 3) learning strategies (e.g., rehearsal, analogies, flowcharting), and 4) metacognitive strategies (i.e., reflecting on their learning processes) (Collins, Brown, & Holum, 1991). Creative thinkers pay close attention to their thinking processes as they engage in these activities, monitoring and evaluating the effectiveness of their thoughts and actions.

Researchers in the area of creativity have identified several techniques that contribute to the generation of original ideas. Creative thinkers are able to examine ideas from various perspectives, make inferences, and elaborate on their thinking (Marzano & Arrendondo, 1986; Raths et al., 1986; Sternberg & Baron, 1985). In addition, they use analogy or metaphors to think through novel problems, reasoning from examples or similar situations to consider possible courses of action (Raths et al., 1986; Sternberg & Spear-Swerling, 1996). As they engage in the process of idea selection, they analyze their ideas through questioning and comparing each new idea to previous ones (Black, 2005; Marzano et al., 1988). After considering possible scenarios, they synthesize ideas through organizing, interpreting, sorting, and summarizing. Finally, they evaluate ideas by judging the logic, value, and worth of the ideas, and generalizing their ideas to new situations (Nickerson, 1984; Paul & Elder, 2004; Raths et al., 1986).

In addition to using these types of techniques, creative individuals possess certain characteristics. They are motivated, flexible in their thinking, and have the confidence to act on their ideas despite the awareness that they do not know for sure how their ideas will play out (Black, 2005). Furthermore, when teachers display these types of creative qualities and engage in creative tasks, the creative achievement of their students also increases (Craft, 2001).

In this book, you will learn content knowledge and "tricks of the trade" that will contribute to your ability to model creative and innovative thinking. You will learn strategies to control and self-monitor your knowledge construction process. We'll introduce you to a variety of ideas to stimulate your ability to generate original ideas. And you'll learn how to use the knowledge you gain to analyze, synthesize, and evaluate your thinking in order to select the best ideas to apply in your classroom. Throughout, we hope that you will develop the attitudes and dispositions necessary for creative thinking: motivation to teach and learn in new and inventive ways, the flexibility to consider multiple perspectives on the issues you face as a classroom teacher, and the self-confidence to move forward into uncharted territory.

Types of Creative Thinking

Creative thinking involves higher-order thinking, which Wegerif (2002) defined as "complex thinking that requires effort and produces valued outcomes. These outcomes are not predictable because the process of higher-order thinking is not mechanical" (p. 2). This is consistent with the way we apply creative thinking in real-life situations. Such complex situations are seldom clearly defined and often involve multiple issues and possibilities. When creative thinking is needed you must be ready to consider multiple possibilities, expect to encounter obstacles, and employ your judgment as you seek the best approach. By involving students in these types of creative thinking tasks, you facilitate and inspire high levels of engagement in the content to be learned and thus promote deep learning.

Creative thinking is not a single process or skill. Rather, it involves many different cognitive skills. Many different types of thinking (e.g., critical thinking, divergent thinking, deductive reasoning) make up creative thinking. For the sake of clarity we describe a few of these specific types of thinking here. However, for simplicity's sake, we will use the term creative thinking throughout the rest of this book to encompass all of these variations. Several types of creative thinking are described next. Which of these terms are familiar to you? How are they similar? Different?

- *Divergent thinking.* A type of creative thinking that starts from a common point and moves outward to a variety of perspectives. To foster divergent thinking, teachers ask open-ended questions to prompt diverse or unique thinking among students. Some examples include: "What predictions can you make about the upcoming hurricane season?" "How might technology in the year 2100 differ from today?" "Based on this rainfall data, what can you infer about the corn production for the upcoming year?"
- *Convergent thinking.* A type of thinking that attempts to bring together thoughts from different perspectives in order to achieve a common understanding or conclusion. Convergent thinking enables students to use sound reasoning and common sense to analyze possible solutions or responses in order to select the one with the most potential, based on a set of criteria. Questions that would elicit convergent thinking include, "How does a sundial work?" "In what ways is a poem like an artistic drawing?" "Which route would provide the quickest way to get from Denver to San Diego?"
- *Innovation.* A type of divergent thinking that aims to produce something that is original and of value. It involves generating and developing ideas, hypothesizing, imagining possibilities, and seeking new solutions. Questions to stimulate innovation include those that prompt students to consider other alternatives, such as "What would happen if . . . ?" "How many different ways can you solve this problem?" Alternately, they may require students to take a different perspective, such as "How would a politician feel about stem cell research? A priest or minister? A parent of a child with disabilities?"
- *Critical thinking.* A type of convergent thinking that determines the validity or value of something. Sometimes called analytical thinking, it involves precise, persistent, objective analysis. Sample questions include: "How are these ideas similar?" "What is the main claim of the editorial? What evidence supports it? What assumptions underlie it?"
- *Inductive thinking.* A type of reasoning that moves from parts to the whole, from examples to generalizations. Students might be asked to answer the following: "What pattern do you observe?" "Where have we seen this before?" "What might cause this pattern?"
- *Deductive thinking.* A type of reasoning that moves from the whole to its parts, from generalizations to underlying concepts to examples. Sample questions include: "What are the similar components of these two objects?" "What are some examples of this principle?" "Is this an accurate example of this rule?" "How does this example relate to the rule?"

Although there are unique aspects to each of these types of thinking, there are also a number of common features. Table 3.1 presents features commonly associated with higher-order or creative thinking, as well as descriptions of how these characteristics manifest themselves in the problems or situations that call for creative thinking.

Summary of Creative Thinking

While "creative thinking" is a phrase that gets thrown around a lot, it's not usually defined, and to make matters even more complicated, it's typically described as either an outcome, or a component, of a variety of different approaches and types of thinking: inquiry learning, interdisciplinary learning, critical thinking, problem solving, informed decision making, knowledge construction, inductive reasoning, reflective thinking, and innovation, to name just a few. In the next section, you'll notice that many of these labels appear as different variations of, or approaches to, authentic

Table 3.1	Characteristics of Creative Thinking
Creative Thinking Is/ Involves:	Implications for You and Your Students
Non-algorithmic	Path of action not fully specified in advance; multiple paths are available
Complex	The entire path is not evident from any single vantage point; multiple vantage points are needed
Multiple solutions	Single solutions are uncommon
Nuanced judgment and interpretation	Conflicting information is often present; interpretations and judgments are needed
Multiple criteria	Presence of multiple criteria can lead to conflicts as each of the various criteria are applied
Uncertainty	Important factors frequently are unknown; given information is not always relevant
Self-direction	Students are expected to make choices based on learning goals and self-monitoring of the problem-solving processes
Imposing meaning	Apparent disorder needs to be structured and contradictions need to be reconciled
Effortful	The elaborations and judgments involved in higher-order thinking require substantial mental work.

Source: Based on Resnick (1987).

APPLY TO PRACTICE

Supporting Creative Thinking with Technology

1. Think about a classroom you have observed lately. Describe one example of students' technology use.
2. To what extent was technology used to develop creative thinking and reasoning skills? Describe the technology and the specific type of thinking skill that was addressed.
3. If the technology was not used to promote creative thinking, can you make suggestions for how to modify the activity to encourage creative thinking? Would a different technology suit the content being addressed more effectively?

instruction. That's because creativity is often developed through an authentic instructional approach. In other words, the characteristics of authentic instruction (autonomous, active, holistic, complex, and challenging) are often considered critical to the development of creative thinking. In the next section, you will learn how to orchestrate classroom activities in ways that enable your students to apply their creativity to solve authentic problems.

Authentic Instruction

You may not realize that the standards documents developed by national professional teaching organizations are designed to help teachers achieve "best practice," that is, the kind of instruction that facilitates and inspires student creativity and learning. Based on a large number of national curricular reports, from a wide range of disciplines (e.g., mathematics, science, social studies, English), Zemelman, Daniels, and Hyde (2005) culled a list of common recommendations made by educational experts and practitioners. These recommendations, captured in Figure 3.1, are based on sound learning theory and are backed by many, many years of educational research. At the heart of these approaches, and as the core of Standard 1, is the

Recommendations of National Curricular Reports	
Instruction is *more effective* and *engaging* when there is LESS:	**Instruction is *less dull* and *tedious* when there is MORE:**
• whole-class, teacher-directed instruction (e.g., lecturing)	• activity, with all the subsequent noise and movement of students
• student passivity: sitting, listening, receiving, and absorbing information	• experiential, inductive, hands-on learning
• presentational, one-way transmission of information from teacher to student	• diversity in teachers' roles, including coaching, demonstrating, and modeling
• valuing and rewarding of silence in the classroom	• emphasis on higher-order thinking; learning a field's key concepts and principles
• classroom time devoted to fill-in-the-blank worksheets, dittos, workbooks, and other "seatwork"	• deep study of a smaller number of topics that enable students to internalize the field's way of inquiry
• student time spent reading textbooks and basal readers	• responsibility transferred to students for their work: goal setting, record keeping, monitoring, sharing, exhibiting, and evaluating
• attempts by teachers to thinly cover large amounts of materials in every subject area	• choices for students (e.g., choosing their own books, writing topics, team partners, projects)
• rote memorization of facts and details	• enacting and modeling of the principles of democracy in school
• emphasis on competition and grades in schools	• attention to affective needs and varying cognitive styles of individual students
• tracking or leveling of students into ability groups	• cooperative, collaborative activity
• use of pull-out special programs	• heterogeneous classrooms where unique needs are met through individualized activities
• use of and reliance on standardized tests	• delivery of special help to students in regular classrooms
	• varied and cooperative roles for teachers, parents, and administrators
	• reliance on descriptive evaluations of student growth, including observational/anecdotal records, conference notes, and performance assessment rubrics

Figure 3.1

Common recommendations from national curricular reports.

Source: Adapted from *Best Practice: Today's Standards for Teaching and Learning in America's Schools,* by Steven Zemelman, Harney Daniels, and Arthur Hyde, 2005. Published by Heinemann, Portsmouth, NH. All rights reserved. Reprinted by permission.

expectation that teachers will develop students' critical and creative thinking skills by engaging them in authentic real-world problems.

When you examine this list of recommendations, it probably is easy to see that, while technology is not required to achieve each item, many of them can be more readily achieved when technology is added to the learning environment. For example, adding computers to the classroom can convert the learning environment into one that is very active and student-driven. Students can spend more time exploring topics of interest and creating innovative products that demonstrate their knowledge in ways that go beyond that which would be required to complete a fill-in-the-blank worksheet. Groups of students, with many different abilities and talents, can work together (either virtually or face-to-face) to research and develop solutions to an authentic problem that is facing the school, community, or nation, such as how to improve the physical accessibility of the local community for individuals with special needs. Additionally, by using Internet resources, students can access the primary documents of a discipline, as well as a multitude of authentic materials (e.g., data from NASA spacecraft, real-time images of approaching weather systems, video of the birth of a baby panda at the San Diego Zoo) that are typical of the materials used by experts in the discipline under study (see Figure 3.2).

There are a lot of different names for this type of approach to teaching and learning including authentic instruction, engaged learning, learning by design, and learner-centered instruction. But, regardless of the specific label used, these approaches are characterized by a common set of principles and strategies. These include such things as 1) learner autonomy and 2) active learning, and tend to be anchored by 3) holistic, 4) complex, and 5) challenging activities. Because ISTE Standard 1 promotes the use of real-world issues and authentic problems to facilitate and

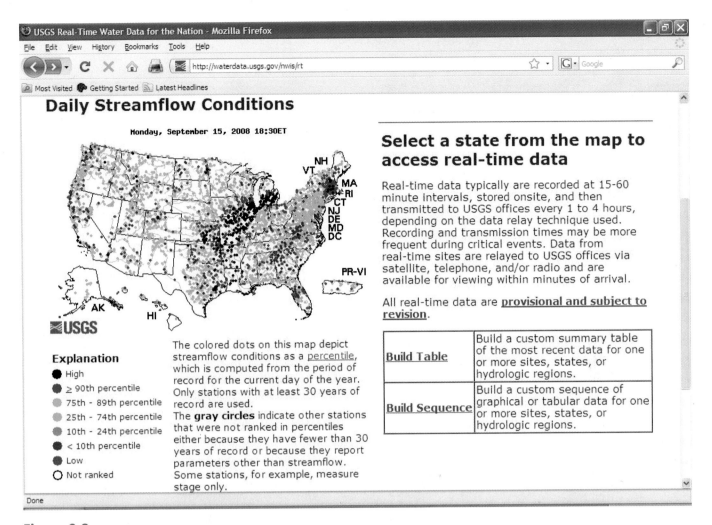

Figure 3.2
The United States Geological Survey provides real-time data for U.S. streams, lakes, groundwater, and precipitation.
Source: Courtesy United States Geological Survey.

inspire student learning and creativity, we will refer to this approach as **authentic instruction**. We discuss each of the five common characteristics listed above and describe how technology can support your efforts to create these kinds of learning experiences for your students.

Learner Autonomy

Authentic instruction provides for, and builds on, learner autonomy. We can support the development of learner autonomy in our classrooms in many ways but one of the basic requirements is that students are able to pursue topics and questions that are interesting and relevant to them. Think about how you feel when you're asked to write about something in which you are really interested, compared to having to write about something you've never heard about before, or worse yet, have heard about, but consider to be a boring topic! You probably weren't very motivated to write about the "boring" topic, were you? But when you were allowed to explore your own interests, and pursue answers to your own questions, then your motivation probably went way up. The level of engagement that results from being able to pursue your own interests is one of the hallmarks of an effective creative task (Egbert, 2009).

There are lots of ways to spark student motivation for learning and fortunately, technology offers some of the most powerful tools available. Yet, technology as a learning object, in and of itself, will not hold your interest indefinitely and is more

THE GAME PLAN

Types of Authentic Instruction

Set Goals

Learn more about different types of authentic instruction. Choose one of the types mentioned in the chapter (learning by design, engaged learning, etc.).

Monitor

Consider to what extent the components of authentic instruction are included. Which component seems to receive the most emphasis? What component is missing?

Take Action

Do an Internet search to locate more information about the approach.

Evaluate and Extend

Would you use this type of authentic instruction in your classroom? How? What do you think you still need to learn? Should you try other strategies to learn more about authentic instruction?

effectively used when it enables you to pursue other interests. In other words, technology tools are more likely to grab and hold students' attention when they are used to support the pursuit and attainment of other meaningful goals. For example, in many authentic approaches (such as project- and problem-based learning), the curriculum is anchored by a "driving question," usually presented in the form of a real-world problem or issue that needs to be solved. These kinds of approaches engage learners as researchers; that is, students learn how to 1) ask important questions that are meaningful to them and to the discipline; 2) design and conduct investigations; 3) collect, analyze, and interpret data; and 4) apply what they have learned to new problems or situations. In these types of approaches, technology can be used to support each step of the process: to gather information, to collect and analyze data, to synthesize results, and to present findings to interested stakeholders. Research has shown that students who participate in these types of curricula develop positive attitudes toward learning.

In order for learners to truly function autonomously they must develop **self-directed learning** (SDL) skills, which is another hallmark of creative and innovative thinkers. In Chapter 2 we introduced you to the GAME plan as a way to guide the development of your own self-directed learning skills. That is, being self-directed means that you are able to set your own learning **G**oals, take **A**ction to meet those goals, **M**onitor your progress toward reaching those goals, and then reflect on, or **E**valuate, the effectiveness of your learning processes and learning outcomes. While we previously discussed how you could use the GAME plan to direct your own learning processes, we now encourage you to consider ways in which you might help your students use the GAME plan as a way to achieve this first principle of authentic instruction, learner autonomy. Table 3.2 outlines how the GAME plan can be used to help students develop SDL skills.

While the ultimate goal is that students will, over time, assume full responsibility for their learning, teachers need to provide guidance and support while students are in the process of *becoming* self-directed. One effective way that you can do this is through the use of **scaffolds**. Simply stated, scaffolds are external supports for learning or solving problems. The general idea behind a scaffold is that it enables you to accomplish something that you could not accomplish on your own. Think about how a painter is able to reach the upper levels on a building because of the use of a scaffold. Similarly, scaffolds enable students to reach higher levels of understanding that would not be possible without them.

Typically, scaffolds enable learners to deal with the complexity of difficult tasks by structuring them in ways that reduce, or constrain, that complexity. At the same

Table 3.2	GAME Plan for Student Self-Directed Learning (SDL)
Steps	**Student Plans**
Goals	• What do my students need to know? • What do my students already know that can help them meet the goals of instruction? • How will I know if they have been successful?
Action	• What content information do my students need access to? • How can my students gain the information and practice the skills they need? • What resources do my students need? • What instructional strategy will I use?
Monitor	• Are my students understanding the content and mastering the skills they need? • What patterns are emerging from my students' responses? • Should I modify my lesson and unit plans?
Evaluate and Extend	• Did my lesson or unit plan work or can it be improved? (If so, should I modify the goals or my instructional strategies?) • What should I do differently in the future?

time, scaffolds help students learn how to accomplish the tasks independently. Scaffolds may assume multiple forms depending on the learning environment, the content, the instructor, and the learners. In addition, they may serve different functions depending on where they are used in the instructional process: at the beginning, to provide entry into the task; in the middle, to support students' inquiry efforts; or at the end, to help students make sense of what they have observed, discussed, or read (Simons & Ertmer, 2005/2006).

While most teachers already use a variety of scaffolds in their classroom instruction (e.g., project guidelines, templates, grading rubrics, etc.), technology offers another means to support students' efforts (see Figure 3.3). For example, one multimedia problem-based learning unit for middle-school students, *Up, Up & Away!*, used scaffolds to support students' initial inquiry efforts (Brinkerhoff & Glazewski, 2004). Embedded within the program was a "Hints" section, divided into two components that matched the two project requirements—designing a balloon that could circumnavigate the Earth and planning a travel route. Each hint began with a question to help students get started: "If I've never designed a balloon before, where do I start?" and "If I've never planned a balloon trip before, where do I begin?"

Scaffolds are important instructional tools, especially in authentic learning environments. Fortunately, software applications, specifically designed to help you scaffold student learning, are available. These include tools that allow your students to highlight or organize material, to schedule tasks and receive reminders, as well as tools designed specifically to support various levels of student proficiency. You can even use common productivity tools, such as word-processing software, to scaffold student learning by increasing or decreasing the number of functions students can use in their work (e.g., thesaurus, dictionary, spelling and grammar check). We'll revisit this idea when we discuss the challenges involved in implementing authentic approaches.

Active Learning

Authentic instruction is based on active, experiential learning. There's an old proverb that says, "Tell me, and I will forget. Show me, and I may remember. Involve me, and I will understand." Few people would argue with the idea that we learn best by doing. While we can certainly learn many things by reading textbooks and by observing others complete a task, the most natural form of learning involves active, hands-on, concrete experience. Think about how you learned to throw a Frisbee, ride a bike, or sing your favorite song. In most cases, you probably just jumped in and gave each of these things a try; interacting with, and manipulating, the objects/tools at hand

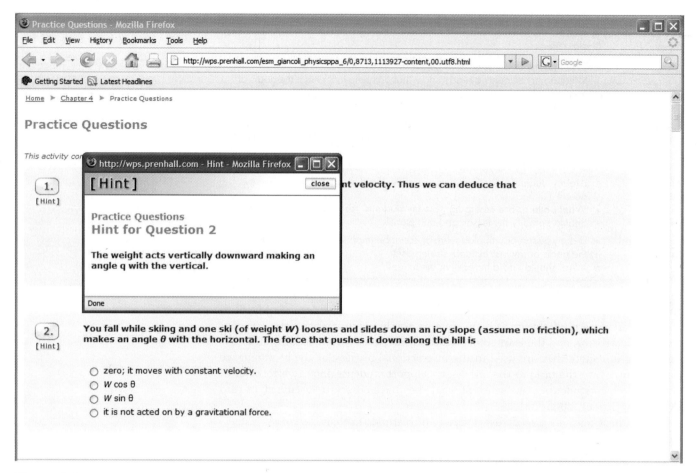

Figure 3.3
Scaffolds may appear in the form of hints.
Source: Screen shot taken from Prentice Hall website based on *Physics*, 6th edition by Douglas C. Giancoli. Copyright © 2005 by Douglas C. Giancoli. Reprinted by permission of Pearson Education, Inc.

and observing what happened. Still, being an active learner doesn't necessarily mean that you have to be *physically* active. What this really means it that you have to be *mentally* active, searching for and manipulating information, synthesizing data, and making interpretations.

Technology supports learning-by-doing in a variety of ways. First of all, technology provides powerful tools (e.g., word processors, databases, image and video editors) that allow you to represent information in a variety of ways (via text, graphics, charts, audio, video) and perhaps, more importantly, to manipulate that information and then observe and interpret the effects of those manipulations. Technology also supports active learning when it is used as a tool to represent and simulate real-world problems, situations, and contexts (see Figure 3.4). For example, through the use of simulation software students can experience what it's like to maneuver *Spirit*, the Mars Land Rover, across the Martian landscape, or to observe, at the cellular level, how cancer cells respond to different types and doses of various drug treatments. Using simulations, learners can engage in activities that would otherwise be too dangerous, expensive, or complex, such as conducting volatile chemistry experiments, navigating a spaceship to the moon, or making risky investment decisions. Simulations can compress time or slow things down so that they are more readily observable, allowing students to repeat the process as many times as needed to understand it.

Technology can also give students access to people, resources, or locations that would be impossible to get to without it. Learners can take virtual field trips to places within their own communities (local museums), across the country (national parks), or around the world (Great Wall of China). They can rocket into space, participate in

Figure 3.4
The ORBITER space flight simulator allows learners to experiment with the physics of space flight without leaving the ground.
Source: http://www.nationalsms.com/docs/1us.pdf. *Courtesy Martin Schweiger.*

critical historical events, or tour the inner workings of the circulatory system. In addition, they can interact with people from other countries and cultures; ask questions of scientists, authors, and other experts; and access real-time data (e.g., census, weather) and primary source documents, all of which allow them to participate in the authentic activities of the discipline.

While activity is necessary for meaningful learning, it is not sufficient. Activity needs to be accompanied by both **reflection** and **articulation** (Jonassen, Howland, Moore, & Marra, 2003). That is, learners need to describe what they have done and explain what resulted and why. This is because when we stop to think about *what* we have learned and to reflect on *how* we learned it, we actually achieve a deeper understanding of the knowledge we have constructed, and are more likely to be able to use that new knowledge in different situations (referred to as **transfer**), which is yet another hallmark of creative thinkers. That is, the active (doing) and constructive (creating) processes work hand-in-hand to build understanding. If you don't engage in both processes you are likely to end up with either incomplete knowledge (observations/facts that can not be interpreted or understood) or inert knowledge (knowledge that is irretrievable when needed).

Holistic Activities

Authentic instruction is holistic. This principle relates to the fact that we gain important skills, including reading, spelling, math, and even technology skills, when we learn them within the context of meaningful activities. This is what businesses sometimes refer to as "just-in-time" training. For example, brief lessons on how to use punctuation will be more meaningful (and therefore more memorable) if they occur within the context of writing a story for an online publication, as opposed to being just one in a series of isolated language arts lessons.

Technology provides the means to situate learning within **real contexts**, and to provide students with the whole picture of an event or process, while still allowing them to focus on the relevant parts (see Figure 3.5). For example, by using videos that allow students to actually view and focus on the red blood cells that carry oxygen from the lungs, learners can more readily understand how these cells work on a molecular level, while still recognizing how they work as part of the circulatory system. By considering the whole system, as opposed to a single part, students are more likely to make far more connections than the teacher would have been able to teach directly.

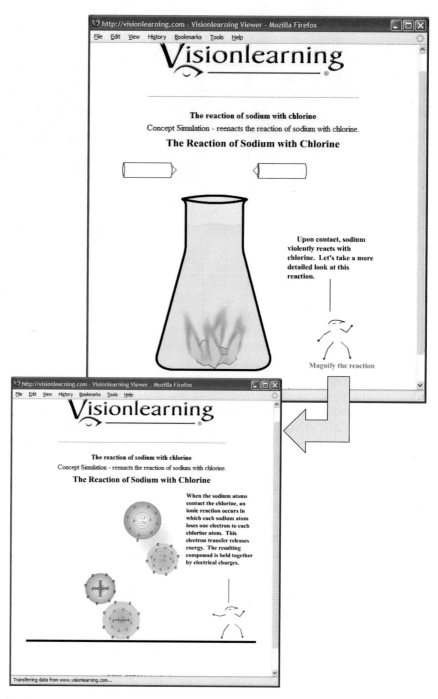

Figure 3.5
Technology allows us to observe events that are too small, too far away, or take too much time to do in real life. This simulation shows a chemical reaction at the lab table and at the molecular level.
Source: Image used with permission. Copyright, Visionlearning, Inc. http://www.visionlearning.com. All rights reserved.

Another way that technology can facilitate more holistic learning is by enabling learners to make connections across multiple content areas. For example, when working on authentic problems, such as determining why fish are dying in a local river, students must work across multiple content areas to investigate the problem, understand the causes, and pose solutions. As part of the problem-solving process, students must conduct both field (science) and library (language arts, information technology skills) research; analyze data and graph results (science, statistics, math, technology), interview local business owners to understand their perspectives (social sciences) on previous actions taken regarding the disposal of waste materials into the river (history), understand local laws and policy issues (government), and create a persuasive presentation to convince local public officials of a proposed course of action (technology skills, language arts). It's easy to see from just this one example how technology can facilitate many, if not all, of the processes involved in solving these kinds of complex problems while simultaneously allowing students to experience the holistic nature of analyzing a problem from a variety of different points of view in order to draw reasoned conclusions. Your students could probably complete this type of activity without technology, but can you imagine how much more difficult it would be and how much more time it would take to do so? Not using technology would also prevent them from using tools, such as probeware and online databases, which might restrict the effectiveness and degree of their understanding.

Complex Activities

Authentic instruction incorporates real-world and complex problems. Previous ideas about schooling placed teachers squarely in the center of the instructional process, serving, primarily, as knowledge dispensers whose main responsibility was to translate complex information into a form that was more readily transmitted to, and absorbed by, the learners. One way teachers accomplished this was by removing the information from its relevant context and stripping it of any "extraneous" details. What resulted, however, was not meaningful learning, but rather artificial understandings of oversimplified ideas, concepts, and situations. Current research has demonstrated that learning is more successful when it is situated within real-world tasks or simulated in a problem-based learning environment (Jonassen et al., 2003). Such experiences are not only more relevant and engaging but also increase the likelihood that students will be able to use what they have learned in new situations, and furthermore, to do so in new and innovative ways.

According to Fred Newmann and his colleagues (Newmann, Bryk, & Nagaoka, 2001), authentic instruction involves more than situating learning within a real context. While an authentic context can illustrate the complexity and richness of a real-world problem, Newmann uses the term **authentic intellectual work** to define, more specifically, how students should work within that context. Authentic intellectual work has three distinct characteristics: 1) construction of knowledge, 2) disciplined inquiry, and 3) value beyond school (see the first two columns of Table 3.3). To the extent that these characteristics are embedded within teachers' expectations for students' work, classroom activities and experiences comes closer to modeling best practice.

Authentic intellectual work starts where the basics end. The real-world aspect implies that students *apply* the basics to tackle projects and problems similar to those that confront adults in their everyday lives (see Figure 3.6). Authentic instruction incorporates assignments that require students to think, develop in-depth understanding, and apply their learning to realistic, important problems. In addition, these assignments are designed to have concrete, practical, aesthetic, or personal value. The goal is to involve students in work that has an impact on others, for example, writing letters, news articles, memos or technical reports; communicating in a

Table 3.3	Using Technology to Support the Key Characteristics of Authentic Intellectual Work	
Construction of Knowledge	**Example: Writing**	**Technology Support**
Assignment involves students in manipulating information and ideas by synthesizing, generalizing, explaining, hypothesizing, or arriving at conclusions that produce new meanings and understandings.	The assignment asks students to interpret, analyze, synthesize, or evaluate information in writing about a topic, rather than merely to reproduce information.	Students access the American Memory collection online from the Library of Congress and evaluate primary documents from the Civil Rights movement, written from different perspectives (e.g., an editorial in the Birmingham Press; Martin Luther King's letter written from the Birmingham jail) prior to writing an opinion piece, stating their own views on the conflict.
Disciplined Inquiry	**Example: Writing**	**Technology Support**
1) *Use a prior knowledge base.* Students must acquire the knowledge base of facts, vocabularies, concepts, theories, algorithms, and other conventions necessary for their inquiry (usually the central focus of direct instruction in basic skills). 2) *Strive for in-depth understanding rather than superficial awareness.* Students use information to gain deeper understanding of specific problems. Such understanding develops as one looks for, imagines, proposes, and tests relationships among key concepts in order to clarify a specific problem or issue. 3) *Express their ideas and findings with elaborated communication.* Students use verbal, symbolic and/or visual tools to provide qualifications, nuances, elaborations, details, and analogies woven into extended narratives, explanations, justifications, and dialogue.	The assignment asks students to draw conclusions or make generalizations or arguments and support them through extended writing.	1) Students record data and information they have found from exploring online simulations as a way to develop deep understanding of genetic processes (natural selection, crossing over, DNA fingerprinting) prior to participating in a debate about genetic engineering. 2) Students create hypotheses about the proposed evolutionary path of the whale, based on one of three hypotheses. Information is gathered through a web-based lab or WebQuest. Students create an argument, with evidence, to support the specific hypothesis chosen. 3) Students use a combination of technology tools to present their ideas/findings via formal written essays, photo essays, video essays, presentation software, web-based portfolios, etc.
Value Beyond School	**Example: Writing**	**Technology Support**
Students make connections between substantive knowledge and either public problems or personal experiences. Accomplishments have practical, aesthetic, or personal value.	The assignment asks students to connect the topic to experiences, observations, feelings, or situations significant in their lives.	Students write for real audiences, such as grade or age peers in distant locations, experts, or interested community members, and create a project website that includes their written work, as well as pictures and links to helpful resources.

Note: We have added the ideas in the technology support column to illustrate how technology can be used to achieve the key components of authentic intellectual work, as outlined by Newmann et al.

Source: Adapted from Newmann, F. M., Bryk, A. S., & Nagaoka, J. K. (2001). *Authentic intellectual work and standardized tests: Conflict or coexistence?*, p. 14–15. Chicago, IL: Consortium on Chicago School Research. Reprinted by permission of the author and Consortium on Chicago School Research.

foreign language; producing a budget; or creating a painting or composing a piece of music.

Technology can be used in many ways to establish authentic contexts for learning and to engage students in authentic intellectual work including the construction of knowledge, disciplined inquiry, and in finding value beyond school. Consider, for example, the last column in Table 3.3 that illustrates some of the ways technology can support each of these components of authentic work.

Challenging Activities

Authentic instruction is challenging. Most of us have experienced the satisfaction and joy that come from completing a difficult task or solving a challenging puzzle. When we see or hear something that we don't understand, we're motivated to figure it out.

Vernier Software

Figure 3.6
Studying flow rate with the Vernier LabQuest.

We might talk to our friends or colleagues, visit the local library or museum, search for information online, or call a related helpline, all with the goal of understanding the phenomenon or solving the mystery. If we can capitalize on these types of natural curiosities in our students, we are more likely to engage them in the topic at hand and to prompt them to take ownership of their learning.

Of course, not every student will find every question or topic equally interesting, or be able to engage in the topic at the same level of sophistication. This is where technology can lend a hand (see Figure 3.7). For example, technology can provide that initial hook that gets students involved in the topic. This might be in the form of a video that captures the faces and voices of real people describing the problems they face in their communities. Or it might be in the form of a game or a simulation that challenges them to complete a task in a limited amount of time or to make decisions about how to avoid an impending disaster.

Once students are engaged, technology can be used to promote and support students' understanding of the content. For example, a variety of computer tutorials are available that provide multiple paths through the same content. In some cases, the computer controls when the student moves on to more advanced concepts; in other cases, learners are given control over the amount of information they receive, the number of practice exercises they complete, and the level of success they obtain before moving on. Because younger, less-sophisticated learners may not know what's best for them, instructionally, it is usually recommended that learners have some, but not all, control over these types of decisions. However, as learners become more capable of directing their own learning, giving them more control over these types of decisions can increase their engagement, as well as their autonomy and self-directedness.

Technology also affords the opportunity to provide engaging and interesting material to students who read at different grade levels—including English language learners or students who read below grade level. Using the concept of **lexiles**, a scale that matches the difficulty of reading material to student ability, students can engage in relevant authentic materials at a level they can understand. For example, a ninth grade student who reads three levels below his grade may be interested in current events related to baseball, pop music, or the country of his birth. Many newspaper, magazine, and web-based articles are written at a level that the student cannot read or comprehend. Software is available that can match the student's interests with reading materials he can read and understand—sometimes providing real-time articles from news services written at different reading levels. Online databases also provide listings of reading materials in almost any content area organized by lexile. In

Figure 3.7
In *Decisions, Decisions,* by Tom Snyder, students learn history and social studies while participating in complex role-playing activities.
Source: http://education.smarttech.com/ste/en-US/Ed+Resource/SAP/history/Elementary/Ready/TomSnyder/Decisions5.htm. Courtesy Tom Snyder.

WEB LINK

Visit the textbook's companion website for a list of resources about and using lexiles.

this way, technology can provide access to interesting and challenging material that is appropriate to the age, interests, and reading level of each student.

Instructional activities that incorporate all of the components of authentic instruction described here (active, holistic, complex, etc.) are naturally going to be more challenging for your students (and for you!). Giving students choices in their learning, as well as responsibility for managing and assessing their learning processes, may cause considerable confusion and frustration at first. When you've got a classroom full of students who are all pursuing different interests, and experiencing a host of different difficulties, you may be tempted to throw in the towel. However, there are lots of strategies and tools you can use to manage the classroom and your students. Many of these strategies are described in Chapter 5. We make note of just two of them here: the use of collaborative work groups and technology-based scaffolds.

Collaborative work groups can ease the challenges of authentic instruction. Although we haven't specifically mentioned that authentic instruction is **collaborative**, this is typically the case. In fact, this is one of the defining characteristics of problem- and project-based learning, two prevalent forms of authentic instruction. Johnson and Johnson (1998) and Slavin (1994) have documented student achievement gains when students work in collaborative small groups. This is likely due to a number of different factors including the opportunity to observe more advanced others think through a problem or perform a task, and thus provide models of the knowledge construction process; the ability to divide complex tasks into smaller, more manageable parts; and the opportunity to receive feedback from, as well as to give feedback to, multiple others. Also, working together in pairs or small groups can benefit students socially as well as cognitively. Learners depend on each other to reach their goals and, in the process, practice their social interaction skills. When done right, the use of collaborative work groups can ease some of the challenges teachers face when students work independently on a host of different projects. Of course, students need to learn how to work together and their initial efforts need to be supported by teachers. Suggestions for managing small groups are provided in Chapter 5.

Although the use of small groups can help teachers address some of the logistical problems they face when implementing authentic learning activities, the primary reason for using them has more to do with what students gain by learning to work with their peers. Both educators and business professionals have increasingly been emphasizing the importance of developing group interaction and problem-solving skills among our future workers. This suggests that, just as these are important skills for *you* to gain, they are also important skills for your *students* to gain.

At the heart of these collaborative activities is the engagement of students in deep conversations about both the processes and the products of learning. When learners work in teams they must achieve a common understanding of the task at hand and then agree upon the methods they will use to complete it. Through these group conversations learners come to understand and accept that there are multiple ways of approaching tasks as well as multiple methods for solving them. This is what transforms these group activities into meaningful learning. And, of course, technology can support these conversations by providing a platform for participation and by connecting learners across the room or across the globe. As stated in Standard 1c, and discussed more thoroughly in Chapter 4, these types of collaborative tools provide a means to illuminate students' thinking, planning, and creative processes.

Scaffolds can ease the challenges of authentic instruction. As noted earlier, another method for addressing the challenging nature of authentic instruction is through the use of scaffolds. While students may feel more motivated to participate in authentic activities due to their holistic and challenging nature, they also may feel more frustrated due to their open-ended nature. Particularly for students who have less experience in inquiry-based methods, scaffolds can help them understand what's involved in the process and what it takes to initiate and complete different inquiry activities. The example, mentioned earlier, of the "Hints" section within a multimedia project for designing a hot air balloon, was employed as a way to help students initiate their inquiry activities. Figure 3.8 provides another example of how a scaffold can help learners get started on a difficult task.

A second approach involves having an expert (the teacher or a more experienced peer) model how to complete a task, investigation, or process. Modeling can prompt students to compare their own approaches with that of the expert, while simultaneously learning the language of the discipline. For example, Alien Rescue (Pedersen & Liu, 2002–2003), a multimedia-based problem-based learning (PBL) program, contains a feature in the software that allows students to view video advice from an "expert" at various stages during the process. The expert verbally describes his problem-solving strategies, such as how he selects relevant information and why he chooses to ignore other information. Pedersen and Liu noted that students were able to transfer these strategies to a new problem, in a different domain, and speculated that enhancing students' thinking during the problem-solving process enhanced their problem solving in the transfer situation.

In general, scaffolds can be used throughout the instructional process and are especially useful in supporting learners' efforts within problem-centered environments. While teachers, themselves, can provide continuous timely support (referred to as "soft" scaffolds) based on their observations of students' ongoing efforts, technological scaffolds (as one type of "hard" scaffold) can be built into many of the planned activities, based on teachers' knowledge of where students are likely to struggle (Saye & Brush, 2002). Even the automatic features of some productivity tools, such as spelling and grammar tools in word processors, list managers in spreadsheets, and autoform filling features in web browsers can be considered scaffolds that can support you and your students depending on how you incorporate them into your classroom activities. If hard scaffolds are put in place to support learners at various stages known to be difficult, the teacher is then free to perform additional soft scaffolding.

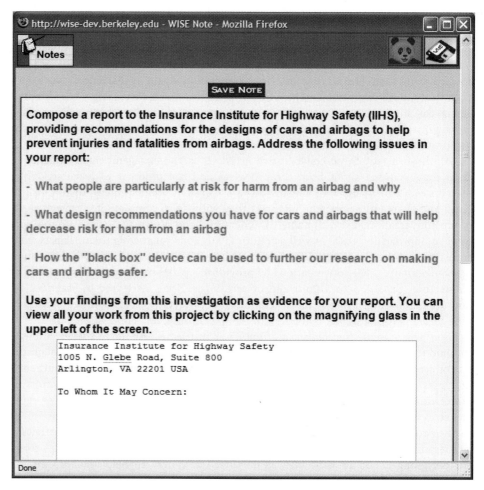

Figure 3.8
Scaffolding can help learners see how to start a difficult task.
Source: http://wise-dev.berkeley.edu/student/topFrame.php?projectID=19530. Courtesy University of California, Berkeley.

Technology Support for Authentic Instruction

Authentic instruction enables you to meet your curricular standards in ways that can engage and support your students' interests, creativity, and motivation. In a problem-centered classroom, your role looks quite different than it does in a traditional, teacher-centered classroom. That is, rather than acting as a knowledge provider you tend to serve more as a resource provider. Furthermore, you engage students' interests by asking thought-provoking questions and providing opportunities for students to construct their own understandings and to be accountable for their own learning.

Table 3.4 summarizes the key components of an authentic approach and lists some of the potential ways in which technology can support teachers' and students' efforts within this type of environment. While we recognize that teachers can create and use authentic approaches and strategies *without* the use of technology, we also recognize that with its addition, the task is, hopefully, less difficult, as well as more stimulating.

There are a variety of ways to incorporate authentic experiences and activities into your classroom including problem-based learning methods, inquiry and discovery methods, inductive methods, role-playing, and simulation, to name a few. Because these strategies often involve exploration, collaboration, and communication, digital technologies can facilitate their implementation. Descriptions of these different methods, and supporting technologies, are presented in Table 3.5. Note that most of the technologies listed with each method can actually be applied across multiple methods.

Table 3.4	How Technology Supports Each Component of Authentic Instruction
Components of Authentic Instruction	**The Role of Technology**
Learner Autonomy	• Supports student interest in a variety of topics; provides the tools needed to pursue the answers to interesting questions • Allows learners to initiate learning on their own via tutorials, simulations, online resources, and discussion groups • Provides tools that support the processes of self-directed learning; setting goals, monitoring progress, reflecting on and articulating learning outcomes
Active Learning	• Engages learners in hands-on, interactive experiences • Provides tools to represent ideas; manipulate information; simulate real-world problems, situations, and contexts • Provides access to people, resources, and places you couldn't access without it • Provides the tools useful for reflection and articulation
Holistic Activities	• Provides the means to situate learning within real contexts • Allows students to observe the relationships between parts and wholes and thus understand how things work together
Complex Activities	• Provides access to authentic documents, real data, and experts that give purpose and meaning to school activities • Allows students to explore information in the context within which it is used • Provides real audiences for students' work • Enables students to communicate ideas in a variety of ways
Challenging Activities	• Increases students' interest in the topic at hand • Promotes and supports students' understanding by providing multiple paths through the information • Provides learners control over their learning processes • Provides access to multiple others, both face-to-face and virtually, for collaborative work • Provides a platform for meaningful conversations with others • Supports development of student independence through the use of scaffolds

APPLY TO PRACTICE

Authentic Instructional Strategies and Technologies

1. Identify a learning objective or outcome from your content area and then select one of the methods of authentic instruction from Table 3.5.
2. Describe a lesson activity that incorporates the specific method you have selected. How would you establish appropriate learning experiences to support the activity? What kind of scaffolds or structures would be necessary for different types of learners?
3. Describe specific ways that technologies could be used to support the successful implementation of your strategy. Why did you choose the specific technology? How is it matched to the skills and knowledge required of the learning objective, your skill level and that of your students, and the specific method you have selected?
4. Solicit feedback from your peers and share your ideas on their lesson activities.

Directed Instruction in Support of Authentic Learning

Despite the benefits of authentic activities, **directed instruction** can still be the best approach under certain circumstances. For example, directed instruction can be preferable when students need just-in-time instruction delivered at the point of need. Students who are working on authentic learning activities may benefit from remediation or practice in prerequisite skills in order to keep up with the pace of the lesson.

Table 3.5	Examples of Authentic Instruction and Potential Supporting Technologies	
Type of Method	Description	Possible Supporting Technologies
Problem-Based Learning	Students are challenged to learn by working cooperatively to find solutions to real-life problems. Curiosity and interest in the process occurs naturally as students work in virtual and face-to-face teams to solve authentic dilemmas.	• Internet for background information • Data collection tools (probes, etc.) to gather data • Simulation software or online models • Spreadsheets and databases to record and analyze data • Presentation software to present ideas and findings
Inquiry/Discovery Method	Puzzling questions spark students' mental stimulation and quickly gets them thinking critically and creatively. Once a situation has been presented, students gather information by formulating their own questions. They research answers in cooperative groups, pairs, or individually.	• Concept-mapping software to map ideas for investigations • Digital cameras or camcorders to gather information • Word-processing software or spreadsheets to create planning charts, timelines, etc. • WebQuests or research using online and other digital resources
Inductive Method	Begins with a question or series of unknown facts or concepts and moves toward known information. Learners actively search for answers to these "unknowns."	• Internet, CD-ROMs, and databases for reference material • Digital cameras or camcorders to record information • Photo and video hardware and software to create and edit images of findings • Spreadsheet and graphing software to create visual representations of findings
Role-Play	Role-play situations require students to take on the characteristics of someone else. Role-play encourages creativity and high levels of thought. This strategy is most successful when students are given time to research the character they must portray.	• Internet search for information about perspectives of different stakeholders • Audio and video recordings of relevant locations, people, etc. • Discussion boards, blogs, and e-mail to communicate with stakeholders, other experts • Single- and multiplayer gaming software
Simulation	Similar to role-play, simulations involve approximating real-life scenarios in the classroom. Students are involved in the reproduction of possible situations. Simulations often include scripted representations that enable learners to closely experience world events.	• Simulation software • Virtual environments • Internet resources to support activity in the simulation • Web- or videoconferencing software to support conversations with experts or other stakeholders

Source: Adapted from Musselwhite, T. (2005). *Creating learner-centered middle school classrooms.* New York: Glencoe/McGraw-Hill. Reprinted with permission of Glencoe/McGraw-Hill and the author.

At other times, students are hindered by their lack of automaticity in the use of certain skills. For example, students who do not know their multiplication tables can be at a disadvantage when performing calculations of the area of a meadow. In these cases, direct instructional methods can provide a useful supplement to authentic learning experiences. Students may find that repeated practice on small chunks of information is the best way to ensure that their skills become automatic. Students who are internally motivated to succeed may also prefer directed instruction as the quickest way to learn new information.

Directed Instruction

Directed instruction encompasses a variety of instructional methods that have at their core the introduction of a topic, an interactive presentation of the content to be learned, and extensive practice to ensure mastery of the targeted information (Magliaro, Lockee, & Burton, 2005). Directed instruction is characterized by the following features:

1. Materials and curricula are broken down into small steps and arranged in what is assumed to be prerequisite order
2. Objectives are stated clearly in terms of learner outcomes or performances
3. Learners are provided with opportunities to connect their new knowledge with what they already know

4. Learners are given practice with each step or combination of steps
5. Learners experience additional opportunities to practice that promote increasing responsibility and independence (guided and/or independent; in groups and/or alone)
6. Feedback is provided after each practice opportunity or set of practice opportunities (Magliaro et al., 2005, p. 44)

The Tools for Use that accompanies this section outlines one popular directed instruction method.

Using Technology to Support Directed Instruction

There are a variety of ways that technology can contribute to directed instruction. Tutorials typically include all of the learning events needed for directed instruction (see the discussion of computer tutorials in Chapter 4). Videos and animations are tools that often improve student attention and increase motivation, and can provide excellent resources from which to structure an introductory activity—often demonstrating an entire concept or skill prior to breaking it down into prerequisite steps.

Drill-and-practice software can provide the repeated practice necessary for basic skills (e.g., math facts, motor skills, spelling) to become automatic. Simulations can model the application of concepts and principles such as the principles of energy and force. Video and animations can also model procedures (e.g., mitosis, building a bridge) and motor skills as with those involved in throwing a bowl on a potter's wheel. Photographs can provide detailed images for analysis.

TOOLS FOR USE

Directed Instruction

Madeline Hunter's (1982) model, *Essential Elements of Instruction,* is representative of common approaches to directed instruction. Hunter identifies several events, outlined below, that the teacher should consider in designing a lesson. Although these considerations are often interpreted as a step-by-step series of events that must be present in each lesson, Hunter emphasized that all events do not need to appear in every lesson:

- *Anticipatory Set:* An anticipatory set is a short introductory activity that prepares students to attend to the new content by focusing their attention and bringing prior knowledge of the content into consciousness. These activities can also provide teachers with an opportunity to diagnose students' initial levels of understanding.
- *Purpose:* The teacher simply states the goal, objective, or purpose of the lesson and why it should be of importance to them. This event further focuses the learners' attention on the relevant content by informing them of what they are expected to learn as a result of the lesson.
- *Input:* The input consists of the factual information and skills students should learn. Hunter suggests that the teacher's role is to determine what information is essential and organize it clearly. Consistent with cognitive approaches to learning, complex information should build on more basic information.
- *Modeling:* The input is accompanied by modeling activities where the teacher highlights the critical attributes that distinguish an idea, concept, or procedure from similar things. Using clear examples and non-examples that are relevant to the students' experiences, the teacher demonstrates the application of the new information.
- *Guided Practice:* The next step is to guide students though the process of applying the information to ensure that they will perform the tasks correctly when they are on their own. Guided practice can range from structured activities where the students "follow along," to more unstructured tasks where the teacher simply circulates around the room to see if students are performing the tasks correctly on their own.
- *Checking for Understanding:* Throughout the lesson, the teacher asks questions to determine how well the students understand the information. Based on the students' answers, the teacher may need to re-teach certain skills or concepts before progressing.
- *Independent Practice:* Guided activities are followed by independent practice where students apply the skill(s) without teacher support. These practice activities enable both students and teachers to determine the extent to which students can perform a task independently. Teachers can assign independent practice activities for homework or in-class but they must be sure to provide students with feedback on their performances.
- *Closure:* The lesson concludes with actions or statements that bring the lesson to a logical conclusion. Closure activities review and reinforce the key points to help students consolidate their knowledge.

APPLY TO PRACTICE

Directed Instructional Strategies and Technologies

1. Consider the directed instruction methods described in this section. Identify and describe when these methods can and should be incorporated into instruction.
2. What technologies can support directed instruction in your area of study (e.g., science, mathematics, language arts, etc.)?

A variety of technologies can be used to help you check your students' understanding. Many computer tutorials or curricular applications include reflection or summary questions at key intervals during the lesson. Students can receive feedback on the questions and may be guided to go back or review material they do not understand well enough. There are interactive technologies, too, that allow for a greater amount of informal formative assessment of student understanding. Whole classes can provide answers to key questions, confidentially or anonymously to boost student confidence and accuracy of response. Students can use infrared responders and wireless handheld devices to "beam" answers to questions you pose. Computer-generated tests can be used for pretests or posttests on the content and you and your students can track and evaluate data from these tests to determine student growth. Students can also provide their own closure through the use of presentations or digital portfolios that include checklists or rubrics of skills and knowledge they are required to master.

What other examples can you think of?

Facilitating Creative Thinking while Meeting Content Standards

Most educators today would agree that two of the primary goals of education are to help students develop creative thinking skills and to become effective problem solvers. And while many schools and teachers have adopted these goals, they are not commonly addressed in the typical classroom. That may be because teachers don't know where to begin to teach these skills. Creative thinking and problem solving are rather "fuzzy" concepts—hard to teach and even harder to measure.

Furthermore, the need to assure that students demonstrate competency on the content standards assessed on state benchmarking tests is one of the major challenges facing teachers today. In the last 20 years, all 50 states have developed content standards. You might be wondering how you can facilitate creative thinking skills while still addressing content and technology standards.

Creative thinking skills are not practiced in isolation; instead, generating original ideas and refining them through analysis, synthesis, and evaluation takes place in the context of responding to some challenge or opportunity. In addition, creative thinkers are self-directed in their approach to solving problems and responding to challenges. They are motivated, flexible in their thinking, and confident in their ability to tackle the task at hand. Authentic instruction provides us with a way to develop both content knowledge and the skills required for creative thinking.

But in order to develop authentic learning experiences for your students, you need to know what content you are required to teach (the curriculum) and the skill level at which your students will be assessed. Standards help determine the specific skills and knowledge that your students will need to master in your classroom, and in some cases, also help to describe expected student behaviors.

Let's look at some standards in more detail. You've probably noticed that standards are often written in fairly general terms so they are frequently accompanied by **objectives** that provide greater specificity. For example, look at Table 3.6 and

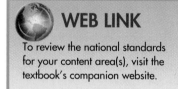

WEB LINK

To review the national standards for your content area(s), visit the textbook's companion website.

THE GAME PLAN

Identifying Content Standards

Set Goals
Learn more about the content standards you may be required to meet when you teach.

Perhaps you may need to contact a teacher or other expert in your chosen field for help in locating the appropriate professional organization.

Take Action
Find out if there is a national organization whose content standards you must meet. Locate its website and review its standards.

Evaluate and Extend
Compare the content standards you found with those located by other students who plan to teach in a similar area. Did you locate the same standards? If not, revise your search strategies to determine which set of standards may be most applicable.

Monitor
Are you locating the standards you need? Do you need to modify your search strategies?

---

note how each science content standard is translated into more specific language through its related objective.

In a content standard or objective, you will generally find two types of elements: knowledge and skills. The knowledge element identifies the discipline-specific facts, concepts, and procedures one must know in order to demonstrate the standard. Content knowledge is represented by the nouns in the standard or objective. In the examples in Table 3.6, the content knowledge is:

- Grade 4: properties of minerals
- Grade 8: rocks, fossils, ice cores, and Earth's geologic history
- Grade 12: the rock cycle; and origin, texture, and mineral composition of rocks

These curricular elements are the basic content addressed in your lessons. In this science example, the basic content addressed in all three grades is related to rocks and minerals, but the facts, concepts, and procedures become more complex as the students mature and progress through the science curriculum.

Table 3.6	Examples of Science Content Standards and Associated Objectives	
Grade	Standard	Objective
4	The learner will conduct investigations and use appropriate technology to build an understanding of the composition and uses of rocks and minerals.	Describe and evaluate the properties of several minerals.
8	The learner will conduct investigations and utilize appropriate technologies and information systems to build an understanding of evidence of evolution in organisms and landforms.	Interpret ways in which rocks, fossils, and ice cores record Earth's geologic history and the evolution of life including: Geologic Time Scale, Index Fossils, Law of Superposition.
12	The learner will build an understanding of lithospheric materials, tectonic processes, and the human and environmental impacts of natural and human-induced changes in the lithosphere.	Investigate and analyze the processes responsible for the rock cycle by analyzing the origin, texture, and mineral composition of rocks.

Source: Adapted from Public Schools of North Carolina. (2006). *North Carolina standard course of study.* Retrieved May 9, 2006, from http://www.dpi.state.nc.us/curriculum.

After identifying the content knowledge, you must determine what your students will do with that content. In other words, what skills must they demonstrate using that knowledge? Do they simply have to recall or define it or will they apply content knowledge in some unique way? A content standard or objective will indicate the type of skill required by the use of a verb. In the examples in Table 3.6, the skills are:

- Grade 4: describe and evaluate
- Grade 8: interpret
- Grade 12: investigate and analyze

When developing lessons aligned with your content standards, it is critical to know what level of skill performance is required of your students. These types of skills are very different and, when combined with the content knowledge, help you to determine what it is your students should be able to do. Based on that information, then, you need to assure that your students have opportunities to both 1) develop those skills during their learning activities and 2) demonstrate those skills during your assessments. One mistake often made by inexperienced teachers is to design activities and assessments at a skill level that is lower than that dictated by the content standard and ultimately assessed on high-stakes assessments. When this happens, students may be aware of content-specific knowledge, but they can't apply it at an appropriate skill level. Adequately covering the content standard does not mean simply exposing students to facts, concepts, and procedures. Students must be provided with opportunities to apply their knowledge at appropriate skill levels.

Standards and objectives are not a prescription; they do not tell you how you must teach in order for your students to achieve them. That is, they do not prescribe the methods you must use nor dictate the materials or resources required to address them. Some content standards specifically mention technology, but as you'll see throughout this book, there are technology tools and resources to help address content standards in all domains regardless of a specific mention.

So let's think about how we could use authentic instruction and technology to develop critical and creative thinking skills around the science standards listed above. As an example, let's consider a lesson for fourth-graders in which they learn to describe and evaluate the properties of minerals. How can you create a lesson that encourages learner autonomy and provides the opportunity for active learning using holistic, complex, and challenging activities?

In order to establish a realistic context for the lesson, the teacher could introduce the fourth-graders to a problem in which a whole box of mineral samples from the geology museum got mixed up and separated from their labels. The museum director needs help from her lab assistants (the students) to straighten out the mess. She asks them for their ideas as to how to accomplish this task. How will they do it? As she facilitates this whole group activity, she records multiple paths to solving the problem and helps the students identify an avenue for investigation.

APPLY TO PRACTICE

Lesson Plans and Content Standards

Find a lesson plan from a website or other lesson planning resource that is relevant to your area of study. Find the standards for your state that are or could be addressed in the lesson you have found. If you need some help, some lesson planning sites are listed on the textbook's companion website and most states include a list of standards for all grades and content areas on their websites.

1. List the content standard(s) addressed by the lesson.
2. Briefly describe the activities in the lesson.
3. Determine how well the activities match the required knowledge (nouns) and the skills (verbs) in the content standard(s). Indicate alignment and potential misalignment.

In the next phase of the lesson, the learners might conduct a web search to learn the basics of mineral identification. The students can be prompted with questions including "What tools will you need?" and "What kind of information do you need about each mineral sample?" The teacher might then refine the problem a bit. She shows the students the labels from the mixed up samples in order to scaffold their learning by making the task more manageable. For the fourth-grade level, five or six minerals would be plenty. The next task for the students is to use a spreadsheet to create a data collection table for each of the minerals in order to assist them with their data collection, analysis, and interpretation. The students might search the web for information to fill in their charts. Finally, the teacher reveals the mineral samples. Using information and tools gathered in the prior stages of the lesson, the students match the minerals with their labels. At the end of the lesson, the teacher asks each group to share their findings for one of the mineral samples. After all the minerals have been identified, she concludes the lesson by asking her students to describe how they went about solving the problem and what they learned in the process. As a follow-up activity, she might want to give them a few more minerals to identify, using the procedures they determined to be successful in their initial investigations.

By establishing a realistic context for students' learning, the teacher provides a holistic, complex problem in which to ground their learning. In order to encourage learner autonomy, students plan, monitor, and evaluate their own learning—learners are given the freedom to design and conduct their investigations. In this process, they practice self-directed learning skills as they plan, monitor, and evaluate their actions. The teacher models the sort of questions students should ask themselves during the self-directed learning process by asking them how they would accomplish their goals, what tools they might need, and what information they need to solve the mineral identification problem. She reduces the challenges of authentic learning by placing her students in collaborative groups where students can pool their knowledge and support each other. Collaborative group work also encourages reflection and articulation as the students explain their reasoning to their team members, and reflect on the reasoning of others. When the teacher presents the mineral labels that the students are to match with the mineral samples, she further reduces the complexity of the problem by constraining their information searches to a manageable number.

Using this approach, the students learn to describe and evaluate the properties of minerals through an authentic learning experience that, as you have learned in this chapter, would help develop their critical and creative thinking skills. Students are given the opportunity to design and conduct an investigation in which they collect, analyze, and interpret data, and then apply what they learned to new problems. By allowing students to decide what information is needed, the instructional time becomes inquiry-driven and the students become active learners. Students have a clear problem to solve, and their understanding of the properties of minerals is rooted in a practical application.

In Part II of this book, we provide additional examples of how you can meet content and technology standards while developing students' creative thinking skills. Guest authors in the areas of language arts, foreign language, math, science, social studies, health/physical education, visual arts, and music provide specific examples of the use of technologies to anchor authentic learning experiences in each content area. Furthermore, Appendix A contains additional information on the role standards play in lesson planning.

Chapter Summary

In this chapter, we described how the components of authentic instruction could be used to facilitate and inspire student creativity and learning. We also described how the principles of authentic instruction could guide your use of technology in the classroom. Specifically, we discussed how different types of authentic instruction (problem-based learning, project-based learning, etc.) promote learner autonomy and active learning by anchoring instruction in holistic, complex, and challenging activities. We discussed the occasional need for directed instruction and explored multiple ways in which technology can support this approach as well as each of the components of authentic instruction.

In the last section of this chapter you considered how to reconcile the goal of helping students meet content standards with the goal of promoting critical and creative thinking in your classroom. Using the example of a science lesson on the identification of minerals, we illustrated how you could design learning experiences that provide opportunities for your students to obtain the skills required in the content standards, and at the same time, develop their creative thinking skills.

In the next chapter, we continue our discussion of specific approaches to using technology to encourage the development of creative thinking skills. You will be prompted to think about ways in which common software applications (word processing, databases, etc.) can be used to support the development of your students' creative thinking skills. We will also consider a variety of ways in which the computer can be used to support meaningful conversations and student reflection and collaboration.

YOUR PORTFOLIO

This chapter described how to use technology to facilitate and inspire student learning and creativity through the use of authentic classroom activities. To demonstrate competency in ISTE NETS-T Standard 1 a-b, add the following items to your portfolio:

1. Reflect on how technology can be used to develop students' creative thinking skills. Consider the recommendations from the national curricular reports (see Figure 3.1) for creating more effective and engaging instruction that can inspire student creativity and learning. Write a brief reflection of a teaching or learning experience that you think best exemplifies a "best practice" lesson. Indicate the role technology played in the lesson and how it supported the tenets of authentic instruction you described above.
   a. What aspects of the lesson worked best?
   b. What aspects would you change if used in the future?
2. Describe a lesson in which you incorporate the principles of authentic instruction. Locate a set of national or state standards that your future students may be required to meet. Select one standard around which to design a lesson.
   a. Identify how you will address each of the 5 components: 1) learner autonomy; 2) active learners; and 3) holistic, 4) complex, and 5) challenging activities.
   b. Describe specific ways that technologies could be used to support the successful implementation of your strategy.

You might want to review the content area chapters in Part II of this book before you complete this activity.

References

Black, S. (2005). Teaching students to think critically. *Education Digest: Essential Readings Condensed for Quick Review*, 70(6), 42.

Brinkerhoff, J., & Glazewski, K. (2004). Support of expert and novice teachers within a technology enhanced problem-based learning unit: A case study. *International Journal of Learning Technology*, 1, 219–230.

Collins, A., Brown, J. S., & Holum, A. (1991). Cognitive apprenticeship: Making thinking visible. *American Educator*, 6–11, 38–46.

Craft, A. (2001). *An analysis of research and literature on creativity and education*. Report prepared for the Qualifications and Curriculum Authority, UK. Retrieved May 6, 2008, from http://www.ncaction.org.uk/creativity/creativity_report.pdf

Egbert, J. (2009). *Supporting learning with technology: Essentials of classroom practice*. Upper Saddle River, NJ: Pearson.

Hunter, M. (1982). *Mastery teaching*. El Segundo, CA: Instructional Dynamics.

Johnson, D., & Johnson, R. (1998). *Learning together and alone: Cooperative, competitive, and individualistic learning* (5th ed.). New York: Allyn and Bacon.

Jonassen, D. J., Howland, J., Moore, J., & Marra, R. M. (2003). *Learning to solve problems with technology: A constructivist perspective* (2nd ed.). Upper Saddle River, NJ: Merrill/Prentice Hall.

Magliaro, S. G., Lockee, B. B., & Burton, J. K. (2005). Direct instruction revisited: A key model for instructional technology. *Educational Technology Research and Development*, 53(4), 41–55.

Marzano, R. J., & Arredondo, D. E. (1986). Restructuring Schools Through the Teaching of Thinking Skills. *Educational Leadership*, 43(8), 20.

Marzano, R. J., Brandt, R. S., Hughes, C. S., Jones, B. F., Presseisen, B. Z., Rankin, S. C., & Suhor, C. (1988). *Dimensions of thinking: A framework for curriculum and instruction*. Alexandria, VA: Association for Supervision and Curriculum Development.

Musselwhite, T. (2005). Creating learner-centered middle school classrooms. New York: Glencoe/McGraw Hill. Retrieved January 6, 2007, from http://www.glencoe.com/sec/teachingtoday/subject/creating_learn_centered.phtml

Newmann, F. M., Bryk, A. S., & Nagaoka, J. K. (2001). *Authentic intellectual work and standardized tests: Conflict or coexistence?* Chicago, IL: Consortium on Chicago School Research.

Nickerson, R. S. (1984). Kinds of thinking taught in current programs. *Educational Leadership*, 42(1), 26.

Paul, R., & Elder, L. (2004). Critical thinking and the art of close reading (Part III). *Journal of Developmental Education*, 28(1), 36–37.

Pedersen, S., & Liu, M. (2002–2003). The transfer of problem-solving skills from a problem-based learning environment: The effect of modeling an expert's cognitive processes. *Journal of Research on Technology in Education*, 35, 303–320.

Public Schools of North Carolina. (2006). *North Carolina standard course of study*. Retrieved May 9, 2006, from http://www.dpi.state.nc.us/curriculum

Raths, L. E., Wasserman, S., Jonas, A., & Rothstein, A. (1986). *Teaching for thinking: Theory, strategies, & activities for the classroom*. New York: Teachers College Press.

Resnick, L. B. (1987). *Education and learning to think*. Washington, DC: National Academy Press.

Saye, J. W., & Brush, T. (2002). Scaffolding critical reasoning about history and social issues in multimedia-supported learning environments. *Educational Technology Research and Development*, 50(3), 77–96.

Simons, K. D., & Ertmer, P. A. (2005/2006). Scaffolding disciplined inquiry in problem-based learning environments. *International Journal of Learning*, 12(6), 297–306.

Slavin, R. (1994). *Cooperative learning: Theory, research, and practice*. New York: Allyn and Bacon.

Sternberg, R. J., & Baron, J. B. (1985). A statewide approach to measuring critical thinking skills. *Educational Leadership*, 43(2), 40.

Sternberg, R. J., & Spear-Swerling, L. (1996). *Teaching for thinking*. Washington, DC: American Psychological Association.

Wegerif, R. (2002). *Literature review in thinking skills, technology, and learning*. Future Lab Series, No. 2. Retrieved June 1, 2006, from http://www.futurelab.org.uk/research/reviews/ts01.htm

Zemelman, S., Daniels, H., & Hyde, A. (2005). *Best practice: Today's standards for teaching and learning in America's schools*. Portsmouth, NH: Heinemann.

Digital Tools That Support Learning

I t's amazing how much a learning environment can change when technology is added to the mix! While technology is not essential to creating authentic, learner-centered instruction, it offers a powerful resource for engaging students in authentic experiences, typically increasing both their motivation and their learning. In the last chapter, you learned about the importance of developing students' creative thinking skills. You learned that creative thinkers generate a variety of original ideas then select the best one by analyzing, synthesizing, and evaluating the various options available. Furthermore, creative thinkers are self-directed, confident in their knowledge, motivated, and flexible in their thinking. You also learned how authentic instructional methods can support the development of creative thinking skills by providing opportunities for students to engage in holistic, complex, and challenging activities that promote learner autonomy and active learning; how directed

ISTE Standards addressed in this chapter

NETS-T 1. Facilitate and Inspire Student Learning and Creativity

Teachers use their knowledge of subject matter, teaching and learning, and technology to facilitate experiences that advance student learning, creativity, and innovation in both face-to-face and virtual environments. Teachers:
c. promote student reflection using collaborative tools to reveal and clarify students' conceptual understanding and thinking, planning, and creative processes
d. model collaborative knowledge construction by engaging in learning with students, colleagues, and others in face-to-face and virtual environments

NETS-T 2. Design and Develop Digital-Age Learning Experiences and Assessments

Teachers design, develop, and evaluate authentic learning experiences and assessments incorporating contemporary tools and resources to maximize content learning in context and to develop the knowledge, skills, and attitudes identified in the NETS-S. Teachers:
a. design or adapt relevant learning experiences to incorporate digital tools and resources to promote student learning and creativity

Note: Standards 1.a and 1.b were addressed in Chapter 3. Standard 2.b is addressed in Chapter 5, 2.c in Chapter 6, and 2.d in Chapter 7.

Outcomes

In this chapter, you will

- Identify digital resources and design learning experiences that use technologies as tutorials, mindtools, and supports for conversations in order to facilitate student learning and creativity.
- Promote student learning by employing computer-based tutorials or creating online tutorials in the form of WebQuests.
- Help students represent, manipulate, and reflect on what they know through the use of databases, concept maps, or when using computer-based simulations or visualization tools.
- Incorporate hypermedia activities in your instruction, such as digital storytelling and website development.
- Use technology as collaborative learning tools in support of knowledge construction and creative thinking in face-to-face and virtual settings.
- Locate and evaluate digital tools and resources found online in support of instruction in face-to-face and virtual environments.

instruction can support authentic learning; how content standards can be taught through authentic learning experiences; and how technologies could support both authentic learning and directed instruction.

In this chapter, you will begin to think about designing learning experiences that incorporate digital tools and resources to promote student learning and creativity. Wegerif (2002) described three primary roles that the computer can serve: computer as tutor, computer as mindtool, and computer as a support for reflection and conversation. This categorization provides us with a starting point for thinking about different ways we can use technology to engage our students in creative thinking. Although we use Wegerif's language—computer—we're not just talking about a desktop or laptop computer. Many of the applications and activities described in this chapter are supported by a range of technologies, from handhelds (PDAs), to calculators, and even to some cell phones! And since we often use the web to locate instructional resources, we'll also discuss strategies to assist you in locating reputable resources that can be used as tutorials, mindtools, and supports for conversations.

STORIES FROM PRACTICE

Using Technology to Support Creative Thinking

I teach high school biology in a unique setting. While my students are probably no different from most freshmen and sophomore students you might know, I teach this course with two other biology teachers using a method we devised a number of years ago, called Team Taught Biology. Technology is a key component to our approach, enabling us to engage students in the biology content in very unique ways. But I need to point out that, for me at least, the computer is not the coolest part of this. It may even be the weakest part. Learning happens when people are *active* and the computer simply allows us to provide more of those opportunities, because we don't have to lecture.

Although I teach biology, my primary goal for my students is not that they learn biology, but that they become independent learners and critical thinkers. And the independent learning happens only if you give them control. As long as I was telling them what to do and when to do it, there was no chance that they would ever become independent learners. As soon as you give students control over their own education, it's terribly empowering. Most people become

terribly motivated when they have control. And we want them to be self-directed learners; we want them to be critical thinkers. And I think in the computer age that's especially important. Because there is so much junk disseminated by computers—especially on the Internet.

The technology allows for another learning alternative, another option, another way of providing information. Right now, we already have two or three primary options for using the computer in the classroom. One is the Internet—we have an activity every single unit, where students can go to the Internet and interact in that environment, demonstrate understanding, come back and report it. We also have computer tutorials, which have eliminated the need for a lecture. That frees us up to be mentoring instead of spouting knowledge. The third way that computers are used is to do labs that can be done in no other way. Computers enable us to present data that are outside the realm of a biology classroom, such as ozone data, or to examine the dotted wings of a butterfly. As far as I am concerned that is the best use of a

computer—when it is used in ways where you couldn't do the lab any other way.

Arranging our classroom in this way, and using technology to support alternative approaches, provides students with the opportunity to pick those types of learning activities that they enjoy the most. It is not total freedom. There are some things that they have to do. But for every individual there is enough of a selection, enough of a choice. They can't do everything. They can't do all the learning activities, so they get to ignore some of them. And they can ignore those things that they dislike.

The best thing about this approach is that it has taken me off center stage. In the traditional classroom, the teacher is the center, the teacher is the active individual. But in Team Taught Biology, we have set up a situation where everybody is active. And I think that while that doesn't guarantee learning, it sure increases the chances that it's going to happen.

Source: Based on Ertmer, P. A. (2003). *VisionQuest: Envisioning and achieving integrated technology use.* Retrieved June 24, 2006, from http://www.edci.purdue.edu/vquest.

Computer as Tutor

In the role of a tutor, the computer is typically used as a teaching machine, that is, to teach new content to students. If you've ever set up a new computer system using the CD-ROM that comes packaged with it or have worked your way through a tutorial to learn a new piece of software, then you've used the computer as a tutor. Although this role for technology is typically associated with directed instruction in which the goal is for students to master new skills or to improve retention of new information, the tutor model can be adapted to teach more abstract and complex reasoning skills. In addition, many existing computer tutorials can be used to prompt student inquiry or to frame student discussion and reflection, even though this was not the original purpose for the software program.

Computer-Based Tutorials

Computer-based tutorials typically provide a complete lesson on a specific topic including 1) presenting new information, 2) providing practice, and 3) evaluating student learning (see Figure 4.1). Computer tutorials, especially when delivered via intelligent tutoring systems, have the advantage of being able to provide sophisticated feedback at the level needed by individual students.

An **intelligent tutoring system** (ITS) is a type of educational software that can track student responses; make inferences about his/her strengths and weaknesses; and then tailor feedback, provide additional exercises, or offer hints to improve performance. The software is said to *act* intelligently, not actually to *be* intelligent. Other names for this type of software include integrated learning software (ILS) and computer-adapted instruction (CAI). Because an ITS uses sophisticated language and branching (i.e., sequencing the way information is presented based on students' previous responses), it can promote the kind of creative thinking desired. For example, Cognitive Tutor is a mathematics intelligent tutoring system, developed by researchers at Carnegie Mellon University, to help middle and high school students learn math. According to the authors (Carnegie Learning, 2006), Cognitive Tutor provides students with the benefits of individualized instruction, ample practice, immediate feedback, and coaching. As an intelligent tutoring system, the program combines individualized computer-based lessons with collaborative, real-world problem-solving activities. To get a sense of how this type of software works, try out Mrs. Lindquist: The Tutor, an ITS designed to help students learn how to write algebraic expressions for algebra word problems. Pay attention to the type of feedback the software provides when you make an error and you will see how "intelligent" it appears to be.

(a)

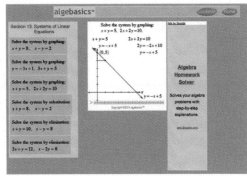

(b)

Figure 4.1

Computer tutorials cover many subjects, including typing (a) and mathematics (b), shown here.
Source: Courtesy of TypingWeb.com; Mark Basse, Algebasics

> **Characteristics of Effective Computer Tutorials**
> - Challenges and problems have meaning for students and provide a range of alternative choices worth discussing.
> - Challenges engage learners with the content of the software, not its interface.
> - A clear purpose or task is evident to the group and is kept in focus throughout.
> - On-screen prompts ask group members to talk together, to reach agreement, and to provide opinions and reasons.
> - Resources for discussion, including information on which decisions can be based, are provided. Opportunities are included to review decisions in light of new information.
> - Students are not prompted to take turns, beat the clock, or establish competitive ways of working.
> - For younger students, audio input or multi-choice answers minimize typing (unless the learners have keyboarding skills). (reported in Wegerif, 2002)

Figure 4.2
Characteristics of computer tutorials that promote creative thinking.

 WEB LINK

To explore *Mrs. Lindquist: The Tutor* and access links to additional information about intelligent tutoring systems, visit the textbook's companion website.

With the right teacher input and software design, a computer tutorial can be an effective way to infuse activities that require and develop creative thinking into the curriculum. For example, the teacher can ask students to work in groups around a computer and then when the software prompts them with a challenge or a question, they can discuss the issue together before reaching consensus about what the response should be. In Figure 4.2, we include a list of specific software characteristics that Wegerif (cited in Wegerif, 2002) demonstrated to be effective in establishing and sustaining effective discussion among students when they were working around the computer. Think about how you could use these characteristics as guidelines to help you select effective software for your classroom. In addition, think about how you could incorporate these characteristics into other approaches and strategies you use in your classroom, with or without the use of computer tutorials.

Just like a teacher, computer tutorials can initiate or frame a meaningful discussion. Unlike a teacher, however, the software will never be intolerant or pass judgment on students' responses. When used as intended, computer tutorials provide opportunities for students to learn new knowledge or skills. When used in more open-ended ways, they can provide additional opportunities for students to engage in activities that support creative thinking (e.g., reflection, meaningful conversations).

THE GAME PLAN

Using Computer Tutorials to Support Creative and Higher-Order Thinking

Set Goals

Learn more about computer tutorials and how you might use them to develop critical and creative thinking skills among your students.

Take Action

Locate a computer tutorial that is designed for your grade level or content area. You may be able to find them in your media center, lab school, a cooperating school, or you may be able to preview software online by using a search engine and entering the term "computer software" or "computer tutorial."

Monitor

Review the software and determine the extent to which the characteristics listed in Figure 4.2 are incorporated. You may want to create a table, rubric, or checklist to guide your work.

Evaluate and Extend

Suggest ways to use the software to increase opportunities for students to engage in creative and higher-order thinking. Identify the type of thinking your activities best address.

WebQuests

One common way of learning new information is through searching the web. The web can provide access to numerous computer-based tutorials, but as you know, it can teach you new content in other ways as well. You can locate information on a variety of topics—how to train your dog to sit, prepare balanced meals, or use video in your classroom, for example. In order to scaffold or support your students' use of the web as a tutor, you might want to create a WebQuest.

A **WebQuest** is an organized format for presenting lessons that utilize web resources (see example in Figure 4.3). The origin of WebQuests is attributed to Dr. Bernie Dodge and Tom March at San Diego State University. As outlined on Dr. Dodge's website (Dodge, 2006), a WebQuest consists of five parts and a teacher page. As you will notice in Table 4.1, a WebQuest contains elements that most educators agree comprise sound instructional design components: 1) an introduction that motivates and prepares the students for the activity, 2) a clear statement of the intended outcome of the lesson, 3) the steps that students should follow, 4) criteria on which they will be evaluated, and 5) concluding activities where students reflect on and extend their learning. You may want to create your own WebQuest using simple web development software, or access one of the many WebQuests available online. Like any lesson plan that you find on the web, you may need to modify WebQuests to meet the needs of your class. However, be sure you credit the original source.

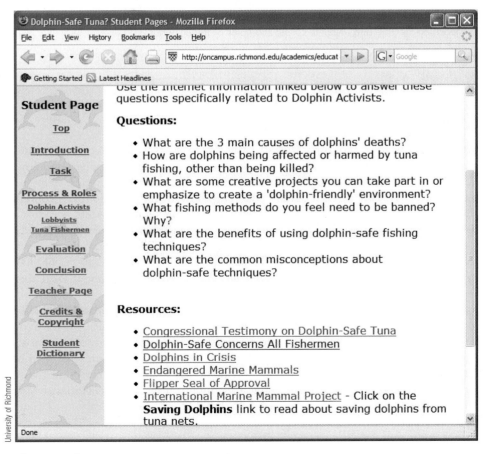

Figure 4.3
WebQuests direct learners to relevant websites to complete the required learning tasks.
Source: http://oncampus.richmond.edu/academics/education/projects/webquests/dolphins/

Table 4.1	Developing a WebQuest	
	The following descriptions are from the WebQuest website at San Diego State University. Visit the textbook's companion website for this URL and other WebQuest resources.	
Component	Purpose	Task
Introduction	The purpose of this section is to both prepare and grab the students' attention.	Write a short paragraph to introduce the activity or lesson to the students. If there is a role or scenario involved (e.g., "You are a detective trying to identify the mysterious poet.") then here is where you'll set the stage. Also, in this section you'll communicate the Big Question (Essential Question, Guiding Question) on which the WebQuest is centered.
Task	The task focuses learners on what they are going to do—specifically, the culminating performance or product that drives all of the learning activities.	Clearly describe what the result of the learners' activities will be. Don't list the steps that students will go through to get to the end point. That belongs in the Process section.
Process	This section outlines how the learners will accomplish the task. Scaffolding includes clear steps, resources, and tools for organizing information.	To accomplish the task, what steps should the learners go through? Learners will access the online resources that you've identified as they go through the Process. In this section, you might also provide some guidance on how to organize the information gathered.
Evaluation	This section describes the criteria needed to meet performance and content standards.	Describe to the learners how their performances will be evaluated. The assessment rubric(s) should align with the culminating project or performance, as outlined in the task section of the WebQuest. Specify whether there will be a common grade for group work vs. individual grades.
Conclusion	The conclusion brings closure and encourages reflection.	Summarize what the learners will have accomplished or learned by completing this activity or lesson. You might also include some rhetorical questions or additional links to encourage them to extend their thinking into other content beyond this lesson.
Teacher Page	The teacher page includes information to help other teachers implement the WebQuest including descriptions of target learners, standards, notes for teaching the unit, and, in some cases, examples of student work.	

Source: Dodge, B. (2006). http://webquest.sdsu.edu.

Computer as Mindtool

Mindtools are computer applications that enable learners to represent, manipulate, or reflect on what they know, rather than to reproduce what someone else knows (Jonassen, 2006). By requiring students to think about what they know in different, meaningful ways, mindtools engage students in critical thinking about the content they are studying. By functioning as intellectual partners with students, mindtools enable them to act smarter than they would without the tools. For instance, in order for students to create databases, they must engage in analytical reasoning; in order to create a web page, they must actively construct representations of their thinking. Students cannot use mindtools without thinking deeply about what they are doing.

Jonassen (2006) described a number of different types of mindtools including databases and concept-mapping tools (also referred to as semantic-organization tools); simulations and visualization tools; and hypertext and hypermedia (referred to as knowledge-building tools). Although other computer applications may also be used as mindtools (e.g., programming software, expert systems, modeling tools), our goal is not to present an exhaustive description of all the possibilities, but to introduce you to the idea of how you can use common software applications as mindtools to promote creative thinking among your students.

Databases and Concept-Mapping Tools

Database and concept-mapping software are computer applications that help students think about, and then communicate, the underlying structure of a content area. Since structure is intrinsic to all knowledge, tools that require students to identify that structure can help increase their understanding of the content.

Have you ever made a grocery list and then organized it by aisles in the store so that you could find the items you needed more readily? On a relatively simple level, you structured your list based on your understanding of two things: 1) how the store (content) was organized (e.g., by food types) and 2) how to classify the items on your list into the different categories. Now, if there were many different ways to classify the items on your list (by quality, supplier, brand names, etc.), and all of them were relevant to your shopping needs, then you would have to think more carefully about how to organize your list.

Databases

Databases are a type of computer software that organizes information. When we use a computer database we can search for information in a variety ways and receive the results almost instantaneously. Although databases are most often used for the purposes of organization and retrieval of information (i.e., as productivity tools), they can also function as mindtools, especially when students are asked to create them. That is because in order to build a database, you must first understand which relationships facilitate its use and then search for, and locate, the information needed to fill it. This requires the integration and organization of a content domain, which requires creative thinking skills. For example, if you were asked to create a database of all the educational videos available in your school library, what are some of the categories you would use to classify each video? Of course, you'd want to be able to locate a video by its title and subject area, and also by grade level. But would it also be important to know the release date or the production studio? And what about being able to relate the information in the video database to information in a teacher database that would allow you to find out if a teacher in an earlier grade level had already used it? As you can see, the planning stage of designing a database is one of the most crucial parts of the process, and it is this aspect that requires students to engage in the creative thinking skills of analysis and evaluation.

Databases have been used to help students understand the organization of a range of content areas and can be used to teach thinking skills. The youngest students probably need help actually developing a database, but you can guide them through the planning process during a group activity. For example, students in a second- or third-grade class can help you classify different types of clip art images you typically use that are then stored in a database. Students from upper elementary grades, and higher, can access, and sometimes add to, a range of databases online.

Collaborative databases are a special type of database that supports a shared process of knowledge building. The goal is to engage students as scientists in the problem-solving process. That is, students generate hypotheses about a given problem situation; gather information through research and observation in order to confirm, modify, or refute their hypotheses; and then seek feedback from others who either collaborate in the investigation or review their published work. An example of this type of collaborative database is the Knowledge Forum, formerly known as CSILE (Computer Supported Intentional Learning Environments).

To help you understand why this is called a collaborative database, picture an environment that consists of text and graphical notes, all produced by students, and accessible through typical database search procedures. Students are given a question, search for and find information, and then record it via notes in the database. Other students then comment on the notes and add new notes. Before students can send a message, however, they must label the message using a limited set of categories (e.g., claim, evidence, counterargument). So, for example, if students post an opinion, they are prompted to support that opinion with evidence, an example, or reasoning. Teachers have used Knowledge Forum effectively in many different areas of the curriculum.

WEB LINK

To visit the *Knowledge Forum* and view examples of other collaborative databases, visit the textbook's companion website.

Wikis

An example of a more public collaborative database is the popular online encyclopedia, Wikipedia (see Figure 4.4). Based on the format of an encyclopedia, this website utilizes a database that can be accessed through web pages by multiple users who create and store information that is then reviewed, revised, added to, and linked to other information.

A **wiki** is a piece of server software that allows users to create, edit, and link web pages quickly, which is what wiki means in the Hawaiian language—quick or fast. According to its creator, Ward Cunningham, a wiki is the "simplest online database that could possibly work" (cited in Wikipedia, 2007). Wikis are a great tool when students need to complete a task together—whether doing research, writing a paper, or planning a presentation. If they aren't all in the same class or if work needs to get done in the evening or on the weekend, wikis allow them to coordinate their efforts much more efficiently than sending a bunch of e-mails back and forth. And they don't have to know web authoring languages or other complicated tools to do so.

Most wikis work the same way. With the click of a button, each student can make changes to a web page. Because changes are attributed to specific users, the community can verify the accuracy of the information or ask for additional details. So, for example, after Emilie creates a wiki page, she simply saves it. Then when her

Figure 4.4

Screen shot of Wikipedia, a popular collaborative database. Courtesy Wikipedia, Inc.

TOOLS FOR USE

Tips for Using Educational Wikis

Consider the following tips when incorporating a wiki in your instruction.

1. *Collaborate.* Wikis work best in support of collaborative projects, so begin by determining a project that addresses your content standards and is suited to student collaboration.
2. *Access.* Determine who will have access to your wiki. For class projects, you may have a private wiki that only students in your class can post to; however, ultimately you may want to share wiki content with other students, parents, the community, or others.

3. *Format.* Determine appropriate formatting of text and other elements to help students understand effective visual communication strategies.
4. *Post.* Set expectations for posting. Let students know how often and how much they should post and what *not* to post, such as contact information.
5. *Notify.* Make sure your wiki is configured to notify the wiki monitor or administrator (probably you!) when changes are made.
6. *Nurture.* Just as when using any new tool, wikis need a little nurturing. Use the wiki in class during instruction, model appropriate use, and guide students to the wiki for appropriate activities.

classmate, Scott, accesses it, he clicks an "edit" button, makes some additional changes, clicks save and it's a web page again, ready for the next student to access and modify. Edit – Write – Save! Following this simple process, it's easy for the students to coordinate their writing efforts.

Wikis have not yet received widespread acclaim as it can be difficult to determine the accuracy and authorship of the information posted, especially in large public wikis. Jaron Lanier, a computer scientist, usually credited with coining the term "virtual reality," suggests that just because these tools give voice to a new "online collectivism," it doesn't mean the collective is correct. The anonymity these tools provide can sometimes erode authority and even accuracy. Just as with any technology tool, you and your students should takes steps to ascertain and evaluate the accuracy of information that a specific wiki contains.

While some teachers are cautious about—or outright forbid the use of—online resource wikis, you can use wikis in your classroom in a variety of ways. For example, you and your students can use a wiki to create your own resources or projects on a closed network, to provide space for group journaling or writing, or to engage students in debates about course topics. Specific websites—including some wikis—are available to help teachers create and use wikis in the classroom.

WEB LINK

Visit the textbook's companion website for a list of sites that support teachers' creation and use of wikis.

Concept Maps

Concept maps are "graphical tools for organizing and representing knowledge" (Novak & Canas, 2006, p. 1). For example, Figure 4.5 presents a sample concept map about the seasons. Concepts (e.g., seasons, amount of sunlight) are included inside of circles or boxes, relationships between the concepts are represented by lines or arrows, and labels are used to describe the relationships (e.g., causes, is determined by). The concepts may also be referred to as nodes and the relationships as links.

There are many ways to use concept maps: Students can use them to access prior knowledge, to organize and represent current knowledge, and to explore new information and relationships. Creating a concept map involves 1) identifying the important concepts in a domain of knowledge, 2) arranging those concepts spatially, 3) identifying relationships among the concepts, and 4) labeling the nature of the relationships among those concepts. Because students have to manipulate information, and think about the relationships among different concepts, creating a concept map encourages convergent thinking. Students are forced to think about how concepts in a domain fit together and to identify additional ideas or concepts that need to be included. There are a variety of software tools that facilitate concept-mapping

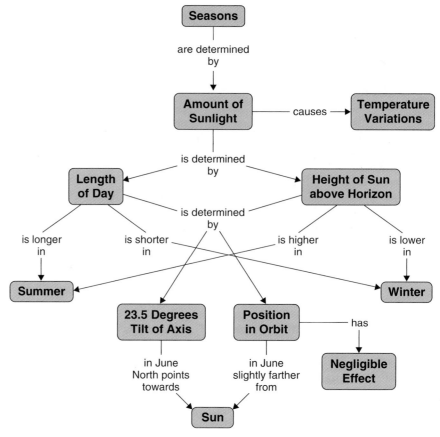

Figure 4.5
Example of a concept map.
Source: Novak & Canas, 2006.

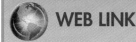

including MindMap, Inspiration and Kidspiration, and SemNet. Interestingly, even though Inspiration was developed for K-12 teachers and students, many scientists, engineers, and other professionals have adopted it as a powerful way to visualize their thinking.

Simulations and Visualization Tools

Simulations provide simplified versions of phenomena, environments, or processes that allow students to interact with, or manipulate, variables and observe the effects of those manipulations (see Figure 4.6). If you've used Oregon Trail, Sim City, or Operation Frog, then you have an idea of what a computer simulation is like. However, not all simulations promote creative thinking (at least not automatically). While simulations have the potential to promote creative thinking, their usefulness will depend on why and how you and your students use them.

One type of simulation software that can be especially powerful is a **microworld**, which allows learners to manipulate, explore, and experiment with specific phenomenon in an exploratory learning environment. Think about some of the video games you or your friends have played. Typically, you must master earlier levels of the game in order to move on to more complex, advanced levels. These adventures occur in a microworld, a lifelike context in which you manipulate objects and observe the effects of your actions on other objects in the environment. As a more academic example, consider that of Interactive Physics, which enables learners to build and test mechanical design models. Through the use of demonstrations, car crashes, and falling objects, students explore such topics as momentum, force, and acceleration. Students

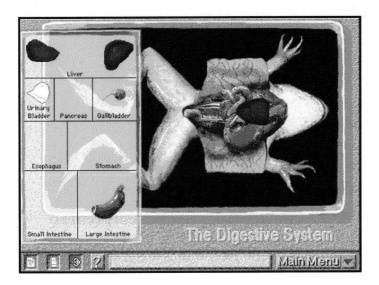

Figure 4.6
Operation Frog allows students to dissect a frog without the frog or the smell. Courtesy Tom Snyder.

can change any aspect of the environment (friction, incline of the surface, etc.) and observe what happens to the other aspects of the environment. This, then, enables them to generate and test hypotheses about relationships among the objects in the microworld. According to Jonassen et al. (2003) microworlds can foster the development of problem-solving strategies, critical thinking skills, and creativity.

Visualization tools allow learners to picture, or represent, how various phenomena operate within different domains. While these tools are often used to help students visualize scientific phenomena, other tools are available that help students understand other types of phenomena, such as the structure of an argument. For example, computer tools are available that enable students to manipulate complex data sets as a way of gaining understanding of *statistical* arguments.

Graphic organizers are a type of visualization tool that can help learners sort or record information. There are many different types of graphic organizers including data grids, tables, diagrams, flowcharts, storyboards, and Venn diagrams. Concept-mapping tools, described earlier, can also be used as graphic organizers. While most of these organizers have been used long before computers were invented, today we have computer software that can simplify the creation of many of them. For example, the ReadWriteThink organization makes a tool available on their website that allows users to create Venn diagrams and the popular Inspiration concept-mapping software includes a Venn diagram template. Organizations that create visualization tools often provide a number of descriptions of how their tools can be used in the classroom. Inspiration Software's newer tool, InspireData, is a data visualization tool that allows you and your students to easily map and manipulate data, such as what you might collect from a survey, and then share that information with the concept-mapping software.

Hypertext and Hypermedia

You are probably very familiar with hypertext and hypermedia from your experiences with websites. **Hypertext** refers to a nonsequential, or nonlinear, method for organizing and displaying text. **Hypermedia** is basically hypertext with media elements (i.e., images, sounds, videos, animations, etc.). While reading hypertext is not likely to lead to noticeable learning benefits, *creating* or *constructing* effective hypertext and hypermedia tends to require creative thinking skills. That is, when developing

WEB LINK

Links to *Interactive Physics* and other microworld resources are available on the textbook's companion website.

WEB LINK

For a list of resources related to visualization tools, visit the textbook's companion website.

Table 4.2	Incorporation of Creative Thinking Skills into Multimedia Development Projects
Type of Skills Needed	**Sample Skills**
Project Management Skills	Creating a timeline for completion Allocating resources and time to different parts of the project Assigning roles to team members Monitoring and evaluating progress toward the goal
Research Skills	Determining the nature of the problem and how research should be organized Posing thoughtful questions about structure, models, cases, values, and roles Searching for information using text, electronic, and pictorial information Developing new information with interviews, questionnaires, and other survey methods Analyzing and interpreting all the information collected to identify and interpret patterns
Organization and Representation	Deciding how to segment and sequence information to make it understandable Deciding how information will be represented (text, pictures, video, audio) Deciding how the information will be modified to meet the needs of the audience (e.g, reading level, age level, context) Deciding how the information will be organized (hierarchy, sequence) and how it will be linked
Presentation Skills	Mapping the design onto the presentation and implementing the ideas in multimedia Communicating information effectively Attracting and maintaining the interest of the intended audiences
Reflection Skills	Evaluating the program and the process used to create it Monitoring the pace and effectiveness of the strategies used Revising the design of the program using feedback

Source: Adapted from Carver, S. M., Lehrer, R., Connell, T., & Ericksen, J. (1992). Learning by hypermedia design: Issues of assessment and implementation. *Educational Psychologist,* 27(3), 385–404. Reprinted by permission of Taylor & Francis Ltd, http://www.tandf.co.uk/journals.

WEB LINK

Visit the textbook's companion website for a list of common tools and services that schools and teachers can use to create websites. Some free web services are included.

hypertext documents students need to think about the conceptual structure of a content area and then reflect on the nature of the links between the content. Designing multimedia products, such as websites, is clearly a complex skill requiring the ability to analyze, evaluate, and synthesize information.

Wegerif (2002) lists a number of different kinds of creative thinking skills needed in order to design effective multimedia presentations (see Table 4.2). Can you think of different ways that you could help your students master each of these important skills?

Creating Multimedia Websites

Websites are the most common form of hypermedia in use today. Many schools and districts are contracting with web services that provide teachers and their students with simple tools to create web pages quickly, sometimes even providing an optional or mandated template for teachers to use. If you've never created a website before, the following discussion will alert you to several things that you and your students should consider. By following these steps, you and your students can benefit from the creative processes involved in analyzing, evaluating, and synthesizing information to create multiple effective paths through a relevant content area (see Figure 4.7).

Define your site. As with any form of communication, it's useful to begin by defining your audience: Who is the primary audience of the site? The secondary audiences? Next, define your goals: What is the purpose of the site? What communication goals do you hope to accomplish? Then, define your content. What information do you want to include? How should the information be linked within and across web pages? And finally, identify your web development tools. Investigate whether your school or school system has a specific content management system or web development software that you are required to use. Each web development system has its unique limitations in the way that content can be displayed.

You should be careful about information you post on your class or school website to prevent identification of individual students. While many schools like to include pictures of students and samples of student work, many will use only a student's

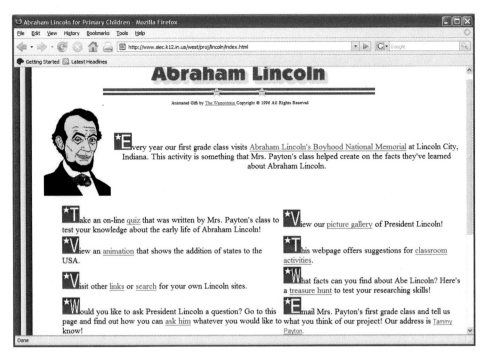

Figure 4.7
Students in first grade at Loogootee Elementary West in Indiana developed this web page as part of their unit on Abraham Lincoln. Courtesy Loogootee Community Schools.

first name or no name at all—using phrases to identify them in pictures such as "students from Mr. Mann's class" or "students from our school." Parents should be made fully aware of the need to provide signed consent prior to including pictures of students or their work on a website. Generally you should not include any information that can identify students and you should *always* have parent and student consent before displaying any pictures of your students or samples of their work. You'll learn more about this in Chapter 10.

Design your site. After you determine exactly what the audience, goals, and content will be, you can begin to plan the structure of your site, determining the most effective way to display and link the content, while also keeping in mind any limitations of the web development tool you'll be using. The web, itself, contains plenty of resources that provide guidance in creating high-quality websites.

One useful way to organize your content is to create a storyboard of your web pages. To storyboard content, create an individual "page" that corresponds to each screen in your program. You can physically represent individual web pages with

APPLY TO PRACTICE

Website Layout and Content

1. Explore several teacher or school websites and make note of what you like and don't like.
2. Summarize your likes and dislikes and why you feel the way you do.
3. Share your perceptions with your peers. Do others like and dislike the same things? What additional ideas did you get from your peers? Are there features from commercial or non-education websites you might consider?
4. Describe how you will use the results of this exploration when you design your own website.

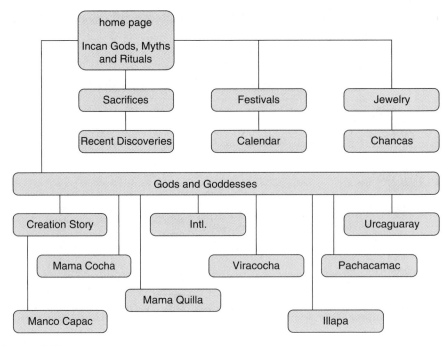

Figure 4.8
This flowchart shows the organization of an educational website on Incan gods, myths, and rituals.

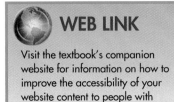

WEB LINK

Visit the textbook's companion website for information on how to improve the accessibility of your website content to people with special needs.

pieces of paper, index cards, or self-stick notes, or digitally by using presentation software, concept-mapping software, or even the drawing tools in most word-processing programs (see Figure 4.8). On each storyboard "page," sketch where you will place your text and graphic elements. After you have some sense of what will be on each page, you should also plan the navigation. Traditionally, this has been done with flowcharts that indicate the hierarchal organization or branching structure of the site. Again, you can use software, such as concept-mapping software, or draw the flowchart by hand. But storyboards and flowcharts don't have to be fancy. They are primarily planning aids. Even very rough sketches of the page layout and the linking relationships among pages will help you plan your site.

TOOLS FOR USE

Top 10 Things to Consider When Creating Websites

1. Keep each page consistent in look and feel.
2. Avoid cluttering the page with too much information, whether text or images.
3. Use consistent styles and names for navigation buttons and keep the navigation buttons in a consistent place on every page.
4. Routinely check to be sure the links to other websites are current, functional, and appropriate to your content.
5. Provide a guide to what is located on the site, either as an outline of pages, an introduction to each page, a site map, or a way to search the site.
6. Include links to any required plug-ins for any multimedia included on your site. Popular plug-in applications include

Acrobat Reader, Flash Player, QuickTime, Real Player, Shockwave Player, and Windows Media Player.
7. Include your name, contact information, the date of the website creation, and the last update, typically at the bottom of each page.
8. Include a copyright notice throughout the site and provide contact information for permission to use copyrighted material.
9. Make sure that student information does not violate students' privacy or compromise safety. Do not include student information unless parental permission is obtained.
10. Check the usability of your site for people with disabilities, such as by having someone familiar with accessible websites visit your site and provide feedback.

Develop the site. Once you have planned your site, you need to actually develop it. Fortunately, there are several tools available that make it easy to do so even if you aren't familiar with common web programming languages.

The simplest solution is to convert your content to HTML for display on the web. **HTML**—Hypertext Markup Language—is the programming language that provides web browsers with instructions on how to arrange information on a web page (see Figure 4.9). Word-processing and desktop publishing software often provide you with the option of saving your document in HTML format. Open a word-processing document and check out the "save as" options you have. One of them is probably HTML or "web page."

Website programs with a graphic interface—sometimes referred to as WYSIWYG, meaning "what you see is what you get"—are available that allow you to quickly create tables, insert pictures, format text, and create hyperlinks much like you would use a word processor. If you've ever created a word-processing document that includes images, you already know the basics of creating a web page. As you know, websites typically consist of text, graphics, and links. You create the text and add graphics, sound files, and movies in much the same way you create a document using word-processing software. Graphics, sound files, and movies need to be in an appropriate digital format and may need to be compressed to a reasonable file size—especially movie files. Documents may need to be converted to PDF format to allow them to be viewed by the widest number of users. After that, it's simple to insert text, links, graphics, movies, and sound. Image manipulation, media compression, text conversion, and web development programs are often easy to use. Typically, they rely on some of the same skills you apply when using other productivity tools such as copying, pasting, and saving as different formats.

Some software, such as Amaya from the World Wide Web Consortium, Netscape Composer, Nvu, or Mozilla's SeaMonkey Composer are freely available online. Commercial web development software, such as Dreamweaver or GoLive, both from Adobe, or Microsoft's Expression Web, offers a variety of sophisticated options but may take more time to learn. Many of these programs include templates that provide predesigned formats that students can use for their web pages. They may also include interactive "wizards" that guide them through website creation using a question and answer format. Most software companies offer online tutorials to guide you through the process of learning their software.

Deliver. As you create your HTML pages, you are creating a series of files that are stored on your computer. You can view them, but you need to upload your files to a **web server** before they will be available for others to view on the web. A web server is simply a computer, connected to the Internet, and running special software that allows it to respond to requests by web browsers. Although many servers are dedicated to that purpose only, any computer can function as a server and be used for other computing tasks as well. There are many server software programs available, including some in the public domain. In addition to web servers, there are other types of servers that have been set up to handle different types of files. For example, there are mail servers, file servers, video servers, and so forth.

Many schools provide teachers with space for their class websites on the school or district server. Often, especially for school and district servers, there is a web master who is responsible for uploading and maintaining pages on the server. You'll need to send your files to the web master and sometimes wait a few days before your pages are available on the web. If this is the case at your school, it will influence the way you use your class web pages.

In other cases, schools that use a hosting service or content management software allow teachers to have access to their web pages at all times. Your hosting service will provide you with specific instructions as to what you need to do to get your web pages onto its server. For example, you may need to use an FTP program to upload your files. FTP means **file transfer protocol** and, as the name suggests, is

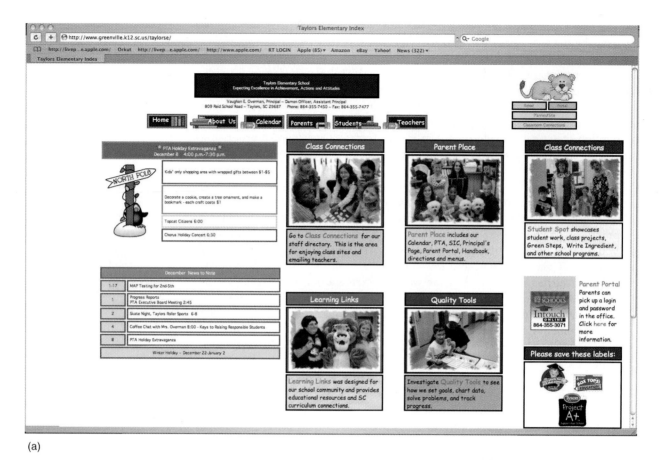

(a)

(b)

Figure 4.9

A school web page (a) created with web development software and the HTML code (b) that underlies it. Courtesy Taylors Elementary School.

simply a way to transfer files from one computer to another. Some services have simple upload pages that allow you to directly transfer files through your favorite web browser. Regardless of the method, it's usually a very simple process, usually no more complicated than sending an e-mail message with an attachment. When you upload your files, make sure you upload your HTML files and all the other files that may be linked to your web pages. Don't forget to upload your images, sound files, and

TOOLS FOR USE

Steps in Web Development

Define
- your audience
- your goals
- your content
- your web development tools

Design
- layout of pages
- menus
- navigation structure

Develop
- convert graphic, text, movie, and sound files to appropriate format
- generate HTML or similar code
- add links to files or pages

Deliver
- upload all files to appropriate servers

APPLY TO PRACTICE

Web Hosting Services

1. Search the web to identify several hosting services. Can you find any that are dedicated to teachers or classroom sites?
2. Share the URLs of web hosting services that you found useful with the rest of your class. Describe why you found the site or tool especially useful.

---

movies, as well as files that you may want available for download such as PDF or Word files.

In the unlikely event that your school or district does not provide you with access to server space, there are many web hosting services available that provide a certain amount of personal server space for free. There are also several free web hosting services just for teachers. Of course, most "free" services are paid for by advertisers who sometimes expose your users to ads as they access your site. If you plan to use a free service for your class website, it's advisable to check with your school administration to make sure it's acceptable to do so.

WEB LINK

Visit the textbook's companion website for a list of common tools and services that schools and teachers can use to create websites. Some free web services are included.

Digital Storytelling

Another popular use of computers as mindtools is through the creation of digital stories. As with other mindtools, digital stories enable learners to reflect, represent, and communicate what they know. Based on the premise of oral storytelling, digital storytelling involves students' creation of a short movie that presents a compelling personal perspective. It may be a story from their own experiences, such as describing the importance of a place or how they overcame adversity—or from their research as when they "become" settlers in the new world. Typically, stories are told from a personal perspective to allow the viewer to see an event, moment, or place from another's point of view; yet effective digital stories also have a theme to which viewers can relate. It has as its basis the writing of a strong personal narrative that begins with a "hook" or "lead" to draw the viewers into the story. They proceed through illuminating specific events or moments in time and conclude with a wrap-up that often is presented in terms of lessons learned.

Throughout the years, digital storytelling has evolved into a recommended series of steps and procedures. Students first develop a personal narrative, then select the most powerful point in their written work to develop into a script. Based on the storyboard, students select images needed to supplement their scripts. Although students may create their own images through digital photography, videotaping, or scanning images, they often select images from those available on the web or from royalty-free clip art collections. The next step involves recording the narration—often the most challenging step. Using readily available software such as iMovie or GarageBand on the Mac or MovieMaker on the PC, students arrange their images, synchronize them with their recorded narration, and output the file as a movie. Some teachers may use more widely available presentation software, such as Microsoft PowerPoint or Apple's Keynote software, for supporting digital storytelling activities, especially with younger students. Presentation software allows even very young students to insert pictures, text, and record audio in support of digital storytelling. As with the development of other types of multimedia, students are required to apply project management skills, research skills, organizational and representational skills, presentation skills, and reflective skills (see Table 4.2).

Each step in creating a digital story is elaborated upon below.

Step 1. Write a Script

Solid writing is at the core of digital storytelling. As with other writing activities, you should provide students with a writing prompt or specific assignment. For example, you may want them to describe a particular place or moment in time that is important to them.

Students need to clearly identify the purpose of their stories and the messages they are trying to convey. They may need to be guided in the development of "hooks" through examining other models of digital stories available online or written works to determine what makes an effective story lead. It's also important for them to learn how to write an effective "wrap-up." Different students learn in different ways so you may want to provide a set of questions to guide them in their writing and storytelling, ask them to draw or otherwise create a visual image of the main point of the story, or have them create concept maps in order to clarify and focus their writing.

Typically, digital movies are 2 to 3 minutes in length so it's a good idea for students to read their stories aloud at this point and time them to make sure they are within the recommended time limit (Jakes & Brennan, n.d.). As they read aloud, students may become aware of grammatical errors or other things they want to change (Buckingham, 2003). This revision process is a natural and appropriate part of self-monitoring.

Step 2. Develop a Storyboard

After students are comfortable with their scripts, they should create their storyboards. Storyboards should contain the narration, a description or sketch of the associated images, any text that may appear on the screen, and a note about any music or sound effects required. At this stage, students begin to visualize what their narratives should look and sound like. As they read over their scripts, they need to identify sections that lend themselves to supplemental images. For each chunk of the script, students need to write or draw a brief description of an image that they want to use to illustrate the idea. At this point, students will not have actually collected the images; instead, the storyboard ensures that their image searches will be productive and effective by focusing their research efforts. Typically, twenty to twenty-five images are needed to illustrate a 2- to 3-minute story (Jakes & Brennan, n.d.).

If your students are not familiar with storyboarding, there are a variety of activities you can use to acquaint them with this process. You might want to have them engage in "backwards storyboarding" by watching a commercial and creating the matching storyboard. Or have them use comic strips as an example of a storyboard, and then create a video movie of the comic strip. Through storyboarding, students learn to think in new ways as they visualize written work.

Step 3. Locate Images

After they have identified the images they want to locate, students can begin researching, finding, or creating images. Students may film full-motion video or they may use still images to illustrate their stories. They may use digital images from their own collections, scan images or graphics that are not in digital form, or download images from the web. When selecting images and video clips, make sure that your students pay strict attention to copyright rules and regulations (see Chapter 10). Fortunately, there are a variety of websites such as Pics4Learning.com, SURWEB, and the American Memory Project from the Library of Congress that provide images and video segments that can be used for such projects legally. Digital storytelling projects provide a wonderful opportunity to teach your students about copyright regulations within the context of a realistic application. However, students should not begin researching images until their scripts and storyboards are well developed.

Step 4. Create a Digital Story

The script and the storyboard are written and the images are located. Now it's time for students to put it all together. Using a variety of commonly available software, students need to record their narrations, load the audio files and images into a moviemaking program, and output the finished products as movie files.

It's commonly accepted that recording the narration can be the most difficult part of the story creation process in terms of classroom management. Students must record their narrations individually in a quiet place—something that can be challenging in a room full of students. One option is to have a parent volunteer, older student, or another student go to a quiet place and record each student's narration on videotape, with the lens cap on (Banaszewski, 2002). The video can then be loaded into the moviemaking program and the audio extracted. Another option is to use microphones such as the Sennheiser PC-130 that eliminate background noise (Jakes & Brennan, n.d.). Experienced teachers recommend that students record their narration in two- to three-sentence chunks so that if they make a mistake, they don't have to go back and record the entire script.

Following this, students will use moviemaking programs to synchronize their sound files with the appropriate images and then output the results as a movie file. Several of these programs are available for free (such as iMovie for the Mac or Movie-Maker for the PC), while others are commercially available. Most of these programs are easy to use and require a minimum of prior instruction. Still, some authors suggest that students work together on a group project prior to producing individual projects so that they become acquainted with the software and production process. And as with the development of other types of multimedia, students are required to apply project management skills, research skills, organizational and representational skills, presentation skills, and reflective skills (see Table 4.2).

After students are satisfied with their sequence of images and accompanying sound files, they **render** their projects into movie files. Rendering can take a while, so some authors suggest that students first render their movies at a low quality so that they can determine if it's satisfactory to them before taking the time to render as a higher-quality file.

Step 5. Share with Others

The final step is to share their movies with others. As students view the movies created by their peers, they develop a deeper understanding of the perspectives of others. One way to structure the class viewing is through following the steps used in "writers workshops" (Banaszewski, 2002). Following the viewing of a digital story, the audience first comments on the things they appreciate about the movie, and then offer suggestions for improvement. The movie's creator simply accepts these appreciations and suggestions without comment. Following the audience's response, the movie's creator can ask the audience questions about things that she or he wonders about relative to the movie. There are also a variety of websites where students can post their movies to share them with a global audience. (See the Web Link.)

If you have limited access to technology, steps 1, 2, and 5 can occur in the classroom using traditional materials, but if you have access to technology more frequently, a variety of software can enhance the process (Jakes & Brennan, n.d.). Prior to script writing, students can use a timeline program to create a timeline of the event (Buckingham, 2003). They can then select one or more moments in time to elaborate on in the digital story. They can create concept maps of the ideas they want to develop, adding details through nodes and links. As they develop their scripts and storyboards, they can use word-processing software to write the scripts, then cut and paste from the scripts into storyboards—which can be as simple as using a table in a word processed document. And with the right equipment, movies can be output to videotape or DVDs to be shown in the classroom using commonly available VCR or DVD players.

As a mindtool, digital storytelling helps students learn to write more effectively through visualizing their stories (Jakes & Brennan, n.d.). As such, it provides authentic, personal learning experiences for your students. Additionally, throughout the process, students learn skills that are important to a variety of content areas such as writing for an audience, researching information, communicating effectively, as well as technology and information literacy skills.

The opportunity to develop a personal story is extremely motivating for students, and the tangible outcome of the process contributes to confidence-building necessary for creative thinking. Students need to be self-directed in their efforts to plan their actions, monitor their progress toward achieving the goals of their projects, and evaluate their efforts. You can help students in the evaluation process by providing them with rubrics in advance that allow them to self-assess their projects. And viewing digital stories can help students identify with the perspective of others.

WEB LINK

There is a variety of software that can support digital storytelling—and a number of websites that provide tips for their classroom use. Visit the textbook's companion website for links to useful sites that support digital storytelling.

Computer as a Conversation Support

While the previous two sections focused primarily on how the computer can be used to increase *individual* learning outcomes, in this section we discuss how the computer, as an interactive tool, can contribute to conversations among learners, and thus contribute to *group and community* learning outcomes. That is, when used as a support and resource for the communicative processes of teaching and learning, the computer can be used to increase creative thinking processes among groups and communities. In the next two sections, we talk more specifically about how the computer can be used to promote collaborative learning outcomes among learners who are both near and far.

Computer as a Collaborative Learning Tool

Imagine if you will, two students working at the computer to complete a simulation game, such as the Oregon Trail or Sim City. As the pair work together, they engage in a heated debate about the pros and cons of different decisions. They make predictions about potential outcomes and then, after some discussion, come to agreement about which steps to take next. In this scenario, the computer acts merely as a prompt or resource for students' conversations, and therefore, as a means to illuminate their thinking. It is this use of the computer, as a mediator of conversation, we discuss here. Whereas in traditional classrooms, teachers may have discouraged students from talking to each other during individual seatwork, here we recognize some of the positive outcomes that can result from the conversations that occur among students as they work through complex problem-solving situations. For example, in a study conducted in the early 1990s, Teasley and Roschelle (described in Wegerif,

2002), observed pairs of students using a simulation, called the "Envisioning Machine," that was designed to teach Newtonian physics. The authors described how the computer program provided a shared focus, the means to uncover the true meaning of the language used to represent the physics concepts being addressed (velocity, acceleration), as well as the means to resolve conflicts by testing out alternative views. In interpreting the results, the authors claimed that it was the *conversation* between the learners, as prompted by the computer simulation, which led to the observed learning gains.

When used as a collaborative learning tool, computers are used not only for stimulating effective language use but also for focusing children's learning activities on specific curricular tasks. What seems to be important here is not the computer software, per se, but the quality of the conversation that occurs around it. This, then, prompts us to think about the teacher's role in an "engaged" classroom and how she/he is responsible for supporting high levels of meaningful conversation.

As noted earlier in our discussions about supporting student collaborations (see Chapter 3), it is important that you prepare your students to work together effectively, whether around the computer or not. As you will learn later in this chapter, many teachers accomplish this by engaging students in a series of conversations that are designed to establish ground rules for collaboration (e.g., listening with respect, responding to challenges with reasons, sharing and reconciling disparate views). Through these activities students learn not only to work together, but also to use language as a tool for collaborative reasoning, problem-solving, and knowledge construction. Research suggests that, *in combination with the right instructional strategies*, the computer can support the development of transferable creative thinking skills (Wegerif, 2002).

Computer as a Conferencing Tool

Communication in an online forum is different from face-to-face (F2F) communication; in some ways worse, and in some ways better. While we lose important information (facial expressions, body language, tone of voice, etc.), we also eliminate information that can cause bias or prejudice (knowledge of age, gender, disabilities, etc.). Computer conferencing can open up many new possibilities for participation. There are many claims that electronic conferencing can be an effective support for the development of creative thinking skills. The reasons for this tend to relate to 1) the ease with which everyone can participate, and 2) the ability to be able to think through your responses before responding. Furthermore, having several conversations occurring simultaneously can prompt more metacognitive reflection. Think about the relative ease with which you participate in multiple conversations with your friends using instant-messenger software. Now, put that into a context where you are all focused on making a decision, or solving a problem, and you can see the potential for developing good thinking (as well as communication and management) skills.

There are a variety of ways in which you can use the computer as a conferencing tool with your students. CSILE, described earlier, is one way. E-mail, listservs, blogs, wikis, newsgroups, and forums all offer additional possibilities. For example, e-pals can connect your students with students in other countries through written exchanges on topics of mutual interest. In a similar fashion, but on a classroom level, Kidlink offers a network run by 500 volunteers in over 50 countries who provide free educational programs related to helping children understand themselves, identify and define goals for life, and collaborate with peers around the globe, individually or through school. Interaction between participants takes place through hundreds of discussion rooms, mailing lists, chat channels, and Kidlink's website (see Figure 4.10). The Global Schoolnet is another example of using the computer to connect students from around the world to explore community, cultural, and scientific issues that prepare them for the workforce and help them to become responsible and literate global citizens.

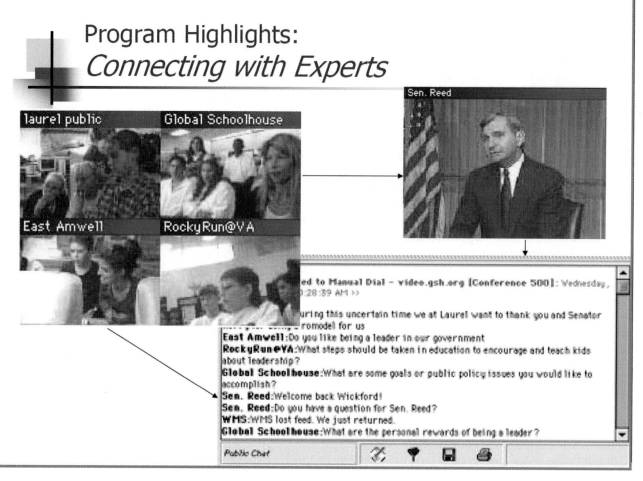

Program Highlights:
Connecting with Experts

Figure 4.10
Kidlink connects kids from all over the world. Courtesy Global SchoolNet.

WEB LINK

Learn more about the projects that use computers as conferencing tools by visiting the textbook's companion website.

Additional conferencing activities that can support collaboration among students include those that focus on the joint collection, analysis, organization, and presentation of information. Typically, students at geographically dispersed sites collect local data and then compare and contrast patterns (e.g., related to health, climate, plant and animal species) across locations. This, then, allows students to look for overarching patterns in the data, requiring creative thinking. For example, Journey North engages students in a global study of wildlife migration and seasonal change. Students share their own field observations with classmates across North America. As one example, students followed the migration of the monarch butterfly as it journeyed north from Angangueo, Mexico to Washington, DC (see Figure 4.11). Other seasonal changes that students have helped track include the first frog heard singing and the first maple syrup sap run.

Videoconferencing and Webconferencing

Videoconferencing and webconferencing tools are becoming more affordable and can be found in many classrooms. Videoconferencing tools can connect teachers and students across designated networks designed specifically to support video or—increasingly—over a high-speed Internet connection. Virtual schools were some of the first schools to employ videoconferencing, especially when the real-time interaction between teacher and student was critical, as when learning a foreign language. Now many districts use this model to provide courses in advanced topics or courses that might not normally meet enrollment requirements in a single school by combining students across a district or state in a single virtual class. Webconferencing tools

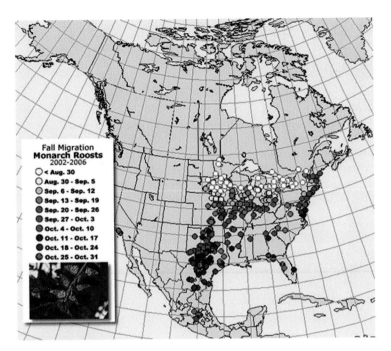

Figure 4.11
Journey North tracks the migration of monarch butterflies across North America. Courtesy Journey North.

TOOLS FOR USE

Considering Webconferencing

You and your students can engage in aspects of webconferencing with a range of investment in time and funds. Multifunction webconferencing tools, such as Horizon Wimba, WebEx, or Adobe Connect, put a multitude of functions at your fingertips. Depending on your needs, you may also be able to use the limited functionality of low-cost or free software such as Skype, Microsoft's NetMeeting, or iChat from Apple. Some common webconferencing features and their educational applications are listed below.

- *Presentation Slides.* Share your class lecture with students at a distance. The most universally accepted presentation software is Microsoft PowerPoint.
- *Desktop Sharing/Shared Control.* With sharing, you or your students can reach out and touch someone's desktop—virtually. This is helpful for guiding students through a complex process or when students are presenting to you or the rest of the class.
- *Document Sharing.* Instead of just posting a word processed, spreadsheet, or other document, document sharing allows real-time collaboration on documents in support of peer-to-peer or small-group work.
- *Web Tour.* So many instructional resources are available on the web that it is important to be able to visit and show websites to your students at a distance.
- *Shared Whiteboard.* Just like a chalkboard or whiteboard in the classroom, you and your students can write, draw, or annotate images displayed on a whiteboard space. You may need to practice your mouse skills, however, to take advantage of the palette of tools available with most whiteboards.

- *Lecture Mode.* You can't always control the quality of phone connections, and some users cannot mute their phones. The background noise from poor connections increases in volume with the number of students connected. Lecture mode can allow you to mute all lines while you're presenting as well as designate individual lines as the primary speaker for questioning or student presentations.
- *Chat.* A chat feature can be helpful for allowing participants to ask questions or otherwise interact without interrupting the audio connection. You may want to establish policies for using chat, however, so students continue to focus on learning outcomes and don't get too distracted with side conversations.
- *Webcam Support.* Having a webcam can increase visual cues for participants that are sometimes missing in text- or audio-based distance learning. Some options for webcams include showing multiple webcams, facial tracking if participants move, as well as webcam shifting that displays the stream of the participant who is currently speaking.
- *Polling, Quizzes, and Surveys.* Take a quick pulse of the opinions in the room or collect formative assessment data to measure student understanding through these features that usually include common forced-choice response types.
- *Recording and Replay.* Did one of your students miss class due to illness or travel? Or maybe one of them would like to review a complex discussion or check the accuracy of his notes. Webconferencings services can offer both audio as well as screen recordings.

THE GAME PLAN

Webconferencing Tools

Set Goals

Learn more about webconferencing tools and investigate ways to use them within an educational context, either for your own professional development or for use by your students.

Take Action

Explore one or more options that are available for conducting web conferences (i.e., meetings or presentations) or webinars (web seminars) over the Internet (e.g., Skype, Adobe Connect, iChat).

Monitor

Make a list of the features available in the program (e.g., video, whiteboards, chat, etc.). What are some of the advantages and disadvantages to each program? Will it be easy to use? Does it have the features you might need?

Evaluate and Extend

Compare notes with your peers. Which program(s) would best meet your current needs? How do you think the program could be used in the classroom?

---

also offer opportunities for synchronous communication. Often supported by common web browsers, teachers or students can host sessions over the Internet that allow others to view presentations, share documents across computers, chat, or take polls. Some webconferencing tools also support live video through the use of inexpensive web cameras, or webcams. Webconferencing tools vary as to whether they support audio through the computer or whether participants use a phone line.

Computer conferencing allows students to engage directly in knowledge creation with others who are not physically present. By providing access to multiple perspectives, students are challenged to think more deeply about the topic at hand. And while it is not intrinsically superior to think together with those outside the classroom, than with those within, it can be more motivating (Wegerif, 2002).

Weblogs

Weblogs, or **blogs** as they are more commonly referred to, belong to the realm of journaling and threaded discussion tools. The following points are designed to help you decide whether and/or how to incorporate weblogs into your classroom.

Use blogs to achieve an instructional goal. Blogs can help students practice and demonstrate different styles of communication, especially through writing. As part of your GAME plan, determine how the use of the blog can meet specific goals. In a writing-intensive class, have students post entries using different forms, such as writing a persuasive paragraph or posting an interview of a friend. A haiku blog posting might be relevant to your instruction, as well as an interesting variation. In terms of communication, you can emphasize design elements to guide the organization of entire blogs, postings by your students, and the incorporation of media. You can also support collaboration and help students develop critical communication skills by guiding their responses to classmates' postings.

Students will need guidance on what and how to post. The blog you use in your classroom may be different than a personal blog as it will have to meet instructional purposes. Help your students understand the form of language that is appropriate, which may require avoiding the use of common Internet acronyms and shortcuts. Set a reasonable goal for posting, perhaps once a week, and use clearly stated writing prompts to guide your students' posts. And by all means, create your own blog as a model for students (see Figure 4.12). The best way to determine the match of a technology to your instruction is to do it yourself.

Just as with any other resource, teach your students to use multiple sources and cite them appropriately. Learning to cite sources is a foundational skill for all

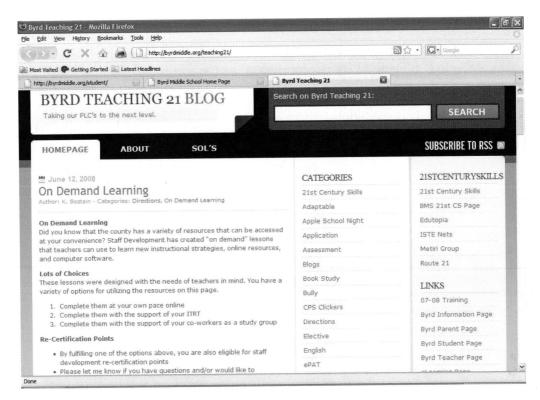

Figure 4.12
Teachers use blogs to communicate with students, parents, and the world. Courtesy Harry F. Byrd Middle School.

students and writing a blog should be no exception, even if the source is a friend, a TV show, or another blog. Using multiple sources can help students not only support the positions in their postings but actually help them better formulate their own opinions and ideas. Determine an appropriate format for citations and require it for postings. Common academic citation styles such as APA or MLA may not be standard for blogging but may be appropriate for young scholars developing their citation skills, especially if you require it in other forms of student work.

The nature of a blog is to share personal reflections, opinions, and feelings. At the same time, blogs and shared discussion spaces have sparked controversy because students have shared personal information, such as pictures and contact information. Help your students understand how to make their blogs personal without revealing personal information. Your students should understand that they can provide personal reflections and voice opinions using a blog but should always refrain from posting personal contact information.

To find exemplary blogs, review trusted resources. Review how other teachers are using the technology by attending conferences, reading journal and magazine articles, or searching the web. In the case of blogs, there are online and print publications that review educational blogs and guide you toward exemplars. There are even some awards available for exemplary blogs. Find and read other blogs and determine what characteristics best suit your teaching style and the requirements of your curriculum.

You shouldn't be surprised that we recommend that you have a GAME Plan for using blogs in your classroom. Just as with any other new technology, you shouldn't select it just because it's a novelty. Whatever technology you decide to investigate, you should have a clear goal that you want to achieve. If being used with students, your goals should be related to your instruction; however, you may have some supporting goals related to your own personal communications and collaboration. Once you've decided to use a technology, continue to monitor how well it is meeting your goal and purposefully evaluate its effectiveness once you've used it, whether after a lesson, a unit, or at the end of the year.

Online Resources

As you noticed in the previous discussion, the web provides access to a variety of sites where the computer is used as a tutor, mindtool, or support for conversation. Fortunately, or unfortunately, anyone can publish on the web through personal or organizational websites, postings on message boards, blogs, wikis, and more. In contrast, printed information often has to undergo strict reviews prior to publication. Academic journal articles are subject to peer review by other professionals in the field. At a minimum, the content found in books, magazines, and newspapers is reviewed by the publication's editor. Even opinion pieces, like "letters to the editor," are reviewed prior to publication (which is not to say this necessarily ensures "fairness" or an unbiased presentation). But this isn't true of information published on the Internet. The ease with which individuals can post and access information creates a critical need to strategically search for and carefully evaluate the information you find on the web.

Productive Searches

You probably have your favorite search engine, such as Google.com, but you should realize that not all search engines work the same. Some use keywords that were provided by the website developer to identify sites that meet your search criteria. Others use software programs to "crawl" the web, searching for specific information on various sites. It's best to experiment with several search engines to find the one that gets you the information you want and need. Each search engine has slightly different guidelines for searching, and a quick look at the "help" or "advanced" search sections of a particular search engine will certainly assist you in perfecting your search strategies. Table 4.3 also provides tips for productive web searching. However, be sure to look beyond the first few results. Sometimes, the sites featured at the top of the list are simply those that have paid a fee to be displayed there. Other search engines will feature the most popular sites at the top of their list. If your search is unsuccessful using one search engine, try another—you may get different results.

Metasearch engines, such as Metacrawler.com and DogPile.com, do not collect information from sites directly but rather compile the results that would appear if you were to use several different search engines. Some authors believe that metasearches are superficial, "barely finding 10 percent of keyword citations from

Table 4.3	Focusing Your Web Search			
Search Tool	Definition/Description	How It Works	How Results Are Generated	Comments
Search Engine	Consists of: 1. The search program (robot, spider, crawler) that creeps around the web, exploring sites and following internal links. 2. The index—a giant catalog of all the search program's results. 3. The search engine software that sorts out the results, ranks, and displays them.	Indexes the pages it discovers	Results based on a mathematical algorithm used to rank relevance	Not all search engines operate the same way. Users need to utilize search strategies appropriate to each engine.
Metasearch Engine	Harnesses the power of multiple search engines.			
Web Directory	Human powered—based on a concept like the yellow pages. Searches keywords provided by web developers.	Categorizes web pages based on content categories	Results are generally restricted to those sites that have been submitted to the appropriate category.	The human-based hierarchical nature of web directories are criticized as offering abridged results.
Hybrid	An increasing number of search tools are blurring the distinction by offering features of both search engines and directories.			

TOOLS FOR USE

Web Searching Tips

When searching for information using search engines (or metasearch engines), you need to structure your search so that you get an adequate, but not unmanageable, number of results, or "hits." Bitter and Legacy (2008) provide the following general tips:

- Search for the singular form of a term. You will get both singular and plural forms returned to you.
- Enter all of the spellings you think might apply for a given term, separating each by a space.
- Enclose a phrase in double quotes (e.g., "technology integration"), otherwise the search engine will find every occurrence of each individual word (e.g., all occurrences of "technology" plus all occurrences of "integration").
- Be as precise as possible. Entering a common word would give you far too many useless sites. Include the word in a specific phrase (enclosed in quotes) to help narrow the search.
- Precede the term with a + mark to indicate that it must be contained in every document.
- Precede the term with a − mark to indicate that you want no documents that contain that word.

- Combine the quotes, +, and − marks to require some terms and prohibit others (e.g., "technology integration" +education −medicine).
- Use wildcard characters (such as *) to substitute for several letters that may vary among the terms you are search for. For example constructivis* would return sites that included both the terms constructivism and constructivist.
- Use Boolean operators AND, OR, AND NOT, and NEAR to narrow searches.
  - AND will give you documents containing more than one term occurring together
  - OR will give you documents that contain one or the other term
  - AND NOT will exclude a term from the search
  - NEAR will find documents that contain the words within a certain number of words from each other.
- Combine Boolean operators and phrases into groupings with parentheses.

each search engine they visit" (Forcier & Descy, 2005, p. 333). Others propose that metasearch engines save time over conducting several individual searches using different search engines as "only about 40 percent of the results found in one search engine may be unique to that search engine. About 60 percent will overlap with results of other searches" (Forcier & Descy, p. 333). You should try a metsearch engine, if you have not already, to see if it meets any of your searching needs.

Despite the fact that search engines are immensely helpful, teach your students to be careful when using them. Some website developers intentionally create web pages that will be placed at the top of search result lists. When done so dishonestly or with the purpose of deceiving the user, this practice is known as **spamdexing** or **search engine spamming**. Some programming methods for spamdexing include hiding text in the coding or directly on the page by incorporating keywords in a tiny font in the same color as the background. No matter the method, proactive strategies for determining the legitimacy of web resources are the best method for preventing students from misappropriating information from misleading websites.

WEB LINK

Visit the textbook's companion website for information and websites for evaluating web-based resources.

Evaluating Information from Online Resources

Students should learn how to verify the legitimacy of content on the Internet. You should also be especially careful to review websites in their entirety before using them with your students.

There are numerous examples of web pages that appear to be valid resources but that provide incorrect and sometimes extremely inflammatory information. Some hate groups have been known to post information about historical events and figures, such as civil rights leader Martin Luther King Jr., that appears to be authentic, at least on the surface. Students who do not take the time to review all of the material closely, who are naïve or do not realize the information is incorrect, or who unknowingly copy and paste information from these websites can turn in projects with information that is not only biased but full of hate speech and prejudice.

Web developers who develop sites with URLs that are just slightly different from a legitimate source are using the practice of **typosquatting**. In this case, an ".org" or a ".net" or other domain suffix may be used instead of the appropriate ".edu" or ".gov" in an attempt to trick unwary students (or others) looking for legitimate information. The White House is one common object of typosquatters. The inappropriate material found on the alternate site can be highly offensive, or sometimes just fictitious. Typosquatting also involves the use of common misspellings of words to prey on the poor keyboarding and spelling skills of students.

A simple web search will reveal many sites that discuss information evaluation techniques. Numerous checklists and rubrics are available that provide useful tools for you. You may already have your own techniques to evaluate the validity and reliability of web information sources. In evaluating web resources, it's useful to answer the standard questions of who, what, when, why, and how.

Who created the website? Is the source credible? What credentials or background does the author have that qualifies him or her to write about this topic? Does the author provide credentials such as occupation, affiliations, years of experience, position, and education?

Search the web for additional information about the author or look for information through other reputable sources. Can you find a personal home page or campus listing for this author? Can you find other publications through a source such as the Educational Resources Information Clearinghouse (ERIC), sponsored by the U.S. Department of Education? Information about the background of the author of a web page is sometimes found on the bottom of a page or through a separate link. Is there a mail-to link or an e-mail address included? It may be a cause for suspicion if the site author is not clearly stated or contact information is not provided.

If the source is a website, look at the URL to learn about the sponsor and location of the site. What does the ending of the URL tell you? Is the page sponsored by a professional organization, school, school district, university, company, government office, or commercial company? What can you find out about the organization? Does the organization have an inherent bias? Does it seem logical that information such as this would reside on this site? It's a good idea to examine the credentials and reputation of the organization or organizations affiliated with a website, just as you examined the credentials of the author.

What is the value of the information? How thorough is it? Does the information appear accurate based on your prior knowledge? Does the information appear to be well researched? Is the information well documented? Are assumptions and conclusions well documented? How current or relevant are the references? Are primary sources of information indicated? Are there references or links to supporting information? If the information resides on a web page, does the page reference only information on the same server? If so, be especially aware of potential biases. Most importantly, does the information agree with other information you have found? It's always a good idea to cross-check information using print and nonprint sources, as well as websites.

When was the information created? What was the date of the original document? When was it last updated? Information such as this helps you determine if the content is up-to-date and timely. If using a website as the source of your information, check to see if the links work properly and lead to related materials. Lots of outdated links often indicate that the site has not been updated in a while.

Why was the website created? What is the purpose of the information? Was it created to sell a product, make a political point, or have fun? Is it to inform, persuade, explain, or entertain? Was it designed to summarize existing research, advocate a position, or stimulate discussion? Who is the intended audience? Does the intended audience impact the content or slant of the information? For what level is the

TOOLS FOR USE

Evaluating Web Resources

Who is responsible for the information resource?
- The name of the author(s) is evident.
- The author's authority, credentials, background, and/or expertise are clearly stated.
- The site includes background information for the author(s), such as previous works, publications, affiliations, etc.
- The name of any sponsoring institution or organization is included along with a current link to that organization.
- The relation between the author(s) and the sponsoring organization is specified.

What about the content?
- The resource provides thorough information that adequately meets the information need.
- The title of the resource clearly conveys its content.
- The source for information is documented; links to the source are included.
- The content is free from spelling and grammatical errors.

When was the information published?
- The information is current, including original date of the document and latest update.
- Linked information is up-to-date; links are active.

Why is the resource published?
- The purpose of the resource is clear and its content reflects that purpose, whether it is to inform, persuade, entertain, or sell.
- Informative or entertaining resources are free from bias. Persuasive or sales sites are easily identifiable.

How useful is the resource?
- Information is presented clearly at the level appropriate to the target audience.
- The resource is logically organized and easy to navigate, including a search box and/or site map if the resource is large.

information written? An examination of the purpose of the information can illuminate biases that may be present in the content.

How is the information presented? Does the information appear to be fact or opinion? Does it make sense? Can you detect any bias? Is the information presented in a thoughtful, orderly, well-reasoned manner? Do the words used tend to evoke strong emotions? Is the information free from errors in writing and grammar?

Chapter Summary

In this chapter, we described how computer software could serve as a tutor, mindtool, and as a support for conversation (Wegerif, 2002). When technology is used as a **tutor**, the software explicitly teaches or provides practice with a specific body of content. When technology is used as a **mindtool**, it serves as an organizational tool, simulation and visualization tool, or knowledge-building tool. As a **support for conversation,** the computer software contributes to conversations among learners, and thus facilitates *group and community* learning. Since the web is a popular way to access computer-based tutorials, mindtools, and conversation supports, we also discussed techniques for productive web searches and evaluation strategies.

Although there are many ways that technology can be used to promote creative thinking skills among students in your classroom, it should be fairly clear from our discussion that simply using technology will not accomplish this goal. Rather, technology needs to be used purposefully in the ways discussed in this chapter and in an environment that explicitly supports students' efforts to be good thinkers. For example, computer tutorials, by themselves, will rarely have enough depth to develop students' creative thinking skills, but when used as the basis for a discussion, students can achieve these higher levels more readily. The same is true for computer tools such as concept maps and simulations: effectiveness as a thinking tool depends on how the tools are used.

In this chapter, we stressed the importance of creating a culture of thinking within an inviting classroom environment. Pay particular attention to the type of questions you ask and the way in which you listen and respond to your students' questions and responses. Continually remind your students that you're interested in their thought processes. Be open to their creative ideas by emphasizing the use of divergent thinking skills. Provide feedback that is informative (including relevant information about the correct response) rather than strictly corrective (informing students that an answer was right or wrong) or comparative (comparing one student to another). Be explicit about the creative thinking skills they are learning, consistent in your expectations for sound thinking, and patient as they slowly achieve new understandings and new approaches to thinking and learning.

As you see, the effectiveness of a lesson will depend, to a large degree, on you, as the instructional leader in the classroom. In the next chapter, we will turn our attention to ways that you can support your students in their collaborative and independent learning efforts through questioning strategies, scaffolds such as project guidelines, modeling technology use, and other techniques that support your students during the process of becoming autonomous, self-directed thinkers.

YOUR PORTFOLIO

This chapter described how to use technology to facilitate and inspire student learning and creativity through the use of authentic classroom activities. To demonstrate competency in ISTE NETS-T Standard 1.c and d and Standard 2.a, add the following items to your portfolio:

1. Reflect on the lesson description you developed in Chapter 3. Identify how technology is used as a 1) tutor, 2) mindtool, or 3) conversation support. Can you generate activities that demonstrate at least one of each type of use?
2. Describe activities for your lesson in which your students use the computer as a collaborative and/or reflective tool to illuminate their thinking.
3. Describe one instance where you engaged in technology-supported learning, either face-to-face or virtually. Did the technology serve as a tutor, mindtool, or support for conversation. Explain why you classified your use of technology as you did.

References

Banaszewski, T. (2002). *Digital storytelling finds its place in the classroom.* Retrieved June 8, 2008, from http://www.infotoday.com/MMSchools/jan02/banaszewski.htm

Bitter, G. G., & Legacy, J. M. (2008). *Using technology in the classroom* (7th ed). New York: Allyn & Bacon.

Buckingham, J. L. C. (2003). *Digital storytelling.* Retrieved June 8, 2008, from http://teach.fcps.net/trt18/Digital%20Writing/DSTunit.htm

Carnegie Learning. (2006). *Math curriculum solutions.* Retrieved June 2, 2006, from http://www.carnegielearning.com/products.cfm

Davis, M. R. (2007). Wiki wisdom: Lessons for educators. *Digital Directions: Trends and Advice for K-12 Technology Leaders.* Bethesda, MD: Education Week.

Dodge, B. (2006). *The WebQuest page.* Retrieved September 26, 2006, from http://webquest.sdsu.edu

Ertmer, P. A. (2003). *VisionQuest: Envisioning and achieving integrated technology use.* Retrieved June 24, 2006, from http://www.edci.purdue.edu/vquest

Forcier, R. C., & Descy, D. E. (2005) *The computer as an educational tool* (4th ed.). Upper Saddle River, NJ: Merrill/Prentice Hall.

Jakes, D. S., & Brennan, J. (n.d.) *Capturing stories, capturing lives: An introduction to digital storytelling.* Retrieved June 8, 2008, from www.jakesonline.org/dstory_ice.pdf

Jonassen, D. J. (2006). *Modeling with technology: Mindtools for conceptual change* (3rd ed.). Upper Saddle River, NJ: Merrill/Prentice Hall.

Jonassen, D. J., Howland, J., Moore, J., & Marra, R. M. (2003). *Learning to solve problems with technology: A constructivist perspective* (2nd ed.). Upper Saddle River, NJ: Merrill/Prentice Hall.

Novak, J. D., & Cañas, A. J. (2006). *The theory underlying concept maps and how to construct them* (Technical Report IHMC Cmap Tools, 2006-1). Florida Institute for Human and Machine Cognition. Retrieved June 7, 2006, from http://cmap.ihmc.us/Publications/ResearchPapers/TheoryUnderlyingConceptMaps.pdf

Wegerif, R. (2002). *Literature review in thinking skills, technology, and learning.* Future Lab Series, No. 2. Retrieved June 1, 2006, from http://www.futurelab.org.uk/research/reviews/ts01.htm

Wikipedia. (2007). *Wiki.* Retrieved November 24, 2007, from http://en.wikipedia.org/wiki/Wiki

Ariel Skelley/Blend Images/Jupiter Images

ISTE Standards addressed in this chapter

NETS-T 2. Design and Develop Digital-Age Learning Experiences and Assessments

Teachers design, develop, and evaluate authentic learning experiences and assessments incorporating contemporary tools and resources to maximize content learning in context and to develop the knowledge, skills, and attitudes identified in the NETS-S. Teachers:

b. develop technology-enriched learning environments that enable all students to pursue their individual curiosities and become active participants in setting their own educational goals, managing their own learning, and assessing their own progress.

Note: Standard 2.a. is addressed in Chapter 4, 2.c in Chapter 6, and 2.d in Chapter 7.

Developing Technology-Enriched Learning Environments and Experiences

Outcomes

In this chapter, you will

- Design learning experiences and lessons that support students' self-directed learning.
- Incorporate technology into learning experiences designed for independent learning, for small-group instruction, and for whole-class instruction.
- Develop, support, and scaffold student learning in a technology-enriched learning environment through the actions you take planning the lesson, during the lesson, and after the lesson.

I n Chapter 3, you learned the importance of using authentic learning experiences to develop students' creative thinking skills. In Chapter 4, you learned to facilitate creative thinking skills by using computers and other technologies as tutors, mindtools, and supports for conversation. As you recall, creative thinkers are self-directed, autonomous learners. They are able to set their own educational goals, manage their own learning, and assess their own progress. However, students may need support while they are in the process of becoming self-directed learners. Scaffolds such as project guidelines, rubrics, and focused questioning can help students learn how to accomplish tasks independently by reducing their complexity to a manageable level. You also learned that collaborative group work eases the challenges of authentic instruction. Research suggests that collaborative learning can improve the effectiveness of most activities (Wegerif, 2002) and the same is true for technology-based activities. In this chapter, you will learn to plan for and manage technology-enriched learning environments—where students work in groups as well as individually—in order to help your students achieve their educational goals, manage their own learning, and assess their own progress.

Supporting Self-Directed Learning

ISTE NETS-T Standard 2.b. requires that you "develop technology-enriched learning environments that enable all students to pursue their individual curiosities and become active participants in setting their own educational goals, managing their own learning, and assessing their own progress"—in other words, to be self-directed learners. Chapter 2 introduced the GAME Plan (see Figure 2.2) as a way to organize yourself during each step of the self-directed learning process. In Chapter 3, we illustrated the similarities between the self-directed learning activities of teachers and students. Here we compile both sets of information to emphasize how you can use the GAME plan to create meaningful lessons that build on, and support, students' self-directed learning. In essence, you should have a GAME plan not only for your own self-directed learning, but for your students' learning as well. In the following discussion, we provide a brief overview of each step, organized by the questions in Table 5.1.

Table 5.1	GAME Plan for Personal and Student Learning	
Steps	Personal Plans	Student Plans
Goals	• What do I want to know or be able to do? • What do I already know about the topic? • How will I know if I have been successful?	• What do my students need to know? • What do my students already know that can help them meet the goals of instruction? • How will I know if they have been successful?
Action	• What information do I need to meet my goal? • What learning strategy will I use? • What resources are needed?	• What content information do my students need? • What instructional strategy will I use? • What resources do my students need?
Monitor	• Am I finding the information I need? • What patterns are emerging from the information sources? • Do I need to modify my action plan?	• Are my students understanding the information and mastering the skills they need? • What patterns are emerging from my students' responses? • Should I modify my lesson and unit plans?
Evaluate and Extend	• Have I met my learning goals? • If not, should I modify my goals or my learning strategies? • What will I do differently in the future?	• Did my lesson or unit plan work? • If not, should I modify the goals, the assessment, or my instructional strategies? • What should I do differently in the future?

Setting Goals for Student Learning

As noted earlier, the first stage of the GAME plan is to set goals. This is true for both your own self-directed learning as well as your students' learning. Strategic learners begin the goal-setting process by analyzing the task at hand. Strategic learners also consider what they already know that can be useful in obtaining their new learning goals. Based on what they know about themselves and the task, they determine the best strategy to achieve those goals. Strategic teachers take a similar approach. When working with your students to set learning goals, begin by helping them identify what they already know and what they need to know about that content in order to determine a strategy to achieve those goals. In Chapter 7, you will learn that by considering your assessments *at the same time* that you set learning goals, you will be in a better position to identify the actions that you need to take to ensure that your students develop the skills needed to meet their goals. When you help your students set goals for learning, you seek to answer questions similar to those posed during your own learning process.

- What do my students need to know?
- What do my students already know that can help them meet their learning goals?
- How will I know if they have been successful?

Taking Action by Providing Learning Experiences

The actions you take in the GAME plan for your students' learning involve designing and arranging experiences that help them meet their learning goals—in other words, developing instructional activities. In Chapter 3, we introduced the principles of authentic instruction as a framework for planning instructional activities that facilitate the development of critical and creative thinking skills. In Chapter 4, we described how technologies could support the development of creative thinking skills by serving in the roles of tutor, mindtool, or support for conversation. The methods you select to facilitate learning will be impacted by the skills and knowledge required by the content you are addressing, the tools and resources you have available, your own teaching style, your students' learning preferences, as well as the types of assessments used to monitor student learning. As you plan the Action you will take to support your students in meeting their learning goals, you will develop lesson plans and associated management strategies. Consider questions such as:

- What content information do my students need?
- What instructional strategy will I use?
- What resources do my students need?

Monitoring Student Progress

Just as you must monitor your own learning goals and actions, you must help your students monitor how well they are meeting their learning goals using a variety of formal and informal means. In Chapter 2, we introduced Schön's (1983) ideas of "reflection-in-action" and "reflection-on-action." The monitoring process involves both forms of reflection. You and your students will reflect "on" their performances in their formal assessments. And you and your students will reflect "in action" as you go about your day-to-day activities in the classroom. You'll make ongoing modifications to your instructional strategies in response to the learning progress of your students. And your students will make ongoing modifications to their learning strategies as they monitor their own progress. As you will learn in Chapter 7, assessments are a part of monitoring, and when they are used to inform instruction or to help students monitor their learning, they are often referred to as **formative assessments**. As you help your students monitor their learning progress, you'll want to consider questions such as:

- Are my students understanding the information and mastering the skills they need?

- What patterns are emerging from my students' responses?
- Should I modify my lesson and unit plans?

Evaluating Instructional Effectiveness

Evaluating the effectiveness of your instruction is a critical component of the GAME plan for student learning. Just because you have provided instruction, or facilitated learning activities, it doesn't mean all of your students met the learning goals. Evaluation is the key to determining how successful your instruction has been as well as which resources and methods will most likely be successful in the future. In evaluating the effectiveness of your instruction, you'll consider assessment data of course, but you'll also want to make note of what you have learned about your teaching. As you learned in Chapter 2, this self-awareness, or reflection-on-action (Schön, 1983) is an important part of a teacher's professional development. In Chapter 7, you'll learn other techniques for evaluating the effectiveness of your instruction. Consider questions such as:

- Did my lesson or unit plan work?
- If not, should I modify the goals, the assessment, or my instructional strategies?
- What should I do differently in the future?

Supporting Students' Efforts to Be Self-Directed

You may want to involve students directly in planning, monitoring, and evaluating their learning activities and sequences. One way that you can involve students of all ages in this process is through the use of KWHL charts (see Figure 5.1). You may be familiar with KWHL charts. A **KWHL** chart identifies what students **K**now, what they **W**ant to know, **H**ow they will learn the topic, and what they **L**earned in the lesson. A KWHL chart can be a useful way for students to actively participate in goal-setting as it can help you identify the gap between what students know and what they need to know. Using a KWHL chart, you can engage students in identifying their prior knowledge on the topic (what they Know) and what they need to know (what they Want to learn). Students and teachers can work together to plan "**H**ow" they will obtain the knowledge they need. These charts are also useful in monitoring learning, as students can be encouraged to list what they have learned in the L column of the charts. Students should be encouraged to evaluate their learning processes as well. After the lesson is over, ask them to reflect on what they have learned about themselves as learners as well as what they have learned about the content.

KWHL Chart

What do you KNOW?	What do you WANT to know?	HOW will you learn?	What did you LEARN?

Figure 5.1
KWHL chart.

STORIES FROM PRACTICE

Creating Technology-Rich Learning Experiences for Second Graders

I'm Janice, and I teach second grade at a large elementary school. While there is a computer lab available in the school, I just tend to use the four computers we have in the classroom. Many people think that trying to use computers with young students is a waste of time, but I think it's just a matter of being really organized. I never wanted to be one of those teachers who had a computer just sitting in the back of the room. . . if the community's going to pay for things, then I wanted to use them, and I wanted to use them for the right reasons. And so I learned, by researching articles, how to find the appropriate curriculum goals and how to utilize the computer as a tool to reach those goals.

For example, I have curriculum objectives that I have selected for students to master

each day. From these objectives, I design a computer-assisted lesson that lasts a minimum of fifteen minutes. I begin by presenting this first as a whole-group activity using a computer and projector. After the concept of the objective has been presented, the students are divided into cooperative groups to complete an activity using the computer as a tool. The project is designed to help the students practice and master the curriculum objectives.

Not too long ago, I realized my ultimate goal was to be the best technology-using teacher possible. So I thought, if I sit around and wait to purchase the latest and greatest technology system, I'm not going to get anything accomplished. And I just realized, I need to use everything I have, so that I can

prove to the administration that I need a better system. If I use everything to its fullest extent and say I need to look further, then— then I have a reason to go to them. . .

My emphasis with my students is on developing their problem-solving skills. I figured that the best way for me to help them develop these was by giving them the opportunity to practice, and reflect on, problem situations that they can attack and solve on their own. Managing my room in ways that allows students to take charge of these situations gives them the kind of practice they need.

Source: Based on Ertmer, P. A. (2003). *VisionQuest: Envisioning and achieving integrated technology use.* Retrieved June 24, 2006, from http://www.edci.purdue.edu/vquest/

Technology-Enriched Learning Environments

Some classrooms have one or two computers, some have clusters of four or five computers (see Figure 5.2), and still others have access to a computer lab. Other schools have laptops, or mobile carts full of computers, which can be checked out for classroom use, or "mini-labs" that are shared by several classes and distributed throughout the school. No matter what technology resources you have available, you will need to know how to "develop technology-enriched learning environments that enable all students to pursue their individual curiosities and become active

Figure 5.2
Possible classroom computer configurations.

participants in setting their own educational goals, managing their own learning, and assessing their own progress."

What can we learn from Janice's use of technology, as described in the Stories from Practice on page 111? Janice finds a way to use whatever technology is available to her in a way that enhances meaningful student learning. She bases her selection of digital technologies on her goals for student learning. She develops techniques that help her students manage their uses of those technologies. And at the end of each lesson, she and her students reflect on what went well and what needs to be improved in the future. It's likely that, like Janice, you also aspire to be the best technology-using teacher possible.

Common Instructional Groupings

Regardless of how the technology is configured in your classroom or school, students always will have the option of working individually, in small groups, or as a whole group. This section focuses on challenges and instructional methods for those common arrangements with specific attention to computer use, although you will have similar considerations for other types of technology such as scanners, probeware, calculators, digital cameras, and other tools.

Individual Use

Students can use computers individually in a variety of settings. Your entire class may be engaged in individual use of the computer, as when you are in a computer lab, or students may use a single classroom computer, one at a time. When computers are used individually, scheduling computer time, coordinating computer work with other instructional activities, and providing technical assistance deserve special consideration.

At times, the entire class needs to work on the same task at the same time. For example, you may want all of your students to complete a computer-based lesson on fractions. Although the whole class may be involved in the same activity, the computer itself would be used individually. At other times, all of your students may need to work individually on their own projects or lessons. For example, students may need to contribute their own autobiographies to a class book.

Under these circumstances, you need access to a mobile cart of computers or a computer lab in order for each of your students to be able to work on an individual computer. Typically, access to a lab or mobile cart of computers is available at an assigned time each week or reserved as needed. For example, each class might use a lab for one hour or one class period each week. When access to computers is available only during specific time periods, you'll need to plan the activities that occur before and after computer use very carefully. If students are to complete a lesson on fractions in the computer lab on Tuesday, you might want them to explore fractions using hands-on manipulatives during class on Monday and follow their computer lesson with an assignment where they apply the skills they learned in the tutorial on Wednesday.

Other times, students will need to work independently on a single classroom computer. A computer-centric learning center can easily support student inquiry at most grade levels when connected to the Internet or networked databases supported by the school's library or media center. A variety of peripherals can also be connected to the computer to support a wide range of content areas. Your one-computer learning station can be connected to a classroom weather station, a digital microscope, a drawing tablet and pen stylus, a variety of science measurement devices including probeware, a piano keyboard, or digital cameras and videocameras. A single computer as a learning station can support the differentiation of instruction and flexible grouping strategies. Students can use software on the computer for initial practice, remediation, or enrichment. When connected to a printer, either directly or via the school's network, you can also print examples of student work that can be stored in portfolios or sent home to parents. The main thing to avoid is using the computer as "a reward." Rather, it should be incorporated as a learning tool for all students to meet both teacher- and student-selected learning goals.

You can still use computers individually even if you have access to only a few computers (or just one), but scheduling computer time requires special attention. Individual students will need access to the available computers at a time when they will not miss other critical class work. Students can be assigned to work on the computers at a set time or they can sign up for a time to use the computer. However, you'll need to take measures to ensure equitable access. For example, if students can only use the computers when they are finished with other work, some students will never have a chance to use them. As you plan your sign-up sheet or rotation schedule, take a look at your classroom schedule and lesson plans to determine when students would be able to work at the computer station without missing other critical activities. Perhaps your class follows the practice of a 90-minute reading block each day. You can schedule that reading block with flexible grouping within a larger 120-minute block to allot 30 minutes extra a day per student. In addition, you have help from a paraprofessional for one hour on Friday afternoons that is reserved for intervention or enrichment activities. If you included computer work in these activity blocks, there would be 3.5 hours available each week. Divide the available time into blocks of a reasonable length. Depending on your students' attention spans, technology skills, and their specific learning needs, reasonable time blocks may be around 30 to 45 minutes. Make sure your students have enough time to focus on the task at hand, but not so much time that they lose interest. To return to our example, if your students were to work for 30 minutes at a time, 22 students could use one classroom computer each week (see Figure 5.3). After you have determined the available blocks of time for computer use, either assign students to time blocks or post the schedule of open time blocks so students can schedule their own computer time. Either way, post the schedule so that students know when they are scheduled at the computer station.

When students need to work individually, whether in a computer lab, with laptop computers in the classroom, with a classroom set of calculators or handheld computers, or on a limited number of classroom computer workstations, both you and your students are responsible for preparing for this limited computer time. In the next section of this chapter, you will learn to plan activities that should occur before, during, and after the scheduled computer time.

When students are working individually, another challenge for you as a teacher will be to provide help when needed. Imagine a group of 20 second-graders all trying to work through a math program together. One student has trouble starting the program, another student's computer won't boot, another has somehow disconnected his mouse, and so forth. When students use the computer individually, they may need help with technical issues as well as the content. As is true whenever students are working on computers, you want them to focus on achieving the lesson goals rather than being distracted by technical issues. The tips provided in the "Technical Support" section of Chapter 8 will help you plan ways to provide computer support as well as assist students as they work through the content independently.

	Monday	Tuesday	Wednesday	Thursday	Friday
9:00 – 9:30	Lori	Roger	James	Karra	Natisha
9:30 – 10.00	Jason	Aniseh	Pupung	Nertha	Mary Alice
10.00 – 10.30	Jong-Gum	Lisa L.	Jeffrey	Ferrell	JW
10.30 – 11.00	Alice	Jason	E-lu	Lisa B.	Andy
2.00 – 2.30	X	X	X	X	Sun-ha
2.30 – 3.00	X	X	X	X	Josh

Figure 5.3
Sample classroom computer schedule for one week.

Small Groups

At other times, the activities that you have planned will benefit from the collaboration that occurs when students work in small groups. Although group size is often determined by practical considerations such as class size and number of computers, it can be difficult for more than four students to work productively around a single computer station. Johnson and Johnson (1991) established guidelines for effective cooperative learning groups back in the 1970s. These guidelines include the need for positive interdependence, individual accountability and responsibility, and a consideration of the group process. For group work to be effective, it's critical to establish classroom norms that support a culture of collaboration.

Students may be tempted to let the most technologically savvy student dominate the computer work, but it's important to establish an atmosphere where dominance by a few individuals is not tolerated. When your students work in groups, take care to ensure that no individual takes a dominant role and no individual takes a completely passive role. Make sure each student gets an equal chance to work on the computer.

Group work is most equitable and productive when specific roles are assigned and the principles of cooperative learning are followed. Depending on the age and abilities of your students, you may want to assign roles to individual students or have the group divide tasks among the members and cycle through them in turn—allowing each student to be the recorder, reporter, and so forth. In order to assign roles, think through the various tasks that are required by the group activity and divide them among the students (see Figure 5.4). For example, if students are conducting research on the web, one student could lead the discussions, one could take notes, one could enter search terms in the computer, and another could track the results of the searches.

Effective collaborative work is characterized by a balance between group responsibility and individual accountability. Clarify whether the tasks can be divided or whether all students must know how to do each task. Often, group members are responsible for both their own individual learning and the learning of other group members. Stress that each individual has something to offer the group and that no one set of skills is more important than another in the functioning of the group. Create an atmosphere of collaboration instead of competition. Stress that each group member has a responsibility to educate the other members on the skills for which he or she has expertise.

Figure 5.4
Students work together at the computer; each student is responsible for a role such as typist, recorder, or reader.

APPLY TO PRACTICE

Student Roles

1. Work with your peers to brainstorm a list of all the possible roles that students can play in collaborative work using technology.
2. Determine the skills and knowledge students must have to participate in each role as well as commonly available technologies that can support them. For example, a "recorder" may capture notes from the group using digital-audio, word-processing, or concept-mapping software.
   - What group behaviors are essential for the group to be successful?
   - What individual behaviors are important to each role?
   - How will you monitor how successful students are in their roles?
3. Compare the list your group created with the lists created by other groups in your class. Merge the lists to create a comprehensive list for your class. Consider adding the master list to your portfolio with a description of how it was developed.

Group work provides an excellent opportunity for the more proficient students to support less proficient students in developing their technological competencies.

Students may need to learn how to support one another. As the teacher, you may need to model effective problem-solving strategies and conflict-resolution skills. Regardless of their ages and abilities, students will need to learn to listen to one another and take turns. As they mature, they also may need to learn how to provide praise and thoughtful critiques. This provides you with an opportunity to help your students develop skills that will be applicable to a wide variety of life's situations.

Students should be evaluated on their abilities to practice group process skills as well as their products. When working in small groups, teachers often conclude the group work with reflection on the group process, as illustrated by Janice in the Stories from Practice. Students should evaluate themselves and each other on the extent to which they took turns, listened to one another, accepted responsibility for the group, and completed their assigned tasks. Even young students are capable of reflecting on their work and making positive suggestions to improve.

TOOLS FOR USE

Group Process Rubric

	1 None of the Time	2 Some of the Time	3 Most of the Time	4 All of the Time
Helping: The students offered assistance to each other.	1	2	3	4
Listening: Group members listened respectfully to each other's ideas.	1	2	3	4
Participating: Group members participated in each step of the process.	1	2	3	4
Persuading: Students exchanged, defended, and rethought ideas.	1	2	3	4
Questioning: Students interacted, discussed, and posed questions to all members of the team.	1	2	3	4
Respecting: Group members encouraged and supported the ideas and efforts of others.	1	2	3	4
Sharing: Students offered ideas and reported their findings to each other.	1	2	3	4

Source: Hall, A. (n.d.) Group Participation Rubric for WebQuest. Phoenix, AZ: Arizona State University at the West campus. Available: http://coe.west.asu.edu/students/ahall/webquest/grouprubric.htm.

You may also want to involve students in establishing a list of rules that can help them monitor and manage their learning during group work. Morrison and Lowther (2002) suggest that group rules include items such as:

- Every team member is important.
- We work as a team and as individuals to accomplish our goals.
- Diversity in opinions is important. We respect the right to be different but work toward consensus.
- We seek solutions to our problems, instead of blaming or criticizing.
- We structure or work according to individual needs.
- We help those who require assistance.

Whole Group

When computers are used for whole-group work, they are typically used as presentation devices. If you only have one or two computers in your classroom, this is one of the most effective uses of a single computer. You can present information slides or websites, students can present their projects, you can demonstrate software and procedures before students go to the lab, and so forth. The ideas are limitless.

To be used as a presentation device, additional equipment will be needed to make the computer screen visible to the whole class. Most popular—and most common—is a **data projector**, which connects to the computer and projects a computer desktop image onto a blank wall, screen, or whiteboard. Data projectors offer excellent resolution, the ability to zoom in, and easy control of projection size. When coupled with an interactive whiteboard or tablet PC, you have an excellent option for whole-class presentation and interaction.

Older technologies include LCD (liquid crystal display) projection panels that can be used to display the images on the computer monitor using an overhead projector. Another option is to split the signal coming from the class computer to display it on a large computer monitor or television. Many computers have "video out ports" that can be used to display the computer images on a television. If your computer lacks such ports, an inexpensive "video scan converter" can be used to transform the computer signal to a signal suitable for display on an older television or NTSC (National Television Standards Committee) monitor (see Figure 5.5). When using a large

Comstock/Jupiter Images

Figure 5.5
A large monitor is being used for instruction in a classroom.

TOOLS FOR USE

Using Interactive Whiteboards

First used in the business community, interactive whiteboards have become a common sight in many classrooms (see Figure 5.6). A new description of a teacher "workstation" might consist of an Internet-connected laptop, whiteboard, projector, and printer and is considered by many to be the basic teaching equipment in a classroom. But not all teachers who have whiteboards take advantage of their many potential benefits. Although little empirical research is available that ties the use of a whiteboard directly to student learning, the whiteboard certainly supports proven pedagogical methods and tools. As you review these ten tips for using a whiteboard in your classroom, keep in mind that the most important consideration is *how* you use the whiteboard to support your instruction.

Project Clear Visuals

The clarity of visuals is a hallmark of the whiteboard. A bonus is the ease with which text, images, and video can be presented and manipulated (e.g., quickly changing fonts, colors, sizes, etc.). This can be helpful for supporting students with a wide range of learning needs and preferences, especially English language learners, some students with special needs, and those with visual learning preferences. Most boards also include handwriting recognition and can insert handwritten notes as legible text into spreadsheets, word processing, and other documents.

Use Any Software

Whiteboards can be used with any software installed on the computer to which they are connected, making them ideal for one-computer classrooms. You can access CD, DVDs, and other videos, and a range of animations and simulations found on the Internet and through stand-alone software. You can even scan in images or hand-drawn student work for use with your entire class. Some interactive whiteboards can also be shared from a distance in support of virtual learning.

Save and Review Work

Important documents, diagrams, or other files created during class can be printed out and distributed immediately or saved as media files that students can access after class. Documents, websites, and images you use in your instruction on the board can be exported to a class website to support absent students, student review, or to keep parents informed of lessons covered in your class.

Interact with Your Instructional Materials

Display and interact with documents, images, video, and animations. You can pause video and circle pertinent features. Still images, such as a diagram of a cell, can be labeled onscreen. Documents can be created and manipulated through highlighting, commenting, or showing changes. One unique feature is the reveal tool that allows you to select portions of the screen to display, or not, that can reveal or cover information on the board as easily as opening a shade or pointing your finger.

Use or Create Templates

Use the built-in templates (e.g., maps, grids, number lines, diagrams, musical staves) and the built-in tools (e.g., timers, rulers, protractors, calculators, probability tools, notepads, cameras) in many different classroom activities. Or, if you wish, scan in your own images or backgrounds.

Involve Your Students

Students can manipulate items directly on the board, adding their own ideas (either typed from the keyboard or handwritten on the board), can underline or highlight text to identify main ideas and key words, can annotate images, or even move items around, as when creating a concept map or diagram. Using the whiteboard can be motivational and mastered by students of all ages.

Support Student Presentations

Present student projects using a variety of software, web resources, and document formats—controlling the presentation (opening and closing files, windows, menus, etc.) entirely from the whiteboard. Teachers use whiteboards with students in most grades, even students in primary grades. In fact, students with less-developed fine-motor skills can often operate the board easily.

Interact with Your Students

Whiteboards support interactive learning environments that promote discussion and opportunities for participation in small-group or whole-class settings. Several boards support classroom response systems through which students can anonymously or confidentially respond to polls or other formative assessments and from which data can be captured, reviewed (immediately, if preferred), or recorded in a gradebook.

Manage Resources Flexibly and Efficiently

You can easily move back and forth between open documents or applications to provide multiple examples, enrichment, or instructional interventions for those students who need them. Less time is spent on resource management than when using a chalkboard or even a computer with only a projector. Many users report using their finger or stylus is easier and faster than using a mouse. Wireless slates, available with some boards, allow you and your students to interact with the board from anywhere in the classroom.

Share with the Greater Teaching Community

Many whiteboard companies offer online communities where you can download lesson plans, presentations, and templates to use in your own classroom. You can post to these communities, too, and may find teachers with similar interests with whom you can communicate and collaborate.

Sources: Bell, 2002; Smith, Higgins, Wall, & Miller, 2005.

Figure 5.6
A single computer connected to a projector and interactive whiteboard can be a valuable resource for supporting your instruction.

television or monitor, make sure that it is high enough for students to see over the heads of other students.

If you don't have a data projector, LCD panel, or large monitor in your classroom, another option may be to check out equipment from some centralized location such as the library or media center. To ensure that you have access to it when you need it, you should always schedule your equipment use in advance. And if possible, you should schedule the equipment to be delivered to your classroom during a planning period or before class to hook it up and make sure it is working properly. If there is one thing that we know about working with technology, it is that things can go wrong! But fortunately, the vast majority of those things can be prevented, or quickly remedied, with just a little thought and preparation—things that are much easier to do when your classroom is quiet than when you have thirty restless students waiting to get on with class (or trying to derail it!).

Of course, when a computer is used for presentations, you need to carefully prepare your materials in advance. Presentation slides need to be developed, websites need to be located and bookmarked, and demonstrations need to be practiced.

APPLY TO PRACTICE

Which Technology for Which Learning Need?

1. Choose one of the technologies described in the Tools for Use: "Choosing Presentation Technologies."
2. Describe a teaching/learning situation in which this tool would be appropriate.
3. List specific learning objectives that the presentation technology could help your students achieve.
4. Combine your ideas with those of your classmates who considered other tools.

TOOLS FOR USE

Choosing Presentation Technologies

Technology	Purpose	Advantages and Limitations
Data Projector	Connects to computer to project image on a screen or blank wall	Resolution options are good—better when using on a screen or interactive whiteboard. The projection size can be huge, great for auditorium settings, but they work well in small spaces too.
Interactive Whiteboard	Used with a data projector, board responds to touch for navigation; use a stylus, marker, or sometimes your finger to "write" on application window; large variety of educational software options	Functionality is great—a very popular tool for teacher and students alike. Professional installation required, and must include use of a data projector. Some boards include portable wireless slates so you can move about the room and still interact with the board.
Interactive Pen Display	Uses the same touch technology as the interactive whiteboard, but in a small screen that connects to computer. Used with a data projector to display on a large presentation screen.	Manipulation is done on the small portable screen; projection can be on any simple screen or even a blank wall if needed.
Tablet PC	A fully functional laptop computer with the interactive pen technology built in. Used with a data projector for presentation.	Offers the portability of a laptop coupled with interactive pen technology in one device. Also includes handwriting recognition.

Summary of Technology-Enriched Learning Environments

Any of these instructional groupings can occur with almost any physical arrangement of computers. Although the national numbers suggest that Internet-capable computers and other technologies are widely available in the nation's schools, you may have little choice in determining what technologies are in your school or classroom. Certainly, school administrators should work to provide equitable access to resources for teachers, staff, and students, but what happens if your class has limited technology? What if there is just a single computer?

As noted earlier, a single computer connected to a display, either a projector or large monitor, can be a valuable resource for supporting your instruction. With this type of display, your single computer can be used to run simulations, model exemplary or completed projects, support a discussion through the use of concept-mapping software or notes created with a word-processing application, guide students on WebQuests or virtual field trips, and connect your classroom to the outside world through e-mail and web resources. Short streaming media clips can help you gain and focus student attention, orient students to an activity or task, or bring in the viewpoint of outside experts. You can use online quizzes or surveys as a group activity to review content or, with wireless responders—infrared, Bluetooth, or FM—students can actually take quizzes and tests or otherwise provide formative feedback through an interactive whiteboard (see Tools for Use) or response system that interfaces with your single computer.

When there are a few computers in the classroom, several students can work on individual projects simultaneously while the rest of the class does some other task, or each computer can be assigned to a group of students for small-group work. One of the computers could be connected to a projector or large monitor for whole-class instruction. When you have access to enough computers for your whole class in a lab, library media center, or using a mobile cart of computers, it might seem easier, or preferable, to have students use them for individual work. However, as noted earlier, there is research to suggest that asking students to work together, especially around a computer, increases the level of conversation in which students engage, which can result in greater learning. You don't want to rule out this type of computer use, just because you have enough computers for students to work individually. Be sure to consider the specific learning goals that students are trying to achieve and then to select your computer-student arrangement to help them best achieve those goals.

APPLY TO PRACTICE

Computer Arrangements

1. Create a description of an instructional activity appropriate for various technology settings. Include a description of how the technology tools will be used within each setting.
   - A one-computer classroom
   - A classroom with five computers
   - A lab or portable lab setting
2. Share your descriptions with your peers. Merge the lists to create a comprehensive list for your class. Consider adding the master list to your portfolio with a description of how it was developed.

Supporting Students' Use of Technology Tools and Resources

The effectiveness of any instructional resource, whether a website, software, video-tape, or textbook, lies partially in the content and design of the resources, but the main impact comes from the way it is used by a skilled teacher. You may need to help students set reasonable learning goals that can be accomplished during the given time. Give students the responsibility for accomplishing necessary preparations before using the technology so that their technology time is not wasted. For example, students may need to collect data to contribute to the spreadsheet that will be built during class time or to draft their autobiographies for the class book. When their time at the computer is over, help your students review what they have completed, identify remaining tasks, and set new goals to accomplish before and during their next computer session. Whether the technology resources are to be used individually, in small groups, or in large groups, it is important to consider what you have to do before, during, and after the lesson to support students in their self-directed learning efforts.

Before Instruction

As a teacher, you know, or will soon know, that preparation is essential! When you use a textbook resource, you read the book carefully and direct your students to the sections that need special attention. You may have them answer certain questions or do certain assignments. Preparing for the use of digital resources requires the same care. Consider how you will scaffold the student's learning activities so that they are able to complete their tasks as autonomously as possible, given their current ability levels.

Plan

Begin by examining, in detail, the resources you plan to use with your students. You may want to perform a trial run of the same tasks that you will ask your students to do and make note of the problems you encounter. As you review instructional soft-ware, determine what sections of it align with your students' learning goals; students may not need to complete the entire program. Also determine the time required to complete the activities. Some activities are easier to stop and start than others. Check whether a game or activity can be saved at any time or only at the end of a level and plan accordingly. You may want to estimate a little extra time if students need to become familiar with the program before they use it for academic tasks.

After you have become familiar with the resources you plan to use with your students, analyze your learners in relation to the skills you want them to acquire. Deter-mine the prerequisite skills your students need in order to participate successfully in the technology-based activities and to learn the content. For example, young students may need help with typing activities. Older students might need a review of math concepts in order to select the best formula to be entered in a spreadsheet. Consider also the attention span of your students. How long can they stay focused and interested in one task? Make sure the learning experience is appropriate for your students and their learning goals.

As you plan your instruction, think about the tasks that students should perform before, during, and after the technology-based activity. Should students collect data for a spreadsheet or create a rough outline of their papers before they arrive at their computer stations? Should they practice the skills they learned in a tutorial after they return to their desks? How will students move from task to task? What procedures will help them manage their own learning? Carefully think through a class activity and determine which parts of the lesson lend themselves to technology use and which ones do not.

Table 5.2 lists activities that typically need to be performed when using a few common software programs. Use the guidance provided in this table to develop your own list of teacher preparation activities for other types of technology-enriched learning experiences.

As you plan your lessons, ALWAYS have a backup plan in case of unexpected technical problems. Some teachers find it useful to set up learning centers or stations where students can work through several activities at one station, with some activities requiring the use of computer technologies and others not. Supplemental activities can be on different but related topics. You may want to assign readings, have students watch a videotape, or participate in experiments to reinforce or broaden their understanding. Of course, you need a backup plan in case you encounter non-technical problems, too, like when you plan to go outside to collect soil samples and it rains. Make sure that all activities clearly relate to specific learning outcomes and are not perceived as unnecessary "busy work."

One challenge you will face is *how much instruction* to provide when using a new application or visiting a new website. Do you need to teach students to use the software or do they already know how? You may be tempted to provide detailed, step-by-step instructions or, conversely, to simply let them "discover" how to operate the program on their own. The ideal amount of instruction to provide will vary, depending on the abilities of your students. Unless the goal of the lesson is to learn the new application, you may want to minimize the amount of time devoted to learning functionality, yet provide enough support so that your students do not struggle unnecessarily. And if you want them to learn technology skills within the context of the lesson, don't forget to make these skills part of your lesson goals.

If possible, teach students skills that generalize across applications as well as skills they need to figure out new digital resources on their own. For example, students should learn to explore the menu structure to determine what options are available within a computer program or website. One good option is to provide students with simple directions to get them started, and then let them have time to discover specific features of the resource on their own while you monitor the success of their chosen strategies. If you choose this option, don't forget to allocate additional time within your schedule for students to explore the capabilities of the resource.

Develop Student Guidelines

When working in technology-enriched learning environments, students will benefit from having guidelines that indicate what they should accomplish during the lesson (their goals for learning), what they are expected to have ready beforehand, and what they should do after their computer time is over, including self-assessment activities. Table 5.3 lists typical preparation and follow-up activities for several types of common software applications from the student's perspective. Use these examples to develop your own list of preparation and follow-up activities for other types of technology-enriched learning experiences.

Table 5.2	Teacher Preparation Required for Software Programs	
Software Type	**Materials**	**Student Groupings**
Tutor		
Tutorial	Select sections of program that match your objectives. Identify necessary prerequisite skills.	Schedule computers for individual use.
Drill and Practice	Identify prerequisite skills and sections to be completed by students.	Schedule computers for individual use.
Mindtools		
Simulation or Problem solving	Identify prerequisite skills and sections of the program that correspond to objectives.	Assign students to small groups for collaborative problem solving. Consider appropriate whole-group problem-solving activities. Schedule necessary equipment.
Database	Develop a sample of what students should generate. Decide what fields are needed, collect data, generate sample report. Create a print or electronic worksheet for students to complete with information that will be entered into the database or let students create their own.	Group students and schedule equipment. When entering data use two or more students so one can read the data while the other one enters it. When manipulating data, use small groups to make predictions and organize and interpret data.
Word processing	Create a sample student project. Assure that directions are clear, planned resources are suitable, and time allocated adequate.	Work individually or if in pairs or small groups, students should take turns entering information.
Spreadsheet	Plan for the data collection process, if applicable. Plan specific data manipulations. Create sample spreadsheets with data. Determine how data will be presented, as a chart or graph. Prepare a template or provide directions for students to create their own.	When entering data use two or more students so one can read the data while the other one enters it. When manipulating data, use small groups to make predictions and organize and interpret data.
Support for communication		
Face-to-face collaborative learning	Choose digital resources that promote conversations and support your learning goals. Plan the roles students in each group will play such as typist, recorder, time manager, and/or subject matter expert. Establish ground rules for collaboration. Develop a worksheet or handout for assessment.	Assign students to pairs or small groups, depending on the nature of the assignment. Schedule equipment.
Discussion lists, blogs, wikis	Set up list, blog, or wiki site and assign appropriate permissions. Establish ground rules for postings. Ensure student safety, especially if using a public space.	Work individually, in pairs, or in teams to post or respond to postings.
Chat, instant messaging	Assign students accounts. Prepare a handout or presentation about appropriate language and safe use of instant messaging. If messages are part of your assessment, determine how you will retain the messages. Ensure student safety, especially if using a public chat room.	Determine who will be chatting with whom, and for what purpose.
Videoconferencing and webconferencing	Determine equipment needed for video and audio transmission such as webcams, microphones, headsets, and adequate bandwidth. Decide on which functions of the resource to employ (such as chat, polls, and document-sharing). Prepare handout or presentation with instructions for participation.	If the conference is essentially a presentation, arrange the room so that all can see and hear the presentation, using projection equipment if necessary. If the conference is interactive, work individually or in pairs at individual computers.

Source: Based on Morrison & Lowther (2002).

Your guidelines should provide enough detail to clearly convey your expectations as to how your students should manage their time, both on and off the computer. Prepare any handouts and assignment sheets needed—either electronic handouts and assignment sheets that students can access from a file server or web page or paper-based copies. Assignment sheets might contain a description of the assigned task, the problem statement, guiding questions, URLs, tips for using technology, and reflection questions. Sometimes you need a series of assignment sheets such as

Table 5.3	Student Preparation and Follow-Up Activities	
Software Type	Before Technology Use	After Technology Use
Tutor		
Tutorial	Complete activities that build prerequisite skills.	Apply skills learned to different but related tasks to solidify knowledge gains.
Drill and Practice	Complete activities that introduce the skills practiced in the lesson.	Continue to practice skills in other ways.
Mindtools		
Simulation or Problem solving	Review rules and procedures for skills that are to be applied.	Synthesize what was learned through discussions or individual reflections.
Database	Determine data fields needed, if not assigned. If sharing data across groups, then all groups should have the same database fields. Determine when to collect data, create data fields, and enter data. Review prior learning and introduce new skills necessary for the activity through readings, research, assignments, tutorials, practice problems. Generate predictions about what the students think they will find.	Discuss findings in whole-class or small-group settings, allowing students to reference their databases during discussions. This may lead to the development of new questions, further analysis, or additional research. Reflect on learning that occurred. Generate a group report that includes reports from the data. Build on the lesson by making connections to other lessons and making additional predictions.
Word processing	Brainstorm and conduct discussions to clarify goals of the task. Identify where to find resources. Review prior learning and skills associated with the task.	Conduct group presentations of products created. Reflect on the process through group debriefing or journal writing.
Spreadsheet	Collect and organize data prior to entering it. Review prior learning on topic and ensure that students have skills necessary to complete the task. Have students read materials, complete tutorials, work practice problems as necessary.	Work with students to interpret and make predictions from the data. Explore activities that further enhance learning or develop critical thinking skills.
Support for Communication		
Face-to-face collaborative learning	Review ground rules for effective collaboration. Set expectations for participation.	Reflect on what worked and what did not work in the collaborative effort.
Discussion lists, blogs, wikis	Review ground rules and instructional goals. Draft postings. Establish goals for reading and responding to others' postings.	Use the information from the products. Reflect on postings and/or responses.
Chat, instant messaging	Review ground rules and instructional goals.	Use the information learned in the chat. Reflect on the chat experience.
Videoconferencing and webconferencing	Check all equipment, connections, and setup. Review ground rules and instructional goals.	Use the information from the conference. Reflect on the experience.

Source: Based on Morrison & Lowther (2002).

general instructions, technical guidelines, resource guides, rubrics, and example projects.

When a computer task is new, it might be helpful to provide your students with step-by-step **technical guidelines**. When preparing step-by-step guides to the use of technology, try to anticipate and minimize the confusion that could occur if students worked from unclear instructions. It's a good practice to 1) perform the task that you are asking the students to do and write down each step you take, 2) prepare your instruction guide following the steps that you recorded, then 3) try to perform the task again, using the instructions you developed, 4) make notes of any steps that were left out or unclear, and finally, 5) correct the instruction sheet as needed.

Make sure you work through the instructions exactly as you wrote them in order to test their accuracy. Develop step-by-step guides only for those tasks students will need. Typically, these would be procedures, activities, and software that are very different from those used in the past. Students will need instructions on how to get started and how to get help when they encounter difficulties (see Figure 5.7).

You can use technology to create your step-by-step guides. You can create a document and insert graphics using word-processing software or develop a series of tutorial web pages linked from your class website. Screen-capturing software is freely available with most operating systems, such as Apple's Grab or the PrintScrn key in Windows. You can capture the activity on your screen using screen-recording software, such as TechSmith's Camtasia or Adobe's Captivate. Screen recordings can play back sequences of actions and are helpful for illustrating processes—such as using menu commands in a video-editing program or creating a series of nested folders (also called directories) on a class file server.

Technical guidelines specific to a particular project can be incorporated into the instructional handouts for that project, while general instructions can be provided through guides that stay with the computer. For younger students or novice technology users, instructions on specific software can be placed near the computers in notebooks or on laminated sheets. Often teachers find that simple step-by-step posters that cover common computer procedures can decrease the number of questions asked. Job aids such as posters and step-by-step handouts support students as they learn a new procedure, and decrease the demand on their cognitive processing while they are learning to perform a new procedure.

When a lesson requires multiple resources, a **resource guide** can assist students in using their time wisely. A resource guide lists the materials and digital resources that are applicable to the lesson. The use of web resources deserves special mention. As you locate sites for use in your lesson, you can simply copy and paste the links into a word-processed document. If this document is loaded on a computer with Internet access, students can open the web pages by clicking on the links in the word-processed document. Another way to ensure that students use their time wisely when searching for information on the web is to create a list of URLs that contain

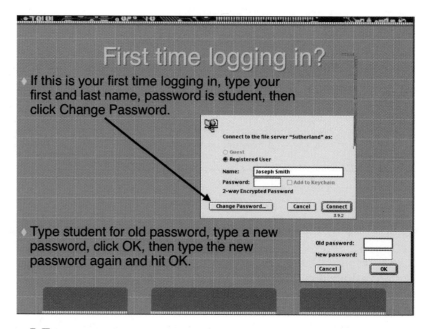

Figure 5.7
Student resource guides help learners with the steps involved in complicated projects, such as logging into a school network.
Source: Laurene Johnson

information relevant to your lesson. Some teachers also create and organize book-marks (or "favorites") in web browsers to help organize student activity on the Inter-net. Another option is to create a web page—one that can be linked from a school or class website—or use a social bookmarking site, such as del.icio.us, that includes those links. Then, all you have to do is to provide the URL of that page to your stu-dents. The advantage of a web-based version is that you and your students would have the page available from any computer with Internet access. You may also want to embed your resources into an instructional activity, such as when using a Web-Quest as described in Chapter 4.

As you prepare materials for your students, it's important to make your expecta-tions of quality clear through rubrics, checklists, or models of exemplary student work (for more information on rubrics, checklists, and assessing quality, see Chapter 7). Let students know the manner in which their finished products should be delivered to you, the expected length, any formatting requirements, and whether they can work with other students or not. **Rubrics** help students determine the critical com-ponents that need to be reflected in the final products. This, then, enables them to set daily goals for completion and to monitor their progress toward realization of the final product. **Exemplars** can further clarify your expectations by providing models of acceptable performance. You may even want to develop a template for students to use as they go through the lesson. A template can illustrate proper formatting, scaf-fold students as they learn to perform the task on their own, save time, and help avoid frustration. For example, you may want to set up a template for a student web page so that students can focus on adding the content rather than on learning the web development program. If students are working with an application that requires detailed setup and formatting, a template can be especially useful.

Prepare Technology

Before you begin your lesson, you'll need to prepare the technology—often compu-ters. If you are using a computer lab, make sure you know how the computers are configured and are comfortable with any lab management software before you bring your class to the lab. Whether you're in a computer lab or rotating students through computer stations in your classroom, computer time is often limited so it's important for students to make the most of the time they have available. If you are using hand-helds, calculators, wireless laptops from a cart, or other portable technologies, deter-mine how the materials will get to the learning area and how the students will access them. Regardless of the setting, the tasks discussed next deserve consideration.

In a lab, turn on computers and open applications. Some computers and software take a while to boot or load, so this simple step can save precious computer time. If students will circulate through computer stations, make sure you direct them to leave the applications open for students who follow. When accessing a file server, you may notice reduced network speed if all of your students log on or download files from a file server at the same time. Some teachers combat this slow down in service by allowing students to sign in before class starts or staggering access to the file server.

Make sure the correct resources are loaded and working properly. You may even incorporate student technology helpers, lab assistants, or parent volunteers to do this with you. Test the software and procedures on the computer that your students will be using. Just because a series of steps works on your home computer, doesn't mean they will work in the lab! Load any other resources your students may need, such as a word-processed list of relevant URLs, a worksheet that students should fill in, or a template.

You'll also need to develop a system for your students to store their work. You may want to create a folder system on the computer's hard drive where students are instructed to store their files in a specific location. Files can be stored by student name or by subject. It's also useful to establish a file naming system to make it easy for you and your students to locate their work. For example high school teachers may want to set up a separate folder for each of their classes and direct students to save their work there, using their last name and the date as the file name. Use a poster or other job aid to remind students how to save their files.

It's a good idea to have a way for students to save their files in more than one location: for example, on the computer's hard drive and on a remote server or removable disk. Different schools will have different options available. There may be a server where your students have file space. If not, use removable media such as zip disks, floppies, or jump drives to back up students' work. As we've said before, things can go wrong! This is especially true when several people use the same computer.

For various reasons, you'll also have to establish procedures for students to move their files from one computer to another. Students may begin a project in class and want to finish it for homework. Or they may begin working on a computer in the lab, and then need to finish it on a different computer in the library. Files can be shared through a school's computer network or moved using removable media devices such as disks, flash, or jump drives. Keep in mind that students may need a way to save large files such as videos or graphics. Students also may need to exchange files with other students, such as when they are working on a group project.

During Instruction

Once your instructional time begins, you'll need to clearly communicate your expectations of what students should do before, during, and after their computer time—before they actually get there. Depending on whether the entire group will work on similar activities or whether students will work independently, you may want to review the procedures with the whole class. You can demonstrate the software or websites used in the lesson, review the rules, and outline the steps before your students go to their computer stations. If students are working independently, these expectations can be conveyed through handouts and posters.

If the entire class will eventually perform the task, it's often useful to demonstrate it to the whole class using a projection system. A demonstration can familiarize students with an interface and reassure them that the procedure is not excessively difficult. If you choose to do a classroom demonstration, make sure you only demonstrate enough of the program for them to get started successfully and do not overwhelm them with more information than they can remember. Online tutorials and screen captures (described earlier in this section) can provide a scaffold to those students who need more guidance on software operations.

In order for your students to make the most of the time they have at the computer stations, let them know exactly what they must complete prior to working on the computers and what they should bring to the computer stations. Do they need paper and pencils for taking notes? Do they need a rough draft? Should they have identified potential search terms? A checklist of things to do prior to working on the computers can be helpful for many students. You may want to work with them to develop their own checklists to help them think through the tasks that should be done to prepare for their computer time. Above all, make sure the link between what they are learning in the classroom and their computer work is very clear! Students should see their computer time as essential to their classroom work rather than an "add on."

Although you might want to create an independent, problem-solving atmosphere in your classroom, let students clearly know what actions they can take on their own and when they should come to you for assistance. You don't want students to rewire peripherals at will. Small problems such as an inappropriate software setting can become a much more challenging problem if students (or even colleagues!) take things into their own hands.

Set up your classroom to make it easy for students to work independently by developing consistent rules and procedures that students should follow when they work on the computers. You don't want progress to come to a screeching halt when printers jam, computers freeze, or the Internet is down. When using technology, things can happen, and both preparation and flexibility are essential. When students are working independently, walk through the computer areas to ensure that they are on task, understand the assignment, and are not having technical difficulties (see Figure 5.8).

Many teachers have found it useful to initiate procedures for students to signal that they need help other than the commonly raised hand. It can be hard to see a hand raised in a classroom full of computers, but most importantly, a raised hand makes it very difficult for students to continue working on the problem while waiting for assistance. As you probably know, many times, a problem can be solved if you just keep at it. Some teachers have signs that are used to signal the need for assistance; others have found that something as simple as a colorful paper cup can be set on top of the monitor to signal that help is needed. Lab management software often includes helpful applications such as chat or instant messaging that allows students to ask questions without interrupting class.

But even with job aids and a signaling system, it's hard for one teacher to get around to a whole class of students who need help! You may want to initiate procedures where students routinely ask their peers on either side of them for assistance before asking you. Identify several computer-savvy students in your class who can serve as peer helpers. You may even want to strategically place "technology leaders" around the classroom. Don't underestimate the ability of your students to provide support to each other!

If you anticipate that your students will need lots of help, especially when they are learning a new procedure that could be difficult, try to solicit extra help. Call on parent volunteers. Arrange to team teach with another teacher, where she helps you in your class in exchange for your help in hers, or combine classes for a period of instruction. See if there are students in your school who could volunteer their assistance for the time that they are needed.

Parents, older students, and other volunteers can supervise students' uses of the computers, just make sure they have clear guidelines as to how to do so. Ideally, volunteers should supervise through coaching, and modeling when necessary, rather than completing the task for your students. Teach your volunteers to ask guiding questions to help the students figure out the answers on their own. If it becomes

Cengage Learning

Figure 5.8
Let your students know you are available for help during computer time.

clear that a student is having great difficulty in performing a task, the volunteer can model the desired behavior. Use your volunteers as a means for students to get individualized attention on tasks that are challenging for them. If your students are very young, you may want parents or older students to help with some of the tasks that may be too difficult, such as typing text into a word processor.

Once the students are working independently, try not to interrupt them to make announcements. If you find that several students have the same problem or you are answering the same question repeatedly, a general announcement may be in order; but, to the best of your ability, try to cluster your announcements and keep your interruptions to a minimum. When a whole-class demonstration would be particularly helpful, lab management software can allow you to block students' access to their computers, and display your own computer or that of one of your students as an example. Lab management software also helps you identify individuals struggling with or going off task so that you can guide them from the teacher workstation or provide individual help at their computers.

Let students know what time they should complete the task well in advance of the finish time so students can allocate their time appropriately. For example, tell students that they have an hour to write an essay, or that they have until 2 o'clock to find information on their report topics. Provide a warning in advance of the finish time, perhaps displaying a countdown timer using software you find online or embedded in interactive whiteboard applications, so that they have adequate time to reach a logical stopping point and save their work.

You may want to involve your students in establishing specific rules for technology use. Don't establish too many rules so they are reasonably enforceable. Rules should include respect for each other's work and modeling positive digital citizenship. Students should learn never to alter or delete any files other than their own. Students should know to use the technology only for the assigned lesson unless they have permission to do otherwise. You can enforce this rule through routinely viewing the "history" of sites accessed by a computer web browser. Develop clear classroom movement patterns so students do not run the risk of tripping over electric and other cables. Other common rules include no food or drinks near the technology. Use the establishment and enforcement of classroom rules as an opportunity to teach students about the safe and ethical use of digital resources. Overall, keep the rules as clear and unambiguous as possible.

After Instruction

As with any other kind of instruction, you should critically evaluate lessons that incorporate digital technologies in order to make them more effective in the future. You may keep a reflective journal, make notes on your lesson plans, or create a series of documents using word-processing software. Keep records of successful activities and procedures, plans for the next time you teach the topic, and other comments that can help you improve on your instruction in the future. Will the lesson continue to be used? Why or why not? Was the software a good investment of time and money? Are modifications needed in the way the digital resources were used in the classroom? What sort of modifications? Were there technical difficulties? Conceptual difficulties? Overall, how well did it work?

Before you begin your reflections, it's a good idea to set up files and folders to manage your notes. You can create your own database of the software, websites, or other digital resources you have used, complete with teaching suggestions, number of copies, handouts for students, and helpful hints. It's worth the time to set up an organizational system for your computer files, just as you would set up an organizational system for your actual classroom. In many schools, grade level or content level teams meet to discuss instruction, the resources used, and the effectiveness of them. "Best practice" ideas and lesson plans are generated by these teams and can be stored electronically for use by all the teachers on the team from year to year.

TOOLS FOR USE

Technology Integration—Steps to Take Before, During, and After Instruction

Before instruction

Plan for technology integration
- Explore the resources to determine what features align with your instructional goals
- Estimate time needed for tasks
- Analyze learners and identify prerequisite skills
- Decide what should be done before, during, and after the instruction
- Plan backup activities in case of technical problems

Develop student guidelines, including instructions, handouts, and rubrics
- Create instructional demonstrations, handouts, and posters
- Develop evaluation rubrics, checklists, and templates
- Create or identify example projects
- Identify resources and create resource guide or WebQuest

Prepare learning environment
- Gather and arrange materials for students' access
- Turn on computers and open applications
- Make sure resources are loaded and working properly
- Develop file storage system
- Model legal software use

During instruction
- Group students
- Let students know what they should do before, during, and after computer time

- Demonstrate tasks that everyone will do
- Provide handouts or tutorials for complicated instructions
- Let students know what they should bring to the computer station
- Make links between class goals and computer time explicit
- Walk through instructional area while students are working
- Guide students through activities or use trained volunteers to facilitate the instruction
- Enforce classroom management procedures
- Keep interruptions to a minimum
- Use prompts to keep the timing of the lesson on track
- Announce stop time in advance
- Monitor or assess student understanding; engage students in self-assessment

After instruction
- Take notes on what happened
- Reflect on what went well and what did not
- Decide how to change the lesson for the next time you teach it
- Set up system to manage suggestions, handouts, reflections, and other materials
- Analyze assessment data
- Plan for reteaching, follow-up, or enrichment
- Put materials away or organize computer files
- Record student progress

THE GAME PLAN

Technology-Enriched Learning Environments

Set Goals
Learn more about how teachers support student learning in a technology-enriched learning environment.

Take Action
Volunteer to assist a local school with technology integration efforts. If possible, try to assist with a lesson at the grade level in which you are interested in teaching.

Monitor
Reflect on the teacher's classroom management strategies. How did he or she support student's self-directed learning? What was done to provide technical training and assistance? What rules and procedures were enforced?

Evaluate and Extend
Make note of things that worked well and things that you would consider changing if you were in charge of the class. What did you learn by working in the classroom? Make a short presentation of the best classroom management techniques you observed and share them with your colleagues. Your peers may have observed different techniques that could be useful.

TOOLS FOR USE

Daily Lesson Plan Template

TECHNOLOGY INTEGRATION FOR MEANINGFUL CLASSROOM USE
Daily Lesson GAME Plan

Lesson Title: **Related Lessons:**

Grade Level: **Unit:**

GOALS

Content Standards:

ISTE NETS-S

☐ Creativity and innovation   ☐ Critical thinking, problem solving, & decision making

☐ Communication and collaboration   ☐ Digital citizenship

☐ Research and information fluency   ☐ Technology operations and concepts

Instructional Objective(s):

ACTION

Before-Class Preparation:

During Class

Time	Instructional Activities	Materials and Resources

Notes:

MONITOR

Ongoing Assessment(s):

Accommodations and Extensions:

Back-up Plan:

EVALUATION

Lesson Reflections and Notes:

Chapter Summary

This chapter focused on planning for technology-enriched learning experiences that support students in setting their own educational goals, managing their own learning, and assessing their own progress. We used the structure provided by the GAME plan to illustrate how you can plan and manage your instruction. Similar to how you use the GAME plan for self-directed learning, you will work with your students to set learning goals, take action to help them achieve those goals, monitor their learning progress, and evaluate both their learning and your teaching. You learned techniques to use digital technologies individually, in small groups, and in whole-group settings. We stressed the importance of preparing materials for students, preparing the computers, and preparing the students for computer use.

All of these elements come together in teacher's daily lesson plans. In the accompanying Tools for Use: Daily Lesson Plan Template we provide a template that you might want to use to note your goals, instructional actions, monitoring strategies, and evaluation plans. Of course, daily lesson plans are typically part of larger unit plans. Lesson planning is addressed in more detail in Appendix A.

In the next chapter, you will learn to "customize and personalize learning activities to address students' diverse learning styles, working strategies, and abilities using digital tools and resources."

 WEB LINK

Visit the textbook's companion website to access observation forms for use when making field visits, especially those focused on technology use.

YOUR PORTFOLIO

To further demonstrate competency in ISTE NETS-T Standard 2b, add the following items to your portfolio:

1. Return to the lesson description that you developed in Chapters 3 and 4. Develop a plan to support students' self-directed learning within your lessons.
   a. Using the lesson plan template provided in this chapter or another lesson plan format of your choice, outline the activities that you and your students will engage in before, during, and after the lesson. If your lesson will span several days, you may want to use the unit plan template provided in Appendix A as well as the daily lesson plan template provided in this chapter. Consider the following:
   - How much time is required to complete the technology-based activity?
   - What prerequisite skills do your students need?
   - What should your students do *before* they engage in the technology-based activity?
   - How will students use the technology? How will you work with the students while they are engaged in technology-based activities? Will they have additional support available?
   - What should they do *after* they complete the technology-based activity?
   b. Develop student guidelines such as instruction sheets, technical instructions, resource guides, and rubrics.
   c. Create a checklist of things that you will do to prepare the computers and other technologies.

References

Bell, M. A. (2002). Why use an Interactive Whiteboard? A baker's dozen reasons! Teachers.net. Retrieved September 13, 2008, from http://teachers.net/gazette/JAN02/mabell.html

Ertmer, P. A. (2003). *VisionQuest: Envisioning and achieving integrated technology use*. Retrieved June 24, 2006, from http://www.edci.purdue.edu/vquest

Hall, A. (n.d.) Group participation rubric for WebQuest. Phoenix, AZ: Arizona State University at the West campus. Retrieved September 13, 2008, from http://coe.west.asu.edu/students/ahall/webquest/grouprubric.htm

Johnson, D. W., & Johnson, R. T. (1991). *Learning together and alone* (3rd ed.). Englewood Cliffs, NJ: Prentice Hall.

Morrison, G., & Lowther, D. (2002). *Integrating computer technology into the classroom* (2nd ed.). Upper Saddle River, NJ: Merrill/Prentice Hall.

Schön, D. (1983). *The reflective practitioner: How Professionals think in action*. London: Temple Smith.

Smith, H. J., Higgins, S., Wall, K., & Miller, J. (2005). Interactive whiteboards: Boon or bandwagon? A critical review of the literature. *Journal of Computer Assisted Learning*, 21(2), 91–101.

Wegerif, R. (2002). *Literature review in thinking skills, technology, and learning*. Future Lab Series, No. 2. Retrieved June 1, 2006, from http://www.futurelab.org.uk/research/reviews/ts01.htm

netbritish, 2008/Used under license from Shutterstock.com

Customizing Student Learning Activities

John Ross and Glenna Gustafson

Students will come to your classroom with different experiences, perhaps knowing different languages, having diverse cultural backgrounds, and having varied levels of access to modern technologies that can support their learning. Digital tools can help you "customize and personalize learning activities to address students' diverse learning styles, working strategies, and abilities using digital tools and resources." The ISTE standard for this chapter, more than any other, truly emphasizes the unique needs, abilities, and preferences of individual students and requires you to use strategies in your classroom that support all of your students and their uses of educational technology. While federal law guides some of these needs, others relate to respect for individuals and their backgrounds. Technology can be a tremendous asset that helps teachers support the diverse learning needs of children. Whether used to capture and report student data, make materials accessible

ISTE Standards addressed in this chapter

NETS-T 2. Design Digital-Age Learning Experiences and Assessments

Teachers design, develop, and evaluate authentic learning experiences and assessments incorporating contemporary tools and resources to maximize content learning in context and to develop the knowledge, skills, and attitudes identified in the NETS-S. Teachers:

c. customize and personalize learning activities to address students' diverse learning styles, working strategies, and abilities using digital tools and resources

Note: Standard 2.a is addressed in Chapter 4, 2.b in Chapter 5, and 2.d in Chapter 7.

Outcomes

In this chapter, you will

- Use data from multiple measures and resources to personalize student learning activities.
- Select and use a broad range of technology resources to adapt instruction to different learning needs and ability levels and to support second language learners.
- Select and use assistive technologies to enable all students, regardless of special needs, to participate in learning.

to students with special needs, or provide access to resources both at home and at school, some technologies do a great job of "leveling the playing field" for students with different abilities, needs, or preferences.

Addressing the learning needs of every student in a class of 20, 30, or more students might sound formidable, but most classes include students with various learning preferences and backgrounds. In addition, in any one classroom, there are students of various abilities, from those designated as gifted and talented to those with learning disabilities. Some classes may also contain students who require physical, mental, or emotional support in order to overcome constraints to learning. In other cases, the obstacles to learning are cultural or related to limited English proficiency, yet these students are often the same age, of comparable maturity, and with similar interests.

In any class you will be faced with developing lessons that address content standards and prepare your students for assessments that will determine how well each has mastered these standards. Yet, individualizing your instruction for diverse learners can be daunting. How can you address curricular needs with this varied pool of students? Technologies, especially networked digital technologies, offer promise for overcoming challenges to customizing instruction that may not have been possible previously.

STORIES FROM PRACTICE

Teaching Every Child Means Reaching Every Child

Fifth grade teacher Brigit Tartaruga is writing her lesson plans for the upcoming week to address science standards related to the rock cycle. Among her class of 27 students, she knows that three of them—Bill, Walter, and Naomi—are in the gifted-and-talented program and will need enrichment activities to stay engaged in the lessons. She also knows that Walter has a history of missing deadlines, not turning in assignments, and being unable to keep his desk or class notebook organized. In addition, she knows that Marina, as an emergent English speaker, will have difficulty

with some of the academic language since her family speaks no English at home. Marina and her family place a lot of emphasis on succeeding in school, however, and she often gets frustrated, sometimes to the point of tears, during long or challenging assignments. Three of Brigit's students, Wendy, Jeffrey, and Mason, have learning disabilities that must be taken into consideration. Wendy has a learning disability that makes it difficult for her to decode unfamiliar words, and Brigit knows that—particularly in science—Wendy can become discouraged with the language in the textbook.

Jeffrey has limited visual capacity and Mason uses a variety of assistive technologies. At this point in the year, Brigit is familiar with Mason's Individualized Educational Plan (IEP) and has worked with his occupational therapist to understand his abilities and how he can demonstrate them through the technologies he uses every day. Of course, scattered throughout the class are those who do or don't like collaborative work, do or don't enjoy using computers, do or don't have strong problem-solving skills, and so on. In other words, it's a pretty typical class.

Using Data to Inform Instruction

Educational practitioners have become highly focused on the use of data to make decisions about the effectiveness of resources, instructional methods, programs, and even schools and those who work in them. This increasing reliance on data for accountability blossomed through the standards movement at the end of the last century and took a giant leap forward with the passage of the *No Child Left Behind Act* (Pub. L. No. 107-110). This influential legislation initiated the development of high-stakes assessments in many grades and tied funding and accreditation to student performance on those assessments. The legal and financial implications of requiring continued improvement of *all* students highlighted the need for educators to better understand, and have access to, data to support instructional decisions.

A few years ago, data collection and analysis in the classroom were limited to tracking attendance and grading students' progress. Although teachers have always collected data through formal and informal assessments, you are entering the teaching profession when there is a greater call for more data collection and more sophisticated analyses of that data. One of the tremendous benefits that networked technologies have brought to the classroom teacher is having easy and immediate access to the many types of student data that once were found in paper-based records stored in disparate locations across the school and district. Greater access to a wide variety of student data provides more opportunities for you to make better-informed decisions about your instruction than was possible for generations of teachers before you. Teachers have always analyzed student performance data, but digital technologies provide easier access to a wider range of data, as well as powerful tools that simplify analyzing and reporting that data. Digital tools also allow you to make connections between state-mandated performance standards, lesson plans, and gradebooks.

State-mandated performance standards are usually assessed through externally developed large-scale assessments. State-administered end-of-course or graduation exams or well-known college entrance exams such as the ACT (from the American College Testing Program) or Scholastic Aptitude Test (SAT) are usually classified as **summative assessments**. Of course, summative assessments to evaluate learning can also be developed by teachers, such as unit tests or final exams. Summative assessments, whether you develop or administer them or not, are usually a final step in the presentation of a lesson, unit, or course rather than part of the instruction. Your students will be required to complete some summative assessments that you have developed as well as some developed by external agents, such as the state, college entrance boards, the military, and others. Grades or scores often associated with summative assessments can carry from low to very high stakes. (Of course, some students may feel *all* grades are high stakes!) Generally, the data from these tests are used to measure the performance of individual students, groups of students, instructional programs, and even the effectiveness of your own instruction. Summative assessments at the end of a unit, semester, course, or year are well established in the culture of schooling. We are sure that you've taken many of these yourself.

You can compare data from large-scale assessments to your own classroom-based assessments and determine how well your instruction prepared your students to perform on these examinations. However, external summative assessments may have little impact on restructuring the learning activities you provide for the students who actually took the assessments as you often don't get the results until those students have moved on to different classes. While their uses may be limited in terms of immediate impact on student learning, they still provide valuable information at many levels—from the individual student level to school and program levels—and should not be discounted. Summative assessments should be considered valuable for the data they provide.

Formative assessments are used during the learning process and provide feedback so you can take steps to adjust your instruction, if necessary, based on your students' needs. Formative assessments also provide feedback to your students—who can use the data to monitor their own learning progress and determine where they may need extra help or enrichment.

Formative assessments can include both formal and informal measures, sometimes using numeric scores, and at other times using percentages or even short narrative responses that provide information about your students. The collection and analysis of these different types of data do more than help you determine student needs. All of these pieces add up to give you an opportunity for determining the effectiveness of your own instructional methods and materials.

You can collect informal data from your students through short surveys, checklists, and other methods. Surveys can be used to collect information about how well students are mastering content as well as information related to their interests, motivation, and learning preferences. Exit polls or exit cards—using paper note cards—are a quick method teachers use to gather informal data from students. This technique is easily supported by a variety of technologies. On exit cards, students quickly note what they have learned during a class or any difficulties they still have. Simple polling software found in lab management software can serve this purpose and can be used both during and after instruction without interrupting it. Students can also respond to quick surveys with online polling software or by "beaming" responses using handheld devices or wireless responders—some of which allow for text entry. The anonymity many of these technologies provide may encourage some students to give you feedback who would otherwise be reluctant to voice their opinions in front of their peers.

Another simple survey-type activity that can be supported by a variety of common technologies is a KWHL Chart, described in Chapter 5. KWHL charts require students to note information they **K**now about a particular topic, information they **W**ant to learn about that topic, **H**ow they plan to learn the information, and then report what they **L**earned after their efforts are completed. Although a useful activity on its own, the KWHL chart can also be used to guide student reflections in a portfolio and provide evidence of student growth.

As a teacher, the data from all types of assessments can be very helpful as you plan, monitor, and evaluate your instruction. Student performance data influence the goals you set for your students and the activities you plan to meet those goals. Data from formal and informal assessments allow you to monitor student learning so that you can adjust students' learning activities, if necessary, based on individual student's needs. Formative assessments also provide feedback to your students who can use the data to monitor their own growth and determine where they may need extra help or enrichment.

You'll learn more about developing, scoring, and reporting classroom assessments in the next chapter. For now, let's consider the ways in which the data from assessments can be used to customize learning activities to meet the unique needs of each of your students.

Using Student Data to Set Goals

All teachers should familiarize themselves with the past performance data of their incoming students. Except for very young students, you will have access to student data from past performances from external assessments such as end-of-course exams, as well as classroom grades, attendance records, behavior and discipline reports, and a variety of diagnostic data for a range of skill and knowledge assessments that may be created by the school, district, or other entities.

Student performance data should influence the goals we set for students and the activities we plan to meet those goals. Although states adopt textbooks for use in most classes, a textbook does not go very far in differentiating activities to meet the diverse needs of your students. A curriculum, whether printed or digital, that gives greater detail is also insufficient for determining what activities and assessments you will use and the tools to support them. All of these tools are helpful, but their use should be guided by the needs of your students. One way to determine those needs is by monitoring and evaluating student data.

It is easiest to use classroom data if they are available electronically, as more and more student records are, but should be used even if available only on paper. Several districts and states are developing online access to student performance data from state-administered assessments. These websites often allow teachers access to all state-administered performance data that can be displayed for individuals or groups of students. Longitudinal reports can show student performance trends over time. Comparisons across content areas may identify weaknesses in one area that are impacting performances in another, such as when limited language proficiencies compound students' efforts to understand science or social studies texts that are above their reading levels. These same data, stripped of student identifiers, can also be reported to parents, community members, and policy makers at the local and national levels through the generation of school report cards (see Figure 6.1). If school or district digital records are not available, you can still create your own summary records to guide your planning using student portfolios or by making annotations in an electronic gradebook.

Monitoring Student Learning

Once students are in your class, you should continue to *monitor* their learning through performances on formal and informal assessments. While end-of-course assessments often come too late to impact learning activities for your current class, many districts and states offer benchmark assessments throughout the year that serve as an indication of potential student performances on the critical end-of-year assessments. These data are often available to you much sooner and some are available online in an effort to provide rapid turnaround in reporting. By reviewing data for individuals, groups, as well as entire classes, you can determine if your students are on track to meet their learning goals or whether some students need supplemental instruction and activities.

While students are in your class, you will probably have the opportunity to compare their performances on your own classroom assessments with results from external assessments. You should compare student performances on external assessments with the grades received in your class, as well as from previous courses, to determine if students are reaching their academic potential. Students with high scores on external assessments but habitually low classroom grades are at risk for continued poor performances in your class or even dropping out of school. These students may have unique learning preferences you are not addressing or may not feel challenged with past or current curricula. A majority of dropouts have reported that they left school not because they could not be successful, but because they did not feel challenged and often felt bored (Bridgeland, DiIulio, & Morison, 2006). In terms of your analysis, these two sources of data—classroom and external assessments—may not be available from the same source and may take some manipulation on your part using spreadsheets or other software.

You also have the opportunity to monitor the effectiveness of your instruction by observing your students during activities and assessments. Note where students are having difficulties, either with the content or with the materials and resources you have selected for the activities, by making annotations in your lesson plan or gradebook. If students have demonstrated mastery of prerequisite content skills through past performances, perhaps the activity is confusing or too difficult. When using technology, the technology itself may serve as a barrier to students who do not have the required skills. For example, students with inefficient Internet search strategies may be inadequately prepared to complete a web activity in which they have unlimited access to resources on the Internet. Instead, preselecting a few online resources or using an academic search engine may support these students and allow them to focus on the content rather than the underlying technology skills.

Evaluating Your Instruction

Reviewing individual student performance data obviously helps you to better identify needs for those individuals. Similarly, reviewing entire class performance is helpful for determining the effectiveness of your instruction. If the majority of a class performs poorly on the assessment of a standard, your instruction may need some revision. Did you adequately address the content standard?

Begin by reviewing your lesson plans. Some electronic lesson-planning software allows you to quickly organize your lesson and unit plans by standard. Did you include the standard in your instruction? Did you address it often enough? Compare

2006-07
NCLB
Report Card

MOUNTAIN STATE MIDDLE SCHOOL

The West Virginia Achieves Report Card is a legislatively mandated publication of a school's progress. The sections in this Report Card are School Accountability, Statewide Testing, Teacher Information (including quality), other school indicators and definitions. Under "Accountability" the checkmarks "√" represent a passing status regarding Adequate Yearly Progress (AYP). The "X" represents needs improvement for standards indicated. A blank space indicates the school is not required to meet AYP because the number of students reporting is less than 50. Elementary and Middle schools are required to use Attendance Rate (greater than 95 percent for AYP) and high schools are required to use Graduation Rate (greater than 80 Percent).

School Profile

School: MOUNTAIN STATE MIDDLE SCHOOL
District:
RESA:

Principal: J. DOE
100 Mountain State Road
Home Town, WV 25310
Phone #:
Fax #:

School Gradespan: 06-08
NCLB Classified: Middle School

Total Enrollment: 863
Percent Low Income: 44.26%
Percent White: 73.35%
Attendance Rate: 96.32%
Dropout Rate: 0.50%
Average Class Size: 25.2

WVEIS Number:

District Profile

District: SAMPLE
RESA:

Superintendent: M. Smith
100 Central Office Road
Home Town, WV 25310
Phone #:
Fax #:

School Gradespan: PK-12
NCLB Classified: District

Total Enrollment: 16,322
Percent Low Income: 38.79%
Percent White: 83.68%
Attendance Rate: 97.83%
Dropout Rate: 2.80%
Average Class Size: 21.4

State Profile

Name: West Virginia Department of Education

Superintendent: Dr. Steven L. Paine
1900 Kanawha Boulevard East
Charleston, WV 25305
Phone #: (304) 558-2699
Fax #: (304) 558-0882

School Gradespan: PK-12
NCLB Classified: State

Total Enrollment: 281,298
Percent Low Income: 49.53%
Percent White: 93.35%
Attendance Rate: 97.20%
Graduation Rate: 84.70%
Number of Graduates: 17,391
Dropout Rate: 2.70%
Average Class Size: 19.7

On The Web:
http://wvde.state.wv.us/

Accountability - Adequate Yearly Progress Status: *Below AYP Status
Needs Improvement in One Or More Accountability Cells

Subgroups	Mathematics		Reading		Graduation/ Attendance Rate
	Participation Rate	Statewide Testing Proficient	Participation Rate	Statewide Testing Proficient	
ALL STUDENTS	√	√	√	√	√
ETHNIC					
White	√	√	√	√	
Black	√	X	√	√	
Hispanic	√	√	√	√	
Asian					
Native American					
STUDENTS WITH DISABILITIES	√	X	√	X	
ECONOMICALLY DISADVANTAGED	√	X	√	X	
LEP					

Targets for State's Middle School Percent of students proficient (mastery level or above)	Reading/Language Arts	Mathematics
	79.2%	70.0%

Previous AYP Status

	2003-04	2004-05	2005-06	2006-07
AYP Status	X	X	X	X

Performance of Students in Each Grade Level (Percentage of Student's Scores At or Above Mastery Level)

	Grade 3		Grade 4		Grade 5		Grade 6		Grade 7		Grade 8		Grade 10		Over All	
	Reading	Math	Reading	Math	Reading	Math	Reading	Math	Reading	Math	Reading	Math	Reading	Math	Reading	Math
School	-	-	-	-	-	-	81.0	71.4	77.9	72.4	79.6	66.5	-	-	79.4	70.2
District	76.7	72.6	83.2	77.5	83.0	83.7	83.6	75.2	82.1	73.8	81.7	67.4	74.9	67.7	80.9	74.0
State	79.1	77.4	82.6	78.9	79.4	80.5	81.9	77.4	81.9	75.6	80.1	71.1	75.0	68.2	80.0	75.6

Performance of Students in Each Sub-Group (Percentage of Student's Scores At or Above Mastery Level) - Reading

	All	Male	Female	White	Black	Hispanic	Asian	Amer. Indian	Low SES	Non-Low SES	Sp. Ed.	Non-Sp. Ed.	L.E.P.	Migrant
School	79.4	74.9	84.4	81.1	72.9	77.8	N/A	N/A	69.7	86.9	37.0	88.3	61.5	N/A
District	80.9	76.3	85.6	81.9	75.7	75.6	81.5	72.2	73.1	86.3	43.0	88.2	49.7	50.0
State	80.0	74.9	85.4	80.4	72.3	75.9	89.6	72.4	72.7	87.9	41.3	87.3	67.3	66.7

Performance of Students in Each Sub-Group (Percentage of Student's Scores At or Above Mastery Level) - Math

	All	Male	Female	White	Black	Hispanic	Asian	Amer. Indian	Low SES	Non-Low SES	Sp. Ed.	Non-Sp. Ed.	L.E.P.	Migrant
School	70.2	71.8	68.5	73.9	56.7	66.7	N/A	N/A	59.8	78.2	30.1	78.5	7.7	N/A
District	74.0	74.2	73.9	75.7	63.6	67.8	82.7	68.4	65.2	80.2	41.4	80.4	49.7	64.3
State	75.6	75.1	76.1	76.2	63.9	70.2	92.4	74.1	67.7	84.1	42.1	81.9	69.2	70.0

Trend Data of Students Performance (Percentage of Student's Scores At or Above Mastery Level)

	Reading				Math			
	2004	2005	2006	2007	2004	2005	2006	2007
School	79.6%	81.4%	81.2%	79.4%	60.9%	72.3%	73.0%	70.2%
District	77.9%	80.4%	80.5%	80.9%	66.8%	73.9%	74.1%	74.0%
State	77.9%	80.4%	80.5%	80.9%	66.8%	73.9%	74.1%	74.0%

Figure 6.1

Online school report cards are a common method for communicating school data to educators, parents, and the general community.
Source: West Virginia Department of Education

your lesson plans with your actual practice. Did you carry out the lesson plan as you intended? Did external events, such as field trips, early release due to inclement weather, or other events prevent students from completing all of the learning activities? Reviewing your instruction in this way may uncover discrepancies between what is commonly referred to as the "written" curriculum—what you intended to teach—and the "enacted" curriculum—what you actually taught.

Next, review your lesson activities and assessments. Did you provide activities and assessments that allowed your students to practice and master the standard? Were they at the required cognitive level? Sometimes, teachers may include the terminology or procedures related to a specific content standard but never get to the actual performance level required. For example, a standard that requires analysis is not adequately taught through activities and assessments that simply require students to recall or remember information.

Also examine the technologies you used to support your instruction and assessment. Were the technologies appropriate for the content? Did the technologies support the skill or knowledge level required by the standard and subsequent assessment? If you use a language arts portfolio and students are required to demonstrate critical thinking, the portfolio artifacts should include items that require the practice and demonstration of critical thinking as indicated by the content standard, perhaps through self-reflection or analysis of exemplars. If a math assessment requires students to calculate the area of an irregularly sided object, then be sure to incorporate technologies that allow students to practice and demonstrate the skills required to understand how to perform the calculations rather than those that perform those calculations for the students.

You should also compare student performances on external assessments with your own grades. Do your grades adequately reflect student performance on external assessments? What trends in your classroom grades indicate a need for adjusting your instruction prior to high-stakes assessments? Determine whether you have established fair and equitable grading practices that truly measure student performances and provide reliable feedback to you, your students, and their parents as to how well they have mastered required standards.

Sharing what you have discovered with your colleagues is a critical step in improving your instructional effectiveness (see Figure 6.2). By posting and sharing lesson plans on a secure server, and comparing them to data from student performances, over time you and the other teachers in your content area and at your grade level can develop "best practice" lessons that have been shown to have the greatest impact. Technology can help conduct analyses and generate reports as well as provide a means to continue a dialog outside of common planning times and staff meetings. Other content experts in your school who are given access to these lesson plans and reports, such as special education teachers, can help to improve these lessons by indicating common accommodations or pedagogies effective with students with different learning needs and preferences. Technology specialists and resource teachers may provide options for different technologies that can support the lessons that teachers at various levels of technology proficiency may choose to incorporate. These same lessons and reports can be helpful for self-study or peer-review, as well as for use in full staff meetings where lesson exemplars are presented, either through live demonstrations or from videotapes, and then discussed.

Summary of Using Data to Inform Instruction

As you have learned in this section, systematic reflection on student data can help you set and revise goals for student learning, monitor the effectiveness of learning activities, and then select and revise instructional strategies. If a student performed poorly on an assessment, is it because that student did not understand the concept? How did the learning activities you selected impact the performance of your students on your assessments? Did you use teaching strategies that motivated and supported

Wadsworth/Cengage Learning

Figure 6.2
Collaborating with colleagues is an effective method for reviewing the effectiveness of your instruction.

the needs of *all* of your students? Or did you misjudge the prior knowledge of your students, their foundational skills, the support they needed during instruction, or the type of feedback required to help them reach mastery? The needs of the students in your classroom will change continually throughout the school year and from year to year. Just because you have worked hard on a lesson, or used a lesson successfully in the past, it does not mean that it will work every year. Over time, the data you collect from a variety of assessments can help you monitor the effectiveness of a lesson and help you both hone your teaching skills and improve the activities you use in your classroom. Digital technologies have become invaluable for collecting, analyzing, and reporting that data and for helping teachers to better evaluate the effectiveness of their lessons and determine areas of strength and need.

This section on using data to inform instruction has covered a number of ways you can find, generate, and review data in order to better meet the learning goals of your students. There should be a clear link between your students' learning goals, the instructional activities you select, the resources you include, the assessments you administer, and the tools that support them. It's not a direct linear relationship. Instruction is a cyclical process that can be modified along the way by backtracking or moving ahead based on what you know from analyzing multiple sources of data related to your teaching and your students' learning outcomes.

Table 6.1 uses the GAME plan to summarize some of the questions you should consider at each step in your lesson planning and delivery. As you reflect on the questions in Table 6.1, the answer to these questions will always include "it depends on what my students need." So, before you can answer these questions, you will need to collect, analyze, and reflect on the appropriate data. (You'll learn more about how to develop, score, and report assessment data in the next chapter.)

Universal Design for Learning

One way that you can customize and personalize learning activities to address students' diverse learning styles, working strategies, and abilities is through adhering to the tenets of universal design. **Universal design for learning** (UDL) suggests that

Table 6.1	Data-Based Decision-Making GAME Plan

Set Learning Goals

- What content standards must I cover?
- What prerequisite skills and knowledge do my students possess?
- What skills and knowledge do they need to gain?
- How will my students demonstrate new skills and knowledge?
- Do my students have the required technology skills to use the tools and resources I've selected?

Take Action

- What activities best support the cognitive level of my students?
- What learning preferences do my students have?
- What tools and resources should I use to engage my students in learning the content standards?
- How can I ensure optimal motivation for learning?

Monitoring

- Are my students making adequate progress?
- What misunderstandings do they have?
- Are the activities well suited to helping students master their learning goals?
- Are the tools and resources promoting student learning?
- What changes to the learning activities should I make?
- Which students need enrichment materials or activities?
- Which students require supplemental materials or activities?

Evaluating and Extending

- Did my students reach their learning goals?
- Did my students reach their academic potential?
- Were there any unexpected levels of student performance?
- Did the activities support or interfere with student learning?
- Did the tools and resources support or interfere with student learning?
- What changes should I make to my approach for my next lesson?
- What changes should I make to my approach before I use these activities and tools again?

teachers can remove barriers to learning by providing flexibility in terms of options for materials, methods, and assessments (Rose & Meyer, 2002). As seen in Hillary's story on page 142, when given alternatives for obtaining and demonstrating knowledge and skills, many students who were once labeled "disabled" can indeed be successful. Although originally developed for students with special needs, the more flexible the teaching strategies, materials, and assessments you use in your classroom, the more accessible they will be to the diverse needs and preferences of *all* the students with whom you work.

But how is technology critical to universal design for learning? While universal design may incorporate some methods and materials that may be fairly low-tech, digital media promises to provide the greatest flexibility in terms of planning, implementing, and assessing learning activities. Unlike the preponderance of print-based and analog audio and video materials that are commonplace in many of today's classrooms, digital media can be created, stored, cataloged, searched, adapted, and even linked together much more easily. Using common software and hardware, teachers as well as students can find information in a variety of formats, transform it so it is easy to see or hear or understand, repurpose or modify it, or generate new information and media that can be used to demonstrate new understandings or skills. By adhering to the tenets of universal design, you can develop instruction and assessments that effectively meet the diverse needs of students.

Neural Networks That Influence Learning

The UDL framework is based on the multifaceted nature of the brain, specifically the recognition, strategic, and affective networks. While research identifies these three

STORIES FROM PRACTICE

Just Your Average Kid

Hillary is just your average teenager. She's a junior in high school and is concerned about taking exams and going to college, well, at least to some degree. At any one time, you may find her talking on her cell phone, working on her laptop, or posting on her blog. There are, of course, the other times when she's helping her teachers and other students better understand how to use technology to support teaching and learning. Hillary and technology are inseparable, but that was not always the case. At an early age, Hillary was diagnosed with multiple learning disabilities. At the age of five, educators at her elementary school suggested to her parents that she be taken out of school. The educators contended that she would never be able to read or write or function in a school setting and that she could never expect to go to college. Among other learning disabilities, Hillary was diagnosed with Developmental Coordination Disorder, severe ADD (attentive deficit disorder), sensory defensiveness, and sensory integration issues. The everyday school activities of reading and writing led to more than frustration—often leading to tears and exasperation.

Measured on tests of intelligence, Hillary scored in the gifted range. Despite the capacity and desire to learn, some of Hillary's inherent disabilities countered attempts by teachers and therapists to fit her into a "traditional" classroom. After many struggles, Hillary's parents found OCR (optical character recognition) software that allowed her to "read" common items such as textbooks and directions for games she wanted to play. The simple task of being able to access print—in what might be considered a nontraditional way—opened up the world to Hillary. Her laptop is now ever present. She'll admit that she might misplace a pencil or a homework assignment, but she *never* misplaces her laptop. She uses it to schedule events and remind herself of appointments or assignments that are due. She uses it for all of her schoolwork. It catalogs her life, not just her schoolwork, and it is the interface through which she interacts with her friends and the rest of the world—sending e-mail, chatting online, updating her blog—just like your average teenager.

primary networks that influence learning, the way that each network reacts to stimuli, prompts responses, and promotes engagement, and the degree of influence each has over the other, can be as unique across individuals as fingerprints and personalities. Still, the growing body of knowledge about these three networks is important for understanding how you can incorporate aspects of the UDL framework into your instruction in order to provide your students with greater access to learning. The following sections explore each network.

Recognition Networks

In order to recognize something, such as a letter, word, picture, person, sound, smell, or other sensory input, you rely on the **recognition networks** of your brain. The recognition networks help you to identify patterns, such as the use of symbols for language or music, the organization of features to tell the difference between people's faces, as well as more subtle patterns such as the use of irony or comedy in a poem. In terms of learning, the recognition networks process "the what" that should be learned.

Similar to the other two networks, recognition networks reside in a general area of the brain, but even the simple task of identifying a word on a page involves a number of different systems and subsystems within this area—in this case, recognition systems that process information related to vision that help you recognize color, shape, orientation, context, and other attributes. Hearing the word at the same time calls into play additional systems related to sound—all of which operate in parallel.

Not everyone has the same capacity for recognizing sensory data. With the many systems and subsystems that operate simultaneously within these networks and the varying capacities that individuals have for recognizing sensory data, it is easy to understand that the dominance of, or damage to, one of these systems can result in a learning preference or even a disability for a particular type of activity or medium. For this reason, supporters of UDL suggest that digital media provide the flexibility needed to reach the widest number of students, students who rely on different strengths and preferences due to the working of their recognition networks.

You can implement teaching strategies that support recognition networks. Examples of these strategies include providing multiple examples that tap into different

Figure 6.3
You can support recognition networks by allowing students to use multiple media and formats.

senses and highlighting critical features whether through the use of labels and arrows on charts and diagrams, physically highlighting passages, or using different font colors, sizes, and treatments within text. You can support recognition networks further by allowing students to use multiple media and formats to access information, practice skills, and demonstrate mastery (see Figure 6.3), as well as providing background context for new information or skills (Rose & Meyer, 2002).

Consider the challenge faced by Brigit, the teacher in the Stories from Practice that began this chapter. As you recall, she was preparing lesson plans to address science standards related to the rock cycle. Based on what Brigit knows about the students in her class, some of them have strengths in auditory processing, others learn best through visuals, while others need to manipulate concrete objects to make sense of the information. In order to support the variety of recognition network strengths present in her class, Brigit could provide her students with several examples of the rock cycle using a variety of media. That is, some students could read a text, others could view an animated movie, while still others may talk through the steps in the process. Students who are overwhelmed by the technical terms may benefit from a website with hyperlinks that allows them to click on each rock type to learn more.

Strategic Networks

The processes you follow to plan, execute, and monitor your actions are related to the **strategic networks**. The actions you take are highly dependent on the outcomes you expect to achieve. For example, if your students are expected to learn the scientific names for the three types of rocks in the rock cycle for a test on Friday they would most likely take different actions than if they were preparing for the state science fair. The resulting actions can either be mental or physical. In terms of learning, strategic networks operate on "how" things can be learned.

Like the recognition networks, strategic networks rely on numerous systems and subsystems, all of which operate in parallel. As you become more familiar with a process, your routines become more automatic until you might be considered an expert.

Experts perform differently than novices in many of the processes related to learning, such as identifying problems; proposing hypotheses; planning, organizing, and selecting strategies; monitoring their own performances; and seeking assistance (Bransford, Brown, & Cocking, 1999).

Think of an activity for which you consider yourself to be fluent, such as riding a bicycle, playing a musical instrument, or even walking and talking. You looked and behaved much differently when you first started any of these activities. Now consider the many types of processes your students may employ to accomplish a single learning goal. A lesson that results in a product such as a paper, web page, or presentation can require both fine and gross motor skills (such as moving about the room, operating a keyboard or mouse, or retrieving and opening a book), speech (such as communicating with lab partners or asking a question), general learning strategies (such as creating a task schedule, monitoring how well you are meeting objectives, or choosing a different strategy if the first one did not work well), and expression (creatively responding to the lesson requirements or incorporating personally relevant information). All of these processes are carried out in the brain by the strategic networks.

You can support the brain's strategic networks by providing opportunities to practice skills with various levels of support and providing ongoing, relevant feedback. Demonstrating concepts and skills through the use of varied models of expert performance can allow students of different abilities to identify with a preferred mode and degree of performance for mastery. Flexibility is the key, and strategic networks, like recognition networks, can be supported by incorporating multiple media and formats to demonstrate mastery (Rose & Meyer, 2002).

Affective Networks

Affective networks relate to feelings and emotions and can influence one's motivation for and engagement with a particular goal, method, medium, or assessment. The affective networks process "the why" of learning. Affective networks are influenced by prior knowledge and past experience so each student has the potential to react differently to any one instructional event. For example, during the rock cycle lesson, students who have lived in or are from Hawai'i might bring in pictures or samples of volcanic rock and tell stories about Pele, the goddess of fire and volcanoes, and how local legends influence the culture of people from these islands. Students from other areas could tell stories from their families that illustrate the influence of geology on human existence, such as living in a coal mining community, visiting Native American tribes in the deserts of the Southwest, or topographical changes on the Mid-Atlantic coastline. In addition, feelings and emotions can be influenced from one day to the next and you or your students may be highly engaged in an activity one day but may be less so the next such as when you are feeling ill, tired, or upset over an argument with a relative or friend.

By offering choices of media and tools within the scope of your required content, you are supporting students' affective networks (see Figure 6.4). Choice can also be offered in terms of student rewards as well as the context in which the learning will take place. You may provide activities at varied levels of difficulty or challenge students at all levels of ability with a variety of engaging materials (Rose & Meyer, 2002).

Universal Design in the Classroom

All three of these networks can influence your performance—and that of your students—in an infinite number of ways. Some of your students' strengths and learning preferences will be obvious and may already be carefully documented so you can design learning activities that meet their greatest needs. Others you will have to discover and monitor as your students mature, build new skills and knowledge, and become experts in both simple and complex skills. Finally, some students may require

Wadsworth/Cengage Learning

Figure 6.4
By offering choices of media and tools, you can support students' affective needs.

daily monitoring, such as when a student's affective response changes due to an emotional event such as receiving a poor grade in another class or having experienced an upsetting event outside of class.

How can you use your knowledge about these three networks in your classroom? Perhaps of greater concern is the question, "How does technology play a role in all of this?" As you may recall, digital media provide greater flexibility than static linear media, such as print-based materials and analog audio and video, for adapting materials to students' needs. In the UDL framework, digital media are key elements for providing flexibility in the development and implementation of three fundamental aspects of the teaching/learning cycle: 1) setting learning goals, 2) providing learning activities, and 3) assessing student progress.

Setting Goals

As a teacher, you develop learning goals for your students that allow them to obtain the skills and knowledge required by curricula and standards. When incorporating universal design for learning based on the operations and limitations of the recognition, strategic, and affective networks, learning goals should:

- allow students to clearly understand the outcomes (recognize "what" should be learned)
- be achievable through a variety of media (provide multiple opportunities for "how" it can be learned) and
- communicate the importance of the goal to students (emphasize "why" the learning is important).

Rather than "dumbing down" the curriculum or providing only a portion of the curriculum to some students, an approach based on UDL should allow all students to meet learning goals through flexible means.

In order to create learning goals that meet these criteria, you should focus on the outcomes—what is it you really want your students to know and be able to do? Once decided, UDL emphasizes that achieving outcomes should not be contingent upon the media used to achieve them. Relying simply on any one medium, such as a printed textbook, immediately imposes barriers on some students. Of course, if students are required to learn a specific skill that is directly tied to a specific medium, such as operating a table saw, dribbling a basketball, or playing the C-minor scale on the clarinet, the medium of instruction becomes less flexible. But for many academic goals, especially those in core curricular areas, there may be a great deal of flexibility to choose which media are used to help students build the knowledge and skills needed to achieve content standards.

In the case of the fifth grade class studying the rock cycle, if the outcome is for students to be able to describe components of the rock cycle, students can achieve this goal through instructional activities that incorporate a variety of media. For example, an instructional goal that required students to describe the rock cycle by reading a chapter in a textbook and answering questions in short answer form, using paper and pencil, imposes learning barriers for numerous students. Students with limited English proficiency could find the academic language used in the static textbook with words such as *sedimentary, igneous,* and *metamorphic* an insurmountable barrier. Students with limited visual capacity or learning disabilities that make it difficult to focus on important details could also find the print-based medium a barrier if they did not have access to alternate versions of the book, such as a CD-ROM or web-based version. Students who might enjoy the tactile experience of handling and manipulating rock samples or those who require greater academic challenges, may find the lesson uninteresting.

Consider the outcomes that could be achieved instead if the student with limited English proficiency used a digital textbook or web page with text at various reading levels, hyperlinks to definitions, graphics, or even audio files of correct pronunciation for difficult new vocabulary. Students with limited visual capacity could use OCR software or documents in the common portable document format (PDF) that allowed them to vary the size of the text or they could have the text read to them using text-to-speech software. Students with attention problems could use a digital version of the textbook in combination with supplemental software that allowed them to highlight key terms and phrases and to automatically generate an outline of the material they selected as important, helping them to focus and organize their learning. Students who prefer manipulating artifacts may take digital pictures of rock samples from a science lab and include them in a presentation. Students who require enrichment activities could draw on several web resources, such as materials from the geology department of a local university that related the rocks found in their area to the cycle described in a primary source. These are but a few examples that demonstrate how an instructional goal focused on outcomes, rather than specific delivery tools, could allow students to use a variety of media and methods to master the same content standards.

In order to engage the affective networks of students, the UDL framework emphasizes setting goals that communicate the importance of the outcome to the students so they understand not only what to do and how they might do it, but also why it is important. According to Rose and Meyer (2002), "students who understand the goals of their schoolwork are more likely to stay focused, monitor themselves successfully, and derive satisfaction from their practice" (p. 88). In order to emphasize the importance of a goal to your students, the goal could be related to prior knowledge, such as information from previous lessons or courses, or past experiences, such as a live or virtual field trip. Highly relevant goals (such as outcomes that are related to or directly affect students, their friends, and family members; the locality; or are drawn from current events) can also engage students' affective networks by increasing motivation. In the lesson on the rock cycle, you might ask students to recall their field trip to the beach in discussing where sand comes from. You can require students to examine the relationship between the beach sand and the sandstone used to build the school. Perhaps you would show a video of how artists in some cultures, such as Navajo, use sands of different colors to create paintings for religious ceremonies.

Individualizing Learning

Once clear learning goals have been set, the UDL framework suggests that teachers utilize instructional strategies that allow individual students greatest access to *active learning*—not just passive information. Teaching methods supported by universal design for learning include:

- Using multiple media and formats to access information, practice skills, and demonstrate mastery.
- Providing students with choices in the media, tools, and context in which the learning will take place.
- Demonstrating concepts and skills through the use of varied models of expert performance to allow students of different abilities to identify with a preferred mode and degree of performance for mastery.
- Providing multiple examples that tap into different senses.
- Providing opportunities to practice skills with various levels of support and provide ongoing, relevant feedback.
- Including activities with varied levels of difficulty to challenge students at all levels of ability with a variety of engaging materials.

Central to these strategies is the use of digital media to provide students with flexibility as they meet the demands of learning goals. These ideas are also consistent with Howard Gardner's idea of multiple intelligences, featured in Figure 6.5.

There are several types of software applications, including and related to word processing, that can support students with a variety of learning styles and abilities (Brodwin, Cardoso, & Star, 2004; Hasselbring, 2000; Quenneville, 2001). **Word-processing** applications are almost universal on personal computers found in schools and offices, and provide a variety of supports to help both your general education students and those with learning disabilities. The ability to quickly create, edit, and revise manuscripts that look professional can benefit everyone. Features built into many word-processing and specialized composition programs can also support a wide range of student learning activities such as highlighting errors in spelling and grammar, creating keyboard shortcuts for common tasks, as well as creating toggle keys paired with sounds for aural identification of keys and shortcuts. **Word-prediction software** can be used to help students identify words quickly based on common usage patterns, arrangement of letters, or suggestions based on grammar (see Figure 6.6). This software supports communication tasks and helps students to overcome limited language skills. Other writing aids and comprehension software, such as concept-mapping software, can support brainstorming, concept organization, outlining, and generating schematics important to clearly formulating and communicating ideas.

Networked **communication tools** offer great flexibility in the methods and settings in which students can communicate with one another as well as with teachers and outside experts. Collaboration and communication are important skills for all students to develop, but these skills are especially important for students with disabilities and those with limited language skills (Hasselbring, 2000). Tools that allow students to communicate asynchronously provide them with the opportunity to develop and communicate their ideas at their own pace, as opposed to class discussions that may discourage participation for those students who need extra time to formulate, refine, and express ideas. These tools also develop social skills that are essential in the classroom and beyond.

Students who need additional information such as definitions, examples, pictures, and other explanations of words and concepts, can benefit from the flexibility of **multimedia tools** with embedded hyperlinks. The linked material may incorporate text, audio, or visual information that helps students with diverse learning preferences find support in a mode that they prefer. Some caution should be used in hyperlinked environments, however, as students can quickly become overwhelmed or highly engaged in material that is unrelated to the instructional goals. Strategies

Gardner's Multiple Intelligences

In his 1983 book, *Frames of Mind*, Howard Gardner proposed the theory that individuals possess multiple intelligences. The seven original intelligences and a recently added eighth intelligence suggest that people learn and express themselves in different ways. According to Gardner (1993), each of us has varying degrees of the culturally and biologically influenced intelligences.

 Bodily-Kinesthetic Intelligence is manifested through physical actions with the body, manipulating objects, touching and feeling objects to better connect and internalize feedback from the environment.

 Interpersonal Intelligence refers to the capacity to be highly empathetic and to connect to with others and to understand their desires, motivations, and needs.

 Intrapersonal Intelligence enables one to be introspective and to have a deep understanding of one's abilities, fears, and motivations.

 Linguistic Intelligence is a capacity to understand and/or communicate effectively through written and spoken languages.

 Logical-Mathematical Intelligence refers to the ability to use strategies for analysis that include detecting patterns, carrying out mathematical processes such as calculations, and testing hypotheses through reason.

 Musical Intelligence includes a preference for processing and expressing one's self in all things musical, such as a strong affinity for pitch, rhythm, and timbre.

 Naturalist Intelligence, the most recently added intelligence, suggests a capacity to relate well to natural environments, and to understand natural laws and processes as well as evolving cultural patterns.

 Spatial Intelligence includes the ability to mentally and physically divide and order space, to use imagery to understand a space and imagine how it might be transformed.

Gardner does not suggest that the theory is prescriptive and will result in a single instructional approach. In fact, he admits that his theory has often been misinterpreted and that inappropriate applications have resulted in a negative perception of the theory by some educators (Gardner, 1995). He does, however, suggest that schools cover too much content in too little depth. Instead, he recommends that teachers take the time to cover material in greater detail through a variety of methods and materials. Gardner says that schools that have most effectively applied multiple intelligences take human differences seriously. Any uniform approach to education—including a uniform approach to assessment—is bound to appeal to a minority and alienate or frustrate the rest.

Figure 6.5
Gardner's Multiple Intelligences.

for combating these problems include creating a list of approved websites that are either bookmarked on student computers or linked from a general class launch page, as well as previewing multimedia materials and providing job-aids to clearly structure student participation. Some software applications may allow you to turn off certain features in order to allow students to focus on academic goals.

A common science objective for a fifth grade class related to the rock cycle is to be able to describe and explain how different topographical formations, such as canyons, valleys, meanders, and tributaries are formed and worn away by the movement of rocks and soil. On one end of the spectrum is to require that all students do library

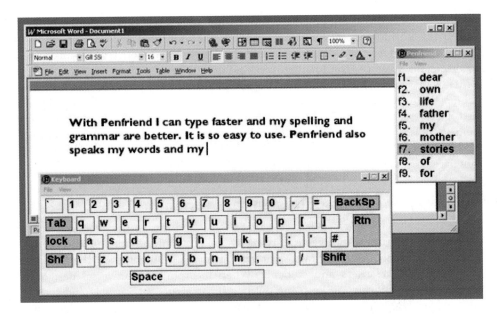

Figure 6.6
Word-prediction software is especially helpful for students with dyslexia.
Source: © Penfriend Ltd 1999–2002

research and write a short paper about the topic. Although some students may do well with this task, others may do better with some other options. For example, students who are struggling readers or English language learners will benefit from the use of visuals and may better understand the natural process by viewing videos or online animations that they can manipulate and review more than once. Notes they take can be organized using concept-mapping software that can generate an outline from which they work on a larger report. Some students may use online communication tools to collaborate, such as creating a wiki with their classmates that identifies important topographical landmarks in the region or state and each contributing to finding information about how they were formed. The wiki can support images, text, and hyperlinks to relevant resources and can track which students have created and edited the content.

Monitoring and Evaluating Student Learning

Knowing that universal design discourages the use of a single medium for setting goals and providing learning activities, you will probably not be surprised to know the same is true for assessing student progress. Student assessments that are limited to a single medium, such as taking a quiz or test with pen and paper, immediately impose barriers that prevent some students from accurately demonstrating their skills and knowledge. Any medium used for assessment will have inherent properties that either support or conflict with students' abilities, preferences, and interests. The challenge is to match assessments with instructional goals and activities in a way that allows students to truly demonstrate their knowledge and skills. As you will learn in Chapter 7, the method and media used for assessment should also be matched to those used for instruction.

Although as a teacher, you will have little control over the format by which standardized "high-stakes" tests are administered, you will have control over the types of assessments that you offer in your classroom. Universal design for learning suggests following similar practices for assessment of student progress as for setting goals and providing learning activities: that is, by incorporating a variety of media that allows students some flexibility in demonstrating mastery of the instructional goals. Unlike high-stakes summative tests, universal design encourages the use of assessments that are closely related to the instruction, both in time and in format.

Digital tools offer several opportunities for embedding assessment strategies within the learning process. Students with access to online curriculum tools may have their progress checked and reported automatically; for others, you may need to take some steps to monitor their progress and understanding. For example, students working on the rock cycle wiki described earlier can be provided a schedule for the posting of information. Edits to the wiki are time stamped and the user identified. Other students who are using digital content may be allowed (or not) to use built-in tools, such as dictionaries and spell-checking tools, to complete their projects. If the objective focuses on describing and explaining, checking and correcting their language may actually be a beneficial pedagogical activity.

Summary of Universal Design for Learning

Universal design for learning suggests that instruction can be designed and implemented for students with diverse learning styles, preferences, abilities, and motivation. Digital media are a key factor for implementing UDL based on the flexibility they offer both teachers and students. When incorporating universal design for learning, it is important to keep the options for students manageable and focused on the learning outcomes, rather than the materials they use. Some students may be required to use technologies to assist them with a significant portion of their learning activities—and you may be required to understand how to incorporate these technologies in order to help these students achieve their learning goals. Some students require the use of assistive technologies, which are the focus of the next section.

APPLY TO PRACTICE

Meeting the Needs of Diverse Learners

1. Select a lesson plan that you have developed or one that is available from a print or online resource. Describe alternative activities and assessments in the lesson plan that would allow you to meet the needs of students with differing abilities. Consider students with the following needs:
   - high-poverty students who do not have the same background experiences
   - students who prefer to learn by doing or through experiential learning
   - students who have difficulties focusing on and deriving meaning from print
   - students with high ability and interest in the subject who require enrichment
2. What type of additional information do you need to meet the needs of these students? What experiences can you draw upon to identify with these students? What resources are available to help you meet these challenges?

Assistive Technologies

Many of you may be asking, "Why do I need to know about assistive technologies? I'm not going to be teaching special education." While that may be true, consider the fact that over 75 percent of students with disabilities spend the majority of their school day in general education classrooms (Boyer & Mainzer, 2003). In the past, these students would have been assigned to classrooms separate from their age-peers who do not have special needs. Recent legislation, such as the No Child Left Behind Act, has mandated that students with disabilities be assessed alongside their peers without disabilities. For many students with disabilities, access to the curriculum will require the use of technology, specifically assistive technologies. The effective use of these technologies can make the difference between successful and unsuccessful educational and social experiences for students with disabilities.

Legal Precedents for Assistive Technology

Assistive technology, or AT, was first defined in the *Technology-Related Assistance of Individuals with Disabilities Act of 1988* (Pub. L. No. 100-407), sometimes referred to as the "Tech Act." This definition has been used in several laws since then, such as the *Americans with Disabilities Act of 1990* (Pub. L. No. 101-336), *Individuals with Disabilities Education Act (IDEA) of 1990* (Pub. L. No. 101-476), and subsequent reauthorizations in 2004 (Pub. L. No. 108-446). Specifically, assistive technology refers to "any item, piece of equipment, or product system, whether acquired commercially or off the shelf, modified, or customized, that is used to increase, maintain, or improve functional capabilities of individuals with disabilities" (Pub. L. No. 108-446). It's important to understand that it is not the device itself that makes it assistive technology, but how it is used to support individuals. Some technologies may be considered assistive technology for some students, but not for others.

The law and its reauthorizations, commonly referred to as IDEA, require that states "ensure that all children with disabilities have available to them a free appropriate public education that emphasizes special education and related services designed to meet their unique needs and prepare them for employment and independent living." In order to qualify for special education and related services, it is not sufficient for a student to demonstrate or be diagnosed with a definable sensory, physical, mental, or cognitive impairment, but that the special education or related services support that student in participating in educational activities (Mendelsohn & Fox, 2002). According to the U.S. Office of Special Education and Rehabilitative Services (2005), more than 6 million students with disabilities between the ages of 5 and 17 were served under IDEA in 2003.

IDEA requires the development of a written **Individual Educational Plan (IEP)** for all students who qualify for special education. The IEP is developed through significant parental involvement, in cooperation with classroom teachers and other school officials, such as guidance counselors, special education teachers, school psychologists, or occupational therapists. Once written, and as the child's teacher, you are required to follow procedures described in the IEP, which may include the use of assistive technology. If assistive technology is prescribed in a student's IEP, find out how you and your colleagues will be trained in order to appropriately incorporate the assistive technology in your teaching.

Some students with disabilities may not qualify for special education but are still covered by Section 504 of the *Rehabilitation Act of 1973* (Pub. L. No. 93-112). Section 504 states that "no otherwise qualified individual with a disability shall, solely by reason of his or her disability, be excluded from the participation in, be denied the

 STORIES FROM PRACTICE

Andrew's Story

Several years ago, I had the opportunity to work with five-year-old Andrew. At age 3, Andrew was involved in a car accident that left him a quadriplegic with limited neck movement. When I met Andrew, he was an inventive five-year old and determined to do everything that other five-year olds could do.

Andrew used a mouth stick to access his toy cars, move game pieces, torment his older sister, and access a traditional keyboard. The mouth sticks were simply lightweight dowel rods with a plastic mouthpiece on one end and a pencil eraser on the other.

Using the mouth stick Andrew was able to turn the computer on and type with surprising quickness. But there was one thing that Andrew wanted to do that all five-year-olds enjoy doing—Andrew wanted to draw a picture. Attempts to adapt the mouse for Andrew's use had not been very successful.

Since Andrew was able to access a traditional keyboard, I decided to try the Mouse-Key features found in the Windows Accessibility Panel. MouseKeys allows the numeric keypad to act as a mouse. I placed colored

stickers over the number keys to indicate the direction the mouse would move and the function of the key—click, double click, lock and drag.

Within ten minutes of showing Andrew how the keys worked we were printing his picture. Today, Andrew is a happy third grader who is in a fully inclusive classroom. He's still using a mouth stick to access the keyboard and annoy his sister.

Source: Glenna Gustafson

benefits of, or be subjected to discrimination under any program or activity receiving Federal financial assistance." Most schools receive federal financial assistance and therefore are required to adhere to the tenets of the Rehabilitation Act.

Section 508 of the Act also requires that electronic and information technology resources be accessible by individuals with disabilities. This is a major concern for publishers and developers of digital resources for schools as the amount of digital media and online services that are used by schools continues to increase—with some states allowing for the adoption of digital materials in addition to or in lieu of textbooks. You and your fellow teachers should be cognizant of how digital media, including software and online resources—even school-generated web pages—are compliant with Section 508. The importance of assistive technology as a valuable resource for helping people with disabilities was reaffirmed with the passage of the *Assistive Technology Act of 1998* (Pub. L. No. 105-394), sometimes referred to as the "AT Act." The AT Act builds upon its predecessor, the Tech Act, by extending funding for assistive technology to states and six U.S. territories. The AT Act supports capacity-building efforts at the state level in order to establish assistive technology services and resources, as well as services that inform the public about and advocate for assistive technology.

Many individuals may find it difficult to distinguish assistive technology from other forms of technology such as instructional or educational technology. Upon examination, all technologies are just tools that make some part of our lives simpler by capitalizing on our strengths and removing barriers. Think about the tools that you have used today, whether they are word processors, Internet browsers, or other tools. Maybe you enlarge fonts for easier legibility or organize tasks in an electronic calendar so you can meet deadlines. What other types of barriers have these tools helped you overcome? Where have you used these tools—in your home, at work, in school? How would your life be different if you did not have access to these tools? As you review the definition for AT, have you been using assistive technologies without realizing it?

By definition, an AT device can include a wide range of tools—an item, a piece of equipment, or a product system. For example, one solution for a student having difficulty holding a pencil might be a simple plastic pencil grip (item). For another student who is unable to use a pencil, a portable word processor (piece of equipment) might be the tool used to assist with the task. And for yet another student, a computer with voice-recognition software (product system) might be chosen to assist with writing.

There are numerous classifications of AT devices based on their function (Bryant & Bryant, 2003; Cook & Hussey, 2002). Table 6.2 provides examples of the types of AT devices commonly found in schools. Keep in mind that individuals may use one or more devices for a variety of functions.

Assistive Technology Continuum

Assistive technology tools can be classified along a continuum that moves from devices that are considered to be "low tech," to tools and devices that are more complex or "high tech." Generally "low-tech" devices are found at the lower end of the

WEB LINK

An extensive list of web resources related to the categories of assistive technology can be found on the textbook's companion website.

WEB LINK

Visit the textbook's companion website for information on some of the disabilities or special needs your students may exhibit as well as examples of assistive technologies available to support them.

APPLY TO PRACTICE

Defining Assistive Technology

1. Now that you've been introduced to the legal mandates behind the provision of assistive technology devices and services for students with disabilities, how would you define assistive technology? Write a definition for assistive technology in your own words. As a general or special educator, where do you see yourself fitting into the process of selecting and using assistive technology for students with disabilities?
2. Place this definition in your portfolio.

Table 6.2	Categories of AT Devices	
Category	Function/Uses	Examples
Mobility and Positioning Aids	Ensure the most comfortable and effective solution for sitting, standing, resting, or moving for an individual.	• Wheelchair • Walker • Stander • Cushions
Sensory Tools	Assist people who are blind, visually impaired, or hearing impaired.	• Hearing aids • FM systems • Auditory trainers • Eyeglasses • Reading devices • Text-to-speech software • Telecommunication devices for the deaf
Daily Living Tools	Increase independence and assist individuals in performing functional living skills or self-help activities such as cooking, eating, bathing, toileting, dressing, and home maintenance.	• Adapted eating utensils • Buttoner • Adapted kitchen tools • Reading magnifiers
Environmental Tools	Assist people to manipulate their environments for daily living, working, schooling, and recreation.	• Electronic systems which control access to lights, home appliances, television, computers, and security systems
Instructional Tools	Assist in the education and instruction of an individual.	• Overhead transparencies and projectors • Audiotape players • Multimedia software and tools • Internet technology • Computer software and hardware
Computer Access	Assist people with using the computer.	• Adapted keyboards, mice, and switches • Functionality settings in the computer operating system
Alternative and Augmentative Communication Tools ("Aug com" devices)	Assist people who may have speech difficulties, are nonverbal, or have difficulty with oral communication.	• Speech synthesizers • Text-to-speech software • Telecommunication devices for the deaf
Motivational Tools	Promote participation in cultural events and leisure time activities for individuals with disabilities.	• Adapted sports equipment • Special prosthetic devices • Audio descriptions of movies • Large print or Braille

continuum (see Figure 6.7). These inexpensive tools often lack moving parts and have limited functionality. Additionally, they require little or no training to use. Often low-tech tools can be found in your desk or kitchen junk drawer and include clothespins, shelf liner, paper clips, sticky notes, and hook-and-loop tape. More complex examples of low-tech tools include calculators, talking picture frames, spell checkers, timers, and battery-adapted toys.

"Mid-tech" assistive technologies use some form of power source, are moderately priced, and may require initial training for use. Mid-tech tools include tape recorders, CD players, portable word processors, leveled augmentative communication devices, and talking dictionaries.

"High-tech" assistive technologies, found at the highest level of the continuum are more complex and expensive. High-tech multifunctional tools often can be customized to meet individual needs and may require extensive training in order to

- environmental controls
- augmentative or alternative communication devices
- speech synthesizers
- voice recognition systems
- FM amplification systems
- text-to-speech software
- word-prediction software
- trackball, mouse stick, and switches
- touch-sensitive pads
- eye-tracking technology
- abbreviation-expansion software

High-tech

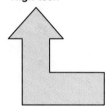

- word-processing software
- prewriting, organization, concept-mapping software
- portable word processors
- large-print word processors
- ergonomic, alternative, programmable, or virtual keyboards
- hyperlinked multimedia
- electronic organizers
- scanning reading pens
- leveled voice output devices
- Telecommunication Devices for the Deaf (TDDs)
- captioning
- text messaging
- American Sign Language software
- Descriptive Video Services (DVS®)
- Closed-Circuit Television Magnification (CCTV)
- Braille notetakers, embossers, and refreshable Braille displays
- talking dictionaries
- audio/video recorders
- CD/MP3/other media players

Mid-tech

- scanning print using an optical character recognition (OCR) scanner
- enlarging print and visuals onscreen
- talking picture frames
- calculators
- timers
- switch toys
- spell checkers

Low-tech

Figure 6.7
The AT Continuum: Examples of assistive technology.

use. Computers, computerized voice-output devices, environmental controls, and software programs are forms of high-tech tools.

Andrew's story demonstrates how several tools can be used in combination. Andrew's low-tech mouth stick, combined with the high-tech modifications made with the MouseKey features found in the Windows Accessibility Panel, made computer access possible for him.

But how do you use this information to improve your instruction and provide greater opportunities for all students to succeed in your classroom? Although selecting assistive technology for students who qualify for special education or related services should be a group decision that will undoubtedly involve all members of the IEP team, there are several simple adaptations that you can make to the computer hardware and software used in your classroom to provide access to all students.

Computer Adaptations

Computer hardware and software can be used by many students who experience physical, cognitive, visual, organizational, or auditory disabilities. The computer and its software can provide students who have diverse learning needs with a means for accessing and interacting with the curriculum. However, some students will need to have adaptations made to the computer to provide more effective computer access.

Positioning

Appropriate positioning of a computer for some students may be as simple as repositioning the user, the keyboard, or the monitor. Students who are provided with the necessary physical supports and clear visual access when working with computers will be able to concentrate on their work better. A variety of commercially designed chairs, desks, and tables are available that can make positioning of the student and computer easier; however, many adaptations can be made at no or low cost. Remember, also, that when working on positioning issues with a student with a disability an occupational therapist may be available to assist you. Additional information about how to arrange your classroom computer workstations in ways that promote students' ergonomic health is included in Chapter 9.

Keyboard Adaptations

Access to the computer can often be improved by adapting or modifying the traditional keyboard, mouse, and monitor. For young students or students with physical or visual difficulties the traditional keyboard may be difficult to use because of the size of the keys. However a few inexpensive alterations can provide access for some students. Several ways that the traditional keyboard can be modified include:

- Placing large, colored alphabet stickers on the keys for easier visual access.
- Using stickers, stick-on felt or rubber pads, or small buttons to mark keys that students might use the most frequently. These changes add visual distinction and texture to the keys.
- Creating a key guard from a piece of heavy-duty cardboard. Cut out only the sections for the keys that the student might need to access. Commercially made key guards are also available.

Commercially adapted keyboards are designed or configured to meet a variety of physical or sensory needs (see Figure 6.8). "Small form factor" or one-handed keyboards, like InfoKeys BAT Keyboard, are designed to provide physical access. Large key or "tactile feedback" keyboards, such as BigKeys provide access to the visually impaired. Some keyboards utilize a variety of keyboard overlays that match functional uses like the Intellikeys. There are also onscreen keyboards, like My-T-Soft, which are software programs that allow text input with a mouse, a touch screen, or a single external button called a switch. Additional adaptations can be made to the keyboard from within the operating systems for both Windows and Mac. For more information on these adaptations, see the Tools for Use box.

WEB LINK

Visit the textbook's companion website for information on alternate keyboards and keyboard adaptations.

Mouse Adaptations

Mouse adaptations can be made in a similar way to keyboard adaptations (see Figure 6.9). By adding a button, pom-pom, or colored sticker to the left mouse button, students will have a visual or sensory reminder of the correct side of the mouse to click. By turning the mouse upside down, students can use the mouse more like a trackball. Use the settings within your operating system's control panel to

Courtesy Glenna Gustafson

Figure 6.8
Keyboard adaptations. From left to right: Alphasmart, a portable word-processing keyboard; Intellikeys, a membrane keyboard; BigKeys with colorful and enlarged key targets; and a traditional keyboard that has been adapted using colored alphabet stickers.

TOOLS FOR USE

Built-in Computer Accessibility Features

As mentioned earlier, additional accessibility features for making the mouse and keyboard more accessible can be found in the Control Panel for Windows and System Preferences in the Mac operating systems. Several of the most commonly listed features are listed in below.

Additional Accessibility Features found in Windows and Mac operating systems are shown in the table below. Tutorials are available from the Microsoft and Apple websites.

Accessibility Features in Computer Operating Systems

Feature	Purpose
StickyKeys	Provides a way for one-handed or single-finger typists to press two keys at once, for example, pressing SHIFT, lifting your finger, and then pressing the D key to make a capital "D."
MouseKeys	This feature on the keys on the numeric keypad is used to control all of the mouse functions for users who have difficulty controlling a traditional mouse.
RepeatKeys	Allows the user to adjust how fast the auto-repeat works. This helps to eliminate a string of unwanted characters when a key is depressed.
SlowKeys	Provides a way to adjust the length of time a key must be held down before the computer interprets a press as input.

Feature	Purpose
Zoom (MAC) Magnifier (WIN)	This display option makes the computer screen more readable by creating a separate window that displays a magnified portion of the screen.
Display Adjustment	These settings offer the user the ability to select their preferred settings for color, size, and text for the computer display.
Voice Over (MAC) Narrator (WIN)	This text-to-speech utility reads what is displayed on the screen—the contents of the active window, menu options, or text that has been typed.

---

deactivate the right-mouse button if needed. Settings can also be found here to select a larger mouse arrow, change the functionality of the right- and left-mouse buttons, and slow down the mouse speed.

Numerous commercial mouse alternatives are available. These include trackballs, track pads, joy sticks, and game controllers. Each of these alternatives provides a different means of physical access.

Courtesy Glenna Gustafson

Figure 6.9
Mouse adaptations. From left to right: a traditional mouse adapted with a pom-pom glued to indicate the left mouse button; a single pillow switch when combined with a switch interface can be used as a mouse alternative; a Biggy trackball provides the user with bright colors; the handle of a joystick can also be adapted to meet a variety of needs.

APPLY TO PRACTICE

Built-in Accessibility Features

1. Choose either the Windows or Mac operating system and explore the accessibility features found in each. If you need more help, visit the Microsoft and Apple Accessibility websites that have tutorials. Links to these sites can be found on the textbook's companion website.
2. A detailed description and list of the accessibility features for each operating system can be found at each of these sites. Print and add to your class notes or portfolio.

APPLY TO PRACTICE

Learning More about Assistive Technologies

Many teachers and those who serve on IEP teams are unaware of the many possible technologies that can support students with special needs. Whether legally prescribed as assistive technologies or not, many students stand to benefit if you understand and monitor AT possibilities.

1. At professional conferences, visit displays or presentations related to assistive technology. Collect artifacts such as brochures, research, or white papers and keep them in a topics file. Add URLs to your portfolio from industry representatives, researchers, and other educators to help you monitor developments in AT.
2. Visit websites for AT in a particular area. Focus on one need at first and research available AT literature, demonstrations, and even sample products that may be available online. You can model your success on other topics, perhaps on an as-needed basis when faced with students with specific learning needs. Add the most promising URLs to your portfolio.

 WEB LINK

For more information on built-in accessibility features, visit the Microsoft and Apple Accessibility websites linked from the textbook's companion website.

THE GAME PLAN

What Every Special Educator Should Know

General and special educators are expected to meet the general technology competencies as set forth by state and national organizations. However, it is critical that special educators have a thorough understanding of assistive technologies in order to assist students with disabilities achieve success in educational and social environments.

Set Goals

The Council for Exceptional Children (CEC, 2003) published a set of competencies to address the knowledge and skills required for certification of special educators. Learn more about these requirements.

Take Action

Review the CEC standards at http://www.cec.sped.org/ps/perf_based_stds/standards.html

Monitor

Using these standards, how would you assess your knowledge about technology and special education?

Evaluate and Extend

If you plan to be a special educator, add one or more goals, based on these standards, to your portfolio.

Chapter Summary

As a classroom teacher you face the challenging task of trying to meet the needs of a variety of diverse learners. We began the chapter with a discussion of how you can use student data to set individual learning goals, monitor their progress, and evaluate your selected learning activities to ensure that you meet the needs of all students. We presented universal design for learning (UDL) and the use of assistive technologies as two ways that teachers can customize and personalize learning activities to address students' diverse learning styles, working strategies, and abilities.

As you learned in this chapter, the universal design for learning framework is a tool to help you make instructional decisions to support students with diverse needs, especially students with learning disabilities, who can be supported via technology. This information should help you develop lessons that are inclusive of all students in the learning environment, and identify, use, and evaluate appropriate technology resources that clearly support all students, regardless of special needs.

Assistive technologies also offer the promise of supplementing and enhancing abilities and compensating for barriers that diverse learners might experience. Greater access to and participation in the educational environment for all learners is the ultimate goal for using assistive technology. In order to meet this mandate, general and special educators need to know how to locate and select the appropriate assistive technologies for a diverse student population.

By using the techniques introduced in this chapter, you should be able to incorporate strategies for equitable use of technology resources in your school and classroom regardless of inherent student characteristics or ability levels. In the next chapter, you will learn techniques for collecting and reporting assessment data, which, as you learned in this chapter, can provide you with the information you need to customize your students' learning activities.

YOUR PORTFOLIO

To demonstrate competency in ISTE NETS-T Standards 2.c, review the lesson plan you have been developing throughout Chapters 3, 4, and 5 and modify it to provide evidence of customizing and personalizing learning activities to address students' diverse learning styles, working strategies, and abilities using digital tools and resources.

1. Reflect on the use of data to inform instruction.
   a. Create a narrative description of how you will consider past performance data in setting student goals.
   b. Make sure that your lesson includes the opportunity for you to monitor student progress throughout your lesson or unit.
   c. Identify the ways that you use data to evaluate student progress and the effectiveness of the lesson and the resources used in the lesson.
2. Create a narrative description of how you can create a learning environment supportive of all students by applying the principles of universal design for learning. Make sure you identify how you will support students' recognition, strategic, and affective networks as you set goals, individualize learning, and monitor and evaluate student progress. If necessary, modify your lesson plan to incorporate these principles.
3. Identify assistive technologies within your lesson and the ways they could support students' special needs, such as visual, hearing, or orthopedic impairments.

   a. Include commonly available technologies, such as word processors and web browsers that allow you to change font sizes for readability, calendar programs that help keep students organized, or concept-mapping software that allows students to organize ideas that can be converted into a text outline with the click of a button.
   b. Also explore specialized tools that may require additional training or support, such as modified keyboards or optional input devices.
   c. Consider the benefits all students may have using technology tools in a way that may be considered assistive regardless of whether they have an IEP or not.

References

Boyer, L., & Mainzer, R. W. (2003). Who's teaching students with disabilities? A profile of characteristics, licensure status, and feelings of preparedness. *Teaching Exceptional Children, 35*(6), 8–11.

Bransford, J. D., Brown, A. L., & Cocking, R. R. (Eds.). (1999). *How people learn: Brain, mind, experience and school.* Washington, DC: National Academy Press.

Bridgeland, J. M., Dilulio Jr., J. J., & Morison, K. B. (2006). The silent epidemic: Perspectives of high school dropouts. Seattle, WA: Bill and Melinda Gates Foundation. Retrieved on September 5, 2007, from www.gatesfoundation.org/Education/TransformingHighSchools/RelatedInfo/SilentEpidemic.htm

Brodwin, M. G., Cardoso, E., & Star, T. (2004). Computer assistive technology for people who have disabilities: Computer adaptations and modifications. *Journal of Rehabilitation, 70*(3), 28–33.

Bryant, D. P., & Bryant, B. R. (2003) *Assistive technology for people with disabilities.* Boston: Pearson.

Cook, A. M., & Hussey, S. M. (2002). *Assistive technologies: Principles and practice.* St. Louis: Mosby.

Council for Exceptional Children. (2003). What every special educator must know: Ethics, standards, and guidelines for special
educators (5th ed.). Arlington, VA: Author.

Gardner, H. (1993). Education for understanding. *The American
School Board Journal, 180*(7), 20–24.

Gardner, H. (1995). Reflections on multiple intelligences: Myths
and messages. *Phi Delta Kappan, 77,* 200–209.

Hasselbring, T. (2000). Use of computer technology to help students with special needs. *The Future of Children, 10*(2), 102.

Mendelsohn, S., & Fox, H. R. (2002). Evolving legislation and
public policy related to disability and assistive technology. In
M. J. Sherer (Ed.), *Assistive technology: Matching device and
consumer for successful rehabilitation* (pp. 17–28). Washington,
DC: American Psychological Association.

Office of Special Education and Rehabilitative Services. (2005).
Guidelines for assessing the functional capacities of an
individual with specific learning disabilities to determine
significance of disability for order of selection purposes.
Washington, DC: U.S. Department of Education. Technical
Assistance Circular RSA-TAC-05-01. Retrieved July 6, 2006,
from http://www.ed.gov/policy/speced/guid/rsa/tac-05-01.pdf

Pub. L. No. 93-112. (Rehabilitation Act of 1973).

Pub. L. No. 100-407. (Technology-Related Assistance for
Individuals with Disabilities Act of 1988).

Pub. L. No. 101-336, 104 Stat. 327 (Americans with Disabilities Act
of 1990).

Pub. L. No. 101-476 (Individuals with Disabilities Education Act of
1990—IDEA).

Pub. L. No. 105-394. S.2432 (Assistive Technology Act of 1998).

Pub. L. No. 107-110. (No Child Left Behind Act of 2001).

Pub. L. No. 108-446 (Individuals with Disabilities Education
Improvement Act of 2004).

Quenneville, J. (2001). Tech tools for students with learning
disabilities: Infusion into inclusive classrooms. *Preventing
School Failure, 45,* 167–170.

Rose, D. H., & Meyer, A. (2002). *Teaching every student in the digital
age. Universal design for learning.* Alexandria, VA: Association
for Supervision and Curriculum Development.

Lisa F. Young/Fotolia

ISTE Standards addressed in this chapter

NETS-T 2. Design Digital-Age Learning Experiences and Assessments

Teachers design, develop, and evaluate authentic learning experiences and assessments incorporating contemporary tools and resources to maximize content learning in context and to develop the knowledge, skills, and attitudes identified in the NETS-S. Teachers:

d. provide students with multiple and varied formative and summative assessments aligned with content and technology standards and use resulting data to inform learning and teaching.

Note: Standard 2.a is addressed in Chapter 4, 2.b in Chapter 5, and 2.c in Chapter 6.

Assessment and Evaluation

When you think about assessments from your experiences as a student, what feelings come to mind? How have different teachers in your school career used assessments? What were their purposes? What were the benefits of those assessments for your teachers? What were the benefits to you as a student?

Maybe you didn't think about assessments as being beneficial when you were a student. But well-designed assessments are a critical part of the teaching-learning cycle and do more than just help determine grades. As you will notice in the Stories from Practice box, assessments can provide valuable information to students, teachers, and the larger community—information that can be used to inform teaching and improve learning. Assessments have a wide range of uses including, but not limited to:

- providing feedback to students on their progress toward achieving learning goals

Outcomes

In this chapter, you will

- Develop assessments and scoring practices that are aligned with content and technology standards.
- Incorporate a variety of appropriate technology-based resources for assessing learning into your instruction.
- Use technology applications to communicate student performance data and report this evidence to parents, administrators, and other stakeholders.
- Use data from multiple measures and resources to assess student use of technology as required by the NETS-S.

- motivating students and providing opportunities to build confidence
- monitoring the progress teachers are making in their curricula
- evaluating the effectiveness of instruction
- determining participation in supplemental or enrichment programs
- providing information to parents, communities, and others in the public about school performance
- comparing students and schools to others or to established criteria
- measuring progress of students or schools over time

ISTE NETS-T Standard 2 requires you to "design, develop, and evaluate authentic learning experiences and assessments incorporating contemporary tools and resources to maximize content learning in context and to develop the knowledge, skills, and attitudes identified in the NETS-S." Standard 2.d further requires you to "provide students with multiple and varied formative and summative assessments aligned with content and technology standards and use resulting data to inform learning and teaching."

STORIES FROM PRACTICE

I recently visited a local middle school to interview teachers and the principal. This middle school—a National Blue Ribbon School as designated by the U.S. Department of Education—is known for its innovative and exceptional use of technology. The school incorporates a web-based gradebook and reporting software that allows teachers to post student assignments and grades as well as communicate with parents online. When asked how this technology had affected her practice, one veteran teacher half-jokingly replied that she had been brought into the technology world "kicking and screaming" and that she would give up her paper-based gradebook only "over my dead body." However, she then went on to elaborate that despite her original reluctance to use the online gradebook, she couldn't imagine teaching without it now. It had helped to break down communication barriers between her and the

parents, many of whom were in two-income families and did not have the opportunity to visit the classroom as often as parents did when she began her career. To her, it had "brought the parents into the classroom." Now she routinely uses the system not only to post final grades but also to inform parents of upcoming assignments and to prompt greater home involvement when students need extra help or encouragement with an assignment. The only negative feedback, joked the principal, had come from the students who groaned that their parents now know "what they did in school" every day and are able to ensure schoolwork is completed and supported at home.

The gradebook program allows teachers to analyze and chart student performance individually, by group, or by class, and to send confidential messages to parents with real-time grade data via e-mail. These data reports

allow teachers to quickly determine whether they need to reteach content to the entire class, a group, or an individual. Some of the teachers in the school described how they post helpful web resources and even their class lecture notes or presentations on the website so that both parents and students can use it to support or supplement instruction outside of class. The veteran teacher reported that the parent of one of her students routinely downloaded her classroom presentations at work and that the whole office would look forward to reviewing them. Not only does she think that this practice provides great public relations for the school, but "it's like that parent's in the classroom getting the same lesson her child did that day."

Source: John Ross

Assessing Student Learning

As you learned in Chapter 6, assessment data can be used to set goals for student learning, monitor learning through formative assessments, and evaluate learning through summative assessments. Assessments, therefore, are an important part of the learning process. How can assessment support learning? Classroom assessments that promote learning (Assessment Reform Group, 1999, p. 7):

- involve sharing learning goals with students
- aim to help students know and recognize the standards for which they are aiming
- involve students in self-assessment
- provide feedback that leads to students recognizing their next steps and how to take them
- are based on the belief that every student can improve
- involve both teachers and pupils reflecting on assessment data

Have you experienced assessments that were specifically designed to facilitate learning? Perhaps you have had projects or assignments reviewed by your teachers or peers prior to being allowed to revise and strengthen them. Perhaps you engaged in simulations that allowed you to practice the steps of an experiment before demonstrating your understanding on an exam. Formative assessments can include videotaped performances, electronic journals, checklists and rubrics, as well as many other formats that allow you to practice or check your understanding prior to being evaluated on the "big test." Formative assessments may or may not have a grade assigned to them but if they do, these grades are often used for the purposes of monitoring student progress or providing a benchmark rather than as a final judgment.

As suggested above, feedback is critical to formative assessment. Your students will benefit most when they receive feedback about the *quality* of their work and suggestions for improvement—not just whether their responses were right or wrong. To improve learning, they must also receive feedback about their progress *during* instruction. **Outcome feedback,** knowing whether a response is correct or not, is the simplest and most common type of feedback, but it provides little guidance to students (Butler & Winne, 1995). Early drill-and-practice software often provided this type of feedback, in which student responses were boldly acknowledged as "CORRECT" or "INCORRECT," but rarely with an explanation why. For formative assessment to achieve maximum benefit, feedback must provide an explanation of why an answer is correct or incorrect, should support students when they are using appropriate strategies and content knowledge, and guide them when they are not. **Cognitive feedback** refers to feedback that helps students develop a better understanding of what is expected for performance, how their current understanding or skill levels compare to those expectations, and how they might improve their performances (Butler & Winne, 1995).

It's important that you don't isolate the assessment strategies and tools that you use in the Monitor and Evaluate stages of your instruction and just "tack them on" at the end. The cycle of instruction is iterative and the stages overlap. As you will learn in the next section, you plan your assessments as you set goals for student learning. In addition, some of the assessments you develop may be part of your instructional actions.

Aligning Assessments with Standards

In education, **standards** define what students should learn or be able to do after instruction. Think of content standards as representing the goals we have for our students. As such, they help shape what we do in the classroom. Typically, teachers create specific learning activities based on general standards that were approved at the state level and then translated into suggested units or objectives at the local level. Standards promote equity by requiring that all students, regardless of gender, ethnicity, or socioeconomic status, have similar opportunities to achieve the same content and performance goals. However, the way in which these goals are met will, by necessity, vary depending on your students' unique needs. Although standards provide a framework within which we, as teachers, operate, there is plenty of room

TOOLS FOR USE

Instructional Objectives

Many school systems require teachers to write instructional objectives, so it is useful to know how to do so. An **instructional objective** describes what your students should be able to do when they have successfully completed your lesson. The addition of the qualifying term, "instructional," places it within the context of your classroom and emphasizes that it should be more specific than a state or national objective that supports a content standard. The instructional objective bridges the gap between the content standard and the assessment measure. In other words, objectives can be thought of as specifications for your assessments. For example, an objective and the associated assessment measure might look like this:

Objective: Given multiple sample checks, locate the bank routing number and customer account number on the checks.

Assessment: Review the five blank checks located in the envelope. Circle the bank routing number and underline the customer account number on each check.

An instructional objective has three parts (Dick, Carey, & Carey, 2005). These parts describe

1. What your students are going to do (the skills and knowledge identified in the content standards and objectives)
2. How the students will do it (the conditions under which they will perform the skills or behavior, including necessary materials and resources)
3. How you will know the students have done it successfully (the criteria for a successful performance)

When considering the first part of an instructional objective, what your students are going to do, content standards help determine the knowledge your students will need and the skill level(s) required to demonstrate that knowledge. The second part of an instructional objective describes the conditions under which your students will perform the skills required by the standards, including the necessary materials and resources. The third part of an instructional objective describes the criteria for a successful performance such as time limits, degrees of accuracy, or percentage correct. Examine the objective below, which contains all three components:

Objective: Using a reproduction of the architect's blueprint of your school (the conditions), locate all restrooms and drinking fountains on the first floor (the performance) with 100 percent accuracy (the criteria).

Although content standards and objectives provide the focus for a good lesson plan, you still must use your experience, knowledge, and other resources to develop a lesson that will help your students effectively build the required content-related skills and knowledge. The standards, objectives, instructional activities, materials employed, and assessment measures are interrelated and should support each other. In other words, they must all be "in alignment."

For more information on converting content standards to objectives, see the textbook's companion website.

for interpreting standards at the local level. In other words, standards do not require every teacher to teach every child in the exact same way.

Standards, also, do not routinely describe how students will be assessed. To be more useful, standards must be converted to something more measurable. One way to do that is to write instructional objectives (see Tools for Use); another way is to develop your assessment instruments. Objectives and assessments are really two sides of the same coin. Objectives describe the skills and knowledge your students must master; assessments provide the specific means for them to actually demonstrate those skills and knowledge. The assessment strategies and tools that you select should be closely aligned with the learning goals you have developed for your students; the content standards you have selected for your lesson and unit plans; and the teaching strategies, activities, and materials used in your lesson. For example, if your students will use science simulation software for an assessment, they must have the opportunity to learn the skills that are needed to perform the simulation, including practice with the software, if necessary, prior to completing the assessment. If your students will compose a letter using word processing software, they must be given adequate practice and experience not just in using a keyboard, but in using a keyboard for letter-writing activities. Regardless of whether you actually create your assessments prior to developing learning activities, assessment and learning activities are closely linked and should be considered together.

Alignment of Standards and Objectives

Let's review a few examples of content standards. Table 7.1 presents mathematics content standards and one supporting objective for three grade levels. The standards

Table 7.1	Examples of Mathematics Content Standards and Associated Objectives	
Grade	Standard	Objective
4	The learner will understand and use graphs, probability, and data analysis.	Describe the distribution of data using median, range, and mode.
8	The learner will understand and use graphs and data analysis.	Approximate a line of best fit for a given scatterplot; explain the meaning of the line as it relates to the problem, and make predictions.
12	The learner will collect and interpret data to solve problems.	Write and interpret an equation of a curve (linear, exponential, quadratic) that models a set of data.

Source: Adapted from Public Schools of North Carolina. (2006). *North Carolina standard course of study.*

in Table 7.1 were selected to demonstrate similar types of skills in each domain, but at different grade levels. For example, the sample standards for mathematics are so similar across grade levels, they use much of the same terminology:

> Grade 4: The learner will understand and use graphs, probability, and data analysis.
> Grade 8: The learner will understand and use graphs and data analysis.
> Grade 12: The learner will collect and interpret data to solve problems.

In these examples, the math standards and objectives relate to data use and graphing. Although the global nature of the standards *suggest* which skills and knowledge are necessary, they fall short in terms of specifics. Greater specificity is provided through the supporting objectives. Although only one objective is listed for each of these examples, content standards often have multiple objectives that, in combination, make up the requisite skills and knowledge your students must develop to demonstrate they have mastered the standards. Together, the standards and objectives make up the **curriculum** that your state asks you to teach. The complete standards and supporting objectives for the eighth grade mathematics example is given in Figure 7.1.

To achieve **curriculum alignment**, you must develop lessons that are matched to the standards. Similarly, you must develop or select assessments that allow students to demonstrate content mastery at the level demanded by the standards. This means a couple of things: first, that your assessments are aligned with your lessons in terms of knowledge and skills, and second, that they are aligned in terms of the format and materials used. For example, if your objective is for students to be able to compose a five-paragraph paper and your assessment is completed in a computer lab

---

Standard 8.1:The learner will understand and use graphs and data analysis.

- Objective 8.1.1: Collect, organize, analyze, and display data (including scatterplots) to solve problems.

- Objective 8.1.2: Approximate a line of best fit fot a given scatterplot, explain the meaning of the line as it relates to the problem and make predictions.

- Objective 8.1.3: Identify misuses of statistical and numerical data.

Figure 7.1
Eighth grade mathematics standard and objectives.
Source: Adapted from Public Schools of North Carolina. (2006). *North Carolina standard course of study.*

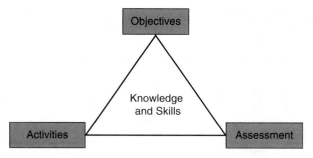

Figure 7.2
Alignment among objectives, activities, and assessment.

using word-processing software, then your instruction needs to provide opportunities for students to practice composing a five-paragraph paper using the word-processing software. If you don't provide access to the appropriate materials, then you cannot expect your students to demonstrate mastery of the objective. By keeping all of these components aligned, you increase the odds that your students will be successful. As illustrated in Figure 7.2, **curriculum alignment** ensures that instructional objectives, activities, and assessment measures are all directed toward student mastery of the same content knowledge and skills.

Developing Assessments

When you develop assessment instruments you need to consider the same three components you considered when writing instructional objectives: 1) the behavior, skill, knowledge, or attitude to be demonstrated, 2) the conditions under which they will be demonstrated, and 3) the criteria that specify the level of performance or knowledge required. As you may know, the behavior, skills, knowledge, or attitudes your students are required to master are outlined in your content standards (see Chapter 3). Performance conditions identify equipment, supplies, or other resources, including technologies, which are allowed during the assessment of student skills. They also include any time limits or other constraints imposed upon students as they are demonstrating the skill. Criteria clearly describe what acceptable performance looks like. Criteria can be conveyed through rubrics, checklists, or a simple list of what an acceptable answer should include (e.g., "Your report should include five sources and no grammatical or factual errors."). When shared with students before embarking on an activity, students can set goals for their own performances and can continue to monitor their performances throughout their learning, whether creating a web page, writing an essay, or preparing a presentation for the class. They can also determine the essential elements of complex projects, making the project seem more approachable even to struggling students.

Whether an intended consequence or not, the assessment activities you select will indicate to your students which skills and knowledge you feel are most important or worthwhile. If you test factual knowledge, students will believe that facts are most important; if you test critical and creative thinking skills, students will pay more attention to developing these skills. So, if your goal is to create a learning environment that promotes deep understanding of content, what type of assessments should you choose? How can you communicate the interest and excitement you have for your content area, or even your interest in lifelong learning, through assessments? Think about the messages you send to your students when you select and use your assessment methods. Do these messages include a focus on meaningful understanding or are they focused on how to pass a test at the end of the year? How do your classroom assessments communicate your expectations to your students?

There is no magic formula to determine the right assessment task or the appropriate technology for every performance goal or assessment task. In fact, a variety of technologies and formats may fit any number of assessment tasks and can be used equally well in multiple content areas. In practice, you should use a variety of assessment formats and tools that are matched to your students' learning goals and that provide an adequate picture of student understanding.

Assessment Formats and Technologies That Support Them

There is little agreement regarding the classifications of assessment formats. In fact, some complex assessments can blur the lines between different formats and include elements of several. We group assessment formats into four broadly defined groups: 1) forced-choice assessments, 2) open-ended response assessments, 3) performance-based assessments, and 4) project-based assessments. Characteristics of each of these four broad categories and the technologies that support them are explored next.

Forced-Choice Assessment Formats

Review the continuum, presented in Chapter 1, that describes the common stages of technology integration through which teachers progress. Remember that one of the first ways that teachers build their skills with new technologies is to replicate familiar strategies. This is true for both instruction and assessment, and in terms of assessment, most people are familiar with forced-choice question formats. These are the customary multiple-choice, true/false, matching, and fill-in-the-blank question formats that are popular in large-scale exams and that have influenced the assessment practices of many teachers.

A benefit of this assessment format is that it can be quick to administer and score. Also, items can be readily developed or obtained in these formats, especially for constructs with lower levels of cognitive demand. It is possible, but difficult, to develop forced-choice questions that accurately assess skills and knowledge at a higher level of cognitive skill, for example when students are required to apply, analyze, or evaluate content parameters. Depending on your level of technology proficiency, and that of your students, there are a variety of technologies that support the inclusion of forced-choice formats in your assessment toolkit.

You will probably have access to a variety of electronic test-item banks, including ones that you and your colleagues develop. Item banks may be available from publishers of state-adopted resources, such as textbooks, or may be available for purchase from assessment vendors. Some states and districts offer online access to item banks that may include items from previously administered large-scale assessments. Test-item banks may provide good formative and summative assessment items for your own classroom.

Items for summative assessments must be kept secure; however, some states and districts are tackling the development of online formative assessments that are available for access by teachers, students, and parents at all times on an on-demand basis.

TOOLS FOR USE

New Trends in Computer-Adaptive Testing

Computer-adaptive testing (CAT) is based on item-response theory (IRT) and has the potential to create an optimal test for every individual (Meijer & Mering, 1999). CAT has been applied to large-scale testing by the military (Fletcher, 1992), admissions testing for higher education (Bennett, 2001), and some statewide assessments (ETS, 2001). CAT assessments attempt to present an appropriate number and sequence of questions based on 1) a determination of the student's level of understanding or proficiency, and 2) the construct being measured. In simple terms, it works like this: A question is presented at a level that is determined to be in the mid-range of the student's ability—although this determination can be difficult. When the student answers a question correctly, the following questions become progressively more difficult. When the student answers a question incorrectly, the following questions become easier. The test continues until some predetermined level of accuracy is established (Wainer, 2000).

These assessments capitalize on the growing number of online assessment systems—both state-based as well as vendor-provided systems—that have been developed since the late 1990s. Beginning with familiar formats, many online assessment systems began by replicating common paper-and-pencil formats, the most popular of which is the forced-choice response (Bennett, 1998).

Of course there is a variety of testing software that supports forced-choice question formats. Scannable test forms, available in several formats, are used in many classrooms. As you probably know, students use a question booklet (or sheet) to read the questions and indicate their answers by filling in the appropriate "bubbles" on a form that can be read by a test scanner. Open-response questions (e.g., essay or short answer questions) can also be included on some forms, but you'll probably still have to grade these responses yourself.

Online testing software is available in many schools and ranges from highly secure formative and summative tests that are matched to state content standards to editable forms you create yourself. Even if your school or district does not have access to a commercial online quiz generator, several free services are available online (see Figure 7.3). Many of these require you to register your students, often using a student identifier, so that results can be e-mailed to you or accessed later. Check with your school first before using any service in which student information is recorded.

A popular new technology that supports the use of forced-choice items is the wireless responder. There are a variety of wireless tools that can be purchased and used with or without additional hardware and software. These small tools look similar to television remote controls and allow individual students to "beam" responses anonymously, or at least confidentially, to questions posed to an entire class. Simple versions allow for students to select from one of four to six buttons (e.g., A, B, C, or D depending on the corresponding answer choice) with more complex versions available that allow students to work out problems or enter calculated responses, such as the solution to a math problem. The students' responses are beamed using infrared or radio frequency to a central source that is connected to a computer at the front of

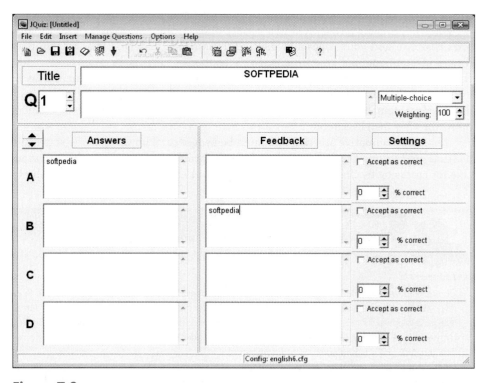

Figure 7.3
Hot Potatoes is popular software for developing questions for students.
Source: © 2003–2008 Half-Baked Software Inc.

THE GAME PLAN

Forced-Choice Assessments

Set Goals

Learn more about one of the technologies used to support forced-choice assessments. Choose one of the technologies presented in this chapter such as item banks, online assessments, or wireless responders.

Monitor

Determine how the assessments match the demands of your content areas. Talk with other students in your class or with practicing teachers to determine how the tools can be used in your own teaching.

Take Action

Review examples of these tools by investigating them online, visiting a school that uses them, reading about them in journals or magazines, or attending an educational conference with a vendor display area.

Evaluate and Extend

Discuss the strengths and weaknesses of the technology with others and determine strategies for incorporating the technology in your classroom.

the room. These systems may also be connected to or built into some type of display hardware such as an interactive whiteboard (see Chapter 5).

Detailed data collection, analysis, and reporting can occur instantaneously. This type of live polling of responses is ideal for monitoring learning through formative assessment and can help you and your students quickly determine content areas that require further instruction or where there are obvious gaps in understanding. Student data can also be stored and tracked over time to give you a picture of individual student growth and the need for supplemental instruction.

Open-Ended Response Formats

Because it is difficult to write high-quality, forced-choice questions that truly tap into higher-order thinking skills, open-ended questions are often employed when students have to demonstrate higher levels of cognitive skill, such as the application or synthesis of rules, procedures, or concepts or to demonstrate creative and original thoughts and ideas.

What does the following bring to mind? "Explain in your own words what is meant by . . . " How about, "Compare and contrast the following . . . "? These are examples of prompts for open-ended questions in the form commonly known as short-answer or essay questions. Responses may be restricted ("in 100 words or less . . . ") or extended for more in-depth responses. You've undoubtedly encountered many of these questions in your career as a student and may have a few yet to experience. Although these formats are familiar, you should consider why and when to use open-ended responses and their implications for your assessment practices.

On the plus side, open-ended questions often take very little time to develop. On the scoring end, however, they usually take longer than forced-choice responses in which there is only one correct answer that can be scored by machine. If not carefully planned and inspected by peers and other content experts, open-ended questions can be less reliable due, primarily, to the subjective nature of scoring them.

Any technology that supports text entry can be used to incorporate open-ended text responses. But this extends beyond word-processing software, as a variety of communication and collaboration tools exist that allow students to respond to your queries. Students can extend their learning through participation in online communications via threaded discussions, e-mail, or even chat software. However, colloquialisms familiar to the chat and IM (instant messenger) world often do not follow standard language usage and may have limited application in settings where proper grammar or formatting is required. Depending on what you are assessing, you may or may not want your students to express IMHO (in my humble opinion), LOL (laugh out loud), or to wink ;-) at each other. In this case, technology may actually lead to superficial assessment activities.

Journaling is a common activity and can be used to facilitate self-reflection and self-assessment. Journaling can be supported by a variety of technologies, such as common word-processing software, designated journaling software, as well as blogs. Many word-processing applications include note and tracking features that allow you and your students to incorporate suggestions, options, and revisions within a single document. They also include tools, such as grammar and spell checkers, that can support students with difficulties in these areas when critical thought outweighs the need for mechanics. The use of grammar, spelling, and other writing tools are an important part of communicating effectively when using information and communications tools in the 21st century.

Both stand-alone and web-based tools can incorporate video, graphics, and other media that allow students to support their text-based entries. Web-based communications such as blogs or threaded discussions allow for an added layer of complexity as you, other students, and even the original author can return to a posting and provide critique, clarification, or demonstration of further understanding or skill. This type of collaborative journal can support peer review as a type of formative assessment. Unique to threaded discussions and online forums is that messages can be sorted and organized by parameters such as the author, date, or subject, making it easy to follow a student's argument, line of reasoning, and can even demonstrate growth over time.

Performance-Based Assessments

There are a variety of ways students can demonstrate mastery through performance. Performance-based assessments are possible in all content areas but may most easily be exemplified by domains that require oral communication skills or the development of psychomotor skills in conjunction with other content knowledge, such as sports, the fine arts, and many lab sciences. Performances can very quickly extend beyond the demonstration of rudimentary skill and can require students to demonstrate very complex behaviors that may exhibit choices based on personal values and creativity.

Oral communication is a ubiquitous teaching and assessment strategy. Teachers ask their students questions to determine prior knowledge, levels of understanding or misunderstanding, or simply to clarify a point. This type of questioning and dialog can be informal or can be used in formal settings, such as in the case of an oral exam or interview. And although this is a book about the use of technology, it's important to emphasize that technology should only be used when it facilitates learning, and not simply as a novelty. Sometimes you'll just want to ask a question. No technology required. But there are some ways that technology can support assessment through dialog, primarily through recordkeeping.

The ease with which digital video can be captured and edited allows it to serve as a tool for demonstrating student skills and knowledge. As demonstrated by the hundreds, if not thousands, of live early morning news shows at elementary schools across the nation, even very young students can master basic video capture and editing to record their progress. Class or small group discussions can be captured and stored in portfolios. Student presentations can be recorded and kept as a record of content understanding. And although this section focuses on technology that supports *student* assessment, the value of using videotape to record your own teaching as a means of evaluating and developing skills (as presented in Chapter 12) cannot be understated.

Technology can provide a means for recording critical early literacy and numeracy development—foundational skills for later learning. In early literacy classes, the assessment technique of "running records" (see Figure 7.4) allows teachers to quickly

Figure 7.4
Wireless Generation uses handheld computers to allow teachers to gather and compile student response almost instantaneously.
Source: http://www.wirelessgeneration.com/reading3d_demo3.html. © 2000–2008 Wireless Generation, Inc.

score student performance on short reading passages to gauge student fluency, expression, accuracy, and confidence. Developed in a print-based world, running records are now supported by handheld computers (PDAs), from companies such as Wireless Generation, that provide the added benefit of quick data reporting. Running records of an entire classroom of students can be completed in less than a class period, and data from these records can then be aggregated and reported almost instantaneously—something that takes much longer to accomplish by hand. You can make changes to your instruction as needed, even daily if necessary, based on real-time data collection. Handheld devices support other literacy assessments as well, such as oral retelling and assessments of phonemic awareness and phonics development. Whether based on formal or informal observations, many student information systems allow you to quickly add notes to student records that can be accessed and recorded on handheld and laptop computers, making student records dynamic.

Project-Based Assessments

Related to performance-based assessments is the creation of products to support **project-** and **problem-based learning**, as introduced in Chapter 3. Although project-based assessments are especially well suited for formative purposes, they are also employed in summative settings, such as the generation of capstone projects at the end of a year or course of study. There are a variety of methods for incorporating project-based assessments in a classroom, as well as many different tools to support them.

Project-based assessments are often linked to a category called **authentic assessments.** In Chapter 3 we introduced you to the concept of **authentic intellectual work** and described how authentic instruction used real-world contexts to engage students in the actual work of a discipline. In an authentic assessment, students are required to demonstrate understanding of concepts and perform skills within the context of that authentic activity, that is, by replicating real-world performances as closely as possible (Svinicki, 2004). In these cases, the assessments may be so intricately embedded or linked to the instruction that it may not be apparent to students that there is a formal assessment. In science classes, students can perform experiments using probes and other measurement devices that scientists use and record their findings in a laboratory notebook—digital or paper; students can demonstrate writing proficiency by using word processing and layout software to create brochures or newspapers; students in math classes can use GPS devices to measure buildings and land forms and generate scale drawings that show the application of concepts such as area.

Wiggins (1998) lists six characteristics of an authentic assessment:

1. The assessment is realistic; it reflects the way the information or skills would be used in the "real world."
2. The assessment requires judgment and innovation; it is based on solving unstructured problems that could easily have more than one answer and, as such, requires the learner to make informed choices.
3. The assessment asks the student to "do" the subject, that is, to go through the procedures that are typical to the discipline under study.
4. The assessment is done in situations as similar as possible to the context in which the related skills are performed.
5. The assessment requires the student to demonstrate a wide range of skills that are related to the complex problem, including some that involve judgment.
6. The assessment allows for feedback, practice, and second chances to solve the problem being addressed.

Project-based assessments, whether taking the form of authentic assessments or not, can also support pedagogies related to **problem-based learning.** As described in Chapter 3, problem-based learning, also called PBL, can help students meet the demands of standards and learning goals that require higher-order thinking skills, such as those related to problem identification, selecting and monitoring strategies for solving the problem, applying knowledge, and evaluating the success of one's efforts. Problem-based learning can also utilize performance-based assessments, as a well-designed problem can easily require students to demonstrate new knowledge and skills through performance with the only limitations being the appropriate fit to the content being explored.

Think of the typical science fair project. This is a project that is often built around a specific problem, whether determined by the student or the sponsoring organization. The problems often meet the requirements for authentic assessment as students are required to perform like scientists in terms of the research they complete and the tools they use. They also usually complete some type of performance in terms of explaining their projects and their new understandings and skills that have been developed. So in this case, you may have an authentic, problem-based project that is assessed via performance and a product!

These distinctions are not as critical as developing assessments that appropriately meet the demands of your curriculum and the needs of your students—it usually doesn't matter if you can explicitly state whether you are engaging in project- or problem-based activities, or both. The bottom line is that project-based learning typically results in some type of product, perhaps a web page or a multimedia presentation, and it may or may not include some type of performance, such as an oral report or class presentation using the products students have created.

Technologies to Support Performance- and Project-Based Assessment

Products and performances can incorporate a wide variety of technologies, from research papers composed using word-processing software to multimedia projects that include graphics, video, and audio. Students may conduct research on the web, use a digital camera to take pictures to support their presentations, create graphics using drawing programs, and demonstrate their knowledge using presentation software. Obviously, there are many tools you can use to support performance- or project-based learning activities. In the following discussion, we'll focus on just a few of the many technologies that can help you assess student learning when using performance- and project-based assessments: 1) concept maps, 2) simulations, and 3) portfolios and work samples.

Concept Maps

As you recall from Chapter 4, concept mapping is a graphic technique for representing student understanding. Concept maps traditionally consist of **nodes** representing concepts and **links** that show the connection between nodes (see Figure 7.5 for an example of one type of a concept map). Concept-mapping software is available for use by young students; however, the concepts that can be addressed and the resulting maps can become extremely complex and thus, are often used more with older students. Concept mapping is not dependent upon technology; but, concept-mapping software is widely available for facilitating the process and a variety of map templates are readily available, including Venn diagrams (see Figure 7.6), plot outlines, timelines, lab reports, and many others. Popular concept-mapping software can also toggle back and forth between the visual map layout and a corresponding text-based outline, allowing students to generate and review content in graphic or text form.

The nodes and links in a concept map help reveal student thinking and can illuminate misconceptions. Your students can compare their maps to those created by experts—including yourself—and this comparison can provide specific cognitive feedback essential to good formative assessment. Although paper-and-pencil concept

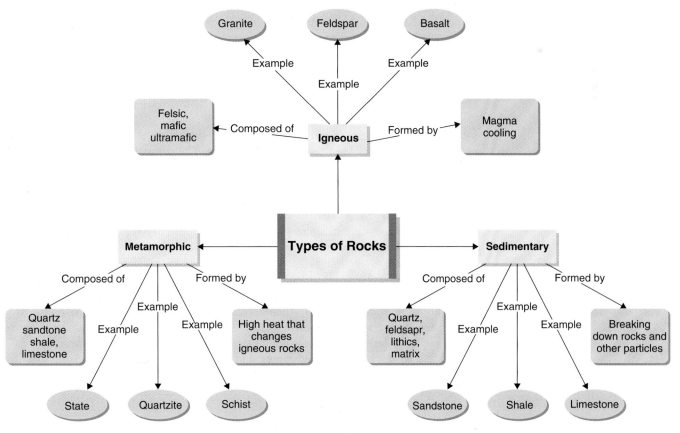

Figure 7.5
Example of a concept map.

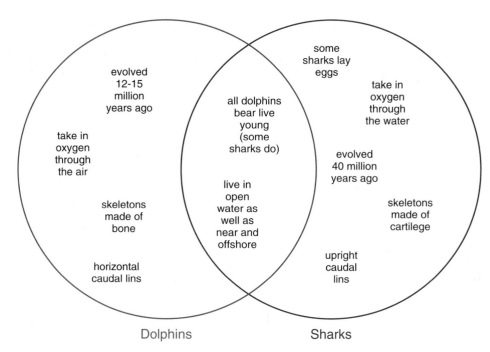

Figure 7.6
Example of a Venn diagram.

maps may also be analyzed for understanding and student misconceptions, the widespread availability of concept-mapping software increases its utility. As such, it has become a popular technology in classrooms at all grade levels.

One concern regarding using concept maps for assessment is how to implement concept mapping consistently across classrooms to generate valid and reliable results. Although technology can support concept mapping, it cannot resolve the human-dependent implementation issue. Concept maps do rate high in terms of utility, however, and can be integrated into many different content areas.

Simulations

Simulation software can provide access to learning activities that might otherwise be difficult or impossible to create in a classroom. The simulations available for use in your classroom range in sophistication from simple animations that can be found free online to sophisticated virtual environments. You can access online simulations of weather-related events or space missions and collect student performance data using an electronic journal or laboratory notebook. Students can access historical simulations and work in small groups to create presentations to give to the rest of the class, complete structured worksheets, or write reflective essays guided by questions you pose.

Simulation software is unique in that it not only provides opportunities for learning but it can support assessment, as well (see Figure 7.7). Simulation software can capture different elements of student performance data, such as the paths they follow through the software and the choices they make. That data can then be analyzed and reported and used to make judgments about skill and knowledge proficiency.

It's easy to imagine how games and virtual environments could be used for assessment as well. You may have to generate scoring procedures for some simple simulations or educational games that do not have data analysis and reporting features built into them. You can combine the use of these software applications with other assessment methods, such as journals or short quizzes, in order to check for students' progress on their learning goals. However, the selection and use of simulations, games, or virtual environments for assessment should meet the same rigor for

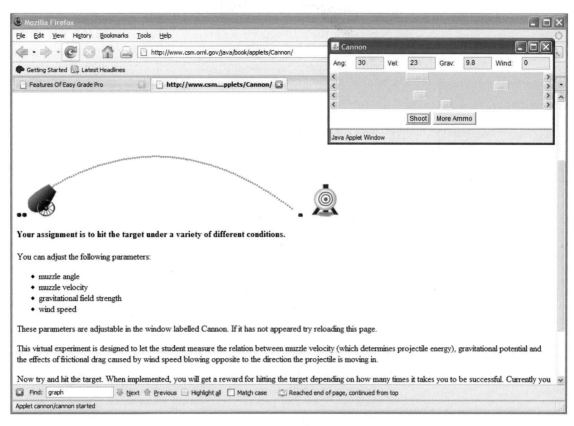

Figure 7.7
This ballistics simulation has a simple form of self-assessment. Once the student correctly manipulates the cannonball to hit the target, the target bursts into flames. Courtesy Oak Ridge National Laboratory.
Source: www.csm.ornl.gov

selecting any technology in your classroom and should appropriately match the needs of the content, your students, and the learning goals they are trying to meet.

Portfolios and Work Samples

As you already know through the development of your own professional portfolio in conjunction with this textbook, portfolios contain examples of work that can be compared to competencies or standards—often through the use of some type of checklist or rubric. There are varying opinions as to the different types of assessment portfolios and what they are called. However, depending on the needs of your students and your school, you may choose to incorporate one of two different types of assessments portfolios or perhaps a hybrid of the two. The first demonstrates growth by incorporating work samples that show a range of student proficiency over time and may be called a **dossier, process, or documentation portfolio**. By including original and revised versions of work, portfolios can demonstrate changes in understanding or proficiency and can show progress over time. The second type of assessment portfolio contains samples of exemplary work and is often referred to as a **showcase portfolio**. This latter form of portfolio is common for assessing entry into a program, such as the Advanced Placement (AP) Studio Art General Portfolio Program used by the College Board, that combines student art work, photographic slides, and a written student reflection to determine whether student applicants receive college credit for their art skills.

Print-based versions of portfolios have made the transition to digital formats, appearing on self-contained storage media such as CDs and DVDs and in web-based portfolios. There is software designed specifically to support portfolio development, but use caution when selecting this software. Be sure you take steps to ensure that students can continue to access their work after they've left your school or classroom. You don't want them to depend on proprietary software that is not readily accessible. By creating student work samples in common digital formats, such as word-processing documents, portable document formats (PDF), graphic files, and HTML pages, you may be able to store these artifacts in a portfolio management system as well as provide copies to students for use in common software applications. In fact, as Helen Barrett from the University of Alaska demonstrates on her portfolio website, just about any type of software can support the development of portfolios. As you learned in Chapter 1, Dr. Barrett has created versions of her portfolio in word processing, database, spreadsheets, and several multimedia applications and has posted them on the web using HTML, graphics, video, and other formats.

When incorporating portfolios in your instruction and assessment, it is important to determine an organizing structure in advance and make it apparent to your students. For example, your own portfolio for this class is probably organized around the ISTE NETS-T. To facilitate learning and student growth, your students themselves should determine what artifacts should be selected. However, the guidelines and criteria for the selection of materials contained in the portfolio should be explained and made clear to your students. And sometimes you may want all students to include a specific artifact or work sample as a means of monitoring their mastery of expected standards.

As you know, portfolios also serve as a means for self-assessment and self-reflection, as it is common that students write or explain why they have selected the artifacts in their portfolios, what those artifacts demonstrate in terms of their learning or understanding, and why they feel they are exemplars. Your students will likely need guidance and practice in creating reflections. (See information about creating self-reflections in Chapter 2.) Reflection provides a natural opportunity for providing cognitive feedback to your students as you review and discuss the portfolio artifacts with them.

Both the process of artifact selection and the subsequent assessment of portfolios rely on some subjective judgment. Also, portfolio use is not standard across classrooms. Your students' portfolios will be highly dependent on your classroom practices, and not all teachers will place the same emphasis on portfolio development, allot the same amount of class time for their development, provide the same access to outside resources or help, or collaborate with students to the same degree in terms of selecting relevant artifacts. However, the main point to remember is that although portfolios pose problems when compared *across* classrooms, one of the primary benefits of portfolio use is that they can help teachers and students *within* a classroom become more systematic in analyzing and learning from one's work samples than would normally occur during instruction (Shepard, 2000).

APPLY TO PRACTICE

Technologies to Support Project-Based Learning

Investigate the use of at least one technology tool, whether presented in this chapter or not, that can be used to support the creation of a project in your area of content expertise and demonstrate student mastery of content standards.

1. Identify a technology you have little experience with and find a sample to use on your own. You may be able to download freeware or trial versions of concept-mapping software, check out software or hardware from the library, or borrow from a local school.
2. Develop a small-scale project using the tool that demonstrates how you might incorporate this into your own teaching. How is the tool helpful? What limitations does it have, if any? What resources or training are required to use it fully?
3. Share your findings with others in your class.

Summary of Assessment Formats

Formative and summative assessments can be classified as forced-choice, open-ended, performance-based, or project-based. This section introduced you to a variety of technologies that can support these formats. But assessments are useless unless you score them to evaluate students' progress and determine whether your students learned what they set out to learn. Common scoring procedures are the focus of the next section.

Scoring Expectations and Practices

Once you've selected an assessment or assessment format, you must determine a method for obtaining an appropriate score for each student's performance. Scores, or grades, receive a great deal of attention in education and you want to be sure that your assessments not only adequately allow students to demonstrate their proficiencies, but that the judgments you make based on those assessments are fair and accurate. Some scoring practices and guidelines are provided below.

Scoring Keys

When an assessment allows you to make an objective judgment as to whether a response is right or wrong, grading is rather straightforward. Your student either got it right or not. When students are required to choose between a limited set of possible answers, as with multiple-choice, matching, and true-false questions, grading guidelines consist of a list of correct responses. These forced-choice assessment formats easily lend themselves to computerized test administration and scoring.

A popular technology for scoring forced-choice responses is a test scanner. These scanners use the famous "bubble sheets" with which you are undoubtedly familiar. You can create multiple test forms to increase security and a grade scanner can score all forms within a few minutes. Test scanners also allow you to do an item analysis of an assessment to determine whether any items were too easy or too hard, which can help you improve the match between your standards, instruction, and assessment.

Some open-ended test formats require constructed responses that also can be judged right or wrong. Short-answer questions and even some essay tests can be scored using keys that consist of a list of acceptable answers. Scoring keys for these open-ended formats should include common variations in wording for each acceptable response. Although this type of test can also be administered and scored by computer, developing a program to score constructed responses is more difficult than developing one to score forced-choice responses.

You may have already taken essay tests that have been scored by a computer without realizing it. At one time, these student responses were scored by multiple human raters who had to undergo intensive training and were reviewed frequently for their consistency and reliability. In several state and national tests, essays are now scored strictly by technology using artificial intelligence. Vantage Learning has developed software it calls IntelliMetric that uses artificial intelligence (AI) and examples of student writing to review and score student writing assessments. The computer scoring has been compared to and often surpasses the reliability of human scoring. The problem is that the scoring engine requires hundreds if not thousands of student samples to provide the best results, so is still impractical for use in most classrooms. However, some states that have shifted to the assessment of student writing online also provide websites that teachers and students can use to practice and receive feedback.

Rubrics and Checklists

This chapter has introduced a variety of assessments that cannot be scored neatly by a completely objective format. Class discussions, observations, open-ended questions and essays, problem-based learning projects, and portfolios offer unique challenges to scoring. Usually, teachers turn to the use of checklists or rubrics to score these types of assessments and to reduce the subjective quality of their judgments.

Checklists are a simple way to score the observation or demonstration of a skill. These can be factual recall skills or more complex skills involving analysis and evaluation. You can create a simple yes-no checklist in which the parameter or skill you are looking for is deemed either present or not. For example, the science lab checklist in Figure 7.8 simply lists standard safety behaviors students should follow.

A more complex checklist can use a scale that indicates the degree to which the parameter you are looking for is present, from a little to a lot. A checklist can help you monitor your students' cognitive development. That is, you can determine gaps in student schema (or patterns of understanding), which can help you determine whether they need reteaching or other supplemental instruction. From a developmental perspective, you can monitor what your students are able to do independently and how their skills develop over time.

You can also use checklists for specific assessments, such as when observing a student demonstrating required concepts during a think-aloud. In the **think-aloud** process, students verbalize what they are thinking when completing a task, such as reading a story, solving a math proof, or even working on complex problems that may require advanced skill in collaboration with others. The think-aloud process helps to generate artifacts of student cognition, as students are actually telling you what they are thinking, the strategies they are using, and questions and concerns they have. The chart in Figure 7.9 shows a simple method for collecting data from a think-aloud protocol used to monitor comprehension of a reading passage. Checks are placed in the corresponding column for each time a behavior is observed. Comments can be inserted in the final column and are not necessary for a simple performance audit.

Checklists can also be used to score projects or performances. In this case, some care should be taken to determine whether the presence of an item on the checklist actually corresponds to student understanding and skill. Are you grading the student or the project? Multiple measures of assessment may help you develop a clear picture of student understanding.

Checklists can be developed and implemented using a variety of technologies, and since their purpose is to quickly and easily collect data, the use of technologies to capture, store, and report that data makes them even more powerful. Some simple checklists may be available for use on PDAs or tablet computers that allow you to

---

Science Lab Checklist

During science labs, please make sure that you

❑ Store backpacks and personal items in the storage area at the back of the room.
❑ Log on to the school network appropriately and keep your password and data files secure.
❑ Do not eat or drink in the laboratory.
❑ Restrain long hair and loose clothing and wear laboratory aprons when appropriate.
❑ Wear gloves and keep exposed skin away from all chemicals.
❑ Send only one lab partner to the supply room at a time.
❑ Close laptops before transporting them and carry them with two hands.
❑ Put all laptops, probes, and other equipment back in their designated storage spaces.
❑ Thoroughly clean all work surfaces and equipment after each use.
❑ Make certain hot plates, burners, gas, and water are turned off before leaving the laboratory.
❑ Frequently back up all lab data on your designated folder, including journal entries and worksheets.
❑ Sign off from the network at the end of class.

Figure 7.8
Science lab checklist.

enter data onscreen with a stylus. And although not every helpful checklist or inventory is currently available for handheld devices, common productivity software, such as word-processing and database software, is supported by many of these devices and can allow you to quickly develop those checklists you use regularly for assessment. Storing the results of checklist data in spreadsheets and databases provides powerful analysis and reporting features. Simple summaries and graphs can be created quickly that give you individual and group profiles, and also can help you determine the need to modify your instruction for reteaching or enrichment. Portable devices can also support many common observation tools, such as checklists of content-based behaviors and interview protocols.

Generally, checklists are rather one-dimensional. Usually, either the students did the tasks or they didn't. Rubrics, however, provide an added dimension that allows both you and your students to determine gradations in quality. Rubrics are common methods for assessing performance-based projects, especially those supported by technology. Rubrics are malleable and can be created for any content area and assessment mode, such as the scoring of projects, essays, portfolios, or live or videotaped student performances.

Rubrics are framed by some type of scale, but the degrees of the scale are clearly described or defined to demonstrate different levels of quality. Generally, a three-, four-, or five-point scale is manageable depending on the complexity of the task, project, or performance to be scored. Too many "quality" levels for a simple skill or too few for complex skills erode the effectiveness of the rubric. Another consideration is whether to begin your rubric scale at no points (0) or 1. Your rubric should relate to the standards or learning goals for the activity, lesson, or project and the descriptions should clearly describe the levels of performance rather than subjective judgments (Brookhart, 1999). For example, a descriptor for an exemplary writing sample that notes that all sentences and proper nouns begin with a capital letter is a clear description of the expected level of performance; whereas, use of the terms "good" or "weak" are subjective and provide little concrete feedback or a justifiable position.

Rubrics can be analytic or holistic (Brookhart, 1999). An **analytic rubric** breaks the assessment down into component categories (see Figure 7.10). For example, an analytic rubric for a student history presentation may include categories about accuracy of information, proper grammar and spelling, writing style, as well as elements of design. A **holistic rubric** may have descriptors that touch on each of these elements but it does not break them down into separate rating scales per category (see Figure 7.11).

Rubrics have become popular due to their valuable pedagogical aspects. Rubrics can help you determine the activities and resources needed in your instruction. Since rubrics define the different degrees of exemplary products and performances, they are likely to delineate the critical skills and knowledge necessary for mastery. For example, a rubric that defines excellence regarding the appropriate citation of Internet resources requires your students to 1) find and evaluate appropriate web-based resources and then to 2) cite them according to an accepted standard. If

Did the student…		
	Check for each instance	Comment
Make predictions Use imagery by describing pictures Link new information to prior knowledge Talk through confusing points Use comprehension strategies		

Figure 7.9
Collecting data using a think-aloud checklist.

Multimedia Project Rubric

Assignment: Interview a friend or relative to create a biographical web page/site. You must collect the following information:

- Date and place of birth
- Your reason(s) for interviewing this person
- Most memorable event in his/her life
- An accomplishment for which he/she is most proud

Your web page/site must contain at least five paragraphs of text, one image, and one hyperlink to a supporting resource. Any quotations must be correctly formatted and appropriately cited.

Score	0	1	2	3
Content features	Several of the required content elements are not included or are inaccurate.	Some of the content elements are not included or are inaccurate.	All of the content elements are included.	All content elements are included and are explained with significant detail and supporting data.
Grammar and punctuation	There are many errors in grammar and punctuation.	There are a few errors in grammar and punctuation.	There are one or two errors in grammar and punctuation.	There are no errors in grammar and punctuation.
Writing style	The writing is very difficult to read throughout with little or no variation in sentence structure and vocabulary is below grade level.	The writing is somewhat difficult to read in some points with little variation in sentence structure and vocabulary is below grade level.	The writing is easy to read with some variation of sentence structures and appropriate grade-level vocabulary.	The writing is both interesting and easy to read with a variety of sentence structures and appropriate and challenging vocabulary.
General design features	The information is difficult to view and text is difficult to read. The use of images, colors, and other media consistently detract from the presentation of the information.	Some of the information is difficult to view and/or text may be difficult to read. The use of images, colors, and other media may detract from the presentation of the information in some instances.	The information is presented clearly with text that is easy to read. The use of images, colors, and other media does not detract from the presentation of the information.	The information is presented in a creative manner with text that is easy to read. The use of images, colors, and other media is imaginative and adds to the presentation of the information.

Figure 7.10
Analytic rubric for multimedia project.

they've never done this before, your rubric reminds you to provide them with this knowledge before they can successfully meet the required criteria.

Another pedagogical value of rubrics is realized when they are jointly developed with students. Although this does take some time and you may not choose this approach each time you create a rubric, the process helps students develop skills in determining what constitutes best performance. Providing students with examples of differences in quality of performance or products can help them grasp the differences between various degrees of acceptable performance—for example, a 3-point and a 4-point performance. Students can then apply this understanding when creating their own products or performances.

Rubrics also provide a mechanism for providing detailed feedback to students (Andrade, 2005). They set expectations at the beginning of your lesson so students can better set their own goals for performance. They also provide support for formative self-assessment and peer assessment so that students can receive critical support for determining their levels of performance and either continuing with or selecting different strategies to complete their projects. Underlining or circling critical elements in the descriptors in a rubric can be much quicker than generating detailed feedback for every student. A descriptor for exemplary performance that notes that "there are no spelling errors" when compared to a descriptor that states "there are 2 or 3 misspelled words" gives the students a real measure for determining excellence.

Multimedia Project Rubric

Assignment: Interview a friend or relative to create a biographical web page/site. You must collect the following information:

- Date and place of birth
- Your reason(s) for interviewing this person
- Most memorable event in his/her life
- An accomplishment for which he/she is most proud

Your web page/site must contain at least five paragraphs of text, one image, and one hyperlink to a supporting resource. Any quotations must be correctly formatted and appropriately cited.

---

3 Points—All content elements are included and are explained with significant detail and supporting data. There are no errors in grammar and punctuation. The writing is both interesting and easy to read with a variety of sentence structures and appropriate and challenging vocabulary. The information is presented in a creative manner with text that is easy to read. The use of images, color, and other media is imaginative and adds to the presentation of the information.

2 Points—All of the content elements are included. There are one or two errors in grammar and punctuation. The writing is easy to read with some variation of sentence structures and appropriate grade-level vocabulary. The information is presented clearly with text that is easy to read. The use of images, colors, and other media do not detract from the presentation of the information.

1 Point—Some of the content elements are not included or are inaccurate. There are several errors in grammar and punctuation. The writing is difficult to read in some parts with little variation in sentence structure and vocabulary is below grade level. Some of the information is difficult to view and/or text may be difficult to read. The use of images, colors, and other media may detract from the presentation of the information in some instances.

0 Points—Several of the required content elements are not included or are inaccurate. There are many errors in grammar and punctuation. The writing is very difficult to read throughout with little or no variation in sentence structure and below grade-level vocabulary. The information is difficult to view and text is difficult to read. The use of images, colors, and other media consistently detract from the presentation of the information.

Figure 7.11
Holistic rubric for multimedia project.

However, Shepard (2000) also cautions that simply providing explicit criteria may not truly promote student learning if students learn to mechanically address the criteria without actually developing the relevant skills or knowledge. She suggests that students be allowed to use self-assessment as a way to understand what the criteria mean, not just to apply them mechanically.

Rubrics can be created using commonly available software applications. There are also websites that not only allow you to enter your descriptors to automatically generate a rubric but that house rubric examples and templates you can use for guidance. The popular Rubistar website by 4Teachers allows you to quickly create, customize, and save a rubric. If you are just starting out with creating rubrics, the Rubistar engine can even suggest descriptors for each level of your rubric for a range of common teaching models, such as the 6+1 Trait Writing Model, or even for specific skills, such as the use of manipulatives or the explanation of mathematical concepts. In addition to using this and similar web-based rubric generators, you may want to collaborate with other teachers in your school or district to develop rubrics based on your state's content standards. Joint development and use helps to improve the validity and reliability of your assessments and rubrics. Rubric templates, examples, and actual rubrics matched to lesson and unit plans can be stored electronically on shared directories or within lesson-planning software.

WEB LINK

Visit the textbook's companion website for resources to help you create rubrics for use in your classroom.

THE GAME PLAN

Rubrics for Assessment

Set Goals
Determine how rubrics and digital exemplars of student work will be accessible to students and parents.

Take Action
Review resources that provide guidance for developing rubrics to identify methods that can be used to share artifacts developed from them. If necessary, visit the resources for rubrics on the textbook's companion website. You may want to consider how you would share artifacts from your own rubric as an example.

Monitor
Determine whether you can successfully generate methods for sharing artifacts based on your own rubric. How can you keep critical information secure? What methods support collaboration and further reflection?

Evaluate and Extend
Extend your findings to classroom settings. Develop guidelines for the sharing of information from rubrics as well as methods for explaining student mastery of content standards to parents.

Summary of Scoring Expectations and Practices

Whether used for formative or summative assessments, scoring practices often involve scoring keys, checklists, or rubrics. Forced-choice and some open-ended assessments can be scored using scoring keys. Other open-ended assessments, as well as performance and product-based assessments, usually require the use of checklists or rubrics. The results of these assessments can be used to provide students with feedback as to their learning progress and provide you with feedback as to the effectiveness of your lesson.

Collecting, Analyzing, and Reporting Student Data

Once you have scored your assessments, you typically need to report the results to a variety of other stakeholders, especially parents and school administrators. Maybe you still own a few handwritten report cards, perhaps from your earliest years of school. These are artifacts of a bygone era. Electronic gradebooks not only save teachers hours of time from having to provide handwritten summative reports at the end of a grading period, but also make it easier to generate early reports to inform parents of student success as well as poor performances. Stand-alone gradebook software may allow you to print progress reports for an entire class in a few minutes, whereas online gradebooks can provide reports on-demand. As you recall from the Story from Practice that began this chapter, online gradebooks can support frequent and consistent communication between home and school, often through secure e-mail or other messaging tools. The greatest boon is the early identification and reporting of student difficulties that can lead to identifying helpful interventions before the problems become insurmountable.

Electronic gradebooks can provide confirmation of trends in student performance early in the instructional process (see Figure 7.12). Although you will undoubtedly have some indication that some students are having difficulties, based on their daily performances and participation, some electronic gradebooks provide visual cues and organizational features to help identify low performing students on a daily basis. Graphing features are common in many electronic gradebooks and student performances can often be visually represented in easy-to-read, colorful line or bar graphs with a few clicks. You can use these features to check the performances of individuals or groups of students over time or to compare performances across groups. You may

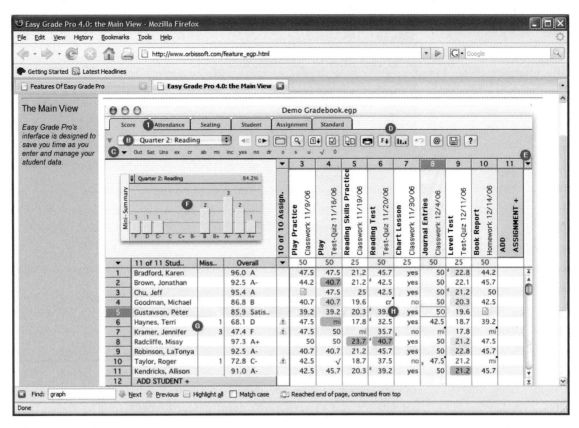

Figure 7.12
Electronic gradebooks typically include powerful graphic analysis tools. Courtesy Edline.

want to track select groups of students, such as students formally designated as "at-risk." Networked gradebooks may allow you and your colleagues, such as an IEP team, to track the progress of an individual student or groups of students across multiple classes using real-time data. Try doing *that* with paper gradebooks!

Unlike paper-based gradebooks, electronic gradebooks provide more than just a place to store grades. They can often support data analysis and reporting, as well. Final grade averages are easily calculated and are often available at all times through the grading period. Different types of grades, such as weighted grades or grades for multipart assessments, are easily included and assigned appropriate significance without the need for a calculator. Using predetermined formulas, student grades in a class will always be calculated the same way, reducing the possibility of error. As long as you set up the weights and averaging criteria correctly, you have less chance for incorrectly reporting student grades.

Online student information systems (SIS) can store and report more than grades. They can help record student attendance. They can present longitudinal data about student performance as well as identify specific student needs. They can link to cafeteria and health records. They can indicate class and transportation schedules, such as the appropriate buses students should ride. Some student information systems can be accessed by teachers and staff throughout the building, sometimes through wireless handheld devices, such as PDAs. Some may even allow you to include a picture of each student. All of these data are important for better understanding how and why your students perform the way they do.

If your school or district has not adopted a networked student information system, you can still use digital technologies to record a great deal of data. Electronic collections of student performance, attendance, and related data can be as simple as keeping records in a directory (folder) on a file server. Even stand-alone (as opposed

APPLY TO PRACTICE

Reporting to Stakeholders

1. Investigate common features of student information systems (SIS). You can do this by investigating product websites, reviewing product descriptions in journals and magazines, visiting a local school that utilizes one, or attending an educational conference and viewing vendor demonstrations. You may even consider asking for a SIS demonstration for you and others in your class from a product representative. It may be best to divide and conquer by having teams or groups of students investigate different products and share their information.

2. As you review various systems, consider the following questions:

    * What technology skills, required by the SIS, are you confident with and which ones would require practice or training?
    * What kinds of data are collected by the SIS? Can you include standards or learning goals and student progress toward those standards?
    * What kind of progress reports can be created for sharing with students in class or with parents, such as in a parent conference?
    * How is two-way communication supported between you and stakeholder groups? Does it provide options for families with limited Internet access or for having to export data in different formats?

3. Compare and discuss your findings with other members of your class.

to networked) electronic gradebooks often include the opportunity to record student attendance and to create anecdotal notes. Records such as these, indicating days when students behave uncharacteristically, can be compared to other records of student data that may be stored in different offices throughout the school. A variety of data are sometimes required to fully understand student performance; new digital technologies often provide a means for schools to share pertinent student data with faculty and staff.

Evaluating Students' Uses of Technology

In a textbook designed to help you develop your technology skills for teaching, it seems natural that you would also consider how you will evaluate the technology proficiency of your students. It is important to know your students' technology proficiencies so that you can plan and implement appropriate learning activities and assessments. Although many technologies have found their way into the classroom, few have had as large an impact on teaching and learning as computers. As you learned in Chapter 1, networked computers and the skills related to them, commonly referred to as information and communications technology, or ICT, have also generated national and international discussions about what it means to be "technology literate" and the role schools play in helping students become so.

The importance of technology proficiency has received greater attention through recent legislation. The latest reauthorization of the *Elementary and Secondary Education Act*, commonly called *No Child Left Behind* (Pub. L. No. 107-110), specifically calls for all students entering high school to be technologically literate. The law falls short, however, on offering any guidance on how students will demonstrate that proficiency, any suggestions for assessments that can be used, or how the data will be collected and reported. Although this legislation makes technology proficiency a national priority for schools, this shifting definition of technology literacy or proficiency is difficult to pinpoint. Specifically, Title II, Part D, Goal 2 (a) of the law reads as follows:

> To assist every student in crossing the digital divide by ensuring that every student is technologically literate by the time the student finishes the eighth grade, regardless of the student's race, ethnicity, gender, family income, geographic location, or disability.

The importance of having students prepared to live and work in a technology-dependent environment has prompted several organizations to make attempts to hit the moving target of defining technology proficiency. As you are well aware, ISTE established technology standards for students (see Figure 1.7 in Chapter 1) and some version of these standards (or the original ISTE NETS-S) have been adopted by many states. These standards provide broad guidelines of what students should know and be able to do with technology.

Once the states adopted the ISTE NETS-S or created their own standards, they then set out to develop assessments to determine whether students could demonstrate them. Early tests mirrored the early computer curricula previously described in Chapter 1 that focused heavily on recall of facts, such as important milestones in the history of computers or the names and functions of hardware components. Just as the rapid evolution of technology changed curricula and the definition of technology proficiency, many state assessment programs for computer literacy or technology literacy disappeared. Some states have dropped their student technology standards altogether and instead have embedded technology proficiencies within content standards. Whether stated or implied, many states also encourage the use of appropriate technologies to support the mastery of content standards rather than isolating technology skill development.

To demonstrate the embedded nature of technology proficiency within content standards and how your assessments can help you monitor and evaluate that proficiency, let's review a few content standards and analyze them for explicit and implied technology proficiencies. Figure 7.13 provides excerpts of English content standards focused on writing at the middle school level from three different states. (Please note that these are not complete standards and have been formatted for consistency of presentation.) Notice that some technology tools are specified in some of the

California	Florida	Texas
Students write clear, coherent, and focused essays. The writing exhibits students' awareness of audience and purpose. Essays contain formal introductions, supporting evidence, and conclusions. Students progress through the stages of the writing process as needed.	The student writes to communicate ideas and information effectively.	Writing/processes. The student selects and uses writing processes for self-initiated and assigned writing. The student is expected to:
• Create compositions that establish a controlling impression, have a coherent thesis, and end with a clear and well-supported conclusion. • Establish coherence within and among paragraphs through effective transitions, parallel structures, and similar writing techniques. • Support theses or conclusions with analogies, paraphrases, quotations, opinions from authorities, comparisons, and similar devices. • Plan and conduct multiple-step information searches by using computer networks and modems. • Achieve an effective balance between researched information and original ideas.	• Writes text, notes, outlines, comments, observations that demonstrate comprehension of content and experiences from a variety of media. • Organizes information using alphabetical, chronological, and numerical systems. • Selects and uses appropriate formats for writing, including narrative, persuasive, and expository formats, according to the intended audience, purpose, and occasion. • Uses electronic technology including databases and software to gather information and communicate new knowledge.	• Generate ideas and plans for writing by using prewriting strategies such as brainstorming, graphic organizers, notes, and logs. • Develop drafts by categorizing ideas, organizing them into paragraphs, and blending paragraphs within larger units of text. • Revise selected drafts by adding, elaborating, deleting, combining, and rearranging text. • Use available technology to support aspects of creating, revising, editing, and publishing texts. • Refine selected pieces frequently to "publish" for general and specific audiences. • Select and use reference materials and resources as needed for writing, revising, and editing final drafts.

Note: These standards have been reformatted for consistency.

Figure 7.13
Comparison of three states' standards and objectives for writing.

objectives in each standard for each state. But many of the other content standards, although not mentioning specific technologies, can easily be demonstrated by writing projects that utilize common technology-supported activities, whether electronic journaling, using a word processor, creating an electronic presentation, developing a web page, or participating in a threaded discussion. The choices you make for doing so are governed by your content knowledge and technology proficiency, as well as the technology proficiency of your students.

Over time, many of these standards for writing—like many content standards—will remain the same. The technologies, however, will change. By selecting technologies appropriate for the assessment of these content standards, you are also providing the opportunity to evaluate your students' technology proficiencies. As you can see from reviewing these example standards, you may do so explicitly or by embedding technology proficiencies in the way you teach and your students learn relevant content.

ISTE NETS-T Standard 2 requires you to "design, develop, and evaluate authentic learning experiences and assessments incorporating contemporary tools and resources to maximize content learning in context and to develop the knowledge, skills, and attitudes identified in the NETS•S." Furthermore, you are expected to "provide students with multiple and varied formative and summative assessments aligned with content and technology standards and use resulting data to inform learning and teaching." Throughout this chapter, we have been preparing you to do this. With the shifting emphasis from isolated technology standards to embedding technology proficiencies in content standards, your decisions for assessing technology proficiency fall in line with assessing students' mastery of your content standards as a whole. As you develop and implement lessons and units, the technologies you select for your activities and assessments should be representative of those embedded in your content domain. Assessing student technology proficiency then becomes part of monitoring and evaluating how well your students achieve your learning goals.

New Trends in Technology-Assisted Assessments of Technology Proficiency

Some interesting assessments of technology proficiency have been developed that rely on some of the capabilities of technology to create unique learning and assessment environments. Most of these assessments occur in one of two different types of simulated environments.

The first type of simulated environment is the re-creation of common software tools based on general features. These simulated applications allow the user to perform common tasks, such as creating and saving documents, creating a calculation in a spreadsheet application, finding information from a digital data source, or creating and sending electronic mail. Not developed solely for measuring student proficiencies, these simulated programs can be used to assess the proficiencies of teachers as well. Although the simulations are generic, many of the skills tested are still basic operational skills and many still incorporate forced-choice question formats. Some do allow users to complete the tasks by more than one strategy, such as using shortcut keys, menu commands, or buttons on a toolbar to complete the same cutting and pasting task.

The second form of simulation truly starts to draw on the power of technology to create assessments that would not otherwise be possible with paper and pencil. These assessments also use simulations of common software, such as web browsers, e-mail programs, and word processors, but students use these tools to tackle complex problems. Not only do they have to demonstrate basic operational skills, but they need to show how they use these technologies to solve the problems. Although not available for widespread use, a few prototype assessment systems of this nature have been developed and offer exciting possibilities for creating highly authentic and engaging assessments in all content areas—not just for determining technology proficiency.

Chapter Summary

This chapter has emphasized the critical role of assessment when developing authentic learning experiences. Assessment is more than the assigning of grades and serves a critical role in monitoring and evaluating the academic progress of your students. In Chapter 6, we discussed the value of using a variety of formal and informal data to inform your instructional decisions. Assessments should be woven throughout instruction to serve many purposes and can take many forms. Just as you will vary your instruction and select multiple methods for presenting your instruction, you will draw upon multiple assessment formats and tools to support them. And although it will be important for you to be able to monitor the technology proficiencies of your students, you may find that the technologies you choose to do so will depend most on making good choices for supporting your instruction and assessment. Assessment data also help you determine the effectiveness of your own instructional choices including the selection of technology-based resources. As a teacher it is important to know whether *how* you teach, with or without digital technology, is effective in helping students learn the intended content.

YOUR PORTFOLIO

To begin to demonstrate competency in ISTE NETS-T Standard 2.d, return to the lesson activities you began in earlier chapters and add your assessment strategies.

1. Develop assessments and scoring guidelines based on the lesson or unit plan, to which technology is a major contributor.
2. Make sure your assessments are clearly connected to the content and technology standards addressed by your lesson as well as the activities contained within the lesson.

References

Andrade, H. G. (2005). Teaching with rubrics: The good, the bad, and the ugly. *College Teaching*, 53(1), 27–30.

Assessment Reform Group. (1999). *Assessment for learning: Beyond the black box.* Cambridge, UK: University of Cambridge School of Education.

Bennett, R. E. (1998). *Reinventing assessment: Speculations on the future of large-scale educational testing.* Princeton, NJ: Educational Testing Service (ETS).

Bennett, R. E. (2001). How the Internet will help large-scale assessment reinvent itself. *Education Policy Analysis Archives*, 9(5). Retrieved January 22, 2001, from http://epaa.asu.edu/epaa/v9n5.html

Brookhart, S. M. (1999). The art and science of classroom assessment: The missing part of pedagogy. *ASHE-ERIC Higher Education Report*, 27(1). Washington, DC: The George Washington University, Graduate School of Education and Human Development.

Butler, D. H., & Winne, P. H. (1995). Feedback and self-regulated learning: A theoretical synthesis. *Review of Educational Research*, 65, 245–281.

Dick, W., Carey, L., & Carey, J. O. (2005). *The systematic design of instruction* (6th ed.). New York: HarperCollins.

Educational Testing Service (ETS). (2001, July/August). People in the know series: Ray Christensen. *Capital News & Views*. 1–3. Washington, DC: State and Federal Relations Office.

Fletcher, J. D. (1992). *Individualized systems of instruction.* Alexandria, VA: Institute for Defense Analyses. (ERIC Document Reproduction Service No. ED 355 917).

Meijer, R. R., & Mering, M. L. (1999). Computerized adaptive testing: Overview and introduction. *Applied Psychological Measurement*, 23, 187–194.

Pub. L. No. 107-110. (No Child Left Behind Act of 2001).

Public Schools of North Carolina. (2006). *North Carolina standard course of study.* Retrieved May 9, 2006, from http://www.dpi.state.nc.us/curriculum/

Shepard, L. A. (2000). *The role of classroom assessment in teaching and learning. CSE Technical Report* 517. Los Angeles: Center for the Study of Evaluation, Standards, and Student Testing (CRESST).

Svinicki, M. D. (2004). Authentic assessment: Testing in reality. *New Directions for Teaching and Learning*, 2004(100), 23–39.

Wainer, H. (2000). Introduction and history. In H. Wainer (Ed.), *Computerized adaptive testing: A primer* (2nd ed.) (pp. 1–21). Mahwah, NJ: Lawrence Erlbaum.

Wiggins, G. (1998). *Educative assessment: Designing assessments to inform and improve student performance*. San Francisco: Jossey-Bass.

8

Wadsworth/Cengage Learning

Selecting and Maintaining Digital Resources

Standard 3.a requires you to "demonstrate fluency in technology systems and the transfer of current knowledge to new technologies and situations." In doing so, you are expected to select and use hardware and software best suited to particular learning experiences—and plan student learning experiences that appropriately use these tools (ISTE, 2008). This involves identifying and solving common hardware and software problems as well. Throughout this book, we have focused on planning and management strategies that support students during their technology-based learning experiences. In this chapter, we will focus on the selection of hardware and software resources best suited to particular learning experiences. We'll also discuss hardware and software maintenance techniques, including techniques to identify and solve common hardware and software problems.

As a teacher, you will encounter a wide variety of classroom technology resources throughout your career. Although the U.S.

ISTE Standards addressed in this chapter

NETS-T 3. Model Digital-Age Work and Learning

Teachers exhibit knowledge, skills, and work processes representative of an innovative professional in a global and digital society. Teachers:

a. demonstrate fluency in technology systems and the transfer of current knowledge to new technologies and situations

Note: Chapter 9 addresses Standard 3.b., 3.c., and 3.d.

Outcomes

In this chapter, you will

■ Select and evaluate hardware and software in response to the learning needs of your students.
■ Identify strategies to support the routine maintenance of computer hardware and software systems.
■ Troubleshoot routine problems as they arise.

Department of Education (Wells & Lewis, 2006) reported that on average, there is one instructional computer with Internet access available to every 3.8 students across the nation, some schools have more than that; others have less. Schools will vary in the type and number of computers and other digital technologies available. They will also differ in how they make those resources available to teachers. You may find yourself in a school with all the technology resources you desire. But it's also possible that you'll find yourself in a school where the technology is scarce and outdated. Many times, students have better resources at home than at school; other times, the only access students have is in school. How will you apply your current knowledge of selecting and maintaining technology systems as you assume the role of an instructional leader in your school?

Have you ever bought a computer before? If not, what about a different technology, such as a television, a car, or a cell phone? What motivated you to make that purchase? What goals did you have for the technology? What needs did you think it could fill? Perhaps you wanted a computer so you could complete homework assignments using word-processing software so they'd be neater and easier to revise. Perhaps you wanted to access the Internet to do research for some of your classes or even to pursue areas of interest outside of school, or maybe you wanted to be able to chat with your friends by e-mail or instant messaging, or to create your own website or blog. Your prior experiences with these technologies will assist you in selecting, using, and maintaining digital resources in your classroom.

STORIES FROM PRACTICE

Keeping Up with New Technologies . . . and the Kids!

It's taken me a while, but I no longer worry about asking my students for help with technology. Just the other day, I was working with my fifth grade class on identifying the main elements of a story we were reading. We were using concept-mapping software to identify elements such as setting, mood, main characters . . . things like that. We did an example together in class first but I had given my students some creative leeway when they were developing their own concept maps, you know, using different fonts, colors, and even including graphics if they wanted. A couple of the students really took advantage of that opportunity and designed some really

beautiful maps, so I wanted to show them to the rest of the class.

We were using laptops in the class and instead of transferring the files I just moved each student's laptop to the projector at the front of the room. Of course, this was a day I was being observed, so there was a little added pressure. When I got the first laptop to the front of the room, I just couldn't get the projector cable to connect. I tried it one way, then upside down, and was just getting really frustrated. Being observed didn't help either. So I asked the student who had designed the map, Jaime, to come up and help me connect his laptop to the projector while I told the rest of the class why

I had selected his example. Of course, Jaime got it connected in just a second and we were able to go on with the lesson immediately.

There was a time when that would have devastated me, but technology changes so quickly you just can't know everything. Now, I tend to learn just enough about a new application to get it started with my class and then the students teach me new ways to use it. Not only does this make things easier for me, it gives the students a chance to shine as well.

Source: Based on unpublished interview conducted by John Ross.

Selecting and Obtaining Digital Resources and Technologies

As a teacher, your role in obtaining new technology resources will vary depending on the school system in which you work, and even on the specific school within that system. Depending on the size of the system and the relative emphasis on technology integration, your school system may have a team of technology support personnel devoted to helping teachers select instructional technology resources. For other schools, you may be able to voice your own needs and influence technology selections by serving on a school or district technology committee that actually reviews software and hardware needs, conducts research for solutions, and makes recommendations for purchase. Even if you don't serve on a technology committee specifically, most schools and districts have policies and procedures that allow classroom teachers to voice their needs for technology resources. Once hired, you should find out the process for requesting technology resources for your classroom including required forms you'll have to complete and to whom you'll have to address your requests, whether a lead teacher, principal, or technology coordinator.

The following sections describe characteristics of hardware and software and suggest some things you should keep in mind as you select technologies to meet your needs and those of your students.

Software Selection

Very often, when people think about purchasing new and emerging technologies, they focus on hardware. We're often inundated with advertisements about the new capacities of hardware and it seems like new hardware continues to gets smaller, faster, and more powerful at an amazing rate. But it's really the software that does the critical work in your classroom. A writing assignment is of little value on a computer without word-processing software. A science lab with probeware is useless without the software that helps to collect, analyze, and report the data you collect via the probes. Even the Internet is inaccessible without a web browser or e-mail program. Although hardware is still a critical consideration, it is usually the software that you should review first in terms of meeting your goals. An acceptable software solution may then influence subsequent hardware purchases.

Another reason for focusing on software first is because as a teacher you may have little influence over the selection of hardware in your school. Many schools and districts buy computers and other technology in bulk from district- or state-approved vendors and you may not get a say in these decisions. Many of these computers are bundled with common software, such as word processors, spreadsheets, and databases, as well as communications software that allows you to access and utilize the Internet, whether through a web browser or via e-mail software. In addition, many schools provide access to instructional content through subscription services, whether an online database of journals and news articles or entire lessons and activities. However, it *is* likely that you will have a say in the selection of software to directly support your classroom instruction.

Computer software can enhance your instruction in several ways. In Chapter 4 we mentioned that computer software could serve as a tutor, as a mindtool, or as a support for conversation (Wegerif, 2002). As you recall, when technology is used as a *tutor*, the software explicitly teaches or provides practice with a specific body of content. When technology is used as a *mindtool*, it serves as a semantic organization tool, simulation and visualization tool, or knowledge-building tool. Mindtools can include word processors, databases, spreadsheets, multimedia or web-development software, concept-mapping software, and other tools that help students and teachers represent, manipulate, or reflect on what they know (Jonassen, 2006). As a *support for conversation*, the computer software contributes to conversations among learners, and thus facilitates group and community learning. Keep in mind that many software titles include components of several categories, and thus could be classified in more than one way. For example, video-editing software may contain a tutorial on techniques to maintain visual continuity as well as serve as a mindtool by providing the means to edit video footage.

The *type* of software you select as well as the actual software program can be influenced by and alternately influence decisions you and your colleagues may make about hardware selection.

Hardware Selection

Based on the best software application to satisfy your goals, you may require different types of hardware. You may select drill-and-practice software that can run on computers that require little in terms of memory and processing power. Or you may select simulation software that requires capturing real-time data through probes attached to handheld devices that then must interface with computer workstations. And maybe you have the opportunity to work with VR (virtual reality) applications that allow your students to solve complex social and historical problems but that require very powerful computers and unique hardware sensors. All of these configurations are found in schools today, so don't eliminate a possibility until you've determined the best fit with your needs.

Hardware comes in all shapes and sizes but it may be easiest to group your decisions about selecting hardware into three categories:

- existing hardware that will address your need without any modifications
- existing hardware that will address your need after modifications
- new hardware that is selected specifically to address the need

Since the late 1980s schools have purchased a great deal of hardware and networking. Most schools and districts purchase large-ticket items, such as computers, printers, photocopiers, and fax machines from a district- or state-approved list. Many schools purchase identical workstations in volume to get the best price, streamline installation, and optimize the limited technical support capacity that most schools face. Whether distributed across classrooms or available in labs, the school you work in is likely to have a substantial base of hardware from which you can select. If your goal can be met by the use of readily available tools, your school may have sufficient existing hardware to meet your needs.

The most common modifications made to existing hardware are increasing the memory and processing power to run desired software. You may have had great success with some math software that was installed on your computers, but newer versions of the software may tax existing configurations and require more memory or processing power. In addition, you may want to capitalize on components of existing hardware that are not normally used or have had limited use to date, such as the use of sound or video. Other software may require the purchase of additional peripherals such as scanners, cameras, and probes, or input devices such as styluses that require you to modify the computer system as a whole, if not simply a single hardware device.

Finally, some applications may require modification of the networking configurations or capacity of existing hardware. This may be the most difficult modification in terms of buy-in from your technical support personnel, but if the instructional benefits warrant these modifications, you should gather your data to support your recommendation. In terms of configurations, you may want to incorporate communications software, such as instant messaging or blogs, in your language arts classroom. This type of access to web-based applications may require a change in the security settings of your school's network. They may also require a change in your school or district's acceptable use policy as many new technologies are often banned from schools before they are accepted in organized instructional activities. You also may help your school determine that even though some learning experiences will require a large amount of dedicated bandwidth, such as video- or webconferencing, they can truly be beneficial to your students. For example, you may want to participate in a series of videoconferences from a university or participate in virtual field trips to remote museums through webconferencing software. If these instructional opportunities offer the best means to satisfy the goals of your instruction, it may be worth the effort to convince technology and administrative personnel to consider modifying your hardware and network infrastructures and the policies that support their use.

Of course, there are times when you will want to recommend acquiring new hardware. When selecting hardware it's often tempting to select the most powerful items with as many features as possible instead of basing your decision on the necessary features. New hardware often contains numerous features you may never use or that you would be better off using on a different device. For example, digital video cameras contain many special effects. Many casual users seldom use the effects and serious users often are more likely to use software-based special effects installed on their computers rather than the effects built into the camera. Even cell phones do so many more things than just operate as phones, but not everyone needs to use all those features. Although it is appealing to have the latest available hardware, it often is more economical to hold back just a little. Size and speed are features that often command a premium price without necessarily increasing your ability to meet your needs.

Selecting Digital Resources and Technologies

Because of the numerous types of technologies available today, there's a strong chance you'll be able to find technology resources that will satisfy your goal. Sometimes you may find an overwhelming number of products that make all kinds of claims of effectiveness in a range of prices from affordable to unbelievable. In order to make the best decisions about software and hardware, you'll need some practical methods for taking action to determine the best solution. Some of the common action steps that support selecting technology-based resources include setting goals for technology use, specifying the requirements for use, locating promising resources, reading reviews and getting recommendations from others, and evaluating the resources to determine whether they are suitable for your instructional needs. The following section presents some practical steps you can follow related to each of these steps.

Set a Goal for Technology Use

Before choosing hardware or software you need to know what you want it to do. Just like that cell phone or personal computer you were asked to think about earlier, you need to determine the goal you have for the new resource. In most cases, this will be defined by the learning needs of your students and curriculum. For example, you may find that some students perform better if they are able to view animations or videos of processes or systems before analyzing their component parts. Your curriculum may have complex topics that are hard for students to visualize, such as understanding the customs or social activities of past or distant cultures. Or you may want to find a safe way for students to manipulate dangerous or expensive chemicals or other substances within a limited timeframe. Finally, there may be some topics that students learn more readily when they are able to work in groups and create a product such as a web page or presentation. Different combinations of technologies can meet all of these learning goals.

Examine the goals that you want your students to accomplish and if and how technology-based resources can contribute to them. Based on the tasks students should perform and the way you want technologies to enhance your instruction, you can determine the requirements for the technologies you need. What content area and grade level is of interest? Do the materials need to be suitable for a particular pedagogy? Do you want to use the technology as a "tutor" to learn new information or will you use it to supplement information you have already presented? Or do you want to use the technology as a tool by which students demonstrate their learning? Perhaps they will use it to create a product, such as a web page or group

APPLY TO PRACTICE

Choosing Technology That Matches Your Goals

1. Identify some of the different needs you will face as a classroom teacher and determine your goals for meeting those needs. These may include goals related to instruction (e.g., develop an activity that allows my students to interact and share ideas with students from different cultural or ethnic backgrounds), goals related to your curriculum (e.g., identify resources to supplement my instruction that students and parents access at home), or goals related to recordkeeping or resource management (e.g., create a tracking system to evaluate the effectiveness of my lessons).

2. Consider the type of software that can help you meet these goals. If the software is instructional, what type is it? How does it match your teaching style? Have you used similar software before? What additional skills are required to operate the software?

3. What hardware is necessary for running the software? Is it readily available or does it require specialized hardware? If new hardware must be purchased, what justifications can you provide for the expense? Do you know how to operate all the hardware involved in satisfying the needs? If not, what additional skills and knowledge do you require?

4. Share your responses with colleagues. For those who selected similar goals, how did your software and hardware proposals align? What differences were there? What additional software or hardware options could you suggest for those with different goals?

presentation, or they can use technologies similar to those used by experts in a specific profession.

Once you've determined your goal, you need to take action by selecting possible technologies to meet that goal. This next step may be a little more complex, especially if you don't routinely keep up with trends and developments in new and emerging technologies. What's possible? How will you know? Where do you find it? Sometimes finding the answers to these questions can be a lot of fun! They may even provide you with an opportunity to improve or enhance your teaching by introducing you to new methods, a range of new resources, or by saving you time and effort. Chances are that other teachers have had the same needs as you and there just may be several different technology resources that have been developed to meet them. The resources you find may be high- or low-tech, but you'll need a process to make the most of your time and that provides you with the best information to make your recommendations.

Specify Requirements

After you've identified a goal for the use of technology, you'll need to consider any requirements or restrictions that will influence your decision. The computers in your school or district may also have specific requirements in terms of accessibility. If you cannot install new software on the school computers you may need to use software that can be maintained at a distance over a network. In addition, you need to consider whether the software can interface with existing software, such as by exporting or importing data or other elements created by the school's word-processing or spreadsheet applications.

Some schools limit computer choices to one version of an operating system, which can be beneficial to technology support personnel who then only have to remain current in the intricacies of a single system. This certainly influences the actual software you purchase, but possibly not the type. For example, if you find concept-mapping software that you'd like to use that is normally developed for the Macintosh operating system, chances are you can find a similar type of concept-mapping software that runs on a Windows-based machine. Or you may find some promising lesson activities for a particular brand of graphing calculator that you then can modify or repurpose to use with the graphing calculators already owned by your school. Sometimes though, you may observe or evaluate some instructional applications that encourage you to request modifying the existing hardware infrastructure at your school.

You also have to consider the requirements of your network. How great of a demand will the new resource place on the school or district's network capacity? As the Internet has become more robust in terms of the content it contains and the applications it can support, many school networks quickly have become overburdened by new applications that were not originally planned for. A recent example of this is the popularity of video streaming services that allow teachers to view and download small video segments for use in class, rather than having to obtain full-length videos and the projection equipment to show them. In some school districts, these services were so popular that school networks were insufficient to handle other important tasks related to managing student data, communications among staff, and accessing other instructional resources. In this case, the network requirements were not considered prior to purchasing the streaming video service.

Of course, the hardware you have available will have requirements that must be met. Besides the operating platform, there may be issues concerning the use of audio or video, memory, or supporting peripherals. Audio in a lab setting is disruptive to learning if headphones are not available. Programs that require so much memory that they slow down or crash computers or don't allow other software to run can be counterproductive as well. Some software may also require peripherals such as scanners or cameras, and if this equipment is already available in your school, you may have to consider whether the new solution will operate on your existing peripherals or require new equipment (see Figure 8.1).

What about student groupings or computer arrangements? Does the new technology match your own learning style and others who will use it? Can you and your students benefit from the new technologies fairly quickly or is extensive training and practice required—for either you or your students? Is the technology strictly lab-based or can you incorporate it into your classroom?

And, finally, is cost an issue? Although these other requirements are truly important factors to consider, some resources you identify that have the greatest potential may still be beyond the budget allotted for their purchase. However, if you truly believe in the potential of new technologies for yielding a high return on investment in terms of significant gains in student achievement, you may find it worthwhile to seek funding for these purchases by writing grants, fundraising, or contacting possible donors. Requirements are guidelines that should shape your decision making, but

Figure 8.1
It is important to consider the needs of all learners when incorporating modern multimedia software.

sometimes the potential benefits of a resource override the limitations of requirements and actually help those requirements become more flexible and accommodating. After you've decided on the requirements for the technology resources to meet your goals, you can begin to identify materials that meet your needs.

Locate Resources

There are many ways to identify technology-based resources that may meet your requirements. First, investigate the resources available to you locally. Determine what software is installed on your classroom computers and school network. Many textbooks include CD-ROMs and companion websites. As you survey the available resources, check with the library media or technology specialists in your school and district to determine what other instructional resources are available to you. Are instructional television programs available for viewing in your class? Are videotapes or DVDs available at the school or through interlibrary loan programs? Check to see if any CD-ROMS, DVDs, and software titles are maintained by the district for use in the classroom. Some schools have web-based resource centers that allow you to search, preview, and schedule instructional media well ahead of time.

Of course, the resources available locally are just a small sample of the resources available to you. As you well know, a massive storehouse of resources is at your disposal via the Internet. For example, museums, historical foundations, government programs, and a wide range of educational nonprofits offer interactive educational programming on their websites. WebQuests are a popular way to organize web-based resources for teaching and learning and you'll find many of them online. Podcasts, which are digital audio files that can be downloaded from the Internet and played back on an MP3 player or computer, also have become popular in education and may be used to support student learning in your classroom. The web provides access to a variety of software that is free or low-cost to the educational community. When selecting resources from the Internet, you can begin by reviewing the links and recommendations at one of the many portals for teachers.

So what do you do if you don't find anything that meets your requirements locally or on the web? Numerous software catalogs will come across your desk and there are innumerable websites that offer educational hardware and software. But before you begin to select software for purchase, check on the specific procedures that you should follow. You may have to fill out forms or make justifications for the purchase of any new technology. Just like hardware, many districts and states maintain a list of approved vendors who have agreed to provide software at reduced prices. The increase in digital resources has prompted some states to maintain a list of software titles that have been adopted at the state level. Whether your state maintains a list of approved software or not, it's important that software be selected as carefully as the other educational resources in your classroom.

After reviewing all these resources, numerous software titles may catch your interest, but in order to determine what is worth purchasing, you should either evaluate the software yourself, find out if others recommend the title, or both. Either way, you'll need some information about your possible selections.

Read Reviews and Recommendations

It's useful to read reviews of the potential technology resources in order to narrow the pool of programs that you actually evaluate. There simply isn't enough time to evaluate all the technologies available. Both software and hardware reviews are readily available in magazines, journals, and on the Internet. Professional organizations and magazines routinely publish these reviews. Book and software distributors (such as Amazon.com) often include reviews by users on their websites. As you're reading, remember that reviews represent a subjective judgment, so make sure you identify who reviewed the technology and what criteria they used to evaluate it. Reviews can be conducted by a wide variety of people—university faculty, teachers,

TOOLS FOR USE

Using Podcasts in Your Classroom

Podcasts are digital audio files that can be downloaded from the Internet and played back on an MP3 player or computer. Although made popular by Apple's MP3 player, the iPod, the "pod" part of podcast simply refers to "play on demand," meaning that you or your students can play it whenever and wherever you want. Free software is available for most computers that can play podcast files, and many different brands of portable media players are now available. Podcasts were originally audio-only files, but newer formats allow the inclusion of images in slide-show fashion or even video, sometimes referred to as "vodcasts."

Here are some things to consider when using podcasts in your classroom.

- *The Player:* If you're going to use podcasts to supplement your instruction, consider the hardware that will be used and the necessary peripherals. Since they are media files, computers will have to be media-ready and will need sound cards, speakers, or headphones. Consider whether you want to play the podcasts for your whole class at one time, or have students access them on their own in a lab or other multi-computer setting. You can also make them available for students to use at home, but find out how many students have the technology needed to access them, and plan alternative options for students who do not have access at home.

- *The Software:* The most common software used to play podcasts on a computer is Apple's iTunes. iTunes is free and available for both Mac and Windows operating systems but is only one option. Additional software is available to play podcasts and a quick Internet search can find several choices. No matter which application you use, you may need to collaborate with your school technology staff to make sure that an appropriate player for podcasts is installed on your computers, as not all media players are able to play podcast files.

- *The Podcast Episodes:* Podcasts are available from a range of providers, whether specifically targeted at schools or not. The iTunes store categorizes podcast episodes and series so you can quickly find education-related podcasts. Another feature is iTunesU, which is a clearinghouse of podcasts from colleges, universities, public radio, and other education-related sources. Most of these series and episodes on iTunes and iTunesU are free.

- *Subscription Service:* Many podcasts available through iTunes or other services add new episodes on a routine basis. That's what makes them podcasts, because you can subscribe to them and they automatically upload to your player when a new episode is available. Even if you don't plan to have routine updates to your podcasts, your students can benefit from this technology in the form of study guides, lecture notes, or student presentations.

students, parents, independent reviewers, and so forth. No matter how well you attempt to identify the criteria on which the software will be evaluated, ultimately, judgments are based on an individual's past experiences, beliefs, and biases. Try to determine how well the reviewer's needs and situation matches your own goals and teaching situation. A reviewer in a large, urban district who used software in a lab setting may not have the same experience as someone in a smaller school with five computers in the classroom. Also try to determine whether the reviewer actually used the software in an instructional setting, or whether they simply reviewed it based on a set of criteria. Keep in mind that just because it is recommended by someone somewhere, it may not be appropriate for your needs. You may want to consider using only nationally recognized sources of software reviews to narrow your pool.

In addition, don't forget to ask your colleagues. What technology do they use and what are the benefits they've experienced? Are there any limitations that they've found? Maybe a group of teachers from your school would be interested in forming a study group that reviewed technology resources throughout the year. Some schools or districts maintain their own databases of technology reviews—especially software—completed by local teachers. However, to facilitate comparisons among products in the database, all the teachers in the school or district must use a common set of evaluation procedures. A local database of software reviews can save individual teachers considerable time, as they may consult it prior to conducting their own investigations. In addition, you may be able to contact the teacher/reviewer and chat about the features of the product. It's quite possible that there are positive (or negative) aspects of the technology that would suit your needs more (or less) than the person who originally reviewed it.

You should also access your virtual community of colleagues as a source of information (see Figure 8.2). You may want to go to an online lesson plan website and

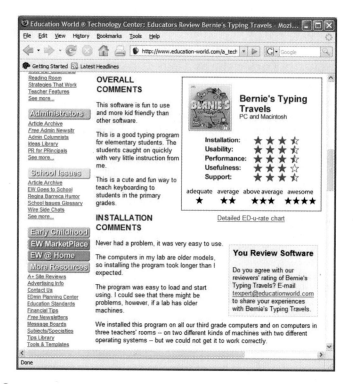

Figure 8.2

Technology reviews by teachers for teachers can provide valuable insights on software you are considering. *Source:* Copyright 1996–2008 by Education World, Inc. All Rights Reserved.

note the hardware and software titles that appear most frequently in lessons related to your grade and subject. If you're interested in a particular technology, locate a teachers' discussion forum and search the archives to see if it has been discussed. If not, and the group or message board lends itself to such discussions, ask for the recommendations of others.

As you collect information from catalogs, product descriptions reviews, and recommendations, you may want to keep records of how the various software titles compare on criteria of interest. Read the relevant reviews in a systematic fashion and create a form, database, or spreadsheet to compile your results (see Figure 8.3). You'll want to collect information on the name, publisher or distributor, grade level, type of software, content area, and cost. Fortunately, much of this information is available in catalogs and selection guides.

Also make note of any ideas you have about where the digital resources fit within your curriculum and lesson plans. In order to determine if a particular software program—whether it's a tutorial on the Vietnam War or a web-based exploration of acids and bases—is appropriate for your classroom, you need to look at your instructional goal or objectives and the capabilities of the digital resource. Would it be used to gain attention and establish a context, to provide the primary instruction in the content, to provide practice and feedback, as remediation, or enrichment? As you begin to identify a small list of products for local review, think about where each product fits in your instruction.

Evaluate Technology

Although others can make recommendations, the best way to determine which resources will enhance your lessons is to try them yourself. In order to evaluate new technologies, you need to gain access to a copy of the product for review purposes, determine the criteria on which you will evaluate the product, and preview the product using your criteria.

Relevant Information from Software Reviews

Title:

Publisher/distributor:

Cost:

System requirements:

Grade level:

Type of software:

Content area:

Instructional goals:

Strengths noted in review:

Limitations noted in review:

Overall rating:

Figure 8.3
Sample form used to compare software reviews and recommendations.

APPLY TO PRACTICE

Find Reviews and Recommendations

1. Survey the wide variety of technology reviews that are available in print and on the web. You may actually have a conference coming up where you can review technology as well. It may be helpful to narrow your search down to a topic of interest. If necessary, you can start at the textbook's companion website for a list of websites that provide reviews of technology.
2. Of the resources you found, which provide the most useful information? Why? What characteristics about these resources were helpful? How much trust can you place in the reviews you've found? Which of these have the credibility and longevity that support that decision?
3. Compare the resources you found with colleagues or classmates. Create a master list and keep it in your portfolio so you can return to it once you are charged with finding new technology for your classroom or school.

Secure a Review Copy

After you have located software or hardware of potential interest, you need to access a copy of the product in order to conduct your own evaluation. This is often easier to do with software than hardware, but some hardware vendors will provide samples of easily portable technologies for review. Local resources and websites should be reviewed to determine if they meet your instructional needs. As you know, it's much easier to publish and distribute a website than other types of software, so be especially careful to explore the entire site before using it with your students (see Chapter 4 for more information about reviewing websites). Since links become outdated quickly, you should probably conduct an additional review of the links just prior to your class time.

Many times, you can download a trial version of commercial software from the publishers' website. Some software vendors will allow free previews of an entire program. Other vendors will provide a free demonstration program containing a subset of a larger program. Often trial versions are limited in some way. For example, you may be unable to save your work, the product may include a "watermark" indicating that it was created with a trial version of the software, or the version may expire after 30 days.

 WEB LINK

See the textbook's companion website for a list of websites that publish reviews of technology.

In other cases, a review product is not available. Some vendors will not allow previews without a purchase order, but will allow the teacher to return the product within a specified time period with no financial obligation. Universities, regional educational centers, and some district offices also may maintain different hardware and software for teachers to review. You may also be able to borrow a product from another teacher for preview purposes or contact the vendor to find out if a school or district near you has purchased the product. If you can't obtain a review copy and you're still very interested in the product, ask for an in-school demonstration of the product by a vendor representative or find out if the product will be on display at an upcoming conference or meeting. As a general rule, if there is no way to preview the software, avoid that software.

Establish Criteria for Review

To evaluate educational software, websites, and other digital resources, begin by determining exactly what criteria you will use. Some school districts have developed **software evaluation rubrics** for their teachers to use. Often, teachers develop or locate their own forms. Based on your needs and requirements, locate or develop a standard form on which to record comments and compare features across multiple programs. There are a wide variety of forms available on the web and elsewhere so you should have no trouble locating one to use or adapt to your needs. You will have specific things you will want to observe in the technology, but in general, you'll want to evaluate items such as the following:

- *Content.* Is the content valid? Does it teach what it says it teaches? Is it up-to-date? What topics and subtopics are covered? Is the vocabulary appropriate for the intended audience?
- *Free of bias and stereotypes.* These may not be intentional, but commercially prepared instructional materials, as well as content on the Internet, may include gender, racial/ethnic, or other biases or may reinforce stereotypes that can disengage some of your students. As you review new technologies, consider questions such as the following: Does it avoid stereotypes and attitudes related to age? Does it avoid racism? Is it inclusive and appropriate for both female and male students? Does it promote recognition and acceptance of diverse cultures, languages, and religions? Is there any objectionable content, bias, or stereotyping present? Is it accessible by students with a wide range of physical capabilities? Does it avoid discrimination of any type? Does the learning resource promote tolerance and diversity?
- *Goals and standards.* When evaluating the contents of new technologies, always relate them to your required learning standards and curriculum goals. What standards or curriculum goals are addressed? Some software companies even take the extra step to provide the match between the skills the software teaches and specific curriculum standards and learning objectives.
- *Intended audience.* For what grade level or ability level is it most appropriate? Is it appropriate for a range of ability levels? Can you set the academic level at which your students work? Does the program adjust the level as your students progress?
- *Instructional approach.* Is the instructional approach compatible with your teaching style? Is it grounded in a well-established learning theory? Are there resource guides or supporting lesson plans available? Does the publisher provide tips for integrating the program/product into the curriculum?
- *Product quality and ease of use.* Is it durable? Are there any parts that will be easy to break or lose? Can students with small fingers use it easily? For computer-based applications, consider the appropriateness of the screen design, use of graphics, animations, sound and other media elements, and the feedback provided. Are the appearance, language, text style, and graphic content appropriate for the intended audience? Is the interface logical and the

THE GAME PLAN

Develop a Technology Evaluation Form

Set Goals

Design a technology evaluation form that meets your specific needs.

Take Action

Collect a variety of technology evaluation forms from magazines, journals, the web, or even from school districts with which you have been associated.

Monitor

Review the forms to determine which ones include criteria that you believe are important.

What are the consistent elements that appear across forms? What unique elements should you also consider?

Evaluate and Extend

Create an evaluation form that you could use to compare educational software. Use the form to review at least 3 different software titles to determine if the form includes useful criteria. Using the form may identify additional criteria or may help you streamline your form.

---

software easy to use? Will training be required before you or your students can use it?

- *Documentation.* Is program documentation online, available as a PDF file, or as a user manual? Does it provide information on installation and use of the program? Does it provide tips on overcoming common problems? Is the documentation well written, logically organized, and easy to use?
- *User support.* How is technical support provided? Is there a "help" option available? Does the documentation, software, or supporting website contain a tutorial to teach users how to operate the program? Does the software or website include a demonstration of the program features? Is there a website that provides technical support? Is phone support available or can you request assistance through e-mail or a website?
- *Teacher support.* Are there lesson plans? Background information? Are the objectives and prerequisite skills listed? Are there suggestions for student groupings or allocating time to the computer task? What about activities or worksheets for students to complete before or after their computer work?
- *Equipment needs and compatibility.* What are the system and memory requirements? Will the resource be compatible with your classroom machines? Platform compatibility issues used to be a bigger concern than they are now; however, some software may still be specific to only one platform. If your school installs software on a school or district-wide network, make sure the resources are compatible with the network server.
- *Cost.* How much does it cost for a single copy? A lab pack? Are site licenses available? If so, how much do they cost?

Preview the Technology

It could take a substantial chunk of time if every teacher in a school were to individually review all the software titles and hardware products of potential interest, so you might want to work with other teachers in your school or grade level to share the workload. Develop a plan to disseminate the reviews to other teachers and administrators. Use the review sheet you created in this chapter or one developed by a school or district. Attempt to identify potential classroom applications of the software or other digital resources and make sure they align with the areas of need. Perhaps you could work with a school or district to develop and maintain a database to provide a centralized source of technology reviews conducted by local teachers.

WEB LINK

See the textbook's companion website for a checklist that you can use to evaluate software.

Attitude questionnaire			
Is it easy to use?	☺	😐	☹
Is it fun?	☺	😐	☹
Did you learn new things?	☺	😐	☹
Would you use it again?	☺	😐	☹
Would your friends like it?	☺	😐	☹
How did you like it overall?	☺	😐	☹

Figure 8.4
Attitude questionnaire for use with young children.

After you have conducted your own evaluation, if you're going to use the product for instruction, you will want to try it with your students. Students are by far the most effective judges of software. You'll need to determine whether it holds their interest and is easy to use, but most importantly, you'll need to determine if they learn from it. It can be hard to look past the production values of the product to clearly see the effects on student learning.

If the resource is available on the web or locally in adequate numbers, you can try it with your entire class. You may want to develop a test on the content to determine if your students learned from the program. Administer the test before and after your students use the instructional product, then compare their scores on the pretest and posttest. You also may want to collect information about their attitudes toward the lesson. Even very young students can tell you whether they liked or disliked a program (see Figure 8.4). If possible, observe them using the software and make note of any problems they encounter.

Based on your review, you can begin to create a list of digital resources and web links to support your classroom instruction. Keep records of the results of the evaluation to use as a basis for purchase or use. Many educators keep a running list of items they'd like to purchase so they have it readily assessable when the opportunity to purchase software occurs.

Obtaining Digital Resources and Technologies

Your school or district will usually have a policy or procedure for requesting and purchasing technology. You'll want to be familiar with the procedures for requesting new hardware and software purchases in your school or district and be sure you know how to voice your needs. As a nonprofit institution, your school or district may be able to obtain hardware and software at a lower cost than you can as an individual. This price might also be reduced further when purchased as part of a site license that allows hardware to be purchased as a class set or for software to be installed on multiple computers. You'll have to check your school or district's policy for purchasing new technology for instruction before buying and installing any software. As you will learn in Chapter 10, most acceptable use policies specify that teachers should not install software without prior authorization.

All software should be considered copyright protected, and its use requires a license. When you purchase a single copy of software for your personal use, the licensing will probably restrict its use to only one computer. So, if you purchase a word-processing or gradebook program and install it on your home computer, you should check the license to see if you can also install it on a school computer. Sometimes you can, sometimes you can't. Unfortunately, there are no standards for software licensing—even for educational software—so you need to be aware of the acceptable and unacceptable uses for every software application you use.

STORIES FROM PRACTICE

No One Will Ever Know

Jim Casey was new on his job as Technology Resource Teacher at the Red River Technical High School. As part of his duties, he had been asked to oversee the school's Career Resources computer lab. The competition for this job had been fierce, and he was feeling relieved that he had been selected.

His predecessor, Robb Blintly, showed Jim around the computer lab he would now have responsibility for supervising. Jim asked an obvious question about software licensing agreements and received a surprising answer: many of the software items in use had not been paid for or properly licensed. He was told that in order to keep up with hardware replacement and software purchases, there was no possible monetary way to do both. As hardware took priority, software purchases were set for a later date. "These are big companies, and our use of their software is minimal," his predecessor confided. "We've always had a few major

items used in the lab that we paid for, but we've also had a number of less common ones that get used as well. The teachers depend on accessing the unlicensed software to teach in at least half of the classes. Plus, we train students to use the software, so when they go out into the workforce they will use the software. Actually we are doing the companies a favor!"

"How do the teachers feel about using illegal software?" Jim blurted out.

"None of the teachers really know the situation. Frankly they'd rather not know," Robb said.

"How much would it cost to get licenses for all of the software?" Jim asked.

"You don't even want to think about that," said Robb. "There is at least $30,000 worth of software in use. But you don't need to worry about it, because no one will ever know."

"But what if the software police come and check?" questioned Jim.

"Oh, that's easy. I have set up the labs so that at any time I can erase the hard drives in an instant, by pushing one button," touted Robb. "I wouldn't worry about it. Like that is ever going to happen."

Over the next few days, Jim thought a lot about his situation. If he took the job, he shouldered the responsibility for the software in illegal use. Also, because a new computer lab had recently been furnished, funds were at an all-time low. If he did not take the job, he would be unemployed, because he had resigned his previous job to take this one. His future course of action was suddenly much more complicated than he had previously imagined.

Source: Adapted from Eastmond, J. N., & Astorga, B. (2001). Ethically Speaking: No one will ever know . . . well, maybe not. *TechTrends*, 45(4), 8–9. Reprinted with permission from Springer Science and Business Media.

Perhaps you are familiar with downloading new software applications or upgrades to existing software from the Internet to your computer. Usually these downloads include a screen with a long list of requirements that you are supposed to agree to by selecting a button. When you select the "I agree" button, do you actually know what you are agreeing to? Do you know whether you can have multiple copies of the program? Can you share it with other teachers? Is there a limit as to how long you can use it? What if it's just for "educational purposes"? Whether purchased over the counter or downloaded from the Internet, you should know the uses and limits placed upon the software by its license.

Sometimes you don't have to pay for software, or pay very little. With increased bandwidth and Internet access, it may be possible for you to quickly and freely download and install software onto a school computer. Two common categories of software of this type are **shareware** and **freeware.** Shareware software often allows you to preview the software for a limited time and then requires purchase, but usually at a minimal cost. Freeware has no cost, but you should not assume it is not copyright protected. Some of these programs require individual registrations or limit the number of copies that may be distributed. Just as with commercial software, you should know the limitations of the licensing agreement of freeware and shareware. Unfortunately, some freeware also contains malicious **spyware**, discussed under security issues in Chapter 10. As a general rule, be careful with what you download and make sure you follow the guidelines for acceptable use.

A unique category of software is **open-source** software, free software that allows users to access and modify the underlying code. Anyone can download this kind of software for free and contribute to its ongoing development. This means that there is a community of users who have a taken an interest in the use and development of the software and some open-source software is often maintained to standards that rival commercial alternatives. Of course, you also can just use the software in your classroom and don't have to worry about becoming a developer, but you can benefit

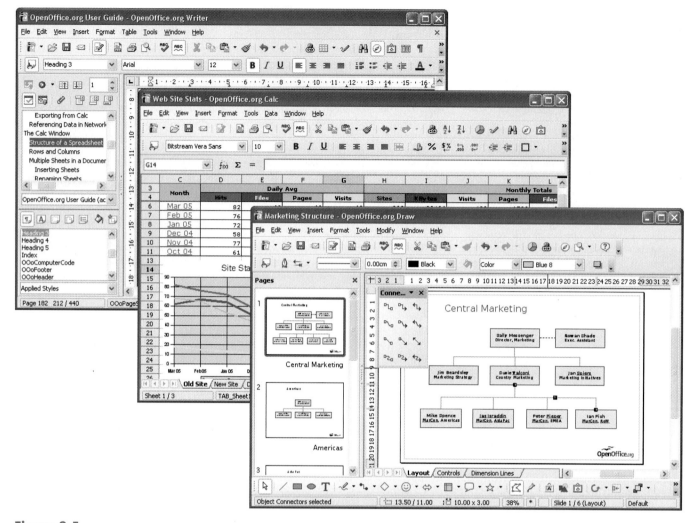

Figure 8.5
Open-source software includes common productivity applications that parallel commercial versions, such as word-processing, spreadsheet, and drawing applications from OpenOffice shown here. Courtesy OpenOffice.org.

from user discussions, online communities, and subsequent improvements to the software.

The underlying philosophy of this type of software is that a community of users will be generated that uses and supports the software and that will give back to other users—all free of charge. Some of the users will create or improve functionality and then make the revised software available to anyone who wishes to use it. There are open-source versions of a wide range of applications, including operating systems, word processors, spreadsheets, databases, and many other types (see Figure 8.5). There is even open-source curricular content, such as that found on Curriki.org and free-reading.net. You may have taken an online course using the open-source course management system called Moodle, or posted comments on the open-source phpBB discussion board.

The open-source movement continues to grow and more digital applications become available or are improved, but many schools have yet to jump on the open-source bandwagon. When you consider that open-source materials are free, you might wonder why more schools don't use open-source software. There are some possible explanations.

The primary caveat when using open-source software is that it does not come with the type of support that can be included in purchased software. Although there is a community of users, and sometimes that community has discussion forums

TOOLS FOR USE

Open-Source Software

There are many open-source applications that can be found for use in an educational setting, from operating systems, common word-processing tools like word processors, course management software, and even open-source content resources. Some examples include

- Linux is a computer operating system, like Windows or Macintosh, that has been available since the early 1990s.
- If you're familiar with the Microsoft Office Suite, you may find OpenOffice to be very similar (see Figure 8.5). It runs on multiple operating systems, is compatible with other productivity software, and contains similar applications, such as a word processor, drawing tools, a spreadsheet, database, and presentation software.
- Amaya, from the World Wide Web Consortium (W3C), Nvu, and Mozilla's SeaMonkey are open-source web design applications you can use to create web pages. Besides HTML code,

some open-source web editors support cascading style sheets (CSS), XML, and other programming languages and codes.

- Teachers in many content areas use concept-mapping tools to support their instruction, and can find open-source versions online, such as FreeMind or CMap.
- If you have taken a class online, you may have encountered the Moodle course management system. Users can post assignments, quizzes, and communicate with others in their class.
- Free-reading.net is an example of open-source content resource, this one in support of early literacy instruction.

For more information about open-source software, including a more detailed definition and the development of standards to support open-source applications, visit the nonprofit Open-Source Initiative online (www.opensource.org).

or other online help, there is no tech support person you can easily contact to ask questions when you run into problems. Schools are notoriously understaffed when it comes to technical support, and sometimes when a problem occurs in open-source software you may have to spend a good bit of time searching through online support materials, looking at the code, or finding other means to get an answer to your question or solution to a problem. For some software, it may be best to have a resident expert to whom you can turn to for support and advice.

The Open Source Initiative, established in 1998, is working to provide guidance to the open-source community. The Open Source Initiative has developed a definition of open source, standards, a certification mark, and maintains a list of licensed open-source software. Although some groups are trying to help standardize what open-source software means and how it is used, there is still a lack of widespread understanding of open source. Although many school and district leaders may be resistant to move away from familiar "brand name" applications to something that is less well understood, as the number of open-source applications and curricular materials increase, it is likely

THE GAME PLAN

Exploring Open Source and Freeware

Set Goals

Examine some of the free software applications available to educators. For example, Google Apps for Education provides web-based word processing, spreadsheet, and presentation programs.

Take Action

Explore the applications and compare them with similar applications with which you are familiar.

Monitor

What are the advantages and limitations of the free applications?

Evaluate and Extend

Do the free applications meet your needs? Would you want to use them in your classroom? Share your findings with your peers.

that more districts will begin to explore the use of open-source materials in their schools.

Maintaining Technology Resources

It would be great if all you had to do was install a piece of hardware or software and then it would operate forever without any problems. Unfortunately that isn't how things work in the real world. Classroom technologies, like all technology, will require routine maintenance. Just as your car runs best with routine tune-ups, so do computers. Your primary areas of responsibility will vary depending on your school's technology configuration and procedures.

Maintaining computer workstations over a network has become a common method to monitor, and sometimes repair, technology from a distance, often resulting in a savings of time and cost. In a networked environment, your district technology personnel can oversee all hardware and software installations, antivirus and antispyware maintenance, and service pack updates from a distance rather than having to physically visit each computer. These identical workstations on a network, sometimes called "cloned" or "ghost" workstations, typically have identical software configurations, password-protected logins, and networked peripherals, such as printers and file servers. This time-saving method also helps network administrators provide a more secure computing environment for you and your students, but requires that you take steps to ensure that you can continue to access proprietary instructional software. In addition, it necessitates that you and your students appropriately store and back up data files from activities and assessments. A common method for maintaining the security of a network is to routinely return all of the networked computers back to their original configurations. This sometimes means removing extra programs and old data files.

Technology support personnel are often overburdened. Although businesses strive to reach tech support ratios of 1:25 (one tech support person for every 25 computers), many districts may have ratios as low as 1:100, with one case study noting a ratio of 1:336 (Gartner, 2003)! So, regardless of the network capacity of your school or district, both hardware and software maintenance is necessary to keep your computer system running properly, to ensure that your system is working with the most current resources, and to ensure that resources purchased in the past will be usable in the future. It's vital that you understand your responsibilities and role in computer maintenance and that you be able to perform routine basic troubleshooting and maintenance.

Solving Routine Problems

Anyone who works with technologies will encounter problems and computer systems are no exception. It is not a question of *if* you will encounter problems, but simply a matter of *when*. Given that you are going to encounter hardware or software difficulties during your career, how will you deal with them? Will you attempt to address the difficulties yourself or will you let somebody else do it for you? If you are in a position to let somebody else address all difficulties for you, most of this section will not concern you. But if you don't develop some skills in this area, you can loose valuable instructional time when small problems occur in your classroom or lab. When there are no experts handy, you'll need to take problems into your own hands, so it's important to have a troubleshooting strategy that allows you to investigate the problem and identify and implement a solution. But don't worry; there are basic troubleshooting techniques that are applicable across a wide variety of technical problems.

Our recommended troubleshooting strategy begins with what you should *not* do. Because the problems you encounter may deal with either hardware or software, you should not assume that you know which one is the source of the cause. The problem may be caused by something that is broken, or it may not be. Again, you should not make any assumptions. Also, the problem may, or may not, be something that is your fault. Once again, watch your assumptions. And, finally, the problem may be with your own computer or software or it may be with your network. One last time, don't jump to conclusions.

A Troubleshooting Model

Now that you know what not to do, let's discuss the steps you should perform when you are troubleshooting. The model we are suggesting involves four major steps: 1) identify the problem, 2) apply a solution, 3) check the results, and 4) repeat as necessary. The steps and sub-steps are described in the following discussion.

Isolate the Problem. Begin by attempting to identify the problem. When you are troubleshooting difficulties, you don't know what the problem is. Instead, you are confronted with one or more symptoms and, based on the symptoms, you hypothesize what the problem is. This step requires you to act like a detective and pay close attention to any clues your computer system provides.

Attempt to isolate the symptoms. Where do they occur? Under what circumstances? When the problem only occurs when using a single software application, you may need to update or reinstall the application. When the problem occurs when using a single document, it may indicate you don't have enough memory to work with the document, or the document itself or an element in the document, such as a graphic you inserted from a website, may be corrupted or damaged. When the problem occurs globally when using any application, don't forget to check cables and connections. How frequently do the symptoms occur? Check to see if you get the same symptoms on more than one computer—an indication it might be a network configuration problem. Can you make them disappear? If so, how? If you're having problems with a website, try using a different web browser on the same machine or even a different computer. If the symptoms no longer exist, the original browser may not be configured correctly or have the proper plug-ins installed. If the site works on your home computer but not at school, the problem may be related to your network. Look for any hints, messages, or clues.

Of course, you should recognize that many problems are routine occurrences and software and hardware developers have supports to help you solve them. Often the biggest challenge is correctly identifying the symptoms. Sometimes error messages provide suggestions as to why the malfunctions are occurring. Error messages may be numbered or contain key terms that you can look up in a manual or online reference. Manuals accompanying your hardware and software generally also contain troubleshooting sections that offer solutions for many of the symptoms you might identify, regardless of whether they include error messages or not. Don't forget to check manufacturer help files online.

Identify the Best Solution. After you have hypothesized what the problem may be, you should identify one or more possible solutions. First, try the tips available in your computer and software manuals or the manufacturer's website. In addition, user groups and discussion forums can be a good source of information. Go to the product manufacturer's site and look for a discussion group. Using the search function, enter a short phrase that describes your problem, for example "iMovie crashes." If you're lucky, you'll find someone who has solved the problem while working with the same combination of software and hardware as you. If your search of product literature and websites doesn't provide some helpful solutions or if you can't get on the Internet with the computer in question, you may need to call a technician or the product help line, if there is one. Be aware that some technical support help lines charge for their services if your product is no longer under warranty.

Another source for possible solutions may be right in front of you. Ask your students or colleagues. Students interested in computers may have experienced this very same problem and found ways to solve it. Tell your students the problem you're experiencing and see if you receive any good suggestions. And don't forget to thank your students if they can help you out. Model good problem-solving and collaboration skills with your students and they'll be more likely to use them later.

Apply a Solution and Check Your Results. Once you've identified possible solutions, try the best one—one at a time! If your solution works, you are done. However, if the applied solutions don't solve the problem you identified, you have incorrectly identified the problem and need to hypothesize another problem statement. However, before applying a new solution, *try to return the entire system to the way it was before you started*. That's the best way to isolate the original problem. If you just keep making changes, one on top of the other, you may compound the original problem. So it's very important to try to put it back to the way it was before trying another solution. Then, once that is done, remember to apply relevant solutions one at a time. After each application, check results.

Repeat, if Necessary. You'll need to repeat this process as many times as necessary until a solution is found. If no solution is found after trying all relevant solutions, seek outside assistance. Walking away and seeking support from someone else can also prevent you from inadvertently making the problem worse by bending a pin, breaking a key, or erasing important data from your computer—something many of us have done when frustrated. As noted earlier, troubleshooting handbooks, help lines, discussion forums, and websites are all useful sources of information; however, these sources of support are most effective if you have narrowed the problem significantly. Your discussions will be most productive if you can tell the support technician what you have already done to try to correct it.

There's one last common error that we can all overlook—human error. Anyone who has provided desktop support or who has monitored a computer help line can tell you dozens of funny stories about people who were convinced their computers were not operating correctly. Very often, the error or malfunction has occurred as a result of the computer doing exactly what it was "told" to do, by the user. That's OK. We've all had our share of human errors. Use the experience to learn more about your computer, possibly after taking a deep breath or trying something new for a while.

TOOLS FOR USE
Four-Step Troubleshooting Process

1. Isolate the problem: Identify the problem that you are trying to solve as specifically as possible. Identify what happens and when it happens.
   - What are the symptoms?
   - Where do they occur?
   - Under what circumstances do they occur?
   - How frequently do they occur?
   - Can you make them disappear? If so, how?
2. Identify one or more possible solutions: Examine software manuals, hardware manuals, online support sites, and software discussion forums to locate potential solutions. Talk to your colleagues or students about the problem. If necessary, call the troubleshooting hotline once you have identified your problem.

3. Apply a solution and check results
   a. Select the best solution, then make one logical change at a time
      - If it works—you are done
      - If it doesn't work, *put it back the way it was!*
   b. Is there another solution for the proposed problem?
   c. If yes, Return to Step 3a—Apply a single, relevant solution, and select another possible solution
   d. If no, make sure things are put back the way they were and return to Step 1—Take a closer look at the problem.
4. Repeat process if necessary: If a solution is not found after trying all relevant possibilities, seek outside assistance.

Hardware Maintenance

Many common problems can be prevented with simple regular maintenance. There are some maintenance tasks you and your students should complete while others will be handled strictly by your school or district technology support personnel. We've broken down the hardware maintenance issues discussed in this section into four distinct areas: routinely servicing current hardware, repairing or replacing things that break, replacing consumables, and adding new hardware.

Routine Servicing

Computer hardware contains electronic and mechanical components. Electronic components have three major enemies: heat, power fluctuations, and unwanted liquids. Most computer systems have fans to exhaust the heat that builds up when electronic components operate. Some newer systems use liquid cooling systems to capture the heat and move it away from the components. Dust and lint limit the effectiveness of fans by covering the components as well as blocking the exhaust vents. At a minimum you should clean the cooling fan vents on a regular basis.

The screens on computer monitors are notorious for collecting dust. How you remove the dust depends on the type of monitor you have, CRT (cathode ray tube—older technology for monitors and televisions) or LCD (liquid crystal display—common in laptops). With a CRT you can moisten a soft cloth with a small amount of diluted isopropyl alcohol, wipe the screen clean with the cloth, and then wipe the screen dry with another soft cloth. LCD screens are more sensitive and require both extra care and an extra soft cloth. Manufacturers recommend gently wiping the dust from the LCD screen without using any cleaner. If the screen is still dirty, then a small amount of diluted isopropyl alcohol or a commercial LCD cleaner can be applied to the soft cloth and then used on the screen. Remember, all of these components are sensitive to static electricity discharges so take precautions including the use of static free tools and grounding.

As for liquids, you should try to avoid the combination of keyboards or laptops with coffee, soft drinks, water—any liquids, basically. The two don't mix well and many schools have strict "no liquid" policies in computer labs and around computer equipment in classrooms.

Power fluctuations also can damage or destroy electronic components. Surge protectors are available to minimize the impact of excess power. Uninterruptible power supplies (UPS) can be used to ensure a constant power supply, balancing out too much or too little power. Electricity from your local power supplier is not the only type of electricity that can damage your computer's components. Static electricity also can cause major problems, especially with chips and printed circuit boards. Before working on electronic components you should discharge any static buildup by touching a metal computer case.

Dust, dirt, and grime are perennial enemies of mechanical components. Depending on the component, these contaminants can come from various sources, including your own hands. Dust can be introduced into media drives when they are inserted into the computer. Dust or other contaminants sticking on a CD, DVD, or floppy disk can easily enter the drive and affect its operation. It's a good idea to examine your storage media before inserting them in their drives and to remove any junk you may find. Rather than carrying these media loose in your backpack, store them in protective containers. Of course, dirt can come from other sources. Dust and grime inevitably will accumulate on your keyboard through regular use. Compressed air can be used to remove dust and lint from the keyboard while isopropyl alcohol wipes do a good job of removing grime (see Figure 8.6). If you use compressed air for dust control, be aware of health and safety risks of misuse. These products should not be accessible to students.

Peripherals often include more mechanical parts than the core components of the computer system. Printers can be affected by the after-effects of paper jams and

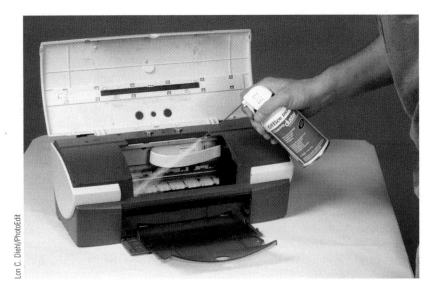

Lon C. Diehl/PhotoEdit

Figure 8.6
Routine maintenance of computers and related peripherals includes keeping all of the components clean.

toner spills as well as wear and tear on gears and rollers. Mice can pick up lint that interferes with their operation. Periodic cleaning can reduce problems with peripherals.

Repairing

In spite of your best efforts, it is likely that some hardware component will break or malfunction. When malfunctions occur there are two choices, repair or replace the component. As a practical matter, the number of components you actually can repair economically is quite limited. Bent pins on a connector can be straightened but most other repairs should be looked upon as temporary, at best. In the overwhelming majority of cases, your choices are between replacing a component yourself and having someone else replace it for you. In general, novice users are capable of replacing pluggable components outside the computer case. These items include the computer mouse and keyboard. Intermediate to advanced users can replace pluggable items within the computer case including circuit boards, memory, and hard drives. Above all, when using your school's technology, follow the procedures in place to ensure you are operating within your limits as outlined in the technical support procedures. You may need to carefully assess the problem and submit a technical support request, or troubleshoot the issue following your system's guidelines.

Replacing Consumables

A common form of hardware maintenance occurs when items are replaced. Many of these items are consumable supplies such as those used by computer printers. Both ink jet and laser printers use cartridges and paper, consumable items that a typical user can replace. Another example includes the light bulbs for computer projectors. With the popularity of using teacher computer workstations that project images to a screen or whiteboard, schools quickly have become cognizant of the high cost of these consumables.

Students should be encouraged to conserve resources during their computer use. For example, they can use the preview function of the print command to determine how many pages will be printed and then print only the pages they need. They can use a small font or reduced line spacing for draft versions of word-processed documents. They can cut and paste text from the websites they use for research purposes in order to restrict the amount printed to only the necessary information (though remind them to gather the information needed to properly cite the sources). And they can use the "draft" mode to conserve ink. You may need to develop guidelines as to how much printing is allowed.

Adding Components

Occasionally you will decide that your computer should be upgraded by adding a new hardware component. In this case, you are increasing your computer system's capabilities rather than replacing an existing component or supplies. For example, you might decide you need additional storage space so you install either an internal or external hard drive to supplement your existing hard drive. We've come full circle back to hardware purchase, covered earlier in this chapter.

Software Maintenance

Maintenance is not limited to hardware components; software also requires maintenance. In many K-12 school settings, software issues are handled at the server level by the network administrator or other technology support personnel. The efficient installation and maintenance of software is one of the greatest advantages of networked environments. There may be situations, however, when you may need to install or update software on your school's computers, such as when existing media plug-ins on a browser must be updated before students can view content you've found on the Internet. In general, software maintenance can involve one or more of the following tasks: installing new software, reinstalling or updating current software, organizing and backing up files, and protecting software from harmful influences.

Installing New Software

The first type of software maintenance involves the acquisition and installation of totally new software. In this case you may purchase the software on storage media, such as a CD-ROM, or you may download the software at a slightly lower cost over the Internet. The latter option is especially attractive if you need the software in a hurry and if you have a high-speed connection for your computer.

Most software has become very easy to install and requires very little knowledge about the workings of the computer. You will often be prompted during the software installation process to review terms of use and select locations on your computer for the installation of the software. Typically, the installation wizards will recommend the best options for you.

Again, you should check with your technology support staff or administration to understand the procedure for installing new software on a school computer. Even if you have purchased software for your own use, you may not be able to install it on a school computer without permission. And once you do, you'll still need to be careful of cloning or ghosting software that your technology support personnel may use to maintain computers on the network and that can inadvertently remove any software you have purchased and installed.

Reinstalling and Updating Current Software

Some common forms of software maintenance include reinstalling or updating software on your computer. A reinstallation may be necessary when existing software has a serious malfunction or a system crash interacts with application software. This doesn't happen often but you definitely will want to keep copies of your original software handy just in case it happens to you. A much more frequent type of software maintenance occurs when you are called upon to install updated versions of existing software. Software producers commonly issue corrections and updates for previously released versions of software. These patches usually are made available to registered users at no charge and most are now routinely delivered over the Internet. Your computer probably checks for new updates routinely and notifies you when they're available. Producers also release "new and improved" versions of prior software and make

Cookies are small text files that are saved to your hard drive when you visit a website in order to personalize your future visits.

For example, when you revisit a site and it . . .

- greets you by name
- displays your last search terms
- offers to sell you products that fit your tastes

. . . this is because of the cookie(s) the site has saved on your computer, and accessed in order to serve you better. You may decide to delete them because they tend to build up over time and begin to compromise your computer's efficiency. If you rely on cookies for your favorite websites, however, you may not want to delete them unless you're absolutely sure which ones you are deleting.

Figure 8.7
What is a cookie?

these versions available to registered users at fees lower than those charged to new users.

File Maintenance

Another form of software maintenance deals with deleting, organizing, or archiving (backing up) individual files. Even in networked environments, it will be your responsibility to manage and organize your own files and to back them up periodically.

Some software programs create and store large numbers of temporary files on your hard drive that should be removed periodically. If left unattended, they can occupy huge amounts of storage space and slow the overall operation of your computer. For example, temporary files are commonly generated when you visit Internet sites. You can use the options in your web browser to delete these temporary Internet files. **Cookies** are Internet files that might or might not be considered temporary (see Figure 8.7). To state it simply, these files store important information about you and your computer when you visit Internet sites. This way, the common Internet sites you visit will remember who you are and your preferences. You may or may not want to remove cookies during your routine maintenance.

Software programs can help you analyze your computer contents and determine if you have unused files or data on your computer that should be removed. You should use caution with these programs or when deleting files in general, however, as sometimes you may inadvertently remove critical files. It's good practice to review any files suggested for deletion.

On other occasions you do not want to delete files on your hard drive but you may want to organize them to make them easier to locate. By using a combination of folders and subfolders (or directories and subdirectories) you can organize your files in a logical, efficient manner. This is a good practice that can help avoid unnecessary file deletion from your computer. Often, you can get very organized by creating a relatively small number of major folders and a larger numbers of subfolders in which to keep your work. For example, you might want to have a folder for all your lesson plans that contains subfolders on specific topics.

Yet another type of file maintenance involves the creation and use of back-up or archive files. There are multiple reasons you may benefit from the use of archive files but often they address one of two needs: 1) you have critical files that would need to be restored quickly in the event of a computer disaster, or 2) you have a large amount of file space devoted to files you use infrequently but which you are not prepared to delete at this time. In either case, archives can be created to contain these files. After the relevant files have been moved into the archive folders, those folders can be moved to a storage media separate from your computer such as a CD-ROM, file server, or external hard drive. This process frees up storage space on your computer and provides back-up protection in the event of computer failure. Although the possibility of a failure might seem remote, archive files serve as a form of insurance that you cannot afford to overlook. It's good practice to routinely schedule a back up of your files. Some software can be used to do this and if your computer is connected to a school or district network, your technology staff may be using this type of software to routinely back up your files whether you realize it or not.

Safeguarding Software

The final type of file maintenance discussed here relates to protecting your software from harmful or malicious influences. These influences can take many forms, but the most common source of harm comes in the form of computer viruses. A **virus** is a computer program that executes and replicates itself and, in the process, has the potential to cause major problems on your computer. Multiple antivirus products are available to detect the presence of viruses on your computer and to offer protection against them. Most antivirus vendors have websites that offer updated versions of their products to their registered users. For these products to be effective you have to consistently download the updates and use them to scan and repair the files on your computer.

Computers connected to the Internet are exposed to other types of intrusive programs that can track your computer activity, add unwanted codes to your computer, and perform unauthorized uploads of private user information to external parties. Firewall and antispyware programs are available to address these problems but,

THE GAME PLAN

Computer Maintenance

You will need to evaluate your role in maintaining the equipment you use in a school, as well as create a different, more extensive plan for managing your personal equipment. To keep your computer operating smoothly, follow these steps to maintain your hardware and software.

Set Goals

Develop a routine maintenance plan for your computer. Your plan should establish a schedule that addresses the four areas of hardware maintenance and the four types of software maintenance discussed in this chapter. For example, how often do you intend to clean dust and lint from your computer? How will you check for updated drivers or virus protection?

Take Action

Examine software manuals, hardware manuals, online support sites, and software discussion forums to locate maintenance information. Search for protective software available from your district. Browse local retailers and online dealers to locate back-up supplies. Acquire the maintenance tools, supplies, and updates you need. Install new hardware and software

according to the manufacturer's recommendations. You may even want to create a chart similar to the Tools for Use: Maintenance Schedule, or schedule reminders for routine maintenance appointments using calendar software.

Monitor

Are you cleaning and servicing all parts of your computer (hardware and software) on schedule? Have you protected your computer from power fluctuations and spilled liquids? When was the last time you updated your virus protection? How long has it been since you checked for application updates for your software? Have any parts of your computer system malfunctioned and, if so, what did you do? Have you installed any new hardware of software?

Evaluate and Extend

Are all parts of your computer (hardware and software) functioning properly? Are you finding the software updates that you need? Do you have extra consumables on hand? Are some supply and information sources better than others?

TOOLS FOR USE

Maintenance Schedule

Be informed of your school system's policies on software and hardware maintenance. Many districts restrict general staff from running virus protection, installing hardware or making changes to the settings. Find out what your responsibilities are in performing technical computer maintenance. Sample tasks are provided below.

Please note: most cleaning chores should be completed with the power off!

Daily Tasks

- Back up all work.
- Exit all applications.
- Log off all users from the network.
- Shut down power to all computers or put into sleep/stand-by mode.
- Shut down power and store any peripherals.
- If used, cover computers and peripherals.

Weekly Tasks

- Move or remove files that have been downloaded to the desktop or temporary folders/directories.
- Empty trash/recycle bin.
- Organize/consolidate folders/directories.
- With the computer powered off, wipe off computers, monitors, keyboards, mice, and mouse pads with appropriate cleaner.
- Dust computers, peripherals, and work areas with lint-free cloth.
- Restock consumables (paper, toner, etc.).

Periodically (may require training or assistance)

- Clean mechanical mice (rollers and balls).
- Routinely create back-up archives.
- Use compressed air to blow dust and dirt from keyboards (do not let students do this).
- Check for wear and tear of all cables and cords.
- If possible, remove dust from inner components of workstation, especially fan blades.

once again, regular updating and use of the programs are needed to ensure ongoing protection.

Among the duties of network administrators is to ensure security of the network system, in part by scanning e-mail messages for viruses, running updated virus protection software, and utilizing antispyware software. Find out how your school or district protects its technology systems and be informed of your responsibilities. Additional information about how to protect your computers against a variety of malicious influences is found in Chapter 10.

Technical Assistance

Let's face it, when it comes to technology, none of us can be expected to know everything about every digital resource we encounter—and we don't have to. When using computer technologies, you may have to accept the fact that you are not the most knowledgeable person in the room when it comes to the hardware and software. And that simple fact is just fine. You can adopt a confident and open attitude that allows you to accept help when offered, even from your students. It's more productive to feel confident in what you do know, and not feel threatened by what you don't know.

Most districts and many schools will have personnel available to set up and troubleshoot equipment. These technology specialists focus on understanding and supporting hardware, software, and networks and have been in school districts much longer than technology integration specialists although they may have little or no teaching experience. Depending on the size of your school, you may have to share the expertise of a technology support person with another school in your district or rely solely on district technology support personnel. Many states also have state or regional service offices that provide some limited technology support to school districts they oversee.

Be sure to establish your own network of volunteers to provide classroom technology support. Parent volunteers can assist you with routine maintenance tasks such as running disk utility software, removing old files, and backing up data. Others may be able to help with more serious problems such as computer malfunctions. Your parent network will change from year to year, so collect information about the technology skills of the parents when you gather demographic information at the beginning of the school year. A simple volunteer form can list technology-related activities for which you may need assistance. College students and other community volunteers, as well as older students in your school, may also be sources of support. Some examples of the work that volunteers can complete are

- cleaning computer monitor screens, keyboards, and mice
- dusting behind computers and wiring
- supervising computer labs
- providing technical assistance to students when working on computers
- providing data entry and word processing

Chapter Summary

Digital technologies can enhance your classroom instruction in numerous ways. You can add realism to a lecture on the circulatory system with a video clip of a beating heart. Your students can engage in a virtual frog dissection by visiting the Whole Frog Project online. They can create their own personal history web pages that include digital pictures, videos, and interviews of relatives and friends. However, effective use of these technologies depends in part on the careful selection of technology resources. In this chapter, you learned to identify your software and hardware requirements, locate resources that meet your requirements, narrow your choices through reading recommendations and reviews, and evaluate resources to determine if they are suitable for your use.

In this chapter, you also learned basic maintenance and troubleshooting techniques and we provided advice on securing technical assistance. At the least, your responsibilities will include managing and organizing your own files, and backing them up periodically. You will most likely assume the responsibility for ensuring that your computer is kept clean and reasonably dust free. Pay attention to the way the computer is wired. Become familiar with basic troubleshooting techniques found within your computer manual. Check on cables, cords, and plugs. Sometimes these have a way of coming loose—and no one likes to have their requests for technical support met with the observation that equipment is simply unplugged.

In the next chapter, we will turn our attention to ways that digital resources can be used to enhance communication and collaboration among students, parents, peers, and the wider community. We'll also discuss how you can model the effective use of computer systems through safe and healthy use.

YOUR PORTFOLIO

To demonstrate competency in ISTE NETS-T Standard 3.a, add the following items to your portfolio:

1. If you have not already done so, identify the software and hardware needed for the lesson that you began planning in Chapter 3. Or select another learning goal and identify the software and hardware needed. Include the following steps:
   a. Identify your goals for technology use. Why do you want to include technologies?
   b. Specify the technology requirements. What operating system do you require? What are the network requirements? What peripherals are

needed? What are your budget limitations? Are there other instructional requirements that constrain the type of technology selected?

    c. Locate resources that might meet your needs, including freeware, shareware, and open-source software.

    d. Read reviews and recommendations for hardware and software that would meet your students' learning or assessment needs. Based on the reviews, which technologies would you select?

2. Locate a software title or website and review it using a software evaluation form of your choice.

3. Develop your own list of troubleshooting tips for common software and hardware problems you encounter.

4. Develop a plan to provide routine maintenance of technology in your classroom. If applicable, include items such as calculators, printers, handheld computers, and other technology, not just computers. Include the steps both you and your students can take and the schedule you will follow.

References

Eastmond, J. N., & Astorga, B. (2001). Ethically speaking: No one will ever know . . . well, maybe not. *TechTrends*, 45(4), 8–9.

Gartner, Inc. (2003). *A report and estimating tool for K-12 school districts: California district case study*. Stamford, CT: Author. Retrieved July 18, 2006, from http://classroomtco.cosn.org/gartner_intro.html

International Society for Technology in Education (ISTE). (2008). *Refreshed ISTE NETS for Teachers Rubrics*. Eugene, OR: Author.

Jonassen, D. J. (2006). *Modeling with technology: Mindtools for conceptual change* (3rd ed.). Upper Saddle River, NJ: Merrill/Prentice Hall.

Wegerif, R. (2002). *Literature review in thinking skills, technology, and learning*. Future Lab Series, No. 2. Retrieved June 1, 2006, from http://www.futurelab.org.uk/research/reviews/ts01.htm

Wells, J., & Lewis, L. (2006). *Internet access in U.S. public schools and classrooms: 1994–2005* (NCES 2007-020). U.S. Department of Education. Washington, DC: National Center for Education Statistics.

Modeling and Facilitating Use of Digital Tools

As a teacher, your scope of responsibility broadens dramatically from yourself and your immediate family to your students and their families, your school and district, and the community in which you live and teach. You also have responsibility to your profession, including colleagues and professional organizations that extend beyond your school and community. These responsibilities will require you to communicate and collaborate with the numerous people who have an interest in the things that go on in your classroom. In addition, your professional responsibilities will require you to model and facilitate the effective use of digital technologies within your classroom and beyond.

Throughout this book, we've shown you how to do just that, but two chapters (in addition to this one) are particularly applicable to ISTE standard 3. In Chapter 4, we discussed the use of digital technologies as tutors, mindtools, and support for conversations.

ISTE Standards addressed in this chapter

NETS-T 3. Model Digital-Age Work and Learning

Teachers exhibit knowledge, skills, and work processes representative of an innovative professional in a global and digital society. Teachers:

b. collaborate with students, peers, parents, and community members using digital tools and resources to support student success and innovation

c. communicate relevant information and ideas effectively to students, parents, and peers using a variety of digital-age media and formats

d. model and facilitate effective use of current and emerging digital tools to locate, analyze, evaluate, and use information resources to support research and learning

Note: Chapter 8 addresses Standard 3.a.

Outcomes

In this chapter, you will

■ Incorporate technology tools and strategies to facilitate communication and collaboration with students, parents, peers, and community members.

■ Model and facilitate the effective, safe, and healthy use of technology tools.

We also provided strategies to effectively locate, analyze, evaluate, and use the information resources readily available on the web for learning and research. In Chapter 5, we discussed how you can develop a classroom environment to support students in setting their own educational goals, managing their learning, and assessing their progress. Throughout, we've stressed the importance of collaboration in developing the skills needed to function in an information economy.

And just as collaboration can be beneficial to your students during the instructional process, there are multiple benefits to professional collaboration—especially when that collaboration focuses on student learning success. Of course, open and respectful communication is a key component of successful collaborations, so in the first part of this chapter, we focus on ways that you, as a teacher, can use digital technologies to communicate and collaborate with the many people who will have an interest in what goes on in your classroom.

Throughout much of this book, we have also focused on how you can model and facilitate effective technology use through your teaching strategies and management practices. In the last section of this chapter, we focus on how you can model and facilitate effective use of digital tools in another way—through the physical arrangement of technology resources and their safe and healthy use.

STORIES FROM PRACTICE

Then and Now

In my first year of teaching 25 years ago, I remember feeling grossly unprepared for the adventure ahead of me. Although I had graduated with honors, my classes had not prepared me for the realities of the classroom. Handling 30 first graders on my own was very different than student teaching. I wasn't sure how to prepare for the first day of class. Other teachers were making posters of classroom rules and nametags for the students. I watched them, and picked up any ideas I could. I tried talking to the other teachers in the building, but they seemed so confident that I was afraid I would seem incompetent if I expressed my insecurities. I desperately wished there was

someone I could talk with about my teaching.

But I absolutely loved my job. The kids were fascinating and my time in the classroom just flew by. So before and after school I'd sit in the library and pour through teacher magazines such as *Instructor.* I spent many afternoons in "teacher stores," selecting resources that would provide me with tips on teaching and classroom management. I spent lots of my hard-earned cash on materials that would help me through the next day in class. I even looked into classes at the local college, simply to give me an opportunity to discuss with peers and professors the day-to-day issues I was facing.

These days, all of these opportunities are available online—anytime, anywhere, with the click of a mouse. I have access to teacher resources, many of which are free. I can talk with peers and more experienced teachers, without worrying about them judging me. I can take college classes or shorter workshops. There are resources that help me learn, and resources that I can use with my students. If I had the online support available to teachers today, those initial classroom experiences would have been very different!

Source: Katherine Cennamo

Professional Communication and Collaboration

You will find that many of the planning, instructional, assessment, record-keeping, and professional development tasks that teachers perform involve some form of communication. You'll have to communicate with your students, establish communication between home and school, and communicate with school and district administrators, staff, and other teachers. And, you'll need to communicate with others to enhance your own professional development.

THE GAME PLAN

Student Collaboration Tools

Set Goals

Investigate technology tools that could support collaboration in your classroom.

Take Action

Visit websites, review teacher publications in print or online, visit schools, and talk with your peers and current teachers to identify potential collaboration tools.

Monitor

Determine the sources of the recommendations you uncovered: Are they from teachers in real schools? Or product developers or vendors?

Do you include only tools that you are familiar with, or have you identified tools for which you may need some training? What additional resources (networking, hardware, tech support) might be necessary to implement your choices?

Evaluate and Extend

Identify the strengths and weaknesses of one or two potential technologies and how you might include them in a classroom. It is just as valid to explain why you would *not* use a collaborative technology. Share with your peers, practicing teachers, course instructor, or technology specialists and consider revisions based on their comments.

But NETS-T Standard 3 goes beyond just communicating; you'll notice that standard 3.b focuses on *collaborating*—not only with your peers, but with students, parents, and community members, too. Collaboration is more than communication and more than cooperation. Cooperation and a lot of communication may be passive, but collaboration requires active participation between you and others. In a truly collaborative relationship, all parties benefit; partners bring different strengths and interests to the relationship and in return, everyone contributes to and gains from the collaboration in some way.

Of course, open and positive communication is a critical part of successful collaborations, but there are other techniques that can enhance school, home, and community relationships as well. The following sections explore ways students, faculty, staff, parents, and the greater community can collaborate to support student success and learning through 1) communicating, 2) volunteering, and 3) extended learning opportunities. In the past, face-to-face meetings were the primary means of collaborating with these critical stakeholders. Today, widely available technology tools provide effective and efficient means of communicating and collaborating with everyone concerned with classroom teaching and learning.

Communicating

As a teacher, you will need to maintain open lines of communication with students, parents, colleagues, and administrators. As part of your teaching responsibilities, you may need to:

- communicate curricular requirements to your students
- report and discuss student progress with students, parents, administrators, and other teachers
- collect student contact, health, or other information from parents and guardians
- notify parents of field trips and special events
- generate forms that require signatures, such as permission forms and acceptable use policies
- keep parents informed of classroom activities and schedules

- create classroom websites
- publish classroom newsletters
- interact with colleagues for professional development

Many school districts have established procedures for contacting parents through report cards, interim grade reports, and periodic portfolios demonstrating student work. Most districts also publish annual summative reports as brochures or special inserts in the local paper; states publicize summaries of student achievement data through online school report cards. Many schools also have procedures for contacting parents on an as-needed basis, such as through attendance records, disciplinary forms, or information from guidance and career counselors. Some schools encourage teachers to contact parents by phone on a regular basis or to distribute "good news" report cards as one way to praise student achievement. All of these communication venues are now supported by networked telecommunications and digital tools.

You also may want to communicate with businesses, community organizations, and other institutions that support teaching and learning. These may include other schools, museums, libraries, research facilities, and colleges and universities.

Many digital tools can be used to support communication with students, peers, parents, administrators, and the larger community. E-mail and mailing lists provide a quick and easy way to convey information or participate in a discussion with a group of people. Word-processing or desktop-publishing programs can be used to create newsletters and weekly letters to parents. Digital video equipment can be used to document classroom activities to share at parent-teacher meetings or classroom celebrations. Presentation software can be used to structure your classroom presentations or to present to parents and administrators. Gradebook programs, spreadsheets, and graphing software can be used to track and convey student progress to students, their parents, and administrators. Students can create podcasts, wikis, blogs, or multimedia presentations to share their learning with others in the classroom and beyond. The ideas are almost endless.

Communication should be regular and two-way (PTA, 1997), meaning that you're not just contacting parents when you have an academic or disciplinary problem to report or not just contacting community members when you want financial support for new technology or other initiatives. Consistent, periodic communication helps everyone better understand the process of schooling and can create greater understanding when you or your school wants support for a new initiative. Unfortunately, learning how to communicate with parents and the community is not a skill always addressed when learning to become a teacher. Review the Tools for Use: Tips for Communicating with Parents and the Community for some general guidelines that can support you in your practice.

One common way to enhance communications between home, school, and the greater community is through the use of a class website (see Figure 9.1). A class website can provide links to homework assignments, supplemental resources, as well as links to district-wide information, such as bus schedules and cafeteria menus. Classroom websites can make resources available to your students outside of class time, providing opportunities to explore upcoming activities and review previous materials. Students who miss class can access materials at their convenience. The website can clarify expectations for parents and publicize your work to administrators and community members.

Depending on the grade level and subject that you teach, you may want to make resources, such as the following, available to your students and their parents:

- presentation slides
- lecture notes
- announcements
- class calendar and due dates
- homework assignments

- online practice tests
- links to resources used in class
- supplemental and enrichment activities students can do at home for extra practice

Of course, this list is just a small sample of the materials that can be made available on a class website. Your class website also can serve as a convenient "storage location" for your own classroom files. For example, you can create a page with links to websites that you use frequently within your instruction. You and others can have access to them anytime, anywhere you have an Internet connection.

Many school systems subscribe to content management systems, such as EdLine or PowerSchool, that they want their teachers to use for their class websites. The examples on the companion website for this textbook include popular content management systems you might find in your school. Using these systems can be as simple as uploading your content into prepared templates. There's little need to know

TOOLS FOR USE

Tips for Communicating with Parents and the Community

Be proactive
- Get to know parents and community members. Don't let a problem be your first contact with them. Create informal opportunities for communication to establish a friendly, cooperative atmosphere for future contacts.
- Encourage ongoing, two-way communication. Let parents and community members know that you welcome their ideas and input and will take their suggestions and concerns to heart.
- Share information about local, state, and federal education initiatives that impact your teaching.

Be informed
- Consider parents and community members as resources. Consult with them about particular problems or education issues, for example, factors that might affect a student's learning or behavior and what approaches and strategies they have found to be helpful.
- Gather up-to-date information about issues from respected sources—newspapers, professional journals and texts, websites, and so forth. Besides helping you design better strategies to meet your school or classroom needs, the information may also be useful to parents and community members. Parents and others often look to teachers for advice on any matter related to school.
- Consult with school and district administrators or resource personnel for information about school policies or preferred practices relevant to the issue at hand.

Be positive
- Hold high expectations for learning and behavior. Let parents know exactly what is expected of their children, what you do to teach and reinforce these skills and behaviors in the classroom, and how they can support their children's learning at home.
- Inform parents about their children's progress toward instructional and behavioral goals, and let them know about nonacademic accomplishments as well.

- Be a goodwill ambassador for your school in the community, recognizing community support and celebrating student and school success.

Be prepared
- Define and document the problem or need that impedes achieving educational goals. What is its source and scope? For behavioral issues, how often and in what context does the behavior occur? How does the problem or need affect the child, the school, and/or the community? What steps have been taken to address it, and with what results?
- Plan a strategy for next steps, soliciting input and support from parents and/or community members. Be ready to suggest concrete options for addressing a problem, including:
  - the goals of the intervention or project
  - what you will do
  - how parents or community members can help
  - how progress toward goals will be measured and communicated
  - next steps based on evaluation of results

Be respectful
- Treat people the way you want to be treated. All parents appreciate those who have their children's best interests at heart.
- Respect cultural and ethnic differences, and try to see the parents' or community's perspective. Even if you disagree with how to approach a problem, seek common ground, assuming that people are doing the best they can with the knowledge and resources at hand to do what's right for their children or community. Let them know that you respect their opinions and are committed to working with them as partners to ensure their children's—and all children's—success in your school.

Source: Adapted from AEL. (2000). *Administrator's Guide to Technology Leadership.* Charleston, WV: Author.

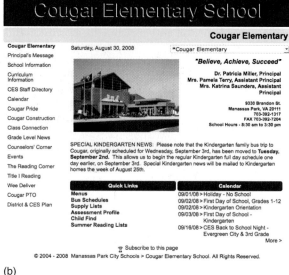

(a)   (b)

Figure 9.1

An example of a class (a) and school (b) website.
Source: © 2004–2008 Manassas Park City Schools

WEB LINK

Visit the textbook's companion website for a list of common tools and services that schools and teachers can use to create websites. Some free web services are included.

HTML or other coding. Even if you don't have one of these systems at your disposal, as you learned in Chapter 4, there are several easy-to-use options for creating a class website.

Often used as an online journal, blogs can also be used in a manner similar to websites or newsletters. The fact that they are easy to create and update with a minimum level of technical expertise makes them a great way to post homework assignments, notes for students, classroom updates for parents, and the wide variety of other information that needs to be conveyed to individuals who have an interest in what goes on in your classroom. The ease with which users can post text, graphics, and other information makes them preferable to some previous web-editing software.

THE GAME PLAN

Creating Your Own Class Website

Set Goals

Investigate the features of technology-based tools that allow teaches to create class websites to communicate with students, parents, or others.

Take Action

Review some of the tools and services listed on the textbook's companion website. Ask practicing teachers at schools you've attended or worked with about technologies they use.

Monitor

What are the common features across these tools? Would you need or want to use all of them? Are there any features you find missing? What training or support might you need to use one of these tools to create your own class website?

Evaluate and Extend

Prepare a plan or example of a class website to communicate with students, parents, and others. Identify the features and how you'd use them. Share your findings with your peers, practicing teachers, or technology specialists to revise your ideas.

THE GAME PLAN

Expectations for Electronic Communications

Set Goals
Learn more about the expectations schools have for their teachers when using electronic communications with students and parents.

Take Action
Review electronic communication policies from schools you find online as well as those who do not post this information online. Schools who do not post this information may have different expectations than those with a well-developed web presence. Review print and online teacher magazines and journals, as well, for discussions about the topic.

Monitor
What commonalities do you find across the policies? What disparities exist? Do some school districts mandate electronic communications? What are some concerns teachers express about using online communications?

Evaluate and Extend
Work with a friend or individually to develop a summary of the issues identified in communication polices that might inform the development of your own policy.

TOOLS FOR USE

How to Look Your Best on a Webcam

It's very easy to look *bad* on a webcam. Often, you're looking down into the webcam, the overhead lights create unflattering shadows, and the color of the monitor background casts an unnatural glow upon your face.

It's helpful to understand how most inexpensive video cameras, such as webcams, work. In order to determine what color should be what, the camera looks for white within the scene. If no white is there, the camera often attempts to make some other light color "white." So when sitting in front of a light-colored wall, the automatic white balance in the camera may want to adjust the color balance to make the wall white, causing unnatural color shifts in your skin tones. For example when sitting in front of a yellow wall, you might become a truly creepy color of blue!

Fortunately, a few simple steps can improve the quality of the image immensely (see Figure 9.2)!

1. Place the webcam at eye level. If you're using a laptop with a built-in webcam, you'll need to raise the entire laptop. Place it on books or another raised surface.

2. Change the background of your monitor to a neutral color and turn it down to a low light level. This will prevent the monitor color from reflecting off your face.
3. Place a white sheet of paper on your desk or keyboard to reflect the light from overhead upward to soften the shadows that are formed when the light source comes from above.
4. Pay attention to your background. A solid medium to dark toned wall works well. Avoid pastel colored backgrounds for the reasons described above. A bookshelf filled with books also makes an attractive background. Experiment with different backgrounds until you find one that is flattering.
5. Solid-colored clothing is usually most flattering on camera. In fact, you may want to wear a white shirt to provide the camera with a spot of white to use to adjust its white balance.

That's it! Take a look at the difference these tips can make!

(a)   (b)

Figure 9.2
As you will notice in the image on the left, it's easy to look bad on a webcam. As illustrated in the image on the right, following a few simple rules can greatly improve a webcam image. Images courtesy Liesl M. Combs.

Although you probably use e-mail every day, it has taken some time for e-mail and other Internet-based communications to take hold in schools. In schools where e-mail communication is common, expectations for its use should be made clear to students and parents. Depending on your schedule, you may tell students and parents that as a general rule you will try to respond to e-mail within a certain time period, such as 24 or 48 hours, two school days, or once weekly during a planning period. You'll just have to monitor how often you use e-mail and how it contributes to student success in your classroom.

You should also have clear expectations about what type of communications will be handled through e-mail. General progress reports, reporting student success stories, or making announcements may be appropriate for e-mail communication. Discussing student performance, whether academic or behavioral, is best left for face-to-face meetings or sometimes a phone call.

Of course, there are many ways to communicate and collaborate with other teachers online. Online communications that allow you to reach out to colleagues and other professionals aren't limited to just the printed word, as some web tools and services offer the option to conduct audio- and videoconferences. You may use these tools if you participate in a telementoring program or if you are collaborating with other teachers to generate curricula, instructional activities, or just share ideas. Some organizations offer computer conferences, book studies, webinars, opportunities to communicate with special guests, and scheduled chats on specific topics related to teaching. Some websites even provide discussion areas especially dedicated to first-year teachers. Many sites require users to "join" in order to fully participate in the discussions. Although a few sites might require a fee, many of them are free. All of these tools can help you connect with others to collaborate and share ideas.

Volunteering

Schools have long relied on volunteers to support their activities. Room mothers, Parent Teacher Associations, booster clubs, and work-sponsored programs are among the groups that provide much-needed moral and financial support to schools.

Digital technologies provide parents and community members new ways to volunteer. Support groups, such as PTAs, are going digital and are organizing and mobilizing with online communication tools. They are developing websites and managing online communications both for their members and for the schools they serve. Parents with technology expertise can also volunteer technology services to you and your school either after school or during class time (see Figure 9.3). Many parents who can't get to school to volunteer because of work or other commitments during the day can now help develop and support class websites; provide online homework help; coordinate functions and meetings; or help advertise events by e-mail, discussion lists, and web pages. Other parents or community members with greater flexibility in their schedules may share technology skills with students and teachers by offering training sessions or providing technical support advice or actual maintenance and repair. In Chapters 4, 5, and 8, we discussed the use of volunteers to help you manage your students' activities during complex, authentic learning experiences and for routine technology maintenance tasks, but the use of volunteers also enhances collaborative school, home, and community relationships.

Parents, community members, and business and industry personnel can also help support student learning in your classroom by sponsoring or participating in **virtual field trips** or telementoring opportunities. Career days and field trips tie into curricular areas and are common events in many schools. When students explore careers, and learn about job requirements, they come to appreciate the connection between schoolwork and potential careers—providing an authentic context to what they are studying and learning. Virtual field trips are the 21st century's version of these familiar events. Students can use audio-, video-, or webconferencing tools to interact with

Figure 9.3
Volunteers support school technology use.

professionals (some of whom may be their parents!) synchronously or they can "tour" businesses, museums, galleries, or other sites at their convenience using images, animations, and videos compiled on websites.

Several websites provide access to ready-made virtual field trips you can use in your classroom. The field trips can focus on a range of topics across a wide range of grade levels and many websites include teacher resources. Of course, you can work with parents, community members, or local businesses or organizations that support education to jointly develop your own virtual field trips for your students. Visit some of the virtual field trip sites on the web in order to get a better understanding of how to create your own.

Some schools, especially senior high schools, provide service-learning or mentorship opportunities where students shadow business and industry personnel to develop their skills—often career-specific skills, but social skills can also be addressed. Using various web-based technologies to support a mentoring program is referred to as **telementoring,** sometimes called eMentoring. Business and industry professionals have the opportunity to participate in telementoring programs through

 WEB LINK

Visit some of the virtual field trip sites listed on the textbook's companion website to plan for or create your own virtual field trip activity.

APPLY TO PRACTICE

Develop a Plan for Tech-Savvy Volunteers

Make preliminary plans for a technology volunteer preparation program to support your class.

1. Make a list of ways volunteers can support needs specific to the grade or content area you plan to teach. Include ways volunteers can provide help with a specific technology or technology-based activity when physically present or by employing technical skills outside of class. Review websites of parent and community groups to determine common technical requests as well as potential volunteering services.

2. Prepare a newsletter, flyer, or set of guidelines for a potential volunteer program. Describe the expectations for participation as well as benefits you hope to achieve for your students, yourself, and the volunteers. List resources necessary to support the program as well as skills volunteers should have.

3. Share your plan with others. Are there similarities? How do their plans differ? What changes should you make to your plan? Revise your plan and record it in your portfolio.

local or national programs. Usually, students receive course credit for participating in these programs and can use technology to record and report their experiences. Blogs, online portfolios, or presentation software can be used by students to demonstrate what they have learned as a benefit from this unique form of volunteering by parents and community members.

Extended Learning

When you create opportunities for learning outside the classroom and beyond the school day for yourself, other teachers, your students, or the larger community, you are extending learning. Schools can provide extended learning opportunities by providing additional learning opportunities on campus or taking them to the home environment.

Homework is perhaps the most common method for extending schooling to the home and its primary purpose is to promote student learning. As we enter the 21st century, many schools can also be found providing web-based material or tools in support of homework. You don't have to create all of your own web-based content but can instead rely on a variety of online resources to support your students in delving more deeply into content that is presented initially in class. These resources include curricular materials as well as those that offer study skills or homework help—some in real time using web-based communications tools. Putting homework help information online also helps parents and agencies that support schools, such as libraries and museums, better organize and prepare their own resources to support what you're doing in your classroom. Of course, one of the best ways to provide links to this information is through a class website, but if not available, you can compile links to helpful information in a document and send it home in print or via e-mail.

Some teachers are using commonly available software to create and post **podcasts** of their instructional sessions for student review. Students often miss class for a variety of reasons, ranging from sports activities to extended illnesses, and podcasts are one means of providing these students with access to information that may be difficult to obtain in another way. Of course, podcasts are also available from a variety of online sources to provide supplemental resources for use in and out of class. If you plan to make podcasts available for students to use at home, first find out how many students have the technology needed to access them, and plan alternative options for students who do not have access at home.

TOOLS FOR USE

Creating Podcasts

Here are some things to consider when creating podcasts for use by your students.

- *Plan, plan, plan.* Just as with developing any instruction, especially one that relies on multimedia, you need to develop an explicit plan before compiling any of the media files into your podcast episode. The steps presented in Chapter 2 in relation to portfolio development will do you well here: define, design, develop, deliver. Carefully consider, then apply, each of these steps in the development of your podcasts.

- *Format is everything.* Whether you're using audio alone or incorporating images or video, you have to make sure they're in the correct format for your podcast. If you're unfamiliar with editing images or video, you can still create helpful audio-only podcasts of presentation notes and study guides for your students. No matter what media you include, make sure it is

converted to a format that can be interpreted by the podcast software you choose.

- *Choose your tools.* Free software is available to help you create podcasts on both Windows and the Macintosh operating systems. Audacity is the tool of choice for audio-only podcasts on Windows, while MovieMaker can be used to incorporate video. On the Macintosh, the freely available GarageBand software allows you to create audio tracks, insert images, and incorporate video. These applications use a timeline on which you apply and arrange your media files.

- *Sharing your podcasts.* Perhaps the easiest method to post your podcasts for your students is through the use of a blog. Most blogging software makes it easy to upload podcast episodes that you can then share with anyone with an Internet connection. And best of all, there are lots of free blogging sites.

Figure 9.4
Students gain technology skills by refurbishing equipment.

Supplying books and other materials for students to use to perform research, develop skills, and create projects is commonplace in virtually every classroom in every school, but some schools go even further by providing laptop computers and handheld devices that students can check out in order to access instructional materials both at school and at home. Other schools loan or sell older equipment at a very low cost for home use. Students can be enrolled in classes or after-school programs that focus on refurbishing this equipment for sale or loan, providing even greater opportunities for extending learning specific to developing technology skills (see Figure 9.4). Older equipment can be a low-cost method for providing access to common productivity tools, such as word processors, so all students' homework can look just as good as their peers while they develop and practice technology skills.

Schools can also provide after-school access to technology by opening their computer labs, libraries, or media centers for students, parents, and community members. In addition, they can extend learning in one area of great need in many communities—technology instruction. Although you probably grew up in a "wired" society, there are still many adults who left school when these technologies were not commonplace and who still need to develop these skills to function well in an information-based economy. During "family computing nights," parents can develop their technology skills and also strengthen the crucial home-to-school connection. Parents can receive valuable technology training or access to digital resources while becoming more familiar with their children's class work and teachers. Some programs provide the opportunity for students to help train parents, grandparents, or other community members on the use of common technologies—helping to strengthen their own technology skills as well as develop a range of social skills. Training for parents can also support responsible computer use and may help allay some concerns parents have about their children using the Internet as an educational resource.

Benefits of Enhanced Collaboration

Through open communication, volunteering, and extended learning opportunities, parents and community members develop a better understanding of your responsibilities as a teacher and become more familiar with the processes and procedures of

STORIES FROM PRACTICE

The Home-School Connection

I've been fortunate to visit a number of different schools from several states that have been recognized for excellence both for technology use and student achievement. For these schools, technology is critical for helping students meet academic goals. I was not disappointed during my two visits to one large high school that had been acknowledged as a Blue Ribbon School from the U.S. Department of Education and an Intel Model School. The faculty and staff had embraced the power of technologies to support their work, and a range of different technologies were used both in class and to support learning once students left the building. Faculty members were adept at using interactive whiteboards in their classrooms and were able to use them in unique ways to connect with learning at home. Software that came bundled with the whiteboards allowed teachers to capture notes taken during class, still images of diagrams or figures, or even short animations that could then be posted to class websites. Both students and parents can review the web-based information. Some students use it for review, while others can view material they may have missed while absent. Parents found it helpful for keeping up with what their children were doing in school. The material could be especially helpful in advanced classes for which parents may have little background or might need a refresher in the content.

Teachers also support homework help in other ways. One teacher added a homework hotline component to her class website. It's basically a discussion board where students posted questions about their homework. At first, the teacher related, she handled most of the questions herself, but she did so from a wireless laptop while watching television or sitting on her deck in the backyard. By the time I visited, her students had taken over the hotline, providing help to others in the class. In her class, getting the right answer was not as important as understanding how to get to the answer, and helping other students online was one way some students better understood the content. During my observation, the teacher was able to begin by reviewing the most troublesome problems as posted on the website and acknowledging some of the best ideas and strategies that were shared. The class discussion was very focused because she already knew the problems her students were having based on a review of the hotline.

Source: John Ross

your school, which may be far different from schools they attended while growing up. The collaborative partnerships that are developed can provide a variety of benefits for students, faculty and staff, parents and the community (Epstein, Coates, Salinas, Sandards, & Simon, 1997).

Communication with your students helps them become more aware of their own progress. Communicating data from groups of students (class, school, state, or national performance data) gives your students the opportunity to monitor and evaluate their learning by comparing themselves to established norms. Students can interact with experts in a variety of career roles when parents and community members volunteer in schools, either virtually or face-to-face. These programs also provide an opportunity for students to develop skills that allow them to communicate and interact with adults and help them develop a greater awareness of the importance of school within a larger context, whether the local or global community.

APPLY TO PRACTICE

Models of Extended Learning

Think of the Internet as an opportunity to extend learning beyond the physical boundaries of the school building and the limitations of the school day. Some teachers have developed websites that are merely informative, while others have truly capitalized on some of the unique advantages of web-based delivery to support student learning.

1. Find an example of a high-quality class website that appears to provide support for learning. What is good about the site? What might you change? What opportunities are presented on the site that you might consider for your own class website?
2. Create a description of the website, seeking permission from the teacher if you would like to use sample text or images, and include a brief statement about what you do or do not like about the site and how you might incorporate some of its features into your own class website.

Students can benefit from the increased opportunities for practice and reinforcement that extended learning opportunities can provide. These opportunities may include increased access to resources, including technology resources, as well as access to people—you, other students, or other experts.

Through communicating with parents and community members, you build greater understanding for your needs and the needs of your students. You can generate support for curricular and extracurricular activities, including the use of technology. You and your colleagues might benefit from the presence of volunteers who provide support for routine management tasks, allowing you to focus more on teaching. Of course, community and business members can volunteer funds and equipment, as well as their time or expertise. Extended learning opportunities provide you with extra support for learning activities beyond class time. You can also benefit personally from the opportunity for professional growth that communication technologies and extended learning opportunities provide.

Parents and community members also benefit through the increased awareness of school programs that open communications, volunteer opportunities, and extended learning provide. Benefits to parents and the greater community include an opportunity to participate in formal and informal teaching and learning. And one commonly cited benefit of extended learning opportunities is the increased access to resources, especially technology resources, when parents and community members share school-based physical and virtual spaces, including hardware, software, and networking. When schools extend learning opportunities to the larger community, they reinforce the important goal of "lifelong learning" for students, staff, parents, and community members.

Modeling and Facilitating Effective Use of Technology Tools

When the computer revolution started in schools, large cumbersome machines—ironically referred to as "personal computers" or "microcomputers"—were often relegated to the realm of computer labs where they could exist on desks or tables designed to accommodate them with ready access to electricity and, eventually, the Internet. But as the revolution continued, a new development occurred. Computers became more common in classrooms.

It seems logical that these powerful resources would be located as close as possible to where learning occurred, but this posed several problems. When boxes of computers started showing up, literally overnight, in classrooms across the nation, teachers had to find space for them—and decide how to use them. We've discussed ways that you can model and facilitate the effective use of digital technologies through your instructional strategies and management practices in many places throughout this book. In this section, we will focus on how you can model and facilitate effective use of digital tools through the physical arrangement of technology resources and their safe and healthy use.

Protecting Students and Technology Resources

The rise in use of educational technology has forced many school districts to insert bulky hardware—such as desktop computers—into spaces that were not designed for them. In the past, classrooms typically were designed as rectangular spaces with the teaching area focused on chalkboards across one wall. Although there were educational initiatives such as "open classrooms" with movable partitions, pods, and mobile or cyclical learning stations, most current classrooms were built to support the most prevalent form of instruction, the lecture. Desks in rows were common, and in many schools, the number of desks in each classroom got larger as student-

Figure 9.5
Many classrooms were not designed to support digital technologies. In this classroom, note the exposed cables and cords, as well as the student working at a table not intended for computer use.

to-teacher ratios increased. Electrical outlets were scarce and classroom phones were almost nonexistent. It's a good thing those days are over.

But are they? School construction is an expensive endeavor and many districts must still make do with older buildings not designed to support digital technologies (see Figure 9.5). The following tips will help you protect both your students and technology resources.

A modern multimedia computer can require more than 400 watts of electrical power, so be aware of the load on your electrical circuits. If you don't have enough electrical outlets for the number of computers in your room, new outlets should be installed by a licensed electrician rather than continually adding cords and adapters that pose a threat to your equipment and your students. Many school districts have licensed electricians on staff. If necessary for short-term use, extension cords should be of sufficient capacity to support the technologies you attach to them.

Dust is the enemy of the computer, so if you still have a chalkboard in your room, ask to have it covered with an inexpensive laminate that allows you to use dry-erase markers and enables it to double as a projection screen. Additional measures that can prevent dust from infiltrating the technology in your room include the use of air filters on your classroom circulation system (usually installed by maintenance personnel), dust covers for equipment, and use of a hand-washing routine.

Air circulation is also important. Computers and their peripherals generate a great deal of heat and require adequate ventilation. Unfortunately, the heat generated by computers and CRT (cathode-ray tube) monitors will also affect the need for air conditioning. Flat-screen displays and laptops generate less heat and use less electricity, with laptops using the least amount of energy and creating the least amount of ambient heat in a room.

Fortunately, newer schools can be designed with modern technologies in mind, and newer hardware continues to get smaller, lighter, and more portable and powerful. Wireless technologies have enabled Internet access to classrooms that would have been prohibitively expensive to connect by physical cables. Even computers in different buildings can be connected to the Internet quickly and relatively inexpensively with wireless technologies. A wireless laptop cart can provide every student in your

Figure 9.6
Computers are often an integral part of learning centers.

classroom with a computer with no wires necessary for power or an Internet connection. Still, regardless of the shape and size of your classroom, or the type of technology you have available, there are some factors you should consider when you decide where to place computers in your classroom in order to facilitate effective use while protecting the technology resources and reducing the possibility of student injury.

If you have only one computer in your room, you probably want it close to the front of the room so that it can be used for presentations, unless it can be moved with ease. You may want it on or close to your desk so that you can use it for class preparation and record keeping; just make sure you can still get to it during classroom instruction. But many times, classroom computers are part of learning centers, so consider whether they need to be close to other work areas (see Figure 9.6).

Keep in mind that computer monitors can be distracting to students working elsewhere in the room. It may be tempting to create a computer cubicle with bookshelves and other furniture; however, make sure you can monitor your students' computer use. Large monitors also can hide students' faces and work. Many teachers find it best to line up computers against a wall so that the monitors are facing into the room. Other students' chairs can be arranged in such a way that their backs are to the computers. This arrangement would allow you to supervise what is on the students' monitors with ease. Even though you may have an Acceptable Use Policy in place (see Chapter 10), it's important to monitor student activity while using technology resources to make sure they are focused on the learning task as well as to ensure they are using appropriate applications and web resources. A classroom full of laptops can make monitoring a little more difficult than five desktop computers across one wall, but by circulating around the room, you still should be able to monitor appropriate use.

Also consider the movement of students within the classroom. You and your students should have enough room to circulate throughout the room without encountering obstacles such as loose cords, cables, raised floor receptacles, and temporary power supplies, such as power poles that provide access to electricity in the middle of the room. Make sure that wires and cables are out of the way of foot traffic and don't present a hazard to either the computers or students. Provide adequate table space for the students' materials. If students will work in groups, make sure there is enough space for several chairs.

Technology-Related Health Practices

As you arrange the computers in your classroom, take care to make the arrangement as ergonomically comfortable as possible in order to reduce the physical strain that extensive computer use may cause. **Ergonomics** refers to the study of and development of furniture, tools, and systems that promote productivity in a safe and healthy way. You may be familiar with desks designed for computer use that have lowered trays for keyboards, padded supports for wrists, and mouse support trays. These are designed to reduce the strain on our bodies when we use the equipment. Ergonomics relates specifically to designing work and learning environments that support the individual.

Computer equipment should be placed on ergonomically correct furniture. You should keep in mind that students come in all shapes and sizes, so what is ergonomically appropriate for one may not be appropriate for all. Chairs can be ergonomically designed to support computer work. Adjustable chairs are optimal, but if unavailable, try to include chairs of various sizes to match the needs of your students. The National Institutes of Health (NIH) offers helpful information about setting up an ergonomically correct computer workstation. Use the Ergonomic Checklist, based on recommendations from NIH (2005), to set up workstations to reduce strain and fatigue for you and your students. Keep the checklist posted near areas where computer work occurs in your classroom.

TOOLS FOR USE

Ergonomic Checklist

Monitor Placement	Chair Adjustment	Desk Height	Keyboard and Mouse Placement
As you begin any computer project, take a minute to make sure that ☐ The monitor is right in front of you about arm's length away with the top of the monitor about eye level. ☐ The monitor is tilted back a little (about 10 to 20 degrees). ☐ The screen is clean. ☐ The brightness and contrast settings are acceptable. ☐ There's no glare on the screen.	While seated in your chair, make sure that you don't stay seated in the same position all the time. ☐ You are not hunched over but are sitting back at an angle of 90 degrees or greater. You should be sitting so that your ankles, knees, and hips are at 90°. Your thighs should be parallel to the floor. ☐ Your feet should be flat on the floor or be supported. Consider creating a footrest by incorporating phone books, crates, or other materials. ☐ If your chair has a backrest, adjust it so it supports the natural inward curvature of your lower back. If necessary, use a slightly inflated beach ball or pillow to provide back support. ☐ If available, armrests should be placed so your shoulders relax naturally and your elbows and lower arms rest lightly on them.	Choose a desk where ☐ The working height of the desk is approximately at the height of your elbows while seated. ☐ The keyboard is approximately 1 to 2 inches above your thighs. ☐ The area underneath you desk is clean and uncluttered so you can comfortably stretch your legs. ☐ If a document holder is used, it is placed at approximately the same height as the monitor and at the same distance from the eyes to prevent frequent eye shifts between the screen and reference materials.	Adjust your keyboard and mouse so that ☐ Your shoulders can relax and your arms can rest comfortably at your sides. ☐ The keyboard is close to you. The mouse is next to the keyboard at the same height. ☐ Your forearms are parallel to the floor. You should not have to reach up for the keyboard or mouse. ☐ If necessary, use the built-in legs found on the bottom of most keyboards to angle the keyboard. A three-ring binder laid on its side also can make a nice keyboard stand. Place a piece of shelf liner on the notebook to help prevent the keyboard from slipping. ☐ A rolled hand towel or a commercially purchased wrist rest placed in front of the keyboard can provide wrist support if necessary. ☐ You do not have to stretch or change the height of your hands to reach the keyboard or mouse. ☐ Do not rest your hand on the mouse when you are not using it. Rest your hands in your lap when not using them.

Source: National Institutes of Health, 2005.

Take care to monitor your own computer use as well as that of your students. Even after taking ergonomic factors into consideration, some **repetitive strain injuries,** such as tendonitis, can occur during computer use due to the sensitive nature of the soft tissues, tendons, nerves, and muscles of the hand that are subjected to repeated motions, awkward positions, or force. **Tendonitis** refers to the inflammation, irritation, or swelling of the tendons, which connect muscles to bone. Another repetitive stress injury commonly associated with keyboard use is **carpal tunnel syndrome,** in which the median nerve of the hand becomes compressed at about the location of the wrist. This can cause numbness, tingling, and pain in the thumb and the side of the hand closest to it. The easiest way to address mild cases of these injuries is to ensure student workstations are ergonomically appropriate, taking special care to make sure that the keyboard is low enough to encourage proper arm and hand placement. Both tendonitis and carpal tunnel syndrome can be treated with braces or a glove-like wrist support that are worn for extended periods. Physical therapy may also be necessary if these injuries become severe. In extreme cases, carpal tunnel syndrome may require surgery.

Different keyboards and input devices (some discussed in Chapter 6 under assistive technology) might be preferable for some of your students, especially if your curriculum requires a good deal of keyboarding. Keyboards that alter the position of the keys to provide a more relaxed presentation matched to natural hand positions can reduce strain for some students as can keyboards with audible clicks when keys are stroked. The clicking signals that the key has been activated and can prevent some students from pressing down too hard while typing. Trackballs, pen styluses, as well as many other input devices allow options for interfacing with the computer that do not rely on a more traditional mouse.

You can also teach your students some simple stretches for your head, neck, and wrists to promote healthy computer use, especially during longer work sessions. The simple stretches presented in Table 9.1 can be done seated or standing.

Table 9.1	Neck, Shoulder, and Wrist Stretches

Side Neck Stretch

- Tilt your head to one side, moving your ear toward your shoulder.
- Hold for 15 seconds.
- Relax.
- Repeat 3 times on each side.

Diagonal Neck Stretch

- Turn your head slightly and then look down as if looking in your pocket.
- Hold for 15 seconds.
- Relax.
- Repeat 3 times on each side.

Shoulder Shrug

- Slowly bring your shoulders up to your ears and hold for approximately 3 seconds.
- Rotate shoulders back and down.
- Repeat 10 times.

Wrist Stretch

- Hold your arm straight out in front of you.
- Pull your hand backward with the other hand—palm facing front, then pull your hand down —palm facing you.
- Hold for 20 seconds.
- Relax.
- Repeat 3 times each.

Source: National Institutes of Health, 2005.

Table 9.2	Avoiding Vision Problems

To avoid vision problems when using a computer monitor:

- Adjust the lights lower than for regular classroom instruction.
- Minimize glare on your screens by avoiding direct sun or overhead lights, using a glare screen, or paint walls a darker color.
- Adjust the brightness and contrast on your screen.
- Adjust the size of text on your screen. Most text applications and web browsers allow you to change the size of text with a menu command or shortcut.
- Blink more often and stay hydrated to keep your eyes well lubricated. People often blink less when doing computer work. If your classroom is especially dry or if the heating system dries out the air, some people may require eye drops to keep their eyes lubricated.
- Take a break, and if you can, go outside into natural light.
- Do eye exercises (see Table 9.3).

Computer monitors challenge our eyes in ways that printed text does not and may lead to **vision concerns** (see Tables 9.2 and 9.3). Unlike most print, text on a computer screen is not presented in uniform levels of light and dark, but with dots of light (called pixels) that make up the images being the brightest in the middle. Unlike the static images on a page, images on a computer monitor are constantly being redrawn. (If you've ever seen a rolling screen when a monitor is not in synch, you might have noticed this.) The **resolution** (clarity of an image or letter related to the number of dots per square inch) of computer monitors is also much less than printed material—which is also why many graphics prepared for presentation on a computer monitor look very jagged or unfocused when printed. Most people read slower on a computer monitor when compared to text for this reason. Software and web designers often follow the guideline of using sans-serif fonts (fonts without the small curls of ornamentation on the extremities of letters) for display on the monitor to improve visibility of text. Older monitors can be fitted with screens to reduce glare but newer flat panel screens may not need this additional equipment.

Table 9.3	Eye Exercises

Palming

- While seated, brace elbows on the desk and close to the desk edge.
- Let weight fall forward.
- Cup hands over eyes.
- Close eyes.
- Inhale slowly through nose and hold for 4 seconds.
- Continue deep breathing for 15–30 seconds.

Eye Movements

- Close eyes.
- Slowly and gently move eyes up to the ceiling, then slowly down to the floor.
- Repeat 3 times.
- Close eyes.
- Slowly and gently move eyes to the left, then slowly to the right.
- Repeat 3 times.

Focus Change

- Hold one finger a few inches away from the eye.
- Focus on the finger.
- Slowly move the finger away.
- Focus far into the distance and then back to the finger.
- Slowly bring the finger back to within a few inches of the eye.
- Focus on something more than 8 feet away.
- Repeat 3 times.

Source: National Institutes of Health, 2005.

APPLY TO PRACTICE

Planning Safe and Healthy Lessons

1. Design a lesson activity that helps students understand the safe and healthy use of technology but that also addresses a content standard from an area in which you excel.
2. Consider requiring your students to develop their own checklists for the safe and healthy use of technology using their own words and examples from their classroom. They can brainstorm ideas or gather information from school-related health and safety tips on the Internet. The result of the activity can be a poster or web page that all students can access to remind them of technology safety.

Some vision problems, such as **computer vision syndrome,** can occur due to the inability of your eyes to maintain focus on items on the screen. These problems are manifest in people who use a computer monitor extensively almost every day. If your students complain of constant headaches, loss of focus, blurring, or sore neck and shoulders during computer use, they may be suffering from computer vision syndrome. The treatment for this vision problem is usually some type of prescription glasses designed specifically for computer use. Reading glasses are usually not appropriate as the distance from eyes to screen is usually farther than to a book held in one's hands. Glare screens and antireflective coatings can help reduce some vision problems but cannot correct computer vision syndrome. If you or your students are going to work at a monitor regularly for two or more hours, you should consider visiting an optometrist who can prescribe computer glasses, if necessary.

Many states require students to meet technology proficiency standards—just like teachers—and safe and healthy use of technology is often a part of these standards. The following Tools for Use presents a list of safety tips for the use of technology in your classroom. You may want to create a similar list with your students as a learning activity to orient them to technology safety as it relates to your class. You can incorporate this activity while teaching students how to use a particular piece of software or hardware or even while covering content standards. For younger students, you may want to consider a "Safety Certificate" they can display or take home to share with their parents. An important aspect of teaching in the 21st century is modeling and facilitating the safe and healthy use of the powerful technologies found in most classrooms.

TOOLS FOR USE

Ten Tips for Safe Use of Technology in Your Classroom

1. Model and monitor appropriate technology use every day.
2. Carefully plan for time to set up and put away equipment.
3. Position computer monitors where they can be observed.
4. Keep aisles and pathways clear to avoid tripping and ease movement of carts on wheels.
5. Keep computers cool with sufficient air circulation by keeping work areas clean and uncluttered.
6. Reduce dust by covering equipment and installing air filters where possible.
7. Carry laptops with both hands with the screen latched.
8. Transport heavy equipment, especially large equipment on carts with wheels, according to the school's safety policy.
9. Put away and lock up equipment when not in use.
10. Report equipment in need of repair in a timely fashion.

APPLY TO PRACTICE

Technology Safety

Depending on the content area and grade you teach, you may need to develop a modified list of technology safety tips that supports specific technologies found in your classroom.

1. Design a top ten list for your classroom. Include the content area and grade that you teach. Some complex technologies used at higher grades, such as in a science or manufacturing lab, may require their own top ten lists—or at least a top five list. If you plan to use particular equipment that requires its own list, create a list that you can use in your classroom. Modify the list so that it is relevant and engaging to your students.
2. Review technology safety lists you may find online or from practicing teachers. Do you need additional information to complete your list? What technologies presented in this book or in your class should be included? How can you use different technologies, such as image- or video-editing software, to make this information more compelling to your students?
3. Share your lists with other students in your class. Are their items different from yours? Why? Do you want to modify your list?

Chapter Summary

In this chapter, you considered ways to use technology tools to enhance communications and collaboration within and beyond your classroom. You learned that open communications are one way to enhance collaborative relationships among schools, homes, and the community. Other ways to enhance relationships include volunteering and extended learning opportunities. Although you may expect to spend most of your time working with your students, other stakeholders, such as parents and community members, can offer a great deal of expertise and help to you and your students. Networked digital technologies have helped to create virtual "classrooms without walls" that have the potential to connect your classroom with others in your school, district, community, or across the globe.

This chapter also provided guidelines and practices you can use to model and facilitate the effective, safe, and healthy use of the technology resources you may find in your classroom or school. We discussed the importance of arranging computers and related tools in a way that protects both students and technology resources. We also provided tips on reducing common health problems that can be associated with extensive or incorrect computer use.

In the next chapter, we focus on protecting your students and technology resources in another way—through modeling and facilitating the legal and ethical use of digital resources and technology tools.

YOUR PORTFOLIO

To demonstrate competency in ISTE NETS-T 3.b, c, and d, prepare the following items for your portfolio. Incorporate artifacts you have created from activities in this chapter.

1. A communications plan that includes a
   a. description of one or two technology-based collaborative tools you could use to support student learning in and beyond the classroom

   b. description of methods for communicating and collaborating with parents, community members, or other teachers, either through a class web page, e-mail, or other communications tools

   c. description of a technology volunteer preparation program to support your class

2. Create a customized list of tips for the safe and healthy use of technology tools in your classroom. Consider the grade level and content area you plan to teach and the technologies commonly associated with locating, analyzing, and evaluating relevant information. Reflect on your role and how you will model effective technology use as well as the responsibilities your students will have for learning in a 21st-century classroom.

References

AEL. (2000). *Administrator's guide to technology Leadership.* Charleston, WV: Author.

Epstein, J., Coates, L., Salinas, K., Sanders, M., & Simon, B. (1997). *School, family, and community partnerships.* Thousand Oaks, CA: Corwin Press, Inc.

National Institutes of Health. (2005). *Ergonomics for computer workstations.* Bethesda, MD: Division of Safety, Office of Research Services. Retrieved June 30, 2006, from http://www.nih.gov/od/ors/ds/ergonomics/computer.html

PTA. (1997). *National standards for parent/family involvement programs.* Chicago: Author.

Safe, Legal, and Ethical Use

ISTE Standards addressed in this chapter

NETS-T 4. Promote and Model Digital Citizenship and Responsibility

Teachers understand local and global societal issues and responsibilities in an evolving digital culture and exhibit legal and ethical behavior in their professional practices. Teachers:

a. advocate, model, and teach safe, legal, and ethical use of digital information and technology, including respect for copyright, intellectual property, and the appropriate documentation of sources

c. promote and model digital etiquette and responsible social interactions related to the use of technology and information

Note: Chapter 11 addresses b and d of ISTE Standard 4.

Outcomes

In this chapter, you will

- Develop instructional activities that adhere to acceptable use policies, appropriate copyright guidelines, and proper citation practices.
- Acknowledge and address issues related to academic integrity such as detecting plagiarism, avoiding cheating, and keeping data secure.
- Create learning environments that protect students and technology resources.

Digital tools generate digital concerns. The ease with which digital tools can be used to find, create, manipulate, and share information can be a boon to teaching and learning. However, these same tools can be used to quickly and easily copy other people's work, capture inappropriate or unwanted images, or spread sensitive information across the classroom, school, or globe. Consider the stories from practice as representing the voice of experience. The following scenarios are based on actual experiences from schools across the nation and are designed to emphasize the relevance of this ISTE NETS-T Standard 4 for all teachers.

As you read the stories, you will see that educators in digital classrooms face some unique challenges, but many of these challenges can be addressed by knowing, modeling, and enforcing computer behaviors that are safe, legal, and ethical. This chapter helps you understand these issues so that you can incorporate appropriate practices into your own work ethic as well as into the culture of your classroom.

STORIES FROM PRACTICE

Voices of Experience

New teacher Jill Bazemore was stunned that her principal had referred to her as a "pirate." She had simply gotten frustrated with the word-processing program on the computers in her classroom. It was so different from the one she had been using in college for several years prior that she had bought a copy of the program she was used to and installed it on the five computers in her classroom. It just made things easier for her. She couldn't believe her principal was talking about being sued. She had actually bought a copy of the program with her own money! Besides, she was just using it in her own classroom.

Based on: *eSchoolNews*. November 1, 2001, "District's $50K 'piracy' settlement spurs policy changes." http://www.eschoolnews .com/news/showStory.cfm?ArticleID=3107

. . .

Mrs. Bell, high school debate coach, quickly rushed to the main office after being called by the principal's secretary. She was annoyed because this was the last week the debate team could practice before going to district finals and she wanted to start working with the students on the team. However, her annoyance quickly changed to surprise when she found two of the best debaters on the team in the office with their parents—all looking extremely upset. It appears these students had observed Mrs. Bell entering her password into the student information system several times and had used her computer while she was out of the room to change grade and attendance records for themselves and several of their friends. The two students were now facing the very real possibility of a court appearance that could result in jail time and thousands of dollars in fines.

Based on: *eSchoolNews*, May 1, 2004, "Students arrested for using teacher's computer to change grades." http://www .eschoolnews.com/news/showStory.cfm? ArticleID=5034

. . .

Social studies teacher Randy Simmons had just finished grading the last of his class's personal history videos when the phone rang. His seventh-grade students had worked in groups and used digital cameras and video-editing software to create short movies that addressed content standards across several curricular areas. He was proud of their efforts and the results. That's why the phone call from his principal was so surprising. It seems that one group of students had used the same equipment to take some extra footage of themselves parodying teachers, the principal, and some of the other students. To make matters worse the students had posted the video on a website. The video became extremely popular on the site and had caught the attention of the local press. He could expect more phone calls from irate parents and community members and possibly a visit from reporters in the morning.

Based on: *eSchoolNews*. November 1, 2003, "'Star Wars Kid' school video puts privacy rights to test." http://www .eschoolnews.com/news/showStory.cfm? ArticleID=4724

Acceptable Use Policies

For many schools, **acceptable use policies (AUPs)** are the first line of defense in preventing unsafe, illegal, and unethical use of a school or district's technology resources. An AUP is a document that clearly outlines what is and is not acceptable behavior, as well as the consequences of unacceptable behaviors. Based on a review of AUPs from schools and districts across the country, educators agree that the primary purpose of school technology, especially the use of the Internet, is to support teaching and learning. Many districts also emphasize that the use of the school or district's technology resources is a privilege, not a right, and that there are rules for expected behavior when using them. Some AUPs may also stress that electronic communications can inadvertently (or sometimes intentionally) be quickly and easily distributed to many people beyond the intended audience and should therefore not be considered private. Individuals who abuse the policies set forth in an AUP often lose access privileges or, at best, are given restricted access to the resources. Consequences of unacceptable use should be consistent with other school and district policies, codes of conduct, or legal codes.

You should never consider your e-mail to be private or confidential. Messages can be intercepted, whether intentionally or not. Seemingly "private" e-mails can be accessed by others many times; even "deleted" e-mail could still be on your hard drive or the service provider's mail server. Be aware that all e-mail written on school or business computers may be the property of the school or business. Schools or districts that provide e-mail services usually emphasize this point in their AUPs to everyone who uses the system including students, parents, and staff members. Some schools don't provide e-mail accounts to students at all, or only provide activity-based e-mail class accounts for a limited duration, such as a grading period or the length of a school-based project.

AUPs are often created by a committee, which may be composed of school board personnel, central-office and building-level administrators, teachers, media and technology specialists, parents and other community members, and even students. AUPs are not just for the use of the Internet and can cover the use of all the tools and resources available for teaching and learning within the school setting. AUPs have been common in schools for years, even prior to the integration of digital tools or Internet use in classrooms. As instructional tools have evolved, AUPs have had to change along with them. In just a few short years, schools have had to consider how their policies should reflect technologies such as e-mail, school-based web pages, instant messaging, peer-to-peer file sharing, cell phones, handheld computers (PDAs), laptops, and camera phones.

Policies will vary from district to district, but AUPs for technology should be consistent with similar policies for other school-related resources and should reflect the basic mission and goals of the school or district. The tone of policies may range from very informal letters to complex documents that read like a legal contract. It is common to have both students and their parents read and sign a district's AUP—which may be part of the student handbook—before students are given access to the school's technology resources. As a teacher, you will most likely be required to read and sign an AUP as well, whether the same as or modified from those for your students. As a teacher, it's important that you not only understand the expectations of your school or district's AUP but that you model expected behaviors described in the policy. Some schools or districts may discuss the AUP at parent nights or technology open houses. This can be especially helpful in areas where parents may be concerned about their children's uses of the Internet and possible access to inappropriate material (see Stories from Practice: Parent Internet Driving School).

Some common elements found in AUPs from schools across the country are an overview, a glossary of terms, the purpose of technology use, the rights and responsibilities of the district, examples of acceptable and unacceptable use, and consequences of unacceptable use. Although the topics may vary from district to district, AUPs often include sections on copyright, issues of academic integrity, and Internet use. See Table 10.1 for some common examples of both acceptable and unacceptable use.

STORIES FROM PRACTICE

Parent Internet Driving School

As the use of the Internet in teaching and learning became more commonplace, faculty and staff at the Nueva School in Hillsborough, California, expected their students to take advantage of this resource both in school and at home. They did so without the use of filtering or other technological means, however. In order to make their Internet experiences positive, new students and their parents attended short trainings at the beginning of the school year called "Parent Internet Driving School" (Abilock, 1997). Every student and at least one of their parents were required to attend the training before they were allowed to use the Internet in this elementary school. During the training, parents and their children learned about the role the Internet plays in the classroom and got to visit common websites used for instruction and to practice using school-provided e-mail accounts. Parents also received information to help them make decisions about Internet use at home, strategies for promoting acceptable use—what is referred to as "techno-parenting," as well as online and print resources that were followed up by regular school communications. This series of short trainings helped to alleviate fears for parents while also encouraging them to support student work outside of the classroom using similar tools and procedures to those being used in the classroom.

Table 10.1	Examples of Acceptable and Unacceptable Uses of School Technology
Examples of Acceptable Use	Examples of Unacceptable Use
<ul><li>Abiding by the policies and procedures of other networks that are accessed</li><li>Being polite and using appropriate language</li><li>Deleting unwanted messages or old data from computers and servers</li><li>Enforcing appropriate use and reporting misuse or security issues</li><li>Respecting copyright and licensing agreements and citing material</li><li>Running virus software on downloaded files, attachments, peripherals, or disks</li><li>Signing correspondence</li><li>Using online time efficiently</li><li>Using the Internet ethically and legally</li></ul>	<ul><li>Altering software by deleting files, downloading programs, or copying or installing unauthorized programs</li><li>Assuming the identity or using the passwords or materials of another</li><li>Conducting commercial activities, advertising products, or taking part in political lobbying</li><li>Downloading text, graphics, or software, or engaging in behaviors that may be considered obscene, abusive, libelous, indecent, vulgar, profane, or lewd</li><li>Gaining access to any pay-for-view site</li><li>Giving out your own or others' private information, such as address, phone, or passwords</li><li>Harassing an individual using the Internet</li><li>Plagiarizing</li><li>Transmitting material that violates any U.S. or state regulation, such as copyrighted, threatening, or obscene material, or material protected by trade secret</li><li>Vandalizing equipment, electronic files, or willfully spreading computer viruses</li></ul>

THE GAME PLAN

Acceptable Use Policies

Set Goals

Learn more about AUPs. Schools and districts list a wide range of acceptable and unacceptable uses for communications technology.

Take Action

Find examples of AUPs from schools across your region or the nation. You can use print-based AUPs from schools you are associated with or search the Internet for a national perspective.

Monitor

Are you finding the examples you need? Have you considered asking for AUPs from friends, colleagues, or former teachers? What other terms might schools use to describe an AUP?

Evaluate and Extend

List commonalities and differences. What types of uses surprise you, as either acceptable or not? What types of uses do you think should be added to your master list? How do you think the lists will change over time? You may want to compile your own table of acceptable and unacceptable uses and an additional list of items you find that seem to be unique to a particular school.

Copyright

One area in which school districts will set AUPs is in the use of copyrighted materials. Information technologies and the ease with which information can be created, duplicated, and shared have had significant impact on copyright law—the law that governs the right to use information. Electronic communications and files are considered a fixed medium (that is, a form of material expression), so items such as e-mail and discussion list messages, web pages, and digital photos are considered copyrighted material. If the material does not explicitly state that it is in the **public domain** (i.e., creative works or information that are not "owned" by an individual but considered part of the common culture) or may be used for educational purposes, you may be violating copyright law when you use it—even if you are using it for an educational purpose.

Although the *Copyright Law of 1976* (Pub. L. No. 94-553, see Figure 10.1) is the most current copyright law, this law precedes the widespread adoption of personal computers in education, so subsequent legislation continues to have an impact on copyright. This section describes issues related to copyright, especially as they relate to the use of technology for teaching and learning. However, due to the constant testing and interpretation of copyright law in the courts and the subsequent evolution of the law, it cannot be considered a definitive authority. It is best to keep track of changes in copyright and state and local interpretations of the law. You can visit the website of the U.S. Copyright Office at the Library of Congress for more information.

In response to the impact of information technology on copyrighted materials, the *Digital Millennium Copyright Act (DMCA)* was passed in 1998 (Pub. L. No. 105-304). The DMCA was a reaction to growing electronic commerce that heightened the penalties for copyright infringement on the Internet, but also impacted education. In particular, the DMCA placed strict restrictions on materials that could be used online for instruction. For example, as a teacher in a brick-and-mortar classroom, you could show a video or images or play sound recordings to the students present, but if you taught the same class at a distance via the Internet, the DMCA severely restricted the amounts of digital media you could use. In fact, you probably couldn't use the same videos, images, and recordings in their entirety that you used with your face-to-face students.

With the number of distance learning opportunities growing quickly at all levels, copyright law was impacted again by the passage of the *Technology, Education, and Copyright Harmonization Act of 2002* (Pub. L. No. 107-273), commonly called the TEACH Act. This revision to copyright law clarified what uses of copyright-protected materials were permissible when used for distance education and also outlined required actions on the part of a school in order to be compliant.

The TEACH Act is limited to certain institutions including some educational institutions. However, to be eligible the educational institution must be a nonprofit organization and be accredited. Public schools are normally nonprofit and accredited, however some charter schools, virtual schools, and institutions of higher education are not and therefore are not eligible to use digital resources as governed by the TEACH Act (see Table 10.2 for an overview of the TEACH Act). The TEACH Act also requires that your district or school develop a policy that is distributed to all

WEB LINK

A link to the U.S. Copyright Office at the Library of Congress is available from the textbook's companion website.

Copyright grants the holder these rights:
- to reproduce the copyrighted work in copies or phonograph records
- to prepare derivative works based on the copyrighted work
- to distribute copies or phonograph records of the copyrighted work to the public by sale or other transfer of ownership, or by rental, lease, or lending
- to perform the copyrighted work publicly (in the case of literary, musical, dramatic, and choreographic works, pantomimes, and motion pictures and other audiovisual works)
- to display the copyrighted work publicly (in the case of literary, musical, dramatic, and choreographic works, pantomimes, and pictorial, graphic, or sculptural works, including the individual images of a motion picture or other audiovisual work)
- to perform the copyrighted work publicly by means of a digital audio transmission (in the case of sound recordings)

Figure 10.1
Copyright Law of 1976.

Table 10.2	The TEACH Act
Your institution must:	**As a teacher, you must ensure copyright-protected material is:**
• Be a nonprofit organization • Be accredited • Have a copyright compliance policy • Provide notice on copyright-protected materials • Prevent copyright-protected material from being transmitted or stored beyond the period of instruction	• Directly related to and is an integral part of instruction • Available only to registered students • Available during a time limited to instructional needs • Used in digital format, if available • Nondramatic in nature or a limited portion of a dramatic work

faculty, staff, students, and parents for the acceptable use of copyrighted materials. This policy dictates how copyright materials will be identified to all who use them. This may be included as part of an AUP. Your district or school should also take steps to ensure that copyright-protected materials, especially those distributed electronically, particularly through online instruction, are accessible to the appropriate students only during the duration of the course and that they are not stored or distributed afterwards.

Your specific obligations as an educator using digital materials under the TEACH Act are to make sure the digital materials are an integral part of the instruction and are used under your supervision. That does not mean that you must be online at all times that your students are accessing a streaming video or downloading a journal article used in your class. You should, however, have the ability to post and remove digital materials in a timely fashion related to their instructional use. You and your school or district must make sure that digital materials are available only to students who are enrolled in the class that requires the materials for instructional activities. This prevents you from posting copyright-protected materials directly to a school website that can be accessed by students or others outside of your class.

When considering all of these stipulations, it is important to note that the materials you use must be legally obtained copies, and if they exist in digital format, you must purchase or obtain them in digital format. For example, you can't digitize your copy of a copyright-protected analog video if it is available in a digital format. You also may use only 1) resources that are performances of nondramatic literary or musical works, 2) limited portions of other works, and 3) the same amount you would normally display in your face-to-face instruction. For example, while your school may have a license to show the entire taped production of "Romeo and Juliet" or the musical "West Side Story" in a classroom setting, you may not broadcast these in distance learning settings because they are both considered dramatic works.

Fair Use and Technology in the Classroom

So what *can* you and your students use in your classroom? It's important to understand whether material falls under the limitations of **fair use**, is in the **public domain**, and may be used in its entirety, or requires licensing, permission, or payment for use.

Fair use refers to the part of U.S. copyright law that allows limited use of copyrighted material without requiring permission from the copyright holder. Fair use guidelines have been established that allow for the limited use of some materials in educational settings. The following four criteria help us determine whether material falls within fair use:

1. the purpose and character of the use, including whether such use is of a commercial nature or is for nonprofit educational purposes
2. the nature of the copyrighted work

3. the amount and substantiality of the portion used in relation to the copyrighted work as a whole
4. the effect of the use upon the potential market for, or value of, the copyrighted work

When considering whether to use material you have found for instruction—whether you have reused a graphic from a website, copied text from an electronic file, or burned an audio file to a CD—reflect upon the guidelines for fair use. If your purpose for using the material is transformative in some way, if it creates something new such as through review or commentary, your purpose may honor the first guideline for fair use. If it is a strict copy, it is probably not fair use under this guideline. For example, if you have created an audio collage of several different actors reciting lines from Shakespeare in an effort to illustrate characteristic features such as alliteration, cadence, or language use, you have transformed the work. Simply playing a movie back in its entirety requires you to honor the copyright restrictions of the work. Transformation also occurs when original works lead to variants through critique, extrapolation, or interpretation.

The material may meet the second guideline if the nature of the work is published and is factual rather than fictional. For example, the use of factual information (mathematical formulas, definition of DNA) that might be found or corroborated across several sources is more likely to be considered fair use than excerpting sections of journals, websites, poems, or other works of fiction and creative nonfiction that might be found on the web. Works that are out of print are also likely to be considered fair use (Stanford University, 2005; University of Maryland University College, 2004).

The acceptable portion of the work you are using in relation to the whole is difficult to judge. There is no set number of words, lines, pages, measures or notes from musical works, or portions or number of graphics, web pages, or lines of code that can be used to measure fair use. While not a strict rule, several guidelines for educators suggest you follow a "10% rule" (Baird & Hallett, 1999). To stay within the guidelines for amount of work, do not use more than

- 10 percent or three minutes of a video, whichever is less
- 10 percent or 1,000 words of text, whichever is less
- 10 percent or 30 seconds of a musical work
- five images from an artist or photographer
- 10 percent or 15 images from a collection, whichever is less
- two copies of a multimedia project

When using materials in your classroom for instruction, you are unlikely to have an effect on the potential market; however, educators should be careful about the term of use of the material. If you use a small portion of a digital work for only one semester or lesson, you are probably not affecting the potential market. But if you use the same material for more than two years or you make more than two copies of a multimedia project you should obtain permission for use from the copyright holder or follow guidelines for the appropriate purchase and licensing of the material. In summary, the use of copyrighted works for educational purposes is more likely to be considered fair use than their use for profit, but you should seek to understand the copyright restrictions common to any material you use regularly. One of the best resources in your school will likely be your school librarian or media specialist.

Public Domain

Materials that have entered the public domain may be freely used and distributed. These materials include those for which the copyright has expired or work created by the U.S. government. Some authors also enter their work into the public domain

APPLY TO PRACTICE

Legal Issues

Keeping up with legal issues as they relate to technology can be especially difficult because of technology's rapid pace of change. Laws normally evolve over time in reaction to new social and technological developments. Laws also change as they are challenged by the courts. It's important that you establish strategies you can use to monitor the changes in copyright law and how these will impact the resources you can access and use in your teaching.

1. Identify print and web-based resources you can use to monitor copyright legislation. List these resources and the links to them in your professional portfolio.
2. Share your findings with others in your class. Review the resources they have found and determine which should be added to your own list.

upon creation. Determining when a copyright has expired has gotten more difficult with the passing of the *Digital Millennium Copyright Act of 1998* (Pub. L. No. 105-304). Generally, all works published in the U.S. prior to 1923 are now in the public domain. Since the passing of the DMCA, most works published since 1977 will remain in copyright for the life of the author plus 70 years. There are some exceptions and you may want to check with your media specialist or the copyright holder if you believe a work may be in the public domain.

Teachers also should be careful with modern interpretations of materials that were originally published prior to 1923. For example, Walt Whitman's "Leaves of Grass" is in the public domain, but the jazz interpretations of the poems by pianist Fred Hersh are not. William Shakespeare's works, such as "Romeo and Juliet" are in the public domain, but many of the film versions are not.

Academic Integrity

Just as you can benefit from the ease with which academic materials and resources may be found, searched, copied, and repurposed, so can your students. Without guidance and training, some of your students may find it all too easy to find and reuse copyright-protected material, regardless of their intentions. The use of other people's identities, such as the use of another student's or even a teacher's password to access sensitive data, also may be alluring to some students. These issues are often addressed through AUPs or honor codes.

Plagiarism

Plagiarism is not a new problem, but digital tools have made this possibility much easier. With extensive resources available on the Internet—both legitimate and otherwise—and through other digital resources such as encyclopedias, newspapers, journals, and curriculum subscriptions, a student can quickly gather and use the work of others and compile it in a digital document. Many students who know how to copy and paste on a personal computer may feel compelled to do so inappropriately when faced with the pressure of meeting an approaching deadline or getting a good grade.

The first line of protection against the inappropriate use of other people's work is to help students understand how to correctly use and cite source material (see Figure 10.2). This can start in very early grades. Some elementary schools have even developed policies that emphasize the importance of properly citing information students have received from other students, their parents, or from media resources such as television programs or websites. Obviously, as students get older and begin to create documents,

Each writing style guide has different ways of correctly citing Internet resources. The proper way to cite information retrieved from the U.S. Copyright Offices is illustrated below, based on the format required by three popular style guides

APA style
U.S. Copyright Office. (2006, July). *Copyright basics*. Washington D.C.: Library of Congress. Retrieved July 7, 2006, from http://www.copyright.gov/circs/circ1 .html#wwp.

Chicago style
U.S. Copyright Office, "Copyright Basics," Library of Congress, http://www .copyright.gov/circs/circ1.html#wwp (accessed July 7, 2002).

MLA style
U.S. Copyright Office. *Copyright Basics*. July 2006. 7 July 2006. <http://www .copyright.gov/circs/circ1.html#wwp>.

Figure 10.2
Citing Internet resources.

graphics, and multimedia projects that draw on source materials, they need to understand how to appropriately cite those materials. They too, must understand copyright and realize that even though they can find text, an image, or sound file on the Internet and quickly incorporate it into a document or movie, it is still protected under copyright law.

Another proactive step to prevent plagiarism is to design activities in ways that avoid the need for heavy reliance on material that easily can be appropriated from other sources. Instead of assigning papers or compositions that simply require students to gather and report information, ask your students to use that information as the basis for a personal reflection requiring analysis and extrapolation. Writing activities can be supported by technologies that can limit access to outside source materials and encourage deeper analysis on the part of students through debate or discussion. Threaded discussions, messaging tools, and online journals are but a few tools that can help students communicate original thoughts rather than simply finding and inserting facts, figures, and the ideas of others. Many forms of digital communication and some electronic documents also can be tracked and time stamped to identify ownership and usage patterns.

Developing skills related to finding, analyzing, synthesizing, and reporting information—whether in traditional formats such as a research or term paper or in a multimedia presentation that combines text, images, audio, and video elements—is a common requirement in the academic careers of most students. Despite your good example and guidance, sometimes you may believe that a student may have used the works of others inappropriately. There are some techniques you can use to investigate the actual source of the material. Keeping samples of work from students that are generated both inside and outside of class, such as through an electronic portfolio, is a good practice for determining the legitimacy of a student's work. This type of student data allows you to quickly compare new works with the consistency of growth demonstrated across time and any inconsistent use of language or rapid advancement in technique can be identified and verified with the student. Any type of strange formatting, such as changes in font, size, color, or unusual characters, logos, or other marks may indicate material that has been copied.

If you feel that a text-based student work may contain the work of others, you can also use software applications or online resources to verify questionable passages. Schools and districts can quickly set up their own electronic warehouse of student papers on which to search or may rely on commercial services that often offer discounts to schools or districts. Sometimes a simple search engine can provide the results of true authorship, and many search engines can search documents in a variety of formats including HTML and portable document format (PDF). Generally, you copy the passage you think may be the work of someone else and paste it into one of the search services or software applications. You can also search some of the many online paper services, sometimes called "paper mills," to look for matching titles or phrases from questionable documents. Another proactive strategy is to not only inform students that this type of service will be used, but require students to submit their own work for this type of scrutiny. This valuable lesson may help them realize just how well they are—or are *not*—doing at avoiding dishonest practices.

Cheating

With pressures to succeed academically from parents, peers, teachers, and society in general, many students may feel compelled to achieve success through dishonest means. As long as there have been tests, there has been cheating, but the digital tools available to students, whether for academic purposes or not, have provided some unique methods for sharing answers and materials. There's no strong evidence that students are cheating more with greater access to technology; however, the methods they use may be different.

Whereas students might once have passed notes in class on folded scraps of paper, they now have the capacity to store questions and formulas on calculators, beam questions back and forth through infrared sensors on handheld computers (PDAs), send instant or text messages to friends across the room or school, or use a camera phone to take a picture of a test and send it to their friends in a later class. While all of these possibilities exist, several simple strategies can help prevent both high- and low-tech cheating.

Simple observation can prevent a variety of cheating methods (see Figure 10.3). Standing and moving about the room during assessments will limit some of the more difficult methods to pull off, such as using a camera phone, PDA, or text messenger. Lab or classroom management software can be used to monitor student activity and block some functionality on student machines. Randomly assigning equipment to

Masterfile

Figure 10.3
Observation is an effective way to prevent cheating during assessments, whether your students are taking a test using a computer or through other means.

classes on test days can prevent some students from storing and sharing information with later classes.

Much like preventing plagiarism, perhaps the best method for preventing cheating is to design assessments that encourage higher-order and critical thinking. Assessments that rely on low-level multiple-choice and identification questions are the easiest forms of assessment for students to compromise. Requiring students to analyze, synthesize, and evaluate information that incorporates relevant facts and data and that requires students to reflect on and interpret their own understandings will help limit sharing of answers—regardless of the technology available.

Keeping Data Secure

Most school personnel are familiar with and have plans for the safeguarding of print-based student information. Lesson plan books, grades, health records, discipline referrals, and other sources of student information are routinely stored in vaults or other secure facilities—sometimes fire-safe vaults. These records can be important to students long after they've left the school system for such important tasks as obtaining additional schooling, employment, citizenship, or even verifying one's age for retirement purposes. Schools have long taken steps to keep this information secure. In fact, they are required to do so by law.

The *Family Educational Rights and Privacy Act* (FERPA, Pub. L. No. 93-380) requires student records to be kept confidential and places strict guidelines on who can have access to those records. Generally, schools must have written permission from the parent or eligible student in order to release any information from a student's education record. However certain agencies, such as other schools, the courts, accrediting agencies, and some officials working in services related to health, safety, and justice systems, may have access to student records without that permission.

As districts and entire states move to large-scale networked services for record keeping, you may have little opportunity to select the hardware and software that will keep these records secure in a digital environment. However, issues concerning your own and student data will arise and you should understand how you and others access that information, whether from your classroom, office, or home, and how it is kept secure.

There are some records, usually those that fall under the label of "directory" information, that can be distributed under certain conditions—even on a web page. See Table 10.3 for a list of common directory information. **Directory information**

WEB LINK

Lab management software has a variety of helpful tools to monitor and control student computer use. Some management software, such as NetSupport School, is available for classrooms—not just labs. Review Chapter 5 and visit the textbook's companion website for references for classroom and lab management software.

Table 10.3	Directory Information

Directory information includes, but is not limited to, a student's

- name
- address
- telephone listing
- date and place of birth
- major field of study
- participation in officially recognized activities and sports
- weight and height of members of athletic teams
- dates of attendance
- degrees and awards received, and
- the most recent, previous educational agency or institution attended

is information which is contained in an education record that generally would not be considered harmful, or an invasion of privacy, if disclosed. Schools may disclose directory information without consent. However, schools must tell parents and eligible students about directory information and allow parents and eligible students a reasonable amount of time to request that the school not disclose directory information about them.

Although school personnel are often cognizant of, and avoid identifying underage students on a web page, of growing concern are publications such as newspapers that routinely post pictures and names of students involved in sports, drama, and other extracurricular activities especially when they have received an honor. Many news agencies replicate print-based stories on the web with pictures and captions. School districts and local news agencies can work together to establish guidelines for appropriate use of identifying information about underage students.

Just because an item is considered directory information, it does not give you carte blanche permission to distribute or post it. Most schools will not post students' names or contact information to the public. Parents also have the right to restrict the posting or distribution of any information about their children, even in yearbooks, school programs, and newsletters. If your school or district chooses to seek this

TOOLS FOR USE

Legal Issues Surrounding the Use of Images of Students and Student Work

Using images of students or examples of their work is an attractive addition to your portfolio; however, it is vital that you understand the legal ramifications before you get started. The same cautions apply to adults as well as children. While students constitute a special protected class, if you wish to include adults in your portfolio, play it smart and seek written consent, respect confidentiality, and be cautious. Remember that images published on the Internet can be viewed by a worldwide audience. Even when the materials will have more limited distribution, the following practices are critical when including student information in your portfolio.

- *Consent:* You may not use photos or videos of others, especially minors, without consent. Specific information regarding the format of use, potential viewing audiences, distribution method, general content and purpose of images must be provided and written consent received prior to production. It is imperative that parental/guardian notification be explicit with written and

dated permission obtained. Some schools seek this permission in their AUP or student handbook.

- *Identification:* Standard practice is to refer to students by first name only. You can also refer to a group of students to avoid identifying individuals, such as "Students in my class . . ." or "Geography students at our school . . ." Adult names may be used in full as needed, but only with their written consent.
- *Student Work:* You should secure parental/guardian permission for including student work in your portfolio. Individuals should not be identifiable. You can maintain confidentiality of identities on student work by using only first names or deleting or blocking out identifiers including city, school, and specific names.
- *Confidentiality:* If your portfolio includes reflections about a student, never refer to that student by name. Use a pseudonym or general term and do not link sensitive reflections about a student to his/her photo or other identifying information.

permission through the use of signed consent forms, whether from a student hand-book or an AUP, you should check with your school administration to verify that all students in your class or organization have indeed granted consent to have pictures or information displayed in class, print, or online.

Password Security

The modern school is full of passwords, identification cards, and other means to ver-ify identity. Teachers and students alike may have identification cards with pictures and magnetic strips, as well as accounts with passwords for e-mail, access to student information systems, and favorite websites and online resources. Some schools may even use biometric devices, such as those that scan fingerprints, to identify students getting on buses, getting lunch, or logging on to a school computer (see Figure 10.4). Keeping track of the way you access sensitive data and making sure that you keep it safe is both ethically and legally pertinent.

In terms of personal information, digital tools have made it easy to have access to an overwhelming amount of information. Often that information is secure and requires you to complete a profile so the system can verify, to some degree, that you really should be allowed to access the information it houses. The number of pass-words you collect can be staggering and confusing. It's tempting to use one or two passwords over and over and to neglect changing them, but this can lead to conse-quences far beyond simple theft of a test document or grade tampering.

There are several steps you can take when required to maintain a large number of user names and corresponding passwords (see Table 10.4). One important step is to change your passwords frequently, at least every several months. This can prevent those people who observe you logging in to your school network or e-mail system every day from exploring the possibility of using your account information, whether for malicious intent or just curiosity.

A common strategy many institutions suggest is to use a mnemonic device such as an acronym created from the first letter of each word in a sentence to create your password. It should be at least eight characters long and use both upper and

Figure 10.4
Biometric devices, such as this iris-recognition technology, help to clearly identify students and staff.

Table 10.4	Tips for Creating Passwords
Do	**Don't**
• Use 8 characters • Mix upper and lower case, numbers, and special characters • Change your passwords often	• Use names, dates, or familiar numbers • Use any real word in any language, either forward or backward • Use a pattern of consecutive letters, numbers, or keys on your keyboard • Write them down or share them with anyone • Enter your password into a website at the request of an e-mail, regardless of who the message may appear to be from

lower case characters as well as numbers and special characters. Consider the following:

1. Begin with the sentence, "My sister Alena likes to skate on ice."
2. Select the first letter of each word, which automatically includes uppercase and lower case letters: MsAltsoi
3. Replace some of the letters with numbers or characters that can either represent the letters or may even sound like the word they stand for. For example: MsA12sk@

There are software programs, some of them shareware, that can help you create passwords and store them in an encrypted format so that others cannot figure them out. If you forget a password, many websites have hint options or links to request a reminder. The system administrator may be able to reset your password or, if necessary, create a new account with a new password.

Internet Safety

Proponents of classroom Internet use view the seemingly unlimited amount of information and the ease of communicating with people all over the world as benefits. But these same characteristics may dissuade some teachers from using Internet resources for instruction due to the possibility of students coming in contact with undesirable websites or individuals. Although many schools have harnessed the Internet to support instruction, students may need guidance in practicing safe, acceptable, and responsible use.

Several federal laws have significant impact on schools and how you, as a teacher, might use the Internet in your classroom. The *Electronic Communications Privacy Act* (ECPA, Pub. L. No. 99-558) was enacted in 1986 and addresses security and confidentiality issues of electronically disseminated communications. In 1998, Congress passed the *Children's Online Privacy Protection Act* (COPPA, Pub. L. No. 105-277) to help safeguard children as they use the Internet. As a result, websites that target children under age 13 must follow specific guidelines regarding the collection of personal information. Not only must they limit the kinds of information they collect, but they also must post notice about the information they collect and how that information is used. If your school or district website collects or stores student information from children under 13, it too must comply with COPPA.

Websites you use in class should have clearly posted privacy policies; if they solicit information from individuals, they must follow the COPPA guidelines. Furthermore, parents or guardians must provide consent for a child to enter personal information on a website. This permission is often required to be in writing—not electronic format—but is a source of contention for software and information publishers who wish to capitalize on the web's ease of distribution. Lobbying and action in courts will continue to test this provision of the law.

The *Children's Internet Protection Act* (CIPA, Pub. L. No. 106-554) amended the earlier Communications Act of 1934 and requires schools and libraries receiving funds from the Universal Service Fund, commonly called the E-rate, to incorporate technology-based solutions that block access to material defined as obscene, pornographic, or harmful to minors. The act, passed by Congress in December 2000, is sometimes called the "Filtering Mandate." Although CIPA does not require that schools actually track how children or adults use the Internet, schools and libraries that receive E-rate funding have to certify to the Federal Communications Commission that they have complied with CIPA in two ways: 1) by installing a technology-based solution to block material deemed objectionable as outlined in the act and 2) by adopting policies to monitor Internet use by students. These policies should address:

- access by minors to inappropriate matter on the Internet
- the safety and security of minors when using electronic mail, chat rooms, and other forms of direct electronic communications
- unauthorized access, including activities that might be considered "hacking," and other unlawful activities by minors online
- unauthorized disclosure, use, and dissemination of personal information regarding minors
- restricting minors' access to materials harmful to them

Protecting Students and Technology Resources

You have probably grown up in a time when digital technologies were prevalent. If you are familiar with using computers for schoolwork, communicating with friends or family, or entertainment, then you are also probably aware that some people may take actions that result in harm to others or to technology resources. The results of these actions can be annoying at the very least, but in the extreme may lead to costly disruption of service or destruction of computers and networks, as well as harming individuals. While there are laws designed to discourage people from harming others or computers and networks, you need to make sure that you and your students become responsible users of technology, especially the Internet. Harm can result through the use of malicious software that affects vast numbers of computers and users directly or via the action of an individual against another individual or group. The software and practices described next in this chapter will continue to evolve, so it is important that you and your students learn what actions you can take to protect yourselves as well as your technology resources.

Malicious Software

It wasn't so long ago that most people considered e-mail to be a novelty. However, e-mail is so prevalent today that even students in kindergarten report having e-mail accounts. If you've had an e-mail account (or accounts) for any length of time, you've already learned the value and ease of sending and receiving messages, pictures, and other information anywhere across the globe. The boom in instant messaging (IM) and text messaging using phones or other web-enabled devices has also increased the ease with which you can communicate with your friends, family, and others. Certainly, messaging technologies will continue to evolve and few barriers may remain to prevent you from communicating with anyone at any time. Unfortunately, just as you can receive junk mail through the postal service, you have probably also received unwanted messages through e-mail. Unwanted messages can also come across cell phones, instant- or text-messaging devices, as well as weblogs (blogs).

The term **spam** refers to unwanted messages across many of these technologies. Once used to describe unwanted messages on early text-based newsgroups, the term became more popular with the increased use of e-mail but may also be associated with other technologies, including facsimile (fax) transmissions, instant-messaging devices, discussion boards, and blogs, among others. Spam can be more than annoying, it can lead to substantial losses to you as an individual as well as to organizations. Unlike junk mail delivered through the postal service, digital spam places most of the cost burden on you, the receiver. Some costs are minor, such as having to take time to delete unwanted messages from your e-mail inbox, but others can be more substantial to you personally, such as when you have to pay to receive an unwanted text message. Multiplied across the hundreds of thousands, if not millions, of recipients of a single spam message, the costs become substantial.

Spam can also include language or pictures that are unsuitable for your students and objectionable to you. These unwanted messages may also be a front for further spamming attacks. Messages that ask recipients to click on a web link to "unsubscribe," check the status of an account, or claim a prize may actually validate that your e-mail address is active and then store it or sell it to others for further spamming attacks. More malevolent intent can ask for sensitive personal information, including credit card numbers or addresses, in order to steal your identity, access bank accounts, or even to attempt face-to-face contact. **Phishing** refers to this type of spam, which may also be called **carding** or **spoofing.** Unfortunately, these messages may seem legitimate and may include logos from well-known and trusted sources (e.g., eBay, PayPal, and Best Buy are some well-known objects of phishing scams). They not only trick children but can be very convincing to adults. The damage caused by phishing has resulted in the introduction of a bill in the U.S. Congress called the Anti-Phishing Act of 2005 (Gross, 2005).

You and your students should be wary of any e-mail that asks for sensitive information. To respond to these messages, you should reply by phone to institutions purporting to have sent you the phishing attempt—not by the means by which it was sent. Some institutions require you to provide answers to questions that only you know as a means of verifying your identity. Pretending to be another person or representing a business is illegal, so phishing attempts can also be reported to the authorities.

Spam can also contain malicious software, sometimes referred to as **malware**, which can cause significant harm to one or more computers as well as a computer network. Three common types of malware are viruses, worms, and Trojan horses. You are probably already aware of computer viruses and may have been the recipient of one (or more!). The term **virus** is often misused to represent a wide range of malicious software types, but is usually most accurately associated with a software program that—once introduced into a computer—can attach itself to another program, replicate itself, and cause damage to software or data on the computer. A virus must be *introduced* to a computer by some action you or another person commits; it can occur by opening an attachment to a message or by sharing an infected document or file over a network or through a portable storage medium (e.g., disk, CD, or thumbdrive).

Related to a virus is a **worm**, which does not need to be attached to another software program. Worms, too, can replicate themselves but can more easily spread themselves across a network, which can result in disruptions of service when a network is clogged with e-mail messages sent as a byproduct of the infection. Worms can also make a computer vulnerable to further attacks or open to manipulation by others by installing a "backdoor" that allows people at a distance to use the computer as a terminal from which to send additional spam or malware. Unlike a virus or worm, a **Trojan horse**, named after the famous giant hollow horse from Virgil's epic poem about the battle of Troy, does not replicate itself. It can, however, cause severe damage to a single computer as it can actually delete all of the data stored on the computer or can cause the computer to turn itself off immediately after booting up. The distinctions among these three most common types of malware become less clear over time as programmers combine or devise new functionality that can be supported by malware.

Viruses, worms, and other malicious software are often the result of the work of an individual and are most often created for personal reasons—the unfortunate sense of accomplishment that can occur when a virus is truly effective in damaging computing resources. These acts are considered illegal and these programmers are often sought out and many have been prosecuted. You may, however, unknowingly install software on your computer that can be equally annoying and dangerous but may not be illegal. These include **spyware** that may record your usage patterns or may even collect sensitive information you transmit using your computer, and **adware** that incorporates the presentation of advertisements as a condition for operating the software.

Adware and spyware are different from the virus-related applications described earlier in several ways. Both are usually created by teams of software developers who see the applications as a legitimate method of collecting information from you to inform marketing and product development decisions. Also, you usually have to actively install some type of software, such as weather forecasting or e-mail software, in order for the spyware or adware to also be installed. While it's pretty obvious that you are installing adware, you often don't know that you may also be installing spyware in addition to the software you originally desired. Both adware and spyware can collect and transmit information back to the company that provided the software. This activity is often described in the Terms of Use for adware, but since you usually don't know you're installing spyware, it doesn't have Terms of Use. At their worst, these programs can transmit sensitive information, such as contact or credit card information, or can become so prevalent that they bog down a computer completely. Spyware appears to infect only Windows-based computers.

Unfortunately, e-mail messages that contain malware often appear to be friendly messages, such as the message "I love you" associated with the famous Love Bug Virus. These messages can appear to come from people you know, but are really the result of the malicious program co-opting the e-mail account of someone you trust. You also may not realize when one of your documents is infected, and you can unwittingly spread viruses or other malicious programs through procedures you thought were appropriate, such as backing up files on a network server or sharing files with colleagues. Malware that is hidden in text files or pictures, called **steganography**, is also extremely difficult to recognize.

The first line of defense against malware is often technological. Hardware and/or software that can prevent unwanted persons, messages, or software from entering a network or computer is called a **firewall.** Firewalls can be installed on a school or district (or larger) network server in order to help protect the entire network, or can be installed on a single computer as a personal firewall. You probably—or should —have firewall software on your own computer right now. Commercial **virus-protection software** is also commonly used to scan files introduced to a computer or for periodic scanning of all files on a computer. Some virus-protection software can also repair infected files and delete malware from your computer. These software programs, as well as spyware blocker software, pop-up blocker software, and security software associated with your operating system should be updated periodically. This update process can be automated (with the Windows Update function in the Internet Explorer program on Windows-based computers and the Software Update program on Apple operating systems being two common methods).

In addition to the use of hardware and software, you and your students should take actions to help prevent infecting your computers with malicious software. Be cautious of opening messages with misspelled words or irregular use of uppercase letters or symbols. You may be required to report suspicious messages to your network administrator, sometimes forwarding the message to the administrator with the routing of the message visible (a feature you can select or view in most e-mail applications). Scan all attachments and don't open any documents that end with the .exe suffix. Some schools and districts do not allow teachers or students to install any software programs and may use software that prevents unauthorized installation or that even uninstalls software that is not approved. Cloning software can be used on networked computers to periodically reset them to their original configuration and applications as well as erase user files stored on the hard drive.

THE GAME PLAN

Protecting Technology Resources

Set Goals
Learn more about malicious software and strategies to protect your technology resources.

Take Action
Find web resources that describe current viruses, worms, and other malware and how to protect your computer from them. Visit the websites for virus protection and personal firewall software vendors as well as sites for Apple Computers and Microsoft to find recommendations for protecting computers that run those operating systems.

Monitor
Review the software installed on the computer(s) you often use. Determine if they are at risk based on what you have found. Do you need additional information? Are there technology experts who can help answer questions about keeping your own computer safe?

Evaluate and Extend
Share your experiences with others. If you use or installed virus-protection or personal firewall software, what were your experiences? Did others have similar experiences?

Threatening or Unlawful Online Interactions

In your classroom or on the school grounds, students acting inappropriately may be easy to spot. Students who threaten or bully others face-to-face can be identified easily and reprimanded, if necessary. But when bullying occurs through the use of social-networking sites such as MySpace.com and Facebook.com, blogs, and other online discussion forums, it can be difficult to prevent or respond to as your school may have little or no authority in the matter. In fact, you may not be aware it is happening. The use of technologies to harass, defame, or intentionally harm another student or group of students is referred to as **cyberbullying**. The consequences of cyberbullying can be dramatic and extremely damaging to the children involved and can result in emotional stress, withdrawal from school, relocation, and even suicide. In 2006, a nonprofit anticrime organization composed primarily of law enforcement officials, Fight Crime: Invest in Kids, reported that one-third of children between the ages of 12 and 17, and one-sixth of children between the ages of 6 and 11 have been victims of cyberbullying. Based on these findings, the organization predicts that more than 13 million children between the ages of 6 to 17 could be victims of cyberbullying.

Some common methods of cyberbullying include:

- *Messaging.* Students can send anonymous messages via e-mail, text messaging, instant messaging, posting on other students' online journals (blogs), or social-networking sites, through chat rooms, or any other messaging method. The messages can be derogatory, hurtful, violent, slanderous, and may contain offensive pictures or graphics.
- *Creating a website.* Students often create websites for school projects and can easily create a website that is hateful to another student or group of students. These websites can include lists such as "Who's Hot" and "Who's Not," similar to the popular yet often malicious "slam books" of classrooms from a bygone era. Cyberbullying websites can also contain highly objectionable language and hurtful statements.
- *Pictures, videos, and other recordings.* Camera phones have made it extremely easy to take pictures of students without their knowledge, such as when changing in a locker room. In addition, digital photos can be readily altered in offensive ways. Videos, pictures, and even audio files can be posted on websites or sent as part of messages.
- *Impersonation.* Students can impersonate another on websites, e-mail, during online games, or by stealing another student's password. The intent in this

case is often to get other students in trouble for acts they have not committed, perhaps by having their rights or access to games or web resources suspended. In some cases the cyberbullies may even pose as "victims" to harassment that they themselves have delivered.

Unfortunately, there may be little you as a school official can do in cases of cyberbullying. Much of what is posted on the Internet is protected by free speech and unless the cyberbully makes a threat of violence or actually commits a crime, there is little that authorities can do. Some of the speech posted on a website may be considered libel, but it is often expensive and time-consuming to prosecute. Most cyberbullying occurs from home and may not be related to school activities.

Schools may not be able to stop cyberbullying unless rules against it are written into the school or district's AUP. A provision in an AUP may include the right to discipline students for their actions off campus that are intended to have an effect on a student or that adversely affect the safety and well-being of students while in school. Regardless, the best strategy to prevent and negate the effects of cyberbullying may be educating teachers, students, and parents. Many of the issues covered in this chapter, such as protecting passwords and appropriate e-mail use, are important for students to understand and follow. Students should also be aware that their actions are easily traced through digital media. Obtaining a domain to post a web page requires a credit card and the name of the owner of that domain is freely available through the domain's WHOIS database. Students should also feel comfortable reporting that they are victims of cyberbullying to their parents and perhaps to school officials, such as their teachers or guidance counselors.

At the point that inappropriate online actions involve adults, the behavior becomes more serious and can lead to **cyberstalking** or engaging with a predator. Sometimes, students participate in online activities that they may not realize are threatening. Obviously, minors should be prohibited from gambling, and online gambling websites must take steps to authenticate the age of their users. However, there are gaming, discussion, and fan websites that students can visit in which they may unwittingly provide sensitive information to others. Children who visit and participate in a website devoted to playing games—even simple games, such as checkers or chess—may actually be communicating with adults who are collecting information from them, such as their interests and hobbies. Building trust with someone who seems to like the same things you do may inadvertently lead to providing contact information. The same is true of chat rooms or social-networking sites, such as the popular MySpace.com or Facebook.com, in which students may provide a good deal of personal information that allows them to be easily identified, all within a context in which they believed they were acting naturally and appropriately.

Educating children about strategies for protecting sensitive information is critical. Students should realize that blogs, chat rooms, and other interactive communication vehicles can be monitored by just about anyone. Even something as harmless as creating a screen name can provide more information than necessary. For example, the screen names, "luv2cheer," "ftblhero42," and "suzeindc" all provide information of interest to online predators. The first is probably a screen name for a cheerleader, while the second is probably a football player who wears jersey number 42. The final screen name gives a location, Washington, D.C., where one might find "Suze" or "Susie." These names, when combined with topics covered during a chat session, can provide a detailed profile of a child.

Some children may also create their own web pages that provide ample information that identifies their ages, genders, and locations. Just by describing their hobbies ("I'm on the Middleboro swim team") or where they go to school, they may inadvertently be filling out their profiles. Posting a phone number, whether online or when using other messaging tools, can immediately pinpoint a child's home location. Entering a phone number in some search engines not only results in a complete address but may actually include a detailed map of how to get there!

Many schools do not authorize the use of chat software on school computers. But as chat rooms, instant-messaging, text-messaging, and other technologies become more prevalent, some educators feel it is important to include technologies that are interesting and commonplace in order to engage students in learning. Regardless of which technologies you use in your classroom, those selected should be based on sound pedagogical principles and provide a strong fit for mastering the required content. When using software, such as chat software, it is best to take a few precautionary steps and inform the students what you are doing. While chat threads often scroll across a window quickly, software is available to "record" entire chat room transcripts. Be aware of common chat room abbreviations and discuss them with your students. You may be surprised to find out the meaning of some abbreviations (see Table 10.5 for a short list). Students should know whether or when they can or cannot use abbreviations (like when writing school papers or taking exams using pencil and paper). You should take steps to investigate unfamiliar abbreviations as they will

Table 10.5	Chat Room Abbreviations

Abbreviations become popular and fall out of use over time—sometimes very quickly. A few abbreviations are given below, but keep track by periodically searching for lists of abbreviations on the Internet, especially if you encounter an unknown abbreviation in student work.

143—I love you
9—someone is watching over my shoulder
99—person watching has left the room
ADDY—address
A/S/L—Age, sex, location
BBL—be back later
CTN—can't talk now

IMHO—in my humble opinion
LOL—laugh out loud
MYOB—mind your own business
NGAAAH—cry of frustration to get attention
POS—parent over shoulder
P911—parent in the room

TOOLS FOR USE

Ten Tips for E-mail Use

Where schools once taught etiquette for writing letters and using the telephone, they now emphasize Internet etiquette, or **netiquette**, for short. There aren't any universal standards, but the following netiquette tips may help you, your staff, and students ease into proper online behavior.

- **Be yourself.** Don't pretend to be someone else or use someone else's password. Protect your own password and log off public machines.
- **Say hello.** Include a salutation and acknowledge the person you're writing to.
- **Describe your message.** Use short, descriptive titles for subject headings and restate the question or issue in a response. Quoting only pertinent material in a reply can save time and may be useful to your audience.
- **Be polite.** Short messages may be seen as brusque, and UPPERCASE letters may be considered shouting. Although you may intend to be ironic or humorous, your text-based messages may lead to misunderstanding.
- **Is it important?** Work out problems face-to-face, not through e-mail. Avoiding issues by sending e-mail merely delays resolution.
- **It's not that funny.** Unsolicited forwards of the newest jokes often are not appreciated and can tie up someone's time and

slow down server response. *Spamming,* or sending unsolicited mail to large groups, is seriously frowned upon, and some service providers may actually revoke your Internet service.
- **Make sure you mean it.** Proofread messages for spelling, content, and meaning. Electronic messages don't always remain private and can be sent quickly to hundreds, if not thousands, of people. Some e-mail has even been used as evidence in court!
- **To attach or not to attach.** Large text or graphics files that require proprietary software can be time-consuming to download and may actually annoy the recipient. Software like Adobe Acrobat may work best for formatting large attachments, and files may be reduced in size by *stuffing* or *zipping* them.
- **Say goodbye.** End with a signature and, if possible, make it a *brief* signature. Contact information can be useful in a signature, but unnecessary quotes, pictures, or HTML formatting may be less appreciated than they're worth.
- **Clean up after yourself.** On public machines, delete message files and quit the mail application to prevent others from using your password or account.

Source: Adapted from: AEL. (2000). *Principal connections: A guide to technology leadership* [CD-ROM]. Charleston, WV: Author.

undoubtedly change over time. Involve your students in developing ground rules for participation and they are more likely to behave appropriately and focus on the learning.

Using Technology to Support Acceptable Internet Use

Based on the requirements of CIPA and growing concerns among educators and parents alike, nearly 100 percent of all public schools reported using blocking or filtering software in 2005 (Wells & Lewis, 2006); most schools have turned to one or more technologies to help keep students safer as they use the Internet for learning. No one strategy can solve all unacceptable use problems and you should not rely solely on technological tools. Training for parents, teachers, and students will help reduce the number and severity of problems you encounter.

Trusted Digital Resources

One method of supporting safe use of the Internet is to use known and trusted digital resources (see Figure 10.5). You can direct your students to acceptable and valid material on the Internet, whether they are web-based references to which your school or district subscribes or are proven free resources.

Subscription content services can also provide valid resources and help support student inquiry in a safe environment. More than electronic encyclopedias, subscription services include content in a variety of web-based formats and many support dynamic content generation by teachers and students as they connect schools to others around the world. Some textbook publishers offer web-based versions of their books as well as activities and materials that are only available online. Some web-based textbooks and content providers also present age- and grade-appropriate

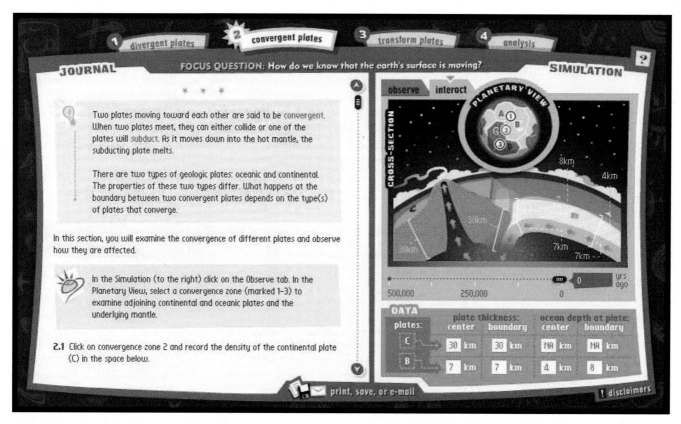

Figure 10.5
Many schools and districts subscribe to trusted online resources.

content at different reading levels, so that students across a range of reading levels have an increased opportunity to master required content. Some content services may also provide lesson planning, gradebooks, and other student information resources so you can have "one-stop shopping" in terms of web-based materials to support your instruction.

Many long-standing print or media companies with a proven track record in education, such as National Geographic or PBS (Public Broadcasting Service), have repurposed their vast print and video archives for web delivery. Many of these organizations now consider web distribution important and so develop materials and tools that capitalize on its unique attributes. Schools that use free resources must weigh the possibility that they may contain advertisements and consider how they want to limit students from leaving the environment for expanded web surfing.

Filtering Software

Filtering software is one of the easiest technology-based solutions to help schools comply with CIPA. While you may not be personally responsible for installing or maintaining filtering software on your school computers, you should know whether your school or district uses filtering software, your obligations for that use, options for reporting inappropriate sites, as well as for unblocking desirable websites that have been blocked.

Designed to help prevent students from coming into contact with inappropriate material when using the Internet, **filtering software** remains a contentious issue for many. Advocates for free speech or those who oppose censorship argue against the limitations these tools place on access to information; however, the increasing amounts of information available on the Internet and the unlimited topics covered have led many schools to use filtering software. The growth rate of information is so quick that filtering software offers one strategy to providing a supportive environment for teaching and learning. Filtering software is also less expensive than evaluating or previewing all the individual sites with which you or your students may come into contact during the school year and over subsequent years.

Unfortunately, filtering software is not always 100 percent effective. Keywords used to ban sites can be derived subjectively and most filtering services do not publish their lists. This is both to protect their proprietary information but to also prevent individuals from subverting their tools by bypassing known sites that are filtered. Filtering software must be updated often to keep pace with the rapid growth of the Internet. Schools or developers of filtering software who claim they prevent students from viewing objectionable material may also open themselves up to litigation if the software is not completely effective (Pownell & Bailey, 1999).

On the other hand, filters can block desirable content and they may not take into account the varying ages, levels of maturity, and individual needs of users—although

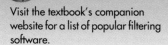

WEB LINK

Visit the textbook's companion website for a list of popular filtering software.

APPLY TO PRACTICE

Web Filters

1. Most public schools use some type of filter to block access to certain Internet sites. What are your beliefs about the appropriateness of web filtering? Under what circumstances, if any, would you support the use of web filters?

2. Search the web to locate descriptions of filtering software. Examine a few of the web filter sites such as Cyber Patrol and Net Nanny and determine what type of content is filtered or blocked and why. Try to determine how that information is blocked and how these practices are monitored and kept current.

3. Does the information you found influence your beliefs about the use of filtering software? Discuss your views with your peers. If there are differing opinions, what evidence can you or your peers provide to support your positions?

filtering software designed specifically for students of different ages does exist. It can be difficult, however, for a district that uses filtering software across the network to allow access to material that may be deemed appropriate to students of different ages and grades. Schools that use filtering software without knowing which sites are being blocked and why may unintentionally censor materials that are constitutionally protected. Some filtering software providers allow schools to customize their installation of the software by adding or removing sites to the general list as well as providing the ability to allow teachers to identify inappropriate sites if encountered accidentally. This often takes place through a website or via e-mail and the inappropriate site can often be removed from access within 24 hours and sometimes much quicker.

Proxy Servers

Proxy servers are software applications that perform several functions, including filtering and storing Internet content. A proxy server can download and save frequently visited websites in a storage area called a cache. This can result in improved network performance because users can view already-downloaded websites without a long wait. A proxy server also acts as a low-level firewall and provides limited protection against network intrusions such as viruses or denial of service attacks. For many districts, filtering software installed on a proxy server is an effective way to protect the network and its users at one point of service that can be easily monitored, upgraded, or repaired, if necessary. Consider, instead, how difficult it would be to combat a network attack in even a small district with a few hundred computers if these tools were located on individual computers. The costs associated with labor alone would be enormous and could effectively shut down instructional computer use for days.

Some proxy servers have features that provide greater management of Internet use on your network by prohibiting unacceptable use. For example, proxy servers may be used to eliminate the use of chat rooms, if desired. They can also prevent the use of software that might overload your network, such as peer-to-peer file-sharing programs that reached their zenith of popularity and notoriety with the music-sharing program *Napster*.

Portable Web Pages

Portable web pages are a classroom-based option that takes the caching idea one step further. With this software, you or your students can visit websites and store them on a local computer for future use. For example, if you were preparing a science unit on nocturnal animals, you can use software to download web pages and their associated files from reputable sources and store them on computers in a lab. Some common web browsers provide this functionality, as well. During class, you can direct your students to use the resources in the web pages already located on the lab computers. Using portable web pages, students spend learning time using valid and reliable material rather than sorting through the mass of information available on the Internet. Students are also prevented from surfing the web and possibly stumbling upon inappropriate material.

This approach has some drawbacks, as well. It is impossible to know about or find all useful material on the web. You may inadvertently leave out valid source material. This method requires more preparation time on your part and for any staff who must prepare machines with the resources. Finally, as web pages rely more on databases, advanced coding languages, and alternate presentation formats such as portable document format (PDF) and Flash animations, not all web pages present information statically and some pages may not download well.

Steps for Safe Internet Use in Your Classroom

You can use a variety of methods to supervise student use of the Internet. While some schools use technological means to monitor or prohibit some uses of the Internet, others view the use of the Internet as providing a number of teachable moments.

APPLY TO PRACTICE

Safe Use of the Internet

Create a plan for safe use of the Internet in your classroom.

1. Find examples from the news media in which teachers or students inadvertently took actions that would not have been considered safe use of the Internet. What were the outcomes? How could they have been avoided?
2. Consider your preferred plan of action for safe Internet practices for your students. Will you rely on a technology solution? Teachable moments? A combination? How is your solution based on your own experiences using Internet resources? What reasons do you have for selecting your solution?
3. Have you ever experienced or been placed in a situation that made you feel unsafe when using the Internet? If so, what did you do? How could you use this experience to help your students make appropriate decisions and take actions to remain safe? Would your answer differ if you were working with third graders versus seventh graders versus seniors in high school?
4. Share your plan with someone in the class and discuss differing perspectives and strategies.

Students are taught to be responsible on the playground, in the cafeteria, and in classrooms, and with the growing reliance on the use of the Internet for many aspects of education, work, and entertainment, many teachers feel it is their obligation to give students the opportunity to learn responsible online behaviors on the Internet. You can do the same by developing short lessons on the appropriate and inappropriate uses of different digital resources including searching the web for instructional materials, sending e-mail, and participating in web-based discussions such as chat rooms and blogs. Some schools involve parents in training sessions at the beginning of the school year or provide technology nights or make presentations at parent organization meetings (such as the PTA or PTO). Parents who know how their children will use the Internet for learning and have the opportunity to practice using the same tools and resources will feel more comfortable with those uses and can support similar appropriate uses at home.

Organize your classroom so that students are guided to use Internet resources—really, all resources—appropriately. Place computers where the monitors can be observed easily. Limit online time and incorporate study aids, work sheets, and activities that are structured to encourage students to stick closely to learning goals. You and your students can also build a class launch page that quickly points students toward appropriate resources and promotes productive use of limited Internet time. Students can also work in groups at the computer to discourage inappropriate use.

Before beginning an Internet-based project, it's helpful to demonstrate successful search strategies and review responsible use practices. Post helpful websites in your classroom or design customized bookmarks that allow students to find common websites quickly. Your school may also use academic search engines or restricted content services. Make sure your students incorporate appropriate citation strategies for both digital and print materials to avoid plagiarism and copyright infringement and know the consequences of illegal use of digital materials. As students practice and follow ethical and legal technology practices in your classes, they will be more prepared to harness these tools for continued productivity and growth in the future.

Chapter Summary

This chapter began with a review of some possible threats to your technology, and to your students using technology, and methods for avoiding or overcoming them. We introduced you to copyright issues and to acceptable use policies in the context of

WEB LINK

See the textbook's companion website for a list of websites and organizations that can help you identify and track legislative actions that relate to the use of educational technology.

safe, legal, and ethical use of the Internet. You also learned strategies for maintaining academic integrity and keeping sensitive data secure. Internet safety was discussed in terms of preventing students' exposure to unacceptable content and individuals. The information in this chapter should help you develop classroom (or school) rules that address issues of privacy, security, and implementation of acceptable use policies.

YOUR PORTFOLIO

To demonstrate competency in ISTE NETS-T Standard 4.a and 4.c, add the following items to your portfolio:

1. Develop a philosophy statement that discusses your commitment to safe, legal, and ethical use of digital technologies. Provide explicit reasons why it is important for teachers and students to consider these issues in teaching and learning. Include specific strategies that you will include in your instruction to advocate, model, and teach safe, legal and ethical use.
2. Identify one aspect of safe, legal, and ethical use that you believe will be important for your students to learn. Develop a lesson that you can use to teach these principles to students at your chosen grade level.

References

Abilock, D. (1997). Parent Internet driving school: Using technology to increase parent involvement in schools. *Technology Connection, 4*(3), 12–13.

Baird, D., & Hallett, K. (1999). Copyright in the academic environment: An introduction. Proceedings of the Mid-South Instructional Technology Conference, Murfreesboro, TN (March 28–30). ERIC Document Reproduction Service No. ED 436 120.

eSchoolNews, (May 1, 2004). Students arrested for using teacher's computer to change grades. *eSchool News Online.* Retrieved June 28, 2006, from http://www.eschoolnews.com/news/showStory.cfm?ArticleID=5034

eSchoolNews. (November 1, 2001). District's $50K 'piracy' settlement spurs policy changes. *eSchool News Online.* Retrieved June 28, 2006, from http://www.eschoolnews.com/news/showStory.cfm?ArticleID=3107

eSchoolNews. (November 1, 2003). "Star Wars Kid" school video puts privacy rights to test. *eSchool News Online.* Retrieved June 28, 2006, from http://www.eschoolnews.com/news/showStory.cfm?ArticleID=4724

Fight Crime: Invest in Kids. (August 17, 2006). 1 of 3 teens and 1 of 6 preteens are victims of cyber bullying. News release. Retrieved February 19, 2007, from http://www.fightcrime.org/releases.php?id=231

Gross, G. (2005). Proposed law aims to fight phishing. *PC World.* Retrieved July 20, 2006, from http://www.pcworld.com/news/article/0,aid,119912,00.asp

Pownell, D., & Bailey, G. (1999). Electronic fences or free-range students: Should schools use Internet filtering software? *Learning & leading with technology, 27*(1), 50–57.

Pub. L. No. 93-380 (Family Educational Rights and Privacy Act–FERPA).

Pub. L. No. 94-553 (Copyright Act of 1976).

Pub. L. No. 99-558 (Electronic Communications Privacy Act of 1986).

Pub. L. No. 105-277, 112 Stat. 2681, Title XIII (Children's Online Privacy Protection Act of 1998-COPPA).

Pub. L. No. 105-304, 112 Stat. 2860 (Digital Millennium Copyright Act of 1998).

Pub. L. No. 106-554, Title XVII (Children's Internet Protection Act of 2000–CIPA).

Pub. L. No. 107-273, Sec. 13301. Educational Use Copyright Exemption (Technology, Education, and Copyright Harmonization Act of 2002–TEACH).

Stanford University. (2005). *Copyright and fair use*. Stanford, CA: Stanford University Libraries. Retrieved June 21, 2006, from http://fairuse.stanford.edu/

University of Maryland University College. (2004). *Copyright and fair use in the classroom, on the Internet, and the World Wide Web*. Adelphi, MD: Author. Retrieved June 21, 2006, from http://www.umuc.edu/library/copy.html#fairuse

Wells, J., & Lewis, L. (2006). *Internet access in U.S. public schools and classrooms: 1994–2005* (NCES 2007-020). U.S. Department of Education. Washington, DC: National Center for Education Statistics.

Wadsworth/Cengage Learning

Diversity and Cultural Understanding

In Chapter 10, we began our discussion of digital citizenship with a focus on legal and ethical behaviors and digital etiquette. In this chapter, we focus on digital citizenship in a different way. As we approach the end of this book, we encourage you to look beyond your personal experiences to develop and model cultural understanding and global awareness in a way that addresses the diverse needs of all learners.

One effect of new technologies is the increasing globalization of our world. Using digital technologies, you are able to communicate with friends across the globe through participation in online role-playing games, discussion forums about your favorite rock band, or meeting people with similar interests through social-networking sites like MySpace or Facebook. Teachers and students, too, are connecting across the globe through the use of electronic pen pals, participation in videoconference-based meetings on activities such as the Model U.N., or taking virtual field trips to historic and cultural sites across the world. These opportunities to communicate and

ISTE Standards addressed in this chapter

NETS-T 4. Promote and Model Digital Citizenship and Responsibility

Teachers understand local and global societal issues and responsibilities in an evolving digital culture and exhibit legal and ethical behavior in their professional practices. Teachers:
b. address the diverse needs of all learners by using learner-centered strategies and providing access to appropriate digital tools and resources
d. develop and model cultural understanding and global awareness by engaging with colleagues and students of other cultures using digital-age communication and collaboration tools

Note: Chapter 10 addressed a and c of ISTE Standard 4.

Outcomes

In this chapter, you will

- Explore methods for supporting the diverse needs of students by creating learner-centered environments.
- Plan and manage classroom activities to ensure all students have access to technology resources.
- Identify strategies you can incorporate in a culturally responsive classroom.

collaborate with individuals of different cultures both develop, and create a need for, greater cross-cultural understanding.

The changing cultural landscape of America's schools will impact your classroom. If trends in census data continue, by 2020 the percentage of minority students—students described as nonwhite—in public elementary and secondary schools will be greater than white students, with Hispanic students comprising the largest minority group. By 2005, the percentage of Hispanic students (19.8) eclipsed the percentage of black students (17.2) enrolled in public elementary and secondary schools. Asian students showed the second largest growth in percentages since 1986, but still only comprised 4.6 percent of students in public schools in 2005 (Snyder, 2008). Further, the percentage of elementary and secondary students in American public schools who speak a language other than English at home rose from 9 percent in 1979 to 19 percent in 2003, with Spanish being the most common home language for these students (U.S. Department of Education, 2005).

The **culturally responsive teacher** is one who understands and capitalizes on the unique cultural attributes of students, including their experiences, as resources for promoting student achievement (Gay, 2002; Villegas & Lucas, 2002). Culturally responsive teachers use a learner-centered approach whereby the culture the student brings to school is understood, nurtured, and leveraged to promote student achievement (Richards, Brown, & Forde, 2006). Culturally responsive teachers exhibit six salient characteristics (Villegas & Lucas, 2002). They:

1. are socially conscious, meaning that one's understanding is influenced by one's culture
2. view students' diverse backgrounds as assets rather than liabilities
3. feel personally responsible for helping schools be more responsive to all students
4. understand how learners construct knowledge
5. know about the lives of his or her students
6. design instruction that builds upon students' prior knowledge and experiences and stretches them beyond the familiar

In these ways, culturally responsive pedagogy is very much in line with the transformative stage of technology integration as described by ISTE (2008) and thus complements other concepts addressed throughout this book. Similar to the tenets of Universal Design for Learning, presented in Chapter 6, and authentic learning, presented in Chapter 3, culturally responsive pedagogy suggests you have to know and understand the learning styles, preferences, and abilities of your students in order to provide successful learning experiences. This translates into the need to provide flexibility in the learning experiences you offer your students. Students come to school with a variety of experiences and knowledge; culturally responsive teachers continually monitor growth in student understanding and skill in order to adjust learning plans and activities to promote student success. As a culturally responsive teacher, it is important to employ a range of resource materials, including books and other print materials, and identify high-quality supplemental materials in a variety of formats including video, animations, and other software-based tools.

Additionally, culturally responsive teachers employ ongoing and culturally aware assessments using a variety of assessment formats, addressed in Chapter 7, to monitor student learning and evaluate instruction. Portfolios and rubrics can play an important role in culturally responsive classrooms, especially when students are given opportunities to identify artifacts they want to include in their own portfolios as well as identifying levels of performance. In this chapter, we will build on the knowledge you've gained throughout this book by focusing on the need to address cultural and socioeconomic diversity and by describing methods for developing social consciousness, learning about the lives of your students, and helping schools become more responsive to all students.

Learner-Centered Strategies

ISTE NETS-T Standard 4.b indicates that you will "address the diverse needs of all learners by using learner-centered strategies." This standard implies that learner-centered strategies, by definition, enable you to consider and meet the diverse needs of your students. We spent a good portion of Chapter 3 describing the key components of learner-centered instruction under the overarching concept of authentic instruction. That is, the components of authentic instruction (autonomous, active, holistic, authentic, and challenging) are those that allow you to create a learner-centered classroom that attends to your students' diverse interests, capitalizes on their diverse talents and interests, and addresses their diverse needs for knowledge and skills. Likewise, culturally responsive instructional methods tend to be holistic, whether through the organization of an interdisciplinary unit that covers multiple content areas, or through the inclusion of complex problems that require students to develop and employ multiple knowledge and skills—personal, moral, social, political, cultural, and academic—within a single activity (Gay, 2002). Simply put, designing and employing culturally sensitive instructional strategies implies creating a learner-centered environment. In this section we briefly discuss how specific components of a learner-centered environment can be structured to support the diverse social, cognitive, and metacognitive needs of learners.

Supporting the Social Needs of Students: Creating a Collaborative Environment

A number of educators have described the importance of creating a classroom environment that is conducive to collaborative inquiry (see Figure 11.1). If we want students to express their own opinions on controversial issues, or to feel comfortable challenging others' points of view, they need to feel assured that they will not be criticized or reprimanded for doing so. Barell (1998) referred to this as an "invitational environment" while Kolodner and her colleagues (2003) described it as a "culture of collaboration." Regardless of the label used, it is important that the underlying values of trust, open communication, and risk-taking are fostered and practiced. When students come to us from disadvantaged or impoverished backgrounds, immersion in safe, interactive learning environments is a powerful way to engage their thinking and motivate their learning. Learner-centered approaches necessitate that we attend not only to learners' *cognitive* needs, but to their *emotional* and *social* needs as well.

So what does an invitational environment look like? What are its key characteristics? According to Barell (1998, p. 15) the following elements are essential:

- *Teacher modeling.* Thinking aloud through problematic situations, sharing both successful and unsuccessful experiences, and modeling the kinds of

Wadsworth/Cengage Learning

Figure 11.1
A collaborative learning environment addresses not only cognitive needs, but emotional and social needs as well.

behaviors and dispositions we want students to gain (e.g., curiosity, persistence, open-mindedness).

- *Questioning.* Using questions that challenge students to go beyond simply finding answers in a book, from a person, or on the Internet; modeling for, and encouraging, students to use critical questioning strategies.

- *Quality responding.* Responding to students' statements, questions, and expressions of feelings in ways that communicate sincere interest in knowing more about their thoughts and feelings.

- *Peer interactions.* Encouraging genuine discussion in which students respond positively to each other, question each other, and openly consider multiple points of view in order to arrive at a conclusion; promoting the idea that all members of the community share responsibility for learning.

- *Group inquiry skills.* Actively supporting the development of students' listening skills, as well as helping them learn how to stay focused on the topic, build on each others' ideas, develop consensus, and so on.

- *Reflective journals.* Using both structured and unstructured journal writing to enable students to share their thoughts and feelings about what they have learned, how they have learned it, and how well they have participated in the problem-solving process. Reflection allows students to abstract from their experiences what they have felt, thought, and learned.

Some of these ideas are probably fairly familiar to you and it's likely that you will be comfortable using or promoting their use in your classroom. However, it's also important to recognize that many of these strategies are skills that develop over a period of time and will not be as easy to implement as you wish. The important thing to remember is to give yourself time and permission to go slowly, expecting your skills to gradually increase over the first few years of your teaching career. Regardless of your initial expertise, students will take their cues from you in terms of how you facilitate a learning environment that is welcoming to all.

Supporting the Cognitive Needs of Students: Promoting Content Learning

Whereas creating a culture of collaboration can help you attend to your students' diverse social needs, creating a culture of thinking can help you attend to their diverse cognitive (intellectual) and metacognitive (reflective) needs. We need to remember that one of the primary reasons we use authentic learning is to promote students' deep understanding of subject-matter content through the process of *doing*. Despite the fact that content learning is one of the key reasons for using an authentic learning approach, it is relatively easy for both teachers and students to lose sight of this goal and to focus, instead, on simply completing the many interesting activities in which they are engaged. The research conducted by Newmann et al. (2001) in the Chicago Public Schools illustrated that even for students in highly disadvantaged schools, their ability to "master the basics," as measured by standardized tests, improved when teachers assigned work that demanded both complex thinking and elaborated communication about issues that were important in their lives.

When using a learner-centered approach, teachers need to be prepared to deal with students' misconceptions and/or inability to make the links between the interesting activities they are completing and the content they are supposed to be learning. One way to address this is to use more direct means for helping students make these connections. The developers of WISE (Web-based Inquiry Science Environments) use the term "making thinking visible" to refer to strategies that enable students to reveal what and how they are thinking within a specific content domain (Linn, Clark, & Slotta, 2003). For example, as part of the WISE approach, students post online responses at various stages in their inquiry, which are saved for accessibility at a later date by either the student or the teacher. Following this, prompts are used to help students connect their ideas to project topics, such as, "How do we use all of this information to solve the problem?" (Linn et al., p. 528). By directly asking students to connect ideas, we help them understand and integrate them into a more coherent whole.

A second way to aid with concept integration is to directly reinforce the learning goals. That is, we can't assume that students are aware of the learning goals they are supposed to be achieving. Kolodner and her colleagues (2003) help make this more obvious through the use of "rules of thumb," which are student-generated rules used to explain their observations during project work. Rules of thumb get posted on chart paper and then are continually tested through additional student-designed experiments. And so, based on students' findings and new observations, they are continually under revision. The teacher guides students' ongoing discussions and challenges students to support their theories with evidence, but refrains from correcting assumptions until students have had the opportunity to test their rules. However, at some point, later in the process, the teacher may need to present the rule through a just-in-time lesson or mini-lecture. As you might guess, lectures aren't common in authentic learning environments but this doesn't mean that they are never used. In fact, sometimes a lecture is the best way to help students understand the content being addressed in an authentic learning activity.

To guard against students becoming more concerned about completing tasks than learning content, it is important to continually help students make links between claims and evidence, questions and information, project design and learning goals. The use of scientific reasoning should be established as part of the classroom culture. Even in disciplines other than science, a culture of "expert" reasoning is important, and can help students become logical thinkers. Posting reminders around the classroom ("Support your claim!" "Present your evidence!") can keep everyone focused on this expectation. Finally, once it is clear what and how students are thinking, it is important to address their misconceptions or biases. Many educators recommend that you begin these activities by asking students to articulate their own beliefs about a phenomenon. Often, students' initial, naïve thinking can play a central role within the inquiry process, especially when teachers can capitalize on the value of failure and refinement.

The strategies described above can support the intellectual, or cognitive, engagement of all students in the authentic learning activities used in your classroom. Thus, regardless of where students enter the process in terms of background knowledge or skills, they have the opportunity to construct deeper understandings through participation in meaningful activities in the learning environment.

Supporting the Metacognitive Needs of Students: Promoting Reflection

An important kind of thinking, first mentioned in Chapter 2, is **metacognition**; that is, the ability to think about our own thinking. Research has shown that reflection, as a form of metacognition, is a vital component of authentic learning approaches. Reflective thinking helps students make connections between their learning goals, the processes they use to achieve those goals, and the content they are learning. It also helps them to better understand processes and explanations so that they can apply them beyond the immediate problem they are solving. It forces them to think about what they are learning and how it applies to the current situation as well as other issues and problems.

In this way, reflection serves as the other half of the activity-construction process, enabling students to make sense of the tasks they have completed. However, when asked to reflect on what they have learned from such activities, students have a tendency to focus on the task, experiment, or the project rather than on conceptual understanding of the key concepts or principles. One way to counteract this is to provide *ongoing* opportunities for students to articulate what they are learning, whether in their small groups or as a whole class. For example, in your role as a facilitator you can ask probing questions, challenge a particular perspective or argument, or offer an alternative hypothesis, thus forcing students to interpret the information they have gathered. By alternating hands-on, investigative work with interpretive or reflective work, students can share what they have learned and benefit from the perspectives of others. Finally, the use of frequent checkpoints and record-keeping devices (e.g., group folders or file directories, digital journals, goal charts, etc.) can keep students focused on their learning goals and provide opportunities for reinforcement or redirection. These techniques can also serve motivational purposes as they allow students to take note of the progress they are making.

While reflection is not a foreign notion to students, teachers need to explicitly promote, guide, and support it among their students. Consider how this book has provided guidance to you on reaching levels of critical self-reflection. Reflection doesn't become a habit unless it is used continually. It's important to leave time in the school day for your students to engage in these types of reflective activities and to guide and support students' efforts until they become comfortable with the process. Luckily, adding reflective thinking activities to the learning environment is a relatively simple thing to do. The strategies for enhancing it are found in some of our most conventional classroom activities—discussions, prompts, and modeling. And, by incorporating these types of strategies, we can greatly increase students' learning.

Another primary goal of authentic learning is to help students develop the skills needed to regulate their own learning, and metacognition is an important aspect of this process. Authentic learning offers teachers many opportunities to teach students self-directed learning strategies that enable them to set their own goals, monitor their progress, and determine next steps toward goal achievement. Although it is unlikely that students will possess these skills initially, early efforts can be supported with specific scaffolds. For example, students can determine daily goals, rate their progress at the end of the day, and then set new goals for the next day. Using problem logs, students can reflect on the strategies used to accomplish specific goals and

APPLY TO PRACTICE

Supporting the Diverse Needs of Students

1. Describe a learning environment that stands out in your memory. It may be one that you remember fondly because of the way it nurtured your own unique learning needs or it may be one that was challenging to you.
2. In your description, describe the degree to which the diverse social, cognitive, and metacognitive needs of students were addressed. Your description may include a variety of methods or structures that do or do not support the following components:
   a. Creating a collaborative environment to support the social needs of students
   b. Promoting content learning to support the cognitive needs of students
   c. Promoting reflection to support the metacognitive needs of students
3. Knowing what you now know, how could that learning environment have been altered to better support the diverse needs of students? If some structures or practices were successful, how could those be applied to other learning environments? What technologies supported, or could have supported, the needs of the students in the classroom?
4. Share your responses and reflect on how you can incorporate these strategies in your lesson and unit plans.

then rate the effectiveness of those strategies based on how well the goals were met. While the intent of these activities is to help students develop important lifelong learning habits, they also provide teachers with valuable insights into students' specific learning needs. Ultimately, giving students ownership in their learning leads to significant benefits for both teachers and students. By helping learners appreciate their accomplishments, understand the processes that enabled those accomplishments (including the strategies that enabled them to overcome obstacles), learners gain important metacognitive skills.

Equitable Access

ISTE NETS-T Standard 4.b also indicates that you will "address the diverse needs of all learners by . . . providing equitable access to appropriate digital tools and resources." But what do we mean by providing access? Early discussions about technology access centered on the lack of hardware and networking for some schools and families. This disparity even took on its own unique label as educational and political leaders across the nation vowed to decrease the **digital divide** among the nation's students. Today, educators recognize that this divide encompasses more than access to a computer or an Internet connection and are better informed about the ways the digital divide might manifest itself in schools. Wiburg and Butler (2003) suggested four components of access that should be considered when tackling the digital divide dilemma:

1. Access to up-to-date hardware, software, and connectivity
2. Access to meaningful, high-quality, and culturally responsive content and the opportunity to contribute to that content
3. Access to educators who know how to use digital tools and resources
4. Access to systems sustained by leaders with vision and support for change via technology

In your role as a classroom teacher, you can directly influence the first three of these components. The final component will become more important to you as you gain experience and serve in positions of leadership, whether as a teacher leader, administrator, or otherwise. You are one of the most important factors in providing access to teaching resources in a way that is sensitive to the cultural and individual needs of your students.

Access to Up-to-Date Hardware, Software, and Connectivity

As technology became more prevalent in America's schools, especially during the push to provide Internet access in every school and at least one "modern multimedia computer" for every five students, the disparity between the technology "haves" and "have-nots" became increasingly evident (U.S. Department of Commerce, 1999). One of the first challenges for schools that were attempting to address the digital divide was to purchase a substantial amount of hardware in order to achieve a student–computer ratio of 5 to 1. Several national and state grant programs during the 1990s helped schools purchase and install enough computers to actually exceed this goal. The U.S. Department of Education (Wells & Lewis, 2006) reported that, between the years of 1998 (when this statistic was first measured) and 2005, the student–computer ratio across the nation improved from 12.1 to 1 to 3.8 to 1.

On the surface it appears that there is at least one computer available for every four students in each school. However, some schools have more computers, so unfortunately, the number of computers in other schools falls below this recommended ratio (Wells & Lewis, 2006). Schools that are most likely to have fewer computers are elementary schools (4.1 to 1), schools in cities (4.2 to 1) or urban fringe areas (4.1), or schools with 75 percent or more of their students qualifying for free or reduced-price lunch (4.0 to 1). Still these numbers are encouraging in terms of identifying the amount of technology available to students (see Figure 11.2). And the increasing availability of lower-cost, highly portable computing devices, such as laptops stored on wireless carts, portable digital assistants (PDAs), and multifunction calculators with probeware, increases the chances that an appropriate hardware device will be available when you and your students need them.

According to the U.S. Department of Education (Wells & Lewis, 2006), virtually 100 percent of all schools across the nation reported some type of Internet connection in 2005, with 94 percent of all instructional classrooms within those schools having Internet access. In terms of overcoming the digital divide, it is also important to consider the *type* of Internet access that is available to schools. An increasing amount of content and media demands high bandwidth, but not all schools can take advantage of these resources, especially if they have slower connections. The percentage of schools reporting some type of broadband connection (which may not

Figure 11.2
The nation's schools have helped students from all backgrounds achieve greater access to technology.

be accessible in all classrooms) is up to 97 percent in 2005. Smaller schools and rural schools were less likely to have high-speed connections but the percentages are very close with 94 percent of schools with less than 300 students and 96 percent of rural schools reporting broadband connections.

These numbers take on greater significance when comparing access to technology and the Internet in students' homes. Across several demographic populations, schools have been a significant factor in increasing the access to computers and the Internet for students who do not have that access at home (U.S. Census Bureau, 2005). In a 2005 report, the U.S. Department of Commerce noted that Black and Hispanic children still have significantly lower home access to computers and the Internet when compared to Caucasians, Asian Americans, and Pacific Islanders. However, children aged 3 to 17, and enrolled in school, reported using computers in school almost as frequently as those who have (and use) a computer at home. Current levels of computer use at school are similar for children from all reported racial groups; however, some differences occur in Internet use when comparing students across racial groups, with the lowest usage levels being reported for use of the Internet at school by Hispanic students (31 percent).

Income and education levels also affect access to the Internet. In general, households with annual incomes greater than $50,000 are more likely to have a computer and Internet access at a rate higher than the national average as are households where the householder has completed some college or associate's degree classes (U.S. Census Bureau, 2005). However, the percentage of all households in all income brackets with access to computers and the Internet is growing, with the largest percentage of growth in households with lower incomes.

Boys and girls appear to have equal access to computers whether at home or school but the way girls and boys use technology differs (National Center for Education Statistics, 2005) and their perceptions toward technology change as they mature (Christensen, Knezek, & Overall, 2005). Girls between the ages of 5 and 17 are more likely than boys to use home computers for e-mail, word processing, and completing school assignments while boys of the same age are more likely than girls to use home computers to play games. The American Association of University Women (AAUW, 2000) reported that the types of computer courses in which girls enroll also differ from boys, with girls less likely to enroll in computer science and programming courses and more likely to enroll in classes focused on productivity tools, such as graphic design, page formatting and design, and online media development. AAUW also noted that despite the increased use of computers in schools and comparable access to them at school and home, girls often report lower self-confidence in relation to technology and less ability to use technology. This finding is corroborated by a longitudinal study of 10,000 Texas public school students (Christensen et al., 2005), where girls in grades 4 and 5 reported enjoying computers more than boys but their perceptions of computers changed beginning around the sixth grade where girls reported less enjoyment using computers than boys. Students' attitudes can be influenced by societal factors, such as friends, the media, and what they do in the classroom. Since young girls entering school report enjoying computers and since just as many girls use technology as boys, both at home and at school, it's not their ability that is lacking. Rather, it is only a perception that develops over time that they are not as capable. The learning environment you create in your classroom and the way female teachers model technology can help combat this perception.

As a group, girls are thought to approach technology differently than boys and many prefer different types of activities (AAUW, 2000). In general, technology-supported activities for girls are more successful when they rely on collaboration and are presented within a relevant context. Technology tasks that are highly structured, such as those related to programming, are preferred more often by boys than girls. When designing group activities, make sure all students have equal opportunities to perform all types of roles, and counter any tendencies to allow boys to monopolize the use of technological equipment and dominate science labs.

Continually alter the ways you pair or group students and make sure all students have opportunities to work with students of other genders, ethnic groups, and abilities.

Above all, ensure that all students, whatever their backgrounds or abilities, have appropriate opportunities to use all of the technology resources available in your classroom. It's important to realize that equitable access to technology does not necessarily mean equal time spent using technology. Each student may require different types of software and hardware for different amounts of time to master curricular requirements. Students with special needs related to writing may need more time to work with software that supports the writing process than those who perform stronger in this area. Gifted-and-talented students who are developing complex projects using multimedia authoring or presentation software may need additional time for editing and programming. Use a variety of technologies that will engage students of different abilities, backgrounds, and learning preferences and allow them to demonstrate their knowledge appropriately. Don't isolate any one student for technology use as a reward or punishment. There is no one formula for determining equitable access. Keep in mind that the driving force behind all of your instructional decisions should be the learning needs of each student.

Access to Meaningful, High-Quality, and Culturally Responsive Content

Providing greater access to computers and the Internet was an important goal, yet the fervor to get schools connected to the Internet and to put five computers in every classroom often outpaced the ability of content developers to create, package, and deliver high-quality content. You have probably noticed that when you turn to the Internet for information, you can be easily overwhelmed by the number of hits returned from a simple web search. And often, much of the content turns out to be pretty useless.

Providing high-quality content is a challenge, especially as you reach out to meet the needs of all of your students, including those who are not part of the dominant culture. In general, English is the dominant language on the Internet, and many pages are written at an advanced level that can confuse, disengage, or frustrate students who have limited English proficiency. In many areas and some states, English is not the most common language spoken and students who are immersed in a program for English language learners may not have the proficiency required to sort through much of the information they find on the Internet. When using digital content, online or packaged on a CD or other resource, you must consider the language abilities of your students.

In addition, many students do not find examples of computer software or Internet content to which they can relate. Girls in particular may have difficulty finding strong role models in terms of characters or software content, although there are several popular titles in which girl characters are prominent (see Figure 11.3). Although computer games are notorious for promoting negative female stereotypes, girls also find it difficult to find positive role models in more traditional instructional materials, including textbooks. Print, as well as software or Internet resources, should portray girls, women, students with disabilities, and people from a wide range of ethnic backgrounds, in a positive light.

Make sure the teams that evaluate and approve instructional materials for your school have a clear policy that encourages them to review for bias. Consider political, religious, and cultural contexts. Also examine the materials for potentially controversial topics and significant omissions. Take care to ensure that they do not reinforce stereotypes and, instead, provide strong role models for students of all genders and ethnic backgrounds. Consider using an evaluation form or creating your own that includes categories that encourage evaluators to consider biases against girls or

Figure 11.3
Use instructional resources with a range of role models to relate to all of your students.
Source: © 2008 Viacom International Inc. All rights reserved. Nickelodeon, Dora the Explorer and all related titles, logos, and characters are trademarks of Viacom International Inc. Courtesy of "Nickelodeon."

boys, students from different racial or ethnic backgrounds, and students with different abilities. This isn't to say that you should never use software that contains subtle biases, but if you do, make sure you use it as an opportunity to explicitly teach students to be aware of such biases.

Access to Tech-Knowledgeable Teachers

This entire book is designed to help you to become a more tech-savvy teacher, so you're on the right path to overcoming this particular contributor to the digital divide. Needless to say, teachers who lack knowledge of how to use technology are

STORIES FROM PRACTICE

Evaluating Software

When I first used this software I just thought about the political issues involved in the simulation, which is based on a mayor running for re-election in a city with a growing immigrant population. The mayor is male, a point I did not even think about until I started my thesis. He does have females on his team of advisors. However, the problems with the simulation go deeper.

The main issue in the mayor's re-election campaign is what to do about the immigrants moving into the city. The first time I used this program, I felt it was a great activity. The second year I used it, I became aware that the choices being made by my students were portraying the immigrants in a negative light. If a group of students made decisions favorable for the immigrants, the mayor either lost the election or much of his support.

It dawned on me that biases were built into the program. Did the designer discuss the possibilities of this program with educators? In fairness to the company, I must point out that an evaluation card is enclosed with the program when it is purchased. The first time I used the program, I gave it glowing reviews! I said that it was a great learning experience for my students because they really got involved in it. I honestly did not think of all the gender and cultural issues that came with the simulation.

I still use the program today, but now I use it in a different way. I encourage students to discuss the biases that are portrayed in the software. We talk about immigration problems, but we also discuss how immigrants contribute positively to the diversity that we should be celebrating. — Carolyn Sue Gardiner, St. Timothy School, Columbus, Ohio.

Source: Eisenhower National Consortium, 2002.

THE GAME PLAN

Gender Equitable Resources

Set Goals

Find resources that encourage technology use for either boys or girls or both.

Take Action

Search for print and electronic resources that provide strategies to encourage boys or girls to use technology for learning, that help you differentiate instruction for learning preferences associated with both genders, or that support initiatives that encourage participation in STEM-related (Science, Technology, Engineering, and Mathematics) career paths.

Monitor

Determine whether the material you collected is free from bias and represents valid positions. If you are finding more material for one gender over the other, what strategies might you use to obtain equal representation?

Evaluate and Extend

Share the resources you have found with classmates, especially with members of the opposite gender to review appropriate materials. Store the best materials or link URLs from important websites to your portfolio along with rationales for why you believe the materials are appropriate.

inadequately prepared to provide their students with meaningful access to technologies that may be readily available in a school. Fortunately, many states have adopted technology standards for teachers that are the same or similar to the ISTE NETS-T standards that are the focus of this book. Other states require teachers to demonstrate at least limited proficiency with a variety of technologies, such as word processors, e-mail, and the Internet.

But one of the most influential factors for how you use technology and provide access to available technologies to your students will be your own beliefs about your role as a teacher and the role of technologies in your teaching. If you've proceeded through the chapters in this book in sequential order, you now know about numerous technology-supported teaching strategies you can employ to engage all students, meet individual learning preferences, and achieve meaningful learning outcomes. But you can't stop here—you need to take steps to provide your future students with access to a tech-knowledgeable teacher throughout your entire teaching career. In the next chapter, we'll explore ways that you can continue to learn about and experiment with new technologies in order to overcome this particular factor in the digital divide.

Promoting Cultural Understanding and Global Awareness

The ISTE NETS-T Standard 4.d indicates that teachers "develop and model cultural understanding and global awareness by engaging with colleagues and students of other cultures using digital-age communication and collaboration tools." Throughout this book you have been encouraged to consider strategies and tools to support collaboration with your colleagues, your students, and their families. Today, digital tools enable you to communicate and collaborate with individuals from around the world as easily as you can communicate with the students in your classroom and the teacher next door. But cultural understanding requires more than simply using tools such as these to communicate and collaborate with those from other cultures. As a culturally responsive teacher, you should take steps to better understand your own culture, the culture of the community within which your school is situated, the culture within the school, as well as the culture of your peers.

If you and your students or colleagues come from different cultures, with different backgrounds, different communication styles, and different experiences with technology, the result can be disconnect and conflict. All parties can feel frustrated, isolated, and erect barriers. You can combat this outcome, however, through awareness of these possibilities and using concrete strategies to determine the cultural and linguistic preferences of the students in your class and avoiding reactions based on stereotypical assumptions. Stereotypes quickly break down when teachers consider the perspectives and needs of each individual.

There are several things you can do to become a culturally responsive teacher who teaches from a perspective of cultural understanding—some of which you can do now and some of which you can do while you are teaching.

Develop an Understanding of Your Culture and the Culture of Others

To get started, most experts in culturally responsive pedagogy agree that one of the first steps you can take is to conduct an evaluation of your own cultural experiences and that of others (Montgomery, 2001; Richards, Brown, & Forde, 2006; Villegas & Lucas, 2002). This requires self-reflection to identify the different cultural groups you belong to whether racial, social, language- or gender-based, or other, and how your experiences in these groups have shaped and continue to influence your life. You should also consider the connection between school and society and how you have been impacted as a member of different school settings.

What Is Culture?

Culture is a complex, intangible concept, yet it shapes how we see the world. Adding to the complexity is the fact that you may associate with different cultures or subcultures, regardless of your background or your physical characteristics. Furthermore, the reasons why you associate with a culture may be different from others. It is not simply your race that helps create your cultural identification. You may identify with a particular ethnic group, but your cultural identity is often a broader characterization than your ethnic identity (LAB, 2002), as members of different ethnic groups may all identify with the same culture. A shared history is important, but even that does not complete your cultural picture. The region in which you (and your close relatives) live or have lived, your educational background, income, gender, and even physical characteristics can help shape your cultural identity, which, in turn, influences the way you behave, the choices you make, your pursuits, and your aspirations—especially in relation to education. The ability of diverse people to identify with the same culture helps to underscore the danger of prescribing blanket beliefs to individuals based on their appearance, background, or locale.

Anthropologists recognize numerous characteristics around which cultures differ. And although different cultures may have different ways of expressing these things, all cultures hold beliefs and exhibit resulting patterns of behaviors in each of these areas (Peace Corp, n.d.). As you read through the following paragraphs, consider your own cultural heritage and how some of those characteristics are evidenced.

Culture is manifest in a wide variety of behaviors and beliefs, some of which are visible and some of which are not. Outward manifestations of culture include styles of dress, greetings, facial expressions and hand gestures. Cultures may have unique music, celebrations, rituals, dances, and art. They may have special eating habits, preferred foods, and housing preferences. Other aspects of culture may be less visible. Cultures may have different views on fairness, personal property, friendship, aging, hospitality, and modesty. They may differ in work ethics, how they value time, the concept of self, ideas about leadership, concepts of beauty, and attitudes toward personal space and privacy. The roles and responsibilities of various family members may differ across cultures. They may have different religious beliefs, values, and

TOOLS FOR USE

Exploring Culture

The following features of culture were extracted from an activity in *Building Bridges: A Peace Corps Classroom Guide to Cross-Cultural Understanding* (Peace Corps, n.d., p. 11). For each feature of culture, think of one example common to people in the country where you were born and compare that with others you know from travel, friendships, or discussions with your classmates.

- Styles of dress
- Ways of greeting people
- Beliefs about hospitality
- Importance of time
- Paintings
- Values
- Literature
- Beliefs about child raising (children and teens)
- Attitudes about personal space/privacy
- Beliefs about the responsibilities of children and teens
- Gestures to show you understand what has been told to you
- Holiday customs

- Music
- Dancing
- Celebrations
- Concept of fairness
- Nature of friendship
- Ideas about clothing
- Foods
- Greetings
- Facial expressions and hand gestures
- Concept of self
- Work ethic
- Religious beliefs
- Religious rituals
- Concept of beauty
- Rules of polite behavior
- Attitude toward age
- The role of family
- General worldview

understandings of the natural world. There may be different rules for polite behavior, social etiquette, and hospitality. All of these cultural beliefs and practices interact in unique ways and influence an individual's general worldview.

Although these aspects of culture may be interesting areas for exploring the similarities and differences among individuals, certain aspects of culture affect cross-cultural communications in ways that are important to establishing collaborative relationships. Different cultures have formal and informal rules that govern speaking, listening, and turn-taking behaviors (LAB, 2002). Some communication patterns that can be manifested differently across cultures include:

- *Conventions for storytelling.* Some cultures rely on personal anecdotes and experiences in storytelling that may not have a clear beginning, middle, or end while others follow strict rules that establish a main topic and then structure the story around it. Consider the influence in the dominant American school culture of the highly structured "five-paragraph essay."
- *Directness in communicating.* Communications in some cultures are indirect and may actually seem ambiguous in comparison to the directness of communication expected in many American classrooms. Indirect communication may relate to topics that are suggested but not spoken as well as conversations with close relatives or friends of individuals rather than the individuals themselves in order to communicate sensitive topics or elicit behavior through indirect influence.
- *When to listen and when to speak.* In the dominant American culture, an eloquent speaker with a firm command of language skills is praised as being intelligent and competent and individuals are encouraged to "speak one's mind," while in other cultures listening and speaking selectively is valued.
- *When and how children should speak.* Some cultures encourage children to speak from a personal perspective in order to understand and explore their world while the dominant American culture uses language with children to socialize them to expected norms, as in "speak only when spoken to" or "children should be seen and not heard."

• *Speaking to an adult or elder.* Questioning an adult in some cultures can be praised as being a "free thinker" or honing one's intellectual skills to be a critical thinker, while other cultures believe it is a sign of poor upbringing and lack of respect.

Schools have their own rules governing communication, patterns of task engagement, and organizing ideas (Gay, 2002). While not true of all schools, the nature of discourse in many schools is often **didactic**, with a single speaker dominating and all others quietly listening. In this type of classroom, communication is often governed by the teacher who decides who will talk, when, and the type of responses desired. Classrooms where students are taught to be direct, precise, and to follow conventions of didactic communication are referred to as **topic-centered**. This highly structured learning environment can be problematic to those familiar with a **topic-chaining** style of engagement and organization. A topic-chaining environment is one that has a strong social context in which time is taken to set the stage for an academic task that is followed through with cyclical and multipart conversations. Conversations and activities can be intense and emotional with emphasis on personal investment. In contrast to didactic communication, a **communal** style of communication may be employed in which listening is participatory and listeners provide prompts, feedback, and commentary to the speaker. In topic-centered classrooms, students who prefer communal communication styles may appear rude or disruptive and teachers may take steps to silence them, negatively affecting their natural preferences for talking, thinking, and academic engagement. In topic-chaining classrooms, students who prefer the structure of didactic communications may appear to lack motivation, be disengaged, uncooperative, or even resistant to an academic task, especially if it involves collaboration with others.

Cultures can also be described as individualistic or collectivist. An **individualist** perspective promotes the autonomy of the individual and measures success by individual accomplishments. On the other end of the continuum, **collectivist** perspectives situate the individual within a larger community and measure the success of the individual as a factor of the whole. People can fall anywhere along the continuum—not just the extremes—and may not exhibit consistent perspectives across all attributes.

Review Table 11.1, the Individualist/Collectivist Continuum adapted from *The Diversity Kit* (LAB, 2002), to determine how different people may view common factors related to education and academic success. Consider the perspective you have based on your own identification and whether you know individuals who might exhibit some characteristics of the opposite perspective. Share your perspective with others and note similarities and differences. A word of caution is in order. Keep in mind that not all persons from any one area, culture, or group will exhibit the same perspective for each factor and that these generalizations are not meant to be definitive descriptions of any one culture.

APPLY TO PRACTICE

Individualist/Collectivist Continuum

1. Rate yourself along the dimensions of the Individualist/Collectivist Continuum as either Highly Individualist, Somewhat Individualist, In Between, Somewhat Collectivist, Highly Collectivist. To what do you attribute your responses? Share your responses with your class.

2. As a variation, collect the responses from an entire class and create a class profile. You can use a variety of technologies to do this, which can then be posted to a class website or discussion area. What trends do you notice? Do responses from different individuals with similar ratings correspond? What about for those with opposing ratings? Knowing these trends, how does this influence how you would interact with others in the class? What about if you had to teach this class?

Table 11.1	Individualist/Collectivist Continuum	
Key Questions	Individualist Perspective	Collectivist Perspective
Why should students achieve their potential?	For the sake of self-fulfillment	In order to contribute to the social whole
What type of work ethic is encouraged?	Students should work independently and get their own work done. Giving help to others may be considered cheating.	Students should be helpful and cooperate with peers, giving assistance when needed. Helping is not considered cheating.
How should praise and feedback be used?	Students should be praised frequently. The positive should be emphasized whenever possible.	Students should not be singled out for praise in front of peers. Positive feedback should be stated in terms of the student's ability to help family or community.
What is the role of the school?	Students should attain intellectual skills in school.	Students should learn appropriate social behaviors and skills as well as intellectual skills.
What is the role of the student in education?	Students should engage in discussion and argument in order to learn to think critically.	Students should be quiet and respectful in class because they will learn more this way.
What is the value of property?	Property belongs to individuals, and others must ask to borrow or share it.	Most property is communal and not considered the domain of an individual.
How should students behave?	Teachers manage behavior indirectly or emphasize student self-control.	Teachers have primary authority for managing behavior, but also expects peers to guide each other's behavior.
What is the role of the parent in education?	Parents are integrally involved with student academic progress.	Parents believes that it is the teacher's role to provide academic instruction to students.

Source: Adapted from *The Diversity Kit: An introductory resource for social change in education,* Table 1, p. 25. Copyright 2002 The Education Alliance at Brown University.

To complete a self-evaluation of your own cultural preferences, it is important to share and learn from others to better understand the complex interactions that help people develop different perspectives. What one culture may view as strange may be considered normal in another culture. Recognizing areas in which people differ is an important step in understanding and appreciating cultural preferences within your school and community. There are no hard and fast rules that can help you determine what instructional strategies and resources will work best for all students who identify with any one culture. It is helpful to know, however, that different people (teachers, administrators, students, and parents) approach many common characteristics of education and society from opposing perspectives.

Working with Students to Develop Cultural Understanding

Although you can conduct a self-assessment of your own experiences right now, once you're in a classroom you'll need to better understand your students' cultures and how those can promote positive learning experiences. Students can create reports of their personal and family histories using presentation software to share with the class. Students can use digital storytelling techniques to tell others about their cultural heritages. Information from family trees, interviews with parents and other family members, and even scanning and incorporating family photos or memorabilia into presentations can help students engage in the process of self-reflection and inform you about who they are. Classroom discussions can be supported with the use of concept-mapping software, and responses to surveys can be aggregated and presented using data-visualization software. Be aware that the process of reflection and sharing can be challenging if not done within an environment of trust and understanding. The goal is to understand what attributes others bring to their educational settings and how prior knowledge and experiences can be leveraged for

STORIES FROM PRACTICE

The Magic of Telepresence

You often hear how technology can expose students to other cultures and connect students across the globe, but the teachers and students in Richland High School in North Richland Hills, Texas, had a unique opportunity to connect with students in England—an experience you might associate more with *Star Trek* rather than public education. In 2001, students at Richland High first connected with a classroom from Moorside School in Salford, Manchester, using digital teleportation. No, they didn't get "beamed up" like in the popular television and movie series. Instead, they used a conference system developed by Teleportec to send a life-size image, consisting of a presenter's upper body and arms, to the opposite classroom which was designed to support interaction with the distant students and teacher. Called "telepresence," the life-size image is created when someone—a teacher or student—enters the unit that has a 30-by-40-inch screen in the background and serves as a "presenter." The person's image is transmitted in real time and projected on to a transparent projection surface. The background is removed from the transmission so it looks like the presenter is sitting in the class and the presenter can see and communicate with the class in the distance—as if he or she were sitting in the room with them.

The first time students at Richland High connected was in October 2001. During the initial part of the transmission, students were excited about the technology and seeing and interacting with peers from a different country. But October was just after the cataclysmic events of September 11th and it was inevitable that one of the students in England would ask the American students how they felt about the events. Of course the students in Texas expressed how sad they felt, but the emotional support they received from their English peers helped to strengthen their social connections and provided a real bond between the two groups. Teachers from the two schools delivered lessons throughout the year using the teleportation system and helped the students in both schools better understand different aspects of culture and history, including presenting information about American Indians as well as discussing the American Revolution from the perspectives of both countries. Without the "presence" of the English students in their classroom, the students from Texas would never have reached such a deep level of cultural understanding.

The system has been used in other schools and classes. A foreign language teacher at Richland High taught her classes to a group of students, from five small schools in her region, who otherwise would not have had the opportunity to study the languages. The system was also used to help connect students and teachers on South Padre Island, Texas, while the Queen Isabella Causeway, which connects the island and the mainland, was being rebuilt after collapsing.

Source: Adapted from McGraw, T., & Burdette, K. (2002). From conference room to classroom: The "magic" of teleportation. *Insight*, 2(4), 73–82.

positive educational outcomes. These types of activities can help both you and your students understand the similarities and differences among the prior knowledge and experiences they bring to the classroom.

Teaching lessons that directly address issues of culture is another way to help students develop respect for diversity. Projects that connect classrooms or even individual students from different schools across the country or the globe are a popular method for introducing students to new and different cultures. The ePals website supports global communication and collaboration among teachers and learners in 200 countries and territories through chat rooms and providing sample project ideas. International E-mail Classroom Connections (IECC) is another organization dedicated to helping teachers connect with other teachers to arrange intercultural e-mail connections among their students.

Many times, cross-cultural projects focus on examining similarities and differences in cultures around a set of common activities such as meals, celebrations, or leisure activities. For example, the Sister School Project, targeted to young children from preschool through fifth grade, connects classes in the U.S. with classes in other countries to explore topics such as typical lunch menus, common nursery rhymes and songs, classroom descriptions, and common recreational activities (American Institute for Foreign Study, n.d.). Classes are encouraged to write letters to each other, work on projects together, or otherwise exchange information about their ways of life.

Building community among diverse learners is an essential element of culturally responsive teaching (Gay, 2002). Cooperative groups require students to develop skills that support collaboration such as listening, speaking, expressing one's own thoughts and ideas as well as respecting and understanding others' perspectives, and reaching consensus. Lab management software with shared workspaces and messaging software can be used within the classroom setting, and shared

WEB LINK

See the textbook's companion website for a list of resources to build cross-cultural awareness and promote connections among students of different cultures.

communications such as a threaded discussion or wiki can be used to support group work beyond the school walls.

Once personal connections have been made, students can use Google Earth to see where others live. They can conduct research online and conduct online "interviews" with students from other cultures. As we've explained throughout this book, learners are most receptive to information that has relevance to their lives. For this reason, establishing a personal connection among students of different cultures can be a powerful means of increasing cross-cultural understanding.

Respecting Cultural Diversity in the Classroom

You should also be aware that culture affects how people react to technology (see Figure 11.4). In some communities that rely strongly on an oral tradition that involves sharing and reflection, disseminating information via mass media—including television and the Internet—can be perceived negatively (Wiburg, 2003). Further, the cultural assumptions implied by a technology and one's cultural response to technology may conflict. Some technologies, such as tutorials or drill-and-practice software, encourage the development of autonomy in the learner that may conflict with students who come from a culture of collaborative communication (McLoughlin,

Monkey Business/Fotolia, Julián Rovagnati/Fotolia, video1/istockphoto.com, vgajic/istockphoto.com

Figure 11.4
Consider the effect of culture on student perceptions and reactions to technology.

1999). In contrast, technologies designed to support group activities may conflict with students of more individualistic preferences. These cultural differences hold true in virtual settings, too, where students may require a great deal of autonomy and self-motivation in order to read materials, view course lectures or media elements, and complete assignments on time, versus being communal and collaborative and being required to participate in group activities through online discussion forums or other group settings (Collis, 1999). As we mentioned earlier in this chapter, content evaluation should involve a consideration of the cultural preferences of your students and their communities.

The atmosphere of your classroom is influenced by both the physical attributes of the classroom as well as the interactions you and your students have with each other. Classroom decorations, bulletin boards, and even the arrangement of furniture should promote positive and purposeful academic engagement. Images used should represent people across a range of ages, genders, places, social classes, and ethnicities that relate to and extend the curriculum (Gay, 2002). Culturally responsive teachers are aware of the strengths and weaknesses of curricula and curricular materials, including cultural biases and distortions that can occur in books, periodicals, videos, software applications, and information on the Internet.

This section has introduced you to ways to develop cultural understanding and global awareness in order to become a culturally responsive teacher who is able to meet the learning needs of students from various cultures. It is not enough to intersperse different cultural elements and artifacts into the curriculum, such as exploring the achievements of a famous person of color, noting the existence of holidays in different cultures, or bringing in food from various countries. Instead, it is the instructional strategies you use to reach students from various backgrounds and experiences that constitute culturally responsive pedagogy.

Review the Tools for Use: Culturally Responsive Instructional Strategies and consider how these instructional strategies, in addition to those presented throughout this section, could be implemented in your classroom. Reflect on technologies you already know that can support these strategies and consider others mentioned in this section that you would like to know more about.

Chapter Summary

In this chapter, we discussed the complex issues related to equitable access to technology and developing cultural understanding to support the learning needs of your

---

TOOLS FOR USE
Culturally Responsive Instructional Strategies

In order to address the learning needs of an increasingly diverse student population in the nation's classrooms, NCCREST (Richards, Brown, & Forde, 2006) describes three components of culturally responsive pedagogy: 1) institutional, 2) personal, and 3) instructional. Consider the following ten strategies you can use in support of culturally responsive instruction.

1. Acknowledge students' differences as well as their commonalities.
2. Validate students' cultural identities in classroom practices and instructional materials.
3. Educate students about the diversity of the world around them.

4. Promote equity and mutual respect among students.
5. Use valid measures to assess students' ability and achievement.
6. Foster a positive interrelationship among students, their families, the community, and school.
7. Motivate students to become active participants in their learning.
8. Encourage students to think critically.
9. Challenge students to strive for excellence as defined by their potential.
10. Assist students in becoming socially and politically conscious.

students. Special attention was paid to explicitly defining and describing a learner-centered classroom. The issue of equity goes beyond simple access to technology and includes actual patterns of use. Although you directly influence equitable access within your classroom, learning continues outside of the school and disparate access at home can become significant as you incorporate instructional technology into your teaching. You are encouraged to be an advocate for equitable access to technology resources in order to better prepare your students to meet the growing technological demands of society.

Access to hardware, software, and connectivity means more than simply having the technology available for your use—it's how you use the technology that's important. You are one of the biggest factors in providing access to learning resources in a way that is sensitive to the individual and cultural needs of your students. Above all, ensure that all students, whatever their backgrounds or abilities, have equitable opportunities to use all of the technology resources available in an interactive classroom with an atmosphere that respects students and provides ample opportunities for students to build on and extend their knowledge and skills. Based on the unique needs of your students, using culturally responsive pedagogies can help you leverage available technologies to meet the learning needs and match the learning preferences of your students.

There is no one formula for determining equitable access, appropriately responding to students' cultural needs, or creating a learner-centered environment. Keep in mind that the driving force behind all of your instructional decisions should be the learning needs of each student. All students will be required to use technology as they matriculate through school and into their careers; you are one of the most important factors in promoting academic success for your students.

YOUR PORTFOLIO

To demonstrate competency in ISTE NETS-T standards 4.b and d, add the following items to your portfolio:

1. A philosophy statement that discusses your commitment to and implementation strategies for addressing cultural diversity and equity issues related to technology use. Provide explicit reasons why it is important for teachers and students to consider these issues in teaching and learning. Include specific strategies that address
   a. creating a collaborative environment that supports the cognitive, social, and emotional needs of students
   b. promoting reflective thinking to support student metacognition
   c. ensuring that all students, whatever their backgrounds or abilities, have appropriate opportunities to use all of the technology resources available in your classroom
2. A reflection on your own cultural experiences. You can do this through identifying the different cultural groups you belong to and reflecting on how these experiences have shaped and continue to influence your life. You should also consider how these cultural influences impact your perception of and reaction to technology, specifically as it is related to using technology to support teaching and learning. You may also want to consider the connection between school and society and how you have been influenced as a member of different school settings.

References

American Association of University Women Educational Foundation (AAUW). (2000). *Tech-savvy: Educating girls in the new computer age.* Washington, DC: American Association of University Women.

American Institute for Foreign Study (n.d.) Global awareness for teachers: Sister School project. Stamford, CT: Author. Retrieved July 20, 2008, from http://www.globalawareness.com/forteachers.asp

Barell, J. (1998). *Problem-based learning: An inquiry approach.* Arlington Heights, IL: Skylight.

Christensen, R., Knezek, G., & Overall, T. (2005). Transition points for the gender gag in computer enjoyment. *Journal of Research on Technology in Education*, 38(1), 23–37.

Collis, B. (1999). Designing for differences: Cultural issues in the design of WWW-based course-support sites. *British Journal of Educational Technology*, 30(3), 201–215.

Damarin, S. K. (1998). Technology and multicultural education: The question of convergence. *Theory Into Practice*, 37(1), 11–19.

Eisenhower National Consortium. (2002). The search for bias-free educational software. *ENC Focus*, 7(4), 45–47.

Gay, G. (2002). Preparing for culturally responsive teaching. *Journal of Teacher Education*, 53(2), 106–116.

International Society for Technology in Education (ISTE). (2008). *Refreshed ISTE NETS for Teachers rubrics.* Eugene, OR: author.

Kolodner, J. L., Camp, P. J., Crismond, D., Fasse, J. G., Holbrook, J., Puntambekar, S., & Ryan, M. (2003). Problem-based learning meets case-based reasoning in the middle school science classroom: Putting learning by design into practice. *Journal of the Learning Sciences*, 12, 495–547.

LAB (2002). *The Diversity Kit. An introductory resource for social change in education.* Providence, RI: LAB at Brown University.

Linn, M. C., Clark, D., & Slotta, J. D. (2003). WISE design for knowledge integration. *Science Education*, 87(4), 517–538.

McLoughlin, C. (1999). Culturally responsive technology use: Developing an on-line community of learners. *British Journal of Educational Technology*, 30(3), 231–243.

Montgomery, W. (2001). Creating culturally responsive, inclusive classrooms. *Teaching Exceptional Children*, 33(4), 4–9.

National Center for Education Statistics (NCES). (2005). Trends in educational equity of girls & women: 2004. *Education Statistics Quarterly*, 6(4). Washington, DC: Author. Retrieved July 20, 2006, from http://nces.ed.gov/programs/quarterly/vol_6/6_4/8_1.asp

Newmann, F. M., Bryk, A. S., & Nagaoka, J. K. (2001). *Authentic intellectual work and standardized tests: Conflict or coexistence?* Chicago, IL: Consortium on Chicago School Research.

Peace Corps (n.d.). *Building bridges: A Peace Corps classroom guide to cross-cultural understanding.* Washington, DC: Author. Retrieved July 20, 2008, from http://www.peacecorps.gov/publications/bridges/index.cfm

Richards, H. V., Brown, A. F., & Forde. T. B. (2006). *Addressing diversity in schools: Culturally responsive pedagogy.* Tempe, AZ: National Center for Culturally Responsive Educational Systems (NCCREST).

Snyder, T. D. (2008). *Mini-digest of education statistics*, 2007 (NCES 2008-023). Washington, DC: National Center for Education Statistics, Institute of Educational Sciences, U.S. Department of Education.

U.S. Census Bureau. (October, 2005). *Computer and Internet use in the United States: 2003.* Washington, DC: Author.

U.S. Department of Commerce. (1999). *Falling through the Net: Defining the digital divide.* Washington, DC: Author.

U.S. Department of Education, National Center for Education Statistics. (2005). *The condition of education 2005* (NCES 2005-094). Washington, DC: U.S. Government Printing Office.

Villegas, A. M., & Lucas, T. (2002). Preparing culturally responsive teachers. Rethinking the curriculum. *Journal of Teacher Education*, 53(1), 20–32.

Wells, J., & Lewis, L. (2006). *Internet access in U.S. public schools and classrooms: 1994–2005* (NCES 2007-020). U.S. Department of Education. Washington, DC: National Center for Education Statistics.

Wiburg, K. M. (2003). Factors of the divide. In O. Solomon, N. J. Allen, & P. Resta (Eds.), *Toward digital equity: Bridging the divide in education* (pp. 25–40). Boston, MA: Allyn and Bacon.

Wiburg, K. M., & Butler, J. F. (2003). Creating educational access. In O. Solomon, N. J. Allen, & P. Resta (Eds.), *Toward digital equity: Bridging the divide in education* (pp. 1–13). Boston, MA: Allyn and Bacon.

ISTE Standards addressed in this chapter

NETS-T 5. Engage in Professional Growth and Leadership

Teachers continuously improve their professional practice, model lifelong learning, and exhibit leadership in their school and professional community by promoting and demonstrating the effective use of digital tools and resources. Teachers:

a. participate in local and global learning communities to explore creative applications of technology to improve student learning

b. exhibit leadership by demonstrating a vision of technology infusion, participating in shared decision making and community building, and developing the leadership and technology skills of others

c. evaluate and reflect on current research and professional practice on a regular basis to make effective use of existing and emerging digital tools and resources in support of student learning

d. contribute to the effectiveness, vitality, and self-renewal of the teaching profession and of their school and community

Professional Growth and Leadership

In Chapter 1, we introduced the notion that teachers progress through stages of technology integration as they become more familiar with technologies that support teaching and learning. Seminal research, which led to the development of one of the first technology integration stage theories, was conducted by researchers associated with the Apple Classrooms of Tomorrow (ACOT) project (Dwyer, Ringstaff, & Sandholtz, 1991). More recently, ISTE, in conjunction with the publication of the new NETS-T, has adopted the idea of teachers progressing through stages of technology integration. Accompanying the ISTE NETS-T is a four-stage rubric (ISTE, 2008) that profiles teachers' behaviors and proficiencies for each standard and substandard in four stages: 1) beginning, 2) developing, 3) proficient, and 4) transformative. A copy of the rubric can be downloaded from the ISTE website.

This entire book has been preparing you to function at the more advanced levels of technology integration—to exhibit leadership by demonstrating a vision of technology infusion that allows you to be

Outcomes

In this chapter, you will

- Identify local and global learning communities where you can explore creative applications of technologies to improve student learning.
- Identify ways in which you can enhance your own technology leadership skills and the skills of others.
- Reflect on published research and your own practice.
- Conduct action research to apply the findings of current research on teaching and learning to your own classroom, as well as share the results with your school and the greater professional community.

one of those dynamic teachers who functions on a day-to-day basis in the "transformative" phase. In this chapter, we focus on techniques that will help you continuously improve your professional practice, model lifelong learning, and exhibit leadership in your school and professional community by promoting and demonstrating the effective use of digital tools and resources.

We begin the chapter with a discussion of ways that you can "participate in local and global learning communities to explore creative applications of technology to improve student learning." We then discuss ways that you can "exhibit leadership by demonstrating a vision of technology infusion, participating in shared decision making and community building, and developing the leadership and technology skills of others." In the next section, we introduce you to techniques for reflecting on your own professional practice "to make effective use of existing and emerging digital tools and resources in support of student learning." In order for you to learn to evaluate and reflect on current research, we discuss the use of published educational research to inform your classroom practice. Finally, we introduce action research as a method of systematically reflecting on both the published research and your own professional practice in order to "contribute to the effectiveness, vitality, and self-renewal of the teaching profession and of your school and community."

Continued Learning through Local and Global Learning Communities

It's important that you think about how you will continue to learn about and explore "creative applications of technology to improve student learning" as you complete your formal education and move into professional practice. On one hand, you can attend formal university classes. In fact, you are probably enrolled in such a class right now. On the other hand, you can pursue informal learning opportunities by searching the web to find answers to your personal questions. You can find reference materials and others to talk with anytime, anywhere, with the click of a button. Both forms of learning are valuable, as well as everything in between! Throughout your career, we encourage you to participate in formal and informal opportunities to enhance your professional practice. As you read the following descriptions of local and global learning communities, try to identify those that you'd like to investigate further.

Local Learning Communities

When you arrive at a new school, be aware of the leaders in technology integration. Are there teachers in your building who can help you? These fellow teachers can be a tremendous source of support and assistance as you work to integrate technology into your classroom. They may be teachers with an interest in technology who have become expert troubleshooters when problems arise with software, hardware, or the network. Or they may be teachers who have had opportunities for professional development in curriculum-based technologies that you have not used before. New teachers are often paired with a mentor teacher. Find out how your mentor teacher can support your technology needs, even if it is through social networking and introducing you to other teachers with similar interests in using technology (see Figure 12.1).

Xaviarnau/istockphoto.com

Figure 12.1
Collaborating with technology specialists or other teachers who use technology is a great way to build skills and community.

If your school or district employs technology specialists, find out what sort of assistance they can provide. Are the specialists available to help you plan lessons that integrate technology? Technical specialists of this type are becoming more common in schools and are often referred to as technology integration specialists, or technology integration teachers. These technology specialists usually have a teaching background and may still teach some classes. They can help you understand the technology tools in your school, as well as assist you in developing teaching strategies, identifying technologies that best match your lesson plan goals, and sometimes even team-teach a lesson with you (see Figure 12.1).

Depending on their age and developmental level, your students can be a source of technical assistance. Many children today grow up surrounded by computer technologies in their homes. Students as young as second or third grade often know a great deal about computer hardware and software. Many of us have heard stories of preschool children being able to use the remote for the television and video player and even being able to log on to child-specific websites. Take advantage of your students' expertise!

Some schools train special teams of student "technology experts" to assist other students when needed. For example, an elementary school established an after-school program to train students to serve as "technology tutors" to other students and teachers in the school (Ertmer & Hruskocy, 1999). Another project, GenYes, originally known as Generation WHY (Generation Yes, 2007), began as a grant-funded project by the U.S. Department of Education. It is now a national organization that helps schools and districts across the country set up their own technology support teams based on lessons they've learned. If you choose to do this, make sure you check with your school administrators regarding the policies for after-school activities and student access to technology resources.

Formal Learning Opportunities

Colleges, universities, professional organizations, and your own school district offer training courses in topics of interest to teachers. Many of these educational opportunities are available online. Some courses include synchronous components where all class members log on at the same time to participate in Internet chats or meetings where students engage in group discussions or share an electronic workspace. Other instruction is available for self-study. For example, software developers, school districts, and other organizations often offer self-paced tutorials on popular software.

Professional Conferences

Attending conferences is another good strategy for increasing your knowledge of new technologies. State conferences may be smaller than national conferences and often the presenters are teachers who have to meet the same instructional requirements as you. Smaller conferences also support a sense of collegiality that allows you to continue conversations by phone or e-mail after they are over. There are also a number of larger national conferences. Besides presentations by nationally recognized education and technology experts, these conferences often have special exhibit areas that allow you to explore new hardware and software. Perhaps the most interesting is the impressive array of vendors that attend these conferences with showroom floors containing row upon row of people ready to show you how their products can be used in the classroom (see Figure 12.2).

A good strategy for attending conferences is to go with one or more other teachers from your school or district and to give each person a specific duty. For example, you might be particularly interested in attending presentations and visiting booths related to videoconferencing. Your friend in literacy and language education may want to focus on new writing tools and products designed to support adolescent literacy skills. Everyone should try to stay focused and gather flyers, presentation materials, and other pertinent information about the topic(s) they've been assigned. Once you are back home, you can review the materials either as a group or individually, allowing sufficient time to truly focus on what you're reading.

Figure 12.2
Attending professional conferences can be invigorating, but it's best to have a plan.

Web-based conferences, webcasts, and webinars offer another option for learning about new technologies from experts and colleagues. Textbook publishers, software developers, hardware vendors, colleges, universities, and professional organizations all sponsor web-based training opportunities. Typically, one or more expert will present on a specific topic using webconferencing software. Participants have an opportunity to ask questions and discuss the topic with both the presenter and other participants. Many times, web conferences include a visual presentation and audio capabilities as well as text-based chat capabilities.

Internet Resources

In today's Internet-connected world, tried-and-true teaching strategies are available for you to access online. In other words, you can actually *use* technology to *learn more about* technology. Now, this is not to suggest that you shouldn't also participate in local professional development opportunities; by all means, you should participate in the various opportunities available to you. But as you well know, the Internet opens up a huge range of opportunities that you may not have locally. "Teacher stores" and bookstores are at your fingertips. You'll find educational journals and magazines; subscription e-newsletters and eZines can deliver useful tips and new ideas to your desktop. You can download lesson plans, or if you develop a lesson that works well, you can post it for others to download. And of course, you have access to a wealth of background resources and readings. If you've never explored the many resources available for teachers, you may want to begin by exploring the sites you locate during the following Apply to Practice activity or the resources listed on the textbook's companion website. As you review the online resources, think about which of these tools could assist you in meeting your professional learning goals.

As you look for learning communities, don't forget to investigate the wide range of listservs, blogs, and podcasts that may be of interest to teachers. In most cases, it's very easy to join a listserv by simply sending a message to a listserv address. Since listservs are often run by a computer with little or no human help, make sure to follow the "subscribe" and "unsubscribe" procedures exactly. Likewise, it's easy to subscribe to podcasts using commonly available software, such as Apple's iTunes. There are also many blogs and wikis—journal-like websites created by and for educators that you can visit at your leisure. However, make sure you don't subscribe to too many things! It can take huge amounts of time just to delete messages or backlogs of podcasts that accumulate, and much more time to review them. Some educational websites and news services, such as eSchoolNews, also provide a review of popular blogs so you can find the information you want a little more easily.

APPLY TO PRACTICE

Participating in Online Learning Communities

1. Explore the instructional options available to you. Locate online classes and workshops that you could take to meet the goals on your professional development plan.
2. Locate and review several teacher sites online. There are some sites listed on the textbook's companion website and many state departments of education also provide lists for teachers in their states.
3. What do you notice about these sites? What are the common and unique characteristics of each? List your two favorite sites and describe why you selected them.
4. Share your favorites with your classmates. Visit the sites recommended by two of your classmates. How do they differ from your favorites?

Professional Communications

One powerful way to learn is through interpersonal communications whether face-to-face, by phone, or online. Through communicating with others, you can seek answers to your questions, as well as serve as a mentor to less experienced teachers. The stories teachers tell about their classroom experiences can inspire you and provide you with a wealth of ideas. You use the Internet to communicate with your distant friends and to establish friendships with individuals whom you've never met based on common interests, and this same network can assist you with lifelong learning opportunities. For example, if you're the only teacher within 200 miles who teaches Japanese, don't worry—there are other Japanese teachers you can chat with online. E-mail, Instant Messenger (IM), message boards, discussion groups, and chat rooms all provide an opportunity to share ideas with colleagues, any time of the day or night.

Exhibit Leadership

WEB LINK

See the textbook's companion website for a list of online resources for teachers.

As you move into professional practice, you have the responsibility to do more than simply keep your skills up to date. Standard 5.b requires you to "exhibit leadership by demonstrating a vision of technology infusion, participating in shared decision making and community building, and developing the leadership and technology skills of others." The growing emphasis in the nation's schools on developing teacher leaders, promoting shared leadership and decision making, and creating communities of practice are a result of the increased complexity of the educational landscape. Today, no one—administrator or teacher—can be expected to possess all the expertise and bear all of the responsibility necessary for managing learning (Elmore, 2000). Teachers must be prepared to actively contribute to and participate in leadership efforts at their schools, including technology leadership efforts.

Throughout this book, we have encouraged you to develop a plan for how you will incorporate digital tools and resources into your teaching and learning; however, implementing that vision will require you to continue to update your skills and reflect on your progress—in other words, to remain a self-directed learner throughout your teaching career. As you learned in the previous section, one way that you can enhance your professional development is through participating in a community of learners. And as you learned in Chapter 3, within a community of learners, decision making is shared across all participants. But as part of the first generation of teachers to enter the teaching profession already comfortable with computers, you have the responsibility to do more than that. As you lead the way and break new ground in the world of technology integration, you and your peers have the opportunity to be the leaders in these efforts—this requires that you help other teachers become technology leaders as well.

Reflect back on the four stages of technology integration that ISTE associates with the new NETS-T, introduced in Chapter 1. Review the indicators for each standard and estimate where you might fall within the four stages: beginning, developing, proficient, or transformative. At what stage do you see yourself now? Since you're likely in the preparation stage of your career, you're probably in one of the first two stages. That's perfectly acceptable. No matter what stage you may be in, there are opportunities for you to embrace a vision of technology infusion by improving your skills, participating in a community of learners in which members share ideas and collaborate to make decisions together, and nurturing the development of technology leadership skills—both yours and others. The action steps outlined in Table 12.1 provide suggestions to help you and your peers move forward on the technology integration continuum. You will notice that there are plenty of opportunities for you to learn from, and to contribute to, the learning of others.

APPLY TO PRACTICE

Action Steps

1. List the steps that you plan to take in the next two years to achieve your goals for developing your skills in technology integration within the classroom. Why do you think those steps would be especially useful for you? What else do you need to know to take those steps?
2. Discuss your steps with a group of peers. Find at least one person who is in the same phase as you are. How is your action plan similar? Different?

Table 12.1	Action Steps toward Becoming a Technology Integration Leader
Phases	**Action Steps**
Beginning	
Embrace vision	• Participate in training on common productivity tools and communications software to support your teaching and learning, such as using word-processing to create lesson plans and student activities; using software to record and report student progress; and using e-mail, a class website, or other online communications tools to connect with students, parents, and other teachers. • Use the Internet, journals, and trade magazines to find lesson activities, research, and technology reviews related to the grade or content area(s) that you teach. • Carve out time in your life to develop your technology skills. Dedicate a chunk of time, such as one afternoon each week, to explore issues related to technology integration.
Build community	• Work with other teachers in your school to explore technologies you believe would be appropriate for classroom use. • Communicate with more advanced technology users, perhaps asking them to observe your classroom, in order to get mentoring and just-in-time support when you need it. • Seek help or input from others who are more technologically proficient when creating lesson plans or activities.
Develop leadership	• Share your experiences with others, in person or via online communications, who are also learning to integrate technology.
Developing	
Embrace vision	• Participate in training on applicable software beyond basic productivity tools. Possibilities include spreadsheets, databases, and graphics or multimedia authoring software. Scanners, probeware, handheld computers, and digital cameras, and digital media players are among the hardware options to be explored. • Incorporate a wider range of curriculum-based software and electronic reference materials such as CD-ROMs, online encyclopedias, or content-subscription services in support of your instruction. • Monitor your classroom instruction in relation to the effectiveness of your technology integration efforts. Investigate and reflect on alternate pedagogies made possible by available technologies.
Build community	• Collaborate with other teachers in your school, both in your own and other disciplines, to explore technologies and develop technology-based lesson activities. • Observe teachers who incorporate technology into their teaching, and follow up with conversations focused on ways to adopt or adapt the activities with your own students. • Share your lesson plans with a critical friend—another teacher, or a lead teacher, or a technology integration specialist—and consider ways to modify unsuccessful activities to increase the possibility of success. Also think about how you could replicate or modify activities that were successful.
Develop leadership	• Discuss and share your experiences in formal collaborative settings, whether during joint planning sessions or other staff meetings. • Document your lessons and activities on a class web page or electronic portfolio.

(Continued)

Table 12.1   Action Steps toward Becoming a Technology Integration Leader (continued)

Proficient

Embrace vision
- Attend technology training for new and emerging technologies that support areas of need for improving student learning in your classroom. Help develop and deliver technology training to other faculty and staff in your school.
- Use a variety of technology-based resources to present and modify content that supports your instruction and meets the diverse needs of your learners.
- Incorporate and evaluate a variety of technology-based methods and materials to identify those that best match the content-based skills and knowledge required of the content area(s) you teach.

Build community
- Collaborate with others by joining professional learning communities online and teacher newsgroups. Share ideas about how to use technology in your classroom to increase the effectiveness and appeal of content-based lessons.
- Participate in virtual observations of teachers and students in diverse settings. Reflect on your own and others' practices; engage in meaningful conversations using discussion boards, e-mail, or videoconferencing tools.
- Participate on technology integration planning committees. Co-teach or co-plan lessons with colleagues who are interested in developing their technology skills. Sign up to be a coach for others in your school, district, or state. Develop a cadre of student helpers who can provide support to developing teachers.

Develop leadership
- Demonstrate lesson activities or share lessons learned from technology-based activities with other teachers in your school at staff or faculty meetings.
- Share your successes with other teachers through print and electronic publications such as school newsletters, listservs, or a school website. Maintain and share your electronic portfolio.

Transformative

Embrace vision
- Continue to attend technology trainings for new and emerging technologies in support of teaching and learning needs in your school. Help to identify training needs in your school or district and help develop and deliver technology training to faculty and staff in your school or district.
- Differentiate your instruction and the technologies you use to optimize student learning in your classroom.
- Participate in long-range projects to monitor and evaluate the effectiveness of existing and potential technologies in support of teaching and learning, such as participating in an action-research project focused on your own teaching or that of a group of colleagues.

Build community
- Use technology to develop or nurture professional collaborative efforts with teachers within and beyond your school and district to explore new and emerging technologies and generate solutions to problems or challenges in teaching and learning faced by members of the community.
- Participate in routine observations of classroom technology integration practices, both having teachers observe your practice and observing the practice of others. Meet in person or use technology to support regularly scheduled discussions about current and promising technologies and technology-based activities.
- Continue routine joint planning sessions with other teachers in your grade or content area or with technology integration specialists and routinely evaluate the effectiveness of lessons in order to identify best practices that can be shared across your school or district. Observe and participate in team teaching or coaching with new teachers developing their technology skills.

Develop leadership
- Communicate with teachers who are working through earlier phases in order to provide mentoring and just-in-time support. Attend and make presentations at professional conferences.
- Write about and publish your experiences both in print publications and on the web. Help others to document their lessons and activities by creating a class web page or electronic portfolio.
- Become a mentor for other teachers. In addition to direct involvement with teachers in your building, offer support throughout the district and beyond.

Reflecting on Professional Practice and Current Research

Standard 5.c requires you to "evaluate and reflect on current research and professional practice on a regular basis to make effective use of existing and emerging digital tools and resources in support of student learning." As you recall, we introduced you to reflection in Chapter 2 as a means of monitoring and evaluating your learning. In this chapter, we'll elaborate on what you learned in Chapter 2, and we'll follow that with a discussion of how you can reflect on current research in order to inform your practice. In the next section, we'll discuss how both of these ideas—reflection on your own practice and reflection on current research—can be combined into a form of inquiry called **action research.**

Reflecting on Professional Practice

In Chapter 2, you learned that effective professionals continually reflect on their practice in order to monitor and evaluate their actions. Reflection should occur both "in-action," in order to monitor your behaviors as you go along, and "on-action," in order to improve your future performance. One effective strategy for practicing reflection "on-action" is to use a video camera to record your teaching.

Videotaping lessons is a time-honored tradition that many teachers have used to help make their teaching more effective. This unbiased mechanical observer can help you determine how effective your lesson activities are, whether you unintentionally favor any students in your class in terms of questioning or task assignment, as well as provide a sometimes painfully accurate record of the pace, quality, and appropriateness of your teaching style and activities. Many student teachers use videotaping during their preservice education but few teachers continue the practice in their own classrooms. That's unfortunate, because even an audiotape can provide insight into your use of common pedagogical practices such as level of language use and questioning techniques.

Videotaped lessons also provide valuable data to help you prepare a written reflection on the events portrayed. Begin with a simple description of what happened in the lesson. After describing the events, try to analyze them to determine how and why you behaved as you did. Pay attention to how the actions of your students impacted your actions, and likewise, how your actions influenced the behaviors of your students. It can be a little difficult, at first, to watch yourself on tape, but you'll soon appreciate its value once it helps you improve your practice and reach the needs of every student in your class.

Teachers are routinely observed, and observation instruments are readily available that can be used to help you develop your teaching skills prior to formal observations. By establishing a schedule for recording yourself periodically throughout the year, you not only provide yourself with the opportunity to practice different pedagogical techniques under less pressure than a formal observation, but you can actually record and demonstrate your own growth. It may seem daunting at first to videotape yourself, but the information you receive from the practice will pay off multifold over time as you learn to hone your craft.

Once you feel comfortable recording your lessons, you may also want to consider receiving feedback from your peers, such as other teachers and administrators in your school. Visiting and observing other teachers is a valuable method for learning new ideas and reflecting on your own practices. While it's not always feasible to be absent from your own class, sharing videotaped lessons is a practical method for building your skills and opening a professional dialog with your colleagues.

Reflecting on Current Research

There are hundreds, if not thousands, of journal and magazine articles that have described some aspect of technology use in education. Literature about the educational uses

TOOLS FOR USE

Videotaping Lessons for Certification

Videotaped lessons are a required element for some certification programs, such as National Board Certification from the National Board for Professional Teaching Standards (NBPTS). The National Board for Professional Teaching Standards has certified more than 55,000 teachers since created in 1987. The process of becoming a National Board Certified Teacher is complex and time-consuming but can lead to financial rewards and incentives in many districts. The National Board also has used portfolios as part of their certification process.

While National Board certification is something you may consider later in your career, the tips and guidelines they provide are useful when recording lessons for your own self-reflection. You can find additional information for selecting materials for a teaching portfolio on their website, available at http://www.nbpts.org/for_candidates/the_portfolio. The following tips are adapted from those materials and can guide your recording of your own lessons and the incorporation of those recordings in a portfolio.

- **Your portfolio should focus on your teaching, not your students' achievement.** The instructional activities you showcase in your portfolio should present challenges you face as a teacher, so you may not want to pick just your best students or class or an extremely familiar lesson. Your lesson should not appear practiced or staged but should represent real interactions with students at an appropriate level to their needs.
- **Choose examples (video, lesson plans, student work, etc.) that accurately represent your teaching.** Collect several examples over a period of time that involve a variety of students with different opportunities to showcase your instructional practices. This will provide you with some choice as to which

examples to include in your portfolio. Student work should reflect your instruction. Select activities that involve some degree of familiar class practice or procedure for students; new or novel activities may not be your best choice.

- **You are the focus.** A best-case scenario is having someone else videotape your class. Regardless of whether this is possible, use a tripod and try to place it on a table or platform. Determine the best angle ahead of time, use as wide an angle on the lens as possible, and keep the camera stationary through taping. All materials and resources integral to the lesson, including text and graphics on a chalkboard, whiteboard, or screen, should be legible on camera. Make a backup copy of every recoding immediately!
- **The action has to be visible.** Lighting is important both for videotaping and digital pictures, so turn on all the lights or open all window blinds or curtains, and do not aim the camera directly into bright light sources, such as a wall containing many windows. If using a projector, try different light settings to capture both information on the screen and interactions in the classroom.
- **Record the best audio possible.** Audio is critical, and difficult, to capture in a classroom setting. Do not use the built-in microphone on the video camera. Instead, use an external microphone connected to the camera, perhaps wearing a wireless microphone in a small-group setting, or using a microphone designed for recording in a large room, such as a PZM® microphone. Place the microphone as central to your teaching area as possible. Eliminate extraneous noises, such as fans, air conditioning units, or even pumps in fish tanks.

of technologies can be grouped into four main categories: opinion articles, descriptive studies, evaluation studies, and formal research studies (ISTE, 2002).

The vast majority of articles that you will come upon can be classified as *opinion* pieces. These include theoretical propositions, curricular ideas, suggestions for using technology in the classroom, articles espousing the wonders of the latest and greatest software, and many similar types of papers. The opinions have more credibility if they are based on the results of well-documented research or evaluation studies. They also have more credibility if they represent the consensus of many people, as is the case with the ISTE standards. But until these opinions are tested, they are just opinions. The opinions may be from very important people or experts in the field, yet they are opinions all the same. Still, opinion articles may provide you with many ideas that you can test in your classroom using the action research methods we describe later in this chapter.

Another common category is **descriptive** papers. Descriptive papers describe the state of something. They can describe what happened to one individual or in one classroom, such as how a teacher's classroom management strategies changed to incorporate Personal Digital Assistants (PDAs). They can also describe the results of large-scale surveys, such as those administered by educational organizations, such as Quality Education Data (QED), the Software and Information Industry Association (SIIA), and the Consortium for School Networking (CoSN). News organizations also provide descriptive reports, such as the popular "Technology Counts" by Education Week that "grades" states for their technology efforts. Most qualitative research reports fall into this category because they focus on a rich description of a specific situation.

There are also formal **evaluation studies**. Evaluation studies are used to determine the effects of an intervention—a product or teaching method. Evaluation reports are a popular method for technology vendors to promote their products and services. Evaluation studies may be well documented and may use a variety of qualitative and quantitative methods to determine the effects of the intervention. However, they do not attempt to test a specific hypothesis and do not need to have a control group.

Formal **experimental research** studies, on the other hand, do test hypotheses and use control groups to determine the effects of an intervention. The results of these studies should be documented well enough for you to determine the extent to which they generalize to other settings. An experimental study should have a control group that is as identical as possible to the experimental group, except for the fact that the experimental group receives the experimental treatment. Randomly assigning participants to the different groups makes the experimental design even stronger, but is not always possible. Sometimes, though, when randomization is not possible, the different groups can be matched in terms of important characteristics, or statistical tests can be run to help make sure the makeup of the groups had little or no impact on the outcome of the research. Studies in which randomization is not possible are often referred to as **quasi-experimental** studies. Statistical techniques are used to determine the extent to which any observed differences between the experimental and control groups may be due to chance alone.

There is a great deal of pressure to conduct "scientifically" controlled studies to determine whether educational interventions "work," by randomizing students into classes, controlling teacher content and presentation, and so forth. The No Child Left Behind Act of 2001 (Pub. L. No. 107-110) calls for the use of "scientifically based research" as the foundation for educational programs. In general, scientifically based research is defined (Eisenhart & Towne, 2003) as research that

- consists of an experimental or quasi-experimental design
- uses empirical methods of data collection that are based on measurements or observations
- uses measurement instruments or observational methods that provide reliable and valid data across multiple measurements and observations
- involves rigorous statistical analyses to test hypotheses
- provides a clear description of the research methods, instruments, and data used in order to allow for replication by other researchers
- has been subjected to peer review by experts who are not associated with the study

However, you need to know that the issue is much more complex than it might seem on the surface. The federal funding for research and development related to technology in educational settings is scarce and most federal funding for technology—such as the e-Rate, Enhancing Education through Technology (Title IID of the No Child Left Behind Act), and several large grant programs—continues to decrease or even be cut altogether. Opponents to continued funding for technology argue that despite all the monies spent on technology, software, networking, professional development, and developing resources, there has been little measurable impact on student achievement—and for many, student achievement is measured by standardized testing. They are no doubt correct. Why would putting computers in classrooms or connecting to the Internet, in and of themselves, increase test scores? You must also consider what the test scores are measuring, and in what format. We would argue that they are asking the wrong question and using the wrong data.

In this chapter, we will provide some guidance on how you can determine research questions that are important to you, such as, "Does this software match the learning needs of my students?", "How does a particular technology tool support my teaching style?", "What are the best methods for helping my students master my curriculum?" From this exploration, you will then also be able to determine what types of data you can collect in your own classroom to help you answer questions like these. But we'll begin by reviewing some of the work of educational researchers that has come before you.

Media-Comparison Studies

Several decades ago, Richard Clark (1983) pointed out that the research being done with media and technology was not useful. He then argued, and continues to emphasize, that what we were doing was comparing one media against another (e.g., film vs. classroom instruction, or film vs. TV, and so forth). Mostly we *were* doing such comparisons. "Why wouldn't you?" you might ask. Because it would be wrong. Clark's basic argument was that media (including digital media) do not influence instruction and learning per se anymore than a delivery truck influences the taste or vitamin content of vegetables delivered by that truck. Basically, media "carries" instruction and can operationally deliver certain teaching and learning techniques (responding, feedback, and so forth) but does not, in and of itself, "teach."

One flaw in such research includes the predictable comparison of technology versus "traditional" instruction. In most cases, the "new" treatment consists of materials that have been designed with much more care than the traditional treatment, so it's no surprise that the new materials appear superior. In many cases, the novelty alone is often enough to give new treatments an edge over traditional methods. Other times, the differences in test scores can be attributed to the fact that one treatment is more carefully designed than the other or the measure of learning is biased in one direction. Another problem with these media-comparison studies is simply a matter of "so now what?" If digital tape is "better" than VHS tapes (and occasionally, it will be, just by chance, if you test it often enough), so what? What does it tell us? In general, for research involving media to be useful, it should either involve the attributes of certain media (for example, is motion better than still images?) or test a theory (for example, do certain media systems make you feel closer to others in a distance learning class?).

For the most part, research has shown that the technology itself doesn't really make much of a difference; instead, it's the way that the technology is used that matters. In other words, it doesn't matter whether students read their biology textbook online or from a book. There's nothing inherent about the technology that makes it unique from another resource. What does matter is the design of the instruction that is delivered to the students and what they do with the information once it has been received. In our example, the design of the text itself matters. The use of titles, summaries, overviews, and clearly labeled pictures can facilitate learners' comprehension of the textbook's content (Kozma, 1991). And it also matters what they do with the information once they have read it. For example, students who have the opportunity to participate in study groups reviewing what they have read, create outlines or concept maps illustrating their understanding of the content, or relate the content to real-world problems or phenomena are better able to understand the content than those who simply read the book. These ideas are consistent with the focus of this book: it's not *what* computer hardware, software, or other digital technology you use that matters, it's *how* you use it.

Granted, different technologies have different attributes, and these specific attributes may matter. In our textbook example, an online textbook may have hyperlinks that allow you to click on a new word the first time it is introduced in the text and then jump to additional information about the topic. The ability to access related knowledge at the point of need may make a difference, but that does not mean that students could not have accessed additional information when using a traditional textbook, for example, by using a dictionary or searching the Internet. However, the ability of a computer to provide immediate feedback through a variety of relevant materials and resources, which then can be quickly incorporated into student products, such as student-generated notes or a portfolio, might increase the likelihood that students will use those supporting resources, deepen their understanding, and increase their motivation for extending their learning.

Obviously it's what teachers and students DO with the computers, connections, and so forth that can make a difference. AND, even if good things happen when you do the right things with the right technology, those "good things" may not be measured by standardized achievement tests. Moreover, it could be argued that even if technologies, well used, never make a difference in test scores, it still would make sense to use them for teaching and learning in the schools so that students "grow up" with the technologies that they will likely use in their future jobs and life outside of school.

Research on the Impact of Technology

That being said, many groups have reviewed the existing literature related to technology use in an attempt to draw conclusions applicable to educational practice.

Summary of Research: CARET

One group that has attempted to summarize the research on learning with technology is the Center for Applied Research in Education and Technology (CARET). CARET was created through a partnership between the International Society for Technology in Education and Educational Support Systems, with support from the Bill and Melinda Gates Foundation (ISTE, 2005a). CARET summarized past and current research findings related to the effects of technology on student learning as follows (ISTE, 2005b).

Technology improves student academic performance when:

- The application directly supports the curriculum objectives being assessed.
- The application provides opportunities for student collaboration.
- The application adjusts for student ability and prior experience, and provides feedback to the student and teacher about student performance or progress with the application.
- The application is integrated into the typical instructional day.
- The application provides opportunities for students to design and implement projects that extend the curricular content being assessed by a particular standardized test.
- The application is used in environments where teachers, the school community, and school and district administrators support the use of technology.

Technology can enable the development of higher-order thinking skills when:

- Students are taught to apply the process of problem solving and are then allowed opportunities to apply technology in development of solutions.
- Students work in collaborative groups while using computers to solve problems.
- Students use technology presentation and communication tools to present, publish, and share results of projects.

Technology improves motivation, attitudes, and interest when:

- Students use computer applications that adjust problems and tasks to maximize students' experiences of success.
- Students use technology applications to produce, demonstrate, and share their work with peers, teachers, and parents.
- Students use challenging, game-like programs and technology applications designed to develop basic skills and knowledge.

Technology helps prepare students for the workforce when:

- Students learn to use and apply applications that are used in the world of work such as word processors, spreadsheets, computer-aided drawing, website development programs, and the Internet.
- Students are provided information regarding the use and benefit of technology and telecommunications for the workplace.

Technology is most effective for low-performing, at-risk, or students with special needs when:

- Students utilize instructional programs that continuously assess individual performance by adjusting the task difficulty to their ability and experience levels.
- Students utilize technology applications selected to address their unique needs, strengths, and weaknesses.
- Students utilize programs that are appropriate to their own language experiences.
- Students utilize technology applications guided by diagnostic educational assessments to determine which programs are aligned with their documented academic needs.
- Carefully chosen technology applications provide immediate student feedback and progress monitoring.

Summary of Research: Apple Computer

Similar to the CARET project, Apple Computer Company (2002, p. 4) summarized the research findings related to the use of technology to raise student achievement:

- Students, especially those with few advantages in life, learn basic skills— reading, writing, and arithmetic—better and faster if they have a chance to practice those skills using technology.
- Technology engages students and, as a result, they spend more time on basic learning tasks than students who use a more traditional approach.
- Technology offers educators a way to individualize curriculum and customize it to the needs of individual students so all children can achieve their potential.
- Students who have the opportunity to use technology to acquire and organize information show a higher level of comprehension and a greater likelihood of using what they learn later in their lives.
- By giving students access to a broader range of resources and technologies, students can use a variety of communication media to express their ideas more clearly and powerfully.
- Technology can decrease absenteeism, lower dropout rates, and motivate more students to continue on to college.
- Students who regularly use technology take more pride in their work, have greater confidence in their abilities, and develop higher levels of self-esteem.

Consumers of Research

While these research findings have been culled from many years of research, they still only represent a starting point for thinking about how to use technology in your classroom. It's important that you don't think of these as definitive answers but rather as guidelines that can and should be adjusted when applied in your classroom with your unique group of students.

Although these results are undoubtedly valid, there is a danger in thinking that the results of one or two studies are the absolute truth. To further complicate matters, many of the studies have conflicting findings. It's important for you to know that research exists, but it is even more important that you know how to be a good consumer of research.

As you examine the research for practical applications that you can use, consider the degree to which the conditions in the study are similar to, or different from, your classroom. Factors such as the following may influence the degree to which the research findings do or do not apply to your environment. When reading a research study, ask yourself the following questions (Bitter & Pierson, 2005):

- Who are the students? What is the age and grade level of the students? How are they like my students?
- What technology is being used? What sort of computers, peripherals, and digital devices are they using? What software applications are being used? How?
- When do they use the technology? Is access limited or not? How often and how frequently do they have access to the technology?
- Where do students have access to technology? Is it available at home and school?
- Why is technology being used? What is the intended purpose? Is it being used to supplement or replace other instruction? What are the instructional goals? How well do those goals match my own?
- How are students and teachers using technology? Are electronic information sources used to supplement direct instructional methods or as a resource within constructivist learning environments? Is it used individually, in small groups, or large group settings? (p. 93)

As you examine the research findings, think about the extent to which the findings apply to your situation. Just because the research was conducted with a different group of students, different content, or different equipment than you have, it doesn't mean that the results would *not* apply to your classroom. But it doesn't mean they do. Look to the research to give you ideas of what *may* be applicable in your classroom, then conduct your own classroom research to determine whether these principles work for you or not.

Teacher as Researcher

One of the best ways to determine what works for your students is to engage in **action research** within your own classroom. Perhaps you have read about the use of blogs for daily journal writing in high school literature classrooms, yet you teach fifth grade. Still, the idea sounds interesting. According to the article you read, students generated more and better stories when they wrote for an audience. Although you teach fifth grade, you still wonder how that would work with your students. Using action research methods, you can investigate whether these techniques work for your students and your curriculum. Action research is also called teacher research or teacher inquiry. No matter which term you use, it refers to the process of systematically collecting data to investigate some issue in your classroom. Action research doesn't just help you—it allows you to "contribute to the effectiveness, vitality, and self-renewal of the teaching profession" and of your school and community, as required by NETS-T Standard 5.d.

Action research can be conducted individually, in collaboration with a small group of peers, or as part of a school-wide endeavor. At one end of the continuum is the teacher who investigates the results of an intervention in his or her own classroom (see Figure 12.3). Other times, teachers in several classrooms work together, often as a grade level or department. And finally, there is school-wide action research. We will focus on the individual teacher-as-researcher, although the methods we discuss can easily be applied to action research projects that involve additional researchers. If you are interested in learning more about action research, you can find some excellent resources about the topic online.

Currently, action research is closely aligned with the reflective-practitioner movement within the teaching profession. When conducting action research, the teacher reflects on his or her own classroom practice in order to identify an area in need of improvement. Although the intervention could be designed to address a problem, it can also be designed to investigate something that you're curious about, or to pursue

WEB LINK

For a list of resources related to action research, visit the textbook's companion website.

Figure 12.3
New and emerging technologies and how they support learning in your classroom makes a great subject for action research.

an opportunity. Perhaps, for example, you want to investigate whether students would benefit from online help sessions before their exams. Just as professional athletes are always working to improve their performances professional teachers should also be looking for opportunities to improve their skills and performances. Action research should be part of your own professional development; as such, it is one way to continue learning so that you can remain a dynamic and responsive teacher.

There are several action research models, and each divides the process into a slightly different number of steps, but the process is essentially the same throughout the models (see, for example, McNiff, 2002; Mertler, 2005; Stringer, 2003). In essence, you identify an area that you want to investigate, you collect data, and you analyze and reflect on the data in order to determine your next step. This process also aligns well with the idea of "data-based decision-making," described in Chapter 6, that is popular today. For simplicity, we will continue to use the GAME plan acronym to organize the steps in the action-research process.

Steps in the Action-Research Process

Action research is a logical extension of the GAME plan that you have been using for your own self-directed learning throughout this book (see Table 12.2). When you use the GAME plan to increase your own knowledge, you identify an area of interest and then take action by seeking information to help you meet your learning goals. As you gather information, you monitor your learning progress to determine if the information you are finding is leading you toward obtaining your learning goals. After you have completed the process, you evaluate your learning progress and processes. You look back and consider whether you obtained your learning goals, whether your strategies were effective, or whether you need to modify either your goals or your strategies.

When you engage in action research, you take this process one step further. You identify an area of interest. You collect information that helps you meet your learning goals. You examine the information you find in light of your learning goals and situation. You evaluate whether this information is sufficient to allow you to meet your learning goals. But then you cycle back through the process, seeking greater insight.

Table 12.2	GAME Plan for Self-Directed Learning and Action Research	
Steps	Self-Directed Learning	Action Research
Goals	• What do I want to know or be able to do? • What do I already know about the topic? • How will I know if I have been successful?	• What do I want to know? • What is already known about the topic? • How will I know if I have been successful?
Action	• What information do I need to meet my goal? • How can I find the information I need? • What resources are needed? • What learning strategy will I use?	• What will I investigate? • What evidence or data do I need to collect? • What research strategy will I use?
Monitor	• Am I finding the information I need? • What patterns are emerging from the information sources? • Do I need to modify my action plan?	• How is it working? • What patterns are emerging from the data?
Evaluate and extend	• Have I met my learning goals? If not, should I modify my goals or my learning strategies? • What will I do differently in the future?	• How did the intervention work? • What will I do differently in the future, based on my research results? • What might I recommend to others?

Establish Goals

As in all forms of self-directed learning, the first step in the action-research process is to determine the focus, or goals, of the investigation. You may want to investigate ways to improve a situation in your classroom. Perhaps your school has received a donation of 25 iPods and you wonder how they could be used to enhance your students' learning. Figure 12.4 lists several questions that can help you identify an area of investigation.

Often, the focus is stated in the form of a question such as "How can iPods be used to enhance my students' learning?" but it can also be stated as a goal statement such as "The purpose of this project is to investigate how iPods can enhance my students' learning." As you identify the goal of your investigation, make sure your focus is narrow enough to be manageable, yet open-ended enough so that it *cannot* be answered with a simple yes or no. Notice that our focus was on *how* iPods could enhance learning, not simply *do* iPods enhance learning. Stating your goal in this way opens up the possibility of identifying more areas of potential interest than a simple yes or no question. You want to allow for a range of insights to emerge. In addition, you want your

---

Starting Points for an Action Research Project

1. I would like to improve. . .
2. I am perplexed by. . .
3. Some people are unhappy about. . .
4. I'm really curious about. . .
5. I want to learn more about. . .
6. An idea I would like to try out in my class is. . .
7. Something I think would really make a difference is. . .
8. Something I would like to do to change is. . .
9. Right now, some areas I'm particularly interested in are. . .

Figure 12.4
Action research question stems.
Source: Adapted from *Madison Metropolitan School District* (2001).

goal to have practical implications for your classroom, in order to be worthy of your time. It should yield potential benefits, to you, your students, and others. And most importantly, you want it to be something that will sustain your interest.

As usual at this stage, you should determine what is known about your area of interest in order to develop a plan to close the gap between what you know and what you want to know. Although some authors suggest that you develop your plan of action based on your own intuition and knowledge, we prefer to build on the knowledge of other researchers, all the while keeping in mind that we, as teachers, are often most knowledgeable about *our* situations. We look to the ideas and research of others as simply a way of expanding our repertoire of possibilities, as data we can use to make our decisions, rather than as Truth (with a capital T!).

Typically, when conducting research, you look to the research literature to see what others know that might be applicable to your situation or interest. If, for example, you were interested in how iPods could be used for student learning, a first step would be to investigate how others have used iPods in the classroom. Opinion pieces and descriptive studies, as well as evaluation and formal research studies, can provide you with ideas worthy of further investigation. As you conduct your investigation, clearly identify what you hope to learn from your research. In other words, how will you know you have been successful? Based on the existing information that you find, seek to develop a plan of action for your classroom.

Take Action

Once you have identified your area of interest and what is known about the topic, you can develop a plan to take action in your classroom. As you work to develop an action plan, consider the following questions:

STORIES FROM PRACTICE

Reflecting on My Classroom Practice

Not long ago our district implemented a new approach to professional development that emphasized teacher research as one of its primary goals. They asked for volunteers to pilot this approach in their classrooms. Because I had already been thinking about some of the things I wanted to improve in my classroom, I decided to sign up.

I have 27 students in my 4th grade classroom, 16 boys and 11 girls. There's a pretty good balance of ability levels, from high to low, although there are more high-ability boys than girls. My students are very active and very social. They ask a lot of questions about everything, but they're not very good listeners.

One of my biggest concerns is my students' inability to work well in small groups. They argue and bicker and have a hard time staying focused. I also have a hard time judging the progress they are making when working in small groups. Some students seem to take charge and put forth full effort while others seem to just let their classmates do the bulk of the work. How do I know that they are actually processing the information and learning?

When I started to think about how to focus this concern into a question that could guide my classroom inquiry, I wasn't sure how to get started. I wanted to know how I could better monitor the success of my students but I wasn't sure what to try. After reading some of the literature about self-directed learning and student self-monitoring, I finally came up with a question that I felt I could investigate in my room.

One of the articles I read mentioned that when students set goals, they are motivated to meet those goals. It also mentioned that when students are allowed to reflect on the progress they are making their motivation and performance increase. So, I decided to give this a try in my classroom. I made up a little survey to measure the students' motivation for the next group project we were going to do about early pioneers, and gave it to them before we started. Then all the students kept a log in which they wrote down what they already knew about pioneers, what they wanted to know, and how they intended to learn what they wanted to know (kind of like a personal KWHL chart). These served as the students' long-range goals.

Then, everyday the students set daily goals that were very specific. At the beginning and end of each class period, I asked the students to check their goals for the day. This really seemed to help focus them on their tasks for the day.

Although the project is not over yet, I have already collected and analyzed lots of data—the motivation surveys (which I'll give again when it's over), the students' logs of their daily goals, as well as their notes about what they accomplished each day. And I should be able to tell if they actually learned more than my previous classes by looking at their test scores and comparing those to the scores from my other classes.

I'm pretty excited about the teacher-researcher approach. It makes so much sense to take a more systematic look at how this new strategy (goal setting) impacts learning before deciding whether it's worth using. If it does, I'll use it again, probably in additional subjects. If it doesn't, then I plan to go back to the literature to get more ideas. Teacher research really helps me feel as though I am in control of my students' learning—and that's a pretty good feeling!

What will you investigate? Will you implement a new strategy? If so, what steps will you take? Or will you focus your study on existing practices? The identification of the intervention itself will probably be the easiest step for you. It is no different than planning any other teaching method.

What evidence, or data, do you want to collect? Perhaps you want to introduce your students to the iPods and ask them to help you brainstorm how they could use them for learning. How would you collect data at this step? Perhaps you could have them work in groups to brainstorm solutions and record those ideas on a flip chart. This flip chart would be your data. You could issue them each an iPod for a month and have them keep a journal of all the ways they find to use the iPod for instruction. You could collect the journals to determine what the students identified. After the iPods were returned, you could examine the number and type of files on each iPod. You could keep your own journal of observations as to how students use them in class. Let's say the iPods also had microphones attached so that students could record classroom lessons or discussions whenever they wanted. You could determine whether the iPods actually included lectures, identify how many, and ask students to self-report how they actually used the iPods at the end of the month-long period. Consider exactly what type of data you need to answer your research question.

As you identify the types of data you need, be aware you can include both quantitative and qualitative data. **Quantitative data** is information that can covert to numbers such as test scores or self-report ratings on opinion scales. **Qualitative data,** on the other hand, typically convert to words and are usually reported in the form of an interpretive narrative. Some forms of data can be used as both quantitative and qualitative data. For example, you may examine journal entries to count the number of times students mention that they used their iPods to listen to a lecture, and also examine their entries to identify the trends in iPod use. For example, music, recorded lectures, books on tape, and data backup may emerge as patterns that can be used to organize the students' patterns of use.

What research strategy will I use? As you plan your data collection, you need to take into consideration the means through which the data will be analyzed in order to ensure that you have collected the necessary information. Quantitative data are usually analyzed statistically while qualitative data are analyzed to identify themes that emerge. In general, you should always plan to collect data from two or more sources as this increases your ability to interpret your results accurately. Consider how you will ensure that you have multiple perspectives represented in the data you collect. See Figure 12.5 for a list of possible data collection methods.

As in your teaching, you'll need to plan what you will do when. One question you may have is when to stop collecting data and go to the next step. In general, you will stop collecting data when you are no longer learning anything new. There is no way to know this for certain in advance so just make your best guess and realize that you may modify your plan as you progress through the study.

Monitor

When you monitor your learning, you ask, "How is this working?" When you monitor an intervention during an action-research project, you ask the same question. And you answer that question through ongoing data analysis.

Quantitative data are analyzed statistically. You can summarize the means, averages, and percentiles. If you've been trained in statistical methods, you may want to use statistical tests, such as *t-tests* and others, to determine the probability that the differences between students' pretest scores and posttest scores can be attributed, at least in part, to the phenomenon you're studying. Spreadsheet programs can help you organize your data and perform statistical calculations.

There are as many ways to analyze qualitative data as quantitative data, but in general, you will read through the data (remember that qualitative data are usually recorded in words) and look for patterns or themes to emerge. Once you have a sense of what the

Ideas for Data Collection

You should collect multiple sources of data, but select the most appropriate data for the question being investigated. Data you can collect include:

- **Interviews** with other teachers, your students, or their parents on the issue you are researching
- **Diaries, journals, or anecdotal notes** that you or your students create to record actions, thoughts, and reflections
- **Memos, minutes from meetings, or notes from the field** if you are engaging in a collaborative project
- **Audio, videotapes, or photographs** from your own teaching or of student interactions and performances that document behaviors over time
- **Questionnaires or surveys** about attitudes, opinions, or learning or other preferences from those directly involved with your issue, whether other teachers, your students, or their parents
- **Checklists** of skills, knowledge, behaviors, procedures, or resources
- **Student records**, such as test results, past grades, attendance, behavior and discipline, and any record of interventions or enrichment activities that students have participated in
- **Samples of student work**, such as papers, projects, web-based communications, portfolios, formal or informal assessments, or recordings of oral reports, presentations, or performances

Figure 12.5
Techniques for data collection.
Source: Based on Ferrance, E. (2000). *Action research.* Providence, RI: LAB at Brown University.

patterns are, you can code your data by identifying instances of these patterns in one form of data (e.g., students' journals) and then look for instances of the same pattern in a different form of data (e.g., observation or interview data). Do the same or different patterns emerge? The data analysis process is iterative. It's useful to keep logs or journals of your findings. You may want to organize your data in tables or draw flowcharts or graphs. As you read through the data, try to summarize what you are learning. Figure 12.6 provides additional tips for analyzing qualitative data.

Throughout the data analysis process, attempt to **triangulate** your data by looking for similar and different evidence in other data sources. When you triangulate qualitative data, you look to see if the same themes emerge from two or more data sources. In our example, you'd want to examine the actual files on the iPods to see if they clustered into the same categories as those reflected in the journal entries. You could also analyze the actual files quantitatively by counting the number of files of each type. Finally, you can triangulate findings across quantitative and qualitative data sources, as when you examine the similarity between findings obtained from students' ratings on an attitude survey (a quantitative source) and comments made during a class discussion regarding the perceived instructional value of using iPods (a qualitative source).

Think about what you can learn from the patterns that emerge. How is your intervention working? What effects can you identify? You may want to talk with others at this point to see if they identify similar themes and patterns as you do.

Evaluate and Extend

Once you have analyzed your data, it's time to reflect on your learning and plan for further action. How did it work? What will you do differently in the future, based on your research? What might you recommend to others?

Analyzing Qualitative Data
When you conduct qualitative research, you collect and analyze your data simultaneously. These processes inform each other. For example, as you analyze your first set of interview data, you realize what new questions you need to ask in your next round of interviews. As you learn more from your data during the analysis process, you generate new ideas for the next round of data collection.

1. **Review** everything you have collected. Make notes as you go.
2. **Look for themes**, patterns, big ideas. Key words and phrases can trigger themes. Determine these themes by scanning the data, not based on your preconceived ideas of what the categories will be.
3. **Narrow the themes** down to something manageable. (3-5 of the most compelling and interesting.)
4. **Revisit** your data and **code** or label information according to the themes in order to organize your ideas. Make sure that you are organizing your data based on what you are actually learning from the data, not on the assumptions you bring with you to your analysis. Some ideas may fit into more than one theme. Create subgroups under each theme.
5. **Write continuously**. Jot down what you are seeing, what questions are emerging, and what you are learning. Keep notes on those new ideas that are unanticipated. Do not be afraid to let the data influence what you are learning as you go deeper with your analysis. Think about creating visual images: a grid, an idea map, a chart, or visual metaphors are all possibilities to help make sense of the data.
6. **Review** your information after it is coded/labeled to see if there is a frequency of certain items and/or powerful, interesting, unusual comments or behaviors which are of particular interest to you. Look for those unique ideas that you had not considered that may influence your thinking. Pay attention to incidents that give you new insights.
7. **Identify the main points** that appear most frequently and are the most powerful. Don't censor the data, even if you don't like what you are learning. Include data that doesn't necessarily reflect change or growth. All of this is part of the learning experience and can still inform our practice.
8. **Write up your major points**. You can write them up by theme, chronologically, or the different modes you used for collecting information. Share your findings with a colleague. Do new questions emerge from this discussion? Jot down ideas for actions you will take as a result of what you are learning.
9. **Provide evidence**. Draw the information together to include some of the evidence that supports each of your themes. The reader should be able to draw conclusions based on the evidence you have presented.

Figure 12.6
A process for analyzing qualitative data.
Source: Adapted from Madison Metropolitan School District (2001a).

A key component of action research is sharing what you learned with others. You may want to discuss your findings with your peers in a grade level meeting or make a formal presentation to the Parent–Teacher Association. You may want to share your ideas in an online discussion forum. And if you choose to, you could even present your results at conferences in your area, post your lesson plans on a website, or publish your ideas in a newsletter. There are multiple ways to contribute to the body of knowledge about teaching and learning and letting others benefit from your research.

In addition to sharing your knowledge with others, you should reflect on your own learning and make a plan for future action based on your findings. Are there other things you'd like to investigate? Do you plan to make a permanent change in your teaching strategies based on the results of your study? Consider what you will do differently in the future based on your research findings. For example, you could

APPLY TO PRACTICE

Develop an Action Research Plan

1. Choose a topic or question that you would like to investigate through action research.
2. Search for literature on that topic to determine what is known about your area of interest.
3. Develop a plan to collect data to investigate your area of interest. Will you introduce an intervention or collect data on an existing phenomenon? Make sure you plan to collect data from several sources to better illuminate the issue.

use the results of your research on classroom uses of iPods to create a proposal requesting an additional donation of more iPods for your classroom. By engaging in action research, you can become a contributor to, as well as a consumer of, research on the use of technology in the classroom.

Technology Support for Action Research

As you can imagine, computer technologies provide wonderful tools to assist in action research. You can use the Internet and other databases to locate existing literature in order to find out what others have to say about your topic of interest. You may want to collect data using portfolios, audiotapes, discussions, interviews, journals, videotapes, surveys, questionnaires, student work samples, and observations, as well as test scores. As you analyze your data, you may want to use qualitative or quantitative data analysis software, spreadsheets, databases, or graphing software. And if you choose to present your findings in team meetings, faculty meetings, newsletters, publications, conference presentations or during in-service training, word-processing and presentation software will be especially useful. As Table 12.3 illustrates, technology can be a valuable part of the entire process. In fact, we can't imagine teaching, or conducting research that will inform our teaching, without technology. Can you?

Chapter Summary

So far in this book, we focused on ways that you could engage in professional growth and leadership as you continue your professional education and move into professional practice. We began the chapter with a description of various local and global learning communities that can contribute to your continued professional growth

Table 12.3	Sample Uses of Technology during Action Research
Steps in the Action-Research Process	Ideas for Technology Use
Goal setting	Conduct searches to determine what the literature says about my topic.
Take action	Develop surveys. Keep journals. Videotape and audiotape classroom events. Scan documents. Organize data collected.
Monitor	Create data tables. Calculate averages and percentiles. Create graphs. Use analysis software to code and look for themes. Create concept maps or flowcharts of trends and themes.
Evaluate and extend	Write up results for a newsletter or publication using word-processing software. Share findings in an online forum. Contribute a lesson plan to a teacher website. Create presentation slides. Add notes to my lesson plans on things I plan to do the next time I teach it. Organize related materials in folders on my hard drive. Make back-up copies of my lesson plans.

and development. In order to prepare you to be a leader in technology integration, we discussed ways in which you could gain the skills needed to make your vision of technology infusion a reality, participate in a community of practice to enhance your technology skill development, and contribute to the technology skill development of others.

In the next section of the chapter, you learned to reflect on your professional practice and the research literature in order to "make effective use of existing and emerging digital tools and resources in support of student learning." We discussed the nature of the research literature that addresses technology use in the classroom, but warned you not to take what you read as the absolute truth. Instead, look to determine your own classroom "truths," knowing that what works in one situation may or may not work in another because of all the varied factors that make teaching so interesting and unpredictable. Existing research studies, evaluation studies, descriptive papers, and opinion pieces provide a rich storehouse of information that you can use to gather ideas that may work for you.

In the final section of this chapter, you learned to use action research to reflect on both the current literature and your own professional practice. Action research is conducted to investigate the potential value of instructional enhancements in your classroom or possible solutions to instructional problems. Often, this involves introducing an intervention and collecting data to observe the effects of that intervention. Interventions are resources or instructional methods that may involve small changes in an individual teacher's classroom or be designed to improve the entire school environment in some way. Since the action-research process can be thought of as a type of self-directed learning, we used the GAME plan acronym to describe the steps in the process. We encouraged you to use action research to "contribute to the effectiveness, vitality, and self-renewal of the teaching profession," your school and community. Fortunately, you can, and should, use the results of research—your research—to inform your educational practice.

YOUR PORTFOLIO

To begin to demonstrate competency in ISTE NETS-T Standard 5, add the following items to your portfolio:

1. Create a comprehensive vision statement that summarizes your plans and hopes for technology infusion in your classroom. Justify your vision statement using findings from the research on using technology to support student learning.

2. Develop a plan for lifelong learning and self-renewal. Identify several specific ways in which you plan to continue learning about creative applications of technology to improve student learning. Discuss how you will use this knowledge to contribute to your teaching effectiveness and the vitality of your school and community.

References

Apple Computer, Inc. (2002). *The impact of technology on student achievement: A summary of research findings on technology's impact in the classroom.* Retrieved June 24, 2006, from http://www.apple.com/education/research/

Bitter, G. G., & Pierson, M. E. (2005). *Using technology in the classroom* (6th ed.). New York: Allyn & Bacon.

Clark, R. (1983). Reconsidering research on learning from media. *Review of Educational Research, 53,* 445–459.

Dwyer, D. C., Ringstaff, C., & Sandholtz, J. H. (1991). Changes in teachers' beliefs and practices in technology-rich classrooms. *Educational Leadership, 48*(8), 45–52.

Eisenhart, M., & Towne, L. (2003). Contestation and change on national policy on "scientifically based" education research. *Educational Researcher, 32*(7), 31–38.

Elmore, R. F. (2000). *Building a structure for school leadership.* New York: The Albert Shanker Institute.

Ertmer, P. A., & Hruskocy, C. (1999) Impacts of a university-elementary school partnership designed to support technology integration. *Educational Technology Research and Development, 47*(1), 81–96.

Ferrance, E. (2000). *Action research.* Providence, RI: LAB at Brown University.

Generation Yes. (2007). *GenYES: Student powered technology integration.* Retrieved January 17, 2007, from http://genyes.com/programs/genyes/

International Society for Technology in Education. (2002). *CARET, Topic: Definition of study types.* Retrieved June 24, 2006, from http://caret.iste.org/RatingStudy.html

International Society for Technology in Education. (2005a) *Center for Applied Research in Education and Technology (CARET).* Retrieved June 24, 2006, from http://caret.iste.org

International Society for Technology in Education. (2005b). *CARET, Topic: Student learning.* Retrieved June 24, 2006, from http://caret.iste.org/index.cfm?fuseaction=questions&topicID=1

International Society for Technology in Education. (2008). *Refreshed ISTE NETS for Teachers Rubrics.* Eugene, OR: Author.

Kozma, R. B. (1991). Learning with media. *Review of Educational Research, 61*(2), 179–221.

Madison Metropolitan School District. (2001a). *Classroom action research: A process for analyzing your data.* Retrieved June 23, 2006, from http://www.madison.k12.wi.us/sod/car/caranalyzeprocess.html

Madison Metropolitan School District. (2001b). *Classroom action research: Guidelines for developing a question.* Retrieved June 23, 2006, from http://www.madison.k12.wi.us/sod/car/cardevelopquestion.html

McNiff, J. (2002). *You and your action research project* (2nd ed.). New York: Routledge.

Mertler, C. A. (2005). *Action research: Teachers as researchers in the classroom.* Thousand Oaks, CA: Sage.

Pub. L. No. 107-110 (No Child Left Behind Act of 2001)

Stringer, E. (2003). *Action research in education.* Upper Saddle River, NJ: Prentice Hall.

Mirek Weichsel/First Light/Getty Images

TECHNOLOGY INTEGRATION IN PRACTICE

T he majority of this book provides general guidance on integrating technology into your classroom. However, in Chapters 13–21, guest authors provide specific examples and guidance for integrating technology into content-specific areas. Having been classroom teachers and continuing to work with classroom teachers, we understand your need to focus on the content standards required by your district or state. The additional chapters provide content-specific guidance that apply to teachers charged with addressing the curricula related to working with English language learners, language arts, foreign language, math, science, social studies, health/physical education, visual arts, and music.

Over the past 20 years, national professional organizations have developed content standards for their content domains, which include the following:

- Expectations of Excellence: Curriculum Standards for Social Studies by the National Council for the Social Studies
- Moving into the Future, National Standards for Physical Education by the National Association for Sport and Physical Education
- National Health Education Standards: Achieving Excellence, Second Edition
- National Science Education Standards by the National Research Council
- National Standards for Arts Education: What Every Young American Should Know and Be Able to Do in the Arts by the Consortium of National Arts Education Associations
- Standards for Foreign Language Learning: Preparing for the 21st Century by the American Council on the Teaching of Foreign Languages.

- National Standards for Music Education by the Music Educators National Conference
- PreK–12 English Language Proficiency Standards by the Teachers of English to Speakers of Other Languages
- Principles and Standards for School Mathematics by the National Council of Teachers of Mathematics
- Standards for the English Language Arts sponsored by the National Council of Teachers of English (NCTE) and the International Reading Association (IRA)

These standards are introduced in each content-area chapter. You may already be familiar with these standards from other courses. There is little doubt these national standards have shaped the way teachers currently address their curricula, design their learning environments, and gauge the academic success of their students.

National and state standards have influenced the creation of state-specific content standards. Furthermore, some districts and schools have developed additional content standards to supplement or support state content standards. As a classroom teacher, it is likely that you will focus, primarily, on developing lessons that meet *state* content standards as these are the standards on which your students will be expected to demonstrate proficiency —usually on high-stakes assessments.

In addition to developing lessons that are designed to help your students meet national and state *content* standards, you may also be expected to help your students meet national and state *technology* standards. Many states have adopted technology standards that are adapted from ISTE's NETS for Students (NETS-S), as discussed in Chapter 1, so we will focus our discussion in the following chapters around these national standards (see Figure 1.7).

You may think it unusual to spend time on standards in a book focused on using technology for meaningful learning, but this book was written with four fundamental premises in mind, as outlined in the Introduction to Part I of this book. One of these premises is that technology is a tool for solving instructional problems. Given this, your choices about technology use will depend on your instruction, which will, in turn, depend on content standards. Furthermore, premise 3 notes that it's more important *how* you use those technologies to solve instructional problems than *if* you use technology at all. There are many different technologies available in most schools; when you are considering the needs of your learners, you must consider how you can help them achieve the required content standards.

In the following chapters, each guest author addresses ways you can use technology to create authentic learning experiences to meet content area and technology standards. Building on the ideas introduced in Chapter 3, content-specific chapters describe strategies and examples of using technology to improve learner autonomy and promote active learning through activities that are holistic, authentic, and challenging.

The potential for technology to help foster students' creativity and higher-order thinking skills receives special emphasis from ISTE and so is addressed within the content-specific chapters. As you know, there are different types of higher-order thinking as well as some commonalities across them. Whether you plan for your students to use technology as tutors, mindtools, or as a support for conversation, you will find a range of content-specific examples in these chapters to help you further understand technology's potential for supporting teaching and learning in your classroom.

The increasing use of technology—not only in teaching and learning but in careers and professions— provides numerous opportunities to support higher-order thinking and creativity. Fortunately, many of the same technology tools used in a wide range of professions and careers are available for use in your classroom. Sometimes these take the form of information and data, other times they include the actual tools that professionals use. And while you may be familiar with word processing software, web browsers, and e-mail, the guest authors emphasize many content-specific tools that allow students to build creative thinking skills by performing as professionals, sometimes by using the same websites and data historians and social scientists have access to, the same image- and graphic-design tools artists and graphic artists use, or unique modeling or simulation software that scientists use in their research.

Throughout the content-specific chapters, you will also find some familiar features, such as Stories from Practice that describe the experiences of real educators, as well as the now-familiar GAME Plan activities that help you to monitor and evaluate your progress toward mastering and demonstrating the ISTE NETS-T. At the end of each content-specific chapter, you are encouraged to add to your portfolio through creating or modifying content-specific lesson or unit plans. Lesson plans are a common portfolio requirement for teachers, and they will be a valuable resource for you as you demonstrate your understanding of both content and technology standards to future employers.

Whether you read only one, or many, of the content-specific chapters, you'll notice how they build upon the ideas presented in the first part of this book. For example, the content-specific chapters address ethical and legal concerns raised when using digital resources, as well as issues related to providing access to learning opportunities for *all* students. In addition, you will notice many important connections to topics covered in Chapter 3 (Supporting Student Creativity with Technology) and Chapter 4 (Digital Tools that Support Learning). Now that you know how important many of these factors are, take the opportunity to read what our guest authors have to say about standards, skills, and technologies.

Wadsworth/Cengage Learning

13

ISTE Standards addressed in this chapter

This chapter provides content-specific suggestions and strategies for addressing both ISTE's National Educational Technology Standards for Students (NETS-S) and the English language arts standards outlined by the International Reading Association (IRA) and the National Council of Teachers of English (NCTE). This chapter also builds on the NETS-T concepts and skills presented earlier, with a special emphasis on skills related to Standard 1 "Facilitate and inspire student learning and creativity." Following an overview of the English language arts standards and how you can address the NETS-S in the language arts classroom, this chapter outlines techniques, tools, and methods for developing authentic learning experiences that advance student creativity and innovation.

Integrating Technology in the English Language Arts Classroom

Sheila Carter-Tod, Ph.D. and Shelli B. Fowler, Ph.D.

For teachers newly entering the language arts classroom, the relationship between technology and language arts pedagogy has varied from complete buy-in—seeing technology as the answer to many classroom difficulties—to skepticism—questioning the role of technology. The reason for such a wide range of responses has to do with teachers' familiarity with technology, their views on the role of technology in learning, and their views on what it means to read and write. Traditionally, concepts of literacy associated with language arts classrooms have focused on texts as written artifacts. Contemporary students, however, are coming to language arts classrooms as "digital natives," as famed gaming researcher Marc Prensky (2001) touts, having been completely immersed and surrounded by technology and digital media for their entire lives. We

Outcomes

In this chapter, you will:

- Identify English language arts standards and explain how technology can support them.
- Discuss how the National Educational Technology Standards for Students can be addressed in an English language arts classroom.
- Understand how authentic learning principles can be addressed using technology in an English language arts classroom.
- Explain how technology can increase learning and facilitate creative thinking in the English language arts classroom.

now teach in language arts classrooms with students whose expectations are that we are familiar with and comfortable teaching technological and visual literacies in addition to teaching traditional reading and writing skills. For this reason, it is important to develop some understanding and guidelines for thinking about why, when, and how to integrate technology into your language arts classroom.

STORIES FROM PRACTICE

Then and Now . . . Trials and Errors I

One of the first semesters that I taught in a computer-integrated classroom, I used the large screen at the front of the class to display notes and students' writing for feedback and discussion. Beyond that, I did not use it during the rest of class time. I still required students to bring paper drafts of their essays for small-group workshops, and we would work awkwardly around the computers to form physically smaller groups in a classroom designed for an entirely different activity. At first, neither the students nor I saw what we were

doing as odd, and the students even adapted further by using floor space and the hallway to conduct these small-group activities. While I was excited to be in a computer-integrated classroom, it did not initially alter the way I presented my instruction. I merely adapted some of my previous instructional methods to a different environment without fully thinking through the capacity of the technology available in the room.

Near the end of the semester, one of my students asked me why we met in the computer

classroom when we so rarely used the computers. I don't remember how I answered that student, but I do remember that her question forced me to rethink my approach to using technology in my classroom. What I needed to work out for both my students and myself was how I was going to transform my use of technology in the classroom from being a tool I used to direct instruction to being more at the center of student learning.

Source: Sheila Carter-Tod

Technology and Content Standards

Language arts classrooms can be technology-rich environments if you help students understand that technology is an integral part of the classroom curriculum. In order to integrate technology in ways that enhance and support language arts content and that create authentic learning environments, you must be fully aware of the standards that govern the use of technology in teaching and learning, whether the NETS-S or local or state technology standards, as well as the standards that govern the discipline of language arts.

With a clear understanding that knowledge and learning cannot be discretely categorized into discernable entities or tidy categories, the International Reading Association (IRA) and the National Council of the Teachers of English (NCTE) (1996) created twelve content standards for English language arts classrooms (see Table 13.1). The standards are content-based, and are designed to reflect existing best practices in language arts classrooms around the country. Although numbered, the standards are not in any specific order and reflect an overlapping of concepts and content. The standards also provide those entering the field with range and flexibility while clearly communicating the parameters and expectations of the discipline. When viewed in conjunction with the NETS-S, the possibilities for integrating technology into the language arts classroom become extremely rich and rewarding for both your students and for you.

It's important to note that since the release of these standards, national and state legislation has been developed that emphasizes the importance of language arts instruction, especially literacy programs such as Reading First (Title I, Part B, Subpart 1 in the No Child Left Behind Act of 2001), that has made millions of dollars

Table 13.1	English Language Arts National Content Standards

1. Students read a wide range of print and nonprint texts to build an understanding of texts, of themselves, and of the cultures of the United States and the world; to acquire new information; to respond to the needs and demands of society and the workplace; and for personal fulfillment. Among these texts are fiction and nonfiction, classic and contemporary works.

2. Students read a wide range of literature from many periods in many genres to build an understanding of the many dimensions (e.g., philosophical, ethical, aesthetic) of human experience.

3. Students apply a wide range of strategies to comprehend, interpret, evaluate, and appreciate texts. They draw on their prior experience, their interactions with other readers and writers, their knowledge of word meaning and of other texts, their word identification strategies, and their understanding of textual features (e.g., sound–letter correspondence, sentence structure, context, graphics).

4. Students adjust their use of spoken, written, and visual language (e.g., conventions, style, vocabulary) to communicate effectively with a variety of audiences and for different purposes.

5. Students employ a wide range of strategies as they write and use different writing process elements appropriately to communicate with different audiences for a variety of purposes.

6. Students apply knowledge of language structure, language conventions (e.g., spelling and punctuation), media techniques, figurative language, and genre to create, critique, and discuss print and nonprint texts.

7. Students conduct research on issues and interests by generating ideas and questions, and by posing problems. They gather, evaluate, and synthesize data from a variety of sources (e.g., print and nonprint texts, artifacts, people) to communicate their discoveries in ways that suit their purpose and audience.

8. Students use a variety of technological and information resources (e.g., libraries, databases, computer networks, video) to gather and synthesize information and to create and communicate knowledge.

9. Students develop an understanding of and respect for diversity in language use, patterns, and dialects across cultures, ethnic groups, geographic regions, and social roles.

10. Students whose first language is not English make use of their first language to develop competency in the English language arts and to develop understanding of content across the curriculum.

11. Students participate as knowledgeable, reflective, creative, and critical members of a variety of literacy communities.

12. Students use spoken, written, and visual language to accomplish their own purposes (e.g., for learning, enjoyment, persuasion, and the exchange of information).

Source: International Reading Association and National Council of Teachers of English. (1996). *Standards for the English language arts.* United States: Author.

available to schools specifically for professional development and classroom materials related to literacy. Materials and instructional interventions used in Reading First programs are based largely on the work of the National Reading Panel, which includes a section—although short—on research focused on the use of technology to support developing literacy.

Table 13.2 on page 316 provides just a few ideas that may help you think about incorporating technology into your language arts classroom in ways that focus on student learning. Using the NETS-S as a guide, Table 13.2 helps you to see how your language arts classroom can become technologically enhanced within the context of the pedagogy of the field. These are suggestions that can serve as a catalyst for your own thinking and application in your own language arts classroom. The example lesson plans at the end of this chapter provide specific examples of how you can design learning experiences that meet both content area and technology standards.

 WEB LINK

For further detailed examples of the alignment of the NETS-S to the national English language arts standards as well as suggestions for assessment, visit the textbook's companion website.

Authentic Learning Strategies Incorporating Technology

Using technology in the language arts classroom can facilitate authentic learning. Yet it is the way the technology is incorporated that can change the very nature of

Table 13.2	NETS-S in the English/Language Arts Classroom

Creativity and Innovation

Students use presentation or multimedia-authoring software to create a multimodal story map based on a story from their classroom reading series that best captures their understanding of the book's characters, setting, problems faced by the characters, and resolutions. Before creating projects, students should engage in classroom work and discussion that helps them to explore the connections between characters and plot in an attempt to identify trends, patterns, and literary conventions like foreshadowing, foils, etc.

Communication and Collaboration

Students create websites, brochures, or news stories for a story or book that they are reading. They connect with other students in the school or district who are reading the same materials, by exchanging e-mail, or participating in online discussions to help gauge different opinions and reaction to the reading. These opinions, reactions, and feedback are incorporated into a class product that appraises the materials they are reading.

Research and Information Fluency

Students conduct Internet searches by collaborating with the school librarian or media specialist, or with teachers from other content areas with the purpose of learning to use the Internet as a source of information. Students follow basic safety rules of the Internet, use keywords and other search strategies to find information, and use search engines and online databases to better understand the types of data each source best provides.

Critical Thinking, Problem Solving, and Decision Making

Students design and develop a class website that supports a research project or other writing project. The writing project should engage students in an analysis of a complex, real-world issue. (e.g., global warming, U.S. port security, causes for and human health risks of increased mercury content levels in tuna). Students are asked to justify the reasons for the resources and tools they include in the project.

Digital Citizenship

Based on the popular Flat Stanley series of books and the Flat Stanley Project website, students create digital versions of themselves using digital photos and send them to relatives and friends in distant places as an attachment to an e-mail. The recipients respond to a couple of questions about where they live, what they do, and how they use technology in their daily lives. The recipients include a picture of themselves or their location, then forward the message to other friends and relatives, copying the student each time so they can track progress of their virtual trip.

Technology Operations and Concepts

Students create individual entries for class biographies using word-processing software. Computer skills like learning to enter, edit, and format text; inserting and editing images and graphics; and opening, saving, and closing files can be covered within the context of addressing language arts concepts related to writing as a process.

---

instruction. As Kajder (2004, p. 6) muses, "If 15 years pondering the role of technology in classroom learning has taught us anything, it has to be that knowledge does not lie within technology; technology is only a tool that helps to unlock the power and the promise of learning." You should focus on how to use technology to engage 21st-century learners, rather than on the technology itself. Incorporating technology into your language arts classroom requires you to make some complex decisions.

This is a lesson that is sometimes learned through trial and error, which the opening Story from Practice indicates; what the teacher did not know at first was that key pedagogical principles, such as authentic, problem-based learning, could guide the integration of technology into teaching. As a teacher, you will need to learn ways to shape "best practices" to your own specific teaching contexts, taking into account local and regional issues, as well as racial, gender, and socioeconomic status stratification issues. The decisions concerning the integration of technology into the writing classroom should always reflect the needs of the learners and the curriculum. The following section presents several questions you should consider to help develop and define your own best practices for integrating technology into your language arts classroom.

THE GAME PLAN

Content Standards

Set Goals

Research the English language arts standards for a state where you plan to seek a teaching position and create an action plan to ensure that you will have the knowledge and skills necessary to help your students achieve those standards. Identify the concepts, knowledge, and skills you will need to ensure that you are prepared to help your students meet the English language arts standards in your state.

Take Action

Explore the department of education website in the state where you plan to seek a position. Review the K–12 English language arts standards in that state and compare them to the state's technology standards. Identify those standards that specifically relate to applying technology in the English language arts.

Develop a plan for how to meet the technology standards in the context of the English language arts.

Monitor

Did you find the information you needed? Do you need to contact the department of education for more information about where to find the English language arts standards or the technology standards for teachers?

Evaluate and Extend

Discuss in class the action plan you developed for meeting the technology standards for instructional personnel. Compare your plan with others. Note the strengths and weaknesses of the various plans. Strengthen your plan by incorporating ideas you have heard in class.

Does using this technology take students beyond what they can do without it?

If your answer is no, then you may not need to use technology. Using technology for any reason other than to enhance learning may come across as an add-on that students may perceive as unnecessary or useless. Such a perception may cause difficulties when you do actually use the technology in ways that enriches the learning experience. Technology can enhance and extend student learning in several ways. Technology can make complex processes clearer through the use of visuals and multiple examples found in online simulations or animations, images or photos from websites or CDs, or graphics or data tables. Technology can help economize time and effort by allowing students to create and manipulate texts quickly and easily. Who hasn't enjoyed the benefits of copying and pasting text, images, and other digital material within and across documents of many formats? Technology can enhance student learning by tracking student activity, such as by using commonly available annotation and commenting functions in word processing software that timestamps changes and shows who made them. Finally, technology also promotes collaboration and communication among students and between you and your students, for example, when using web-based tools, such as a discussion board or a wiki for supporting class work.

Is this particular form of technology allowing all learners in the classroom the opportunity to attain the goals or aims of the curriculum?

If the technology does not further the goals of your standards-based unit or lesson plan, then it may not be the best tool for that particular situation. As you've learned throughout this book, technology should offer a means by which we reach our learning goals, rather than simply an end in and of itself. When incorporating authentic learning, you will likely have to create opportunities for students with varying levels of technological experience.

Consider classroom discussions, a common activity. When students are asked a question during an in-class discussion, many appear shy or hesitant to speak up.

Often, some students will need extra time to formulate their thinking before they are ready to articulate their responses. Providing alternate opportunities for student responses, such as through wireless responders, lab management software, instant messaging, and other confidential methods can promote authentic responses. Devices such as wireless responders allow teachers to determine overall comprehension—as well as specific learning needs—as the class progresses, and do so in a way that can encourage more class discussion, prodding even shy students to get involved. Students who may be hesitant to raise their hands in response to a skills question or correction can actually test their knowledge of that skill without feeling judged for not responding in "standard" English. Wireless responders provide English language learners a sense of safety (via anonymity) and can help them to "speak up" or respond.

Using a blog or wiki, and providing a few open-ended prompts before or after a class discussion, allow students to digest and synthesize readings more fully. Contrary to the idea that pre-class discussion prompts will leave students with nothing left to say, prompts actually give many students the confidence to speak up because they feel more prepared. Conducting post-class follow-up using a blog or wiki provides a time-stamped log to help students monitor their own learning while providing you with a clearer sense of student understanding of assigned readings. Blogs, wikis, and digital portfolios also provide excellent opportunities for students to reflect on their thinking over time, as well as share their work with you and others. The longitudinal record of reflection on work, sharing, and discussion can be an advantage to high-achieving students as well as to those who may find traditional classroom discussions challenging or intimidating.

Does integration of this technology rigorously complement, or provide alternatives to existing curriculum (Kajder, 2004, p. 7)?

There are many forms of technology that can be integrated into your language arts classroom that may allow students with different learning preferences to exceed the level of work possible without technology. Concept-mapping software, such as Inspiration or the web-based Cmap, allows students to quickly generate visual diagrams that can help organize their thinking. Some helpful templates for the language arts classroom are included in many concept-mapping applications, such as Venn diagrams, character webs, and story maps. There is a variety of free or low-cost concept-mapping tools available, some that integrate with interactive whiteboards, and some that allow students to quickly toggle back and forth between their graphic maps and a text-based outline that can serve as a guide for writing.

Some students find storyboarding an effective way to create a digital narrative (Lambert, 2002). Additionally, it is a critical step in the process of digital storytelling. While some multimedia presentations and videos may contain little evident writing in the final product, the processes of researching, outlining, storyboarding, and writing a script are excellent writing activities that support the generation of high-quality products. Storyboarding and script writing are common practices for professional videographers and multimedia developers and require organization, processing, and writing skills that are easily supported by technology. In this case, simply by incorporating technology, you may motivate students by providing alternatives that allow them to succeed. As a result, they may become more invested in the particular assignment.

Simply incorporating specific word-processing software features, note-taking software, or scaffolding software, such as Kurzweil 3000 or Read & Write Gold, into the writing process (see Figure 13.1) may help students with the process of summarizing key points as they learn to identify and extract main points in documents. Auditory Word Processors, or speech-recognition software such as Dragon Naturally Speaking, may give verbal learners a "jumpstart" on a writing assignment by allowing students to speak ideas and early drafts. Once written, text-to-speech software allows students to hear what they've written from an objective voice. This software also provides

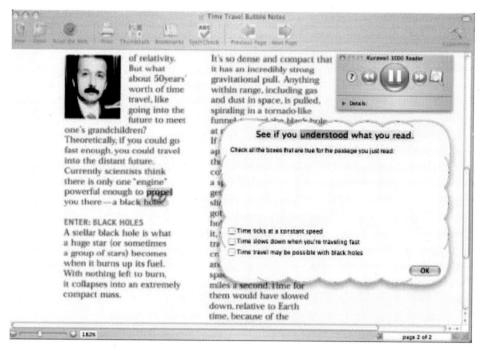

Figure 13.1
Many software tools provide a range of scaffolding supports for the English language arts classroom.
Source: Kurzweil Education Systems.

auditory learners with wonderful opportunities for revision. Rudimentary speech-recognition and text-to-speech software are built into common computer operating systems.

Is there a way to measure the success of students' technology use as well as students' success with the content of the assignment?

Since the goal of integrating technology into language arts classrooms is to enhance learning, assessing whether that goal is achieved is critical. This may entail creating ways of evaluating an assignment that measures student proficiency with a particular technology, such as a word processor for composition. In contrast, there are times when you may have to develop methods to evaluate the assignment that do not penalize those students who have limited technological skill or access. The use of digital portfolios is popular for both students' self-evaluation and teacher evaluation of student writing. If using technology is not an integral part of creating writing samples for a portfolio, then students should be given alternate methods to add their samples to digital portfolios, perhaps through keeping a paper-based portfolio or scanning handwritten samples. Often, when technology skills are measured along with content skills, rubrics can be used to increase students' awareness of their skills and provide teachers with methods to report to school administrators who require documentation of student learning.

Technology and Creative Thinking Skills Instruction

Multimodal literacy is fast becoming a concern for all contemporary language arts instructors. Based on an extensive review of the research on technology in language arts classrooms by NCTE, the "Research-based Policy Statement on Multi-Modal Literacy" articulates the following research-supported assertions concerning the

STORIES FROM PRACTICE

Then and Now . . . Trials and Errors II

When given another opportunity to teach in the computer classroom, I began my planning with my own analysis of what I saw as the relationship between technology and learning. This allowed me to reevaluate and revise my lesson plans in terms of overall learning objectives for the course. Previously, I had rarely used the computers, but now I was focusing on the learning goals for my students rather than the technology itself. It was not until I was willing to rethink the ways in which I viewed my overall approach to instruction in a computer-integrated classroom that my students and I began to experience a more authentic learning environment.

For example, one of the objectives of the course was to help students understand how they, as authors of their texts, needed to make specific decisions about a given essay in light of feedback from various readers. This is often a difficult task because as writers we want to please every reader—having our essay be everything to everyone who encounters it. I

have often found that this task is better understood not in a discussion of the process but instead by looking at essays and the comments that a writer has made about the decisions he or she made revising the text.

To begin this process, I first had students gather all of the feedback they had received either in groups or in conferences with me, or from other individuals who had read their essays, and I asked them to compile that feedback electronically. While working in the computer classroom, we first looked at an essay that had been marked up through hyperlinks by a professional writer who discussed the revision decisions she had made based on the feedback she had received. Next, giving them a list of websites of student work that included reflection on the revision process, I had them read through the comments and see what general patterns they noticed about the choices made by the author. When the students began to see how audience and purpose really drove the

choices that the authors made, they began to better understand how to do the same thing with their own writing.

In that class, and in subsequent classes, we discussed how they might create the same sort of electronic markup of their own decision-making process, and in doing so, create a "history" of their own revision processes. The wonderful thing about having done this was that it led nicely into another objective for the course, which was to help students learn to reflect on the decisions they made as writers to help them see what they were learning about writing in the process of producing essays. This small adjustment to my lesson plan not only helped me to make the work I was doing in the computer lab more focused on the needs of my students, but it also served to encourage the students to be active and reflective participants in their own learning process.

Source: Sheila Carter-Tod

incorporation of technology and multimodal literacy for English language arts students:

- Students who use computers when learning to write are not only more engaged and motivated in their writing, but they produce written work that is of greater length and higher quality (Goldberg, Russell, & Cook, 2003).
- A media-literacy curriculum can lead students to higher reading comprehension scores, writing longer paragraphs, and identifying more features of purpose and audience in reading selections (Hobbs & Frost, 2003).
- Online discussions of literature foster greater student engagement than traditional discussions, and student participants are able to use transcripts to develop metacognitive capacities (Carico, Logan, & Labbo, 2004).
- Use of the Internet for several years can augment student autonomy, enhance motivation, improve the quality of group work, and decrease adversarial qualities in teacher–student relationships (Schofield & Davidson, 2003).

These research findings help to reinforce the point that when technology is incorporated in an effective way, it can indeed facilitate creative thinking skills in the language arts classroom. With greater access to new technologies for teaching and learning, you may be encouraged to promote student generation of new media texts. Selfe (2004, p. 43) defines new media texts as those "created primarily in digital environments, composed in multiple media (e.g., film, video, audio, among others), and designed for presentation and exchange in digital venues." He further notes that because new media texts can incorporate both text and visual elements and can be interactive, they would require the author and participant to use multiple literacies related to seeing, listening, and manipulating, not just reading and writing. Cope and Kalantzis (2000, p. 5) concur that new media texts require us, teachers and students, to embrace a broader definition and pedagogy of multiliteracy, one in which "Meaning is made in ways that are increasingly multimodal—in which written-linguistic modes of meaning are part and parcel of visual, audio, and special patterns of meaning."

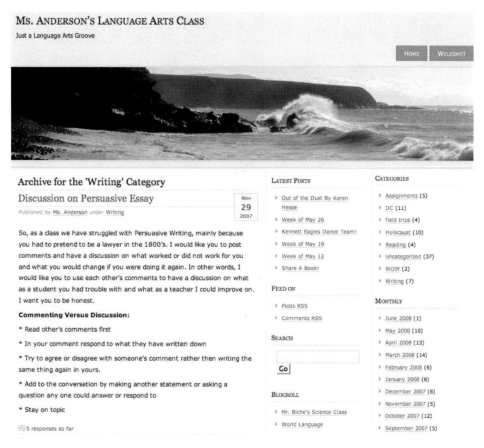

Figure 13.2

New digital tools, such as blogs and wikis, make it easy for teachers and students to communicate on the web.

Source: http://www.terms4kms.com/anderson/?cat=3. Courtesy Julie Beal.

Creative thinking skills play a major role in most language arts classrooms and are clearly included in many of the national English language arts standards. The language of the standards includes several examples of student activities that are designed to develop and nurture creative thinking skills, such as evaluate, synthesize, and apply language and communication skills in a variety of settings; create original works in both print and nonprint form; and act as professionals in a variety of literacy communities.

Evaluate, Synthesize, and Apply Language and Communication Skills

Numerous technology tools allow students to evaluate, synthesize, and apply language and communication skills. Although text, and especially English text, still predominates on the Internet, tools that allow students to view, create, edit, and distribute information across the Internet as images, sounds, animations, and videos are becoming accessible to many students. These powerful tools make it easier for students to explore their creativity and express themselves to a range of audiences in ways that were, at one time, difficult. Now students can post their feelings and thoughts on the Internet using easy blogging or wiki software (see Figure 13.2). They can take and edit digital images and videos and post these on websites to communicate with others. As a language arts teacher, these are also tools that you and your students can use to tap their creativity, align your language arts instruction with student learning preferences, and give students an opportunity to express their language arts skills in a variety of ways. It's important to note that language arts teachers have long addressed creativity in available print and nonprint forms.

Figure 13.3
Many authors and fans of authors have created websites to supplement their writing.
Source: http://www.tiffany-trent.com.

The national language arts standards address topics such as visual language, technological and information resources, and print and nonprint texts.

Create Original Works

Students in the language arts classroom can use a variety of technology-supported tools to create original works in both print and nonprint form. For print, you might logically think of the use of word-processing, journaling, and note-taking software to support activities in your language arts classroom, but many of these applications offer supports to scaffold students as they create print—whether these student products remain in their print-based form or are incorporated into projects using other media. Tools for checking spelling and grammar, embedding notes, and tracking changes can guide student learning and support self-monitoring during creation. Many of these tools can also help students bridge between print and other forms of literacy through the ease of embedding and linking information in a variety of formats, such as images, media objects, and hyperlinks.

Act as Professionals in Literary Communities

The greater access to digital tools similar to, or the same as, those used by professionals helps students of varied levels of language proficiency create projects that can look just like those created by their peers—which can motivate struggling

THE GAME PLAN

Identifying Web-Based Resources

Set Goals

Find online resources you can use for a range of activities in an English language arts classroom. You may need resources to help students develop skills related to multimodal literacy or applying language skills.

Take Action

Review the web resources on the textbook's companion website. Conduct other searches on your own for resources of interest to you.

Monitor

How well do the resources meet stated goal(s)? Are there clearinghouse websites or sites that review online English language arts resources? Did you find resources you did not know existed that might be helpful to you in the English language arts classroom?

Evaluate and Extend

Select the best resources you have found and include a list of them in your portfolio. Share your list with other English language arts students to compile a master list that covers a range of grade levels and competencies.

students. These tools often contain wizards, widgets, examples, help, and even access to user groups and forums that allow students to explore the capabilities of the applications and to stretch their creative potential. Using digital tools, such as page-layout, video-editing, web-authoring, and other multimedia software, advanced students can create print and nonprint projects that demonstrate levels of proficiency that rival those of professionals. Students with varied learning preferences may find different multimedia authoring tools more closely linked to their learning preferences, and these tools may serve as a springboard for creativity in skills related to language arts.

And while discussing the professional presentation of student learning, technology tools—especially communications tools—allow students to demonstrate one final measure of creativity, and this is acting as professionals do in a variety of literacy communities. A wider range of literacy communities are more accessible to students than just a few years ago. Students not only can access books by their favorite authors, but can often find websites, blogs, and podcasts about and sometimes by authors whose work they enjoy (see Figure 13.3). Crafting exemplary websites, presentations, videos, and other multimedia also requires students to develop and demonstrate a range of print and nonprint literacies. As they develop these skills they are truly a part of a range of literacy communities that will require them to draw upon an understanding of print and nonprint texts, of themselves, and of the cultures of the United States and the world.

WEB LINK

View the textbook's companion website to review a list of the software, hardware, and Internet resources mentioned in this chapter as well as additional resources for the English language arts classroom.

Chapter Summary

Although we began this chapter by stating that there has been a range in teacher response to the use of technology in the language arts classroom, we want to end by pointing out that where you decide to locate yourself on that technology integration continuum should be done with some consideration. By weighing the advantages and disadvantages of any technology in terms of your personal goals, the required curriculum, the learning goals for your students, access to technology, and your own comfort with the technology, any decision that you make will be one that is sound. The research, best practices, examples, and lesson plans in this chapter are designed to help you take the steps necessary to make those decisions and reach your goals.

YOUR PORTFOLIO

To demonstrate your understanding of creating learning experiences in the English language arts classroom that address the National Educational Technology Standards for Students, create a lesson plan for common activities in your English language arts classroom using the GAME Plan template available on the textbook's companion website, or one of your choosing. Your topic may address skills related to multimodel literacy, as presented in this chapter, or more familiar activities related to composition or literature.

1. Identify the national English language arts content standards that relate to your lesson. Review the state-specific content standards you discovered earlier in the chapter and determine appropriate assessments you can incorporate in your lesson based on the achievement standards.

2. Research and select appropriate technologies that can support the activities in your lesson. Identify technology standards (such as NETS-S) addressed by your lesson. List all hardware and software required for the lesson and consider any preparation or prerequisite skills you may need to address before the students can complete the lesson.

3. If using the GAME Plan lesson template, include justifications for your technology application and reasons why you selected it in the section labeled Lesson Reflections and Notes. If you are using a different lesson plan template, include this information either on the template or in a separate file. Your justifications may relate to your skills or familiarity with the technology or the skills of your students, the match between the intended outcomes of the technology and your lesson, or even accessibility concerns.

References

Carico, K. M., Logan, D., & Labbo, L. D. (2004). A generation in cyberspace: Engaging readers through online discussions. *Language Arts*, 81(4), 293–303.

Cope, B., & Kalantzis, M. (Eds.). (2000). *Multiliteracies: Literacy learning and the design of social futures.* London: Routledge.

Goldberg, A., Russell, M., & Cook, A. (2003). The effect of computers on student writing: A meta-analysis of studies from 1992–2002. *Journal of Technology, Learning, and Assessment* 2(1), 1–51.

Hobbs, R., & Frost, R. (2003). Measuring the acquisition of media-literacy skills. *Reading Research Quarterly*, 38, 330–356.

International Reading Association and National Council of Teachers of English. (1996). *Standards for the English language arts.* United States: Author.

Kajder, S. (2004). Plugging in: What technology brings to the English/language arts classroom. *Voices from the Middle*, 11(3), 6–9.

Lambert, J. (2002). *Digital storytelling: Capturing lives creating community.* Berkeley, CA: Digital Dinner Press.

Prensky, M. (2001, September/October). Digital natives, digital immigrants. *On the Horizon*, 9(5), 1–6.

Schofield, J. W., & Davidson, A. L. (2003). The impact of Internet use on relationships between teachers and students. *Mind, Culture, and Activity*, 10, 62–79.

Selfe, C. L. (2004). Students who teach us: A case study of a new media text designer. In A. E. Wysocki, J. Johnson-Eilola, C. L. Selfe, & G. Sirc (Eds.). *Writing new media: Theory and applications for expanding the teaching of composition* (pp. 43–66). Logan: Utah University Press.

For Further Reading

Gura, M., & Reissman, R. (Eds.). (2001). *Making literacy magic happen: The best of learning & leading with technology on language arts.* Washington, DC: International Society for Technology in Education (ISTE).

Montgomery, K. Z., & Wiley, D. A. (2004). *Creating e-portfolios using Powerpoint: A guide for educators.* Thousand Oaks, CA: Sage.

Prensky, M. (2001, November/December). Digital natives, digital immigrants, part 2: Do they really think differently? *On the Horizon, 9*(6), 1–6.

Selber, S. A. (2004). *Multiliteracies for a digital age.* Carbondale, IL: Southern Illinois University Press.

Standley, M., & Ormiston, M. (2003). *Digital storytelling with Powerpoint: Teaching powerful storytelling.* Eugene, OR: Visions Technology in Education.

Standley, M., & Via, S. (2004). *Digital storytelling with iMovie: Teaching powerful storytelling.* Eugene, OR: Visions Technology in Education.

Swenson, J., Rozema, R., Young, C. A., McGrail, E., & Whitin, P. (2005). Beliefs about technology and the preparation of English teachers: Beginning the conversation. *Contemporary Issues in Technology and Teacher Education [Online serial], 5*(3/4), 210–236. Retrieved September 28, 2008, from http://www.citejournal.org/vol5/iss3/languagearts/article1.cfm

Yancey, K. B. (2001). Digitized student portfolios. In B. Cambridge, *Electronic portfolios: Emerging practices in student, faculty, and institutional learning.* (pp. 15–30). Washington, DC: AAHE Press.

TECHNOLOGY INTEGRATION FOR MEANINGFUL CLASSROOM USE
Daily Lesson GAME Plan

Lesson Title: Creating a story map	**Related Lessons**: Before, during, and after reading comprehension strategies
Grade level: Elementary	**Unit**: Elements of a story

GOALS

Content Standards:

1. Students read a wide range of print and nonprint texts to build an understanding of texts, of themselves, and of the cultures of the United States and the world; to acquire new information; to respond to the needs and demands of society and the workplace; and for personal fulfillment. Among these texts are fiction and nonfiction, classic and contemporary works.
3. Students apply a wide range of strategies to comprehend, interpret, evaluate, and appreciate texts. They draw on their prior experiences, their interactions with other readers and writers, their knowledge of word meaning and of other texts, their word identification strategies, and their understanding of textual features (e.g., sound–letter correspondence, sentence structure, context, graphics).
6. Students apply knowledge of language structure, language conventions (e.g., spelling and punctuation), media techniques, figurative language, and genre to create, critique, and discuss print and nonprint texts.
8. Students use a variety of technological and information resources (e.g., libraries, databases, computer networks, video) to gather and synthesize information and to create and communicate knowledge.

ISTE NETS-S

- ☐ 1. Creativity and innovation
- ☑ 2. Communication and collaboration
- ☐ 3. Research and information fluency
- ☑ 4. Critical thinking, problem solving, & decision making
- ☐ 5. Digital citizenship
- ☑ 6. Technology operations and concepts

Instructional Objective(s): Students create a story map to illustrate their comprehension of the main characteristics of a story, including the story's title and author, genre, characters, setting, problems faced by the characters, and resolutions. Older students may be able to also identify more complex literary conventions like foreshadowing, foils, etc.

ACTION

Before-Class Preparation: Students read a story or book from their classroom reading series, either individually or during whole-group instruction. Encourage students to use comprehension strategies before, during, and after reading, such as predicting outcomes, connecting to prior knowledge, and summarizing. Before completing this activity the first time, students will need explicit instruction about the elements of a story used in a story map: title and author, genre, character(s), setting, problem, resolution. A completed story map from a recently read story can serve as an example.

During Class

Time	Instructional Activities	Materials and Resources
15–20 minutes	In a small-group or whole-class instructional setting, begin the activity with comprehension questions commonly asked after reading. Review the essential elements of the story and elicit detailed responses from students. If conducting the story-map activity for the first time, ensure students understand the elements of a story used in a story map: title and author, genre, character, setting, problem, and resolution.	Book or story
30–45 minutes	Using presentation or concept-mapping software, students create a document that describes the elements of a story in the story map. A template is helpful for younger students or when using presentation software (i.e., a six-slide presentation). Students use text, or graphics where appropriate, to identify each of the elements. More advanced or experienced readers may be able to create their own concept maps without a template.	Book or story Presentation software Concept-mapping software (optional)

During Class		
Time	Instructional Activities	Materials and Resources
10–20 minutes	Students share their story maps with each other, identifying critical examples of each story map element and noting similarities and differences across maps.	Book or story Presentation software Concept-mapping software (optional)

Notes: This is an activity to promote comprehension and can be included in many units in the early literacy classroom.

MONITOR

Ongoing Assessment(s): For struggling readers, conduct the activity in a small group and closely monitor their responses as they create their story maps. Use probing questions or encourage collaboration for students who encounter difficulties. Completed maps are graded for accuracy and can be stored in student portfolios or other records.

Accommodations and Extensions: Depending on the age and readiness level of the students, this activity can be conducted in small- or whole-group instruction. The activity can also be used for an intervention lesson for struggling readers, but templates should be created or choices should be provided from which the student can select so the student focuses on the comprehension activity and not the technology use. Incorporating images in the map or including terms in other languages can support the needs of English language learners.

Back-up Plan: The activity can be completed using a sheet of paper that is divided into six areas or with a paper-based handout you create using word-processing software.

EVALUATION

Lesson Reflections and Notes: Variations of this activity can be completed each time students finish reading a story or unit. If reading several stories within a single unit, a master story map can be completed as a table or graphic organizer that allows students to compare elements across stories within the same unit as well as identifying similarities and differences between stories.

TECHNOLOGY INTEGRATION FOR MEANINGFUL CLASSROOM USE
Daily Lesson GAME Plan

Lesson Title: Parts of a speech: Famous Examples

Grade level: Middle Grades

Related Lessons: Parts of a speech: Writing a Speech

Unit: Exploring Oration: The Voice, Style, Content, and Context of Speeches

GOALS

Content Standards:

2. Students read a wide range of literature from many periods in many genres to build an understanding of the many dimensions (e.g., philosophical, ethical, aesthetic) of human experience.
3. Students apply a wide range of strategies to comprehend, interpret, evaluate, and appreciate texts. They draw on their prior experiences, their interactions with other readers and writers, their knowledge of word meaning and of other texts, their word identification strategies, and their understanding of textual features (e.g., sound–letter correspondence, sentence structure, context, graphics).
4. Students adjust their use of spoken, written, and visual language (e.g., conventions, style, vocabulary) to communicate effectively with a variety of audiences and for different purposes.
8. Students use a variety of technological and information resources (e.g., libraries, databases, computer networks, video) to gather and synthesize information and to create and communicate knowledge.

ISTE NETS-S

☐ 1. Creativity and innovation

☑ 2. Communication and collaboration

☑ 3. Research and information fluency

☑ 4. Critical thinking, problem solving, and decision making

☐ 5. Digital citizenship

☑ 6. Technology operations and concepts

Instructional Objective(s): Students will identify the beginning, middle, and ending of a speech, and describe characteristics of its intended audience, tone, and style. Students will also describe choices a writer makes related to the parts of a speech.

ACTION

Before-Class Preparation: Identify speech examples from the media center or Internet. Create a handout or guiding questions with time allotments, if necessary, to organize student discussions and written responses. Depending on the method for the compiled project (word processing, presentation, or web page), you may have to create a template for student responses.

During Class

Time	Instructional Activities	Materials & Resources
20–30 minutes	Begin with a general definition of what makes a speech, when and why one delivers a speech and a brief overview of the key terms in the lesson. Generate student definitions for each term using concept-mapping software or a graphic organizer. Include examples of speeches students may or should be familiar with, such as Lincoln's "Gettysburg Address," King's "I Have a Dream" speech, or an acceptance speech for a student government election.	Audio/video/Internet speech resources Concept-mapping software or graphic-organizer template
20–30 minutes	Choose a specific speech for students to listen to while following along with the text version. The chosen speech will probably need some contextualization so it may help to preselect links for students to see that help them to grasp fully both the social and historical context of the particular speech. Then, as a class in a large-group discussion, expand the student-generated concept map or graphic organizer by having the students identify the terms with examples from the speech.	Audio/video/Internet speech resources Concept-mapping software or graphic-organizer template

During Class

Time	Instructional Activities	Materials & Resources
30 minutes	In small groups, have each group analyze the beginning, middle, or end of the speech, using their textbook and other print reference materials, online databases, or websites you have identified to determine reasons for the content and language the orator or speechwriter chose, as well as the tone and style used in the speech. Remind the students that the parts are interrelated and they may find that while they work with the explanation for their sections, they will need to refer to other sections as well. All students take their own notes from the discussion.	Audio/video/Internet speech resources Textbook, online databases, or Internet resources Paper/notebooks, word processor, note-taking software or other for student notes
30–45 minutes	Each group will write 1–3 paragraphs that explain what they felt may have been the writer's motivation or thinking for composing that section and using the particular tone or style giving examples from the speech. Student writing samples can be compiled in a summative word-processing document, class presentation, or wiki.	Word processor Presentation software or wiki (optional)
30–45 minutes	Play the speech again, following along with the text as before. After this experience with the speech, have students read and discuss the posting on each section by their classmates. As a class, discuss how thinking about the decisions that the writer may have made for each part of the speech better helps them to understand the meaning of the speech.	Audio/video/Internet speech resources Student writing samples in word processor, presentation software, or wiki

Notes: Video and audio recordings of King's "I Have a Dream" speech are available online from several sources. Using a speech in the public domain that is available for view on the Internet allows students to access and review the speech both in and out of the classroom.

MONITOR

Ongoing Assessment(s): Monitor student responses during class discussion to ensure all students respond to and demonstrate understanding of key concepts and terms. Encourage participation through probing questions and use of wait time.

If possible, determine group membership ahead of time and give each member of the group a specific role. Roles can be changed over time. Some students may need a handout or series of guiding questions with a timeline from which to organize their discussion and subsequent written response. All students should take notes and keep a copy of their final written responses for their portfolios or other records.

Accommodations and Extensions: Technology selection and the amount of independence depend on the readiness of the students. Some students may be able to construct concept maps or graphic organizers on their own or in small groups. Others may succeed best if the teacher creates the map with whole-class input. The technology used for reporting out—word processor, presentation, wiki, and so forth—is also dependent on the technology skills and knowledge of the student as well as available software to complete the project. Using a word processor allows students to reuse the material in other applications.

The logical companion lesson to this is to have students write their own speeches. Artifacts from this lesson can inform that activity.

Back-up plan: Analog video and audio recordings are available for many famous speeches from most school media centers.

EVALUATION

Lesson Reflections and Notes: Students are evaluated through group participation in class discussions, note-taking, and final paragraphs. Students should record notes and final paragraphs in their portfolios or other records.

The lessons in this unit have the potential to expose students to materials or situations that may be new to them culturally and provide explicit connections to other content areas. You may want to extend the lesson across several classes. It is helpful to keep a journal of content covered, how well it was received, what may still need to be covered, and how you might need to modify the unit to best suit your individual class.

When choosing materials that may be culturally new to some students, it will be important to approach your speech choice and discussions with a sensitivity that allows all students in your class to feel equally comfortable. Having students write their own speeches allows them to explore and express their own sense of voice and identity in both their writing and delivery of speech. Be conscious of your role, encourage, and foster that voice because it will be what makes the speeches theirs. Their specific voice and style in their speeches is unique to them as that of any orator.

This unit may also tie into a specific time of year or more globally studied framework like Black History Month, Women's Month, or Native American Heritage month—all of which would help to introduce speeches by people whom students may not otherwise have an opportunity to hear.

TECHNOLOGY INTEGRATION FOR MEANINGFUL CLASSROOM USE
Daily Lesson GAME Plan

Lesson Title: Putting Beliefs into Words and Stories: A Personal Essay for "This I Believe"

Related Lessons: Persuasive Essay, Journalistic/ Informative Essay

Grade level: High School

Unit: Essay writing

GOALS

Content Standards:

1. Students read a wide range of print and nonprint texts to build an understanding of texts, of themselves, and of the cultures of the United States and the world; to acquire new information; to respond to the needs and demands of society and the workplace; and for personal fulfillment. Among these texts are fiction and nonfiction, classic and contemporary works.

3. Students apply a wide range of strategies to comprehend, interpret, evaluate, and appreciate texts. They draw on their prior experiences, their interactions with other readers and writers, their knowledge of word meaning and of other texts, their word identification strategies, and their understanding of textual features (e.g., sound–letter correspondence, sentence structure, context, graphics).

5. Students employ a wide range of strategies as they write and use different writing process elements appropriately to communicate with different audiences for a variety of purposes.

8. Students use a variety of technological and information resources (e.g., libraries, databases, computer networks, video) to gather and synthesize information and to create and communicate knowledge.

ISTE NETS-S

☑ 1. Creativity and innovation

☑ 2. Communication and collaboration

☐ 3. Research and information fluency

☑ 4. Critical thinking, problem solving, & decision making

☑ 5. Digital citizenship

☑ 6. Technology operations and concepts

Instructional Objective(s): Students analyze and compose with a clear sense of audience and purpose by identifying, analyzing, and practicing the following genres: personal essay, memoir, and narrative. Students describe the choices a writer makes related to these forms.

ACTION

Before-Class Preparation: Review the This I Believe website from National Public Radio (http://thisibelieve.org/educationoutreach.html). This lesson requires students to write a personal essay that they turn into a digital story. Lessons on the This I Believe website were originally developed by Dottie Willis of the Jefferson County Public School System in Louisville, Kentucky, for use by teachers and students across the nation.

During Class

Time	Instructional Activities	Materials and Resources
15–20 minutes	In a whole-class setting, introduce students to the This I Believe website, its history, purposes, and other features relevant to the lesson. This can be accomplished in a computer lab or using a single-teacher workstation to project information for the class.	Computer with Internet connection This I Believe website
20–30 minutes	Using examples from the website, discuss the differences between a personal essay, which is focused on a belief or insight about life that is significant to the writer, and the two other forms of personal writing: the personal narrative and the memoir.	This I Believe website has charts that cover each genre

During Class		
Time	**Instructional Activities**	**Materials and Resources**
30–45 minutes	Individually or in pairs or small groups, have students create documents that list the similar and different characteristics of each genre using at least one example of each genre from the website. They can do this in a table or an expanded Venn diagram, and it can be recorded in a student portfolio or writer's notebook. Students should identify the author's main purpose and supporting details that contribute to that purpose from each example.	Word-processing software Drawing or concept-mapping software (optional)
1 or 2 class periods and/or homework	Individually, students compose a personal essay that is to become the script for their digital story from one of the following prompts or one you provide: • All of us are works in progress with a long way to go before we reach our full potential. In what skill or area are you still working to make progress? • Our society uses the word hero in many different ways. How do you define a hero, and who is a hero in your life? For homework, have students identify personal artifacts (pictures, awards, hobby materials, etc.) that support or contribute to their personal essays.	Word-processing software
50 minutes	Students create storyboards for their essays, incorporating descriptions of personal artifacts—either ones they've already found or ones they need to find.	Word-processing, concept-mapping, or presentation software
1 to 3 class periods	Digitize images either by scanning or taking digital pictures. Some students may also want to create digital images to support their essays. Record narration using the script. Depending on the availability of equipment (scanners, cameras, microphones, software, etc.), groups of students may work through these steps simultaneously. Compile digital files into story and export as a movie.	Scanners, digital cameras, image-editing or drawing software Audio-editing software, such as GarageBand or Audacity iMovie or MovieMaker
1 class period	Students share their digital stories with the rest of the class, describing how their essays match the characteristics of personal essays identified earlier and the significance of the topics they selected and the relationship of the imagery.	

Notes: Story files can be posted on a single server, stored on a web page, or placed on workstations or laptops around a room gallery style. The essays and the artifacts used to create them are appropriate for student portfolios, sharing with parents, and may support college application preparation. Personal essays are often included in college applications, so this activity can help college-bound students organize their thoughts and actually prepare for some applications.

MONITOR

Ongoing Assessment(s): Students will generate comparison charts of the three types of genres that can be assessed and stored in a student portfolio, writer's notebook, or other record. Use your standard grading and feedback processes to evaluate the personal essays. The essays can be evaluated both in terms of how well students understand and produce the concepts of the personal essay as well as in terms of key concepts of grammar and correctness that may have been covered in class. Digital stories can be scored using a rubric with input from students based on characteristics of personal essays they have identified from the website.

Accommodations and Extensions: Help students focus on the content and learning goals by identifying examples of each type of essay on the website in advance, perhaps even creating a bookmarked list or adding appropriate pages to a social bookmarking page. Students who have difficulty beginning or organizing a written composition may benefit from the use of concept-mapping software that converts the map to a text-based outline.

Back-up Plan: Identify several print-based examples of each genre from the textbook or other resources if Internet access is limited.

EVALUATION

Lesson Reflections and Notes: The writing of the personal essay can extend over several class periods. Depending on your preferred methods, essays may go through several drafts as well as class workshop(s). Provide individual feedback and guidance as well as in-class opportunities for students to share, comment on, and revise their essays.

Rob Marmion/Used under license from Shutterstock

Integrating Technology in the ELL Classroom

Jill Robbins, Ph.D.

The number of students entering the nation's classrooms who do not speak English continues to increase. These students may be referred to by a range of labels, such as Limited English Proficient (LEP) students, Culturally and Linguistically Diverse (CLD) students, English Speakers of Other Languages (ESOL), or—the term used in this book—English Language Learners (ELLs). ELLs are the fastest growing population of students in the country (Vialpando, Yedlin, Linse, Harrington, & Cannon, 2005) Over the ten-year period of 1995–2005, the rate of growth of ELLs enrolled in the nation's classrooms far exceeded the rate of growth of the entire student population (56% vs. 2.6%, respectively) (Batalova, Fix, & Murray, 2007). These rates of growth are not consistent across states, with some states, like North Carolina, showing an increase of 372 percent of ELL students. As this population continues to grow, the purpose of Title I of the No Child Left Behind Act (Pub. L. No. 107-110) was

14

ISTE Standards addressed in this chapter

This chapter provides content-specific suggestions and strategies for addressing both ISTE's National Educational Technology Standards for Students (NETS-S) and the TESOL (Teachers of English to Speakers of Other Languages) standards. This chapter also builds on the NETS-T concepts and skills presented earlier, with a special emphasis on skills related to Standard 1 "Facilitate and inspire student learning and creativity." Following an overview of the TESOL standards and how you can address the NETS-S in the English Language Learners (ELL) classroom, this chapter outlines techniques, tools, and methods for developing authentic learning experiences that advance student creativity and innovation in the ELL classroom.

Outcomes

In this chapter, you will
- Identify TESOL standards and explain how technology can support them.
- Discuss how the National Educational Technology Standards for Students can be addressed in a classroom with ELL students.
- Understand how authentic learning principles can be addressed using technology in a classroom with ELL students.
- Explain how technology can increase learning and facilitate creative thinking in a classroom with ELL students.

intended to ensure that "all children have a fair, equal, and significant opportunity to obtain a high-quality education and reach, at a minimum, proficiency on challenging state academic achievement standards and state academic assessments." As the number of ELLs increases in the nation's classrooms, you likely will be responsible for helping these students obtain this high-quality education, regardless of the grade level or content area you teach.

English language learners come into our classrooms with a range of backgrounds and experiences: they may have never been in an English-speaking environment before, their previous schooling may have been inadequate or nonexistent, and they may have extremely limited literacy in their language of origin. However, 57 percent of ELL adolescents were born in the United States, with 30 percent of all ELL adolescents being members of a third generation of U.S.-born students (Batalova et al., 2007). These students are often from families with low incomes and lower levels of formal education (August & Hakuta, 1997), so many may have not been in an educational situation where technology is frequently used, and they may not have access to a computer at home. Thus, teachers of ELLs who want to incorporate technology may face greater challenges than colleagues with native English-speaking students. But as we've noted throughout this textbook, technology opens up a world of possibilities for these learners by providing scaffolds for their learning, enhancing their abilities to communicate in English, and providing access to resources that can empower them to achieve greater academic success.

Technology and Content Standards

ESL (English as a Second Language) Standards for Pre-K–12 students have been developed by the Teachers of English to Speakers of Other Languages (TESOL) to embrace the content areas of language arts, mathematics, science, and social studies. TESOL does not intend that these standards stand alone. Instead, they are designed to work in tandem with standards in other content areas and provide a scaffold for providing access to those content areas for ELLs. In order to acquire academic language skills in English, the ELL must master the discourse of these content areas and develop the associated critical-thinking skills necessary for advancement to higher levels of education. Table 14.1 shows the basic TESOL standards as published in 2006.

When reviewing how these standards might relate to content areas, we need to consider the importance of language in learning. Learning in the content areas is highly driven by language and the TESOL standards acknowledge the central role language plays in accessing and meeting the standards of all content areas. It is not sufficient for students to be able to converse in English for them to be able to access content and be successful in their learning pursuits. There is a difference between the language used for social communications and that used for academic purposes, what one researcher describes as basic interpersonal communications skills (BICS)

Table 14.1	TESOL Pre-K–12 English Language Proficiency Standards

Standard 1: English language learners communicate for social, intercultural, and instructional purposes within the school setting.
Standard 2: English language learners communicate information, ideas, and concepts necessary for academic success in the area of language arts.
Standard 3: English language learners communicate information, ideas, and concepts necessary for academic success in the area of mathematics.
Standard 4: English language learners communicate information, ideas, and concepts necessary for academic success in the area of science.
Standard 5: English language learners communicate information, ideas, and concepts necessary for academic success in the area of social studies.

Source: Teachers of English to Speakers of Other Languages, Pre-K–12 English Language Proficiency Standards. http://www.tesol.org/s_tesol/seccss.asp?CID=113&DID=1583

versus cognitive academic language proficiency (CALP) (Cummins as cited in Reed & Railsback, 2003). Although many students can develop fluency in conversation within two to five years, it can take four to seven years to develop fluency in academic language, with many factors influencing that estimate, including the age of the student and language proficiency level when the student enters school and the support they receive for developing language skills. So although your students may be able to use some English to welcome you, talk with other students in the cafeteria, and respond to simple requests, they may not be ready to master the academic language required to understand even the most rudimentary concepts related to mathematics (hypotenuse, tangent, parallel), science (mesosphere, cumulus, precipitation), social studies (democracy, amendment, citizenship), or even technology (Internet, wiki, blog)!

One commonly endorsed theory about second language acquisition suggests that people move through a predictable sequence of stages (Reed & Railsback, 2003) (see Table 14.2). Knowing where ELLs are on this continuum can help you identify the learning experiences and resources you use to support them in their learning. For example, a student in the earliest stage, the silent/receptive stage, may be responding to your instruction as best they can by pointing, gesturing, or smiling. Their silence does not necessarily denote a lack of interest or understanding. Although an ELL student is responding to your questions or participating in class, it can take from five to seven years before they have reached the final stage on the continuum, the advanced language proficiency stage, in which they can participate fully in the academic discourse in your class.

Table 14.2	Stages of Second Language Acquisition		
Stage	**Development Period**	**Vocabulary Size**	**Characteristics**
Silent/Receptive or Preproduction	10 hours to 6 months	Up to 500 "receptive" words (words they can understand but may not be comfortable using)	Involves a silent period in which the student may communicate by pointing, nodding, gesturing, saying "yes" or "no," or performing a simple act (standing up).
Early Production	Additional 6 months	1,000 receptive and active words (words they understand and can use)	Students speak in one- or two-word phrases and can respond to simple questions (yes/no, either/or, who/what/where questions).
Speech Emergence	Additional 12 months	3,000 words	Students use short phrases, simple sentences, and some dialogue. Longer sentences may have grammatical errors that interfere with communication.
Intermediate Language Proficiency	Additional 12 months	6,000 words	Students are beginning to make complex statements, state opinions, ask for clarification, and share their thoughts.
Advanced Language Proficiency	Up to 5-to-7 years	Students have developed specialized content-area vocabulary.	Students can speak English using grammar and vocabulary similar to native English speakers of the same age.

Source: Based on Reed & Railsback, (2003).

THE GAME PLAN

Content Standards

Set Goals

Research the TESOL or ELL standards for a state where you plan to seek a teaching position and create an action plan to ensure that you will have the knowledge and skills necessary to help your students achieve those standards. Identify the concepts, knowledge, and skills you will need to ensure that you are prepared to help your students meet the ELL standards in your state.

Take Action

Explore the department of education website in the state where you plan to seek a position. Review the K–12 TESOL or ELL standards in that state and compare them to the state's technology standards. Identify those standards that specifically relate to applying technology in the

ELL classroom. Develop a plan for how to meet the technology standards in the context of learning English.

Monitor

Did you find the information you needed? Do you need to contact the department of education for more information about where to find the TESOL or ELL standards or the technology standards for teachers?

Evaluate and Extend

Discuss in class the action plan you developed for meeting the technology standards for instructional personnel. Compare your plan to others. Note the strengths and weaknesses of the various plans. Strengthen your plan by incorporating ideas you have heard in class.

Compounding the complexity of language in academic success are the academic experiences of students in their home languages (L1) as well as their ages and maturity levels. Some ELLs come to this nation from rigorous academic programs in which they were highly successful. Their parents may be highly skilled professionals with high expectations for their children's success. Others may have little or no schooling and may not be able to read or write in their home languages; they may have never gone to school and could have had little exposure to books or other educational resources, especially modern digital technologies. Adolescent ELLs may enter a classroom with limited English proficiency, but will still have the same social interests, challenges, and desires of other students at this age. Choosing learning activities and the resources to support them will be different for each of these situations (see Table 14.3).

Authentic Learning Strategies Incorporating Technology

There are a variety of instructional program tools that can be used to support authentic learning experiences for ELL students (August & Hakuta, 1997; Linquanti, 1999; Reed & Railsback, 2003; Vialpando et al., 2005). These programs overlap in terms of characteristics, including the degree to which students' native languages are incorporated into instruction, the language requirements for teachers, and necessary resources. You also may have little say in determining the programs your school adopts to address the needs of ELLs in your school, but it's important to understand that no single approach will fit the needs of all ELLs. Just as you are encouraged to differentiate instruction and create learning experiences that support the needs of other students, you and your school should consider the needs of your specific ELLs before selecting a program or programs and should compare those needs with available resources—especially teachers trained to support the various programs.

Experts in English as a second language do not universally agree, but the literature on ELL models suggests they can be organized into four main types of programs (Linquanti,

Table 14.3	NETS-S in the ELL Classroom

Creativity and Innovation

Students brainstorm using a whiteboard (or shared online whiteboards with students at distant locations) to activate background knowledge on topics in a social studies classroom. Students can collaborate to review websites that provide content knowledge, using online translators if necessary, or can create graphical organizers of images that relate to shelter, food, and clothing of different cultures being studied.

Communication and Collaboration

Students create digital stories that tell their personal histories or family stories. They include audio files of interviews with parents or family members (in English or their home language) or relevant songs. Pictures and other family memorabilia can be scanned or photographed for inclusion. The digital stories can include narration by the students in English and their home languages and can be shared with their classes or even posted on a class website.

Research and Information Fluency

Students carry out research and prepare information summaries by paraphrasing or restating what they read. When students identify digital images that will become part of their projects, they request permission from copyright owners to use the images.

Critical Thinking, Problem Solving, and Decision Making

Students research water use in their own homes and across their regions through Internet resources and e-mails with experts and authorities. They propose conservation measures that can be undertaken by peers and families by creating web pages or posters created by desktop-publishing software that can be printed and posted around the school.

Digital Citizenship

Students brainstorm issues for a debate on school-related controversies using online chat and social-networking sites. Following research conducted—including visiting social-networking sites and reviewing privacy and confidentiality policies, students collaborate to create a proposition statement for their debate and model the use of these communications tools either with chat, instant messaging, or a wiki.

Technology Operations and Concepts

Students acquire English-language keyboarding skills and basic operations (open, save, edit, copy, paste, etc.) and use them in the course of process writing on assignments within the four content areas. ELLs can transfer knowledge of systems they used in their home countries to similar systems in the English-language environment, for example, students with experience using game consoles can transfer knowledge of menus and programs to navigating operating systems and common software applications.

1999; Reed & Railsback, 2003). The first category of instructional programs includes **native-language instruction** in which students are taught academic subjects in their own language. This method requires a teacher to be fluent in the students' language. These include bilingual programs as well as immersion programs that may require students to develop proficiency in both their native language (L1) and English (L2). A second category of programs involves the students' **native language as support** for learning. In these programs, the primary instruction is usually presented in English and aides or paraprofessionals translate unfamiliar vocabulary or clarify lessons in the students' native language. There are several programs targeted at nonnative speakers that use **English as a second language.** Teachers specifically address grammar and the conventions of English to support communication and content acquisition. The fourth category of programs is often referred to as **sheltered instruction** but also may be called content-based instruction or Specially Designed Academic Instruction in English (SDAIE). Grade-level content is presented in English in ways that are engaging to students at a level at which they can comprehend while also promoting English language development. Two well-established methods of this variety include the Sheltered Instruction Observation Protocol (SIOP) and Cognitive Academic Language Learning Approach (CALLA). These methods require teachers to have depth of knowledge and skill both in language acquisition as well as content-specific pedagogies and may require significant differentiation of instruction and modification of learning resources to meet the needs of students for mastering content and improving English language acquisition.

When considering technologies to support instruction for English language learners, you should consider many of the same factors you will consider when developing learning experiences for your other students. What are the standards my instruction must address and my students must master? What prior knowledge and experiences do my students bring to the learning environment? What resources are available to support my instruction? What instructional strategies will I use? What steps can I take to monitor student learning? Was my instruction effective? What should I do differently in the future?

Learner autonomy is a natural outgrowth of the use of technology. Technology allows students to engage in independent study, to collaborate in new ways, and to produce creative, original projects. As mentioned previously, one method for structuring content-based ESL instruction, the Cognitive Academic Language Learning Approach (known as CALLA), encourages teachers to combine three elements into planning every lesson: language, content, and learning strategies. When students are guided to develop a repertoire of learning strategies, they are more likely to be able to handle the academic language associated with authentic grade-level content subjects. CALLA lessons are in line with the TESOL English Language Proficiency Standards because they support the learning of content at the same time as language skill and awareness, with the support of metacognitive strategies. Teacher modeling of the strategies is the key to CALLA instruction, and can be seen in the sample lesson plans at the end of this chapter.

English language learners, especially, are empowered when given the knowledge of how to use technology to support active learning, a component of authentic learning (see Chapter 3). The ease of creating and editing documents in word-processing software, with its correction features, dictionaries, thesauruses, and other features provides plenty of opportunities for ELLs to engage in active learning experiences that support articulation of their own thoughts and ideas. These tools, along with common productivity tools like presentation and web-editing software, improve the quality and quantity of their written work. These tools make it very easy for ELL students to create documents or web pages that incorporate images and text at any level of English acquisition.

Students can use word-processing, journaling, or blogging software to create either a learning log or a dialogue journal (Vialpando et al., 2005). When using a learning log, students write about what they are learning in their classrooms. They can pose questions or use the logs to explore areas of confusion. Technology-supported learning logs allow students to integrate images, hyperlinks, and other resources to support their learning. The dialogue journal takes the learning log activity further, because when teachers respond to their students in written dialogue, they model proper language use and promote language growth. You may want to provide a prompt for the students or have the students generate the focus of their entries on their own. Technology used for dialogue journals should be secure in order to protect the students' confidentiality.

Hypertext links in reading materials are an added benefit to ELLs. They can provide instant explanations of unknown words, and search features let the reader expand on any concept with images, video, and additional text. Common to web-based resources, hyperlinks can also be embedded in word-processing documents, presentations, and PDF files. These tools can also be accessed by a variety of text-to-speech tools, some freely available on computer operating systems. The scaffolding opportunities provided by multimedia tools in the classroom and delivered via courseware give English language learners easy access to models of correct language use and can promote fluency and comprehension. The computer will repeat material as many times as it takes for students to comprehend.

Software such as DynEd's Clear Speech Works (see Figure 14.1) targets the English learner's particular challenges in pronunciation based on the native language, thus allowing learners to work independently on overcoming problems in

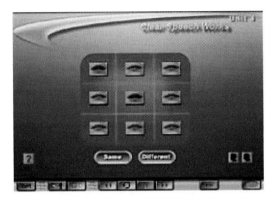

Figure 14.1
DynEd's Clear Speech Works allows students to regulate their own learning and work at their own pace.
Source: Courtesy DynEd International, Inc.

pronunciation. An on-screen tutor models lip and tongue movements for the sounds of English, and students choose to practice pronouncing vocabulary for areas of study in which they have an interest.

ELL writers, like all writers, do better when they have a sense of their audience. Technology expands the potential audience beyond the teacher to classmates, family, and the world at large. Writers also do better when they are part of a community. A variety of ways to connect with others through visual, auditory, and textual exchanges has increased the opportunities for collaboration with other students on active learning projects. For example, students in writing classes can exchange their work using a school network and then use text chat to give each other feedback. A rubric is helpful

STORIES FROM PRACTICE

Communicating with the World

I teach English as a Second Language (ESL) in one of the largest community college systems in the United States, Northern Virginia Community College. Its six campuses are located in the suburbs of Washington, DC, an area that is a powerful magnet for people from around the world. As a result, our school is very diverse with our students representing 150 different countries. Teachers and students alike relish this diversity. At the beginning of each semester, I am eager to discover where my students come from. I teach higher-intermediate ESL writing classes, and my classes are always made up of a very diverse group of students. For example, in a class of 25 students, I might find anywhere from 15 to 23 different countries represented. I am always very pleasantly surprised at how cohesive these classes become. Despite their very different backgrounds, my students seem eager to work with each other. Since class hours are limited to five hours a week, I try to find ways to extend communicative opportunities beyond the classroom. I do this for two reasons. First of all, I want my students to be exposed to as much English as possible, and, second, I want them to get to know each other well. I

have found that wikis are very appropriate for my dual purposes.

A wiki is a website that can be created and edited by a community. It is an ideal environment to help students become better writers in an authentic setting. When students write exclusively for their teachers, they don't feel motivated because the reason for writing is not authentic. My first wiki project was a joint endeavor with a colleague, Don Weasenforth, who teaches ESL in a community college in Dallas, Texas. After introducing themselves through short autobiographies with photos posted to the wiki, the students in our two classes worked together to write essays about attractions in their respective cities. They helped each other organize, revise, and proofread the essays. In the process, they all improved their mastery of the English language, and they also learned a great deal about the two cities. The second project went beyond the first to include students from an EFL (English as a foreign language) class in Yakutsk, Siberia, taught by Larissa Olesova. The theme of this project was global warming, a topic of great current interest. The students gathered and shared information in the wiki

about initiatives in their respective cities to halt or slow down global warming, to become "greener." They then composed two sets of essays, the first classifying the various initiatives and the second comparing and contrasting these initiatives. In both wiki projects, students had a genuine need to communicate and a real interest in the subject matter and were, therefore, very motivated to engage in the writing activities. They were also very conscious of the quality of their writing. Since they were writing for audiences in distant locations, they made a conscious effort to write as clearly and as accurately as possible.

I have also carried out collaborative electronic projects with classes in California, New York, Virginia, Norway, France, Korea, China, and Hong Kong. All have focused on collaborative writing with a strong emphasis on the concept of audience. I have found the wikis to be very useful for writing classes. Students have been very excited, in particular, by the opportunity to go beyond the walls of the physical classroom.

Source: Story from Christine Meloni, Northern Virginia Community College, Alexandria campus.

for guiding these writing exchanges and evaluating each type of writing assignment. Interactive tools such as wikis, blogs, and text or video chat bring the world into the classroom for English language learners.

Development of Oral Skills

English learners should be encouraged to explore the use of recording equipment to improve interpersonal communication skills. Skits, monologues, or role plays can be recorded using digital video cameras, audio recorders, or a multifunction digital camera, and viewed as an aid to self-assessment and to increase awareness of how the student is seen by others. Small digital audio recording devices, used to record and play back teacher instructions or a conversation, can assist ELLs with the transition to mainstream classes. Students can listen repeatedly to the instructions and clarify unknown phrases by questioning a more proficient speaker.

Students can find and link to conversation partners via the Mixxer, an online language exchange database provided by Dickinson College, which hosts a global community of over 13,000 members. The Mixxer helps ELLs find exchange partners using Skype webconferencing technology by narrowing their searches according to native language and one of 28 available target languages.

Technology can also support vocabulary development through the incorporation of holistic vocabulary practice using graphic organizers (Vialpando et al., 2005). When using these commonly available tools, such as Inspiration, you select key vocabulary and images that support them (see Figure 14.2). Some concept-mapping applications include clip art files with many images or allow you to import images—including images you've taken with your digital camera. During the activity, students demonstrate their understanding of the vocabulary terms in a variety of ways, such as pointing to the images or text, dragging images to their correct labels, or creating the labels themselves. You can encourage deeper understandings and promote comprehension by having students organize the items in a semantic web that shows the relationship between them.

Technology and Creative Thinking Skills Instruction

As you learned in Chapter 4, technology can support creative thinking skills instruction when it is used as a tutor, a mindtool, or in support of collaboration. There are certainly opportunities to incorporate technology in these three ways with English language learners. As a tutor, ELLs can engage in WebQuests on a variety of topics

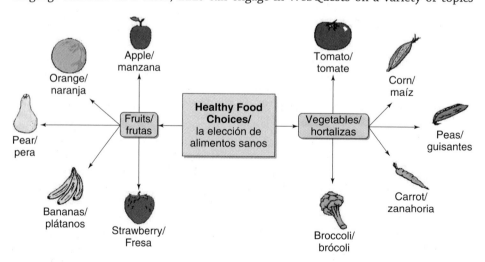

Figure 14.2

Concept-mapping software provides a range of activities for representing vocabulary and promoting comprehension.

that allow them to access English language resources at a variety of levels. Students can complete a WebQuest in response to problem statements related to environmental challenges, such as dependence on fossil fuels or the lack of clean drinking water. These are challenges that face students across the globe and can help ELLs make connections with their countries and peoples of their homes or families' homes.

As students develop English proficiency, they may need some help in manipulating data to show what they have learned in other content areas. Data collected in a spreadsheet can easily be converted into tables or graphs that help visualize math concepts. Graphic organizers can also be used as mindtools to provide multiple representations of concepts that can help ELLs access academic language that might be difficult to understand in a static textbook. Digital storytelling, mentioned in Table 14.3, is another method of using technology as a mindtool that allows ELLs to incorporate oral and written language with imagery. This approach is sometimes referred to as the language experience approach (Vialpando et al., 2005). In this approach, students can create their own reading materials based on the vocabulary and concepts with which they are familiar by relating them to their own experiences. With your help or help from a paraprofessional or volunteer, students can create digital stories following a field trip, class project, or dramatic or musical program that includes relevant vocabulary. The relevance of the story to the students' lives will promote engagement and motivation.

Dialogue Journals, described earlier, are an example of using technology to support conversation, but the examples don't stop there. Students can use text to discuss topics with other ELLs or English proficient students who can scaffold their learning in a peer-to-peer setting. Class web pages that provide access to homework assignments, homework help, or links to enrichment material can be a valuable asset to ELLs and their parents who may need opportunities to access content outside of the school day in order to promote enduring understandings and to encourage English use outside of school for reinforcement.

CALLA instruction, mentioned earlier, is an ESL approach that emphasizes English language learners' need to acquire the higher-order thinking skills and associated academic language necessary for success in their educational careers. CALLA Content and Learning Strategies are easily integrated with technology instruction. One example is the use of *Planning* by the learner before embarking on a new task using technology. Taking a moment to stop and envision the most effective way to complete the given assignment will save both time and energy for the student and the teacher. The metacognitive knowledge learners gain using CALLA will apply to their work in other content area classes. At the end of each technology lesson, ask students to evaluate for themselves how well they completed the assignment, and what strategies they used to overcome the challenges they faced. This self-evaluation guides the learners toward acquiring knowledge about themselves as learners and the particular strategies they should use in future assignments, not only in English class, but in all of their subjects.

Technology allows students to develop the skill of synthesis when they gather information and construct a message to inform others of a point of view. For example, students in an English for Global Issues course can be tasked with learning about a small, little-known country. They can conduct Internet research to find out about the country's economy and plan a tour for visitors, followed by an oral pitch to their classmates to visit the country. They could also present information about an endangered species or resource in the country to raise their classmates' awareness of issues beyond what they could learn merely through the experience of a tourist. After finding information and images on the web, students could use software to organize and edit digital images. Some might create a poster for the country, while others might create an electronic presentation. The TESOL standards addressed through this activity include communication of information and ideas related to science, social studies, and language arts.

For ELLs, technology opens doors to greater potential to produce creative works, because it frees them from basic editing of text to new, multimodal avenues of

WEB LINK

View the textbook's companion website to review a list of the software, hardware, and Internet resources mentioned in this chapter as well as additional resources for English language learners.

expression. Video, audio, and digital images enrich their products and provide a more even playing field with native-speaking peers. Technology can also connect ELLs with a wide range of resources for multilingual and multicultural research, shrinking the world and erasing national borders. Students can explore the web without concern for their pronunciation differences and take on avatars or pseudonyms without identifying their ethnicity. On a smaller scale an individual can create a virtual identity and a global audience for creative works shared via websites, blogs, wikis, and podcasts. Technology can allow students to produce a symphony without touching a single string or a lined sheet of paper.

Chapter Summary

Technology opens up a path to discovery and increased knowledge and proficiency for English language learners. Previous constraints such as linguistic ability, economic resources, and physical borders are diminished when ELLs are given the tools with which to explore the world digitally and to create their own environments for learning. Moreover, knowledge of how to apply technology to solving problems, communicating, and expressing themselves creatively empowers English language learners to achieve success in the wider academic arena, thus setting the stage for higher education and better career opportunities.

YOUR PORTFOLIO

To demonstrate your understanding of creating learning experiences for English language learners that address the National Educational Technology Standards for Students, create a lesson plan for common activities in your classroom using the GAME Plan template available on the textbook's companion website, or one of your choosing. Your lesson plan may address but is not limited to one of these functions of technology to support English learning:

- Gathering information
- Expressing ideas and opinions
- Sharing experiences
- Convincing or persuading

1. Identify the national TESOL standards that relate to your lesson. Review the state-specific content standards you discovered earlier in the chapter and determine appropriate assessments you can incorporate in your lesson based on the achievement standards. Include in your plan a strategy for incorporating language awareness and more than one of the language skills.
2. Research and select appropriate technologies that can support the activities in your lesson. Identify technology standards (NETS-S) addressed by your lesson. List all hardware and software required for the lesson and consider any preparation or prerequisite skills you may need to address before the students can complete the lesson.
3. If using the GAME Plan lesson template, include justifications for your technology application and reasons why you selected it in the section labeled Lesson Reflections and Notes. If you are using a different lesson plan template, include this information either on the template or in a separate file. Your justifications may relate to your skills or familiarity with the technology or the skills of your students, the match between the intended outcomes of the technology and your lesson, or even accessibility concerns.

References

August, D., & Hakuta, K. (1997). *Improving schooling for language-minority children: A research agenda*. Washington, DC: National Academy of Sciences.

Batalova, J., Fix, M., & Murray, J. (2007). *Measures of change. The demography and literacy of adolescent English learners*. New York: Carnegie Corporation of New York.

Linquanti, R. (1999). *Fostering academic success for English language learners: What do we know?* San Francisco: WestEd.

Pub. L. No. 107-110 (No Child Left Behind Act of 2001).

Reed, B., & Railsback, J. (2003). *Strategies and resources for mainstream teachers of English language learners*. Portland, OR: Northwest Regional Educational Laboratory.

Vialpando, J., Yedlin, J., Linse, C., Harrington, M., & Cannon, G. (2005). *Educating English language learners: Implementing instructional practices*. Providence, RI: National Council of La Raza and The Education Alliance at Brown University.

For Further Reading

Chamot, A. H., & O'Malley, J. M. (2004). *The CALLA Handbook: Implementing the Cognitive Academic Language Learning Approach*. Reading, MA: Addison Wesley.

Hill, J. D., & Flynn, K. M. (2006). *Classroom instruction that works with English language learners*. Alexandria, VA: Association for Supervision and Curriculum Development.

McLester, S. (Ed.). (n.d.). *The art of digital storytelling*. Digital media in the classroom. Retrieved September 5, 2007, from www.ebookhost.net/tldmc2/ebook.html

TECHNOLOGY INTEGRATION FOR MEANINGFUL CLASSROOM USE
Daily Lesson GAME Plan

Lesson Title: My Roots and My New Home

Related Lessons: Self-introduction, Family Descriptions, Places in the World

Grade Level: Elementary

Unit: Living in the Global Village

GOALS

Content Standards:
- English language learners communicate for social, intercultural, and instructional purposes within the school setting.
- English language learners communicate information, ideas, and concepts necessary for academic success in the area of social studies.

ISTE NETS-S

☐ 1. Creativity and innovation

☑ 2. Communication and collaboration

☑ 3. Research and information fluency

☑ 4. Critical thinking, problem solving, and decision making

☑ 5. Digital citizenship

☑ 6. Technology operations and concepts

Instructional Objective(s): Students learn how to gather information about their country of origin and their current place of residence on the Internet and present it using presentation software. Using the WebQuest method, the teacher provides a structured framework for web searching and a template for the presentation product.

ACTION

Before-Class Preparation: Find or develop a WebQuest page with the assignment instructions and links to resources students can use for finding information about countries and cities. Include sources for images, such as National Geographic. Arrange for lab time if computers are not available in the classroom. Set up a template in presentation software for the final product that students will create, including these slides:

    a. Title slide
    b. Slide showing the name of home country and space for an image; spaces for data on size, population, political system, etc.
    c. Slide with information on the student's journey to the current place of residence
    d. Slide showing the name of current home/residence and space for image; spaces for data on size, population, political system, etc.
    e. Changes student has observed in lifestyle, foods, or education with spaces for images
    f. Summary slide with space for image and reference list including original location of images and data used in the presentation

Upload the template for the presentation and link it to the WebQuest page. If the teacher doesn't have access to online pages, save to a network or on machines students will use in completing the assignment. Make sure that all supporting files, if sound or video is used in the presentation, are included in the uploaded folder containing the presentation.

Create the checklist of skills used for self-evaluation.

Internet resources:
Internet 4 Classrooms' Guide to Using WebQuests: http://www.internet4classrooms.com/on-line_quest.htm
National Geographic videos: http://video.nationalgeographic.com/video/player/places/index.html
National Geographic Music Videos from around the world: http://video.nationalgeographic.com/video/player/music/index.html

During Class

Time	Instructional Activities	Materials and Resources
30 minutes	Introduce the assignment with a model of the final product showing your home state or city or previous location, compared to your current place of residence. If you have grown up in the same area, use a friend or relative's location for comparison to the city or town in which you live. Explain your own goal in making this presentation and how you met the problems you encountered: "I wanted to show how different my home is from where I'm teaching now. I thought I could do that with pictures of the countryside around my house, but I couldn't find any good ones. Instead, I decided to show pictures of the kinds of things I did as a child; like skating on a open lake, and contrast that with what I do for exercise now, working out in a gym."	Computer with Internet access Projector and screen or large monitor Sample presentation based on teacher's template WebQuest page created by teacher
	Walk students through the presentation and point out places you made a decision or dealt with a formatting or language problem. Model the strategies you used for problem solving when discussing these: "I wasn't sure what the population was of my hometown, and I couldn't find it in the atlas. So I decided to look on the city's website. It had all the numbers I needed." Point out where the information was found for each slide. Make links to original information active in the presentation if the computer used for display has Internet access.	
	Introduce the WebQuest page, using a school site or a file saved locally. Show students how to click on the links to get to a source for data on countries, and then how to search within the resource. Ask students to suggest a country to search for data on, and follow the WebQuest instructions for the data needed about each location. Explain that the location of each piece of information should be saved for the reference list at the end of the project. Show how to modify the template for inclusion of audio or video files (e.g., use the Insert menu in PowerPoint) and how to add more pages if needed.	
5 minutes	Instruct students to use the strategy of Planning for a few minutes before beginning their research. Provide a worksheet where students can outline the points they want to include in the presentation. Next ask students to choose a resource where they will start to look for the information.	Planning worksheet
40 minutes	Let students open the WebQuest page and begin searching for the content about their hometown and current place of residence. Make sure all have successfully downloaded the template for the presentation and saved it to a local drive or flash memory drive. Allow students time to compete their research outside of class if necessary.	Computers with Internet access Presentation software
60 minutes	When students have their presentations ready, give each one time to show and explain their presentation. If you have the equipment, videotape the students so they can watch themselves later and complete a self-evaluation of their presentation. Complete an evaluation yourself to provide positive feedback, and give a feedback form to *only a couple of students* to complete while their classmate is presenting. Giving everyone a feedback form may mean there is no one left looking up at the presenter – they're all looking down at the paper – so they have no one with whom to make eye contact!	Presentation software Computer with large monitor or projector and screen
10–20 minutes	Ask students to reflect on what they have learned from this project. Guide this with a checklist of skills they developed such as web research, information and media manipulation, and oral presentation skills. Students should indicate their level of confidence with the skills as well as those they need to practice more. Did the application of learning strategies make the task easier? ("Remember stopping to *Plan* before you began your research – how did that help you?") Expand on the activity by discussing how students can use these skills in other academic work, such as social studies class, when they have to give a report about a country.	Checklist of skills addressed

Notes: Students from the same country can collaborate on a presentation and share information they gather from the online resources. Information about the current place of residence can be shared among all class members.

MONITOR

Ongoing Assessment(s): Review student presentations in progress to make sure they are using the template properly. Check on comprehension of the assignment and when projects are complete, ask students to run automatic spelling and grammar checks before giving their presentations. Students can record commonly misspelled words for later review.

Accommodations and extensions: Students with poor keyboarding skills can dictate the captions they want for images they include in the presentation and have the teacher or another student type in the text. Some students with poor keyboardking skills may be able to record audio tracks.

Back-up plan: For the event in which the network is down, prepare a folder with images of the countries represented by the students that they can access on the local computer drives. Have CD-ROM or print versions of an atlas or encyclopedia available for research on places and demographic information.

EVALUATION

Lesson Reflections and Notes: Students can work in peer groups or pairs for feedback on their planning document. Collect the self-evaluation forms from each student. Summarize student comments about the lesson in your own reflection.

TECHNOLOGY INTEGRATION FOR MEANINGFUL CLASSROOM USE
Daily Lesson GAME Plan

Lesson Title: Radio Free ESOL

Related Lessons: Writer's Roundtable, In the Movies, Good Eats

Grade Level: Middle grades

Unit: Your Culture, Our Culture

GOALS

Content Standards:
- English language learners communicate for social, intercultural, and instructional purposes within the school setting.
- English language learners communicate information, ideas, and concepts necessary for academic success in the area of language arts.

ISTE NETS-S

☐ 1. Creativity and innovation

☑ 4. Critical thinking, problem solving, and decision making

☑ 2. Communication and collaboration

☑ 5. Digital citizenship

☑ 3. Research and information fluency

☑ 6. Technology operations and concepts

Instructional Objective(s): Students create a short radio advertisement for their favorite singer or group's latest release. The advertisements are aimed at convincing listeners to listen to the singer's work and provide some information about the singer's background. The "radio" ads can be combined and made into a single page of podcasts at Odeo.com or LoudBlog.com.

ACTION

Before-Class Preparation: Obtain enough headsets so each computer workstation has one. Check to make sure they all function with the computer and that the computer has been properly set up for the type of microphone used. Set up a page for the class to share on Odeo or LoudBlog. Make sure all the computers have iTunes or another music download service, such as http://music.download.com linked to a start page or downloaded to the local drive.

Internet resources:
Odeo Online Studio: http://studio.odeo.com/create/home
LoudBlog: http://www.loudblog.com/

During Class		
Time	Instructional Activities	Materials and Resources
20 minutes	Introduce the assignment by demonstrating a podcast you have made about your own favorite singer. In the podcast, encourage the listener to try listening to the singer, and explain what kind of music they can expect to hear in the newest release. Show students how you created the podcast with recording software on the computer or via the Internet. Model planning for your research on the singer ("I want to tell about James Taylor; I think he's from North Carolina but I'm not sure"). Explain how you found information on the singer and downloaded or linked to a sample of the singer's work	Computer with speakers Podcasting software, such as Audacity or Garage Band, or access to a blogging website such as Odeo Online Studio or LoudBlog
40 minutes	Instruct students to plan who they will research by making an outline of what they already know about the singer on a worksheet. Include spaces for the singer's name, home town, the language in which he or she sings, and the type of music the singer makes. In each podcast, students will tell about the singer's background, state why they like the singer, and tell which their favorite song is. Then, they should convince the listener to listen to a sample of the song. This is a good opportunity to discuss fair use and copyright of music with your students, especially if posting these podcasts to a website.	Electronic or paper worksheet
60 minutes	Allow students time to record and upload their podcasts. Give students a chance to sit at the computers and listen to their classmates' podcasts. Have students self-evaluate by answering questions such as, "What did you learn by making the radio spot? Which of your classmates convinced you to listen more to the singer they like? What did they say that made you decide to listen to the singer?" Expand on this activity by asking students to record their opinions on other areas in which they are interested, such as school rules, the cafeteria's selections, or sports teams.	Computers with microphones and headphones Podcasting software

Notes: Students can convey much information about their home cultures by their choices of music. This lesson may open up a discussion in the class about the cultures from which the students came and could be expanded into lessons focusing on the musical heritage of several of these cultures.

MONITOR

Ongoing Assessment(s): Monitor the students' recordings to make sure they are including the information required. As students search for the music they want to share, guide them to narrow down their searches to a particular song available online which can be linked to their podcasts.

Accommodations and Extensions: Students who cannot speak clearly can create a visual presentation about the singer, using PowerPoint or Word. Students with hearing disabilities can choose a visual artist to present.

Back-up plan: For students who are not familiar enough with popular music to have a personal favorite, collect samples of some artists who produce music for their age group, or of your favorite artists, for the students to choose from.

EVALUATION

Lesson Reflections and Notes: Review student outlines. If time is limited, have students share their outlines with a partner. Students can share their justifications with others to improve their podcast outline. Compile student responses to self-evaluation activity to modify or refine the activity.

TECHNOLOGY INTEGRATION FOR MEANINGFUL CLASSROOM USE
Daily Lesson GAME Plan

Lesson Title: A Day in the Life of Our Class

Related Lessons: Personal Narratives, Using Google Maps, Recording sound in Garage Band or Audacity, Fair Use Rules for Copyrighted materials

Grade Level: High School

Unit: Aspects of Culture

GOALS

Content Standards:
- English language learners communicate for social, intercultural, and instructional purposes within the school setting.
- English language learners communicate information, ideas, and concepts necessary for academic success in the area of language arts.
- English language learners communicate information, ideas, and concepts necessary for academic success in the area of social studies.

ISTE NETS-S

☑ 1. Creativity and innovation

☑ 2. Communication and collaboration

☐ 3. Research and information fluency

☑ 4. Critical thinking, problem solving, & decision making

☑ 5. Digital citizenship

☑ 6. Technology operations and concepts

Instructional Objective(s): Each student creates a digital story, possibly including a map, conveying one particular day in his or her life, to be combined in a class wiki. Music, images, and text are combined to create a multimedia expression with emotional impact and a clear message about the meaning of that day in the student's life. Students gain knowledge of the elements of digital storytelling and manipulation of video, still images, sound files, and text while editing in an online community.

ACTION

Before-Class Preparation: This activity requires a couple of handouts that can be in print or electronic form. The handouts will vary in detail depending on the needs of your students. Create handouts that detail the digital storytelling process as well as any instructions required for creating or editing a wiki entry based on the software you use.

Create a wiki for the class and link to examples of stories from digital storytelling websites. Check with your technology staff about access to wiki software, as some may provide it. Others may or may not allow you to use free wiki software, such as PBWiki. Determine how students can access the wikis and help them create their accounts prior to the lesson.

Collect the tools necessary for the project: computers equipped with sound cards, microphones, and headsets; a GPS unit for storymapping (optional); and images of the school to be used in the wiki home page. Have a digital camera available to take pictures of students if they want these for inclusion in their story. Create a page of instructions (include guidelines for fair use of copyrighted materials) for students and upload it to the wiki.

During Class		
Time	**Instructional Activities**	**Materials and Resources**
30 minutes	Introduce the project by displaying digital stories and the class wiki. "We're going to create a wiki with digital stories from your lives. A wiki is a website that a group creates together." Play examples of digital stories and use the digital storytelling handout to identify elements that provide structure and give each one emotional impact (e.g., combinations of images and music or voice-over narration). Have students identify the critical message from the examples. Students will be asked to identify a day in their lives they would like to chronicle on the wiki. Suggest days the students might focus on: graduations, weddings, moving days, first dates, first day at a job, or a visit to a special place. Immigrant students may want to focus on their first day of school in the U.S. or the day they left their home country.	Digital storytelling websites: www.storycenter.org www.coe.uh.edu/ digital-storytelling/ www.storymapping.org/
20 minutes	Give students time to access the wiki and explore the examples using their handout. Ask students to make notes about elements that strike them as particularly effective and identify the critical message from each example.	Computers with Internet access Headphones
15 minutes	Refer to the print or electronic digital storytelling handout to help students plan and organize their wiki entry. Sample information to be included are: • the parts of the day being described (morning, afternoon, evening) • critical events (before, during, after) • the ultimate understanding students want the viewers to remember from their stories • images the students already have • images the students want to obtain • sounds or songs to support the presentation	Print or electronic worksheet Paper or word-processing software
15–30 minutes	Students share their personal story ideas in pairs or small groups (up to 3 works best) and gather feedback to revise or clarify their stories. If they have images or audio files, they can share those, as well as receive feedback on additional media that might support their story. Students should focus on telling their stories, regardless of the media they incorporate.	Student work samples
1 or more class periods	Students create their digital stories in word-processing software first—at least creating an outline of their stories for those students with limited language or technology proficiency. This allows students to check spelling and grammar and conserve time when moving to the upload stage. They can also scan or find images, create or find audio files, and store them in a word-processing document or file folder to organize their information. Circulate between students to help them manage files and overcome challenges in presenting the story.	Computers with Internet access Word-processing or presentation software Image-editing software Audio-editing software
15 minutes	Instruct students in how to upload material to the wiki. A print or electronic handout with instructions can be helpful.	
60 minutes	When students have completed the stories, set aside a time for the class to watch them. Provide a self-evaluation sheet with questions about what the student learned from the project. Expand on the lesson by asking students what other writing projects they would like to share on the wiki. How can they use the digital storytelling technique in their other courses?	

Notes: Be prepared to deal with emotional issues that may arise from students' expression of a pivotal day in their lives. This unit is best suited after the class has been together long enough to form an environment in which students feel it is safe to express their emotions and reveal their life experiences.

MONITOR

Ongoing Assessment(s): Check to see that students are including the basic elements of digital storytelling as they are working on the project. If a student seems to have an unbalanced amount of the elements, such as more images than text, or all text and little sound or images, suggest ways to increase elements that will improve the story's impact on the viewer.

Student products, such as the outline and written narration, can be used as benchmark assessments. Final projects should be evaluated using a checklist and self-reflection.

Accommodations and Extensions: Students who have trouble keyboarding may want to dictate the text to accompany their stories and have the teacher or a classmate type them. Or they may record a voice-over narration of the story using software such as Garage Band or Audacity.

This activity can be completed using presentation software, if access to a wiki is prohibited or beyond the technology proficiency level of the students.

Back-up Plan: Download local copies of the sample digital stories in case the network is down or they have been moved or deleted by the time you want to show them. If you have technology support in your school, ask for a local copy of the wiki on the school's server, so students can still upload their materials even if Internet access is not available.

EVALUATION

Lesson Reflections and Notes: Collect feedback from pairs or small groups. Identify any major issues that require reteaching or additional information. Collect story drafts as well as final wiki entries. Compile comments from self-evaluation sheet to refine or modify the activity.

15

ISTE Standards addressed in this chapter

This chapter provides content-specific suggestions and strategies for addressing both ISTE's National Educational Technology Standards for Students (NETS-S) and the national standards for foreign language learning. This chapter also builds on the NETS-T concepts and skills presented earlier, with a special emphasis on skills related to Standard 1 "Facilitate and inspire student learning and creativity." Following an overview of the national standards for foreign language learning and how you can address the NETS-S in the foreign language classroom, this chapter outlines techniques, tools, and methods for developing authentic learning experiences that advance student creativity and innovation in the foreign language classroom.

Integrating Technology in the Foreign Language Classroom

Greg Kessler, Ph.D.

Human communication has always been interlinked with technology. Early tools for writing allowed messages to be archived and transported. The printing press contributed to an exponential increase in literacy and altered the distribution of language and information. Most recently, computers have dramatically altered linguistic interaction. The creative use of Internet technologies has also played an important role in advancing authentic learning in language teaching (Levy, 2006). Computer-assisted language learning (CALL) in the classroom, in the computer lab, or as homework in the home setting provides teachers and students with great flexibility (Hanson-Smith, 1999). Today's technologies offer teachers a variety of tools and solutions that can be inspiring. However, they may also be overwhelming for some teachers. Establishing solutions for meeting standards can help to maintain the inspirational nature of these evolving technologies.

Outcomes

In this chapter, you will

- Identify foreign language standards and explain how technology can support them.
- Discuss how the National Educational Technology Standards for Students can be addressed in a foreign language classroom.
- Understand how authentic learning principles can be addressed using technology in a foreign language classroom.
- Explain how technology can increase learning and facilitate creative thinking in a foreign language classroom.

STORIES FROM PRACTICE

Engaging Teachers

A few years ago I was teaching practicing teachers to use Internet resources and web-authoring tools for teaching language. I was surprised to find myself working with a number of very experienced teachers who had never used computers before entering my session. They had been told to use technology in the past, but never told why it would be useful. They had never been helped to understand how technology may be beneficial—specifically for language instruction. It appeared that many of them had developed distrust for the use of technology for instruction. They also felt that they already had enough obligations and using technology was something they just didn't have time for.

Through the use of simple web-authoring tools, such as a "What you see is what you get" (WYSIWYG) editor, they quickly realized that creating and using Internet resources was within their grasp. By the time they left the training session, they were able to make engaging interactive language-based activities using Hot Potatoes software. They had also been able to record themselves and integrate their own and other pre-recorded audio into their activities. They left energized and ready to take advantage of the technology resources they had at their schools. Most importantly, they began to "want" to engage in this kind of activity. I have received e-mail from a number of them assuring me that they continue to use these skills. From using a mouse to creating interactive multimedia in a couple of hours, they found a variety of easy-to-use software for use in their foreign language classroom.

Source: Greg Kessler

Technology and Content Standards

Language instruction is typically divided into five or six skill categories: writing, reading, listening, speaking, grammar, and (often) culture. Although there may be a temptation to limit the use of technology to the receptive skills of listening and reading, language teachers today can use technology to address all of the language skills categories quite effectively. In fact, it seems that the integration of technology may be improving students' oral performances in unexpected ways, particularly in comparison to the traditional language classroom in which a majority of instruction (and expectation) is based upon written and grammatical evaluation.

With the integration of easy-to-use audio and video technologies, teachers and students can engage in various forms of technology-supported communication, instruction, and evaluation that directly influence oral production. By focusing on authentic language materials and communicative tasks foreign language teachers are also likely to engage in a form of instruction that is learner-centered while integrating skill instruction. Recognizing the standards that guide foreign language learning will help you to better meet the needs of your students, regardless of the technologies you use in your classroom. Review the national standards for foreign language learning in Table 15.1 and consider ways that technology can be used to support the teaching and learning of each standard.

Language teachers are typically aware of software that is specifically designed for instruction of the language(s) they teach. Although these may offer some language-focused instruction, often these programs do not offer students the rich and varied exposure they can receive when used in combination with other commonly available software. Software that is intended for broader application can provide a familiar environment from which to engage many students and often offers greater flexibility than language-learning software. For example, word-processing software offers multitudes of instructional possibilities, including interacting with text, video, audio, and images. Students can utilize text as a model for their own writing. They can use commenting and reviewing features to conduct an ongoing interactive dialogue with other users of a document. They can do a number of other things as well. A creative teacher simply needs to identify potential uses and their appropriate inclusion in instruction.

Some examples of software that are commonly used in language instruction are found in Table 15.2. This table provides examples of how the ISTE NETS-S can be addressed in the foreign language classroom. It is important to note the wide range of technology available to teachers—including but not limited to computers—that

Table 15.1 **National Standards for Foreign Language Learning**

Communication: Communicate in Languages Other Than English

- Standard 1.1: Students engage in conversations, provide and obtain information, express feelings and emotions, and exchange opinions
- Standard 1.2: Students understand and interpret written and spoken language on a variety of topics
- Standard 1.3: Students present information, concepts, and ideas to an audience of listeners or readers on a variety of topics

Cultures: Gain Knowledge and Understanding of Other Cultures

- Standard 2.1: Students demonstrate an understanding of the relationship between the practices and perspectives of the culture studied
- Standard 2.2: Students demonstrate an understanding of the relationship between the products and perspectives of the culture studied

Connections: Connect with Other Disciplines and Acquire Information

- Standard 3.1: Students reinforce and further their knowledge of other disciplines through the foreign language
- Standard 3.2: Students acquire information and recognize the distinctive viewpoints that are only available through the foreign language and its cultures

Comparisons: Develop Insight into the Nature of Language and Culture

- Standard 4.1: Students demonstrate understanding of the nature of language through comparisons of the language studied and their own
- Standard 4.2: Students demonstrate understanding of the concept of culture through comparisons of the cultures studied and their own.

Communities: Participate in Multilingual Communities at Home and Around the World

- Standard 5.1: Students use the language both within and beyond the school setting
- Standard 5.2: Students show evidence of becoming lifelong learners by using the language for personal enjoyment and enrichment

Source: American Council on the Teaching of Foreign Languages. (1999). *Standards for foreign language learning: Preparing for the 21st century.* Alexandria, VA: Author.

Table 15.2 **NETS-S in the Foreign Language Classroom**

Creativity and Innovation

Students create original works in the languages they are studying, such as biographies, historical guides, and short works of fiction using word-processing, web-authoring, and digital audio and video tools that can be accessed by a computer, CD player, or an MP3 player.

Communication and Collaboration

Students use computer-mediated communication tools, such as e-mail, chat, and text messaging to develop written fluency by communicating with other students, their teacher, and others with greater language proficiency.

Research and Information Fluency

Students use government websites from foreign countries and mapping software, such as Google Maps, to plan a (hypothetical or real) visit to a country in which the language they are learning is spoken.

Critical Thinking, Problem Solving, and Decision Making

Students use Internet resources, currency calculators, and word-processing or document layout software, to research and create a brochure for visitors to a country in which the language they are learning is spoken.

Digital Citizenship

Students use the Internet and other digital materials to explore and better understand cultural and human issues in countries where the language they are studying is spoken, comparing, for example, variations in dialect, pronunciation, and language use in Spanish-speaking countries, such as Spain, Central and South American countries, Puerto Rico, Cuba, and even communities within the United States.

Technology Operations and Concepts

Students use word-processing software to write in different languages, to conduct peer reviews, and to create documents that include cultural artifacts, such as digital images of landmarks, persons in native dress, and foods.

WEB LINK

For additional examples of commonly available technologies and how they can support foreign language instruction as well as detailed examples of the alignment of the NETS-S to the national standards for foreign language learning, visit the textbook's companion website.

THE GAME PLAN

Content Standards

Set Goals

Research the foreign language standards for a state where you plan to seek a teaching position and create an action plan to ensure that you will have the knowledge and skills necessary to help your students achieve those standards. Identify the concepts, knowledge, and skills you will need to ensure that you are prepared to help your students meet the foreign language standards in your state.

Take Action

Explore the department of education website in the state where you plan to seek a position. Review the K–12 foreign language standards in that state and compare them to the state's technology standards. Identify those standards that specifically relate to applying technology in foreign language instruction. Develop a plan

for how to meet the technology standards in the context of foreign languages.

Monitor

Did you find the information you needed? Do you need to contact the department of education for more information about where to find the foreign language standards or the technology standards for teachers?

Evaluate and Extend

Discuss in class the action plan you developed for meeting the technology standards for instructional personnel. Compare your plan to others. Note the strengths and weaknesses of the various plans. Strengthen your plan by incorporating ideas you have heard in class.

can be utilized to maximize the potential of CALL. The lesson plans at the end of this chapter provide specific examples of how you can design learning experiences that meet both content area and technology standards.

Authentic Learning Strategies Incorporating Technology

The first question that must always be asked when considering the use of CALL for teaching is whether the instruction could be done equally well without the use of CALL. If the answer is yes, then it is probably not worthwhile to use the technology. However, when we focus on authentic instruction, the benefits of CALL become exceedingly evident. As you learned in Chapter 3, authentic instruction involves learner autonomy, active learning, and holistic, complex, and challenging activities. Let's explore a few ways that these characteristics of authentic instruction can be achieved in the foreign language classroom.

The ultimate goal of foreign language education is the successful autonomous use of language. Learner autonomy, both as a self-reflective student and ultimate language user, can be influenced intentionally through language instruction. Autonomy is sometimes misunderstood as being "teacherless," but this is not the intent. As Little (1999, p. 14) clarifies, learner autonomy does not mean that students do things "on their own, but rather for themselves." Technology can be used in many ways to help learners achieve autonomy in a target language, such as supporting the development and delivery of audio- and text-based language through word processing, online discussions, and the use of digital audio and video. Collaborative and self-reflective activities allow students to develop their own systems of critiquing their developing language skills.

Another goal for language instruction is for students to express themselves effectively in a target language. This includes the ability to formulate and effectively present their ideas. Digital tools and resources are available to support the development of student-centric language projects, such as by investigating language, skills, and knowledge related to areas of student interest, whether courses of study or hobbies and other interests. Whether students are interested in automobiles, finance, musical entertainment, or cooking, they can draft their own dialogs that incorporate language artifacts they find online. Through the use of communicative language teaching students can be empowered to engage in authentic tasks that illustrate varied and meaningful use of the target language.

Students should be challenged to perform effectively in the target language, and there are a variety of projects you can incorporate in your instruction to help them do so. Tasks need to be designed so that students explore language creatively and in varied ways. Students should not be limited to objective decisions, but engaged in the learning process in a manner that motivates them to strive for autonomy as a language user.

Information gap is a common language teaching technique in which each student in a group has a different portion of a set of information. All of the information is necessary to complete the desired task and the students face the challenge of conveying this information to one another in the target language. Such activities can range from simple interactions such as putting together the pieces of a puzzle to complex activities such as synthesizing research data. This authentic use of language in a task-based context contributes to successful language learning and can be accomplished with a range of commonly available technologies, especially those that support dialog and discussion.

Technology increasingly provides opportunities for people to interact with one another in varied and flexible ways. Since language learning is fundamentally tied to interaction and communication these technologies always have something new to offer. Students can collaborate across networks, geographies, language backgrounds, political affiliations, and any other barriers that keep humans from communicating with one another. Students who work collaboratively in a task-based language-learning environment are likely to benefit from the language negotiation with peers and construction of knowledge that such tasks require.

Web-based collaborative writing tools and environments such as blogs, discussion forums, wikis, shared whiteboards, and webconferencing tools allow students to collaborate as they construct knowledge and refine language skills. Through collaboration students are exposed to more of the target language and encouraged to produce more language. They are also likely to engage in extensive negotiation of meaning, which has been determined to be effective toward their overall language learning (Long, 1996). Through this kind of social interaction and negotiation of meaning they are also likely to develop a better sense of social presence and self-reflection upon the purpose of their language learning.

Problem-based learning activities can be designed that focus on the needs and interests of individual students and allow students to use the target language in a meaningful context. Students can utilize prior knowledge from their first language to assist them in accomplishing the task set before them in the target language. Many technologies can be used to support problem-based learning, but those that allow students to manipulate and manage all aspects of the environment may be the most appealing. Environments such as wikis that allow all contributors to participate in an egalitarian manner encourage participation. Such technologies, along with virtual environments, can also support role-playing and simulation activities. Through the use of avatars within appealing contexts, students can imagine themselves in other personas, perhaps personas that are uniquely inclined toward learning the language in question (Heift, 2007).

Although the bulk of this discussion surrounding technology in instruction currently revolves around computers, it needn't be solely limited to the use of computers. There are a number of additional technological resources, with which you may be familiar, that can maximize the learning potential of your classroom. Some of

STORIES FROM PRACTICE

Language Learning in a Gaming Context

Dr. Douglas Coleman at the University of Toledo has been experimenting with gaming as a tool for second language learning for decades. He has released a few prototypes and actual games intended specifically for this purpose. Included are a variety of games that support a language-learning context. For example, Dr. Coleman has used various incarnations of Sims™ software in the language classroom as a means of providing students with a meaningful problem-solving task. Although it might be ideal to have the software menus in the target language this is not necessary. The goal is to have the students engage in the target language together as they collaboratively interact with the software. Thus, the computer is enabling the communication to take place, but not actually engaged in exchanging the target language with the students. The tasks are inherently appealing, and even engrossing. As a consequence, students use the language in ways that can be very impressive and—sometimes—unanticipated by their teacher. By providing a meaningful context that motivates students to communicate with one another in order to continue to participate in the appealing environment, Dr. Coleman has inspired many language students.

these are intended to work in conjunction with computers and others as stand-alone technologies. Some newer tools for the language classroom include the use of Global Positioning System (GPS) technology along with the concept of geocaching. **Geocaching** is an activity in which participants use a GPS receiver to locate items that have been hidden. Typically this requires a negotiation of coordinates as a participant narrows in on the object she seeks—usually physically in real time, but geocaches can be virtual as well. Virtual caches can be conducted with some of the new Internet-mapping software, such as Google Earth, that can include satellite images of distant locations and the ability to embed text and hyperlinks to other resources. This provides an opportunity to create a scavenger-hunt-type activity that also incorporates aspects of information gap.

Cultural inquiry activities can provide students with motivation to collaborate. Students work in groups to collect, organize, and present various aspects of a target culture. This may include specific historic events, art forms, famous individuals, or other cultural information. Students may be assigned specific topics or allowed to choose their own. Some example topics may include:

1. The food of Mexico
2. Origami and Japan
3. Famous immigrants from Italy
4. French poetry
5. Russian dance
6. The fall of the Berlin Wall

Students take on the role of the teacher as they present their cultural information to the class. Students may collect images, sounds, videos, text, and even print media that help to illustrate the cultural presentation.

CALL has been steadily moving toward more collaborative and authentic activities that empower learners and guide them toward the goal of becoming autonomous language users. Providing students with the opportunity to not only participate in, but to play a role in, designing their own instructional materials can be motivational (Kessler & Plakans, 2001). Engaging in simulated, or even real-world tasks, through web-based communication allows students to take responsibility for their own work and make better-informed decisions. Encouraging students to take more responsibility for their learning helps guide them toward successful autonomy (Little, 1999).

Technology and Creative Thinking Skills Instruction

Creative thinking skills are important for students to develop in any learning area. It is important that teachers recognize the potential for using technology to support these skills. As you will recall from Chapter 4, computers and related technologies can be used as tutors, mindtools, and supports for conversation. Likewise, Computer-Assisted Language Learning (CALL) is commonly divided into three types of activities: Tutorial CALL, CALL for Critical Thinking, and CALL for Communication. Each of these categories of CALL use can support instruction that develops creative thinking skills.

Tutorial CALL

Tutorial CALL involves activities in which a student interacts primarily with a computer, with the computer serving as a type of automated tutor (see Figure 15.1). This type of CALL is typically associated with grammar instruction but can also serve as effective instruction in pronunciation, writing, reading, and listening at various levels. Using the computer as a tutor can provide students with extensive exposure to accurate forms of language as well as opportunity to gain beneficial automated feedback. Some examples include La Chaise Berçante, a CD-ROM that teaches French through the culture of Canada and Quebec; the Learn Language Now! series by Transparent Language with titles in 15 languages; and the popular Rosetta Stone series found in and out of classrooms.

CALL for Critical Thinking

The notion of computers aiding in the development of critical thinking, rather than as tutor, further encourages authentic learning (Bikowski & Kessler, 2002). CALL for Critical Thinking refers to the range of materials that may be utilized in various critical thinking activities. The Internet provides access to a wealth of authentic linguistic content for any target language that can be used to support critical thinking. Education, government, and commercial sites all offer authentic language content that can provide students with the extensive exposure that will help them to critically explore a target language.

Similarly, authentic cultural content can help your students develop a better understanding of the target language and culture. Obtaining information about a target language and/or culture via the Internet has greatly enhanced language learning.

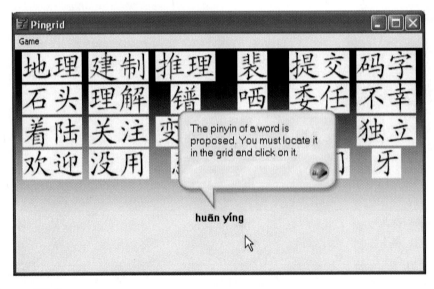

Figure 15.1
A variety of tutorial software applications are available for the foreign language classroom.
Source: Courtesy Emmanuel Haton

Rather than relying solely upon your experience within the target culture, your students can compare a breadth of information to develop a more comprehensive awareness. Students have the opportunity to gain valuable and unique insight into aspects of the language and culture in which they are interested. Utilizing a varied set of materials, including multimedia, text, images, and audio, students are able to develop a holistic understanding of the target culture. Such materials may include authentic samples of the target language, authentic content about the target culture, grammar references or pronunciation guides. This information will likely serve to enhance their subsequent language learning. (See Chapter 11 for more information on using communication tools to develop cultural understanding.)

Another recent development in Internet-based self-access study is the online learning lab (see Figure 15.2). Traditional language labs have been moving online in the past few years, allowing students to do self-study tasks from home, a library, or another convenient location. The ability to record and play digital audio over the Internet is revolutionizing language learning. Language teachers who are familiar with the variety of digital audio and video recording, editing, and playing software and procedures will be well-positioned to integrate these extremely useful materials into their classes. Such integration includes identifying useful authentic audio and video materials and providing an instructional context in which these materials can be explored by students. Such context may include follow-up discussion that reviews the material or considers alternative perspectives, outcomes, or related scenarios.

Teachers may also utilize these technologies to make their own recordings for students. Such recordings can integrate photos and narration into a video or animation demonstrating the target language and culture. It may also involve video that is shot on location in the target culture, thus exposing students to material they would otherwise not be able to access. Teachers may also choose to use these technologies for student projects. Students can create their own video projects that focus on a topic of interest reflecting the target language and culture. These kinds of projects can be most effective when collaboratively performed by teams of students. This allows them to reflect upon the ongoing development of the project and critically assess their work.

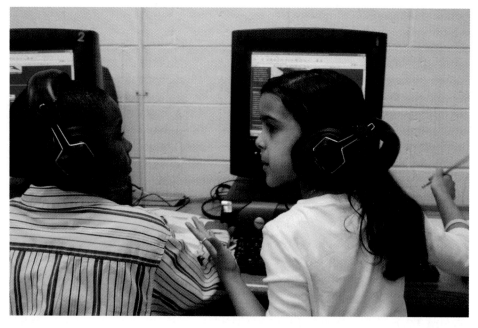

Figure 15.2
Using online learning labs provides access to speakers of languages from across the globe.

CALL for Communication

CALL for communication involves the use of technologies sometimes referred to as computer-mediated communication (CMC) tools. Tools such as e-mail; text chat or messaging; and audio-, video-, or webconferencing support new dynamic forms of human communication. Many of these tools not only offer enhancement to the traditional language classroom, but also influence the very nature of our use of language. Some researchers suggest that CMC has served as a democratizing force in human communication (Kiesler, Siegel, & McGuire, 1984). Herring (1993) explored roles of power, gender, and hierarchical conventions within the new means of communication. People are able to communicate across expanses of time and space in new and exciting ways.

Text-based chat allows you and your students to write to one another in a real-time manner. Voice chat tools allow you and your students to speak to one another individually or in small groups without the use of telephones and associated expenses. Video chat allows you and your students to share additional visual information as you speak with one another from diverse locations. These technologies can be integrated into the language classroom just as they have become integrated into our daily lives.

Teachers can use communication tools to connect their language students with native speakers or classes of students studying their native language. For example, a high school Spanish class in Ohio can interact and even collaborate on projects with a high school English class in Chile. Communication may take place in one or both languages (depending on the level of the students and the purpose of the interaction) and final projects may also be monolingual or bilingual. Students may share insights into actual language use in their countries or regions as well as cultural aspects that might otherwise be overlooked by other sources. Such exchange projects, typically using e-mail as the medium of communication, have been very popular with web-savvy language teachers. Recently, newer mediums have enhanced these interactions. Language students can now communicate with one another using voice and video technologies. These mediums can also be used to present the final products of such exchanges.

One comprehensive way to integrate these technologies is through the use of course management systems such as Blackboard, Angel, Desire2Learn, and Moodle. In addition to communication, these web-based systems allow teachers to manage students' assignments, grades, and other typical aspects of instruction. They allow teachers to create and manage various CMC activities. By utilizing web boards or discussion forums—communication tools commonly integrated into course management systems—your students can participate in discussions and reflections about their interaction with materials upon immediate use rather than later when they are in the classroom. This immediacy offers students the chance to further improve their communicative competence by engaging with the language at a time when it is relevant and they are consequently motivated.

The Role of the Teacher in CALL

Language teachers have had commercial materials available for use in computer labs for decades. Many of these directly address standards-related issues. More recently, as technologies have become more transparent and easier to use, language teachers have found a wealth of new materials available to them. They have also begun to create and customize their own materials for their students' unique needs. Many of these can be shared online with other language teachers while others are created and maintained collaboratively. Becoming familiar with a variety of authoring tools allows teachers to design materials that meet their students' needs at any given point in a program of study or individual lesson. This kind of customized design can increase motivation among students and contribute to their increased participation in various communicative activities in the target language. Often, commercial software does not offer the same individualized characteristics.

THE GAME PLAN

Identifying Web-Based Resources

Set Goals

Find online resources you can use for a range of activities in a foreign language classroom. You may need resources to help students understand a target language or culture or want to incorporate authentic linguistic content.

Monitor

How well do the resources meet stated goal(s)? Are there clearinghouse websites or sites that review online foreign language resources? Did you find resources you did not know existed that might be helpful to you in the foreign language classroom?

Take Action

Review the web resources on the textbook's companion website. Conduct other searches on your own for resources of interest to you.

Evaluate and Extend

Select the best resources you have found and include a list of them in your portfolio. Share your list with other foreign language students to compile a master list that covers a range of grade levels and languages.

You can utilize a handful of easy-to-use, yet powerful tools to create custom language-learning activities for your students. These include automated "What you see is what you get" (WYSIWYG) exercise generators, audio and video software, and course management systems. Each of these tools will allow you to cater to the unique needs, abilities, and levels of your students. Among the most common and accessible authoring tools is Hot Potatoes (see Figure 15.3), which allows teachers to make matching, crossword, multiple-choice, multiple-selection, sentence-order, and Cloze exercises. Readings, movies, audio, and hyperlinks can easily be incorporated into these exercises as well, making them uniquely suited for your language classroom. Authentic media can be reviewed through the use of these exercises, or they can serve as schema-building materials as students begin interacting with new or challenging content. Like any browser-based materials, exercises developed in Hot Potatoes can be delivered via the Internet, a school-based intranet, CD, e-mail, or posted on a course management system. This flexibility ensures that no matter how limited your resources, you have multiple opportunities to integrate these materials into your classroom.

Further power over the materials you provide your students can be gained by learning to use audio- and video-recording and editing software. Software, like the freely available Audacity or Garage Band, allows teachers and students to easily record themselves and share files. They can also use authentic audio material and edit it into accessible chunks for instructional delivery. Video-editing software, such as Movie Maker and iMovie, allows teachers to do similar things with video. Students can also use these programs to create projects that demonstrate their proficiency with the language or explore cultural aspects while using the target language.

Figure 15.3
Hot Potatoes is an authoring application that allows you to create a range of materials for your students.

STORIES FROM PRACTICE
Creative Uses of Technology

Chris Houser and Patricia Thornton (2006) of Kinjo Gakuin University in Japan have been using cell phones with their language students. They observed that most of their Japanese students did not use computers regularly, but did rely on their cell phones on a daily basis. They also noticed that they were text messaging friends and family with great alacrity. The teachers decided to utilize this resource and began engaging in text messaging as a form of homework for their students. They then began distributing exercises among their students through their cell phones, based in the animation software Flash. They have found that this approach motivates students and that they are able to do a lot of additional out of class work while commuting on the subway.

Technology also empowers teachers to share their success stories and challenges with peers. Presentation software has become ubiquitous and you can utilize it to document and present your experiences to other teachers and administrators in your school or district, to parents, and at local and national conferences. This exchange of information is critical for the ongoing success of language teaching programs. Further, there are a number of resources that can be utilized in order to stay professionally connected, informed, and involved. A sample of these would be the Computer-Assisted Language Instructors' Consortium (CALICO), which hosts a very active member discussion list; the International Association for Language Learning and Technology (IALLT); and WorldCALL, an emerging international community of CALL professionals. These organizations contain free resources and opportunities to increase your professional involvement with language professionals across the world.

As has been illustrated in this section, you can choose from a range of technology tools that support CALL. However, it is important to note that although each of these forms of CALL may appear to some to take place solely between the student and the technology, there is a vital role for you—the teacher. You must make important decisions determining which content is most appropriate at all points in instruction. You must also determine the appropriateness of materials for students' levels and ages and how well the materials support the learning goals you have designed for your students.

In-class activity may also involve teachers introducing CALL technologies to students. The need to explicitly demonstrate how CALL resources should be used by students has been addressed by Hubbard (2004), who recognizes that all too frequently teachers simply tell students to perform a certain CALL-related task without preparing them to do so. This can lead to a breakdown during the task that impedes language learning. It is imperative that students be taken through a step-by-step process of how to perform the expected tasks prior to the assignment. It may also require that teachers prepare print-based or digital handouts or guides to assist students. Consequently, teachers must become extremely well acquainted with the materials before using them with their students.

WEB LINK

View the textbook's companion website to review a list of the software, hardware, and Internet resources mentioned in this chapter as well as additional resources for your foreign language classroom.

Chapter Summary

Technology in the foreign language classroom is constantly improving. In our rapidly progressing technological world, there are new developments daily that may influence future language instruction. These developments continually make active participation for both teachers and students more accessible. We are able to both use and produce technology solutions for the classroom. This reality presents us with exciting opportunities to reflect upon current or past practice and strive for more effective or efficient classroom practices. Although we are not all capable of staying current in all areas of technological development, we can adopt the core skills and considerations presented in this chapter to utilize any potential technological development.

YOUR PORTFOLIO

To demonstrate your understanding of creating learning experiences in the foreign language classroom that address the National Educational Technology Standards for Students, create a lesson plan for common activities in your foreign language classroom using the GAME Plan template available on the textbook's companion website, or one of your choosing.

1. Identify the national foreign language standards that relate to your lesson. Review the state-specific content standards you discovered earlier in the chapter and determine appropriate assessments you can incorporate in your lesson based on the achievement standards.

2. Research and select appropriate technologies that can support the activities in your lesson. Identify technology standards (NETS-S) addressed by your lesson. List all hardware and software required for the lesson and consider any preparation or prerequisite skills you may need to address before the students can complete the lesson.

3. If using the GAME Plan lesson template, include justifications for your technology application and reasons why you selected it in the section labeled Lesson Reflections and Notes. If you are using a different lesson plan template, include this information either on the template or in a separate file. Your justifications may relate to your skills or familiarity with the technology or the skills of your students, the match between the intended outcomes of the technology and your lesson, or even accessibility concerns.

References

Bikowski, D., & Kessler, G. (2002). Making the most of discussion boards in the ESL classroom. *TESOL Journal*, 11(3), 27–29.

Heift, T. (2007). Learner personas in CALL, *CALICO Journal*, 25(1), 1–8.

Herring, D. (1993). Gender and democracy in computer-mediated communication. *Electronic Journal of Communication*, 3(2), 1–16.

Houser, C., & Thornton, P. (2006). Computer-assisted language learning: Mobile technology—Teaching ESOL on the fly (Academic Session). Tampa, FL: TESOL 2006.

Hubbard, P. (2004). Learner training for effective Use of CALL. In S. Fotos & C. Browne (Eds.), *New perspectives on CALL for second language classrooms* (pp. 45–68). Mahwah, NJ: Lawrence Erlbaum.

Kessler, G., & Plakans, L. (2001). Incorporating ESOL learners' feedback and usability testing in instructor-developed CALL materials. *TESOL Journal*, 10(1), 15–20.

Kiesler, S., Siegel, J., & McGuire, T. W. (1984). Social psychological aspects of computer-mediated communication. *American Psychologist*, 39(10), 1123–1134.

Levy, M. (2006). *CALL dimensions: Options and issues in computer-assisted language learning.* Mahwah, NJ and London: Lawrence Erlbaum Associates.

Little, D. (1999). Developing learner autonomy in the foreign language classroom: A social-interactive view of learning and three fundamental pedagogical principles. *Revista Canaria De Estudios Ingleses*, 38, 77–88.

Long, M. (1996). The role of the linguistic environment in second language acquisition. In W. C. Ritchie & T. K. Bhatia (Eds.), *Handbook of language acquisition. Vol. 2: Second language acquisition* (pp. 413–468). New York: Academic Press.

For Further Reading

Brophy, J. G., & Magee, P. (1999). The medium is the message—The product and the process of interactive multimedia development (MCE Working Paper 14124). Dublin, Ireland: School of Computing, Dublin City University. Retrieved September 29, 2008, from http://www.computing.dcu.ie/research/papers/MCE/1999.html

Egbert, J., & Hanson-Smith, E. (Eds.). (1999). *CALL environments: Research, practice, and critical issues.* Alexandria, VA: TESOL.

Kessler, G. (2006). Assessing CALL teacher training: What are we doing and what could we do better? In P. Hubbard & M. Levy

(Eds.), *Teacher education in CALL.* Amsterdam/Philadelphia: John Benjamins.

Opp-Beckman, L., & Keiffer, C. (2004). A collaborative model for online instruction in the teaching of language and culture. In S. Fotos & C. Browne (Eds.), *New perspectives on CALL for second language classrooms* (pp. 225–252). Mahwah, NJ: Lawrence Erlbaum.

Warschauer, M. (1996). Computer-assisted language learning: An introduction. In S. Fotos (Ed.), *Multimedia language teaching* (pp. 3–20). Tokyo: Logos International.

TECHNOLOGY INTEGRATION FOR MEANINGFUL CLASSROOM USE
Daily Lesson GAME Plan

Lesson Title: Recognizing and Organizing Letters in an Alphabet

Related Lessons: Alphabet Song, Colors, Numbers

Grade Level: Elementary

Unit: Letters, Colors, and Numbers

GOALS

Content Standards:
- Standard 1.2: Students understand and interpret written and spoken language on a variety of topics
- Standard 4.1: Students demonstrate understanding of the nature of language through comparisons of the language studied and their own

ISTE NETS-S

- ☐ 1. Creativity and innovation
- ☐ 2. Communication and collaboration
- ☐ 3. Research and information fluency
- ☑ 4. Critical thinking, problem solving, & decision making
- ☐ 5. Digital citizenship
- ☑ 6. Technology operations and concepts

Instructional Objective(s): Students listen to the Alphabet Song in the target language and identify the letters as they are presented. Using a Hot Potatoes Jmix (sentence order) activity, students drag and drop letters in the proper order as they listen to the song. When completed, this script will let students know which letters are not in the correct order by returning them to the position below the lines. The Alphabet Song is available in most languages and serves as a fun way to introduce the letters.

ACTION

Before-Class Preparation: Students are oriented to using the mouse to drag and drop the letter images. Students have previously been exposed to the target language alphabet. The teacher has created the very simple exercise using Hot Potatoes software (approximately 5 minutes of preparation time) and made it available to the students on individual computers, a school file server, or class web page.

During Class

Time	Instructional Activities	Materials and Resources
5 minutes	Students listen to the alphabet song first and then open the exercise in a web browser.	Hot Potatoes (to create activity) CD, cassette, or online audio recording Speakers Computers with web browser
10 minutes	Students drag the letters into the correct order based upon their recollection of the song.	Computers with web browser
10–20 minutes	Students listen to the song again and complete the order of the letters. (Repeat as necessary.)	CD, cassette, or online audio recording Speakers Computers with web browser
10 minutes	Student results are shared with the class. Teacher identifies errors and repeats the portion of the song that reflects any errors.	CD, cassette, or online audio recording Speakers Computers with web browser
10–15 minutes	Students sing the alphabet song together with the teacher recording it for potential reflection.	CD, cassette, or online audio recording Speakers

Notes: Students can work independently if enough computers are available. If not they can be grouped in pairs or rotated through computer workstations. Times may vary for languages with less familiar or more complex alphabets. This example uses Spanish for illustrative purposes since the written form of the alphabet is very similar to English. Hot Potatoes software allows the use of any written font to be used in this manner.

MONITOR

Ongoing Assessment(s): Students should be able to identify the letters and organization of the alphabet by the end of the lesson. They will also begin to practice accurate pronunciation of the letters. The productive stage of this activity will provide the teacher with opportunities to identify areas of difficulty that may require additional attention. The final recording of the students singing the alphabet song together can serve as a documentation of development for portfolio assessment. The teacher may want to group students (boys, girls, A versus B side of the room, etc.) during repetitions of the final singing to better monitor individuals.

Accommodations and Extensions: All students should be able to participate in this activity if it is performed as a group project. ELL students can complete this activity for English.

Back-up Plan: Students listen to alphabet song while identifying characters in a book and then sing the song as a group.

EVALUATION

Lesson Reflections and Notes: This is a simple and fun activity for the teacher learning to use the Hot Potatoes software.

TECHNOLOGY INTEGRATION FOR MEANINGFUL CLASSROOM USE
Daily Lesson GAME Plan

Lesson Title: Famous Person Digital Collage	**Related Lessons:** WebQuest
Grade Level: Middle grades	**Unit:** Culture

GOALS

Content Standards:
• Standard 2.1: Students demonstrate an understanding of the relationship between the practices and perspectives of the culture studied
• Standard 2.2: Students demonstrate an understanding of the relationship between the products and perspectives of the culture studied

ISTE NETS-S

☑ 1. Creativity and innovation

☑ 2. Communication and collaboration

☑ 3. Research and information fluency

☑ 4. Critical thinking, problem solving, & decision making

☑ 5. Digital citizenship

☑ 6. Technology operations and concepts

Instructional Objective(s): Students create digital collages of famous persons representative of a country/culture in which their target language is widely spoken. Students justify the individual(s) and the artifacts they select.

ACTION

Before-Class Preparation: Students need to have access to computer with reference tools, such as access to an Internet search engine, encyclopedia, or other database with varied cultural artifacts. Students should be familiar with one of the software tools that may be used for creating the digital collage: presentation software, web-authoring tools, video editor, word-processing, or other software that allows a variety of media to be integrated.

During Class

Time	Instructional Activities	Materials and Resources
15–30 minutes	Orient students to the project and activate prior knowledge by raising their awareness of famous people in their own culture: artists, entertainers, political, historical figures, etc. Students search using digital research tools (search engines, encyclopedias, databases, etc.) to identify famous people in the target culture(s).	Computer workstations with reference tools Internet access (optional)
10 minutes	Students pair or group (small group to whole class) to share the famous people they have identified and determine which may be worthy of further investigation. Students must identify persons from a range of backgrounds (the arts, politics, science, athletics, etc.), time periods, and both genders. Students should justify the reasons for their selection.	Checklist created by students identifying important characteristics of each person and justifications for inclusion.
30–60 minutes	Students work in pairs or small groups to collect information and various digital artifacts related to the famous person they have chosen. Students should collect at least 3 pertinent artifacts and explain why these are representative of the person they are studying. They construct their projects using multimedia-authoring software (see Before-Class Preparation for options). All sources should be appropriately documented.	Computer workstations with reference tools Internet access (optional) Multimedia-authoring software
5–10 minutes per group	Groups present famous person collages to the class.	Computer workstation Projector or large monitor

Notes: Students may be grouped in a variety of ways, but it may be best to group them according to their particular interest in the persons identified.

MONITOR

Ongoing Assessment(s): Monitor student decision-making during the brainstorming session. Students' lists of persons and justifications can be collected. Monitor students as they progress through the task to ensure they identify appropriate artifacts and work within time constraints. The synthesis of information as well as target language skills can be evaluated during the presentation of the final product.

Accommodations and Extensions: Students with limited technology skills may be paired with those with greater facility. English language learners can complete the activity for English-speaking persons.

Back-up plan: Students use magazines, musical recordings, and other traditional cultural artifacts to construct their famous person cultural collages.

EVALUATION

Lesson Reflections and Notes: A checklist can be used to evaluate the final product.

TECHNOLOGY INTEGRATION FOR MEANINGFUL CLASSROOM USE
Daily Lesson GAME Plan

Lesson Title: Cultural Documentary	**Related Lessons:** WebQuest, Famous Cultural Artifacts, Famous Persons
Grade Level: High School	**Unit:** Cultural Awareness

GOALS

Content Standards:
- Standard 1.1: Students engage in conversations, provide and obtain information, express feelings and emotions, and exchange opinions
- Standard 1.3: Students present information, concepts, and ideas to an audience of listeners or readers on a variety of topics

GOALS

- Standard 2.1: Students demonstrate an understanding of the relationship between the practices and perspectives of the culture studied
- Standard 2.2: Students demonstrate an understanding of the relationship between the products and perspectives of the culture studied
- Standard 4.2: Students demonstrate understanding of the concept of culture through comparisons of the cultures studied and their own.
- Standard 5.1: Students use the language both within and beyond the school setting

ISTE NETS-S

- ☑ 1. Creativity and innovation
- ☑ 2. Communication and collaboration
- ☑ 3. Research and information fluency
- ☑ 4. Critical thinking, problem solving, & decision making
- ☑ 5. Digital citizenship
- ☑ 6. Technology operations and concepts

Instructional Objective(s): Students will use the target language to collaboratively design, develop, and present a short documentary about a country in which the language they are studying is spoken. The final project can use presentation software, or can be a podcast combining still images and audio, or a video. Throughout this production they are strongly encouraged to use the target language in their small groups.

ACTION

Before-Class Preparation: This is an activity for students with strong technology skills, as they must have at least rudimentary understanding and skill with using digital audio- or video-editing software. Students uncomfortable with using a digital video camera can use a digital camera, scanner, or obtain images from digital reference resources. Students should also have a thorough understanding of the effective use of search engines and other resources and how to cite materials appropriately.

Determine student groupings and have groups select a country or region and read introductory information to prepare for the project. This information may come from the textbook, other class reference materials, and may occur throughout the semester or year prior to this cumulative activity.

Students construct a list of questions they would like to answer or critical issues they plan to explore in their documentary. Students bring these preliminary plans with them to class to share with classmates.

The class will create a rubric to evaluate the project by identifying the value of potential topics, measures of quality of the presentation, and appropriate language use during production and presentation.

During Class

Time	Instructional Activities	Materials and Resources
20–30 minutes	Students share lists with their group. Each is evaluated based upon the supporting documentation presented with it and the merit that it offers to the final product. Students must reach consensus on the items to be included and their justification for inclusion. This portion of the activity continues until all artifacts are assessed or there is a group consensus that enough critical resources have been identified to produce a storyboard and script.	Student lists and notes for storyboard
20–30 minutes	Students create a storyboard for their documentary using presentation, concept-mapping, or word-processing software. Each segment of the storyboard should contain text or graphics that describe the visual and aural components of the documentary. As they negotiate the timeline, they are encouraged to communicate in the target language.	Software for storyboarding (presentation, concept-mapping, or word-processing software)
10 minutes per group	Storyboards are shared with the teacher to determine appropriate topics and length.	Storyboard
1–2 hours	Students conduct research in order to compose a draft script for their documentaries, with 1 or 2 students composing each segment of the storyboard and identifying potential artifacts. Students should conduct peer reviews of their script segments with their group using the rubric, and sharing drafts with the teacher.	Presentation or word-processing software

During Class		
Time	Instructional Activities	Materials and Resources
1–2 hours	Students create or find media elements for their documentaries based on their storyboards and scripts, perhaps taking digital pictures, creating digital images, or finding and editing images and video.	Internet or other digital reference tools Digital cameras or video cameras Scanner for print-based artifacts
30–60 minutes	Students record themselves narrating their scripts, giving each student an opportunity to speak. Narration can be recorded in segments.	Audio- or video-editing software
1–2 hours	Students use audio- or video-editing software to construct their documentaries by putting all of their media elements artifacts into the timeline and adding any transitions, effects, or other information.	Audio- or video-editing software Presentation software (optional)
15–20 minutes per group	Students present their rough draft documentaries to at least one other student group and the teacher, sharing the storyboard, script, and other notes and information created during the project. Suggestions for elaboration, enhancement, or other improvements are made.	Media player Draft documentary Storyboard Script evaluation rubric
1–2 hours	Students refine their projects.	
10–20 minutes per group	Students present their documentaries to the entire class in the target language. Discussion and questions are encouraged.	Media player Projector or large monitor Evaluation rubric

Notes: Students are grouped according to the country or culture they will be exploring. Groups are no smaller than two individuals and no larger than five. Each group must have access to a computer, and ideally a computer for each student is helpful, but not necessary. Groups may benefit from access to a digital video camera, but this is also not necessary as videos can be made from still images, pre-existing video, animations, text, sound files, and many other authentic products of the target culture students can locate.

MONITOR

Ongoing Assessment(s): Students' use of the target language should be assessed throughout the process of identifying resources, gathering resources, synthesizing information, eliminating redundant or ineffective information, and presenting. A formal assessment of language abilities can be made during presentation of the project as well as in response to the student-generated language within the project itself.

Student-written language can be assessed through the review of the storyboard, script, and final project.

Accommodations and Extensions: Depending on the skill and knowledge of the students, documentaries may be limited to 5 or 10 minutes and no more than 3 topics. Some students may need an outline or template from which to create their storyboards or scripts. Giving students parameters, such as identifying at least one critical economic, social, and political issue to be explored in the documentary and lengths for each topic can help organize and focus students.

Back-up Plan: If video editing is beyond the reach of all students, some students can create digital presentations with images and text or complete a WebQuest based upon target cultures.

EVALUATION

Lesson Reflections and Notes: While student engagement can be high during multimedia projects, efforts should be made to continually emphasize the content and purpose of the activity. Focus is on language use and developing an understanding of culture. Students can meet these purposes through a range of different types of technology use, from very minimal to extensive.

Blend Images/Jupiter Images

ISTE Standards addressed in this chapter

This chapter provides content-specific suggestions and strategies for addressing both ISTE's National Educational Technology Standards for Students (NETS-S) and the content standards of the National Council of Teachers of Mathematics (NCTM). This chapter also builds on the NETS-T concepts and skills presented earlier, with a special emphasis on skills related to Standard 1 "Facilitate and inspire student learning and creativity." Following an overview of the NCTM content standards and how you can address the NETS-S in the mathematics classroom, this chapter outlines techniques, tools, and methods for developing authentic learning experiences that advance student creativity and innovation in the mathematics classroom.

Integrating Technology in the Mathematics Classroom

Gilbert J. Cuevas, Ph.D.

Common technologies found in schools today have tremendous potential to support instruction in the mathematics classroom. For example, spreadsheets, graphic calculators, and a variety of free online manipulatives can help students visualize information, data, or math concepts quickly and easily, improving their understanding of mathematics content. These technologies are tools that can facilitate the learning of mathematics.

Integrating technology into classroom learning experiences requires analyzing and determining tools and strategies that will best help students master curriculum standards. Software should support basic skills, higher-level thinking strategies, as well as students' ability to assess their progression and attainment of skills. You can use technology in your mathematics classroom to perform

Outcomes

In this chapter, you will

- Identify mathematics standards and explain how technology can support them.
- Discuss how the National Educational Technology Standards for Students can be addressed in a mathematics classroom.
- Understand how authentic learning principles can be addressed using technology in a mathematics classroom.

Outcomes *(continued)*

■ Explain how technology can increase learning and facilitate creative thinking in a mathematics classroom.

calculations; collect, analyze, and represent numeric information; create or use models and simulations; and scaffold learners to higher levels of abstraction and problem solving (Alagic, 2003).

You won't always need technology to address every content standard or lesson, but the increased access to technology in the nation's schools and the many powerful math-specific applications available to you and your students make these tools a more viable option for supporting teaching and learning in many situations. The National Council of Teachers of Mathematics (NCTM, 2000, p. 24) notes that "technology is an essential tool for teaching and learning mathematics effectively; it extends the mathematics that can be taught and enhances students' learning."

STORIES FROM PRACTICE

The Trout Pond

I was observing a teacher teaching her eleventh-grade class a lesson that dealt with the use of iteration, recursion, and algebra to model and analyze a changing fish population. The students used graphing calculators to set up equations and tables and to investigate a recursive function (one of the competencies in this particular state requirement for algebra). This data was incorporated into presentation software to demonstrate student findings. The activity the teacher presented was adapted from the Trout Pond Population lesson, found on NCTM's Illuminations website.

The following situation was presented at the beginning of the lesson:

Each spring, a local trout pond is restocked with fish. That is, the population decreases each year due to natural causes, but at the end of each year, more fish are added. The trout pond is an important source of income to the community, as it draws visitors from across the region who not only fish but also visit local restaurants, shops, and hotels. Here's what you need to know.

- There are currently 3,000 trout in the pond.

- Due to fishing, natural death, and other causes, the population decreases by 20 percent each year, regardless of restocking.
- At the end of each year, 1,000 trout are added to the pond.

After students have had ample opportunity to investigate the situation, she asks the following questions:

1. Will the trout population in the pond grow without bound, level off, oscillate, or die out?
2. Let the word NEXT represent the population next year, and NOW represent the population this year. Write an equation using NEXT and NOW that represents the assumptions given above.
3. The town council assumes that 2,000 fish are required to supply people in the town and visitors. What must the town council do to provide an adequate supply of trout for the town and visitors if the number of visitors to the pond increases by 10 percent each year? Explain why you think your

conjecture about long-term population is reasonable.
4. Based on your findings, what steps, if any, should the town council take to continue, halt, or modify their restocking practices? Prepare a response to the town council for their next meeting.

This one problem provided a springboard for addressing a variety of math concepts and skills that required a range of cognitive processing skills. The students worked in pairs using graphing calculators to develop their responses and appropriate equations. Data from their calculations were imported into presentation software and the students presented their answers to the class who served as "the town council" for the purpose of the lesson. The remaining class members provided input at the conclusion of each pairs' presentation on the accuracy of the solution, the level of detail that supported their positions, the methods selected to support their positions, and the quality of their presentations.

Source: Gilbert Cuevas

Technology and Content Standards

As a context for the discussion of technology and mathematics standards, it is important to address the question: What is the nature of the mathematics we are to teach students? While there are many descriptions regarding the nature of mathematics or what mathematics is, there is a view that underlies present standards: Mathematics is a science of patterns, order, and relationships (Mathematical Sciences Education Board, 1989). This is quite a different vision from the commonly held perspective of mathematics as an academic subject that emphasizes computation and rules without the understanding of why these rules work. This view of mathematics communicates the notion of a discipline that stresses problem-solving strategies and making sense of ideas and procedures. This point of view does not imply that computational skills are not addressed. According to the National Council of Teachers of Mathematics (NCTM) (2000) "developing computational fluency requires a balance and connection between conceptual understanding and computational proficiency. On the one hand computational methods that are over-practiced without understanding are often forgotten or remembered incorrectly (Hiebert, 1999; Hiebert & Lindquist, 1990; Kamii, Lewis, & Livingston, 1993). On the other hand, understanding without fluency can inhibit the problem-solving process (Thornton, 1990)."

It is within this context that the NCTM Principles and Curriculum Standards are framed. First, NCTM (2000, p. 11) identifies principles that describe exemplary features of mathematics education organized under six themes:

- *The Equity Principle.* Excellence in mathematics education requires equity—high expectations and strong support for all students.
- *The Curriculum Principle.* A curriculum is more than a collection of activities: it must be coherent, focused on important mathematics, and well articulated across the grades.
- *The Teaching Principle.* Effective mathematics teaching requires understanding what students know and need to learn and then challenging and supporting them to learn well.
- *The Learning Principle.* Students must learn mathematics with understanding, actively building new knowledge from experience and prior knowledge.
- *The Assessment Principle.* Assessment should support the learning of important mathematics and furnish useful information to both teachers and students.
- *The Technology Principle.* Technology is essential in teaching and learning mathematics; it influences the mathematics that is taught and enhances students' learning.

There is at least one notion to be derived from these principles concerning the integration of technology into mathematics teaching and learning: Students need to have opportunities to experience well-structured, challenging, and worthwhile activities that address important mathematics topics.

The standards also address the mathematical content the students should know and the processes they should be able to use to develop a comprehensive and rich understanding of mathematical concepts and competencies. The *content standards*—number and operations, algebra, geometry, measurement, and data analysis—specifically describe the content that students should learn. The *process standards*—problem solving, reasoning and proof, communication, connections, and representation—focus on different ways of gaining and using content knowledge. The process standards are derived from the ways in which students should learn mathematics content as well as the processes mathematicians commonly use. The integration of technology in mathematics teaching and learning should address the process as well as the content standards. The NCTM content standards are presented in Table 16.1.

There are obvious connections between the NCTM standards and the ISTE NETS-S, and certainly technology tools exist to help students develop and demonstrate mastery of both types of standards. According to NCTM (2000), electronic technologies such as computers and calculators are essential tools for teaching, learning, and doing mathematics that can furnish visual images of mathematical ideas, facilitate the organization of data, and analyze that data efficiently and accurately. Technology tools enable students to focus on decision making, reflection, reasoning, and problem solving. Table 16.2 presents some ideas for standards-based math

Table 16.1	NCTM Content Standards
	Instructional programs from pre-kindergarten through grade 12 should enable all students to
Number and Operations	• understand numbers, ways of representing numbers, relationships among numbers, and number systems • understand meanings of operations and how they relate to one another • compute fluently and make reasonable estimates
Algebra	• understand patterns, relations, and functions • represent and analyze mathematical situations and structures using algebraic symbols • use mathematical models to represent and understand quantitative relationships • analyze change in various contexts
Geometry	• analyze characteristics and properties of two- and three-dimensional geometric shapes and develop mathematical arguments about geometric relationships • specify locations and describe spatial relationships using coordinate geometry and other representational systems • apply transformations and use symmetry to analyze mathematical situations • use visualization, spatial reasoning, and geometric modeling to solve problems
Measurement	• understand measurable attributes of objects and the units, systems, and processes of measurement • apply appropriate techniques, tools, and formulas to determine measurements
Data Analysis and Probability	• formulate questions that can be addressed with data and collect, organize, and display relevant data to answer them • select and use appropriate statistical methods to analyze data • develop and evaluate inferences and predictions that are based on data • understand and apply basic concepts of probability
Problem Solving	• build new mathematical knowledge through problem solving • solve problems that arise in mathematics and in other contexts • apply and adapt a variety of appropriate strategies to solve problems • monitor and reflect on the process of mathematical problem solving
Reasoning and Proof	• recognize reasoning and proof as fundamental aspects of mathematics • make and investigate mathematical conjectures • develop and evaluate mathematical arguments and proofs • select and use various types of reasoning and methods of proof
Communication	• organize and consolidate their mathematical thinking though communication • communicate their mathematical thinking coherently and clearly to peers, teachers, and others • analyze and evaluate the mathematical thinking and strategies of others • use the language of mathematics to express mathematical ideas precisely
Connections	• recognize and use connections among mathematical ideas • understand how mathematical ideas interconnect and build on one another to produce a coherent whole • recognize and apply mathematics in contexts outside of mathematics
Representation	• create and use representations to organize, record, and communicate mathematical ideas • select, apply, and translate among mathematical representations to solve problems • use representations to model and interpret physical, social, and mathematical phenomena

Source: National Council of Teachers of Mathematics, 2000.

activities that address each of the NETS-S. The sample lesson plans at the end of this chapter provide specific examples of how you can design learning experiences that meet both content and technology standards.

Authentic Learning Strategies Incorporating Technology

Authentic learning is learner-centered, "where the emphasis is on learning as opposed to teaching" (Wagner & McCombs, 1995, p. 32). Authentic learning activities include cooperative-learning assignments, problem-solving tasks, open-ended projects, and opportunities for self-reflection. The trout pond lesson presented at the beginning of this chapter is an example in which a problem statement goes

Table 16.2   NETS-S in the Mathematics Classroom

WEB LINK

For further detailed examples of the alignment of the NETS-S to the NCTM Principles and Curriculum Standards, visit the textbook's companion website.

Creativity and Innovation

Students apply their math skills to replicate math-based activities in industry and business, such as designing scale models using computer-aided design or geometry software, developing budgets and forecasting trends with spreadsheets, and using real-world data to track and project environmental influences on trade and commerce.

Communication and Collaboration

Students collaborate with their teacher and other students through the use of a class web page that includes discussion software. Students ask questions of their teacher and other students and help their classmates better understand math concepts they are studying or help each other with homework problems.

Research and Information Fluency

Students turn to the Internet to find reliable sources for math-related information and tools. Students can create a web page or set of bookmarks for the class for commonly visited and helpful math websites.

Critical Thinking, Problem Solving, and Decision Making

Students use data trackers such as handhelds, probes, and other devices to collect data that can be represented in multiple representations and manipulated to better understand math concepts, using tools such as Geometer's Sketchpad or Mathematica.

Digital Citizenship

Students understand that technology can be used to better understand the world around them, such as exploring digital images to understand math concepts or collecting data from their community or from data sets on the Internet that they can manipulate and use to answer real-world questions.

Technology Operations and Concepts

Students choose and use appropriate math-specific hardware and software, such as spreadsheets and databases, data trackers, calculators, and simulation software, to solve problems and develop an understanding of math concepts.

THE GAME PLAN

Content Standards

Set Goals

Research the mathematics standards for a state where you plan to seek a teaching position and create an action plan to ensure that you will have the knowledge and skills necessary to help your students achieve those standards. Identify the concepts, knowledge, and skills you will need to ensure that you are prepared to help your students meet the mathematics standards in your state.

Take Action

Explore the department of education website in the state where you plan to seek a position. Review the K–12 mathematics standards in that state and compare them to the state's technology standards. Identify those standards that specifically relate to applying technology in the teaching of mathematics. Develop a plan for how to meet the standards for teaching mathematics.

Monitor

Did you find the information you needed? Do you need to contact the department of education for more information about where to find the mathematics standards or the technology standards for teachers?

Evaluate and Extend

Discuss in class the action plan you developed for meeting the technology standards for instructional personnel. Compare your plan to others. Note the strengths and weaknesses of the various plans. Strengthen your plan by incorporating ideas you have heard in class.

beyond simple calculation and places students squarely in the center of their learning. Student technology use moves beyond routine problem solving and moves into the domain of "nonroutine" tasks, such as exploring number concepts and solving complex problems. Technology-based instruction is well suited to incorporating many of these strategies in your own classroom (Kahn, 1997).

In reviewing research on the use of technology in math classrooms, Guerrero, Walker, and Dugdale (2004) reported that students in elementary grades are more likely to use computers and computer-based math applications rather than calculators; however, the use of calculators increases as students get older. More important than which tools are used, however, is the way these tools are used in your classroom. These same researchers found from the Trends in International Math and Science Study (TIMSS) data that when teachers used technology for what might be considered nonroutine ways, student achievement was positively affected. Routine use of computers can include drill-and-practice software and low-level problem solving. This important finding—that the way technology is used impacts student achievement—is consistent with an analysis of data from the 1996 National Assessment of Educational Progress (NAEP) (Wenglinsky, 1998), where eighth grade students who used computers for uses *other than* drill and practice showed significant gains in their average test scores. Technology used in nonroutine ways can deepen students' mathematical learning and foster achievement in math.

Clements (1998) identified three implications concerning the integration of technology in mathematics learning. First, you should decide how to combine computer- and paper-based lesson activities. Paper-based lessons are appropriate for many situations, especially those where the foundational skills may be important for students to develop or when technology exists but requires a level of proficiency beyond that of the students. Sometimes it is also appropriate to do some early planning or brainstorming on paper before moving into a computer-based setting.

Second, technology tools should be viewed as mathematical tools. There are some activities for which technology provides support that could not otherwise be accomplished—or it would be too difficult or time-consuming to accomplish. Consider the use of a geometry program, such as Geometer's Sketchpad (see Figure 16.1), that

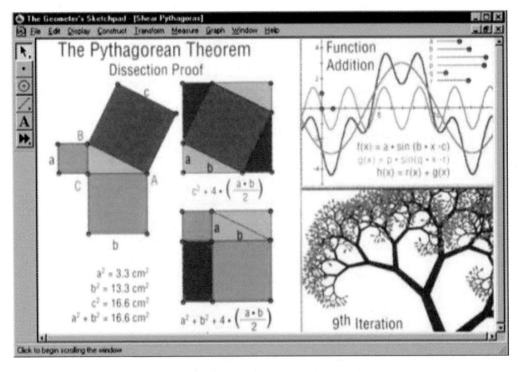

Figure 16.1

Many software tools provide a range of scaffolding supports for the mathematics classroom.
Source: Courtesy Sparrowhaw and Heald

STORIES FROM PRACTICE

Computers as Mathematical Tools

My eighth grade students worked on a Web-Quest our fifth grade teachers created called "How Cool is Hot? How Cool is Not?" I introduced the WebQuest one day by presenting relevant weather-related terms using concept-mapping software and reviewed some of the important technology skills they'd need, such as organizing a spreadsheet to create an appropriate scatterplot. When they came to class the next day, they were assigned to work in pairs and taken to a computer lab for the duration of one class period of 110 minutes, since our school is on a block schedule. There, they worked gathering the information they needed to complete their projects.

The students were required to find 5 pairs of cities using websites we identified for the activity that could be found in a bookmark file on each computer. The students used a spreadsheet to record latitude, longitude, and average high and low temperatures for each city during a month of their choice. With this information, they were to find degree distances and create three scatter plots to compare the data and draw conclusions about relationships between temperature and location (latitude/longitude). Students were also asked to compare average highs and lows from our own city with those at the greatest distance from the cities they identified.

Source: Gilbert Cuevas

allows the user to quickly create regular and irregular shapes, view their measurements, and manipulate them with the click of a mouse. Spreadsheets and data visualization tools, such as InspireData, can allow even elementary students to quickly collect, manipulate, and represent data visually. Some of the ways technology-supported activities can support mathematical connections are by linking multiple representations, relating and integrating mathematical topics and ideas, and connecting mathematics to the real world (Alagic, 2003).

Finally, Clements suggested that teachers need to view computers as devices for developing student mathematical thinking. For example, one of the components of algebraic thinking deals with the representation and analysis of mathematical situations. This can play out in elementary grades when students are introduced to the idea of equations and the processes involved in the solution of equations. Many web-based resources, such as the NCTM's Illuminations website, contain activities that can be used to help students develop mathematical thinking. The Illuminations website offers a range of lessons organized by grade band and standard and can easily be searched to find relevant activities for use in your mathematics instruction.

Moyer, Bolyard, and Spikell (2003) defined a virtual manipulative as "an interactive, Web-based visual representation of a dynamic object that presents opportunities for constructing mathematical knowledge" (p. 373). They elaborated further on what constitutes a "dynamic virtual model." Moyer et al. distinguished static from virtual models in that ". . . virtual static models are not true virtual manipulatives. Static models look like physical concrete manipulatives that have traditionally been used in classrooms, but they are essentially pictures and learners cannot actually manipulate them" (p. 373). A range of web-based manipulatives are also available that allow students to input and manipulate data and view the consequences of their actions in math-specific ways. You can easily find online balances, functions graphers, and 2-D and 3-D modeling software. Utah State University maintains the National Library of Virtual Manipulatives to help you identify online manipulatives for every grade level and a wide range of mathematical concepts and activities.

In a survey of teachers' uses of computers, Becker (2001) indicated at least four general instructional strategies that emphasized authentic learning through the integration of technology and mathematics. Placing these in the context of the NCTM standards, these are 1) use of online manipulatives, 2) exploration or problem-solving lessons and activities, 3) development of mathematics concepts using virtual manipulatives or software, and 4) use of data-exploration activities. There are numerous websites containing data sets that you can use in your mathematics classroom, such as Project GLOBE (Global Learning and Observations to Benefit the Environment) sponsored by organizations such as the National Aeronautics and Space Administration (NASA), the National Science Foundation (NSF), and the U.S.

Department of State. In addition, both physical and virtual graphing calculators are available to capture and analyze data.

Technology and Creative Thinking Skills Instruction

In learning mathematics students can demonstrate creativity through the ways they solve problems and the manner in which they represent geometric ideas or algebraic concepts. In general, creative thought is characterized by relative originality and flexibility (Gardner, 1993). The research on creativity indicates that there are certain kinds of classroom environments that tend to facilitate creative thinking. These classrooms are places where learners express curiosity, self-confidence, engagement, and imagination—characteristics critical to the sort of authentic learning experiences described earlier. Creative environments promote tolerance and freedom for students to pursue solutions to mathematical tasks (Prawat, 1991). The use of technology in mathematics learning can give students opportunities to develop ideas and skills in an environment that promotes creative thinking. Some familiar activities in geometry classrooms—tessellation and isometric drawings—are well suited to technology support and can provide students with contexts within which they can be creative.

"A tessellation is a tiling of a plane using one or more shapes in a repeated pattern without holes or gaps" (Van de Walle, 2006). Tessellations are common in art and architecture with M. C. Escher's works perhaps being some of the most famous; however, many artists create tessellations in print, fabric, and other materials. In grades K–5, students can use the drawing tools that are common features of most operating systems or specialized tools, such as the Patch Tool available on NCTM's Illuminations website (see Figure 16.2) to create patterns of shapes that can be repeated (a tessellation). The Shodor Foundation website contains a tessellation tool for students in higher grades. Starting from a rectangle, triangle, or hexagon, students can bend the lines or move the corners to modify the polygon, but always creating one that can be tessellated. A resulting tessellation might look like the design found in Figure 16.3. In addition, many software applications found in mathematics classrooms, such as the Geometer's Sketchpad and Cabri Geometry, as well as several freely available web-based tools, are also able to support the creation of tessellations.

To help students reflect on their work and address creative thinking in mathematics, ask them to explore which regular polygons tessellate and why. Encourage your students to determine a pattern among the polygons that they tessellate. Ask

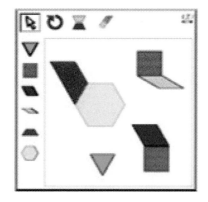

Figure 16.2
Tessellations developed with the Patch Tool from NCTM's Illuminations website.

Figure 16.3
Tessellations developed with tools from the Shodor Education Foundation.

the students to predict which regular polygons will and will not tessellate and why. Follow up by having the students develop their own concise definitions for a regular polygon tessellation.

Students can develop perspective, visual perception, and creative thinking using isometric dot paper or an isometric grid to draw solid shapes built with cubes. An electronic version of isometric paper and activities can be found on NCTM's Illuminations website (see Figure 16.4), while many of the software applications mentioned previously can be used to create isometric drawings. Your school may also have access to computer-aided design (CAD) software or software for creating three-dimensional drawings, such as Cabri 3D or Google SketchUp. There are online guides, lesson ideas, and user groups devoted to using Cabri 3D.

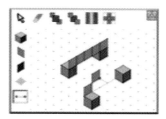

Figure 16.4
Isometric Drawing Tool from NCTM's Illuminations website.

These web-based spatial visualization and reasoning activities give students opportunities to develop geometric concepts and skills as well as creative approaches to the solutions of the given problems. These lessons also provide opportunities for students to reflect and reinforce creative thinking through discussions. For example, students may be asked to compare the differences between front-right-top representations and isometric drawings, or to describe when the two different types of drawings might be most useful.

There are also web-based resources that present novel problem-solving tasks that give students opportunities to use reasoning, representation, and communication skills. A WebQuest activity, such as the Computers as Mathematical Tools story presented earlier, is one example of a novel problem you can find or even create yourself. Public Broadcasting Service (PBS) develops a range of educational resources on a website called PBS Kids that includes unique material as well as material from popular PBS television shows. You can find interesting math games, such as Fun Brain: 13 Ways to Find One Half on this site. In this game-format activity, students use problem-solving skills to explore different fractional representations (e.g., one-half, one-fourth, etc.). Students are given a grid and asked to indicate which of the different shaded areas represent one-half or other fractions. An activity such as this could be used as an introduction to the fractional benchmarks.

Depending on the access to and familiarity with common software applications available to you and your students, you can use a range of technologies to support mathematical problem solving, both in your math classroom and in other content areas. Students can create timelines in history that are developed to scale. Students can import digital images, such as pictures of the Parthenon, into math software to explore architectural and mathematical principles, such as the use of the Golden Rectangle (Garofalo & Bell, 2003). And student work can be presented in class or beyond by incorporating math models, graphs, tables, and a variety of other technology-generated artifacts that are included in reports, presentations, or student web pages. There are certainly ample tools and methods for developing and demonstrating creativity in the mathematics classroom using technology.

Technology-based activities need to give students opportunities to practice creative thinking skills. In effective mathematics teaching, worthwhile mathematical tasks are used to introduce important mathematical ideas and to engage and challenge students intellectually. "Well-chosen tasks can pique students' curiosity and draw them into mathematics . . . . Regardless of the context, worthwhile tasks should be intriguing, with a level of challenge that invites speculation and hard work" (NCTM, 2000, p. 18). Well-designed tasks invite students to think mathematically, formulate and communicate new ideas, justify procedures, and defend the reasonableness of their answers. These activities require students to make decisions or judgments based on facts, information, logic, and/or rationalization. They require learners to justify all decisions and reasoning based on the mathematical ideas and skills being learned. Students' responses to those tasks can give teachers great insight into their thinking and mathematical knowledge.

In developing instruction that promotes creative thinking skills, you may turn to software that helps teach students new concepts as well as allowing them to practice them. This aligns with the concept of computer as tutor presented in Chapter 4. A range of websites is available to support student practice of mathematical concepts. Some of these include AAA Math, coolmath4kids.com, and Math Playground. There is also software that provides higher levels of tutoring, such as individualized instruction through branching, customized to student responses, practice opportunities, individualized feedback, and coaching. Cognitive Tutor, developed by researchers at Carnegie Mellon University, is one such intelligent tutoring system designed to help middle and high school students learn math.

Many computer applications make claims for individualized tutoring but provide little more than drill and practice, a routine use with little connection to improved student achievement. Although drill and practice can be helpful for building foundational skills, moving toward creative thinking skills requires more individualized learning, not just feedback that tells students the correct or incorrect status of responses or gives scores.

Some educational gaming experts (Scanlon, Buckingham, & Burn, 2005) also caution that some animated math games, while popular, often provide very little opportunity to develop higher-order math skills and focus more on achieving the objectives of the game. These gaming experts note that games can be motivational in three ways: 1) representational motivation in which the players are engaged with the setting, characters, and plot behind the game, 2) ludic motivation in which players are engaged with the challenges provided by the rules of the game, and 3) communal motivation which occurs through interacting with others in the gaming environment. Unfortunately, many math games do not capitalize on the opportunity to motivate students by engaging them in rule-based challenges or through engagement with other participants. Keep your critical eye open as you review math games and evaluate the potential they have to focus on math objectives and promote creative thinking skills development.

One of the ways technology can support the development and practice of creative thinking skills is by helping teachers and students represent complex mathematical concepts and understanding, in other words, using the computer as a mindtool. Complexity is relative, in relation to the developmental level of the students with whom you work. Addition and subtraction can be complex concepts to young students so you might use the online manipulative, the Broken Calculator, to demonstrate multiple methods for combining numbers and functions to generate the same result. Older students have a wealth of applications available to demonstrate their understanding of mathematical concepts and making their knowledge more transparent, many of which are presented in this chapter. Many of these tools make it easy for students to demonstrate the steps in their thinking and record the strategies they have used to address problem solving. Never has the phrase "show your work" been supported by so many options.

When learning challenging new ideas, it is helpful for many students to interact with different representations, such as diagrams, graphs, models, and animations (Cox & Brna cited in Alagic, 2003). Many students have difficulty connecting multiple representations of the same concept, such as connecting the verbal, graphical, numeric, and algebraic representations of mathematical functions. The use of graphic-based manipulatives that demonstrate the connection between data in a table to graphs and curves of best fit can be effective for helping students make these connections (Alagic, 2003). It is important, however, that you select technology tools that provide representations that allow your students to make the connections between their current knowledge and the new content and skills they are required to master. Tools that are too complex or that present information in a way in which the students have no background experience can actually negate the benefits of using multiple representations.

A range of technologies, some of them specific to math content and some not, also allow math teachers to use the computer as a support for conversation. Consider the conversations that could have taken place around the opening Story from

THE GAME PLAN

Identifying Web-Based Resources

Set Goals
Find online resources you can use for a range of activities in a mathematics classroom. You may need resources to help students develop mathematical thinking or to formulate and communicate new ideas.

Take Action
Review the web resources on the textbook's companion website. Conduct other searches on your own for resources of interest to you.

Monitor
How well do the resources meet stated goal(s)? Are there clearinghouse websites or sites that review online mathematics resources? Did you find resources you did not know existed that might be helpful to you in the mathematics classroom?

Evaluate and Extend
Select the best resources you have found and include a list of them in your portfolio. Share your list with other mathematics students to compile a master list that covers a range of grade levels and math-related content areas.

Practice in this chapter. Analyzing the trout populations in a nearby tourist attraction and its impact on local economy was communicated via common productivity tools, in this case, presentation software. The Computers as Mathematical Tools story used ubiquitous web tools and browsing software to inform the math-specific use of spreadsheets.

Specific communication tools, such as a class website with discussion software, can also support communication beyond the classroom. One math teacher who set up a "homework hotline" on her class website was surprised to find out how quickly her students took over helping each other with difficult homework problems. The digital "paper trail" of responses that both she and her students could review also helped her to understand who was having difficulties, what difficulties those were, and who may need some enrichment material to keep engaged in class. Students, too, quickly found out that the homework hotline was a tool for helping people develop the skills to answer the questions, not simply providing the answers, since all of their responses were available for everyone to view. The discussions held on the hotline went far beyond answering the question and allowed students to communicate about mathematics using the vocabulary of mathematics.

WEB LINK

View the textbook's companion website to review a list of the software, hardware, and Internet resources mentioned in this chapter as well as additional resources for the mathematics classroom.

Chapter Summary

There are many forms of technology available for use in the classroom besides computers, such as calculators, probeware, and handheld devices. They are reshaping the types of problem-solving tasks students can pursue. Settings for problems can be more realistic and address worthwhile mathematical content. Students can learn more mathematics more deeply using appropriate forms of technology. Students have access to many tools that professionals use to support math in the workplace. These include not only computational tools, but include a range of applications in the arts, science, and history that allow for the application of mathematics in these settings.

Keep in mind these three important ideas when planning to integrate technology in mathematics teaching (NCTM, 2000): First, *technology enhances mathematics learning*. With the technology resources available, students can examine examples or representational forms of selected concepts. Second, *teachers need to select appropriate technology uses to enhance their students' learning opportunities*. We need to remember that the use of technology does not guarantee instructional success; as with any teaching resource or tool, it depends on how well it is used. And third, *technology influences what mathematics is taught*. With technology, students can explore mathematical topics that otherwise would be either too cumbersome or impossible to address. For example, how can students understand the relationship between theoretical and experimental probability? With a computer simulation program, this idea is quickly and clearly communicated.

Implementation of the NCTM standards implies certain critical shifts in the environment of the mathematics classroom. Instruction and learning must move toward classrooms as community of learners where students can explore mathematical topics in depth and connect those topics to real-life situations. The use of technology plays an important and essential part in the success of meeting the intent of the standards.

YOUR PORTFOLIO

To demonstrate your understanding of creating learning experiences in the mathematics classroom that address the National Educational Technology Standards for Students, create a lesson plan for common activities in your math classroom using the GAME Plan template available on the textbook's companion website, or one of your choosing. Your lesson plan may address, but is not limited to, using image-manipulation program, a vector-based drawing application, page-layout software, web-design software, animation software, or a digital-video application.

1. Identify the national mathematics standards that relate to your lesson. Review the state-specific content standards you discovered earlier in the chapter and determine appropriate assessments you can incorporate in your lesson based on the achievement standards.

2. Research and select appropriate technologies that can support the activities in your lesson. Identify technology standards (NETS-S) addressed by your lesson. List all hardware and software required for the lesson and consider any preparation or prerequisite skills you may need to address before the students can complete the lesson.

3. If using the GAME Plan lesson template, include justifications for your technology application and reasons why you selected it in the section labeled Lesson Reflections and Notes. If you are using a different lesson plan template, include this information either on the template or in a separate file. Your justifications may relate to your skills or familiarity with the technology or the skills of your students, the match between the intended outcomes of the technology and your lesson, or even accessibility concerns.

References

Alagic, M. (2003). Technology in the mathematics classroom: Conceptual orientation. *Journal of Computers in Mathematics and Science Teaching*, 22(4), 381–399.

Becker, H. J. (2001). *How teachers are using computers in instruction?* Paper presented at the 2001 Meeting of the National Educational Research Association, Irvine, CA.

Clements, D. H. (1998). *From exercises and tasks to problems and projects: Unique contributions of computers to innovative mathematics education.* Retrieved November 5, 2005, from http://forum.swarthmore.edu/technology/papers/papers/clements/clements.html

Gardner, H. (1993). *Multiple intelligences: The theory in practice.* New York: Basic Books.

Garofalo, J., & Bell, R. (2003). Digital images in mathematics and science instruction: The golden rectangle. *School Science and Mathematics*, 103(7), 351–353.

Guerrero, S., Walker, N., & Dugdale, S. (2004). Technology in support of middle grade mathematics: What have we learned? *Journal of Computers in Mathematics and Science Teaching*, 23(1), 5–20.

Kahn, B. (1997). Web-based instruction (WBI): What is it and why is it? In B. H. Kahn (Ed.), *Web-based instruction* (pp. 5–23). Englewood Cliffs, NJ: Educational Technology Publications, Inc.

Mathematical Sciences Education Board, National Research Council. (1989). *Everybody counts: A report to the nations on the future of mathematics education.* Washington, DC: National Academy of Sciences Press.

Moyer, P., Bolyard, J., & Spikell, M. (February, 2003). What are virtual manipulatives? *Teaching Children Mathematics.* Retrieved September 5, 2007, from http://my.nctm.org/eresources/view_media.asp?article_id=1902

National Council of Teachers of Mathematics (NCTM). (2000). *Principles and standards for school mathematics.* Reston, VA: Author.

Prawat, R. S. (1991). The value of ideas: The immersion approach to the development of thinking. *Educational Researcher*, 100, 3–10.

Scanlon, M., Buckingham, D., & Burn, A. (2005). Motivating maths? Digital games and mathematical learning. *Technology, Pedagogy, and Education*, 14(1), 127–139.

Van de Walle, J. A. (2006). *Elementary and middle school mathematics: Teaching developmentally.* New York: Longman.

Wagner, E. D., & McCombs, B. L. (1995). Learner-centered psychological principles in practice: Designs for distance education. *Educational Technology*, 32(2), 32–35.

Wenglinsky, H. (1998). *Does it compute? The relationship between educational technology and student achievement in mathematics.* (ERIC No. ED 425 191). Princeton, NJ: Educational Testing Service.

For Further Reading

Dodge, B. (2002). *A WebQuest about WebQuests.* Retrieved December 15, 2005, from http://WebQuest.sdsu.edu/WebQuestWebQuest-hum.html

TECHNOLOGY INTEGRATION FOR MEANINGFUL CLASSROOM USE
Daily Lesson GAME Plan

Lesson Title: Data Analysis Integration

Related Lessons: Graphing Data, Alternate Data Visualizations

Grade Level: Elementary

Unit: Data Analysis

GOALS

Content Standards:
- formulate questions that can be addressed with data and collect, organize, and display relevant data to answer them
- select and use appropriate statistical methods to analyze data
- develop and evaluate inferences and predictions that are based on data
- understand and apply basic concepts of probability
- use the language of mathematics to express mathematical ideas precisely
- create and use representations to organize, record, and communicate mathematical ideas
- use representations to model and interpret physical, social, and mathematical phenomena

ISTE NETS-S

- ☐ 1. Creativity and innovation
- ☑ 2. Communication and collaboration
- ☐ 3. Research and information fluency
- ☑ 4. Critical thinking, problem solving, and decision making
- ☐ 5. Digital citizenship
- ☑ 6. Technology operations and concepts

Instructional Objective(s): Students will use a spreadsheet to collect, analyze, and interpret data.

ACTION

Before-Class Preparation: Reserve computer lab. Obtain small bags of varied colored candies and small cups for students, one bag for every student if there are enough computers or one bag for every pair of students.

During Class

Time	Instructional Activities	Materials and Resources
10 minutes	Students open the spreadsheet software, which defaults to creating a new spreadsheet. Students label the columns A through D with the headings: color, number, percentage, probability. Distribute bags of candy and cups while students are setting up their spreadsheet.	Spreadsheet software Bags of candies Cups
10–15 minutes	Students separate candies by color and enter the number of candies per color in the appropriate columns in their spreadsheet.	Spreadsheet software Bags of candies Cups
15–20 minutes	Students create functions to calculate percentages (e.g., what percentage of the candies in your bag is red?) and probability (e.g., what is the probability you would pick a green candy out of your bag?).	Spreadsheet software Bags of candies Cups
5–10 minutes	Students use the graphing function of the spreadsheet to create a pie graph displaying the total or percentage of different color candies in their bag. Students familiar with the spreadsheet software can label each section of the pie graph and may change the color of the sections to match the colors of the candies. Spend time discussing how graphs convey data quickly, perhaps drawing in examples from news or other sources.	Spreadsheet software Web browser (optional)
Blink of an eye	Eat the candy!	

Notes: If necessary, students should be paired prior to the lesson. Try pairing highly proficient spreadsheet users or more tech-savvy students with novice users.

MONITOR

Ongoing Assessment(s): Check for understanding throughout the lesson by having students check their understanding with their partners. In a lab, select examples from student computers to display to the class at each step.

Accommodations and Extensions: Have students consider other materials they may collect and organize, such as types of music, movies, and so forth, in their home. With or without a computer, they can calculate the probability that certain types of media will be played at their house. The limited use of English can allow English language learners to use both their native languages and English for column and graphing labels.

Back-up Plan: The activity can be completed on paper, but allow for more time, especially for creating functions—perhaps limiting functions to totals depending on the age/grade of students. Students can draw bar graphs rather than generate pie graphs using the software.

EVALUATION

Lesson Reflections and Notes: Students will likely be highly engaged in this lesson, perhaps simply by including the manipulatives (candy!). Many students have so much fun they don't realize they are learning how to use spreadsheets as well as to calculate percentages and probabilities, so take some time to emphasize these new skills after the feasting.

TECHNOLOGY INTEGRATION FOR MEANINGFUL CLASSROOM USE
Daily Lesson GAME Plan

Lesson Title: At Home in Your Future

Related Lessons: Compound Interest, Saving for Your Future

Grade Level: Middle Grades

Unit: Everyday Math

GOALS

Content Standards:
- compute fluently and make reasonable estimates
- use mathematical models to represent and understand quantitative relationships
- analyze change in various contexts
- formulate questions that can be addressed with data and collect, organize, and display relevant data to answer them
- develop and evaluate inferences and predictions that are based on data
- recognize and apply mathematics in contexts outside of mathematics

ISTE NETS-S

- ☐ 1. Creativity and innovation
- ☑ 2. Communication and collaboration
- ☑ 3. Research and information fluency
- ☑ 4. Critical thinking, problem solving, and decision making
- ☑ 5. Digital citizenship
- ☑ 6. Technology operations and concepts

Instructional Objective(s): Students compare housing costs in a location they choose and project an annual income necessary for purchasing or renting and maintaining the housing.

ACTION

Before-Class Preparation: Bookmark U.S. Census Bureau web pages, real estate websites, or search engines (such as Google Housing or Yahoo! Real Estate). Download pertinent reports, such as the most current *Income, Poverty, and Health Insurance Coverage in the United States*. It is helpful to set the purchasing options in advance, and some students may require a spreadsheet template for some of the activities.

During Class		
Time	**Instructional Activities**	**Materials and Resources**
15–20 minutes	Students are asked to pick a time in their future, such as 10–15 years from now, and make a few predictions or projections about what their life might be like, especially as it relates to housing needs. Where do they plan to live? Will they have a family, and if so, how big might it be? What type of employment do they expect to have? What level of education does that require? Students write a brief scenario (one paragraph) or fill out a checklist on a worksheet of these and similar items. Using this information, students identify the type of housing they might need in a location that they can research and compare. For example, a student who plans to be married with 2 children might select a house with 3 bedrooms and 2 bathrooms. If necessary, have students consider the number of bedrooms and bathrooms at their home as a point of comparison.	Paper or electronic worksheet Word-processing software
15–20 minutes	Students conduct research on real estate websites or real estate search engines. Students should identify at least 5 different houses to compare, and should record data such as cost, square footage, number of bedrooms and bathrooms, and any other desired information. A spreadsheet is optimal, but this activity can be completed with a calculator and a print-based handout with a table or graphic organizer to help organize the data. Students should include the sources for their information. Using this information, students should determine the average housing price for their 5 choices.	Computer with Internet access Spreadsheet software or calculator
30 minutes	Students should then determine possible options for purchasing housing at the average price they have identified based on the length of the mortgage, lending rates, and down payments. They can either research information such as mortgage rates online or you can provide them with specific data for possible scenarios. For example, students can calculate total expenditures and monthly payments when purchasing the home over 15- or 30-year mortgages at rates of 5, 7, or 9 percent with down payments of 0-, 10-, and 30 percent of the purchase price. If using a spreadsheet, graph the results of the different scenarios for comparison.	Spreadsheet software or calculator
15–20 minutes	Students should calculate an approximate income necessary for purchasing and maintaining the home for the different scenarios using a budget and the commonly recommended figure of 30 percent of their income for housing.	Spreadsheet software or calculator
20–30 minutes	Students then use data from the U.S. Census Bureau, such as the Annual Social and Economic (ASEC) Supplement from the Current Population Survey to determine mean earnings for different levels of educational attainment. They may also find the most current report on *Income, Poverty, and Health Insurance Coverage in the United States* helpful, as it provides data on factors that influence income, such as gender, type of household, age bracket, region, and metropolitan status.	Computer with Internet access
30 minutes to develop report; 1 or 2 class periods for report out and discussion	Students prepare a report or presentation with their findings and the impact the data may have on different scenarios. They should report on the type of housing they've chosen and its cost, the amount of their projected down payment, and the type of mortgages they have selected, as well as reasons for the selection. They should report the annual income they have projected with a 30 percent housing budget. The data and different scenarios will provide ample opportunities for individual and whole-class discussion. For example, students may want to consider how location impacts housing price for similar size houses. They may want to explore differences in reported incomes, such as men versus women, and how these impact decisions they've made. Certainly, they should report on the level of education they project needing—based on given income data—to purchase their housing selection and how this aligns with their career plans.	Word-processing or presentation software Graphs and data tables exported from spreadsheet software

Notes: This activity can also be completed in pairs or small groups.

MONITOR

Ongoing Assessment(s): Student work is assessed at different stages of the project. Students must accurately create the spreadsheet (or other documentation), calculations, and graphs. Depending on reporting preferences (individual written report vs. class presentation), a checklist or rubric will be used to assess the final report.

Accommodations and Extensions: The complexity of the lesson can be reduced or increased to match students at different grade or technology proficiency levels. The full lesson is complex and suitable to students who work well independently, often require challenging enrichment activities, and are proficient with the technology. The lesson can be extended further by having students develop scale drawings of model housing units, such as their own, using CAD software or geometry software, such as Geometer's Sketchpad, and calculating areas to form as a basis for comparison.

Standardizing options (such as identifying one housing type of 3 bedrooms and 2 bathrooms) and limiting the number of parameters to investigate (such as one mortgage rate over 30 years) will reduce the complexity of the lesson and allow students to focus on the math concepts. Students just becoming familiar with spreadsheet software can simply conduct the research on 5 housing choices, record their data, calculate the average price, and a classroom composite graph can be made. Student groups can also be randomly assigned to different scenarios so that the class can explore a range of options at the conclusion of the lesson.

Back-up Plan: Data tables and reports from the U.S. Census Bureau can be downloaded beforehand and stored in a project folder or printed out. Real estate prices can also be obtained from newspapers or paper-based real estate guides obtained from real estate agencies or many retail locations.

EVALUATION

Lesson Reflections and Notes: Emphasis should be placed on using math skills to make informed decisions. While students may enjoy the real estate research, they should be encouraged to consider the complete activity and how their decisions at each stage are related.

TECHNOLOGY INTEGRATION FOR MEANINGFUL CLASSROOM USE
Daily Lesson GAME Plan

Lesson Title: Function Reflections

Related Lessons: Quadratic Functions, Geometric Transformations

Grade Level: High School

Unit: Geometric Transformations

GOALS

Content Standards:
- understand patterns, relations, and functions
- represent and analyze mathematical situations and structures using algebraic symbols
- specify locations and describe spatial relationships using coordinate geometry and other representational systems

ISTE NETS-S

- ☐ 1. Creativity and innovation
- ☑ 2. Communication and collaboration
- ☐ 3. Research and information fluency
- ☑ 4. Critical thinking, problem solving, and decision making
- ☐ 5. Digital citizenship
- ☑ 6. Technology operations and concepts

Instructional Objective(s): Using Geometer's Sketchpad (GSP), students will investigate the reflections of given quadratic functions on a coordinate system.

ACTION

Before-Class Preparation: Reserve computer lab. If the students are not familiar with the Geometer's Sketchpad, have 1–2 sessions with them to help them use the software.

	During Class	
Time	Instructional Activities	Materials and Resources
15 minutes	Have students plot a quadratic function such as $f(x) = x^2 - 3x + 7$. Using the **Graph New Function** command, create $g(x) = -f(x)$ and then $h(x) = f(-x)$.	GSP Graph paper to sketch the functions shown on the computer screen.
10–15 minutes	Plot the original function and the two new functions. Ask students if they know which is which. Have students write algebraic descriptions of the transformations.	GSP Graph paper to sketch the functions shown on the computer screen.
15–20 minutes	Further exploration: have students graph a new quadratic equation and graph both $g(x) = -f(x)$ and $h(x) = f(-x)$. Have the students write their conjectures concerning the relationship between the coordinates of a given point in the pre-image to the corresponding point of the image.	GSP Graph paper to sketch the functions shown on the computer screen.

Notes: Adapted from *Exploring Algebra 2 with the Geometer's Sketchpad*, Curriculum Press (2007).
Students should have some proficiency using the Geometer's Sketchpad. If you do not have access to the GSP, you may use an online public-domain version—GeoGebra: http://www.geogebra.org/cms/index.php?option=com_content&task=blogcategory&id=71&Itemid=55

MONITOR

Ongoing Assessment(s): Check for understanding throughout the lesson by having students check the graphs they have sketched from the screen results. In a lab, select examples from student computers to display to the class at each step.

Accommodations and Extensions: Allow English language learners to use both their native languages and English for column and graphing labels. Have students respond to questions such as: Do you think g(x) will match plot A or plot B? Which plot will h(x) match? Explain why you paired them up the way you did.

Back-up Plan: The activity can be competed on paper, but allow for more time. Students can sketch the functions on graph paper. For students who have not worked with the GSP, include a pre-lesson on the use of the tool. This lesson can also be carried out on a graphing calculator.

EVALUATION

Lesson Reflections and Notes: You need to emphasize questions that help students focus on explanations and conjectures, for example, explaining how points on the function pre-image are mapped onto the image.

ISTE Standards addressed in this chapter

This chapter provides content-specific suggestions and strategies for addressing both ISTE's National Educational Technology Standards for Students (NETS-S) and the National Science Education Standards. This chapter also builds on the NETS-T concepts and skills presented earlier, with a special emphasis on skills related to Standard 1 "Facilitate and inspire student learning and creativity." Following an overview of the National Science Education Standards and how you can address the NETS-S in the science classroom, this chapter outlines techniques, tools, and methods for developing authentic learning experiences that advance student creativity and innovation in the science classroom.

Integrating Technology in the Science Classroom

Brian Giza, Ph.D. and Judy Reinhartz, Ph.D.

Preservice and in-service science teachers are constantly in search of innovative ways to engage their students. In science, the emphasis on hands-on learning often causes teachers to overlook the use of technology in the inquiry process. However, technology can serve many important purposes that supplement inquiry in the science classroom. For example, technology can give learners otherwise unobtainable access to locations and insight into science processes. Technologies such as digital video, photography, and live interactive clips can transport the viewer to Arctic regions, to other planetary surfaces, to the highest mountains or the depths of the ocean, or into previously unexplored microscopic worlds. When students are given nearly immediate access to rain forests, or the cornfields of the Midwest, the hustle and bustle of a city, the beauty

Outcomes

In this chapter, you will

- Identify science standards and explain how technology can support them.
- Discuss how the National Educational Technology Standards for Students can be addressed in a science classroom.
- Demonstrate how authentic learning principles can be addressed using technology in a science classroom.
- Explain how technology can increase learning and facilitate creative thinking in a science classroom.

of star-forming regions, or other exotic locations, the challenge is not just to show the learner these once-unfamiliar locations, but to help them ask and answer questions about them. It is not sufficient to merely use technology to give students access to information, but more important to help them understand how what they are viewing fits into their world, to provide them with context, and to stimulate their interest for continuing their learning. Technology can mediate an understanding of our place in our world and the cosmos, bringing the universe alive with sound and images for all to experience and enjoy.

In the first decade of the 21st century, the question becomes, how do science teachers use technology in their classrooms to promote learning for all their students? One part of the answer lies in teachers' abilities to *communicate* with their students, parents, administrators, and community members using technology, print, and electronic media. Another part of the answer is to use technology to *acquire* and *interpret data*. Data acquisition is a common task in science, and there are many kinds of tools that are appropriate for this task. Another answer is to use technology for *organizing* and *analyzing data*. Finally, there are tools that help in *making decisions* about data and communicating or describing these decisions. Or to state it even more simply, technology is what we use to obtain, organize, understand, and communicate data about our world. That is why technology is so important to science, the discipline that focuses on exploring and understanding our world. This chapter begins with a general discussion of terms, relating them to both the National Science Education Standards (NSES) and the ISTE NETS-S. Some specific examples provide prospective teachers with opportunities to reflect upon standards-based instructional practices.

Technology and Content Standards

Science and technology learning are deeply linked. Rodger Bybee (2003), a longtime leader in science education, stated that science teachers have an obligation to provide all students with opportunities to develop an understanding of science and technology. The American Association for the Advancement of Science (AAAS) has promoted a problem-based and student-centered approach to using technology in science. As stated in Chapter 3 of the Benchmarks for Science Literacy online, students

> must use different tools to do different things in science and to solve practical problems. Through design and technology projects, students can engage in problem-solving related to a wide range of real-world contexts. By undertaking design projects, students can encounter technology issues even though they cannot define technology. (AAAS, 1993, n.p.)

You may already know that National Science Education Standards include more than just science content standards, and provide standards for teaching, professional

STORIES FROM PRACTICE

Technology in the Science Lab

Classification is a fundamental concept in science, and technology can be used to support these inquiry-based skills. I've found, however, that it is important to carefully structure and manage science labs, especially when technology is thrown into the mix. In one of my labs, my students study insect images and use image-editing software to create a virtual insect collection based on sets of characteristics decided upon during small-group discussions. I've found that small groups (three to four) are better than large groups for the kinds of social interactions that translate into effective learning outcomes for my students. In these small groups, my students take on the following roles:

- **Designers:** Designers use a graphics or image-editing program to design insect "tools" such as mouth- or leg-parts that fulfill a task such as cutting,

sucking, or grasping. Depending on their skills, students may either draw digital images or find images online or in a CD-ROM image library that they can then manipulate.

- **Taxonomists:** Taxonomists copy, paste, and assemble the digital images of the insect tools into groups according to common characteristics, whether by type of mouth parts, size, color, or number of wings. This can be done with drawing or image-editing software or even with drawing tools in common word-processing software.

- **Ecologists:** Ecologists develop short descriptions of the niches that the insects might occupy, based upon the adaptations available in each organism's tools. Ecologists conduct research using print, online, and other information sources, and organize all

of the material found and created by the group to produce reports to share with the rest of the class.

Together, each group develops a rich ecology report that they present to the class —part of an instructional unit on diversity in accordance with NSES Grades 5–8 Content Standard C. The goal is to develop a scheme for classification, which provides an understanding of how scientists created the current taxonomical scheme. This activity empowers my students to ask and answer questions, while I provide guidance during the lesson. It's also important to let every student take on each role. I can do this by using these roles in a series of activities across different topics. This not only allows all students to better understand the science content standards but to work on their technology skills.

development, and assessment, as well as standards for science education programs and systems. The Science Teaching Standards are consistent across grade levels, and have much that is philosophically in common with the ISTE NETS for Teachers and for Students. The National Science Education Standards for students vary in detail by grade and science area. There are eight categories of content standards that are presented across three grade-level groupings: kindergarten through fourth grade, fifth through eighth grade, and ninth through twelfth grade (see Table 17.1). You'll note that the first two science content standards cross all grade levels while the remaining content standards are presented in grade-level groupings. These groupings are done because, according to the National Committee on Science Education Standards and Assessment—a committee with representatives from major national science and education organizations that developed the standards—"major conceptual and procedural schemes need to be developed over an entire education, and the unifying concepts and processes transcend disciplinary boundaries" (1996, p. 104).

The major strands in the National Standards for Grades K–12 are presented in Table 17.1 on page 390. Table 17.2 on page 391 presents selected science-learning activities that illustrate the NETS-S. The lesson plans at the end of this chapter provide specific examples of how you can design learning experiences that meet both content area and technology standards.

WEB LINK

For further detailed examples of the alignment of the NETS-S to the National Science Education Standards, visit the textbook's companion website.

Authentic Learning Strategies Incorporating Technology

Simply memorizing facts is not the goal of science teaching. Teachers need to prepare lessons and use technology tools in ways that promote a deep understanding of science that allows students to generalize their knowledge to unique situations. Each student should be prepared to ask and find solutions to questions, not just regurgitate answers. The National Science Education Standards were developed in light of a vision for change—a change in emphasis from instruction that relies on lower

Table 17.1	National Science Education Standards		

Unifying Concepts and Processes in Science
Content Standards Grades K–12

- Systems, order, and organization
- Evidence, models, and explanation
- Change, constancy, and measurement
- Evolution and equilibrium
- Form and function

Science as Inquiry
Content Standards Grades K–12

- Understanding of scientific concepts
- An appreciation of "how we know" what we know in science
- Understanding of the nature of science
- Skills necessary to become independent inquirers about the natural world
- The dispositions to use the skills, abilities, and attitudes associated with science

Physical Science

Content Standards Grades K–4	Content Standards Grades 5–8	Content Standards Grades 9–12
• Properties of objects and materials • Position and motion of objects • Light, heat, electricity, and magnetism	• Properties and changes of properties of matter • Motions and forces • Transfer of energy	• Structure of atoms • Structure and properties of matter • Chemical reactions • Motions and forces • Conservation of energy and increase in disorder • Interactions of energy and matter

Life Science

Content Standards Grades K–4	Content Standards Grades 5–8	Content Standards Grades 9–12
• Characteristics of organisms • Life cycles of organisms • Organisms and environments	• Structure and function in living systems • Reproduction and heredity • Regulation and behavior • Populations and ecosystems • Diversity and adaptations of organisms	• The cell • Molecular basis of heredity • Biological evolution • Interdependence of organisms • Matter, energy, and organization in living systems • Behavior of organisms

Earth and Space Science

Content Standards Grades K–4	Content Standards Grades 5–8	Content Standards Grades 9–12
• Properties of earth materials • Objects in the sky • Changes in earth and sky	• Structure of the earth system • Earth's history • Earth in the solar system	• Energy in the earth system • Geochemical cycles • Origin and evolution of the earth system • Origin and evolution of the universe

Science and Technology

Content Standards Grades K–4	Content Standards Grades 5–8	Content Standards Grades 9–12
• Abilities to distinguish between natural objects and objects made by humans • Abilities of technological design • Understanding about science and technology	• Abilities of technological design • Understanding about science and technology	• Abilities of technological design • Understanding about science and technology

Science in Personal and Social Perspectives

Content Standards Grades K–4	Content Standards Grades 5–8	Content Standards Grades 9–12
• Personal health • Characteristics and changes in populations • Types of resources	• Personal health • Populations, resources, and environments	• Personal and community health • Population growth • Natural resources

Science in Personal and Social Perspectives

Content Standards Grades K–4	Content Standards Grades 5–8	Content Standards Grades 9–12
• Changes in environments • Science and technology in local challenges	• Natural hazards • Risks and benefits • Science and technology in society	• Environmental quality • Natural and human-induced hazards • Science and technology in local, national, and global challenges

History and Nature of Science

Content Standards Grades K–4	Content Standards Grades 5–8	Content Standards Grades 9–12
• Science as a human endeavor	• Science as a human endeavor • Nature of science • History of science	• Science as a human endeavor • Nature of scientific knowledge • Historical perspectives

Source: National Science Education Standards, 1996, Tables 6.2, 6.3, 6.4, 6.5, 6.6, and 6.7. National Academies Press. Reprinted with permission from the National Academy of Sciences. Courtesy of the National Academies Press, Washington DC.

Table 17.2 NETS-S in the Science Classroom

Creativity and Innovation

Students go online to gather data from websites such as the Globe project (www.globe.gov). They analyze and present the data visually using spreadsheet programs, making predictions of weather trends for the upcoming year in various locations. They compare data collected from the website with data they have collected locally to compare and contrast trends using charts, graphics, and text and post their final projects to a class website.

Communication and Collaboration

Students conduct experiments using simulation software or visit distant locations such as a desert, arctic region, or rainforest, using virtual reality simulations. Students test hypotheses and use the simulation software to determine outcomes based on the manipulation of variables, such as limiting natural resources such as light, heat, or water. Working in teams, students communicate their results as an audio book that includes their own voices narrating the results of their explorations. They make the audio book available for download in digital audio or enhanced audio (image plus audio/video) formats for viewing on portable devices, social spaces, or local computers.

Research and Information Fluency

Students use peripherals such as light gates or probeware to collect real-time data during experiments that can be graphed using graphing calculators—either handheld or software-based emulations—to solve problems or answer questions related to energy and motion.

Critical Thinking, Problem Solving, and Decision Making

Students use resources and problems at NASA educational challenge/contest websites to research, develop, collect data upon, and test their solutions to problems/challenges such as building a propeller, constructing and collecting data on a model passive solar dwelling, building a robot, and so forth.

Digital Citizenship

Students explore their roles in the world as "digital citizens" by working on year-long group and individual projects that monitor and submit data online to projects such as the Monarch watch, bird surveys, air and water resource monitoring, and so forth. A number of links to activities of this kind may be found at pathfinderscience.net. Emphasis should also include safe and appropriate use of technological resources.

Technology Operations and Concepts

Students build a solubility tester using simple (and common) electrical components (9 volt battery, LED, capacitor, wires). They use their instruments in laboratory activities to explore water pollution via various common effluents (salt, alcohols, oils). They use a spreadsheet application to organize and analyze their data.

levels of cognition that focus on factual recall to one that is based on inquiry within the context of other disciplines that relate science to personal, social, and historical perspectives.

This emphasis on inquiry within contexts external to science aligns well with authentic instruction. A range of hardware and software tools are available to

THE GAME PLAN

Content Standards

Set Goals

Research the science standards for a state where you plan to seek a teaching position and create an action plan to ensure that you will have the knowledge and skills necessary to help your students achieve those standards. Identify the concepts, knowledge, and skills you will need to ensure that you are prepared to help your students meet the science standards in your state.

Monitor

Did you find the information you needed? What steps did you take to get the information requested in the GAME Plan for content standards? How did you navigate the website for the state department of education? Do you need to contact the department of education for more information about where to find the science standards or the technology standards for teachers?

Take Action

Explore the department of education website in the state where you plan to seek a position. Review the K–12 science standards in that state and compare them to the state's technology standards. Identify those standards that specifically relate to applying technology in science. Develop a plan for how to meet the standards for teachers in the context of science.

Evaluate and Extend

Discuss in class the action plan you developed for meeting the technology standards for the instructional staff. Compare your plan to others' plans. Note the strengths and weaknesses of the various plans. Strengthen your plan by incorporating ideas you have heard in class.

---

support this type of science instruction that incorporates authentic instruction and encourages active, experiential learning. Students should become creators of information, not mere users of technology (Burns, 2005/2006). This is the rationale behind inquiry-based approaches. Developing science skill sets with the help of technology motivates students to: 1) pose questions, 2) select methods for answering these questions, and 3) implement approaches for testing the accuracy of these answers. In these ways, inquiry-based learning supports facets of authentic instruction, such as having students obtain information, formulate ideas, and create products.

Modern science education strategies include web-based resources. Such approaches send students on a quest for science information on the World Wide Web, and with the advent of Web 2.0 collaborative tools, students have the ability to, for example, share a search while participating in online collaborative work groups (Alexander, 2006). The goal of finding information is as old as education itself—what has changed is where students go to get this information. Fifty years ago, students reached for encyclopedias and other print materials; today they go online, often to the Wikipedia, the fastest growing repository of information on the web and one to which users have the ability to contribute—with all the attendant concerns about information validity.

Science classrooms are also an appropriate venue for a popular learning design for the web called a WebQuest (Dodge, 1997; March, 1998), which is a guided inquiry activity using web-based resources (see Chapter 4). There are several ways to use WebQuests. As the teacher, you can make them or obtain them for use in your classroom. The other is to have your students build them as part of an inquiry lesson. Both forms of WebQuests are useful, with the teacher-created version being most useful when a teacher has limited time, and desires to keep the learners on task. Still, when students construct their own WebQuests and build them from prior knowledge, they integrate what they learn in a meaningful way. The knowledge that they acquire stays with them longer and is more generalizable to new contexts. This is a fundamental tenet of authentic learning and is well integrated into the science-learning literature (Wheatley, 1991).

THE GAME PLAN

Identifying Web-Based Resources

Set Goals

Find online resources you can use for a range of activities in a science classroom. You may need resources to help students develop skills related to scientific inquiry or science reference materials. (*Clue:* Review the NSE Standards for ideas for science topics.)

Take Action

Review the web resources on the textbook's companion website. Conduct other searches on your own for resources of interest to you.

Monitor

How well do the resources meet stated goal(s)? Are there clearinghouse websites or sites that review online science resources? Did you find resources you did not know existed that might be helpful to you in the science classroom?

Evaluate and Extend

Select the best resources you have found and include a list of them in your portfolio. Share your list with other science students to compile a master list that covers a range of grade levels and science content areas.

Tools can be used in more than one way, of course. Digital cameras, data collection probes, and digital microscopes are usually considered different forms of technology (cameras as productivity tools, and digital microscopes and probes as technology research tools), yet a teacher may actually consider all three as forms of data collection and analysis tools. For example, when these tools are used for observing and acquiring data, they are simply acquiring data that can be stored and analyzed later. When a digital camera is used to observe metamorphosis by taking a sequence of images over time (see Figure 17.1), it has much in common with a pH probe—both are being used to acquire incremental data during a science laboratory exercise.

2/28/2002 7:44:28 AM Brassica Chrysalis

2/28/2002 7:48:30 AM Brassica Chrysalis

2/28/2002 7:50:31 AM Brassica Chrysalis

2/28/2002 7:53:33 AM Brassica Chrysalis

Figure 17.1
Webcam images of a butterfly emerging from a chrysalis.
Source: Photos © 2004 by B. H. Giza.

The photographs in Figure 17.1 were generated in a science laboratory activity at the fourth-grade level in which the teacher was helping students study metamorphosis by way of a webcam, in accordance with NSES K–4 Content Standard C, *Life cycles of organisms*. In the activity, a *brassica* butterfly chrysalis is placed in a Petri dish in front of an inexpensive computer-connected webcam. Using software that is often provided with many cameras, images are automatically recorded at regular 30-minute intervals over a period of a week. As the chrysalis nears final development, the image intervals are shortened to every few minutes. This kind of remote monitoring can be very useful since butterflies rarely exit from a chrysalis during class time.

With an automated image acquisition tool of this kind, students see the changes that take place, providing them with a broader overview of the entire process, including the movement of the chrysalis prior to its opening. Time delay/shifting imaging is useful in many other biological activities, such as studying plant taxis. A webcam can easily be set up to capture and document plant taxis responses, such as phototaxis or chemotaxis (a **taxis** is a response that a plant makes to different chemical or light stimuli). Examples might be to set up a webcam to photograph two plants in a box, one in strong light, one in weak light, or to study the germination of seeds. These initial activities may be easily adapted to more sophisticated experiments at the secondary school level, with the camera's images being used to compare data using spreadsheets or statistical methods (e.g., what is the average area of leaves produced per watt of light). Modern spreadsheets even have the ability to resize and place colored backgrounds on cells, providing patterns that afford visual reinforcement directly in the input page in addition to the charting module provided with the spreadsheet.

A motion detector is another tool that can be applied in useful and often creative ways (see Figure 17.2). Almost every instrument manufacturer has its version—

Figure 17.2
Motion detectors allow students to record data.
Source: http://www.vernier.com/innovate/innovativeuse86.html

whether it is Vernier, Pasco, Cambridge Physics Outlet, or another vendor—and each provides the user with a few common features, such as the ability to measure motion and record the data about that motion in a computer software interface. Simple (and common) exercises such as matching the shape of a curve in a graph (which is done by moving toward or away from the detector at appropriate speeds and accelerations) can be enhanced by a challenge such as "motion detector etch-a-sketch" in which the curves generated by student motions are imported into an animation program and superimposed to generate an image. Student teams must try to match an agreed-upon drawing and inculcate a deeper understanding of motion, acceleration, and graphical representations of physical phenomena.

Science educators should also seriously think about the number of ways in which spreadsheets can be used. These tools for organizing and calculating information to solve "what if" scenarios are perfect for inquiry science. A good example of a science spreadsheet lesson can be found by searching on the term "spreadsheet" at the Science NetLinks website. Among the lesson plans returned will be one for middle school science from NASA on the use of spreadsheets for calculating your weight on various planets (Johnson-Palmer & Terry, 1996). This simple, application-level activity is a good introduction to ways of entering and evaluating data. Spreadsheets are useful in activities as diverse as classic science or science-fair experiments in which lighting or fertilizer conditions are plotted against plant growth, or for making sophisticated ballistics predictions about paths and distances of objects thrown by catapults/trebuchets. Modern spreadsheets include the ability to conduct t-tests or more sophisticated statistical functions, and free, open-source versions (e.g., CALC from OpenOffice.org) have many of the features needed in today's science classroom.

Technology and Creative Thinking Skills Instruction

It is not uncommon to see technology promoted as a path to improving the rigor of instruction. Fortunately, technology is well suited to supporting problem-based and inquiry learning approaches that are authentic and well integrated with both the ISTE and National Science Education Standards. But using technology in the classroom is more than showing a video, conducting an online research, and/or word processing. It means having an understanding of the theoretical underpinnings of instruction and how technology can be most effectively used to develop creative and critical thinking skills. The key concept to keep in mind is that technology tools can be adapted to support learning in a number of ways. An educator can envision these new ways of using tools by considering: 1) the science-learning task and 2) how a technology tool might be adapted to that task.

One approach in determining technology tool use in the classroom is to consider how the tool will be used both in terms of its task and in terms of the cognitive level of the instructional outcome. Borich (2006) indicated that questioning strategies and learning activities can be classified as either Type 1 or Type 2 outcomes. Type 1 outcomes include the learning of facts, rules, and action sequences. Type 2 outcomes include the learning of concepts, patterns, and abstractions. The same kind of grouping can be used for the use of technology in the classroom by considering whether it is being used to learn or reinforce facts, rules, or learning sequences (Type 1), or to facilitate the learning of concepts, patterns, or abstractions (Type 2). Often tool use may begin at a Type 1 level and proceed in later activities to a Type 2 level.

Consider the use of podcasting in instruction. Providing Internet-based lessons in rich media format for students to use for a review, for homebound students to access basic information, or for parents to use while helping their children with homework is a technology-enhanced form of direct instruction (Type 1 use). Providing an opportunity for students to interact and integrate audio or video materials in a cooperative and interactive online environment (Type 2 activity) is much more powerful. Integrating technology into science education strategies such as inquiry learning or problem-based learning is one way to build toward Type 2 outcomes.

For science learning to be more meaningful, the technology tool is best used when it supports Type 2 learning outcomes, which permits the user to generalize and use knowledge creatively. The instructional approach commonly referred to as "direct instruction" is often used to reach Type 1 outcomes. Activities at the Type 2 level are most effectively taught using authentic learning experiences that develop a deeper understanding of a concept through problem solving. Strategies that promote reasoning, creative, and evaluative skills become an essential component of the "hands-on, minds-on" science instruction.

But what does technology mean in the context of science education? How does a teacher help students understand that technology is the use of tools to extend and support human abilities? One way is to encourage students to view and use tools in new ways, for example, asking them to design and build a microscope or a balance prior to using one (Giza, 2007). This hands-on approach to engaging students in exploring both science and the tools of science has been updated in innovative ways. For example, locations abound on the web that provide science educators with technology—"physlets," interactive Java, or Flash-based physics simulations that may be used to explore concepts such as optics. The web locations where these physlets are found may vary over time, but they can often be located by entering terms such as "optics physlet" or "momentum physlet" into an Internet search engine.

Technology is applied science, and when technology is used in the teaching of science it can be of great benefit, such as when using it to bring science to a learner's cultural context. For example, your students may be required to study sound. Recording sound is not difficult today, with portable recording built into many personal devices (phones, handheld devices, MP3, or other digital audio recorders). It is also easy to import sound from recording devices into computers. There are a number of software programs that can be used to analyze sound, ranging from free, open-source tools like Audacity to sophisticated laboratory-based products like Vernier's Logger Pro. Software programs like WAVEPORT are ideal for the science classroom (see Figure 17.3).

You may want to add a cultural context to a lesson on sound or waves, by integrating it into an activity in accordance with NSES Grade 5–8 Content Standard A that relates to understanding and performing scientific inquiry (NRC, 1996, p. 143). Folktales associated with "spirits of the wind" abound in many cultures including the *Banshee* of Irish legend, or *La Llorona* of Latin culture. You can begin by asking students to record the sounds of the wind in various locations and continue by exploring how those sounds are generated, as well as using computer software to describe the sounds in terms of timbre, pitch, and amplitude. Then, you can add an additional activity in which students conduct an Internet search about sound as an element of a fable. A leading question might be, "Why are folktales often associating sounds of howling and crying with forests or wooded river beds?" (You might want to note that resonance is a significant factor in the sound produced as air passes over an open tube, whether it is a woodwind musical instrument or a hollow log.) In this kind of enriched multimedia research exercise, science is contextualized in a way that reinforces its content. Integrating science and social contexts can be of particular value to recent immigrants or English language learners (ELLs) (Giza, 2005; Hansen, 2006). As multimedia graphics and animation tools become more accessible and easier to use, their classroom application has naturally become a potential source of new instructional activities and curricula (Latham, 2005; Mayer & Moreno, 2002; Sperling et al., 2003).

We would like to remind you that one possible misuse of technology is to reinforce one particular instructional modality, instead of differentiating learning to meet the needs and learning styles of diverse students (see Chapter 6). Using a variety of instructional strategies provides a richer set of experiences for all students. By rethinking how technology can be applied, and constantly striving to use it to build a

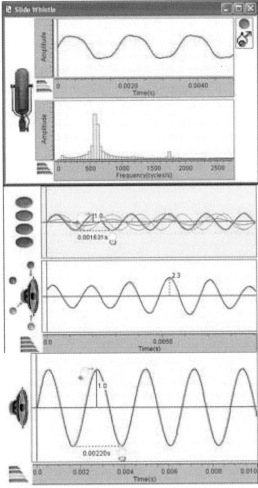

Figure 17.3
Tools such as WAVEPORT software make sound capture and editing easy in the science classroom.
Source: Courtesy of PASCO scientific WAVEPORT® Software. http://www.pasco.com/featured-products/waveport/index.cfm

WEB LINK

View the textbook's companion website to review a list of the software, hardware, and Internet resources mentioned in this chapter as well as additional resources for the science classroom.

deeper understanding, educators will have a wider range of tools for planning and delivering instruction to reach the largest number of diverse learners. For Tomlinson and McTighe (2006), technology is one way to help educators "work smart." The use of technology can bring together instructional design and strategies in creative ways that work to promote the development of student science knowledge, understanding, and skills.

Nevertheless, there is also a danger in going too far, by losing sight of the science learning in the rush to use the latest tool. Burns (2005/2006) summed up the situation by asserting that "schools have conflated technology use with instructional quality" (p. 49). It is important to remember that technology can facilitate the asking and answering of questions, and those questions should have an appropriate instructional meaning and context. Emphasis on the learning outcome and not upon the tool or process used to get there should always be paramount.

Chapter Summary

The future of technology in science education is bright—as long as tools are used appropriately. As the World Wide Web continues to grow and provide ever-increasing instructional resources, specific web-based strategies, such as WebQuests, can be used to inspire critical thinking and contextualize learning in ways that are powerful supports to science-learning experiences. Web-based collaborative tools, such as wikis, can be used to support cooperative learning among science students, or they might be equally useful in facilitating lesson study by teachers within a school or a district. The knack for using technology tools successfully in science classrooms is to focus on the content to be taught, the science inquiry processes, and mastery of the technology delivery system. For tomorrow's science teachers, it is essential to become accomplished at infusing technology into the science curriculum. For technology use to expand into science classrooms at all levels, it is essential that you are aware of the specific digital tools and resources that are available and how to implement them.

YOUR PORTFOLIO

To demonstrate your understanding of creating learning experiences in the science classroom that address the National Educational Technology Standards for Students, create a lesson plan for common activities in your science classroom using the GAME Plan template available on the textbook's companion website, or one of your choosing. If you work with younger students, you may want to address teaching scientific inquiry through the active construction of ideas and explanations. If you work with older students, you may want to address science from a personal or social perspective, such as developing an understanding of population growth, environmental quality, or natural and human-induced hazards.

1. Identify the national science content standards that relate to the science lesson you have selected. You may also want to review the assessments described in the National Science Education Standards document to determine appropriate assessments you can incorporate in your lesson.
2. Research and select appropriate technologies that can support science activities in your lesson. Identify technology standards (NETS-S) addressed by your lesson. List all hardware and software required for the lesson, and consider any preparation or prerequisite skills that you may need to address before presenting the lesson to students.

3. If using the GAME Plan lesson template, include justifications for your technology application and reasons why you selected it in the section labeled Lesson Reflections and Notes. If you are using a different lesson plan template, include this information either on the template or in a separate file. Your justifications may relate to your skills or familiarity with the technology or the skills of your students, the match between the intended outcomes of the technology and your lesson, or even accessibility concerns.

References

Alexander, B. (2006). Web 2.0: A new wave of innovation for teaching and learning? *Educause Review, 41*(2), 33–44.

American Association for the Advancement of Science (AAAS). (1993). *Benchmarks for science literacy online.* Section A, para 2. Retrieved March 17, 2006, from http://www.project2061.org/publications/bsl/online/ch3/ch3.htm

Borich, G. (2006). *Effective teaching methods, 6e.* Upper Saddle River, NJ: Prentice Hall.

Burns, M. (2005/2006). Tools for the mind. *Educational Leadership, 63*(5), 48–53.

Bybee, R. W. (2003). The teaching of science: Content, coherence, and congruence. *Journal of Science Education & Technology, 12*(4), 343–358.

Dodge, B. (1997). *Some thoughts about WebQuests.* Retrieved August 18, 2005, from http://edweb.sdsu.edu/people/bdodge/

Giza, B. H. (2005). The ALE Approach: Integrating art, music, and drama across the content areas. In A. Macias (Ed.), *Working with English language learners: Perspectives and practice* (pp. 123–130). New York: Kendall-Hunt Publishing, IA.

Giza, B. H. (2007). Modeling Leeuwenhoek's microscope with disposable camera lenses. *Science Scope, 31*(2), 48–51.

Hansen, L. (2006). Strategies for ELL success. *Science and Children, 43*(4), 22–25.

Johnson-Palmer, J., & Terry, K. (1996). Classroom tour of the solar system. *Athena Space Curriculum.* National Aeronautics and Space Administration. Retrieved July 25, 2007, from http://vathena.arc.nasa.gov/curric/space/planets/sstour.html

Latham, S. A. (2005). Learning communities and digital storytelling: New media for ancient tradition. In *Proceedings of society for information technology and teacher education international conference 2005* (pp. 2286–2291). Norfolk, VA: AACE.

March, T. (1998). Why WebQuests? An introduction. WebQuest for learning website. Retrieved August 10, 2005, from http://www.ozline.com/WebQuests/intro.html

Mayer, R. E., & Moreno, R. (2002). Animation as an aid to multimedia learning. *Educational Psychology Review, 14*(1), 87–99.

National Research Council (NRC). (1996). *The National Science Education Standards.* Washington, DC: National Academy Press.

Sperling, R. A., Seyedmonir, M., Aleksic, M., & Meadows, G. (2003). Animations as learning tools in authentic science materials. *International Journal of Instructional Media, 30*(2), 213–221.

Tomlinson, C. A., & McTighe, J. (2006). *Integrating differentiated instruction understanding by design.* Alexandria, VA: Association for Supervision and Curriculum Development.

Wheatley, G. H. (1991). Constructivist perspectives on science and mathematics learning. *Science Education, 75*(1), 9–21.

For Further Reading

Brown, D. (2004). *Tracker, open source physics java video analysis.* Retrieved March 17, 2006, from http://www.cabrillo.edu/~dbrown/tracker

Crowther, D. (2005). Here we grow again. *Electronic Journal of Science Education.* [Online] Retrieved March 17, 2006, from http://unr.edu/homepage/crowther/ejse/crowedit4.html

Donovan, M. S., & Bransford, J. D. (2005). Scientific inquiry and how people learn. In M. S. Donovan & J. D. Bransford (Eds.), *How students learn: Science in the classroom* (pp. 397–419). National Research Council. Washington, DC: National Academies Press.

Gaskill, M., McNulty, A., Brooks, D. (2006). Learning from WebQuests. *Journal of Science Education and Technology, 15*(2), 133–136.

McLellan, H. (1992). *Narrative and episodic story structure in interactive stories.* East Lansing, MI: National Center for Research on Teacher Learning. (ERIC Document Reproduction Service No. ED 348 012).

National Research Council (NRC). (2000). *Inquiry and the National Science Education Standards.* Washington, DC: National Academy Press.

Robin, B. R., & Pierson, M. E. (2005). A multilevel approach to using digital storytelling in the classroom. In *Proceedings of society for information technology and teacher education international conference 2005* (pp. 708–715). Norfolk, VA: AACE.

Vidoni, K. L., & Maddux, C. D. (2002). WebQuests: Can they be used to improve critical thinking skills in students? *Computers in the Schools, 19*(1), 101–117.

Wenglinsky, H. (2005). *Using technology wisely: The keys to success in schools.* New York: Teachers College Press.

TECHNOLOGY INTEGRATION FOR MEANINGFUL CLASSROOM USE
Daily Lesson GAME Plan

Lesson Title: Scientist for a Day	**Related Lessons:** Life Cycle of Organisms
Grade Level: Elementary	**Unit:** Organisms

GOALS

Content Standards:

Science as Inquiry
- Abilities necessary to do scientific inquiries
- Understandings about scientific inquiry

Life Science
- The characteristics of organisms
- Organisms and environments

ISTE NETS-S

☐	1. Creativity and innovation	☑ 4.	Critical thinking, problem solving, and decision making
☑	2. Communication and collaboration	☐ 5.	Digital citizenship
☐	3. Research and information fluency	☑ 6.	Technology operations and concepts

Instructional Objective(s):

Students assume the role of various scientists, one geologist, and one zoologist or botanist, to observe, record, and describe the inhabitants, both living and nonliving, in a designated plot of ground.

ACTION

Before-Class Preparation:

Prior to the lesson, take time to walk around outside the school. Identify several areas where the students can observe and that will elicit a variety of responses from each group. Although each group of students selects the plot of ground where they carry out their observations, guide them to those areas containing a variety of organisms and nonliving things.

Prepare the instructions for the Outdoor Observation:
- Step 1: Decide which person is to serve as the geologist, the botanist, the zoologist, and the sampler/data recorder.
- Step 2: Stay within the area designated by the teacher.
- Step 3: The sampler/recorder tosses the hoop into the air. Wherever the hoop lands, that is the area that your group is to observe.
- Step 4: The geologist observes the rocks and soils of the area. The botanist observes the plant life in the area, and the zoologist observes the animal life within the area. The sampler/data recorder records the data. Be sure to count the number of organisms or rocks within your area.

Create a blog for students to enter a description of the activity and their findings.

During Class

Time	Instructional Activities	Materials and Resources
20 minutes	Lead a class discussion by beginning with the following: Today we will learn how to observe like a scientist. We will also learn about three different types of scientists: the botanists, the zoologists, and the geologists. Some of you will take on the role of a specific type of scientist, while others will record data. Have students write a short summary describing the jobs of the botanist, the zoologist, and the geologist.	Computer with word-processing software Checklist

During Class		
Time	**Instructional Activities**	**Materials and Resources**
20 minutes	Ask students to distinguish between living organisms and nonliving things. There are some very general rules to follow when trying to decide if something is living or nonliving. Listed here are the six rules used by scientists: • Living organisms are made of cells. • Living organisms obtain and use energy. • Living organisms grow and develop. • Living organisms reproduce. • Living organisms respond to their environment. • Living organisms adapt to their environment. Ask students, "Which scientist(s) study living organisms? Which scientist(s) study nonliving things?" Students complete an online quiz distinguishing living organisms from nonliving things.	Computer with Internet access Living versus Nonliving Quiz http://www.usoe.k12.ut.us/curr/science/sciber00/7th/classify/living/quiz/livingqu.htm
15 minutes	Review the instructions for the Outdoor Observation. Each person has a specific job during the time of observation. After the group discussion, divide the students into groups of four. Assign or allow students to select a job: the botanist, the zoologist, the geologist, and the sampler/data recorder. Accompany the class outside and direct the groups to four different areas near the school.	Student lab notebook Checklist
30 minutes	The random sampler/data recorder tosses the hula hoop into the air. Wherever the hoop lands designates the plot of ground the group is to observe. The geologist observes the rocks and soils of the area. The botanist observes the plant life in the area, and the zoologist observes the animal life in the area. The students count the number of organisms and rocks within the area. The sampler/data recorder records the data. The data will be used to create a graph. Each scientist writes his/her observations in their lab notebook. The sampler/data recorder records the number of living organisms and nonliving things found within the observed plot. After the observation period is complete, the students return to the classroom. Group members compare their findings and record the information in their lab notebook.	Hula hoop Student lab notebook
20 minutes	Demonstrate the process of data reporting by creating a bar graph with spreadsheet software using the following sample data: *Rocks—10, Grass—33, Ants—15*. Direct students to title their graphs and label the axes. The X-axis should be labeled *Observed Living Organisms and Nonliving Things* and the Y-axis should be labeled *Number of Living Organisms and Nonliving Things*. Discuss the proper method for creating the scale with the students. If a rubric is utilized to assess the graph, inform the students of the grading system.	Computer with spreadsheet software Smart board Rubric
45 minutes	Student groups create a blog entry describing the activity and their findings. Students are to choose one other group's findings and write about the differences in the data from that group as compared to the data from their group. Students are to speculate why these differences could have occurred.	Computer with Internet access Rubric

Notes: Groups should be comprised of 4 students: one biologist, one zoologist, one geologist, one sampler/data recorder. The jobs of the sampler and data recorder can be performed by the same student.
Once outside, demonstrate the proper procedure for selecting the plot of ground, by gently tossing the hula hoop.

MONITOR

Ongoing Assessment(s): Students should be monitored to ensure they are focusing on their observations and data collection. Students use a teacher-generated rubric to identify components of the graph.

Accommodations and Extensions: Provide guidance to groups having difficulty distinguishing between living organisms and nonliving things found within their plots of ground.

MONITOR

If some students need assistance in constructing their graphs, consider placing them with a partner within the group to complete the task. Provide digital cameras for each group to create a virtual catalog of the living organisms and nonliving things found in their plots of ground. Using the Internet and field guides, have groups identify the scientific names of the living organisms observed.

Back-up Plan: Students can tour the school, categorizing living organisms and nonliving things and collecting data needed to complete the activity. Predetermined categories may be necessary to limit the amount of data collected. Graphing can be demonstrated using an overhead projector and completed using graph paper.

EVALUATION

Lesson Reflections and Notes:
Completed activity is graded using a checklist for the job summary and the lab notebook, and a rubric for the graph and blog.

TECHNOLOGY INTEGRATION FOR MEANINGFUL CLASSROOM USE
Daily Lesson GAME Plan

Lesson Title: Can the Trash!	**Related Lessons:** Waste management, Composting
Grade Level: Middle grades	**Unit:** Reduce, Reuse, Recycle

GOALS

Content Standards:
Science as Inquiry
- Abilities necessary to do scientific inquiry
- Understandings about scientific inquiry

Life Science
- Populations and ecosystems

Personal and Social Perspectives
- Populations, resources, and environments
- Natural hazards
- Risks and benefits
- Science and technology in society

ISTE NETS-S

☑ 1. Creativity and innovation   ☑ 4. Critical thinking, problem solving, and decision making

☑ 2. Communication and collaboration   ☑ 5. Digital citizenship

☐ 3. Research and information fluency   ☐ 6. Technology operations and concepts

Instructional Objective(s):
Students will receive a general overview of the world's environmental dilemmas, thereby understanding the global implications of their actions.

ACTION

Before-Class Preparation:
Ask parent volunteers or other teachers to collect their waste paper in a separate bag for a period of three days. Please be specific and inform them that no food is to be placed in this bag, only paper products such as construction paper, copy paper, newsprint, or empty food containers, such as pizza boxes.

During Class		
Time	**Instructional Activities**	**Materials and Resources**
15–30 minutes	Read the poem by Shel Silverstein, "Sarah Cynthia Sylvia Stout Would Not Take The Garbage Out". Lead the students in a discussion concerning the implications of the poem, the mounting garbage, and the concept of garbage disposal. Introduce the idea of the world's garbage and its size and volume. Communicate to the students that our world is in danger from pollution of the air, water, and land, overwhelming the delicate balance of nature of the planet. Many species of plants and animals face extinction at an alarming rate. Until all of the people of the world are educated and informed, this destruction will continue. Because they, the students, are the leaders of tomorrow, it is their task to become responsible users and protectors of the environment.	Poem by Shel Silverstein, "Sara Cynthia Sylvia Stout Would Not Take The Garbage Out" from *Where the Sidewalk Ends* Other suggested readings: *The Garbage Can* by Linda Ann Nickerson and *Thank you, Mr. Garbage Man* by Erin Elizabeth Kelly-Moen
20 minutes	Have students determine • how their purchasing and disposal methods affect their personal environmental impact • their carbon footprint	Computer with Internet access Websites, such as The Personal Environmental Impact Calculator http://ans.engr.wisc.edu/eic/RecyclingForm.html Carbon Footprint Calculator http://www.carbonfootprint.com/calculator.aspx
10 minutes	Demonstrate the process of categorization using a small bag of waste paper and separate plastic bags. Observe safe practices by wearing plastic gloves and washing the hands after the process is complete. Mass one of the categorized bags with a spring scale or large digital balance, demonstrating the use of the measuring instrument.	Bags of garbage collected over a period of three days. Plastic gloves Spring scale or large digital balance
5 minutes	Demonstrate how to calculate the weekly volume (volume of waste paper/3 days × 7 days), the monthly volume (weekly volume × 4 weeks), and the yearly volume (weekly volume × 52 weeks).	Interactive whiteboard
20 minutes	Working in pairs, students sort and categorize the waste paper collected over the three-day period. Have students use separate plastic bags for specific categories, such as newsprint, construction paper, and copier paper. Make sure the students wear plastic gloves while they are involved in the sorting process. Caution them to wash their hands after the waste paper is categorized. Students collect data by massing the separate bags using a spring scale or large digital balance. Have students create a bar graph to display their data. The X-axis should be labeled with the categories and the Y-axis should be the volume. If a rubric is utilized for assessing the bar graph, share the expectations with the students at this time.	Bags of garbage collected over a period of three days. Spring scale or large digital balance Plastic gloves for each student Personal computers or student lab notebook Computer with spreadsheet software Rubric
15–30 minutes	Students calculate the weekly, monthly, and yearly volumes of each type of material. Students will write a two-paragraph summary, based on their calculations, as to the possible effects on the environment of the amount of waste paper accumulated in a year.	Calculators (not needed if personal computers are used) Computer with word-processing software
30 minutes	Utilizing their findings, have students create a public service announcement that highlights reasons to recycle. If a rubric is utilized for assessing the announcement, share the expectations with the student.	Computer with video-editing software such as iMovie (Apple) or Movie Maker (Windows) Rubric

Notes:

MONITOR

Ongoing Assessment(s): Use a checklist to ensure active student participation in the investigation. Periodically check the data collected on the personal computer or in the student lab notebook. Students use a teacher-generated rubric to identify components of the graph and public service announcement.

Accommodations and Extensions: Some students will need assistance in constructing their graph or writing their summaries. Students collect newspaper and magazine articles and share them with the class. Have students create posters using desktop-publishing software about the different issues of the environment, using the articles and making their own illustrations. Connect with one or more classrooms in another state or country to compare recycling procedures and volume of garbage collected and recycled. Schedule a class trip to a recycling center. Have students use recycled paper when appropriate.

Back-up Plan: Have students design signs for each classroom in the building to remind them to turn off the lights and turn off the water when not in use. Enlist other classes and start a recycling program at the school.

EVALUATION

Lesson Reflections and Notes: Grade the activity using a rubric for each completed component. Incorporate student suggestions for new categories of trash separation into the lesson.

TECHNOLOGY INTEGRATION FOR MEANINGFUL CLASSROOM USE
Daily Lesson GAME Plan

Lesson Title: Calamity on Coal River

Related Lessons: Acid/Base Titrations, Stoichiometry

Grade Level: High School

Unit: Chemical Reactions

GOALS

Content Standards:

Science as Inquiry
- Abilities necessary to do scientific inquiries
- Understandings about scientific inquiry

Physical Science
- Structure of atoms
- Structure and properties of matter
- Chemical reactions

Science and Technology
- Abilities of technological design
- Understandings about science and technology

Science in Personal and Social Perspectives
- Environmental quality
- Natural and human-induced hazards
- Science and technology in local, national, and global challenges

History and Nature of Science
- Science as a human endeavor
- Nature of scientific knowledge

GOALS

ISTE NETS-S

☑ 1. Creativity and innovation
☐ 2. Communication and collaboration
☑ 3. Research and information fluency

☑ 4. Critical thinking, problem solving, and decision making
☐ 5. Digital citizenship
☑ 6. Technology operations and concepts

Instructional Objective(s): Students are presented with a short scenario concerning the release of an unknown quantity of liquid into holding ponds that empty into the Coal River. Students must determine the identity of the unknown liquid, and propose a method for cleanup and disposal, including the amount of neutralizing agents necessary.

ACTION

Before-Class Preparation: Prepare the memo describing the scenario as a handout to student teams. Try to authenticate the letterheads for a more realistic effect.

MEMO
To: All Lab Teams
From: Lab Supervisor (Teacher)

The Department of Environmental Protection (DEP) has contracted our lab to identify an unknown liquid that was released into two holding ponds that empty into the Coal River. The DEP also wants us to propose a method for cleanup and disposal. We will receive $150,000.00 beyond their normal fee of $200,000.00 due to the urgent nature of the case. A courier from the DEP will deliver a sample of the unknown liquid to us tomorrow. Due to contamination when collected, only a small amount of the liquid is viable. Be very careful with your samples, as you will not be able to obtain another.

Before you begin the lab work, I must approve your procedure. Provide me the following items as soon as possible:

- Detailed plan for your procedure
- Concept map of your experimental design
- Detailed list of the equipment and materials you will need with itemized and total costs for the accounting department

You will have one week to complete this task. Use your time wisely and stay under our $275,000.00 budget. Remember to observe lab safety precautions and waste disposal methods as discussed in our recent lab safety meeting.

Prepare the unknown solution; varying concentrations of hydrochloric acid. Some suggested concentrations are as follows: 6M—add 500mL of HCl to 1 liter of water, 3M—add 250mL of HCl to 1 liter of water, 1M—add 83mL of HCl to 1 liter of water, 0.5M—add 41mL of HCl to 1 liter of water, and 0.1M—add 8.3mL of HCl to 1 liter of water. Only one sample to a lab group. Each group receives a different concentration for different results.

During Class

Time	Instructional Activities	Materials and Resources
25 minutes	Conduct a lab safety briefing before beginning this scenario; include basic lab safety and waste disposal. Students take notes in their notebooks.	Student lab notebooks
20 minutes	Distribute the memo to the students and discuss the task for their teams.	Memo
20 minutes	Have student teams brainstorm various ways of approaching the problem. Guide the teams to the formulation of a problem statement.	
60 minutes	Each group prepares a background search or short abstract of the Coal River and its current pollution problems.	Computer with Internet connection Word-processing software The Coal River Group website, http://www.coalrivergroup.com, and American Rivers website, http://americanrivers.org
90 minutes	Student teams formulate detailed plans of their procedures and create concept maps of their experimental designs. Once approved, teams receive their samples of unknown liquid.	Computer with word-processing software and concept-mapping software, such as Inspiration

	During Class	
Time	**Instructional Activities**	**Materials and Resources**
90 minutes	Student teams provide detailed lists of the equipment and the materials needed with itemized and total costs for the accounting department. To determine the cost of the equipment and materials, have teams use online catalogs of science materials.	Computer with spreadsheet software Online science materials catalog, such as Flinn Scientific, http://www.flinnsci.com
Several class periods	Student teams conduct analyses of their samples. Have students use digital cameras to capture their work in the lab. If only one camera is available, take photos of the students as they perform their lab work. If more are available, assign each team a camera.	Student lab notebooks Probeware (pH) Calculators Digital camera
Several class periods	When completed, teams prepare a portfolio to present to the DEP that includes the following: • Cover Sheet: Must contain the name of the company, team name, the problem addressed, and date. • Report of Analysis: Students prepare reports summarizing the procedures their team used to analyze the samples. • Analysis and Findings: Students report their findings about the identity of the unknown liquid and its concentration in each sample, including calculations and a discussion of the multiple trials. • Data Table • Graph • Invoice: Students prepare detailed invoices showing all costs, services, and employee hours spent on this project. • Suggestions and Improvements: Students prepare memos to the lab supervisor that include suggestions for reducing costs and improving the analysis procedures. Be aware that this is an open-ended section and provides the students with opportunities to exhibit what they have learned.	Computer with word-processing and spreadsheet software Calculators
Several class periods	Student teams create presentations for the DEP detailing the suggested methods for cleanup and disposal. Be sure to have students include the photos taken during their analyses. You may want to have them present to a larger audience than their own classmates. Send invitations to your guests with a short narrative explaining the project.	Computer with presentation software Video projector Interactive whiteboard, if available

Notes: Students need to have prior knowledge of stoichiometry, acids, bases, and titration techniques. Several tutorials are located online. If you are located near a river, it may be more effective to localize this scenario.

MONITOR

Ongoing Assessment(s): Observe students to see if they are active participants in the experimental process. Periodically check student lab notebooks. Students must keep lab notebooks during the entire project. These are their rough drafts of information and proof of their investigations.

Accommodations and Extensions: Consider assigning students to a team to ensure equity. Some student teams may need more guidance in creating an experimental design. Since several jobs exist within a team, purposefully assign these jobs to accommodate the students' skill levels. Student teams can create web pages of their presentations and findings. Using drawing tools and software, teams can create maps and pictures of the lab equipment to accompany their presentations.

Back-up Plan: Student teams design and develop scenarios utilizing concepts from chemistry textbooks, articles from local newspapers, and local television news. The scenarios are reviewed by other teams and revised for class use.

EVALUATION

Lesson Reflections and Notes:

Create a rubric to assess students' progress. Some areas to assess may include:

- Excellent technique was used throughout the lab procedure
- Data and observations were recorded accurately, descriptively, and completely, with no serious errors
- Analysis and Interpretation items are performed clearly, concisely, and accurately, with correct units and properly worked calculations
- Graphs are drawn accurately and neatly
- Recognition of the connections between observations and the related chemistry concepts are expressed in an exemplary manner
- Sound reasoning and logic are evident throughout the report
- Suggestions and recommendations are concise and accurate and offer new insights

18

ISTE Standards addressed in this chapter

This chapter provides content-specific suggestions and strategies for addressing both ISTE's National Educational Technology Standards for Students (NETS-S) and the curriculum standards from the National Council for the Social Studies. This chapter also builds on the NETS-T concepts and skills presented earlier, with a special emphasis on skills related to Standard 1 "Facilitate and inspire student learning and creativity." Following an overview of the curriculum standards and how you can address the NETS-S in the social studies classroom, this chapter outlines techniques, tools, and methods for developing authentic learning experiences that advance student creativity and innovation in the social studies classroom.

Integrating Technology in the Social Studies Classroom

David Hicks, Ph.D.; Melissa Lisanti, MA, NBCT; Peter Doolittle, Ph.D.; Adam Friedman, Ph.D.; Richard Hartshorne, Ph.D.; Kathy Swan, Ph.D.; Mark Hofer, Ph.D.; and John Lee, Ph.D.

History of Magic was by common consent the most boring subject ever devised by wizard kind. Professor Binns, their ghost teacher, had a wheezy, droning voice that was almost guaranteed to cause severe drowsiness within ten minutes, five in warm weather. He never varied the form of their lessons, but lectured them without pausing while they took notes, or rather, gazed sleepily into space. Harry and Ron had so far managed to scrape passes in this subject only by copying Hermione's notes before exams; she alone seemed able to resist the soporific power of Binns' voice. (Rowling, 2004, pp. 206–207)

Historical thinking is a very close relative to active, thoughtful, critical participation in text- and image-rich democratic cultures. Consider what good historical thinkers can do . . . they are informed, educated, thoughtful, critical readers, who appreciate investigative enterprises, know good arguments when they hear them, and who engage their world with a host of strategies for understanding it . . . Thomas Jefferson could hardly have wanted better citizens than these thinkers. (Van Sledright, 2004, pp. 222–223)

Outcomes

In this chapter, you will

- Identify social studies standards and explain how technology can support these results.
- Discuss how the National Educational Technology Standards for Students can be addressed in a social studies classroom.
- Demonstrate how authentic learning principles can be addressed using technology in a social studies classroom.
- Explain how technology can increase learning and facilitate creative thinking in a social studies classroom.

T his chapter provides examples and insights into the ways digital technologies can be effectively used in the teaching and learning of social studies within your standards-based classroom. We believe that teaching requires an informed and creative mind; as you read this section, you should consciously examine and reflect upon how you can build on and/or adapt these ideas and applications for yourself as you design instructional units that thoughtfully and appropriately utilize technology as a partner in your social studies classroom.

Technology and Content Standards

Before embarking upon a study of the possibilities and potential for the integration of digital technologies within the social studies, it is necessary to first understand a little about the nature of social studies and identify the curriculum standards that define and guide the teaching of social studies at both the state and national level. This begins by asking the question: what do the two opening quotes have to do with standards and integrating technology within the social studies?

In short the opening quotes provide a context for ongoing calls to actively use digital technologies as a partner within the social studies classroom. Although the first quote comes from a work of fiction the description of experiences Harry and his friends have in their history lessons may well resonate with many of you. The teaching of social studies has been observed by generations of students and researchers as clinging to a very specific pattern of teaching: the teacher talks and students listen, read, and answer questions in textbooks. Students are then expected to memorize facts and details that, for the most part are "removed from their intrinsically human character" (Goodlad, 1984, p. 212). What is often lost or forgotten in such teaching is the recognition that "the primary purpose of the social studies is to help young people develop the ability to make informed and reasoned decisions for the public good as citizens of a culturally diverse, democratic society in an interdependent world" (National Council for Social Studies, 1994, p. 157). Such a mission cannot be achieved if students are treated as passive consumers of information. As the second quote illuminates, wise practice within the social studies classroom should include preparing students to actively engage in inquiry, perspective taking, and meaning making in order to develop the habits of mind that are important for the rights and responsibilities of 21st-century citizenship. In response, a growing number of social studies educators contend that the social studies classroom should be the ideal space to prepare young citizens to critically explore their world (the past and present) through the use of digital technologies in the standards-based classroom. That is, having access to current knowledge resources, digital archives, and experts—with a great number of these available via the Internet—can only benefit a teaching field that 1) advocates teaching and learning social studies from a constructivist perspective, 2) stresses the importance of teaching students to develop the knowledge, skills, and dispositions to ask questions and gather data as part of the process of inquiring into past and present issues, and 3) recognizes the importance of establishing clear standards and performance expectation for students.

The National Council for the Social Studies (NCSS) released their national standards in 1994. The standards sought to define the social studies and provide curriculum standards and performance expectations for students. Within the standards, the Social Studies is defined as

> the integrated study of the social sciences and humanities to promote civic competence. Within the school program, social studies provides coordinated, systematic study drawing upon such disciplines as anthropology, archeology, economics, geography, history, law, philosophy, political science, psychology, religion, and sociology, as well as appropriate content from the humanities, mathematics, and the natural sciences. (NCSS, 1994, p. vii)

The National Standards for Social Studies are made up of ten thematic curriculum standards (see Table 18.1). As presented in Table 18.1, a number of key themes such as times, continuity, and change (NCSS II); people, places, and environments (NCSS III); individual development and identity (NCSS IV); and production, distribution, and consumption (NCSS VII) are clearly linked to specific social science disciplines, while other themes represent an integration of disciplines. Although the standards draw from and support all the social sciences disciplines, in keeping with the above definition of social studies, the ten thematic standards are designed to be interrelated, whereby, "to understand culture . . . students need to understand time, continuity and change; the relationship among people, places, and environments; and civic ideals and practices. To understand power, authority and governance, students need to understand the relationship among culture; people, places and environments; and individuals, groups and institutions" (NCSS, 1994, p. 15).

The NCSS has long recognized the potential role of technology as a powerful resource to support the teaching and learning of social studies. Specifically they contend "integrated social studies teaching and learning include effective use of technology that can add important dimensions to student learning" (NCSS, 1994, p. 165). The growth of digital technologies, alongside the ever-increasing number of computers and level of Internet access within schools, continues to bolster calls to appropriately utilize digital technologies as a partner in the standards-based classroom. Table 18.2 provides examples of the ways that social studies teachers can address

Table 18.1	National Council for the Social Studies Curriculum Standards
NCSS Thematic Strand	**Disciplinary Connections to School Courses**
1. Culture	Geography, History, Anthropology, and multicultural topics across the curriculum
2. Time, Continuity, and Change	History
3. People, Places, and Environment	Geography
4. Individual Development and Identity	Psychology and Anthropology
5. Individuals, Groups, and Institutions	Sociology, Anthropology, Psychology, Political Science, and History
6. Power, Authority, and Governance	Government, Politics, Political Science, History, and Law
7. Production, Distribution, and Consumption	Economics
8. Science, Technology, and Society	History, Geography, Economics, and Civics and Government
9. Global Connections	Geography, Culture, Economics and multicultural topics across the curriculum including Natural and Physical Sciences and the Humanities.
10. Civic Ideals and Practices	History, Political Science, Cultural Anthropology and Global Studies and Law-related Fields

Source: NCSS. (1994).

WEB LINK

For further detailed examples of the alignment of the NETS-S to the national social studies standards as well as suggestions for assessment, visit the textbook's companion website.

Table 18.2   NETS-S in the Social Studies Classroom

Creativity and Innovation

Widely available video-editing software allows students to craft their own digital documentaries on any of the NCSS standards. Concept-mapping software allows students to create their own understandings and representations of a variety of concepts. Students can use a range of software to develop timelines that incorporate media elements.

Communication and Collaboration

E-mail, online-discussion, and collaboration software have dramatically widened access to other communities around the world. Communication tools allow students multiple opportunities to engage in dialogue on all of the NCSS standards.

Research and Information Fluency

Digital archives have made primary source materials available in vast quantities. The National Archives and Library of Congress are described in detail in the chapter. WebQuests are available on many topics or can be created by a teacher or groups of teachers.

Critical Thinking, Problem Solving, and Decision Making

Resources that engage students in "doing history" are described in the chapter. Sites like the History Inquiry Project and Historical Scene Investigation engage students in the complex decision-making processes utilized by historians. Simulation software such as the popular Decisions, Decisions and role-playing software also promote the development of student decision-making skills.

Digital Citizenship

Socials studies students must develop historical inquiry skills that support their verification of resources, especially resources found on the Internet. Social studies students can investigate, track, and debate the issues and ever-changing laws relating to the use of new and emerging technologies, including cell phones, social-networking websites, instant-messaging software, and filtering software.

Technology Operations and Concepts

Students can use widely available word-processing software to engage in the writing process across all social studies standards. They can access basic information on the Internet on a variety of topics.

THE GAME PLAN

Content Standards

Set Goals

Research the social studies standards for a state where you plan to seek a teaching position and create an action plan to ensure that you will have the knowledge and skills necessary to help your students achieve those standards. Identify the concepts, knowledge, and skills you will need to ensure that you are prepared to help your students meet the social studies standards in your state. Describe any explicit purpose or rationale given for teaching social studies within your state standards.

Take Action

Explore the curricular standards of the National Council for Social Studies and those from the department of education website in the state where you plan to seek a position. Review the K–12 social studies standards in that state and compare them to the state's technology standards. Identify those standards that specifically relate to applying technology in the social studies curriculum. Develop a plan for how to meet the standards for teachers in the context of social studies.

Monitor

Did you find the information you needed? Do you need to contact the department of education for more information about where to find the social studies standards or the technology standards for teachers?

Evaluate and Extend

Discuss in class the action plan you developed for meeting the technology standards for instructional personnel. Compare your plan to others. Note the strengths and weaknesses of the various plans. Strengthen your plan by incorporating ideas you have heard in class.

each of the ISTE NETS-S in their classrooms. The lesson plans at the end of this chapter provide specific examples of how you can design learning experiences that meet both content area and technology standards.

Authentic Learning Strategies Incorporating Technology

The recent shift from viewing technology-as-teacher to technology-as-partner in the social studies classroom recognizes that the key to supporting and improving citizenship education does not rest with simply giving teachers and students access to online and CD-ROM knowledge resources, digital archives, and experts via the Internet. Rather it requires teachers to be ready, willing, and able to organize instructional strategies that leverage digital technologies as developmental tools to be used by students as a resource stimulus for inquiry, perspective taking, and meaning making, and not solely as a conduit for the transmission of knowledge. As presented in Chapter 3, teachers who create instructional settings that support authentic learning strategies often operate from a constructivist philosophy. Doolittle and Hicks (2003) suggested that implementing digital technologies as a developmental tool within a constructivist social studies classroom becomes probable when:

- Teachers and students are prepared to implement technology as a tool for inquiry.
- Teachers use technology to create authenticity, which facilitates the process of student inquiry and action.
- Teachers use technology to foster local and global social interaction such that students attain multiple perspectives on people, issues, and events.
- Teachers facilitate student knowledge construction by using technology to build on students' prior knowledge and interests.
- Teachers enhance the viability of student knowledge by using technology to provide timely and meaningful feedback.

So how can teachers begin to organize and implement such student-centered strategies in the social studies classroom? Although we will present some ideas and accompanying resources—many of them freely available web-based resources—for how to meet each of these strategies, please note that what is offered here are simply examples, and do not form an exhaustive list of all the quality social studies resources that are available. You should seek to identify further resources that build on these initial ideas and develop authentic learning strategies for the social studies classroom.

Strategy 1: Teachers and students are prepared to implement technology as a tool for inquiry.

Although a growing number of students and teachers may be acquainted with such tools as word processors, presentation tools, and web browsers, the idea of using these tools as a way to support student-centered teaching and learning is still very new for many students and teachers. The use of digital repositories as an inquiry tool becomes problematic if students are not prepared to conduct searches of the Internet and databases and more importantly to evaluate the trustworthiness of these resources. Time needs to be spent helping students become productive, critical, sensitive, and sophisticated users of digital resources, especially those found on the Internet. Preparing students to engage in inquiry requires that they be taught how to be discerning and critical users of information resources such as the Internet (see also Internet Resources and Search Strategies in Chapter 4).

Numerous lessons and high-quality media elements are available online that contribute pedagogical ideas for utilizing digital technologies to support inquiry in the

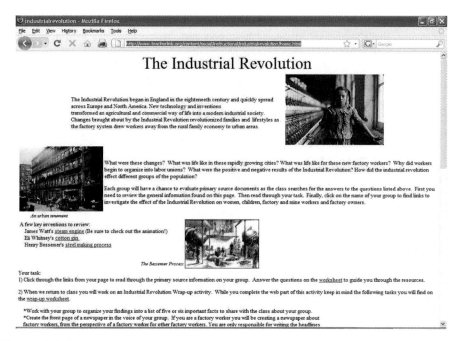

Figure 18.1
Numerous lessons and high-quality media resources are available online to support the social studies class.
Source: Courtesy University of Virginia, Center for Technology and Teacher Training, www.teacherlink.org

social studies. For example, Teachers' Domain from Boston's public broadcasting station, WGBH, incorporates videos, animations, images, and other materials from their popular television programming to support lessons for sciences and social studies teachers. Similar types of materials are available from the national Public Broadcasting Service (PBS) as well as other education-oriented broadcasters, such as the Discovery Channel and the History Channel. Museums, colleges, and universities, too, offer resources for the social studies teacher designed to promote inquiry. For example, the Center for Technology and Teacher Education at the University of Virginia has developed a collection of instructional lessons that are available online (see Figure 18.1). These standards-based lessons clearly model various approaches to using a range of technologies within the inquiry-based social studies classroom. Specific lessons in the overall collection make use of web-based resources, graphing calculators, spreadsheets, databases, presentation software, and geographic information systems. The lessons cover subject matter in all major disciplines including history, geography, political science, economics, and behavioral sciences. Pedagogical approaches featured in the lessons include critical thinking, map skills, questioning, research, classroom discussion, simulation, spreadsheets, lecture, problem solving, writing, and virtual field trips. Several of the lessons make use of primary historical sources from Digital History Libraries housed at Virginia Center for Digital History (VCDH). The overall collection of lessons promotes student-centered and active learning and targets the diverse needs of learners.

The NCSS 2007 Annual Bulletin entitled *Digital Age: Technology-Based K–12 Lessons for the Social Studies* provides a collection of standards-based lessons that use digital technologies as a partner in the social studies classroom. All the lessons are based upon a unifying lesson plan template (see NCSS Bulletin Template). The Bulletin includes lessons from across the K–12 spectrum and correlates lessons to both the ISTE NETS-S and the NCSS curriculum standards. The lessons are designed to address diverse learning needs, and they provide students with opportunities to obtain information, formulate ideas, and create products that are designed by learners.

Another powerful model that teachers use to engage their students in inquiry-based social studies lessons is a WebQuest, whose creation is often attributed to Bernie Dodge at San Diego State University. A WebQuest is an example of how web-based resources can be utilized to support structured inquiry-orientated lessons, whether your students search the entire web or work within a limited set of web resources that may be housed on a school server, organized through a class web page or series of favorite bookmarks, or even commercially provided content services including those from textbook and other content providers. Dodge's website allows you to search and locate examples of social studies WebQuests for all grade levels while also providing a template and instructions to design your own WebQuest to engage students in relevant and meaningful questions that can be explored by navigating to specific online sources. (For more information on WebQuests, see Chapter 4.)

Strategy 2: Teachers use technology to create authenticity, which facilitates the process of student inquiry and action.

The ability to access authentic social studies materials and engage in authentic inquiry is vital if students are to make real-world connections within the social studies classroom. The development of digital historical libraries and archives is changing the way teachers and students can access learning materials. Today, students can access books, maps, primary sources, newspapers, fact books, visual materials, and many other forms of information through CDs, DVDs, and online library collections and archives. Three well-known digital archives that have pedagogical portals to support the teaching of all the NCSS thematic strands are Digital History at the University of Houston, the National Archives, and the Library of Congress' American Memory website (see Figure 18.2). These archives continue to digitize their collections, and teachers and students can search and locate key historical resources.

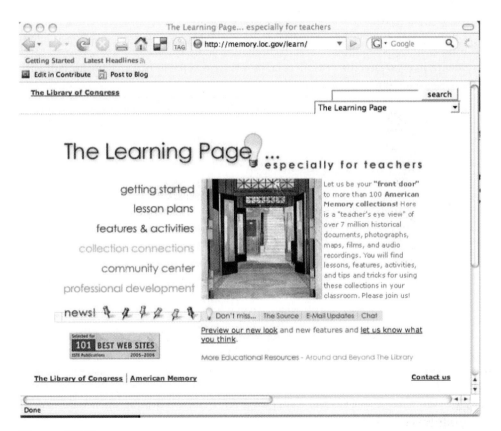

Figure 18.2
The American Memory website is one resource for authentic social studies materials.

Learning how to successfully negotiate such archives is vital prior to working with students. There is nothing more frustrating for students as they begin to search digital archives than either 1) not knowing how to efficiently search and use key words to explore various collections, and/or 2) subsequently locating sources and bookmarking the sources only to find the next day you cannot locate them again because they were actually searching a relational database. Preparing your students to search and save sources by working with them on tutorials such as "How to use Library of Congress resources" is vital and necessary to ensure student success.

Beyond digital archives and libraries, there are a number of powerful websites that teachers are currently using to allow students to ask questions and explore all NCSS thematic strands. For example, websites such as the CIA World Fact Book, the Constitution Finder, and Elections Around the World are powerful resources to conduct comparative political studies using authentic materials. Such sites provide teachers and students with access to a wide range of resources that previously would have been exceptionally difficult to access for use within the social studies classroom.

As digital technologies continue to evolve, a whole new level of authentic inquiry and activity is developing within the social studies classroom. For example, Google—the popular search engine company—has developed Google Earth, a stand-alone geographic search tool that brings together maps, satellite imagery, and layers of geographic information, to allow users to conduct local, national, and international searches. Users appear to "fly" around the earth to explore and address NCSS III: People, places, and environments. Students can use satellite images of their own communities before flying to identify, explore, and compare data from other countries and cultures. Layers and layers of new information continue to be added to Google Earth, with some of the most impressive focusing on the physical and human geography of Africa, provide by the National Geographic Society. You, too, can add layers and embed links to instructional activities or even other resources in Google Earth, such as linking to streaming videos, pictures, or other websites that help provide greater context and depth of knowledge about the people and places students explore during their map inquiries. These technologies serve as powerful resources to teach students how to become critical citizens who are capable of engaging in authentic inquiry and actions.

Strategy 3: Teachers should use technology to foster local and global social interaction such that students attain multiple perspectives on people, issues, and events.

Technology provides social studies teachers the potential to provide their students with unprecedented access to people, ideas, and events. Bringing the world into the classroom through online media including newspapers and news networks supports the teaching of current events and provides multiple perspectives on peoples and cultures from around the world. You and your students can contact students from down the block or around the world. The Newseum's Today's Front Pages allow students to compare and contrast news stories and the reporting of significant events from around the world.

In addition, a number of sites, including the International Education and Resource Network (IEARN), ePals classroom exchange, and the Global SchoolHouse Foundation support international links and collaborative time-sensitive and relevant school-based projects that foster research, collaboration, and cooperation. A variety of digital tools are available for you to use to create local and global connections with other students, teachers, and content experts. Whether you're joining an established community, such as the examples given here, or drawing upon local experts such as professionals from museums, libraries, or parents of your students, digital communication tools can help broaden your students' experiences. Such projects create opportunities for students to explore and revise their conceptions of people,

STORIES FROM PRACTICE

Building Oral Histories

At Rocky Gap High School, in southwest Virginia, students are using technology to go beyond simply accessing information to using technology to build on prior local knowledge by creating the Bland County History Archives (see Figure 18.3). The archive is the result of ongoing work by students in social studies who have collected oral histories from their community. As part of the process students have scanned historical documents and photographs, transcribed oral histories, and uploaded these resources into an online searchable database that has developed into an award-winning online historical archive of their Appalachian community. In addition to the website, students plan to create a CD and short video of samples from the project. The melding of students' prior knowledge, personal interests, technology, and history of place at the community level has resulted in the development of an ongoing, evolving local history project.

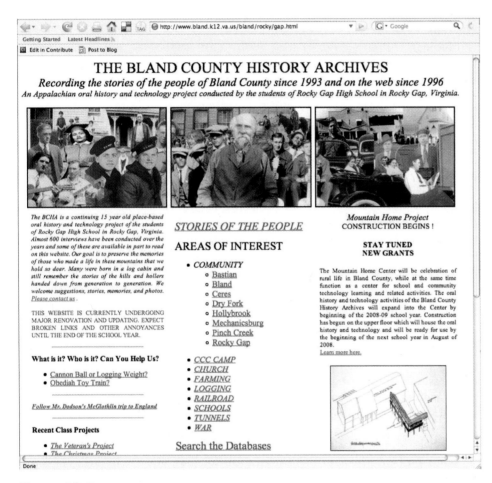

Figure 18.3
Students at Rocky Gap High School built and maintain the Bland County History Archives.

places, and environments over time and space. (For more information on using technology to develop global understanding, see Chapter 11.)

Strategy 4: Teachers should facilitate student knowledge construction by using technology to build on students' prior knowledge and interest.

The integrated nature of social studies continues to offer numerous opportunities for teachers to help diverse learners explore their own interests and questions and complete social studies projects. Social studies is ultimately the study of people, places, and events throughout the ages; it is a subject that explores existential issues of life and death over time and space. Tapping students' interests with regard to exploring questions related to the human condition is something that social studies teachers should nurture. Now as never before, digital technologies serve as powerful portals for students to examine and follow their own interests within the social studies classroom as consumers of information and data. For example, if students begin to ask questions about the U.S. elections and how the electoral college works, the website "270 to Win" provides access to historical electoral interactive maps that reveal the results for every presidential election in U.S. history. The site also provides the opportunity to examine strategies for winning the electoral college in upcoming presidential races. Similarly, merely learning the origins of one's first names and surnames can begin to intrigue students and open up opportunities to explore their own histories and genealogy and numerous resources exist to allow students to begin such investigations.

Strategy 5: Teachers enhance the viability of student knowledge by using technology to provide timely and meaningful feedback.

An essential part of the instructional process is the need for knowledge assessment. This requires providing timely and ongoing feedback with regard to the viability of students' essential understanding of the knowledge and skills taught within the social studies classroom. During this era of standards, a number of resources have been developed that allow students to assess their developing understandings. For example, the Online Regents Exam Prep Center, the Interactive Quizzes site by Tami Maloney, and History Teacher.net all provide access to online social studies multiple-choice questions that, when taken, provide students with immediate feedback. Many states are developing formative assessment and benchmark testing systems that allow students to assess their knowledge throughout the school year. Some states allow access to practice tests only during school with results available only to teachers while some states have developed systems that allow teachers, students, and parents to access formative assessment items outside of the school day and campus in order to help them set their own learning goals for better performance on high-stakes assessments that occur toward the end of the year (Axelson, 2005). The popularity of handheld wireless responders allows teachers to quickly create formative assessment opportunities through the creation of forced-choice questions that allow students to anonymously "beam" their answers to a teacher workstation during class. Often used for short quizzes or polling, software associated with these class performance systems provides real-time data analysis to help you determine strengths and weaknesses in student understanding.

In addition, games and simulations are designed to allow students to test their ideas, hypotheses, and knowledge and receive immediate feedback based on their choices and actions. You may want to include some educational games in your social studies classroom, such as the Government Printing Office's Place the State, interactive games on Ben's Guide to U.S. Government for Kids, and the Interactive History Content Games. These online games are designed to be quick and interactive. More complex educational games and simulation software are available offline, such as Making History: The Calm Before the Storm, a PC-based World War II single- or multiplayer-simulation game by Muzzy Lane Productions; and Decisions, Decisions by Tom Snyder Productions. These games and simulations provide rich opportunities for students to examine ideas, make choices, and evaluate the viability of their choices. Such games and simulations are important because they are designed in a way that students take on roles, make decisions and choices, and are provided with feedback pertaining to the outcomes/consequences of their initial choices. As James Gee (2003) noted, "When players do this, two things can happen: On the one hand, their presupposed perspectives on the world might be reinforced . . . On the other hand . . . video games can challenge players' taken for granted views about the world (pp. 140–141).

Taken together, all of these strategies place students at the center of their learning and serve as a break from the typical transmission model of social studies. The authentic learning strategies above clearly begin to provide opportunities to foster creative thinking skills in the social studies classroom. However, it is important to look more closely at how digital technologies can facilitate autonomous creative thinking within the social studies classroom.

Technology and Creative Thinking Skills Instruction

As has been made clear throughout this chapter, designing instruction to support wise practice in the social studies classroom involves adding to and going beyond teacher-centered instruction toward considering a "shift from an emphasis on a 'story well told' (or, the story as told in the textbook), to an emphasis on 'sources well scrutinized'. . . [Where students] pose questions, collect and analyze sources, struggle with issues of significance, and ultimately build their own historical interpretations" (Levstik, 1996, p. 394). The ability to appropriately use both teacher-centered and student-centered instruction requires that teachers develop a sense of pedagogical purpose and confidence with regard to believing that a student's abilities to learn history and social studies and to think historically are skills that "educators can nurture, not an ability whose development they must wait for or whose absence they must lament" (Barton, 1998, p. 54). If students are to engage in the types of authentic creative thinking required of 21st-century citizens then there is a need to go beyond simply providing access to the resources, documents, and materials and to design strategies and scaffolds that model the habits of mind required to engage in such thinking in the classroom. Currently there are a number of digitally supported instructional projects that specifically model the "doing" of history and allow students to practice and explore creative thinking and problem solving in ways that would not be possible in the everyday social studies classroom.

History Matters is a product of the Center for History and New Media housed at George Mason University in Fairfax, Virginia. History Matters offers a range of resources, including 1,000 primary documents in text, image, and audio, and an annotated guide to 850 of the best U.S. History websites. Designed for teachers of U.S. History survey courses, History Matters provides an excellent starting point for investigating American history. Two additional online resources encourage students to develop inquiry skills within the context of doing history. Do History allows a student to take on the role of historian and piece together elements of the past to form an understanding of what happened in the life of a New England midwife, Martha Ballard. In addition, this web-based resource allows students to form an understanding of the complexity of history and the realization that there is no one interpretation of a historical event. The History Inquiry Project introduces students to the concept of historical inquiry and provides tutorials and resources to help facilitate the teaching and learning of historical inquiry for teachers and students. Similarly, the Historical Scene Investigation (HSI) project (see Figure 18.4) looks to help bridge the gap between the potential of web-based historical documents and the creative thinking scaffolds necessary to prepare students to engage in open-ended historical inquiry. Using the metaphor of a crime scene investigation popularized by the popular *CSI: Crime Scene Investigation* television series, case-based exercises guide students to analyze selected historical documents to solve a historical problem or question.

These resources provide models of historical inquiry that you can incorporate into your social studies classroom. Using the framework from the HSI project, your students can become historical detectives using materials you gather from your media center, library, or classroom. Students can even pose their own problems for inquiry based on events or situations of local interest. Students can investigate evidence you compile through a combination of print and digital resources. Your students can search for clues using a range of tools including Internet databases and

H.S.I.
Historical Scene Investigation

Home   About HSI   Open Cases

When Elvis Met Nixon

Becoming a Detective

http://www.archives.gov/exhibit_hall/when_nixon_met_elvis/part_1.html

Why was this photograph of Elvis Presley and President Richard Nixon taken in December of 1970?

Investigating the Evidence

There are a series of documents that follow. It is your job to determine the type of evidence included within this file, the credibility of each piece of evidence and how the evidence fits together. Finally, you will be asked to come up with a plausible explanation of why the photograph was taken and how you came to that particular conclusion.

- Document A: Letter from Elvis Presley to President Nixon, December 21, 1970
- Document B: Photo of Nixon and Presely in the Oval Office, December 21, 1970
- Document C: White House agenda for meeting, December 21, 1970
- Document D: White House Memorandum, December 21, 1970

Figure 18.4
Students can develop inquiry skills in a social studies context at websites such as the Historical Scene Investigation.
Source: College of William and Mary School of Education. http://web.wm.edu/hsi/cases/elvis/elvis_student.html

other web resources, digital cameras and video cameras, as well as handheld or laptop computers. Students can compile their data using productivity tools, such as word processors, note-taking software, databases, and spreadsheets. Once students crack the case, they can present the data they have collected and support their positions with presentations, web, or multimedia-authoring software—including pictures and video elements they have collected and edited.

The availability of word-processing tools, image- and video-editing software, web-development tools, as well as concept-mapping software on school computers is opening up possibilities for teachers and students to shift from being consumers of information to creative producers of information. These common software applications offer the potential of changing the ways students can craft and present their work. For example, presentation software, such as PowerPoint or Keynote, affords

THE GAME PLAN

Identifying Web-Based Resources

Set Goals

Find online resources you can use for a range of activities in a social studies classroom. You may need resources to help students conduct historical inquiry or attain multiple perspectives on people, issues, and events.

Take Action

Review the web resources on the textbook's companion website. Conduct other searches on your own for resources of interest to you.

Monitor

How well do the resources meet stated goal(s)? Are there clearinghouse websites or sites that review online social studies resources? Did you find resources you did not know existed that might be helpful to you in the social studies classroom?

Evaluate and Extend

Select the best resources you have found and include a list of them in your portfolio. Share your list with other social studies students to compile a master list that covers a range of grade levels and social studies content areas.

both teacher and student the chance to develop professional presentations that use historical resources and maps. In addition, presentation software can serve as a tool to develop motivational and interactive review games and quizzes based on popular game shows, such as *Jeopardy, Hollywood Squares*, and *Who Wants to be a Millionaire* in the social studies classroom.

Even without the use of such templates, presentation software or multimedia-authoring software can be used to create interactive quizzes. For example, individual slides can contain a multiple-choice question, and upon answering the question students can be directed to different feedback slides based on their answer selections. Wireless responders, used with or without an interactive whiteboard, take these quizzes one step further by allowing students to beam responses to questions that can be analyzed and reported in real time—with or without revealing student identities. While the teacher can create the quiz, a more meaningful option is for students to create the questions (either individually or in groups) based on specific time period or standard, and the questions can then be combined for the entire class to review. By allowing "expert" groups of students to create the questions and appropriate answer choices, students are actively and creatively thinking about the subject matter and engaging in creative thinking. Plus, you will be surprised at the difficulty of the questions that students create, as they often enjoy stumping their classmates.

The availability of intuitive, user-friendly video-creation software, such as Windows Movie Maker or iMovie, has also opened up a new avenue through which teachers and students can create meaningful projects that fuse images, music, video, and narration as they develop digital accounts of events in order to demonstrate their deep understandings of a topic. Teachers and students can literally become a mini Ken Burns overnight. These digital historical documentaries or digital historical narratives can be shared on the web or distributed on CD or DVD. Student-created digital movies provide teachers and students with the opportunity to explore topics that are personally relevant while providing opportunities for the writing process, content investigation, collaborative and authentic assessment, as well as 21st-century technology skills.

A number of websites provide explanations and models of why and how to develop digital history narratives for the social studies classroom. For example, Documenting the Historical South Digital Library at the University of North Carolina, Chapel Hill is an excellent resource for teachers and students beginning to embark

STORIES FROM PRACTICE

Digital Movies in the Social Studies Class

I had the opportunity to speak with one of our graduates in his second year of teaching about his use of technology in his Social Studies classroom. He had developed a digital movie using Movie Maker software in order to introduce and review the French Revolution with his students. He told me that developing a short digital movie would allow him to capture the feeling of upheaval and change during this tumultuous period of history.

Movie Maker comes standard on just about any computer, including the one his students had. For his movie on the French Revolution, he put a high charged song, P.O.D.'s "Boom," in it as background to images and quotes from the period. The final movie was broken down into six main events and in three minutes it covered the early 1770s to the fall of Napoleon in 1815. The movie moved very fast but it was intended to capture the emotion of that period. This was a period when roughly 40,000 people were executed in public, a government changed hands almost monthly, and France was at war with its neighbors on several occasions. It was probably appropriate to make the text, images, and music as chaotic as the era. The video allowed him to introduce the topic in a very relevant way. The students responded positively right away and were excited about the opportunity. It was also used for review at the end of the unit.

While reflecting on the lesson, he suggested he might change some things about the lesson if he did it again. For example, he would have assessed the students on the topic before they started to make the film, and established clear checkpoints to help them move through the stages of creating a digital video. He probably shouldn't have let them mess with music until halfway through the project, because many of the students just wanted to focus on finding a good song and they took way too long to choose one. From a technology standpoint, it would have helped to make sure projects were complete and in Windows Media form *before* class to help with presentations.

Source: David Hicks, Virginia Tech, Blacksburg, VA.

WEB LINK

View the textbook's companion website to review a list of the software, hardware, and Internet resources mentioned in this chapter as well as additional resources for the social studies classroom.

on digital historical narratives. Similarly the Digital Directors Guild provides a space in which K–12 educators can explore digital moviemaking, its place in the curriculum, and its impact on student learning. Housed within the site is an expanding matrix of student-created digital movies including examples across all grade levels and content areas, including an expanding database of classroom projects and reflections.

Taken together, these resources serve as powerful exemplars of how social studies educators are utilizing digital resources to create sophisticated learning environments that 1) use technology as a learning scaffold, and 2) foster active engagement by students and the building of viable strategies for engaging creative thinking practices that are part of the process of "doing" historical inquiry. An important stage in the doing of history is not simply analyzing historical documents, but working with evidence to create accounts of the past. How such accounts/interpretations are prepared and presented by students is becoming more dynamic and creative as a direct result of the emergence of digital technologies and associated software.

Chapter Summary

This chapter has emphasized the potential power of technology to augment and enrich standards-based social studies curriculum. Incorporating technologies for their own sake is an awkward proposition, unlikely to yield deeper results than frustration or amusement. Instead, social studies instruction designed around student inquiry and meaning making will seek to harness the potential of technology: 1) access to volumes of information and historical sources, 2) outlets for creativity and production, and 3) tools for research and analysis, among others. As always, social studies teachers carry the profound responsibility of designing instruction that meets the needs of diverse learners and prepares them to participate in a democratic system during an information age that is as fraught with tension as it is rich in resources. By successfully integrating technology as a tool for social studies inquiry, providing scaffolds for understanding issues of ethics, and preparing students to navigate in a complex digital age, social studies teachers can equip students with knowledge and skills to depend on far beyond their school years.

YOUR PORTFOLIO

To demonstrate your understanding of creating learning experiences in the social studies classroom that address the National Educational Technology Standards for Students, create a lesson plan for common activities in your social studies classroom using the GAME Plan template available on the textbook's companion website, or one of your choosing. You may want to focus on one of the specific strategies described in this chapter, such as historical inquiry, or you may want to help students access digital resources that they can use across different activities.

1. Identify the national social studies content standards that relate to your lesson. Review the state-specific content standards you discovered earlier in the chapter and determine appropriate assessments you can incorporate in your lesson based on the achievement standards.
2. Research and select appropriate technologies that can support the activities in your lesson. Identify technology standards (NETS-S) addressed by your lesson. List all hardware and software required for the lesson and consider any preparation or prerequisite skills you may need to address before the students can complete the lesson.
3. If using the GAME Plan lesson template, include justifications for your technology application and reasons why you selected it in the section labeled Lesson Reflections and Notes. If you are using a different lesson plan template, include this information either on the template or in a separate file. Your justifications may relate to your skills or familiarity with the technology or the skills of your students, the match between the intended outcomes of the technology and your lesson, or even accessibility concerns.

References

Axelson, M. (2005). *Online, standards-based, formative assessment conference proceedings.* Charleston, WV: Edvantia, Inc. Retrieved July 26, 2006, from http://www.edvantia.org/publications/index1.cfm?&section=publications&area=publications&id=664

Barton, K. (1998, April). *"That's a tricky piece": Children's understanding of historical time in Northern Ireland.* Paper presented at the annual meeting of the American Educational Research Association, San Diego, CA. (ERIC Document Reproduction Service No. ED 426 915).

Doolittle, P., & Hicks, D. (2003). Constructivism as a theoretical foundation for the use of technology in social studies. *Theory and Research in Social Education,* 31(1), 72–104.

Gee, J. P. (2003). *What video games have to teach us about learning and literacy.* New York: Palgrave Macmillan.

Goodlad, J. (1984). *A place called school.* New York: McGraw-Hill.

Levstik, L. (1996). Negotiating the history landscape. *Theory and Research in Social Education,* 24, 393–397.

National Council for the Social Studies (NCSS). (1994). *Expectations for excellence: Curriculum standards for social studies.* Washington, DC: Author.

Rowling, J. K. (2004). *Harry Potter and the order of the phoenix.* New York: Scholastic Paperbacks.

For Further Reading

Bennett, L., & Berson, M. J. (2007). *Digital age: Technology-based K–12 lesson plans for the social studies.* Washington, DC: National Council for the Social Studies.

Cantu, D., & Wilson, W. J. (2003). *Teaching history in the digital classroom.* New York: M. E. Sharpe.

Diem, R. (2000). Can it make a difference? Technology and the social studies. *Theory and Research in Social Education,* 28(4), 493–501.

Friedman, A. M. (2006). World history teachers' use of digital primary sources: The effect of training. *Theory and Research in Social Education,* 34(1), 124–141.

Lee, J., & Clarke, W. (2003). *High school social studies students' uses of online historical documents related to the Cuban missile crisis.* Paper presented at the annual meeting of the Society of Information Technology and Teacher Education (SITE), Albuquerque, NM.

Means, B., & Olsen, K. (1994). The link between technology and authentic learning. *Educational Leadership,* 51(7), 15–19.

Thornton, S. J. (2005). *Teaching social studies that matters: Curriculum for active learning.* New York: Teachers College, Columbia University.

Van Sledright, B. (2004). What does it mean to think historically, and how do you teach it? *Social Education,* 68(3), 230–233.

TECHNOLOGY INTEGRATION FOR MEANINGFUL CLASSROOM USE
Daily Lesson GAME Plan

Lesson Title: American State and National Sites and Symbols

Related Lessons: American History Sites and Symbols

Grade Level: Elementary

Unit: American Sites and Symbols

GOALS

Content Standards (NCSS Thematic Strand):
- Culture
- People, places, and environment

ISTE NETS-S

- ☐ 1. Creativity and innovation
- ☑ 2. Communication and collaboration
- ☑ 3. Research and information fluency
- ☐ 4. Critical thinking, problem solving, and decision making
- ☐ 5. Digital citizenship
- ☑ 6. Technology operations and concepts

Instructional Objective(s):
- Students will identify key American state and national sites and symbols
- Students will provide relevant supporting information (in the form of questions) of the images they identify and answer questions posed by other students.

ACTION

Before-Class Preparation: Familiarize yourself with Flickr (http://flickr.com) a web-based photo-sharing site in which individual users can upload and organize digital images. Accounts are free, and a teacher can create a group for a class so that each student can store his/her images in one location. A group can be made public (for the world to see) or private (only for individuals invited to the group). Regardless of the option the teacher chooses, it is strongly recommended that the teacher set up a group prior to implementing this lesson.

After an image is uploaded, it is given a unique URL, and can be given a **tag**, which is a keyword used to describe it. A unique feature of Flickr—and one particularly applicable to elementary social studies—is that each image can be given notes as well as commented upon. Using a **note**, a student (or teacher) can select a particular part of an image and describe it in further detail, and it is only visible when the user scrolls their mouse over that particular selection. There is also space for multiple users to provide comments on an image.

It should be noted that this lesson format is for the introductory lesson in Flickr, and as such, describes setting up individual student accounts and becoming familiar with the site. As Flickr can be used at different times throughout the school year, the start-up time will likely decrease. Students should already be familiar with searching the web, and, in a previous lesson, will have brainstormed and located sites and symbols that represent what it means to live in America and be an American. These images will now be used to support this lesson.

During Class

Time	Instructional Activities	Materials and Resources
20 minutes	Students open the Flickr website and select one state and one national image (previously uploaded) related to sites and symbols. The students then add tags and develop annotations or questions in the form of notes. The annotations should provide the name and location of the site and differentiate between a state or national site or symbol (or both). Questions can be about the image itself or the time period studied.	Computer with Internet connection
20 minutes	Students share their annotations and/or answer the questions posed by their classmates in the form of comments.	
10–15 minutes	A slide show is created by the teacher from the individual images that have been uploaded and shown to the class. Students reflect on individual images.	

Notes: This lesson was adapted from Richardson (2006). For further reading, see the chapter entitled, "Fun with Flickr: Creating, publishing, and using images online" (pp. 101–109) in: Richardson, W. (2006). *Blogs, wikis, podcasts, and other powerful web tools for classrooms.* Thousand Oaks, CA: Corwin Press.

MONITOR

Ongoing Assessment(s): During the lesson teachers should informally assess students' understanding of the objectives, specifically students' abilities to develop appropriate tags, as well as create appropriate questions based on the uploaded images.

Accommodations and Extensions: Teachers may want to have all students on computers or could use 4–6 computers and have students rotate through various activities that both require and do not require computer access. Another option is to use a single computer and the teacher to lead the class in a direct instructional activity.

   Using digital images can support participation by some students with special needs and English language learners (ELLs). ELLs can provide tags in more than one language to strengthen their language learning.

Back-up Plan: If an image-searching site is blocked at your school, provide a selection of images on a web page or the school's hard drive. This can be done individually, in pairs, or in groups. In the event that Internet access is not available the day of the lesson, teachers should print images, and have students comment upon and notate them with pen and paper. Also, if the teacher has images saved on his/her computer, this can be done as a whole-class activity.

EVALUATION

Lesson Reflections and Notes: Assessment of student learning should be ongoing. Teachers should informally assess student work throughout the activity. A rubric that differentiates exemplary, middle, and beginning level questions and answers should be used to evaluate student work.

TECHNOLOGY INTEGRATION FOR MEANINGFUL CLASSROOM USE
Daily Unit GAME Plan

Unit Title: Civil War Voice Wall Project

Related Lessons: Major Events in the Civil War, Places Made Famous by the Civil War

Grade Level: Middle grades

Subject: Social Studies

GOALS

Content Standards (NCSS Thematic Strand):
* Time, continuity, and change

ISTE NETS-S

☑ 1. Creativity and innovation

☑ 2. Communication and collaboration

☑ 3. Research and information fluency

☑ 4. Critical thinking, problem solving, and decision making

☑ 5. Digital citizenship

☐ 6. Technology operations and concepts

Instructional Objective(s): The purpose of this lesson is to engage students more deeply in their study of the Civil War and to enable them not only to learn the key content (i.e., Abraham Lincoln, Jefferson Davis, etc.), but also to understand the multiple perspectives of different people who lived through the war. To this end, the project emphasizes research, writing, and technology skills throughout its three phases.

ACTION

Before-Class Preparation: Identify or create the rubric to assess the final project. The rubric should emphasize content objectives and provide guidelines for effective communication via audio and video. Due to the complexity of the project, it will save time to use a teacher-created or previously created rubric rather than having students create the rubric. Create handouts and identify exemplars from the Internet, DVDs, or other video resources to introduce the project.

Date	Schedule of Lessons	Materials and Resources
Day 1	Students are introduced to the activity by being charged with directing a short (5–7 minute) documentary about important Civil War characters. Their assignment is to create documentaries that can be used by the rest of the class to learn about the character they have been assigned. Review the rubric that will be used for the final assessment of the movies and the introductory handout that lists each character and the types of information to be included in the movie. If available, show brief clips from a previous class or those found on the Internet, DVDs, or other video resources.	
Week 1	**Research Phase:** After being assigned a partner, student pairs select a character from the project introduction handout that provides guidelines on the type of information to research. Topics to include are: • Character: Who is the character? When and where did your character live? • The Events: What events led up to the defining moment for your character? What were the complications and obstacles? What were the turning points? • The Defining Moment: What was the key moment in your character's life? • The Resolution: What happened? How was the situation resolved? • The Conclusion: What was the impact of the character's resolution? Why is it still important to remember this today? Students begin their research with print materials, such as their textbook, encyclopedias, books, novels, and primary source documents. Students can take written or electronic notes, the latter of which can be stored on a file server and backed up on portable data storage. Once the groups have developed a general understanding of their characters, students spend time in a computer lab to corroborate and expand upon their research and to collect images to incorporate into their stories. Bookmark useful websites for students to support their Internet research. Students keep a careful list of where they found their information and images so they can properly cite them in their projects.	Handouts (paper or digital) of major characters in the Civil War Print resource materials
Week 2	**Writing Phase:** Once students have found information to support the research guidelines, students begin the writing phase using a storyboard organizer, such as concept-mapping or presentation software. Students can choose to write from a first- or third-person perspective. Before beginning any writing, the groups should be able to identify the defining moment for the character. This would serve as the central theme of the story. Student work can be saved to portable storage or printed out each day so that students can take their work home with them, exchange copies with peer editors, and work with parents in the evening on revising their work. Students should both contribute to the writing process and reach consensus on material that is included in the movie, including the selection of images, music, or sound effects they want to include.	Concept-mapping or presentation software to organize storyboard
Week 3	**Production Phase:** Students use video-editing software, such as Windows Movie Maker, iMovie, Photostory, or Garage Band to create their movies. Each student should record part of the narration. Images are added to support the narration. Students are encouraged to add sound effects, music, and effects and transitions to their movies, but emphasis should be placed on creating accurate, high-quality content.	Computers with video-editing software Microphones Headphones Rubric
1 class period	**Premiere:** During the premiere, have each student group introduce their own film. Take time to celebrate and congratulate each pair after their movie is shown. Students can take notes for each character during the premiere, or can be given a CD of all of the movies or access to them on a file server.	Computer with speakers and projector

Notes: Pairs are best for this activity so that each member has a chance to work on the computer. Groups should be no larger than 3 students.

MONITOR

Ongoing Assessment(s): Several artifacts are created that should be monitored, such as student research notes, storyboard, and script.

Accommodations and Extensions: Students may need guidance in identifying relevant images and sounds. Students should constantly be reminded that the emphasis of the lesson is on finding and communicating accurate information, not on flashy graphics, transitions, or other aspects of the technology.

Back-up Plan: Students with limited technology proficiency or limited access can present their research findings as an oral report.

EVALUATION

Unit Reflections and Notes: The final movie is assessed using a rubric introduced at the beginning of the lesson. Students' content knowledge about each of the characters will be assessed via a unit test.

TECHNOLOGY INTEGRATION FOR MEANINGFUL CLASSROOM USE
Daily Lesson GAME Plan

Lesson Title: Lakota Winter Counts

Grade Level: High School

Related Lessons:

Unit: Nature of History/Native Americans

GOALS

Content Standards (NCSS Thematic Strands):
- Culture
- Time, Continuity, and Change
- Individuals, Groups, and Institutions
- Civic Ideas and Practices

ISTE NETS-S

☑ 1. Creativity and innovation

☑ 2. Communication and collaboration

☑ 3. Research and information fluency

☑ 4. Critical thinking, problem solving, and decision making

☑ 5. Digital citizenship

☑ 6. Technology operations and concepts

Instructional Objective(s):
- Students will describe the methods used by Lakota Indians to record historical events.
- Students will compare the Lakota method of historical record keeping to that of other cultures studied, including Aztec, Chinese, and Islamic cultures.

ACTION

Before-Class Preparation: Teachers will need to review background material on the Lakota Winter Counts (see http://wintercounts.si.edu from the Smithsonian. Sections appropriate for students are titled "What are Winter Counts?" and "Who are the Lakota?").

Lakota Winter Counts were a method of historical record keeping used by Lakota Indians. Various Lakota tribal groups would designate one member, called a keeper, to keep the historical record. Their job was to identify a memorable event, not necessarily the most important, but most memorable, and produce a drawing of the event. This event would be recorded along with previous years' drawings and arranged in order to keep track of successive years. A year for the Lakota was the time from the first snowfall to the following first snowfall. Each year was marked as a winter, giving rise to counting the successive winters with drawings.

ACTION

The following resources from Smithsonian provide additional background (listed online at http://wintercounts.si.edu/html_version/pdfs/biblio.pdf)

Burke, C. E. (2000). Collecting Lakota histories: Winter Count pictographs and texts in the National Anthropological Archives. *American Indian Art*, 26(1), 82–89, 102–103.

DeMallie, R. & Parks, D. (2001). Teton. *Handbook of the North American Indians: Plains*. Vol. 13: Pt 2 (pp. 794–820). Washington, DC: Smithsonian Books. Academic overview of the Lakota tribes.

DeMallie, R. & Parks, D. (2001). Tribal traditions and records. *Handbook of the North American Indians: Plains*. Vol. 13: Pt 2 (pp. 1062–1073). Washington, DC: Smithsonian Books. Scholarly overview of the winter count traditions of the Plains Indians.

During Class

Time	Instructional Activities	Materials and Resources
10–15 minutes	Introduce the Lakota Winter Counts system of historical record keeping. Use the Smithsonian website to display images from specific winter counts.	Computer with large monitor or projector and screen http://wintercounts.si.edu
10 minutes	Show examples of other cultural efforts to record successive years in calendar form. These can include Aztec and Christian solar calendars as well as Chinese and Islamic lunar calendars. When working with students on this brief overview teachers should explain to students that the Lakota Winter Counts is unique in that a human event is used to mark a year. Other calendars do not use human events, but instead use celestial movements.	Computer with large monitor or projector and screen http://webexhibits.org/calendars/ http://www.azteccalendar.com/
20 minutes	In this part of the activity students will select an event from their lives in the past year. In the tradition of the Lakota Winter Count keepers, students should select an event that is memorable and make a drawing of the event. Each drawing should be interpreted with a one-paragraph annotation of why they selected that event.	Word-processing software with drawing tools or drawing software Images can also be hand drawn and scanned or photographed
20 minutes	After students have created one drawing representing a memorable event in their lives, divide students into pairs and assign each student a year in U.S. (or local, state, or world) history. The years can be successive years or deliberately selected nonconsecutive years. Each student pair should select an event from their year that they think is memorable for everyone and illustrate that event in methods similar to their personal events. Teachers may need to provide students with supporting materials for their assigned year.	Word-processing software with drawing tools or drawing software Images can also be hand drawn and scanned or photographed
10 minutes	All the student illustrations should be arranged in the tradition of a Lakota Winter Count, using the Smithsonian Lakota Winter Counts website as a reference for helping students understand how to arrange their drawings. Drawings can be arranged using presentation or image software that allows for the creation of slide shows. Hand-drawn or printed counts can be hung in the classroom for display.	Computer with large monitor or projector and screen http://wintercounts.si.edu

Notes: The Smithsonian website uses Flash. Teachers may want to have all students on computers or could use 4–6 computers and have students rotate through various activities that both require and do not require computer access. Another option is to use a single computer and the teacher to lead the class in a direct instructional activity.

MONITOR

Ongoing Assessment(s): During the lesson teachers should informally assess students' understanding of the objectives, specifically students' abilities to describe the Lakota Winter Counts system and their understanding of the similarities and differences between the winter counts system and other calendars.

Accommodations and Extensions: This activity can be easily adapted for English language learners and for students with learning disabilities. One strategy is to provide adapted texts to accompany the winter counts.

Teachers might wish to include a culminating assignment in which students describe the Lakota Winter Counts and how it differs from other calendar systems. This activity could be made more authentic by requiring students to write proposals for how a system

MONITOR

such as the winter counts might be used in their school to record the history of events in the school. In addition to the actual proposals, this work should include a description of the winter counts system as well as two or three other calendar systems.

Back-up Plan: In the event that Internet access is not available the day of the lesson, teachers should print copies of the Winter Counts website as well as text resources that can provide background information for students.

EVALUATION

Lesson Reflections and Notes: Assessment of student learning should be consistent and ongoing. Teachers should use questioning to monitor student understanding, specifically about the Lakota winter counts system and their understanding of the similarities and differences between the winter counts system and other calendars.

Monkey Business/Fotolia

Integrating Technology in the Health and Physical Education Classroom

Craig P. Tacla, Ph.D., James A. Krouscas, Ph.D., and Kerry Redican, Ph.D.

Like many people, you may have decided to teach health and physical education because you are good at sports, enjoy competition, or value leading a healthy and physically active lifestyle. Teaching health and physical education can be enjoyable and rewarding; but you may require some guidance when working with students who do not have your same level of interest and motivation. National and state standards clearly identify goals and objectives associated with each grade level and provide specific assessment ideas to assist teachers with the task of illustrating how their program will meet these suggested guidelines.

ISTE Standards addressed in this chapter

This chapter provides content-specific suggestions and strategies for addressing both ISTE's National Educational Technology Standards for Students (NETS-S) and the National Standards for Health and Physical Education. This chapter also builds on the NETS-T concepts and skills presented earlier, with a special emphasis on skills related to Standard 1 "Facilitate and inspire student learning and creativity." Following an overview of the National Standards for Health and Physical Education and how you can address the NETS-S in the health and physical education classroom, this chapter outlines techniques, tools, and methods for developing authentic learning experiences that advance student creativity and innovation in the health and physical education classroom.

Outcomes

In this chapter, you will

- Identify health and physical education standards and explain how technology can support them.
- Discuss how the National Educational Technology Standards for Students can be addressed in health and physical education classrooms.
- Understand how authentic learning principles can be addressed using technology in health and physical education classrooms.

Outcomes *(continued)*

■ Explain how technology can increase learning and facilitate creative thinking in health and physical education.

Although most health and physical educators are equipped with content knowledge and a variety of effective teaching techniques, many know very little about the practical applications of technology in their teaching. For this reason, it is important to discuss how, when, and why health and physical educators should incorporate technology.

Technology and Content Standards

Health education and physical education are two components of a school health program model often referred to as a Coordinated (or Comprehensive) School Health Program (CSHP) (Birch & Kane, 1999; Centers for Disease Control and Prevention, n.d.). The CSHP is comprised of eight different but related components (see Figure 19.1) that provide a framework to coordinate health-related services and programs within a school as well as providing connection to, and a point of entry for, external services that serve young people, such as health care workers, the media, and community organizations that address health issues. Health and physical education classes are arguably the most critical components of this model for helping students learn about and set the foundation for a life of healthy living. They are also the two components over which you, as a teacher, will have the most control.

The Joint Committee on National Health Education Standards has identified guidelines for what is taught in health education and what students should be able to demonstrate in K–12 health education (see Table 19.1). These standards are excellent recommendations and can help teachers structure learning experiences and activities that are meaningful and challenging to students and can provide the planned, sequential curriculum that is a key component of the Comprehensive School Health Program. When implementing these standards, new and innovative practices within health and physical education must be considered. One area in particular that can benefit from the utilization of technology is the health-related fitness of our young people.

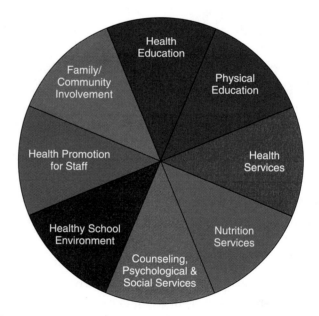

Figure 19.1
Coordinated School Health Program.
Source: Centers for Disease Control.

Table 19.1	National Standards for Health Education Developed by the Joint Committee on National Health Education Standards

1. Students will comprehend concepts related to health promotion and disease prevention to enhance health
2. Students will analyze the influence of family, peers, culture, media, technology, and other factors on health behaviors
3. Students will demonstrate the ability to access valid information and products and services to enhance health
4. Students will demonstrate the ability to use interpersonal communication skills to enhance health and avoid or reduce health risks
5. Students will demonstrate the ability to use decision-making skills to enhance health
6. Students will demonstrate the ability to use goal-setting skills to enhance health
7. Students will demonstrate the ability to practice health-enhancing behaviors and avoid or reduce health risks
8. Students will demonstrate the ability to advocate for personal, family, and community health

Source: Joint Committee on National Health Education Standards. (2007).

Table 19.2	National Standards for Physical Education Developed by the National Association for Sport and Physical Education

1. Demonstrates competency in motor skills and movement patterns needed to perform a variety of physical activities
2. Demonstrates understanding of movement concepts, principles, strategies, and tactics as they apply to the learning and performance of physical activities
3. Participates regularly in physical activity
4. Achieves and maintains a health-enhancing level of physical fitness
5. Exhibits responsible personal and social behavior that respects self and others in physical activity settings
6. Values physical activity for health, enjoyment, challenge, self-expression, and/or social interaction

Source: National Association for Sport and Physical Education. (2004).

Following public outcry by the health community in the United States, public health experts proposed a change in focus for physical education. *Healthy People 2000* (U.S. Public Health Service, 1990) and the more recent *Healthy People 2010* (U.S. Public Health Service, 2000) reported a need for physical activity as a method of chronic disease prevention. Included in these reports are national goals for the promotion of physical activity and the need for quality physical education in the schools. In light of these reports the National Association for Sport and Physical Education (2004) revised its national content standards for physical education (see Table 19.2). The new standards for K–12 physical education programs specifically outline critical components of a physically educated person and highlight the role of physical activity within one's maintenance of good health.

The health and physical education standards rarely mention technology or its use in the classroom specifically; however, health and physical education teachers have long used a variety of technologies to help support their teaching and promote student learning. Although the underlying goal of health and physical education has remained relatively constant over time—that of helping young people become physically fit while developing the skills and knowledge that allow them to establish and maintain a healthy lifestyle—the tools and resources available to teachers and students to support health and physical education have evolved and expanded, just as in other disciplines. In addition to Internet resources, data tools, and presentation software that can be found in all types of classrooms, health and physical education teachers also have access to a range of technology tools designed specifically for health and fitness, including pedometers, heart rate monitors, and digital fitness equipment. Review Table 19.3 for examples of how the NETS-S can be supported in health and physical education classrooms. The sample lesson plans at the end of this chapter provide specific examples of how you can design learning experiences that meet both content area and technology standards.

 WEB LINK

For information related to the standards for physical education programs and further examples of the alignment of the NETS-S to the national standards for health education and national standards for physical education, visit the textbook's companion website.

Table 19.3	NETS-S in the Health and Physical Education Classroom

Creativity and Innovation

Students use word-processing and presentation software to report on a personal health or fitness activity, such as recording dietary, exercise, sleep, and work patterns over a specified period. Students can use spreadsheets to track and graph lifestyle changes, such as the progress they have made using a physical fitness regimen or tracking healthy weight management.

Communication and Collaboration

Students communicate with health and fitness professionals on topics of interest, such as routinely reviewing web pages and blogs of college or professional athletes or athletic programs, investigating health issues through frequently asked questions on local and national web resources, or using an Ask an Expert feature.

Research and Information Fluency

Students use Internet resources and instructional software to develop a healthy personal nutrition program and monitor their daily habits, or they create a physical fitness routine to meet desired goals and record their physical activity in a log or website.

Critical Thinking, Problem Solving, and Decision Making

Students use digital video to capture and analyze their own as well as team performances in physical activities. Students participating in golf or tennis can analyze their swings while students participating in team performances can evaluate the effectiveness of tactics and strategies during team play.

Digital Citizenship

Students use technology to develop, monitor, and support a healthy and fit lifestyle, including researching the principles of fitness or activities and sports of interest, monitoring their own nutritional habits, or using exercise equipment to reach personal health and fitness goals.

Technology Operations and Concepts

Students use a range of technology tools designed to support sport and fitness, including heart monitors, pedometers, stethoscopes, electronic blood-pressure devices, in addition to instructional software.

THE GAME PLAN

Content Standards

Set Goals

Research the health and physical education standards for a state where you plan to seek a teaching position and create an action plan to ensure that you will have the knowledge and skills necessary to help your students achieve those standards. Identify the concepts, knowledge, and skills you will need to ensure that you are prepared to help your students meet the health and physical education standards in your state.

Take Action

Explore the department of education website in the state where you plan to seek a position. Review the K–12 health and physical education standards in that state and compare them to the state's technology standards. Identify those standards that specifically relate to

applying technology in health and physical education. Develop a plan for how to meet the technology standards in the context of the health and physical education.

Monitor

Did you find the information you needed? Do you need to contact the department of education for more information about where to find the health and physical education standards or the technology standards for teachers?

Evaluate and Extend

Discuss in class the action plan you developed for meeting the technology standards for instructional personnel. Compare your plan to others. Note the strengths and weaknesses of the various plans. Strengthen your plan by incorporating ideas you have heard in class.

Authentic Learning Strategies Incorporating Technology

Without question the most pressing issue facing physical education today is the lack of physical activity among young people. It has been well documented that low levels of physical activity among adolescents is a growing trend with serious implications. For example, according to the 1996 surgeon general's report (U.S. Department of Health and Human Services, 1997), the percentage of young people who are overweight has more than doubled in the past 30 years, and inactivity and poor diet cause at least 300,000 deaths a year in the United States. Needless to say, low levels of physical activity are an issue of epidemic proportions.

In light of these figures, you may be wondering what the connection is between technology and physical activity. After all it would seem that young people need less time in front of a computer or television and more time exercising. Granted, there is no substitute for vigorous physical activity. If young people are to reap the rewards of a physically active lifestyle they must abandon a sedentary lifestyle and instead embrace physical activity and movement. However, technology can make a difference in getting young people (and adults) to make healthier choices, especially in the area of physical activity. Technology itself can motivate students and many technology resources are available to support better understanding of the critical components of health and physical education and how these can be made relevant to individuals. Therefore, in this section we will discuss how technology can be used by teachers to support authentic learning designed to increase physical activity among students and meet health and physical education standards.

Especially in the physical education classroom, it is easy to create activities that promote active or experiential learning, which are commonly associated with authentic instruction. However, you should not confuse physical activity with truly authentic active learning. In Chapter 3 of this book, you learned that active learning is anchored by holistic, complex, and challenging activities. Furthermore, to be truly focused on each learner, the activities should promote student autonomy. This means that students should engage in instructional activities that are relevant and interesting to them. You may have your entire class actively involved in a team sport or game, but for some students the activity may not be interesting or challenging, or it may be frustrating because it is beyond their current skills. This, then, makes it difficult for many students to understand the relevance of and become engaged in the activity.

For many health and physical education teachers, a good place to start in creating authentic instruction is the development and implementation of personal health and fitness plans. A personal health and fitness plan can be developed for students at many grade levels and can be administered in health or physical education classrooms. The goal is to help students develop a plan that is relevant to them while addressing the major components of your curriculum, whether that be the development of motor skills, promoting physical activity, or practicing health-enhancing behaviors and reducing health risks. A personal health or fitness plan meets the five criteria of authentic instruction described in Chapter 3. It promotes learner autonomy, because your students identify and monitor their own goals and strategies for achieving them, in other words they engage in self-directed learning. It leads to truly active learning, not just activities, as your students must implement strategies and monitor their effectiveness. It is holistic, as students obtain information from a variety of sources as well as about themselves, such as information that leads to understanding their current health profile or levels of physical activity and goals for fitness. It is realistic, because students formulate ideas about their own health and fitness and the best method for improving or maintaining positive attitudes toward a healthy and active lifestyle. Finally, it is challenging, as students must address the one critical question central to all health and physical education, "What must I do to develop and maintain my own healthy lifestyle?"

A variety of technologies are available to help students develop and monitor a health or fitness plan. In order to implement this organizing activity in your health or physical education classroom, your students will 1) gather information to create personal health or fitness goals, 2) develop and implement a plan with strategies for meeting personal goals, and 3) monitor or evaluate the success of their plans.

Perhaps the most helpful information-gathering tool is the Internet. Never before has such a wealth of health and fitness information been freely available from reliable sources. Colleges and universities, government organizations, and well-known health and fitness organizations routinely provide and update web-based information on a full range of health and fitness information that your students can tap into to guide the development of their personal plans. For a general overview of health and physical education curricular issues, you can turn to websites such as PE Central or HealthTeacher. PE Central is known as the premier website for health and physical education teachers, parents, and students. Its goal is to provide the latest information about developmentally appropriate health and physical education programs for children and youth. HealthTeacher was created to meet the National Health Education Standards and the Center for Disease Control's Core Health Topics. It contains more than 250 ready-to-use lesson ideas for health educators.

Before beginning their Internet research, you and your students may want to visit the Evaluating Internet Health Information website from the National Institutes of Health (NIH). This site catalogs other sites that discuss the importance of and procedures for evaluating the health information on the web and includes an audio tutorial from the National Library of Medicine. The NIH, along with other government organizations such as the Centers for Disease Control and Prevention (CDC), host a number of additional health-related websites that provide research or best-practice information. The NIH website provides links to information related to child and teen health, men's health, minority health, seniors' health, women's health, and wellness and lifestyle. Visitors to the CDC website can find information for developing and applying disease prevention and control, environmental health, and health promotion and education activities.

Weight management is an issue with which many children and young adults grapple. Online calorie calculators, body-mass-index calculators, and exercise calculators like the ones offered at The Calorie Counter, Keeping Kids Healthy, or research-based information from the federally sponsored Weight-Control Information Network (WIN) can help your students form goals for appropriate weight management using their own data (see Figure 19.2). Online calorie calculators easily determine and count the number of calories for several thousand different food products. Calculators like these also allow your students to determine how many calories they are burning while performing moderate or vigorous types of physical activity. Often, they can simply choose an activity from a dropdown menu, enter their weight in pounds, and indicate how long they spend doing the activity. The exercise calorie calculator will then tell them how many calories are burned in that time period. Other helpful websites include the MyPyramid site sponsored by the U.S. Department of Agriculture or the Fast Food Fact Finder. MyPyramid is designed to help you choose the foods and amounts that are right for you and the Fast Food Fact Finder site gives nutrition information for just about everything on the menu at several of the largest fast food restaurants.

Once students have gathered general information about health and fitness, they'll need some personal information in order to design and implement relevant and realistic goals. They can utilize one or more health assessment technologies just for this purpose. Health assessment technologies come in primarily two forms: electronic assessment devices and assessment screening software. There are many affordable, noninvasive forms of assessment technology available for use in the K–12 classroom. Some of these include sphygmomanometers, thermometers, bioelectrical impedance devices, and breathalyzers. Each one of these devices can be purchased for $100 or less and one device could be used by multiple students if the learning activity is

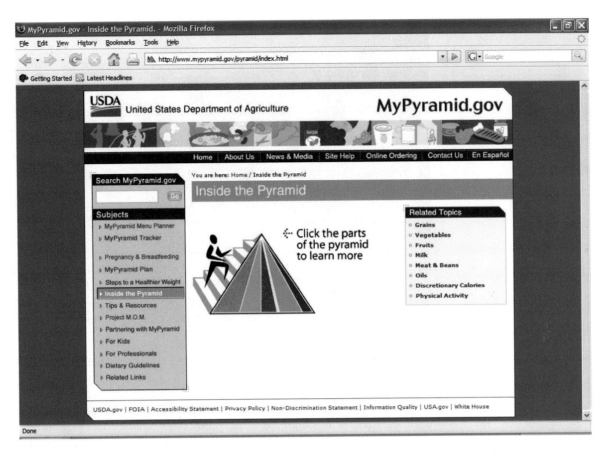

Figure 19.2
Valuable health-related websites are available from many reputable government and education institutions.
Source: http://www.mypyramid.gov/pyramid/index.html

THE GAME PLAN

Identifying Web-Based Resources

Set Goals

Find online resources you can use for a range of activities in a health or physical education classroom. You may need resources to help students research and develop a personal health or fitness plan.

Take Action

Review the web resources on the textbook's companion website. Conduct other searches on your own for resources of interest to you.

Monitor

How well do the resources meet stated goal(s)? Are there clearinghouse websites or sites that review online health or physical education resources? Did you find resources you did not know existed that might be helpful to you in a health or physical education classroom?

Evaluate and Extend

Select the best resources you have found and include a list of them in your portfolio. Share your list with other health and physical education students to compile a master list that covers a range of grade levels and curriculum goals.

carefully developed and implemented. It must be noted that the intention is not to diagnose but to help students learn how to gather important physiological information to determine personal health and physical statistics (see Figure 19.3). So, the real focus here is the process not the outcome.

Figure 19.3
Elementary school pupils undertake a physical sports task and log the results into a laptop computer.

Sphygmomanometers are used to measure blood pressure and can be operated by students who are trained to use them. Sphygmomanometers report systolic blood pressure, diastolic blood pressure, and pulse. There are normal ranges for systolic and diastolic blood pressure and pulse that students can find in textbooks or online. Students can note the data and determine if any kind of follow-up is necessary.

Students can utilize **heart rate monitors** during a range of physical activities, such as fitness training, inline skating, running, or walking (Fiorentino, 2002). The heart rate monitors are small and can be worn on a wrist like a watch. The monitors not only help students identify their heart rates but also tell students when they reach their target heart rates during exercise and how long they have been in that target heart rate range. Data from the heart rate monitors can be uploaded to a computer so an activity level history can be recorded and even graphed. Some heart rate monitor companies include websites with resources for students and lesson plans that help teachers understand how to incorporate them into their curricula.

Bioelectrical impedance devices are used to electrically determine one's body composition (the amount of lean cells in body mass versus fat cells). It is common for a bioelectrical impedance device to have an LCD screen illustrating a person's weight and percentage of body fat. Although a range can be used as a reference point, it should be pointed out that a skinfold assessment performed with calipers by a trained expert is a more accurate form of analysis than a bioelectrical impedance device. Body fat percentage calipers are used to assess the percentage of body fat. A fold of skin is positioned between the calipers and slightly compressed. A readout will show the percentage of body fat. Like the other measures, there are ranges associated with these values that require interpretation, but calipers utilized by a trained individual continue to be a highly accurate measure of one's percentage of body fat.

An increased awareness in health-related physical fitness has yielded an increased production of assessment tools and packages. One commonly available assessment tool is the Fitnessgram, which assesses important aspects of a student's health-related fitness—not skill or agility. Students are not compared to each other, but to health fitness standards, carefully established for each age and gender, that indicate good health. Once the assessment has been done, the Fitnessgram report provides personalized feedback in the health-related fitness areas of aerobic capacity, body composition, muscular strength, muscular endurance, and flexibility.

Paired with the Fitnessgram is the Activitygram, which records a three-day recall of physical activity. It assesses each 30 minute block of time between the hours of 7:00 am and 11:00 pm. Students are asked to enter three pieces of information about each activity: 1) the type and name of activity, 2) intensity of activity, and 3) length of activity. The Fitnessgram/Activitygram 8.0 software allows teachers to maintain a centralized database of fitness testing scores for all their students, to create an individualized fitness report on each student for parents and/or caregivers, to write the report in English or Spanish, and to maintain an activity log for students. It also provides teachers with the option of using a handheld computer for data entry.

Once information has been gathered and plans have been developed, many commonly available productivity tools can be used to craft the plan and document implementation. Word processing documents can provide a synthesis of the information students have found to provide context for personal goals. Spreadsheets or databases can be used to track student progress toward fitness goals. Spreadsheets have the added benefit of quickly converting data into graphs that can easily help you and your students identify their progress. Finally, you may want your students to report on the progress they have made at the end of a grading period. Again, word processing software can easily import graphs of student data as can presentation software that can be shared with families or the rest of the class.

One unique method for combining outdoor activity with technology for authentic learning is the strategy of **geocaching** (Schlatter & Hurd, 2005). Geocaching uses Global Positioning System (GPS) receivers to search for and find small hidden treasures—the cache—that can be located anywhere in the world. The Geocaching website contains guidelines for developing and finding geocaches as well as the location of thousands of caches across the globe. Teachers can create their own geocache on school property or within the local community. Students use the GPS information to find the caches, which are never buried, but may be placed in such a way as to make them unobtrusive to people passing by. The GPS units are accurate up to 30 feet, except in places where national security is of concern, so once the students find the general area, a little sleuthing is in order.

Linking the physical activity of the geocache hunt with instructional activities in other content areas can engage the students cognitively. You could create a series of caches that require students to use math to find the next cache or that requires students to identify and record attributes of historical or biological significance for the surrounding location. Physical education classes can incorporate speed caching in which teams compete against the clock to find one or more caches. Another twist is a 21st-century approach to an exercise circuit, in which teams are required to perform a physical task at each cache in a series, such as having each person complete 10 jumping jacks at one and jogging in place for three minutes at another. In addition to the physical activity, students learn how to read maps, understand coordinates using longitude and latitude, develop communication and cooperation skills, as well as learn how to use this rapidly evolving and useful technology (Schlatter & Hurd, 2005). This can be a fun and interesting way to engage students in authentic learning using technology.

Technology and Creative Thinking Skills Instruction

Creativity may not be the first thing that comes to mind in the health and physical education curriculum, but creativity is an extension of authentic instruction that promotes the development and demonstration of higher-order thinking skills. Creativity often occurs as students are challenged to evaluate new information, synthesize what they have learned, and apply new knowledge and skills to novel situations.

In fact, physical education teachers are actually charged with addressing curricular standards that support creativity. Standard 2 of the National Standards for Physical Education developed by National Association for Sport and Physical Education requires students to demonstrate "understanding of movement concepts, principles, strategies, and tactics as they apply to the learning and performance of physical activities." Highly successful athletes are admired for the creative and innovative ways they apply strategies and tactics to solve performance problems under pressure. This requires more than psychomotor skills and taps into creativity and higher-order thinking. Standard 6 explicitly states that students should value "physical activity for health, enjoyment, self expression, and/or social interaction." Activities supporting these standards can include the use of technology.

As you read in Chapter 4, in order to address creative thinking skills, critical thinking, and problem solving, teachers often turn to authentic problem-based learning. In problem-based learning, students are challenged to identify and solve problems. Problems grounded in real-world situations not only provide greater relevance to students but can increase motivation for developing the skills and knowledge necessary to solve them. It is also important to connect new knowledge and skills with prior learning, so students can understand the continuum of skills and knowledge you are presenting throughout your curriculum.

Seifried (2005) described three methods for promoting the type of higher-order thinking skills that contribute to creative thinking within health and physical education classes. Using the Guided-Discovery Method, you support your students through a series of questions designed to help them discover answers related to a concept from your curriculum. Depending on the age and background knowledge of your students, these questions can begin at a very low level of cognition but gradually build to complex concepts such as competition and motivation within the setting of a team activity or the effects of peer pressure and personal values in a potentially unhealthy social activity such as being pressured to smoke. In the Divergent Teaching Method, students propose multiple solutions to problems and are challenged with understanding and evaluating the solutions proposed by others in an effort to expand their own problem-solving strategies and compare the effectiveness of their solutions against others. Finally, the Self-Check Method requires students to compare their performances to criteria that are selected by the teacher or another authority. In the classroom, this can play out through the use of benchmarks of performance, rubrics, or standards set by organizations, such as the President's Challenge Physical Activity and Fitness Awards Program. Although these strategies can be used in many settings, Seifried (2005) endorsed the use of videos of student activity as a means for supporting each of these types of instructional methods directed toward the development of higher-order thinking.

Video Recordings

With the acquisition of digital cameras, digital video-editing software, and portable computing devices, teachers are beginning to utilize digital video as a way to engage their students in alternative forms of reflective assignments and self-evaluation projects (Fiorentino, 2004). Some of the reported benefits of using video include the ability to review performance immediately, zoom in or focus on skills or critical sections of the body during performance, vary camera angles to address individual or group performance, and simply play the video over and over (Trinigy & Annesi, 1996).

Video can be used to help introduce new skills, from discrete practice drills to their strategic application in games or team events. Video can be especially helpful to demonstrate activities or skills that occur in unusual settings, such as aquatic activities or those that occur outside (Anderson, Mikat, & Martinez, 2001). Teachers can also create digital libraries or playbooks that contain both still images and video (Anderson, Mikat, & Martinez, 2001). These images could be combined with scanned or electronically created diagrams that highlight critical features of a play in a team sport, such as basketball, or the proper execution of dribbling and passing a soccer ball.

Besides demonstration, video has long been used to monitor and assess student performance. Reviewing tapes following extracurricular team games is a common activity, but this same type of activity can promote individual growth within the classroom. Video can be used to capture baseline data of student performance (Anderson, Mikat, & Martinez, 2001), as well as benchmark performances over time, and compared later to a final performance. Video can be used in this manner by students as artifacts in a digital portfolio identifying growth over time or mastery of a new skill. In order to promote the development of student creative thinking skills in relation to physical performance, students should be required to critique and reflect on their own performances of a motor skill. For example, following students' performances of a motor skill, students would engage in a self-analysis project where they set subsequent performance goals. Teachers are provided the opportunity to review the digital video and offer individualized feedback to the student. This form of individualized instruction is highly needed as large class sizes in physical education prevent teachers from frequent interactions during the skill development component of a lesson.

Video can be used not only to support student skill and knowledge development but also to demonstrate creative aspects of physical activities. Gymnastics and dance are physical activities that certainly have a high creative expression component. Students studying formal dance or gymnastics can use video to record and analyze their own practices and performances. Digital video can be edited quickly to allow students to create portfolios of their best creative efforts. Students of all ages, but especially younger students, can demonstrate movement concepts and principles in ways besides formal dance or competitive-level gymnastics that can be captured by video or still images.

Photographs

As an alternative to digital video, digital photography is a less expensive way for many schools to gain some of the benefits described above (see Figure 19.4). Still photos of small groups of students can be included in journals, assessment activities, rubrics, or as the impetus for discussion (Ryan, Marzili, & Martindale, 2001). A good recommendation is to take pictures of small groups rather than individuals. The individuals within the group can still assess their own performance, but the images of the other students in the photograph provide additional opportunities for reflection and comparison. Taking pictures of every student performing every critical skill may also be impractical. By displaying these pictures or importing them into word-processing or presentation software, you can challenge your students to higher levels of understanding about the skills and their own mastery through probing questions, such as "Explain how your kicking technique is similar to or different from other students in this picture. Explain how you'd improve your technique or help someone else with their technique" (Ryan et al., 2001).

Pedometers

In physical education, teachers commonly use fitness and skill development as the measures of their students' success. As physical education began to take seriously the need for increased physical activity it was also necessary to implement a mechanism of student accountability to assess whether appropriate levels of physical activity were met. One affordable instrument providing such accountability is the pedometer. A **pedometer** is a small device that can be fastened easily to a belt or the waistband to measure the number of steps an individual takes. Typically, people accomplish the majority of their activities on land, and pedometers are commonly used for measuring physical activity levels in youths and are widely accepted by researchers and practitioners (Crouter, Schneider, Karabulut, & Bassett, 2003; Kilanowski, Consalvi, & Epstein, 1999). Although other devices such as the heart rate monitor are also utilized, none have the advantages of the pedometer. According to Beighle, Pangrazi, and Vincent (2001), pedometers offer three advantages:

1. Data can be stored permitting the assessment of the frequency, intensity, and duration of physical activity.

ilumus photography/Fotolia

Figure 19.4
Students can take digital photographs of themselves and classmates to record performances of many different skills.

2. Data are provided at specific times of the day, which is useful to determine physical activity patterns.
3. The device is unobtrusive.

Pedometers can be used to help students set realistic fitness goals that are based on their current fitness levels. Individualized fitness or activity goal setting is made possible because many pedometers not only count steps but are now able to convert steps into distance and caloric expenditure. Other more expensive pedometers even have the capability to record activity time. These higher-end pedometers are capable of recording cumulative activity using a start-and-stop fashion, but differ from a typical stopwatch. These pedometers will start recording time engaged in activity once the individual starts the activity and will stop recording time with the end of the activity (Cuddihy, Pangrazi, & Tomson, 2005). The increased functionality requires students to input personalized information such as weight and/or length of step, but these recent advances in pedometers open a variety of instructional opportunities never before realized by physical educators.

Websites, such as PE Central's Log It and Gmaps Pedometers, support and extend the use of pedometers in your classroom. Features of Log It include a virtual hike across the United States, feedback about daily physical activity goals, the ability to compare your progress to others', and the ability to view your own weekly and monthly progress. Gmaps Pedometer allows anyone to create and track mileage anywhere on the globe using Google's online mapping technology. Students can find their communities on the map by entering their street addresses and can then map out walking, running, hiking, or bicycling paths. After finding mileage, you can also estimate calories burned as well as print your route or save it as a favorite.

Technologies in Health Classes

The technologies in this section have focused primarily on use in the physical education classroom, but many of the activities and related technologies mentioned so far can be utilized in health programs, as well. Certainly, the personal health and fitness plans described at the beginning of this chapter require students to identify and solve real-world problems, made more real by their relation to each student's individual health goals. Further, the application of problem-based learning to more global health issues supports the development and demonstration of higher-order thinking skills. Many commonly available technologies are available to support this type of instruction.

Instruction designed to support the development of creative thinking skills in the health classroom should include problems that challenge students to analyze, synthesize, and evaluate information. Activities that address these levels of cognition include using concept-mapping software to compare and contrast student nutrition habits with recommended guidelines (analysis), conducting research on the spread of common infectious diseases and using a spreadsheet to predict the impact on health in the community and country over the next ten years (synthesis), or creating a web page or presentation that criticizes or defends the portrayal of different lifestyle choices on personal and community health (evaluation).

Chapter Summary

Many health and physical education teachers believe that technology plays an important role in their ability to deliver effective lessons. This chapter has presented a sample of the resources you may use to quickly and efficiently integrate various forms of technology into your teaching. You may find that, as a new health and physical education teacher, you might have to take it upon yourself to become the leader in the identification and application of emerging technologies in your school or district. You may need to communicate the instructional importance of technological tools to other teachers, administrators, students, and parents. In doing so you should provide practical examples of how the advances in technology not only save you time but also increase the quality of your instruction and maximize student learning. Make sure you collect or develop examples now and save them in your portfolio for later use.

Few would argue the fact that health and physical education are an important function in today's society. Combating low levels of physical activity and fitness levels is of utmost importance. In order to accomplish the goal of preparing competent, proficient, and active adults, consider using the technological tools available to support health and physical education and continue to monitor and evaluate future technologies that hold the potential to enhance student and teacher performance.

YOUR PORTFOLIO

To demonstrate your understanding of creating learning experiences in the health and physical education classroom that address the National Educational Technology Standards for Students, create a lesson plan for common activities in your health and physical education classroom using the GAME Plan template available on the textbook's companion website, or one of your choosing. Your lesson plan may address, but is not limited to, using Internet resources, commonly available productivity software, or health-related measurement devices.

1. Identify the national health and physical education standards that relate to your lesson. Review the state-specific content standards you discovered earlier in the chapter and determine appropriate assessments you can incorporate in your lesson based on the achievement standards. Include in your plan a strategy for emphasizing the connection between health and physical education and how the activity promotes the attainment of personal goals.

2. Research and select appropriate technologies that can support the activities in your lesson. Identify technology standards (NETS-S) addressed by your lesson. List all hardware and software required for the lesson and consider any preparation or prerequisite skills you may need to address before the students can complete the lesson.

3. If using the GAME Plan lesson template, include justifications for your technology application and reasons why you selected it in the section labeled Lesson Reflections and Notes. If you are using a different lesson plan template, include this information either on the template or in a separate file. Your justifications may relate to your skills or familiarity with the technology or the skills of your students, the match between the intended outcomes of the technology and your lesson, or even accessibility concerns.

References

Anderson, M., Mikat, R. P., & Martinez, R. (2001). Digital video production in physical education and athletics. *Journal of Physical Education, Recreation, and Dance, 72*(6), 19–21.

Beighle, A., Pangrazi, R. P., & Vincent, S. D. (2001). Pedometers, physical activity, and accountability. *Journal of Physical Education, Recreation, and Dance, 72*(9), 16–19.

Birch, D. A., & Kane, W. M. (1999). A comprehensive approach to health promotion. *Journal of Physical Education, Recreation, and Dance, 70*(1), 57–59.

Centers for Diseases Control and Prevention (CDC). (n.d.) *Healthy Youth! Coordinated School Health Program.* Retrieved May 12, 2007, from www.cdc.gov/HealthyYouth/CSHP/

Crouter, S. C., Schneider, P. L., Karabulut, M., & Bassett, D. R. (2003). Validity of 10 electronic pedometers for measuring steps, distance, and energy cost. *Medicine & Science in Sports & Exercise, 35*(8), 1455–1460.

Cuddihy, T. F., Pangrazi, R. P., & Tomson, L. M. (2005). Pedometers: Answers to FAQ's from teachers. *Journal of Physical Education, Recreation, and Dance, 76*(2), 36–55.

Fiorentino, L. H. (2002). Preparing professionals to use technology. *Journal of Physical Education, Recreation, and Dance, 73*(6), 21–22, 27.

Fiorentino, L. H. (2004). Digital video assignments: Focusing a new lens on teacher preparation programs. *Journal of Physical Education, Recreation, and Dance, 75*(5), 47–54.

Joint Committee on National Health Education Standards. (2007). *National health education standards: Achieving excellence,* 2nd ed. Atlanta, GA: American Cancer Society.

Kilanowski, C. K., Consalvi, A. R., & Epstein, L. H. (1999). Validation of an electronic pedometer for measurement of physical activity in children. *Pediatric Exercise Science, 11,* 63–68.

National Association for Sport and Physical Education. (2004). *Moving into the future: National standards for physical education.* Reston, VA: National Association for Sport and Physical Education.

Ryan, S., Marzili, S., Martindale, T. (2001). Using digital cameras to assess motor learning. *Journal of Physical Education, Recreation, and Dance, 72*(8), 13–18.

Schlatter, B. E., & Hurd, A. R. (2005). Geocaching. 21st-Century hide-and-seek. *Journal of Physical Education, Recreation, and Dance, 76*(7), 28–32.

Seifried, C. (2005). Using videotaped athletic contests within Mosston's teaching methods. *Journal of Physical Education, Recreation, and Dance, 76*(5), 36–38.

Trinigy, J., & Annesi, J. (1996). Coaching with video. *Strategies, 9*(3), 23–25.

United States Department of Health and Human Services. (1997). *Physical activity and health: A report of the surgeon general.* Atlanta, GA: U.S. Department of Health and Human Services, Centers for Disease Control and Prevention, National Center for Chronic Disease Prevention and Health Promotion.

United States Public Health Service. (1990). *Healthy people 2000: National health promotion and disease objectives.* Washington, DC: United States Government Printing Office.

United States Public Health Service. (2000). *Healthy people 2010: National health promotion and disease objectives.* Washington, DC: United States Government Printing Office.

For Further Reading

DerVanik, R. (2005). The use of PDAs to assess in physical education. *Journal of Physical Education, Recreation, and Dance*, 76(6), 50–52.

Fiorentino, L. H., & Castelli, D. (2005). Creating a virtual gymnasium. *Journal of Physical Education, Recreation, and Dance*, 76(4), 16–18.

Hatano, Y. (1993). Use of pedometer for promoting daily walking exercise. *International Council for Health, Physical Education and Recreation*, 29, 4–28.

LaMaster, K., Barnes-Wallace, L., & Creeden, K. O. (2002). Using technology in elementary physical education. *Journal of Physical Education, Recreation, and Dance*, 73(8), 12–13, 55.

Luke, M. D., & Sinclair, G. D. (1991). Gender differences in adolescents' attitudes toward school physical education. *Journal of Teaching in Physical Education*, 11(1), 31–46.

Palmer, S. E., & Hildebrand, K. (2005). Designing appropriate learning tasks. The Environmental Management Model. *Journal of Physical Education, Recreation, and Dance*, 76(2), 48–55.

Pangrazi, R. P., Beighle, A., & Sidman, C. L. (2003). *Pedometer power*. Champaign, IL: Human Kinetics.

Williams, E. W. (2002). Using your personal digital assistant to store lesson plans. *Journal of Physical education, Recreation, and Dance*, 73(3), 16–18.

Woods, M., Karp, G. C., Shimon, J. M., & Jensen, K. (2004). Using WebQuests to create online learning opportunities in physical education. *Journal of Physical Education, Recreation, and Dance*, 75(8), 41–56.

TECHNOLOGY INTEGRATION FOR MEANINGFUL CLASSROOM USE
Daily Lesson GAME Plan

Lesson Title: Muscular Strength and Muscular Endurance

Related Lessons: Aerobic and Anaerobic Exercises

Grade Level: Elementary

Unit: Fitness Components

GOALS

Content Standards:

1. Comprehend concepts related to health promotion and disease prevention to enhance health.
3. Demonstrate the ability to access valid information and products and services to enhance health.
7. Demonstrate the ability to practice health-enhancing behaviors and avoid or reduce health risks.

ISTE NETS-S

☑ 1. Creativity and innovation

☐ 2. Communication and collaboration

☐ 3. Research and information fluency

☑ 4. Critical thinking, problem solving, and decision making

☐ 5. Digital citizenship

☐ 6. Technology operations and concepts

Instructional Objective(s): Students will be able to identify the differences between muscular strength and muscular endurance and will create a digital story describing some of their favorite ways for building muscular strength and muscular endurance by creating a relevant activity or exercise routine.

ACTION

Before-Class Preparation: Print out handouts for back-up plan.

During Class

Time	Instructional Activities	Materials and Resources
10 minutes	Have each student draw a picture of his or her favorite exercises and tell how this exercise affects the body. If available, students may find pictures or images of their favorite exercises in print or online resources.	Paper and Pencil Optional: magazines or computers with Internet access
10–15 minutes	Review the key points related to muscular strength and endurance, include benefits and examples of ways students can exercise and follow a conditioning program to build muscle strength and endurance. Emphasize that the goal is to lay the groundwork for a lifetime of fitness that helps them enjoy and perform common physical tasks, including participating in their favorite sports and fitness activities.	Presentation can support lecture and provide examples
1–2 class periods	Students find images or take pictures of each other completing exercises designed to build muscular strength and endurance. Compile the pictures in a document that can serve as a reference for students for creating an activity or exercise routine. Software used can include word-processing or presentation software. Students can even create their own activity guides with guidelines for how often they should complete the activities they have included and use it to record their activities.	Digital camera Word-processing or presentation software

Notes:

Muscular strength is the maximum amount of force a muscle can produce in a single effort.
- Muscular strength is built by doing maximum resistance exercises only a few times.
- Resistance exercise is an exercise in which a force acts against muscles.

Muscular endurance is the ability of the muscle to continue to perform without fatigue.
- Less resistance and more repetitions builds muscular endurance.

Benefits:
- Helps a person perform everyday tasks, such as carrying schoolbooks, climbing stairs, and lifting objects.
- Helps maintain correct posture.
- Reduces the risk of low back pain.
- Reduces the risk of being injured.
- Helps a person enjoy physical activities without tiring.
- Improves body composition by increasing muscle mass and decreasing fat tissue.
- Improves self-image because muscles are firm and the body is toned.
- Keeps bone dense and strong.
- Make the surface of joints less susceptible to injury.

Muscular strength and muscular endurance are built through a conditioning program that may use weights but can also include exercises such as sit-ups, push-ups, etc. Muscular strength and endurance are kept through a continuous program, such as training two to three days a week.

MONITOR

Ongoing Assessment(s): Check for student understanding about muscle strength and endurance, the benefits of exercise to promote strength and endurance, and age-appropriate methods for completing exercise to build strength and endurance.

At the completion of the lessons, students should create an exercise or activity routine using the exercises they've developed and track their activities. Students can be assessed for maintaining their routines over a given period of time.

Accommodations and Extensions: Students may require additional instruction on available equipment, exercises, and activities. This activity can be used to organize a series of lessons on exercises or to review after the exercises have been taught.

Depending on the age of the students and availability of technology resources, the teacher may have to compile a group exercise routine.

Pictures taken by students can be enlarged and posted in gym or other exercise areas as reminders of how to complete exercises or use equipment correctly as well as the benefits of the exercises.

Back-up Plan: If computer access is limited, the presentation slides can be printed out and distributed to students.

EVALUATION

Lesson Reflections and Notes: Seek permission from parents to take pictures of students, especially if used for posters or other public display.

TECHNOLOGY INTEGRATION FOR MEANINGFUL CLASSROOM USE
Daily Lesson GAME Plan

Lesson Title: Body Composition

Related Lessons: Aerobic and Anaerobic Exercises

Grade Level: Middle grades

Unit: Fitness Components

GOALS

Content Standards:

1. Comprehend concepts related to health promotion and disease prevention to enhance health.
7. Demonstrate the ability to practice health-enhancing behaviors and avoid or reduce health risks.

ISTE NETS-S

☐ 1. Creativity and innovation

☑ 2. Communication and collaboration

☐ 3. Research and information fluency

☑ 4. Critical thinking, problem solving, and decision making

☐ 5. Digital citizenship

☑ 6. Technology operations and concepts

Instructional Objective(s): Students will be able to identify the concepts related to body composition. Students will be able to understand how to assess and influence body composition.

ACTION

Before-Class Preparation: Bring in food labels.

During Class

Time	Instructional Activities	Materials and Resources
5–10 minutes	Capture students' questions, concerns, assumptions, or stereotypes related to being overweight or obese using a KWHL chart or concept-mapping software. Collect and quickly review responses with students at the end of allotted time.	Word-processing or concept-mapping software
10 minutes	Define and discuss components of body composition (e.g., muscle, bone, fat, and other tissue that comprise the body). Discuss diseases related to being overweight or obese (e.g., cardiovascular disease, type 1 or type 2 diabetes, etc.). Discuss current statistics related to rate of obesity and adolescent obesity. Address specific questions, concerns, assumptions, or stereotypes identified by students during introductory activity.	Presentation software can support lecture and provide images of diseases
10 minutes	Discuss healthy eating behaviors as a component to disease prevention. Emphasize the connection to appropriate fuel sources for the human body and the importance of leading a physically active lifestyle.	Presentation can support lecture and provide images of muscle, bone, and fat
15 minutes	Handout and discuss the components of food labels (e.g., serving size, calories, total fat, saturated fat, etc.).	Option: Have students find food labels or food manufacturers' websites online
1–2 class periods	Students will bring in food labels from the foods they eat. Compile these food labels and have students input data into online calorie calculators and exercise calculators. Students can use presentation software to discuss how their bodies use the various types of food as fuel and how many calories are expended during the various moderate to vigorous activities they enjoy.	Presentation software; Calorie calculator website / Exercise calculator website or software

Notes:
Body Composition describes the percentages of fat, bone, and muscle in human bodies.

Diseases Related to Being Overweight or Obese
Cardiovascular Disease: According to the American Heart Association, buildup of plaque on the arteries (atherosclerosis), partly as a result of high cholesterol and fat diet, is a leading cause for cardiovascular diseases.
Type 2 Diabetes Mellitus: It is the most common form of diabetes, in which either the body does not produce enough insulin or the cells ignore the insulin. Insulin is necessary for the body to be able to use glucose for energy.

Components of Food Labels
Serving size of a food product is a confusing term, as it is found both on the Food Pyramid and on Nutrition Labels and has two related but different meanings. Make sure to explain both definitions to your students.
Calorie is a unit of food energy. In nutrition terms, the word calorie is used instead of the more precise scientific term kilocalorie which represents the amount of energy required to raise the temperature of a liter of water one degree centigrade at sea level.

Total fat is the number of fat grams contained in one serving of the food. Fat is an important nutrient that your body uses for growth and development, but you don't want to eat too much. The different kinds of fat, such as saturated, unsaturated, and trans fat, are listed separately on the label.

Cholesterol and sodium numbers tell you how much cholesterol and sodium (salt) are in a single serving of the food. Too much cholesterol can lead to heart disease. You call it salt but the label calls it sodium; either way too much can lead to high blood pressure, and uncontrolled high blood pressure can lead to stroke, heart attack, heart failure, or kidney failure.

Total carbohydrate tells you how many carbohydrate grams are in one serving of food. Carbohydrates are your body's primary source of energy. This total is broken down into grams of sugar and grams of dietary fiber.

Protein tells you how much protein you get from a single serving of the food. Your body needs protein to build and repair essential parts of the body, such as muscles, blood, and organs.

Vitamins and minerals lists the amounts of vitamins and minerals in a serving of food. Two especially important and commonly listed vitamins are vitamin A and vitamin C. Each amount is given as a percent daily value. Other vitamins may be listed on some labels as well. Also listed are important minerals that are in a serving of the food. Again, each amount is given as a percent daily value.

MONITOR

Ongoing Assessment(s): Check for student understanding about components of body composition and the dangers associated with being overweight or obese.

At the completion of the lessons, students should be able to determine how various food sources affect their bodies and the importance of leading a healthy and active lifestyle.

Accommodations and Extensions: Students may require additional instruction on components of health-related fitness. Depending on the age of the students and availability of technological resources, the teacher may have to compile supplementary instructional materials.

Back-up Plan: Students can conduct the activity with paper and pencil and calculators, but more time should be allotted.

EVALUATION

Lesson Reflections and Notes:
In order to address the topic of body composition with middle school students a positive learning environment must be established. Students must respect the feelings of others when discussing such a personal subject.

TECHNOLOGY INTEGRATION FOR MEANINGFUL CLASSROOM USE
Daily Lesson GAME Plan

Lesson Title: Cardiovascular Endurance

Related Lessons: Aerobic and Anaerobic Exercises

Grade Level: High School

Unit: Fitness Components

GOALS

Content Standards:

1. Comprehend concepts related to health promotion and disease prevention to enhance health.
7. Demonstrate the ability to practice health-enhancing behaviors and avoid or reduce health risks.

ISTE NETS-S:

- ☐ 1. Creativity and innovation
- ☐ 2. Communication and collaboration
- ☐ 3. Research and information fluency
- ☑ 4. Critical thinking, problem solving, and decision making
- ☑ 5. Digital citizenship
- ☑ 6. Technology operations and concepts

Instructional Objective(s): Students will be able to identify benefits of cardiovascular endurance using appropriate terminology. Students will create daily physical activity plans and record their actual activities.

ACTION

Before-Class Preparation: Print out handouts from presentation software for back-up plan. Bookmark websites or create screen shots in case Internet access is unavailable.

During Class		
Time	**Instructional Activities**	**Materials and Resources**
10 minutes	Students identify activities that impact heart rate and breathing. They record them based on when and where they routinely conduct these activities. Students can use a graphic organizer or simply list the activities.	Word-processing software or graphic organizer
10–15 minutes	Present key concepts and terminology related to cardiovascular endurance using presentation software or displaying information from health-related websites. Link the benefits of exercises that promote cardiovascular endurance with activities students identified or those available to them during school, in organized sports, or other afterschool venues.	Presentation software Computer with Internet connection
45 minutes	Students identify goals for cardio exercise and create daily health plans to record and monitor their activities. If possible, they can create records of activity for the past three days using Activitygram software. They can search fitness, health, or sports sites online to develop reasonable goals that support their interests. Students can create their plans using a variety of software, with spreadsheet software being well suited to this activity.	Health/fitness websites Optional: Activitygram software Spreadsheet (or other) software
Ongoing	Students maintain records of their cardiovascular activities over a period of time, such as a month, semester, or year. Students monitor their goals and adjust their plans based on their success.	Software used to create health plans

Notes:

Cardiovascular endurance is the ability to perform prolonged, large-muscle, dynamic exercise at moderate-to-high levels of intensity.

Benefits of cardiovascular endurance include:

- **Helps the heart and lungs function more efficiently.**
- **Improves metabolic rate.** Physical activities that promote cardiovascular endurance burn calories. They raise the resting **metabolic rate** for up to twelve hours.
- **Promotes healthful aging.** Physical activities that promote cardiovascular endurance activate antioxidants. **Antioxidants** are substances that protect cells from being damaged by oxidation. Antioxidants also tie up free radicals. **Free radicals** are highly reactive compounds that damage the body. Free radicals are believed to be one cause of aging.
- **Improves insulin sensitivity.** Activities that promote cardiovascular endurance improve **insulin sensitivity**, which helps with metabolism of carbohydrates, fats, and proteins. Risk of developing diabetes is lowered.
- **Improves the muscles' ability to use lactic acid. Lactic acid** is produced by muscles during vigorous activity and is one of the factors that cause body cramps. Cardiovascular endurance activities lengthen the time people can exercise without becoming tired.
- **Increases the level of high-density lipoproteins and decreases the level of low-density lipoproteins. HDL** ("good" cholesterol) carries cholesterol to the liver for breakdown. **LDL** ("bad" cholesterol) carries cholesterol to body cells. This reduces the risk of heart diseases.
- **Improves the function of your immune system.** People with good cardiovascular endurance may reduce their chances of getting ill.
- **Protects against some types of cancer.** For example, cardio activities speed up the movement of food through the gastrointestinal tract. A person is more likely to process food regularly. This decreases the risk of colon cancer.
- **Improves psychological well-being.** Cardio activities allow the release of beta-endorphins into the blood stream. **Beta-endorphins** are produced in the brain and create a feeling of well-being.

Activities for building cardiovascular endurance include **aerobic exercise** for at least 30 minutes. These activities can include running, swimming, jumping rope, cleaning house, basketball, bicycling, and many others.

MONITOR

Ongoing Assessment(s): Review student understanding during opening activity and lecture using questioning. Identify misconceptions in prior knowledge and check for understanding of key concepts and terminology.

Monitor daily physical activity plans. Have students monitor their own plans.

Accommodations and Extensions: Students can create their plans using a variety of software, including word-processing or spreadsheet software, or can create journals using journaling software, a blog, or website. If handheld computers are available, students may be able to update their activity logs at the end of class with these devices.

Back-up Plan: Use pictures or point out sports/fitness equipment within the gym or classroom that promote cardiovascular endurance. Presentation can be printed for student note taking if display is not available. Students can print daily health plans on a weekly basis to record with pencil if computers are not readily available—transferring their records to the software they have selected once each week.

EVALUATION

Lesson Reflections and Notes: The plan can be expanded to include dietary and other health and fitness components to serve as the basis for a semester- or year-long activity that encourages students to develop and live healthy lifestyles.

ISTE Standards addressed in this chapter

This chapter provides content-specific suggestions and strategies for addressing both ISTE's National Educational Technology Standards for Students (NETS-S) and the National Visual-Arts Standards. This chapter also builds on the NETS-T concepts and skills presented earlier, with a special emphasis on skills related to Standard 1 "Facilitate and inspire student learning and creativity." Following an overview of the National Visual-Arts Standards and how you can address the NETS-S in the visual-arts classroom, this chapter outlines techniques, tools, and methods for developing authentic learning experiences that advance student creativity and innovation in the visual-arts classroom.

Integrating Technology in the Visual-Arts Classroom

**Tammy McGraw, Ed.D. and
Nancy Lampert, Ed.D.**

Outcomes

In this chapter, you will

- Identify visual-arts standards and explain how technology can support them.
- Discuss how the National Educational Technology Standards for Students can be addressed in a visual-arts classroom.
- Understand how authentic learning principles can be addressed using technology in a visual-arts classroom.

Technology's impact on the visual arts and art education is not a recent phenomenon. Throughout history, technology has shaped the tools, techniques, and media of creative expression and visual representation. Each new technology challenges people to reconsider long-held beliefs about art and the production of art. The debate surrounding 17th-century Dutch master Johannes Vermeer's alleged use of the camera obscura is not unlike current debates about digitally enhancing photographs. Do these technologies enable artists to *cheat* or simply realize the full potential of their talents? These issues compel us to rethink our beliefs about art and artists. As an art educator, you will be challenged constantly with new

Outcomes *(continued)*

■ Explain how technology can increase learning and facilitate creative thinking in the visual-arts classroom.

technologies. This chapter shows why it is important to analyze each new technology carefully and embrace the ones that can enhance student learning, improve instructional practice, or support meaningful student assessment.

Specific tools and software titles change over time; the ones mentioned in this chapter are merely representative examples of broader categories of digital tools and media (see the textbook's companion website for examples). Each category has unique capabilities and processes. Technology will continue to change rapidly; however, just like Vermeer's alleged use of the camera obscura, technology always will play a part—occasionally controversial—in the world of art. The goal of art educators is to help students understand the different technologies that can maximize the learning experience and produce high-quality art.

STORIES FROM PRACTICE

Then and Now

As an art teacher, I always believed that students should be exposed to the world's great works of art and that these works are the best models from which to learn. Unfortunately, teaching in a rural community 20 years ago—hours away from even the smallest museum—left me with few options for sharing great artwork with my students. One option was my personal art books. I held them up and passed them around the class. Sometimes, I had to explain how the art might look if it were in color—a learning challenge for even my most visual students. Each year, when I prepared my classroom budget, I wanted to request visual resources in the form of photographic slides or Shorewood Fine Art Reproductions. Each glass-mounted slide was $3.75; Shorewood prints were $9.50. It cost $2.75 to have the print mounted and an additional $2.25 to have it laminated. I also had to add $3.50 for packaging and handling. Finally, I would call UPS to determine the exact shipping charges, which had to be reflected in my budget. I eventually came to the conclusion each year that, due to the cost of other consumable classroom materials, the slides and prints would have to wait. Fortunately, I taught long enough to find a solution to the problem. In 1993, I convinced the division's Gifted-and-Talented Program Coordinator to purchase a laser-disc player along with a National Gallery of Art laser disc containing 1,645 paintings, drawings, sculpture, and prints, accessible through a HyperCard navigation program. Although $750 now may seem like an enormous fee for accessing a museum's collection, it was a real bargain in 1993. Today, the world's greatest art collections are available on the web, along with extensive resources for students and teachers.

Source: Tammy McGraw

Technology and Content Standards

The National Commission on Excellence in Education (1983) is often credited with initiating the intense focus on content standards; however, the No Child Left Behind Act of 2001 brought content standards and assessments into the consciousness of educators everywhere in the nation. Visual-arts teachers—like their counterparts in other content areas—feel increased pressure to ensure the quality of their art programs and provide evidence of that quality through appropriate assessments.

Six national content standards for the visual arts are applied across grades K–12, specifying what students should know and be able to do in the visual arts (see Table 20.1). Related achievement standards denote students' expected understandings and proficiencies at the completion of grades 4, 8, and 12. Significantly, these standards focus only on student-learning *outcomes*. They do not provide a roadmap for achieving these results or limit the technologies that can be used; instead, they

Table 20.1	National Visual-Arts Standards

1. understand and apply media, techniques, and processes
2. know art structures (elements and principles) and art functions
3. choose and evaluate ideas, subjects, and symbols
4. understand the art of diverse times and cultures
5. reflect upon and assess art
6. connect visual arts with other disciplines

Source: The National Visual Arts Standards, Copyright © 1994, National Art Education Association, 1916 Association Drive, Reston, VA 20191-1590.

challenge educators to explore current and emerging technologies that can expand visual-arts learning and creative expression.

The National Educational Technology Standards for Students (NETS-S), like the visual-arts standards, can be addressed easily in a visual-arts classroom. Table 20.2 presents examples of how NETS-S might be introduced or reinforced in a technology-rich visual-arts classroom. As you look at these examples, think of other activities that might address the standards. Could the activities relate to one or more of the national visual-arts standards? Use the information in Table 20.2 to generate further ideas for meeting other visual-arts standards and the NETS-S. Are there additional state or local standards to be considered? The sample lesson plans at the end of this chapter provide specific examples of how you can design learning experiences that meet both content area and technology standards.

WEB LINK

For further detailed examples of the alignment of the NETS-S to the national visual-arts standards, visit the textbook's companion website.

Table 20.2	NETS-S in the Visual-Arts Classroom

Creativity and Innovation

A middle-school art teacher assigns a video essay to her students. One student researches the life and work of Marc Chagall. She taps a variety of resource CD-ROMs and the web to obtain additional images depicting Chagall, his work, and life in the 20th century. Since Chagall was born in Russia, she downloads music by 20th-century Russian composer Sergei Prokofiev from an online music site. She narrates the three-minute video, describing Chagall's life, his work, and how his work compares to her own art. Now feeling that she really understands Chagall and his art, she returns to the *Green Violinist* and uses a 2-D animation program to bring the violinist to life—dancing to a tune that she composed in GarageBand. She posts her animated short on YouTube.

Communication and Collaboration

Art students create a class website that features student artwork, blogs, and a local arts calendar. The site has downloadable print publications, such as the school newsletter produced with desktop-publishing software. Three times a year, students invite a visual-arts professional to participate in a live chat so students can learn more about various careers in the visual arts. A recent guest donated proceeds from the sale of one of her paintings to help students purchase an island in Teen Second Life. Students plan to use the island as an environment to display their digital artwork.

Research and Information Fluency

A teacher asks her elementary art students to create a mural at the entrance of their new school, but there is much debate about what should be painted. The teacher works with her students to design a simple survey they will administer to other students and staff. The students use a spreadsheet application to collect and analyze the data, creating charts for a school-wide presentation.

Critical Thinking, Problem Solving, and Decision Making

A local parent–teacher organization sponsors an animation workshop for sixth-grade students. The workshop is conducted by AnimAction, an organization that works with students to produce animated public-service announcements. The students choose tobacco use and prevention as a topic. They consult various sources, including the local chapter of the American Cancer Society, for information. Using a variety of traditional and digital tools and media, each team creates a 30-second animated public-service announcement, which is broadcast by local television stations.

Digital Citizenship

A group of middle-school art students develop a website on contemporary art and identify several virtual museum collections that could be incorporated into their site. They search for information on copyright and fair use to determine if they can link directly to a Bruce Nauman work at the Art Institute of Chicago. The museum does not permit framing, but its policy on linking is unclear. After searching the web for typical agreements on linking, they e-mail the Art Institute's webmaster requesting permission to link to the image.

Technology Operations and Concepts

An art student takes a photograph of a landscape with a digital camera and uploads the image to a desktop computer system. Using Adobe Photoshop, he manipulates the image to create a surrealistic landscape. He saves and uploads the image to his web-based portfolio. He prints a finished copy for display in the school and e-mails it to his home computer.

THE GAME PLAN

Content Standards

Set Goals

Research the visual-arts standards for a state where you plan to seek a teaching position and create an action plan to ensure that you will have the knowledge and skills necessary to help your students achieve those standards. Identify the concepts, knowledge, and skills you will need to ensure that you are prepared to help your students meet the visual-arts standards in your state.

Take Action

Explore the department of education website in the state where you plan to seek a position. Review the K–12 visual-arts standards in that state and compare them to the state's technology standards. Identify those standards that specifically relate to applying technology in the visual arts. Develop a plan for how to meet the technology standards in the context of the visual arts.

Monitor

Did you find the information you needed? Do you need to contact the department of education for more information about where to find the visual-arts standards or the technology standards for teachers?

Evaluate and Extend

Discuss in class the action plan you developed for meeting the technology standards for instructional personnel. Compare your plan to others. Note the strengths and weaknesses of the various plans. Strengthen your plan by incorporating ideas you have heard in class.

Authentic Learning Strategies Incorporating Technology

To state the obvious, the learner should be the most important factor considered when designing effective classroom strategies; however, students' individual needs, capabilities, experiences, and interests often are overlooked. Barbara McCombs (2000) suggested that the principles of authentic learning, which she calls learner-centered instruction, are essential to designing technology-supported practices that meet all students' needs. The American Psychological Association (APA, 1993, 1997) specifies 14 principles that influence learning for all. The Learner-Centered Psychological Principles are organized into the following four domains that we use as a framework for addressing authentic learning strategies in a visual-arts classroom:

- cognitive and metacognitive factors
- developmental and social factors
- motivational and affective factors
- individual-difference factors

Cognitive and Metacognitive Factors

Most good visual-arts teachers employ authentic learning strategies such as active learning, collaboration, and reflective practice. You learned in Chapter 3 that active learning is a hallmark of authentic instruction and that activity must include reflection and articulation. Good teaching strategies and classroom-management techniques require little change to accommodate new technologies; on the contrary, new technologies offer interesting ways to approach these strategies. Metacognition refers to thinking about one's own thinking and is a method of reflection on one's learning. Visual-arts teachers often incorporate metacognitive instructional practices by asking students to reflect on a project and determine what worked and what needed improvement—or by challenging students to identify which pieces to include or eliminate from their portfolios.

Metacognitive strategies help students apply learning in one area to new contexts; this empowers them to take greater control over their own learning. These strategies also can enable students to predict their performances on various tasks and monitor their current levels of understanding (Bransford, Brown, & Cocking, 2000). With an image-manipulation tool, such as Adobe's Photoshop, students can 1) consider the anticipated results of certain functions, 2) decide whether to perform a particular function, and 3) undo the function if the results are not acceptable. For example, a student wants to apply an artistic filter to her image. She reviews what she knows about the various options (e.g., colored pencil, cutout, dry brush, fresco, sponge). She remembers seeing Henri Matisse's cutouts at the National Gallery of Art —large, beautiful shapes with bright colors. After considering all possible techniques, she decides to apply the cutout filter but is immediately disappointed with the results. Why? She expected the image to be converted to large, brightly colored shapes; instead, the shapes are much smaller than expected, and the color is predominantly brown. Rather than simply undoing the action and moving to another filter, she explains the problem to her teacher. They discuss settings that can be adjusted and discover that the filter is set to produce seven levels. After discussing the matter with her teacher, the student determines that selecting fewer levels would create larger shapes. The student adjusts the filter to four levels and produces much larger shapes. She is pleased with the results and moves on to address the issue of color.

This scenario illustrates one way in which digital tools can support metacognitive strategies in the classroom. This same scenario also illustrates other important considerations such as the role of a learner's prior knowledge and experience. Can you identify other ways visual-arts technology supports metacognitive strategies? How do you think about your own thinking and learning? How do you evaluate which strategies are working for you or if you need to try different ones?

Developmental and Social Factors

New technologies have had a tremendous impact on the social factors that influence visual-arts learning. Networked technologies have changed learners' social interactions, interpersonal relations, and communication practices. These technologies can support many of the authentic instructional methods addressed in Chapter 3, such as supporting the work of collaborative workgroups, helping students explore the driving question in a problem-based learning activity, or supporting inquiry and discovery. The World Wide Web, in particular, provides unlimited opportunities for finding exemplars from artists and museums across the globe, communicating with other artists and students of art, as well as allowing your students to share or display their work. The web allows student art exhibitions—including still images, animation, and video—to be displayed digitally for anyone in the world to access.

New software permits learners to explore how artwork looks in various settings or with different display options such as wood or metal frames. QuickTime Virtual Reality (QTVR) (see Figure 20.1) allows learners to view a sculpture from various angles rather than from one vantage point. As a result, students can experience sculptures as three-dimensional objects as the artists intended.

Perhaps the web's most profound impact upon learning is the capability of displaying and sharing artwork on a worldwide stage. Desktop-publishing software, such as Adobe InDesign, and web-publishing software, such as Adobe Dreamweaver or one of many freely available web editors, have simplified the production and distribution of classroom products while greatly expanding students' communication and design capabilities. Students of every age can maintain online portfolios at little or no cost. Artsonia.com has an extensive gallery of student work, and families can purchase items with their child's artwork imprinted on them.

The web can also facilitate sharing of artwork created with traditional media. Through the Memory Project, high school art students create portraits of children who have been abandoned, orphaned, abused, or neglected. Teachers access a website

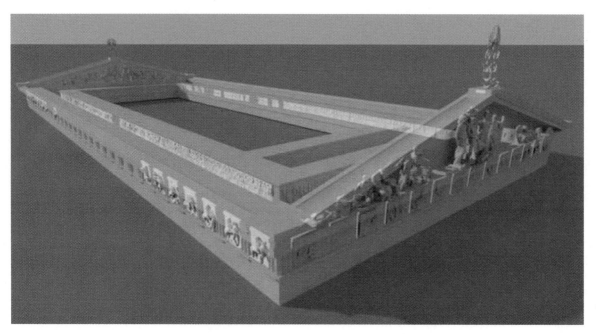

Figure 20.1
New software tools, like QuickTime Virtual Reality software, can allow students to view art work from many perspectives while in your classroom. This is a Virtual Reality rendering of the Parthenon.
Source: Courtesy USC Institute for Creative Technologies

to download digital photographs of children from which high school students will work. The finished portraits are delivered to the children.

These advances are important, but consider the issue of collaboration. Today's learners want to be connected—not just to their classmates—but to others who share similar goals and interests. Online collaborative art spaces such as SITO have existed for more than a decade; however, a rapidly growing number of social networking sites indicate an increasing demand to be connected. MySpace.com, which consists of more than 200 million user pages, is an extensive network of member profiles, groups, photos, blogs, videos, and music. While member profiles are the most prominent feature of MySpace, sites such as Buzznet.com place a greater emphasis on sharing users' content. Many new social networks are emerging around specific interests, making it even more likely that the visual arts could flourish in such a community. Despite the potential benefits social networking technologies bring to visual-arts education, you must also be constantly aware of the risks associated with these services and how you can reduce these risks for your students (see Chapter 10).

Photo management tools such as Flickr and Picasa are becoming increasingly sophisticated in how they enable users to organize and share images and offer a good model for supporting communities of learners. These sites go beyond merely sharing photos on the Internet by employing tools that can support online communities. For example, users attach comments or tags to describe their photos, as do others who view those photos. The resulting metadata make it much easier to find and share the images with family and friends, as well as unknown individuals who possess similar interests. Furthermore, the site's interface facilitates easy posting of the images to most blogs, further supporting conversation and community. TheBroth.com, like many social networking and media sharing sites, has profiles, friends, blogs, tagging, and other features. On the other hand, TheBroth is also a massive multiplayer environment that emphasizes real-time collaboration on digital artwork.

Networked technologies are changing the relationship between artist and consumer. Visit some social networking sites, collaborative workspaces, or even online game environments on the web. How could similar networked technologies support the social aspects of visual-arts learning?

THE GAME PLAN

Identifying Web-Based Resources

Set Goals
Find online resources you can use for a range of activities in your visual-arts classroom. You may ask your students to visit some of the world's greatest art collections or investigate belonging to or creating their own art-specific online communities.

Take Action
Review the web resources on the textbook's companion website. Conduct other searches on your own for resources of interest to you.

Monitor
How well do the resources meet stated goal(s)? Are there clearinghouse websites or sites that review online visual-arts resources? Did you find resources you didn't know existed that might be helpful to you in the visual-arts classroom?

Evaluate and Extend
Select the best resources you have found and include a list of them in your portfolio. Share your list with other visual-arts students to compile a master list that covers a range of grade levels and skills.

Being connected is only one consideration in designing technology-supported experiences for learners. Students no longer want simply to consume media—they want to manipulate, adapt, generate, and disseminate it. This perspective will shape dramatically how students view the creative process. One recent work of art that exemplifies this interaction is F2T (Free to Talk) created by Frank Plant and Thomas Charveriat. F2T is a unique installation featuring sculpture, robotics, SMS (Short Message Service), and hip hop music. Viewers send text messages from their mobile devices to Rapper, the main feature of the installation. Upon receipt of the message, the SMS is analyzed and frequently used words are identified. Rapper is then activated and begins to perform a rap based on the message. Other elements in the installation, with accompanying lights and sound, are set into motion as Rapper sings. When the song is completed, a souvenir printout is generated with the original SMS and the lyrics to the song composed and performed by Rapper.

Increasingly, art is not just produced by a talented few but becomes something everyone can explore and improve upon. This will likely result in continuous examination and assessment of intellectual property laws. Again, other models outside the visual arts may better illustrate our evolving thinking about collaboration and how we view the act of improving someone's work. Wikis, for example, encourage users to create and edit web page content through a standard browser. What other tools can you identify for increasing active participation and collaboration in the visual arts?

Motivational and Affective Factors

Some would argue that the visual arts already are more suited than other disciplines to promote learner motivation and emotional aspects of learning. Certainly, many students are given a good deal of autonomy—a characteristic of authentic instruction—in terms of pursuing topics that are interesting to themselves and therefore increase personal relevance. The novelty of new technologies alone is enough to interest many students; however, technology's ability to adapt personal preferences could prove to be an exceptional motivational tool, especially when it is used to allow students to achieve meaningful goals.

Recent advances in video production present unique opportunities for learners to exercise control, or autonomy, over their own learning (see Figure 20.2). Affordable digital video cameras capable of producing high-quality video have become widely available in schools and many homes. Inexpensive and easy-to-use video-editing programs enable learners easily to import video clips and still images, edit them, insert

Spencer Grant/PhotoEdit

Figure 20.2
Digital video is within the grasp of many art students.

titles, create transitions and special effects, and export them for distribution in a variety of formats including DVD or the web.

Video production is but one activity in the visual-arts classroom that can support authentic learning as it encourages students to 1) explore areas of interest through authentic tasks that mirror those in the real world, 2) improve planning skills by developing scripts and storyboards, 3) collaborate with other students in small groups, and 4) use various media creatively to communicate ideas. Students can develop decision-making skills by selecting and editing video clips, choosing still images, or considering the advantages of voice-over narration versus background music. Furthermore, video production can foster the critical analysis and reflection necessary for self-assessment and learning. It is easy to motivate learners who are producing a video documentary on a topic meaningful and relevant to them.

Many other technology-enhanced experiences in a visual-arts classroom can facilitate learner control. Identify a learning objective and generate a list of alternative experiences that could achieve the same objective. Consider ways these alternatives enable learners to demonstrate what they have learned.

Individual-Difference Factors

A visual-arts classroom is often viewed as a place where learners' individual differences, prior experiences, and personal expressions are celebrated. Although this may be true in many cases, visual-arts teachers—like all teachers—need to understand their students' diverse needs, interests, and capabilities. Technology offers many solutions that can help visual-arts teachers attend to the needs of all learners.

Traditional and digital media offer visual-arts teachers many ways to enhance instruction. For example, a teacher could film herself demonstrating traditional woodcut printmaking. She could import the video to her computer and use a video-editing application to add narration and title slides that present the process in numbered steps. By digitizing and posting the demonstration to a website, students would be able to access it as often as needed.

These same strategies can be used to provide meaningful, individual feedback to students. For example, the teacher could require her students to work in teams to videotape each other demonstrating a process. She could use video-editing tools to embed her recorded comments in the videotaped demonstration, allowing students to review the teacher feedback as often as needed. The videos also could be a good tool for facilitating discussion between the student and teacher.

The web's vast resources can help overcome potential linguistic, cultural, and socioeconomic barriers. Language translation tools allow learners to access information in their native languages; likewise, students can look up artifacts from around the world, broadening their understandings of the contributions of different cultures. Socioeconomic differences in art production can be reduced and perhaps even eliminated. In the past, consumable art supplies, such as watercolor paper or film, have been beyond the financial reach of many students. Digital tools allow all students to create high-quality products.

Technology and Creative Thinking Skills Instruction

Many researchers and theorists have studied creative thinking. Although each defines the construct in a slightly different way, most generally describe it as thinking focused on the generation of multiple ideas and evaluation of various alternatives (Ennis, 2002; Jones et al., 1995; Paul, Elder, & Bartell, 1997; Perry, 1999). E. P. Torrance (1969) defined creativity as "the process of sensing problems or gaps in information, forming ideas or hypotheses, testing and modifying these hypotheses, and communicating the results" (p. 4). The use of technology in visual-arts classrooms inspires students to evaluate gaps in information, form ideas, and communicate the results.

Aesthetic and Critical Inquiry

The aesthetic and critical inquiry that occurs in visual-arts classrooms actively challenges students to develop responses to open-ended questions (Lampert, 2006b). When students focus on open-ended problems that have more than one possible solution, they engage in the process of evaluating many alternatives—key components of creative and critical thinking (Lampert, 2006a). Technology facilitates this inquiry through the sheer volume of aesthetic and critical comparisons it brings to students' desktops. Before digital technology, art teachers were limited to whatever photographic slides, posters, and images in books they could locate. Now, they and their students can search the Internet for countless images to be viewed on display devices varying from computer monitors to data projectors. For example, imagine a discussion about the aesthetics of whether functional forms, such as vessels, should be considered art, craft, or both. The students instantly can search a wealth of digital images of vessels—from ancient and contemporary cultures all over the world—to aid their discussion. Through digital images, contemporary handmade teapots displayed at a crafts museum could be compared with ancient teapots used in a Japanese tea ceremony, teapots depicted in 18th-century European paintings, teapots students have brought from home, or even those shown on a shopping search engine. To supplement the discussion, students could research the history and use of the vessels. As students discuss the information they have retrieved and reconcile the opposing viewpoints of classmates, they link the ideas of other students with their own thoughts on these complex aesthetic issues. Such linkages help students create complex cognitive networks. Further inquiry into the content area eventually stabilizes these networks (King, 2002).

Concept Mapping and Creative Thinking

Hypertext concept-mapping applications, such as Eastgate System's Tinderbox or the popular Inspiration and Kidspiration applications, are also tools that can help stimulate creative thinking (see Figure 20.3). They are a common example of the use of a computer as a mindtool, as described in Chapter 4. Concept-mapping applications

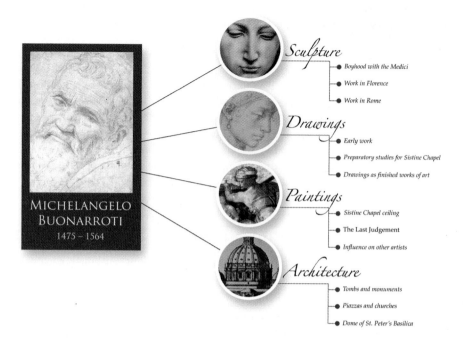

Figure 20.3
Creative thinking can be stimulated with the use of concept-mapping software.

motivate students to discover new connections between ideas for topics they are researching—such as the topic of how various artists have depicted the landscape. For example, middle school students studying 19th-century landscape painting might use concept-mapping software to create links between information on 19th-century oil painting techniques, 19th-century farming techniques, and 19th-century textile production to compare and contrast manual production techniques of that era. This type of inquiry-based activity is similar to classroom discussions of multiple viewpoints—an activity that helps to develop elaborated cognitive networks on content.

One art student who used concept-mapping software said the following: "With hypertext, it is a deeper kind of thinking than I would normally do. Like in biology, I never remember the stuff I take notes on. But, creating the [concept] web myself, instead of just taking the teacher's notes, is more fun. I am linking and researching something I am interested in" (Taylor, 2006, para. 19).

Critical Awareness of Visual Culture through Production

Our society seems to be inundated with image-based information. This elevates the importance of visual literacy as a fundamental part of a child's education and calls for heightened critical awareness of visual culture through production. Much of the visual media today is technological—the Internet, television, music videos, video-games, and so forth. Consequently, K–12 art students often are interested in producing their own videos, websites, and animations. Production experience increases students' ability to view, understand, analyze, and interpret the pervasive visual media that surrounds them. As students produce their own visual media, they experience open-ended problem solving by choosing imagery, content, effects, and sound from a wide range of options. During critiques, students can compare and contrast their own media with that of classmates. This cycle of production and critique supports a range of critical thinking types, such as divergent thinking in which students explore open-ended questions, as well as convergent thinking when students are asked to provide constructive feedback to others or analyze given techniques or products in order to guide the development of new work or new artists. This prompts them to reflect on the outcomes of production choices, which heightens their visual literacy and their awareness of the effects of visual media in contemporary culture (Freedman, 2003).

Visual Exploration

As suggested previously, image-manipulation programs support new forms of visual exploration. They include the ability to add and delete individual layers of information (e.g., graphic elements, text, background images, etc.) without starting from scratch and can encourage learners to experiment with multiple options before committing to a course of action. This promotes creativity, flexibility, and a willingness to try various solutions. The history palette in Photoshop enables learners to review each action carefully and undo those actions at a precise point in the development of their work. These programs also help students study and manipulate lighting effects far beyond what art classes had been able to do with natural light and spotlighting. Scanning software, when used in conjunction with image-manipulation programs, lets students create digital compositions of original images without altering them, broadening the range of materials students have to work with.

Research

Websites and image databases allow learners to search, retrieve, and interact with vast image collections, many of which are accessible only electronically. Research on the web, however, has moved beyond keyword searches. Content-based search engines consider the characteristics of the image itself. The Hermitage website uses IBM's experimental Query By Image Content (QBIC) technology, which allows visitors to search for artwork with similar visual attributes, like color or layout. Content-based search engines, while still an emerging technology, are particularly promising for the visual arts.

Technological advances also are sparking new interest in the study of art and art history, challenging students to explore sometimes-controversial issues. Technologies not usually associated with art, such as CAT scans usually associated with use in medicine, have been used recently to study ancient treasures (Ghysels, 2003) made of wood, bone, ivory, and other fragile materials. The CAT scans show that precious stones, secret messages, and other items of intrigue are hidden inside these ancient treasures.

Teachers are adapting these technological advances for classroom activities. Dan Rockmore, a Dartmouth mathematics professor, has analyzed the authenticity of artwork attributed to Rembrandt (Trivedi, 2005). Rockmore's software produces a statistical summary that reveals an artist's mathematical signature. Like handwriting, he asserts the mathematical signature is unique and should be consistent from painting to painting. Advances such as these can provide new information for teachers that will enable them to help students better appreciate the techniques of great painters and understand what makes a Rembrandt a Rembrandt.

Execution

Technology has tremendous potential to expand what constitutes fundamental skills and basic techniques in an art classroom. Technical execution becomes less of a barrier when students can use vector-based applications, such as Adobe Illustrator, to generate a perfect circle, produce a gradient without effort, or convert any scanned image into an editable and scalable vector path. Drawing software empowers students to create perspective drawings with greater complexity and accuracy than they might be able to accomplish manually. With paint programs, K–12 students can study color theory without mixing paint; create color wheels and charts showing

Vartanov Anatoly/Used under license from Shutterstock

Figure 20.4
Art instruction can benefit from hardware as well as software tools.

primary, secondary, and tertiary colors; and overlay semitransparent digital colors to simulate color mixing. Animation software can help students create paths and transitions; similarly, page-layout applications can assist them with placing page elements consistently. Although technology eliminates some barriers related to technical execution, it does not replace knowledge, talent, and contextual understanding.

The benefits of certain tools for the visual-arts classroom—such as graphics tablets (see Figure 20.4), large flat-panel displays, digital cameras, and color printers —are apparent because they support the highly visual nature of art activities, but pervasive technologies such as cell phones also hold creative potential. Cell phones that can capture and display digital images are becoming standard gear for many young people. The interest in developing creative content for mobile devices is also increasing. For example, Ithaca College hosts the CellFlix Festival, a competition that offers a $5,000 prize to the creator of the best film shot with and presented on a cell phone. Other forms of technology that have plummeted in cost include digital cameras, digital video cameras, removable storage media (e.g., Compact Flash, SD, USB "jump" drives), and inkjet-compatible papers, such as canvas, inexpensive papers that look and feel like canvas, digital rag (100% cotton paper), backlit display film,

STORIES FROM PRACTICE

Pushing the Limits

Some of the most interesting uses of digital tools and media occur when pushing the limitations of the tool. In 1998, I worked with a student competing in the ThinkQuest competition. He and his teammates wanted to create a website to teach others about animation. Although a number of animation applications were available at the time, he chose Avid Cinema (a video-editing application similar to iMovie) to create very sophisticated clay-animation sequences. He shot still images with an Apple QuickTake 100 digital camera, imported them into Avid Cinema, and animated them by stringing thousands together into a movie. While Avid Cinema never was intended to be a clay-animation studio application, it worked perfectly for a learner who understood how to apply the tool skillfully to solve a particular problem. His greatest challenge, on the other hand, was finding a way to store thousands of 640-by-480-pixel images!

Source: Tammy McGraw

TOOLS FOR USE

Lesson Activities

Following is a short list of lesson activities you can consider including in a visual-arts classroom. Research any of the ideas that you are unfamiliar with and add topics that you don't see here. Consider technologies you and your students can use to complete these activities.

- Design business card and CD and DVD covers
- Color exercises
- Digital collages
- Digital drawings and paintings
- Digital manipulation of scanned artwork
- Digital movies
- Digital portraits created from scanned and manipulated photos
- Digital portfolios
- Greeting cards with original illustrations
- Internet research
- Line, shape, and balance exercises

- Logo design
- Mosaic designs
- Music videos
- Newsletters
- Posters for school events
- Posters on various artists
- Posters on travel locations
- Presentations with a projector
- Stained-glass designs
- Tessellations
- Web galleries
- Websites on art topics

foils, linen, polysilk fabric, and iron-on transfer paper. New media offer extraordinary opportunities for personal expression and learning.

Chapter Summary

This chapter has introduced a number of ways in which technology has and will continue to affect visual-arts education. It has described how various technologies can 1) increase learning and facilitate creative expression, 2) support mastery of visual-arts standards, 3) create authentic learning experiences, and 4) promote creative thinking. Perhaps most significantly, the chapter has underscored the importance of evaluating the potential of each new technology for enhancing student learning, improving instructional practice, and supporting meaningful student assessment.

WEB LINK

The textbook's companion website contains a list of web resources for visual-arts teachers, including links to software and hardware, museums, and educational sites designed for the visual-arts classroom.

YOUR PORTFOLIO

To demonstrate your understanding of creating learning experiences in the visual-arts classroom that address the National Educational Technology Standards for Students, create a lesson plan for common activities in your visual-arts classroom using the GAME Plan template available on the textbook's companion website, or one of your choosing. Your lesson plan may address, but is not limited to, using an image-manipulation program, a vector-based drawing application, page-layout software, web-design software, animation software, or a digital video application.

1. Identify the national visual-arts standards that relate to your lesson. Review the state-specific content standards you discovered earlier in the chapter and determine appropriate assessments you can incorporate in your lesson based on the achievement standards. Include in your plan a strategy for

incorporating art-history research, aesthetic inquiry, and art criticism along with the use of art-production software.

2. Research and select appropriate technologies that can support the activities in your lesson. Identify technology standards (NETS-S) addressed by your lesson. List all hardware and software required for the lesson and consider any preparation or prerequisite skills you may need to address before the students can complete the lesson.

3. If using the GAME Plan lesson template, include justifications for your technology application and reasons why you selected it in the section labeled Lesson Reflections and Notes. If you are using a different lesson plan template, include this information either on the template or in a separate file. Your justifications may relate to your skills or familiarity with the technology or the skills of your students, the match between the intended outcomes of the technology and your lesson, or even accessibility concerns.

References

APA, Task Force on Psychology in Education. (1993). *Learner-centered psychological principles: Guidelines for school redesign and reform.* Washington, DC: American Psychological Association and Mid-Continent Regional Educational Laboratory.

APA, Work Group of the American Psychological Association's Board of Educational Affairs. (1997). *Learner-centered psychological principles: A framework for school redesign and reform.* Washington, DC: American Psychological Association.

Bransford, J. D., Brown, A. L., & Cocking, R. R. (2000). *How people learn: Brain, mind, experience, and school.* Washington, DC: National Academy Press.

Consortium of National Arts Education Associations. (1994). *National Standards for Arts Education: What every young American should know and be able to do in the arts.* Reston, VA: Music Educators National Conference.

Ennis, R. (2002). *A super streamlined conception of critical thinking.* Retrieved January 13, 2006, from http://faculty.ed.uiuc.edu/rhennis/SSConcCTApr3.html

Freedman, K. (2003). *Teaching visual culture.* New York: Teachers College Press.

Ghysels, M. (2003). CT scans in art work appraisal. *Art Tribal, 4,* 116–131.

Jones, E., Hoffman, F., Moore, L., Ratcliff, G., Tibbits, S., & Click, B. (1995). *National assessment of college student learning: Identifying college graduates' essential skills in writing, speech and listening, and critical thinking.* Washington, DC: National Center for Education Statistics.

King, A. (2002). Structuring peer interaction to promote high-level cognitive processing. *Theory into Practice, 41*(1), 33–39.

Lampert, N. (2006a). Critical thinking dispositions as an outcome of art education. *Studies in Art Education, 47*(1), 215–228.

Lampert, N. (2006b). Enhancing critical thinking with aesthetic, critical, and creative inquiry. *Art Education, 59*(5), 46–50.

McCombs, B. L. (2000). *Assessing the role of educational technology in the teaching and learning process: A learner-centered perspective.* The Secretary's Conference on Educational Technology. Retrieved January 13, 2006, from http://www.ed.gov/rschstat/eval/tech/techconf00/mccombs_paper.html

National Commission on Excellence in Education. (1983). *A nation at risk: The imperative for educational reform.* Washington, DC: Government Printing Office.

Paul, R., Elder, L., & Bartell, T. (1997). *California teacher preparation for instruction in critical thinking: Research findings and policy recommendations.* Sacramento: California Commission on Teacher Credentialing.

Perry, W. (1999). *Forms of ethical and intellectual development in the college years: A scheme.* San Francisco: Jossey-Bass.

Taylor, P. G. (2006). Critical thinking in and through interactive computer hypertext and art education. *Innovate, 2*(3). Retrieved March 5, 2006, from http://www.innovateonline.info/index.php?view=article&id=41&action=article

Torrance, E. P. (1969). *Creativity.* Belmont, CA: Dimensions.

Trivedi, B. P. (2005). The Rembrandt code. *Wired, 13*(12). Retrieved January 5, 2006, from http://www.wired.com/wired/archive/13.12/rembrandt.html

TECHNOLOGY INTEGRATION FOR MEANINGFUL CLASSROOM USE
Daily Lesson GAME Plan

Lesson Title: Art That Speaks!

Related Lessons: Virtual Gallery Walk, My Self Portrait

Grade Level: Elementary

Unit: Art and Me

GOALS

Content Standards:

1. Understand and apply media, techniques, and processes
3. Choose and evaluate ideas, subjects, and symbols

ISTE NETS-S

☑ 1. Creativity and innovation

☑ 4. Critical thinking, problem solving, and decision making

☑ 2. Communication and collaboration

☐ 5. Digital citizenship

☐ 3. Research and information fluency

☐ 6. Technology operations and concepts

Instructional Objective(s): Students will interpret the meaning of a painting and animate a figure to explain the scene through words and facial expression.

ACTION

Before-Class Preparation: Reserve computer lab. Bookmark museum sites. Using CrazyTalk software, create an example based on Adriaen Brouwer's Youth Making a Face housed in the National Gallery of Art, Washington.

During Class

Time	Instructional Activities	Materials and Resources
15–20 minutes	Show students Youth Making a Face by Adriaen Brouwer. Guide them through a discussion of the painting and ask them to think about why the boy is making a face and what he might say if they were able to ask him.	Museum websites
5–10 minutes	Show them an animated example with your interpretation of the scene.	CrazyTalk software
15–20 minutes	Ask each student to find artwork that contains at least one person or animal that can be "brought to life."	Computer with Internet connection or CD-ROM library of images
20 minutes	Have students write a script in first person, read it to a classmate, and refine the script based on feedback.	Word-processing software
20–30 minutes	Have students record their scripts and animate their images.	CrazyTalk software

Notes: Students should work in pairs to refine scripts.

MONITOR

Ongoing Assessment(s): Check for understanding by having students share scripts and animated images with their peers. Check to see that the audio and character movements are in sync.

Accommodations and Extensions: Have students think about how they could change the scene by altering the emotional expression of the characters.

Back-up Plan: If the technology fails, students can prepare scripts for the characters and practice speaking for the audio recording.

EVALUATION

Lesson Reflections and Notes: To support students that have difficulty with the writing component, consider pairing students or having the class develop one or two scripts as a whole for this segment of the lesson to emphasize the animation activity.

TECHNOLOGY INTEGRATION FOR MEANINGFUL CLASSROOM USE
Daily Lesson GAME Plan

Lesson Title: Ad Campaign

Related Lessons: Elements of Design

Grade Level: Middle grades

Unit: Major Artists

GOALS

Content Standards:

1. Understand and apply media, techniques, and processes
2. Know art structures (elements and principles) and art functions
3. Choose and evaluate ideas, subjects, and symbols
5. Reflect upon and assess art

ISTE NETS-S

☑ 1. Creativity and innovation

☑ 2. Communication and collaboration

☑ 3. Research and information fluency

☑ 4. Critical thinking, problem solving, and decision making

☑ 5. Digital citizenship

☑ 6. Technology operations and concepts

Instructional Objective(s): Students research artists to determine information about their lives, artistic output, characteristics of style, and influences and then create an ad campaign to promote their artists. Students select one piece of work by the artist to focus their research. Students create a logo and one-page ad campaign with the intention of "marketing" the artwork and artist to other students.

ACTION

Before-Class Preparation: If time permits prior to class, create a "sample" marketing advertisement for an artist and artwork of your choosing. Otherwise, make a selection and use it to focus your opening discussion.

Identify online and print-based resources students can use to conduct their research. To optimize time and organize students, preselect a limited number of artists (10–12) and one or two works per artist.

Prepare the art work review handout. Examples of viewing guides can be found online. This handout should present questions students should ask themselves when reviewing their selected art work. Questions may include:

- What is the subject of the art work?
- Is there anything significant about the art work that draws your interest?
- Does it tell a story? Create a mood?
- How are different design elements incorporated into the work of art (elements such as line, color, space, texture, balance, composition, etc.)?

During Class

Time	Instructional Activities	Materials and Resources
15–20 minutes	Using your sample advertisement or selected art work, conduct a mock "marketing presentation" as if your students were prospective design clients. Using your handout as a guide, discuss with your students design elements and how these may represent or relate to the artist and work of art you are presenting. Determine elements of the art work that most appeal to the students in the class.	Sample marketing presentation or work of art Museum websites
1–2 class periods	In pairs, students select (or are assigned) an artist and art work to research. Students collect and record research about the artist using journaling, word-processing, or other software, citing all resources. From their research, they compile lists of 7–10 pertinent facts about the artist and the art work. Students also review their artwork using the guiding questions handout. Responses are recorded and stored with their research notes	Museum or art-related websites Journaling or word-processing software
1–2 class periods	Students create a logo and one-page "marketing presentation" to share with the class. Presentations should be digitized but do not have to use only digital materials, perhaps creating 3-D displays that can be photographed with a digital camera.	Drawing or image-editing software. Word-processing or presentation software can also be used. Scanner or digital camera (optional) Other art supplies
1 class period	Students present their designs to the rest of the class, describing how their designs best match the lists of facts they found in their research as well as how they relate to their artwork selections. Students should include their lists of facts and references. Students in the class should provide feedback on the "marketing campaign."	Student projects

Notes: Student projects are digitized to include in portfolios or on class websites.

MONITOR

Ongoing Assessment(s): Monitor student research to ensure students are finding appropriate information. Collect and review their final fact list and references, and completed artwork review handouts. The final products are best assessed through the use of a rubric.

Accommodations and Extensions: Students with requisite background knowledge on art and artists may be allowed to select their own subjects and artwork. Others may need explicit instruction and fewer choices.

Back-up Plan: Technology facilitates this lesson but print materials and nondigital art materials can be used to complete the lesson.

EVALUATION

Lesson Reflections and Notes: In some classes, students may be able to provide feedback by completing rubrics for completed projects. In others, this type of feedback may best be handled through a teacher-led group discussion.

TECHNOLOGY INTEGRATION FOR MEANINGFUL CLASSROOM USE
Daily Lesson GAME Plan

Lesson Title: Pop Art Portraits | **Related Lessons:** Monet and the Impressionists, Op Art

Grade Level: High School | **Unit:** Color

GOALS

Content Standards:

1. Understand and apply media, techniques, and processes
2. Know art structures (elements and principles) and art functions
3. Choose and evaluate ideas, subjects, and symbols
4. Understand the art of diverse times and cultures

ISTE NETS-S

☑ 1. Creativity and innovation ☑ 4. Critical thinking, problem solving, and decision making

☐ 2. Communication and collaboration ☐ 5. Digital citizenship

☐ 3. Research and information fluency ☑ 6. Technology operations and concepts

Instructional Objective(s): Students will

- study Andy Warhol's portraits of Marilyn Monroe and discuss the effect of repetition, symmetry, and contrast on a single image
- understand the expressive qualities of color
- understand layers and produce a multilayered image
- create self-portraits in the style of Andy Warhol

ACTION

Before Class Preparation: Reserve computer lab and digital cameras. Bookmark websites.

During Class

Time	Instructional Activities	Materials and Resources
15–20 minutes	Show examples of Andy Warhol's serigraph portraits of Marilyn Monroe and guide students through a focused discussion. Some of these can be found online or in art reference books. An interview with Andy Warhol can be found on the Web Exhibits website.	Websites with Andy Warhol's portraits of Marilyn Monroe http://webexhibits.org/colorart/marilyns.html
10–15 minutes	Go to the Web Exhibits site and allow students to adjust the colors on the Marilyn print to explore how color affects the mood of the portrait.	http://webexhibits.org/colorart/marilyns.html
10–15 minutes	Place students in pairs and have them take photographs of each other with a digital camera. Emphasize composition (e.g., head and shoulders, looking directly into the camera, etc.) Download images to the computer and open in Photoshop.	Digital camera Image-editing software that supports layers, such as Photoshop or Fireworks
5–10 minutes	Use the select tool to select and delete the background and replace it with an intense color. Adjust the image threshold in layer one so that only the essential shapes are visible. Discuss how this effect is similar to Warhol's serigraph technique.	Image-editing software that supports layers
10–15 minutes	Select each area that should be a single color and paste into a separate layer. Color and name each layer.	Image-editing software that supports layers

During Class		
Time	Instructional Activities	Materials and Resources
10 minutes	Copy the completed image and paste it onto a new background. This can be repeated multiple times to explore symmetry and repetition. Modify the color of the images through hue and saturation adjustments.	Image-editing software that supports layers
10 minutes	Print the finished image on a color printer and prepare it for display.	Color printer

Notes: Students should work in pairs to capture images using digital cameras. This lesson is best suited for students with some familiarity of Photoshop (or your preferred image-editing software), its tools and palettes.

MONITOR

Ongoing Assessment(s): Check to see that students are working in layers and can use the tools to manipulate the images as required (e.g., threshold, hue, and saturation) to create the desired mood/effect.

Accommodations and Extensions: Have students consider how they might use similar tools and techniques to create a portrait in the style of pop artist, Roy Lichtenstein. What processes would be similar? What would be different?

Back-up Plan: If the technology fails, students can use traditional art supplies to plan the color scheme for their portraits.

EVALUATION

Lesson Reflections and Notes: Final evaluation should include an evaluation of the effective and accurate use of the software. Students should justify final color choices and may present other combinations they tried but discarded. You can conduct a discussion with the class on the characteristics of portraits that make good settings for this treatment.

Lonnie Duka/PhotoLibrary

ISTE Standards addressed in this chapter

This chapter provides content-specific suggestions and strategies for addressing both ISTE's National Educational Technology Standards for Students (NETS-S) and the Music Content Standards outlined in the National Standards for Arts Education. This chapter also builds on the NETS-T concepts and skills presented earlier, with a special emphasis on skills related to Standard 1 "Facilitate and inspire student learning and creativity." Following an overview of the Music Content Standards and how you can address the NETS-S in the music classroom, this chapter outlines techniques, tools, and methods for developing authentic learning experiences that advance student creativity and innovation in the music classroom.

Integrating Technology in the Music Classroom

John D. Ross, Ph.D.

Whether you've thought about it or not, your understanding and appreciation of music have probably been heavily influenced by technology. You've undoubtedly listened to recordings of your favorite performers and compositions from different genres and styles. If you are a musician, you have probably been recorded many times yourself, whether performing or practicing alone or in ensembles. Not too long ago, music teachers would visit classrooms with portable record (LP) players, which eventually gave way to cassette tapes, then compact discs (CDs), and now even MP3 players. The use of visual media has also progressed from the passive viewing of filmstrips and films on large reels to an affordable and helpful pedagogical tool. Video recordings, now often digital, have become an integral tool for helping young musicians evaluate and critique their performances.

Outcomes

In this chapter, you will

- Identify music standards and explain how technology can support them.
- Discuss how the National Educational Technology Standards for Students can be addressed in a music classroom.
- Understand how authentic learning principles can be addressed using technology in a music classroom.
- Explain how technology can increase learning and facilitate creative thinking in the music classroom.

Many helpful music-specific technologies that support student and professional musicians are also available for use in music classrooms. Essential tools for all musicians, such as metronomes and tuners, went digital decades ago. Students interested in music theory and history have at their disposal a range of information resources on CDs, DVDs, and online. These resources have the benefit of providing students with examples of music from cultures and locations from around the world that were previously very limited, exposing students to many new genres and styles. Software is also available for learning to read, compose, and arrange music, as well as developing sightsinging and eartraining skills. Even the world of marching bands took a digital step forward with the development of software for drill design that includes animation and three-dimensional views of patterns of motion. And finally, a multitude of digital instruments are used not only in classrooms, but on stages across the world by students and professionals alike.

STORIES FROM PRACTICE

Composition in the Music Classroom

If my students' reactions were any indication, one of the most rewarding learning activities they completed was writing their own songs. I first implemented this activity in a beginning band class with students who had limited performing capability. Still, they were exposed to, and had a rudimentary understanding of, the elements of music (i.e., pitch, rhythm, meter, dynamics, and form) through the simple melodies from their method books. Students began composing simple 4- to 8-measure melodies in late October—just a few months after receiving their instruments for the first time! Each of my four classes voted on their "favorite" student melody to represent their class in "our song."

I would arrange each melody differently so I could introduce different musical elements, forms, and styles. I would often include a round with one slower tempo, one IV-V-I

cadence, harmony in thirds and sixths, and always finished with a rock- or pop-based rhythmic accompaniment—one that the percussion students would help me compose. The students also suggested and voted on a name, often some variation of the school mascot, the Cougars. I began this process with paper and pencil and was glad to receive a keyboard and computer with a sequencer the second year. It saved me a lot of time in arranging and dramatically reduced the time required to get the parts back to the kids so we could practice. The first year we played "our song," we got a standing ovation and had to play it again immediately for the proud parents. Every year, whenever we'd have a "student choice" day in class, we undoubtedly had to play "our song."

Based on this early success, I continued to include composition with my students. As

you might guess, increasing access to technology made it easier for them. My jazz students could slow down digital recordings to transcribe improvised solos and compose their own solos for the same songs. When working on Elliott Del Borgo's composition for band, inspired by Dylan Thomas's famous poem "Do Not Go Gentle Into That Good Night," my high school students used a range of digital tools to create visual art, poems and short stories, and even more musical compositions that reflected our discussion about elements such as timbre, tone, meter, dynamics, and expression in both the poem and the composition. In this way, my students were able to relate the elements of music, composition, and performance to other subject areas that will stay with them longer than simply learning their individual parts for the song.

Technology and Content Standards

Following the trend of the creation of content standards in other curricular areas during "the era of standards," national content standards for music were developed in the 1990s by the Consortium of National Arts Education Associations under the guidance of the National Committee for Standards in the Arts. Each set of Fine Arts

Table 21.1	Music Content Standards

1. Singing, alone and with others, a varied repertoire of music
2. Performing on instruments, alone and with others, a varied repertoire of music
3. Improvising melodies, variations, and accompaniments
4. Composing and arranging music within specified guidelines
5. Reading and notating music
6. Listening to, analyzing, and describing music
7. Evaluating music and music performances
8. Understanding relationships between music, the other arts, and disciplines outside the arts
9. Understanding music in relation to history and culture

Source: From National Standards for Arts Education. Copyright © 1994 by Music Educators National Conference (MENC). Used by permission. The complete National Arts Standards and additional materials relating to the Standards are available from MENC: The National Association for Music Education, 1806 Robert Fulton Drive, Reston, VA 20191; www.menc.org

standards includes a set of content standards and then a range of achievement standards for three grade clusters: 1) kindergarten through fourth grade, 2) fifth through eighth grade, and 3) ninth through twelfth grade. In addition, four content standards are identified for prekindergarten students. Involving students in music education at an early age is critical for later success and can influence whether some students develop essential musical skills at all.

The content standards are global statements describing music skills that students at all grades should be able to do, such as singing, performing, improvising, and composing. The achievement standards provide greater specificity about the types of skills and knowledge that students should possess for each content standard. See Table 21.1 for a list of the nine content standards for music.

In reviewing the nine national content standards for music, it is important that these nine types of skills be addressed in both general and specialized music classrooms for students of all ages. Elementary school students should sing and play some instruments, whether recorders, percussion, or others. And at a level appropriate to their development, they should be able to read basic music notation, identify different song forms (e.g., rounds, ostinatos, ABA form, etc.), and determine the quality of performances, including their own. As students' skills progress and they enroll in specialized ensembles, these same nine skill areas still should be addressed. Singing remains a critical skill for band and orchestra students, and many choral students are required to play instruments, particularly percussion-like instruments that include their hands. Students of all ages can compose or arrange simple melodies or rhythmic accompaniments, which often can be combined with improvisation. Improvisation itself is a critical skill not restricted to jazz but can be found in most musical genres from melismas in Gregorian chant and the figured bass lines in the Renaissance and Baroque periods through current folk and popular music. At every grade, music students can develop the critical listening and analysis skills that are tempered by their understanding of the elements of music, how these relate to other disciplines, and how history and culture influence music creation, performance, evaluation, and acceptance.

Rarely do the music standards mention technology specifically, but as you well know, musicians are often surrounded by and integrate a variety of technologies in their practice and performance. Some technologies may be used for multiple purposes and support more than one skill. This chapter is not intended to cover all possible technology tools available for teaching and learning in every type of music classroom. However, it provides you with background on a range of tools and their uses that you can then draw from and build upon in your own classroom. Table 21.2 illustrates how each of the NETS-S can be supported in a music classroom. The sample lesson plans at the end of this chapter provide specific examples of how you can design learning experiences that meet both content area and technology standards.

 WEB LINK

For further explanation of the achievement standards and how these standards can be assessed, as well as detailed examples of the alignment of the NETS-S to the music content standards, visit the textbook's companion website.

Table 21.2	NETS-S in the Music Classroom

Creativity and Innovation

Digital tools allow students to work as professionals through the use of practice and accompaniment software, recording devices, and digital instruments that support their practice and monitor their musical growth. Students listen to and observe performances by professionals on CD, DVD, and online and use hardware and software to support composition, analysis, and sequencing of musical elements.

Communication and Collaboration

Students use telecommunications appropriately to communicate with other students and teachers. Students can send recordings of their performances to others to demonstrate proficiency or seek constructive feedback. Students use appropriate digital instruments as well as recording and broadcast media to communicate musical thought and expression.

Research and Information Fluency

Students use online and other digital resources to learn about musical styles from different genres, cultures, and time periods. Students use CDs, DVDs, websites, and other sources of recordings and musical notation to expand their learning and to compare differences in the treatment of musical elements by different cultures as well as compare differences in interpretation by performers.

Critical Thinking, Problem Solving, and Decision Making

Students use a range of digital tools to support their musical growth. Performers use practice software and recording devices to monitor their progress and make informed decisions about strategies for continued improvement. Students use professional standard notation software for composing and arranging as well as musical instruments and recording technologies used by professionals.

Digital Citizenship

Students demonstrate appropriate care and use of digital instruments and equipment, such as sound systems including microphones, audio and video recorders, and computers. Students demonstrate their understanding of copyright and fair use, licensing, and royalties when selecting music to perform in different settings or including music in presentations. Students use technology to support their practice outside of class to develop their skills and increase motivation.

Technology Operations and Concepts

Students demonstrate common basic skills related to technology, such as opening and saving files, cutting, pasting, and other basic operations when using music productivity tools related to notation, composition, and arranging. Students use common audio and video recording devices as well as MIDI instruments.

THE GAME PLAN

Content Standards

Set Goals

Research the music standards for a state where you plan to seek a teaching position and create an action plan to ensure that you will have the knowledge and skills necessary to help your students achieve those standards. Identify the concepts, knowledge, and skills you will need to ensure that you are prepared to help your students meet the music standards in your state.

Take Action

Explore the department of education website in the state where you plan to seek a position. Review the K–12 music standards in that state and compare them to the state's technology standards. Identify those standards that specifically relate to applying technology in music

education. Develop a plan for how to meet the technology standards in the context of music.

Monitor

Did you find the information you needed? Do you need to contact the department of education for more information about where to find the music standards or the technology standards for teachers?

Evaluate and Extend

Discuss in class the action plan you developed for meeting the technology standards for instructional personnel. Compare your plan to others. Note the strengths and weaknesses of the various plans. Strengthen your plan by incorporating ideas you have heard in class.

Authentic Learning Strategies Incorporating Technology

Music programs have a long history of relying on the apprentice model of instruction, an approach that focuses instruction on the specific needs of the learner. Students at all levels still rely on attending private lessons with a master teacher in order to develop the fine points of performance, whether singing or playing an instrument. This one-to-one process can produce tremendous results in terms of student growth, but it is costly and time-consuming. In whole-class settings, music teachers are able to provide instruction for a large number of students, many who may be unable or unwilling to attend private lessons. These classes, however, traditionally have large enrollments—often much larger than that of a teacher in a core curricular area. It can be quite challenging to help students fine-tune the psychomotor skills required for musical performance, while at the same time address the highly creative aspects of musical interpretation in a 50-minute class with 85 students. This is the reality of teaching music, however—at least how it has been for this author. So how can you provide the individual attention students need to develop their musical skills and knowledge within a large group setting?

Instruction in Musical Performance

As related in the Stories from Practice about a master teacher, you can help your students attain the skills required for musical performance if you provide them with methods and supports that will enable them to continue to learn and grow musically when you're not around. In other words, you can help them learn to practice, and there are a variety of technologies available to do just that.

For many years, music textbooks and method books have been paired with recordings. Once provided on vinyl records and cassette tapes, recordings of master performers are now available on CDs, DVDs, and the Internet. Students can hear performance techniques for most instruments as well as music from various cultures, from African drumming to Appalachian fiddle techniques. Beginning trumpet students can listen, in the comfort of their own bedrooms, to examples of simple melodies and fingering exercises played with exemplary tone and phrasing by a master teacher. Vocalists in a show choir can hear all of the parts of a composition they are working on, or can isolate their individual parts or even just the accompaniment with no vocal parts. Some professional performers produce their own instructional recordings. For example, your students can learn from a video by jazz saxophonist, Gerry Mulligan, or play along with a CD-ROM from B. B. King. There are also helpful lessons and demonstrations online from different reputable sources on a range of

STORIES FROM PRACTICE

Lessons from a Master Teacher

One of the most critical lessons I learned in teaching students to sing or play an instrument came from one of my teachers during a private lesson. I've been able to use that advice throughout my career as a music teacher. Having studied with my saxophone teacher, Doug Graham, for almost four years and while preparing for my last hurdle, my senior recital, we discussed my future and the inevitability of his not being available for weekly lessons. While these lessons often challenged, and sometimes even tormented, me they always helped me progress down the path of musical proficiency. I was very focused on my upcoming performance, when Doug told me, "I'm not teaching you to perform. I'm teaching you to practice." It was a bit of a surprise at first, but this statement became a critical component of my philosophy as a music educator. I've worked with hundreds of students—from elementary grades through senior citizens—who have all focused on performing something somewhere, whether in their living room or at Lincoln Center in New York. Still, I have always tried to focus my instruction on helping them to develop the skills they can use once I'm not around. Indeed, I was teaching them to practice.

Source: John Ross

topics. Consider having young drummers observe common drum set techniques from vodcasts (video podcasts) by Little Kids Rock or tune in to a number of other musical podcasts from educational institutions that post to Apple's iTunes U. You and your students can also create your own digital recordings that can support practice at home and in class, such as accompaniments used in elementary music classes to standard warm-up exercises for vocalists.

Instrumentalists can use microphones to interact with practice software, such as smartmusic, eMedia, or Band-in-a-Box. Vocalists can interact with practice software, too, such as the Singing Coach series from Carry-a-Tune Technologies. This interactive software captures and displays a student's vocal performance, both visually and aurally, and can contain a number of tutorials and exercises. Some applications also include a wide range of professional recordings of individuals and ensembles performing band, choir, and orchestral literature that students can play along with at home. More advanced versions of practice software can track and notate problems with student performance, as well as record the student performance with or without the accompaniment that can be stored, e-mailed, or burned to a CD for later review.

The newest generation of practice recordings includes features that allow students to manipulate the recordings themselves—something difficult or nearly impossible to do with analog recordings. Digital recordings can be played at different tempos without affecting pitch, so when students are learning a new song they can slow down the tempo of a song they are practicing and gradually increase the tempo to performance speed as they advance. Some multimedia packages include visuals that scaffold student learning. Students can view keys highlighted on a keyboard or finger placement on the fretboard of a guitar. Music notation can also be displayed on a computer monitor that then is highlighted as the music is performed—the 21st century's version of "follow the bouncing ball."

The usefulness of practice software can be debated, with opposing positions focusing on the inability of the computer-driven accompaniment to truly replicate the physical and emotional synthesis that musicians experience when performing together. However, these innovative methods for helping students practice on their own carry many benefits that are hard to dispute. They can bring exemplary models of performance into a student's home at little cost, which is especially useful for students who do not have access to private lessons. They also incorporate tools that professional musicians routinely use in good practice, such as metronomes and tuners, and by allowing for playback at varied speeds help students develop good practice habits. And, perhaps most importantly from the perspective of a seasoned music teacher, they can make practicing fun! Students can begin playing some of their favorite songs very quickly and may feel like they are truly performing without having to hire a rhythm section to drop by every night. Practicing is essential for the young musician and these new digital tools can be far more motivational and rewarding than sitting in your room alone and singing the alto part from a cantata or playing the upbeats from the trio of the march your school band will play a month from now (see Figure 21.1).

Learning to Read and Write Music

Students who learn and perform music undoubtedly need to be able to read and write the standard systems of notation. The youngest music students may not use the traditional notation system of notes and rests, staves and clefs, and related dynamic and tempo markings. Guitar students may be required to read tablature to play some of their favorite songs. Advanced students will explore unique additions to the notation system more familiar with compositions from the 20th century and beyond. Regardless of the notation system that you have to address in your instruction, digital software is most likely available that can support the level of instruction you must address.

The content standards in the early grades often link music with more holistic conceptions of musical notation and may encourage students to draw, dance, or otherwise describe elements of music, such as fast versus slow tempos, or high versus low

Figure 21.1
Technology supports practicing, student engagement, and motivation.

pitches. Students in the early grades can also experiment with music composition and arrangement through the generation and reorganization of sounds, whether explicitly musical or not. Multimedia software—both stand-alone and online—is available to support this early music development, with some designed specifically to address the national music standards. Presented as a series of games, elementary students can explore the activities in the software developed by Kid's Music Stage, such as Alice in Vivaldi's Four Seasons, or in software featuring the characters Piano-mouse and friends from pianomouse.com. Interactive websites, such as Creating Music, also provide age-appropriate musical games and activities for these young students. The activities in this type of software can introduce students to classical repertoire, musical instruments, form, structure, and a range of other musical skills. They can go beyond simple drill-and-practice to provide an interactive musical environment with realistic sounds that students can manipulate. By providing immediate aural and visual feedback, a positive learning environment is afforded these young students (Kersten, 2006). For a complete lesson resource, packages from Sibelius (e.g., Groovy Music, Starclass) contain lesson plans, recordings, and related resources for helping young students learn about music notation and complete developmentally appropriate compositions and arrangements.

More advanced students can benefit from the variety of sightsinging and eartraining software that is available (see Figure 21.2). Software applications, such as

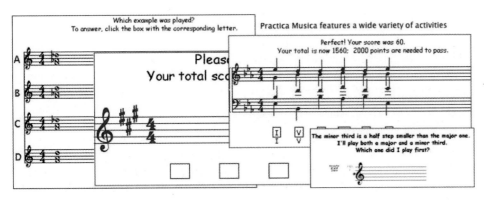

Figure 21.2
Sightsinging and eartraining software helps students develop critical musical skills.
Source: Courtesy ARS Nova, www.ars-nova.com

Practica Musica or Auralia, combine visual presentation of notes and/or rhythms with the critical aural presentation of the sounds the symbols represent. This pairing of visual and aural stimuli was not available with print-based resources, because these resources required someone to perform the exercises, making them impractical for very young students or students without keyboard skills. With the wide range of software applications available now, students of all levels can practice sightsinging and eartraining skills across many difficulty levels on their own or in classroom settings.

As these programs have become more advanced, new features have been added that lead to a more sophisticated level of student skill development. Very complex rhythms and multipart examples can be presented that the students not only listen to but can "perform" for the computer, either by tapping keys or actually singing back to the computer using a microphone. Some programs allow you to edit the musical examples, so your students can practice most needed skills or passages related to the repertoire they are currently studying. Several include increased levels of difficulty and tracking and reporting of student performance.

Understanding Different Musical Styles and Genres

Audio and video recordings have long been a critical component of music classrooms. Leonard Bernstein was lauded for using the promising new educational technology of television in the early 1960s to broadcast his famous "Young People's Concerts" with the New York Philharmonic to explore musical styles and genres and to help create a more musical literate populace. These valuable recordings, as well as excellent recordings by numerous talented professional musicians from across the globe performing just about any musical genre you can imagine, became available in videocassette and then DVD formats. Unlike the music teachers of Leonard Bernstein's time, or even those for a few decades after that, you and your students have the opportunity to find and explore musical performances from both well-known and unknown musicians from across the globe performing music from virtually every time period, genre, and style. Although some of these are available on CDs and DVDs, a wealth of free web-based resources are available from highly trusted sources designed to support music educators at all levels. Some sites include lesson plans aligned to music content standards with links to recordings or videos. Others may require a little preparation on your part and allow you to customize activities for use in your own classroom—using textbooks, method books, or other literature.

THE GAME PLAN

Identifying Web-Based Resources

Set Goals

Find online resources you can use for a range of activities in your music classroom. You may need resources to support skill development such as sightsinging or eartraining, or you may be looking for engaging web resources for younger students exploring musical styles and performances from different cultures.

Take Action

Review the web resources on the textbook's companion website. Conduct other searches on your own for resources of interest to you.

Monitor

How well do the resources meet stated goal(s)? Are there clearinghouse websites or sites that review online music resources? Did you find resources you didn't know existed that might be helpful to you in the music classroom?

Evaluate and Extend

Select the best resources you have found and include a list of them in your portfolio. Share your list with other music students to compile a master list that covers a range of grade levels and musical skills.

A quick trip around the web can unearth a variety of these resources, such as Arts-Edge from the Kennedy Center with complete lesson plans in music, dance, theatre, and the visual arts for every grade as well as connections to interdisciplinary units. Several professional music organizations develop and provide educational resources, such as San Francisco Symphony Kids, DSOKids from the Dallas Symphony Orchestra, and the New York Philharmonic's Kidzone! websites that have a wide range of music games, audio and video recordings, and informational activities related to composers, performers, instruments, and many other music-related topics. The Silk Road Project was started by cellist Yo-Yo Ma in order to provide opportunities to explore musical traditions from cultures and communities located across Eurasia. Or consider the multimedia offerings of the River of Song website from the Smithsonian Institution and PBS. This extensive resource explores music traditions along the Mississippi River. With just a few clicks more, you and your students can find websites with information about and audio and video examples of just about any musical genre or style from any time period.

Technology and Creative Thinking Skills Instruction

When working in a large class or directing a performing ensemble, it can be challenging to address the more creative aspects of musical performance, such as style and interpretation—whether your class focuses on music appreciation or performance. But many of the technology tools described in this chapter can provide supports for your music curriculum that can help you address creative aspects of music with your students. These tools can help students relate content and musical selections in your classroom to music they may be interested in outside of class and to make informed decisions about music they do or do not prefer. There are also many tools available to support the development of sound practice habits that allow students to make positive musical growth and to achieve advanced levels of performance. Whether focusing on composition and arranging, performing, or relating music to other disciplines, styles, and time periods, there are tools available that can help your students develop and hone creative skills.

Some of the tools already described for teaching music can also be used by students to demonstrate their learning and mastery of creative thinking skills. The following section introduces additional technologies that can be used in music instruction with an emphasis on how they are used by students to demonstrate creative thinking skills and musical knowledge.

Performing and Recording Music

Student performance is critical in the music classroom at all levels. Whether in class or a more formal setting, student performances are the expected outcomes for many music programs. Certainly, there are a range of instruments that have progressed from being electronic to actually being digital. But many of the ways your students would perform on digital keyboards, strings, percussion, and even wind instruments are similar to their analog counterparts. One critical element about digital instruments that is unique, however, is the use of the digital music language, MIDI, which stands for Musical Instrument Digital Interface. This communications protocol allows a wide range of digital instruments—and analog instruments played into digital converters—to generate digital data that can be stored, manipulated, and "played" back by a variety of tools and instruments.

MIDI takes both composition and performance to a new level, especially through the use of sequencers and sequencing software. With sequencing software, a desktop computer can become a recording studio, and with the ease of creating websites and burning discs, performers of all ages are writing and publishing their music to share with anyone who will listen. Your students can have access to a range of sequencing software from those used by professionals to scaled-down versions designed for young musicians. Free programs like Audacity and GarageBand can also be used as sequencing tools and can incorporate additional digital media such as pictures or video. With a USB interface, such as Fast Track USB, your students can record their own instrumental performances right into these applications. Software such as Traktor DJ and Mixman Studio can be used to change sequences entirely, by altering tempos, adding and deleting tracks, and adding a number of effects, including "scratching," first made popular by DJs in dance clubs and on MTV using turntables and, ironically, analog recordings.

Most sequencers allow for the display of lines of sounds or music, usually called tracks, in several formats, including music notation, a series of bars (see Figure 21.3), or even actual sound waves. Most sequencers also include a "piano roll" function that allows users to see the visual notation scroll across the screen. This visual organization of the tracks allows for quick editing—through copying, cutting, and pasting —in addition to a range of sound-specific functions, such as quickly adjusting volume or muting tracks. Early students can "compose" simple soundscapes to illustrate concepts related to tempo, rhythm, or timbre, while more advanced students can create incredibly complex compositions in a range of styles.

Recording is a well-established use of technology that allows students to demonstrate musical proficiency and growth. Recording media have progressed over time from analog reel-to-reel and cassette tapes, to Digital Audio Tape (DAT) recorders and digital file formats that can be burned to CDs or DVDs or shared online. Students can record practice sessions, sometimes using the practice software described earlier in this chapter, or can record sections of required music for assessment purposes. Having students record performances outside of class saves instructional time

Figure 21.3
Sequencing software provides visual notation in a variety of formats. Groovy Music from Sibelius is shown here.
Source: Sibelius Groovy screenshots and images ©2006 Avid Technology, Inc. Used by permission. Sibelius, Sibelius Groovy Music and Groovy Music Shapes are trademarks of Avid Technology, Inc.

and allows you to review and provide highly specific feedback to each student, even recording your comments on a separate track so the students can hear both their performances and your comments at the same time. Recordings of ensemble performances, whether in class or during actual performances, can also be used as a pedagogical tool when students critique their own performances and provide strategies for improving them. Recordings also give students a record of performance over time that can be included in a portfolio. It's sometimes difficult for students to remember at the end of the year what they sounded like back in September, but a series of recordings demonstrating growth can really give students positive feedback and increase their motivation.

It's not uncommon to visit a school program and see an army of moms and dads with videocameras in the auditorium. Now that digital recording has jumped into the 21st century, you and your students can share their performances with family members and friends, regardless of the geographic distance. Software such as Audacity and GarageBand, mentioned earlier, can be used to create podcasts and vodcasts of student performances so even a grandparent across the country can hear them. Video performances can be uploaded to sites such as YouTube or Google Video. These files are converted to the Flash player format that makes them accessible to most computer users. A big caveat is needed here, however, as all performers must obtain permission to post copyrighted music or only post music that is in the public domain. Just because you've performed a song in concert, it doesn't mean you have the authority to disseminate that performance.

Notating Music

Sequencing software often provides some form of musical notation; however, powerful software exists that is specifically designed to allow students to write any type of musical notation. Sometimes the distinction between sequencing and notation software is blurred as some applications can do both. Through a MIDI interface, compositions can be created using a computer keyboard, mouse, or musical input device, such as a digital keyboard. Once entered, all musical elements can be modified and revised, such as transposing sections or an entire composition, duplicating or adding lines, or changing playback tempos. Students can construct simple one-line melodies or extremely complex multipart scores with extended notation for dynamics, articulation, and performance techniques developed since the beginning of the 20th century.

Popular music notation programs, such as Cakewalk, Finale, and Sibelius, are powerful tools used by music professionals around the world as well as being available to, and used by, music students. Simpler notation programs are also available for younger students, and some music notation software, often with limited functionality, is available as freeware or shareware that can be downloaded from the Internet. Your students can use music notation software to write basic counterpoint, recreate common musical forms such as a round or fugue, create rhythmic accompaniments, or compose entirely unique compositions. Students with a high degree of proficiency can have their compositions included in school performances, with a score and all parts being generated from a computer running commonly available music notation software. Your composition students may even consider sharing performances of their original compositions on the Internet through sites such as the Podsafe Music Network, where other users of this site can download and use them for podcasts and other presentations.

Demonstrating Understanding of Different Musical Styles and Genres

Students demonstrate much of their understanding of musical concepts and skills through performance; however, the music content standards also require music students to develop skills for understanding different musical styles and genres. In your classroom, you may help students to 1) develop critical listening skills related to analyzing and evaluating music; 2) relate the common elements of music to other disciplines in and outside of the Fine Arts; and 3) develop their understanding of the influences of history and culture on music styles, genres, and performances. Several web resources have already been mentioned to support research in these areas. In order to demonstrate their knowledge, students can use a variety of multimedia software that allows both visual and aural presentation of musical examples and related artifacts. For example, an elementary class can work together to identify instruments their families have at home or instruments they have seen on television or in other media. The students can take pictures of the instruments with digital cameras or find pictures in digital libraries or scan them from print publications, such as catalogs. Students can research and write short descriptions of the instruments and the pictures and text can be combined with short recordings of friends, family, or the students themselves performing on the instruments they've identified. You can help students combine all of this work in presentation software, on a class web page, or in other multimedia authoring software.

Older students can research favorite performers, composers, or music from different places or periods of history to generate similar multimedia reports. A variety of short videos can also be incorporated demonstrating either a musical performance technique, an interview with a performer, or the role of music in celebrations in a different or related culture. Podcasts found online can be incorporated for demonstration, as well. Students can present these materials to the music class or, if you work with teachers from another discipline, they may provide this information in a history, social studies, or language arts class to enrich their understanding of a particular culture or writing form. The critical aspect of these demonstrations is the appropriate selection and use of sounds and musical elements to represent the aural aspect of music—something very difficult to address in print alone.

Both you and your students can find free music online to support presentations and projects. You can download free music files directly from websites or use peer-to-peer file sharing programs, such as Morpheus or eMule. File sharing got a bad reputation during the days of Napster where users downloaded copyright-protected files, but there are legal download sites for teachers and students, such as the Audio Archive. Helping students to understand when and how to do this legally can be an important aspect of digital citizenship. Most sites clearly describe how the music resources you acquire can be used. To find answers to frequently asked questions, activities to use in your instruction, and updated information about copyright in the music classroom, visit the Music Education Copyright Center website from MENC.

Solving Real-World Problems and Students Acting as Professionals

You could argue that students in a music classroom are often being creative. Creativity is an essential element in music instruction and performance, but if your methods limit the types of activities your students participate in and the opportunities they have in which to express that creativity, you can end up with a music class that relies on rote memorization, uninspired regurgitation of information, and very little creativity. As has been mentioned throughout the examples given in this chapter, the creation of digital tools—including musical instruments as well as hardware and software—allows students to work as professionals. Activities that challenge students to make decisions and create products similar to professionals often require creative thinking skills. Music-notation software allows students to use the same tools as professionals to arrange and compose music. They can also use these tools to analyze compositions to better understand techniques that professional composers employ. Schools can also set up digital recording facilities that allow students to analyze their own performances. Students can perform published compositions as well as their own creations that can be recorded digitally, and these recordings can be edited through sequencing software and mass-produced for dissemination by CD or as MP3 files on a portable digital player.

In terms of supporting creative musical performance, the digital tools described in this chapter allow students to develop good practice skills using the same or similar tools that professional musicians use. Practice software and digital performances can help bridge the gap between solo practice and professional input, as these live or recorded performances can be shared with professional performers. Students can bring recordings to professionals who offer private lessons or coaching. High-speed Internet connections have been used to bridge the geographic distance between students and noted performers, as when students in West Virginia performed for noted performer and composer Mark O'Connor in New York City over a broadband Internet connection in 2000.

Evaluation, Synthesis, and Application to Create Original Works

Music students at all levels are routinely required to develop and utilize creative thinking skills, such as evaluation, synthesis, and application. Obviously, these skills are involved in musical performances with or without digital tools, whether the performance involves younger students singing or clapping together in class or an advanced ensemble performing a difficult repertoire. But digital tools can support the development and demonstration of creative thinking skills further.

Evaluating musical performances, whether one's own or those of others, often takes place in music classes. Digital recordings, both audio and video, are extremely helpful for allowing students to develop these skills. An individual student performing in an ensemble of 4, 40, or 140 students may be so enveloped in sound that he or she misses critical missteps, such as incorrectly performed rhythms, pitches, bowings, or vocalizations. It's hard to argue with a recording, though. You should know that some students may have difficulty listening to or watching themselves perform —maybe you do as well—so it's important to introduce it early in your instruction and make it a routine practice. Begin with recording whole-class or ensemble performances and gradually work up to recording individuals or asking students to record themselves at home.

As music students mature, they synthesize techniques and methods they've learned and apply them in performances. But the nonperforming elements of music education also are important to developing a well-rounded music student. Crow (2006) noted that many young students are already creative with their music, capturing and sharing the music they like to listen to on MP3 players, creating playlists, and even mixing, sequencing, and looping tracks to emulate what they hear and see from their favorite performers in the music industry. As a music teacher, you can capitalize on this aspect of creativity with students from a range of ages.

Young students can synthesize and apply musical concepts with simple sequencers that allow them to combine musical phrases or more simple sounds. These young students can "compose" simple compositions according to parameters that increase incrementally, such as replicating a meter based on groupings of three with a strong first beat, or combining loud and soft sounds to simulate a crescendo. Older students using sequencing software or sound loops can also emulate music from a range of styles, including that which they find most interesting, thus using their natural interest to promote understanding of characteristics of music, such as pitch, rhythm, dynamics, and others.

Researchers (Gall & Breeze, 2005; Jennings, 2005; Reynolds, 2005) identified positive attributes and some trade-offs music teachers might consider when using multimedia composition and sequencing software. The ease with which students can interact with the software and change the interface (e.g., from sound bars to

WEB LINK

View the textbook's companion website to review a list of the software, hardware, and Internet resources mentioned in this chapter as well as additional resources for the music classroom.

traditional notation) allows many students to quickly become engaged with the tasks of composition that might not be possible when using traditional instruments with which students may not have sufficient facility or technique. The visual notation common to this software is also often easier for novice musicians to manipulate as compared to standard notation. Software-based projects can encourage students to collaborate and communicate about their compositions as well as incorporate singing, rhythmic performance, and using musical language to describe their work. Long compositions are easily stored, sometimes in sections, which makes it easy for students to retrieve and review their work, which in turn makes it easy for them to get back to work at the start of a new class session. Students are also able to bring in pre-recorded samples that may be more engaging and relevant to their own interests, such as different drum tracks.

Multimedia presentations can also require students to evaluate, synthesize, and apply not only musical skills but skills across the curriculum. These skills can be demonstrated through the creation of static information displays, such as web pages or presentation software, or used to augment a student's live "performance" through a class presentation, discussion, or debate. These same presentations can also be recorded and used for assessment, placed in a student portfolio, or played later at an assembly or meeting for other students, parents, and the community.

Chapter Summary

Digital tools are available to support the development of skills and knowledge addressed by the national music content standards at every level. Professional quality tools are readily available for schools so your students can address the real-world problems faced by professional musicians. Digital tools are available to support and enhance music instruction in even the earliest grades. They are also often available to students once they've left your music classroom, so they can continue to nurture their musical interests and develop their musical skills. Truly, with the range of tools available to support almost every aspect of music teaching and learning, you are more likely to be faced with considering *which* tools to choose in your classroom rather than whether a tool is available.

YOUR PORTFOLIO

To demonstrate your understanding of creating learning experiences in the music classroom that address the National Educational Technology Standards for Students, create a lesson plan for common activities in your music classroom using the GAME Plan template available on the textbook's companion website, or one of your choosing. If you work with younger students, you may want to address developing foundational rhythmic or music reading skills. If you work with students who perform, you may want to create a lesson that requires them to demonstrate mastery of a new technique or passage.

1. Identify the national music content standards that relate to your lesson. Review the state-specific content standards you discovered earlier in the chapter and determine appropriate assessments you can incorporate in yourlesson based on the achievement standards.

2. Research and select appropriate technologies that can support the activities in your lesson. Identify technology standards (NETS-S) addressed by your lesson. List all hardware and software required for the lesson and consider

any preparation or prerequisite skills you may need to address before the students can complete the lesson.

3. If using the GAME Plan lesson template, include justifications for your technology application and reasons why you selected it in the section labeled Lesson Reflections and Notes. If you are using a different lesson plan template, include this information either on the template or in a separate file. Your justifications may relate to your skills or familiarity with the technology or the skills of your students, the match between the intended outcomes of the technology and your lesson, or even accessibility concerns.

References

Crow, B. (2006). Musical creativity and the new technology. *Music Education Research, 8*(1), 121–130.

Gall, M., & Breeze, N. (2005). Music composition lessons: The multimodal affordances of technology. *Educational Review, 57*(4), 415–433.

Jennings, K. (2005). Hyperscore: A case study in computer mediated music composition. *Education and Information Technologies, 10*(3), 225–238.

Kersten, F. (2006). Inclusion of technology resources in early childhood music education. *General Music Today, 20*(1), 15–26.

MENC. (1994). *Performance standards for music: Strategies and benchmarks for assessing progress toward the national standards, Grades PreK–12.* Reston, VA: Author.

Reynolds, N. (2005). The computer as scaffold, tool and data collector: Children composing with computers. *Education and Information Technologies, 10*(3), 239–248.

For Further Reading

Ajero, M. (2006–2007). The 21st-century recital hall: How Internet audio and video can provide an alternative stage. *American Music Teacher, 56*(3), 58–59.

Katz, M. (2004). *Capturing sound: How technology has changed music.* Berkeley: University of California Press.

Lamb, A., & Johnson, L. Turn up the music with digital technologies. *Teacher Librarian, 34*(2), 55–58.

Richmond, F. (Ed.) (2005). *Technology strategies for music educators.* Boston, MA: Technology Institute of Music Educators (TI:ME) Publication.

Watson, S. (2005). *Technology guide for music educators.* Boston, MA: Technology Institute of Music Educators (TI:ME) Publication.

TECHNOLOGY INTEGRATION FOR MEANINGFUL CLASSROOM USE
Daily Lesson GAME Plan

Lesson Title: Instruments of the Orchestra | **Related Lessons:** Popular and Traditional Instruments

Grade Level: Elementary | **Unit:** Musical Instruments

GOALS

Content Standards:

8. Understanding relationships between music, the other arts, and disciplines outside the arts
9. Understanding music in relation to history and culture

ISTE NETS-S

☐ 1. Creativity and innovation	☑ 4. Critical thinking, problem solving, and decision making
☑ 2. Communication and collaboration	☑ 5. Digital citizenship
☑ 3. Research and information fluency	☑ 6. Technology operations and concepts

Instructional Objective(s): Students identify and describe critical features of instrument families—both visually and aurally—and work in collaborative groups to develop short multimedia presentations about the instrument families of the orchestra.

ACTION

Before-Class Preparation: Develop presentation template with title slide; one slide each for strings, woodwinds, brass, and percussion; and a slide for references and credits. If necessary, identify student groups prior to lesson. Identify and bookmark appropriate websites.

During Class

Time	Instructional Activities	Materials and Resources
15–20 minutes	Distribute and review the assessment rubric. Provide examples of slides at different levels of the rubric, including those demonstrating different design elements, proper grammar, and the appropriate citation of references. Each instrument family slide must contain at least the following: • A picture or pictures of instruments from the family • Names of at least 3 instruments in the family • Common materials used to manufacture the instruments • At least one sound file of one instrument from the family	Rubric Presentation examples
At least two 45–50 minute sessions	Organize students in work groups. Students work collaboratively on their presentations, going through the processes of research, note taking, writing, development, and review.	Bookmarked websites Magazines and reference books Presentation software Scanner (if available) Digital camera (if available)
15–20 minutes	Students peer review a presentation from one other group and complete a rubric as feedback.	Draft rubric
Allow 10–15 minutes per group	Students present their presentations to the class. Leave plenty of time for each group to play their audio files. During presentations, ask probing questions, such as identifying similar and different instrument examples across the groups. Use the audio examples to check for understanding from students not presenting. Presentations and completed rubrics can be included in student portfolios.	Student presentations Rubrics

Notes: Groups of four students work well for this activity. If access to computers is limited, students can rotate through workstations, some working on Internet research, research with magazines and books, scanning (if necessary), and design of the presentation.

MONITOR

Ongoing Assessment(s): Students will use a teacher-generated rubric to identify content-specific requirements for the presentation as well as the quality of the presentation including appropriate grammar and language usage.

Accommodations and Extensions: Students who are speakers of other languages can incorporate their language into the presentation in addition to English. Students with special needs will be class experts who can provide guidance to the rest of the class in terms of how to make their presentation more accessible to students with limited visual or aural abilities, such as selecting appropriate color choices (foreground and background), font selection and size, and descriptions of aural elements.

Students with a musical background can include pictures of their instruments or instruments from their homes. Some students may be able to include recordings they make themselves or perform in class.

Back-up Plan: Students can collect pictures of instruments from magazines and use books available in the classroom for their research and can create a paper-based version of their presentation.

EVALUATION

Lesson Reflections and Notes: Consider how you might share the student presentations, whether for portfolios, parent conferences, or open-house visits. Presentations could be shared on CDs, as digital movies, or posted to a secure website.

TECHNOLOGY INTEGRATION FOR MEANINGFUL CLASSROOM USE
Daily Lesson GAME Plan

Lesson Title: The Elements of Music

Related Lessons: The Elements of Art, The Elements of Writing

Grade Level: Middle Grades

Unit: Form and Functions Across the Arts

GOALS

Content Standards:

3. Improvising melodies, variations, and accompaniments
4. Composing and arranging music within specified guidelines
5. Reading and notating music
6. Listening to, analyzing, and describing music

ISTE NETS-S

☑ 1. Creativity and innovation

☑ 2. Communication and collaboration

☐ 3. Research and information fluency

☑ 4. Critical thinking, problem solving, and decision making

☑ 5. Digital citizenship

☑ 6. Technology operations and concepts

Instructional Objective(s): Students work in pairs to create short (4–12 measure) compositions comprised of sequences that demonstrate their understanding of the elements of music: pitch, rhythm, dynamics, timbre, and form. This is a summative activity that can be completed in parts throughout the year or at the end of the year.

ACTION

Before-Class Preparation: Determine 2 to 4 examples students will complete for each element of music. Some examples include:
- Pitch: consonance, dissonance, melody, harmony, cadence
- Rhythm: meters, strong versus weak beats, repetition, sequences
- Dynamics: crescendo/decrescendo, sforzando, subito
- Timbre: strike, bow, male versus female voices, percussive sounds, sounds from nature, man-made sounds
- Form: binary, ternary, 12-bar blues

Develop a checklist for the activity. Identify examples from past literature, the textbook, and recordings, or create your own examples. Determine whether the activity will be completed in parts throughout the year or as a summative activity at the end of the year.

Set up workstations to include sequencing/notation software, digital recordings/loops, headphones, and microphones. Internet resources, such as the Podsafe Network, can also be used for source recordings.

During Class

Time	Instructional Activities	Materials and Resources
Throughout the year	Students explore the elements of music in general music, music appreciation, or specialized music courses. The elements are related to songs they sing, recordings they hear, or repertoire they perform.	Recordings Literature, method, or textbooks
20–30 minutes	Review and use explicit examples to demonstrate the characteristics of an element (or the elements) of music. The discussion can require students to compare examples or ask students to recall or perform examples they have encountered earlier.	Recordings Literature, method, or textbooks
10–15 minutes	Review the checklist and requirements for the activity. For example, students may be required to select 2 examples of an element from a longer list. If so, try to ensure each example is selected at least once. Discussion of the appropriate use of copyrighted material should be included.	Checklist
30–60 minutes	Provide direct instruction on using the sequencing/notation software and peripherals. The amount of time spent on this segment depends on the students' familiarity and experience with the sequencing/notation software. If necessary, students will need to be shown how to: • find musical or sound sequences on the hard drive or file server • record musical or sound sequences • import sequences into the software • edit, copy, and paste sequences or parts of sequences • save their work to an appropriate storage medium	Computer workstation Sequencing/notation software Headphones Microphone Internet access (if available) Projector/screen (if using teacher workstation)
20–30 minutes per example	Students compose their examples for the elements of music. Emphasize that students are to focus on illustrating the element of music rather than composing long or complex examples. Students should record their justifications for why their composition is a good example.	Computer workstation Sequencing/notation software Headphones Microphone Internet access (if available) Word-processing software
45–60 minutes per element	Students present their examples to the class and justify why their compositions are representative of the characteristic. Students can also describe any problems they faced or creative decisions they made in creating their compositions. Students should compare compositions from other students in the class that illustrate the same characteristic.	Computer workstation Sequencing/notation software or media player Speaker Projector/screen (for whole-class display)

Notes: Students can complete this activity as individuals or in pairs. Larger groupings are not recommended.

MONITOR

Ongoing Assessment(s): Students should be closely monitored to ensure they are focusing on creating a representative example of the element rather than lengthy compositions. A timer can be employed to help students monitor time spent. Peer review can be used to ensure the examples are easily understood.

Accommodations and Extensions: Student choice can be supported by allowing students to select 2 examples per element from a longer list. If access to workstations is limited, determine a method for rotation that may include students working on different lesson activities offline.

   The use of recordings for this activity provides an opportunity to discuss digital citizenship and the fair use of music that may be copyrighted or within the public domain.

   Students can export their compositions as sound files and embed them in word-processing or presentation software, in which they can record their justifications for why their compositions are representative. These documents can be saved in student digital portfolios.

Back-up Plan: Students can identify examples from the textbook, method book, or repertoire and can perform them in whole or small groups. Students can also improvise examples based on those found in their literature.

EVALUATION

Lesson Reflections and Notes: The activity will be evaluated by a checklist.

TECHNOLOGY INTEGRATION FOR MEANINGFUL CLASSROOM USE
Daily Lesson GAME Plan

Lesson Title: Practice Guides

Related Lessons: Listening Guides

Grade Level: High School

Unit:

GOALS

Content Standards:

2. Performing on instruments, alone and with others, a varied repertoire of music
5. Reading and notating music
6. Listening to, analyzing, and describing music
7. Evaluating music and music performances
8. Understanding relationships between music, the other arts, and disciplines outside the arts
9. Understanding music in relation to history and culture

ISTE NETS-S

☑ 1. Creativity and innovation

☑ 4. Critical thinking, problem solving, and decision making

☑ 2. Communication and collaboration

☑ 5. Digital citizenship

☑ 3. Research and information fluency

☑ 6. Technology operations and concepts

Instructional Objective(s): Students conduct web research to develop practice guides for solo and ensemble literature to share with their peers. Each practice guide should contain information about the composer, the time period and style in which the composition was written and how those influenced the composition, and at least three challenging passages with suggestions or exercises for improving their performances. These passages may involve expression, articulation, fingering/bowing, ornamentation, phrasing, or other elements of music (e.g., pitch, rhythm, dynamics, form, and timbre) unique to the composition. This activity can be completed over a 6-to-9-week period concurrently with other instruction.

ACTION

Before-Class Preparation: Develop a checklist of required criteria for each practice guide and determine a timeline for completion. The timeline can be determined with the students. Find or create examples of completed practice guides. If necessary, create a template for the web page or wiki entry. Designate equipment (i.e., digital recorders, digital instruments, computer workstations, etc.) for recording or notating examples used in the practice guides.

During Class

Time	Instructional Activities	Materials and Resources
30–45 minutes	Share and discuss checklist of required criteria and the examples of completed practice guides. Provide or determine the timeline collaboratively so students understand their weekly requirements. Timeline should include time for the presentation of drafts and revisions.	Checklist Timeline Practice guide examples Web software
Weekly	Review drafts of the practice guides. Class time should be allotted to allow students to conduct research as well as to scan, record, or create examples in notation software.	Word-processing software Internet research Scanner Digital recording equipment Notation software

During Class		
Time	**Instructional Activities**	**Materials and Resources**
Final week	Students enter revised information into web pages or wiki. Allow time for students to review each other's work, especially those who perform in the same medium. Students can present their practice guides to the class, actually performing passages they have included in their practice guides.	HTML or wiki software Storage space on class or school server

Notes: Some of the content of this project can be completed outside of class time as homework (in support of home practice), but weekly class time should be provided for research and technology use as well as to monitor student progress. Students who study with and incorporate suggestions from private teachers should attribute that information.

MONITOR

Ongoing Assessment(s): Weekly progress checks should be conducted in relation to the predetermined timeline.

Accommodations and Extensions: Some students may need help determining appropriate passages to include in their practice guides. Suggestions for mastering these passages can come from method books, etudes, or other material used in class. Students with limited web skills can create their practice guides using word-processing software. Students requiring help with recording, creating graphics, or using notation software can work in pairs.

The lesson should include discussions about the appropriate and fair use of copyrighted material in support of digital citizenship.

Elements of the practice guide may be related to content objectives in social studies, history, language arts, and foreign language classes. Some compositions and passages may also have connections to science or math content standards.

This lesson model can also be used in general music or music appreciation classes to create listening guides for music from any genre. Listening guides could include information about the performers as well as any pertinent social or historical information. Instead of providing practice suggestions for challenging passages, students can support the development of critical listening skills by describing important or unique treatment of different elements of music (e.g., pitch, rhythm, dynamic, form, and timbre).

Back-up Plan: Students can conduct historical research using reference books from the library and can keep written notes in their practice folders. Manuscript paper may be necessary. This project can also be completed with word-processing or presentation software.

EVALUATION

Lesson Reflections and Notes: Completed projects will be graded using a checklist or rubric.

The practice guides are best presented on a website in which they are cataloged and searchable, either using a database-driven site or wiki. Over time, different students may add to or revise the practice guides. Revisions should reflect appropriate attribution to previous authors.

Appendix
Lesson Planning for the Content Areas

You probably wouldn't have gotten where you are today if you did not plan your actions. You most likely planned your semester schedule, when you would do homework, when you would perform your other work, and when you would eat, sleep, and socialize. In planning your life, you might have a monthly calendar that you use to keep track of the "big picture." But you probably also have a daily schedule where you plot out exactly what you will do when. You also may have "to do" lists that remind you of what you need to accomplish on any given day. As a teacher, you will engage in similar levels of planning. Curriculum plans, sometimes called curriculum maps, provide an overview of the year. Unit plans span several days or weeks. Daily lesson plans provide a "road map" for your day-to-day activities in the classroom (see Chapter 5). They provide a checklist of items that you must remember to collect for the class, a reminder of what you want to say

to the students, and a record of what works (and what doesn't) from year to year. You need to see both the "big picture" of what you are trying to accomplish and the details that must be attended to on a day-to-day basis. All of these levels of planning—curriculum plans, unit plans, and daily plans—fall under the broad umbrella of "lesson planning."

In the next few sections, we will provide an overview of curriculum plans, unit plans, and daily plans, then discuss how technology can make the lesson-planning process more efficient and effective (see Figure A.1).

Curriculum Overview

At the most global level, you will probably look at the entire school year to plot out what topics will be addressed at what

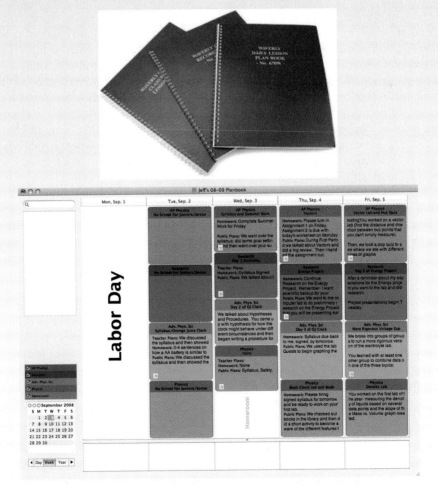

Figure A.1
Sample planning tools.
Source: Courtesy of Waverly Publishing Co.

STORIES FROM PRACTICE

Curriculum and Technology Alignment

It came as no surprise that Dogwood Elementary, outside of Memphis, Tennessee, was recommended to me as a school worth visiting to observe exemplary technology integration. Students and teachers from all grades were very comfortable with accessing and using available technology. I watched a second grade class follow what were obviously well-established procedures for getting laptops from a mobile cart and using them to access approved websites to gather data to create concept maps for a science concept. Fifth grade students were equally well equipped to use spreadsheets to graph data they had collected previously and to use these graphs to support their positions in a class discussion.

The a-ha moment for me came later while spending time with school principal, Susan Pittman. I told her how much I enjoyed my visit and how impressed I was by how well integrated technology was throughout the school. Susan told me that she and her teachers worked hard to achieve that success by spending time each year revising their curriculum maps for all grades. However, their process was different from most other schools I had visited. While many schools complete a curriculum alignment process, the faculty at Dogwood Elementary had purposefully considered the technology skills and tools they wanted their students to master and included those in their curriculum maps. This process

helped teachers better understand what technologies they could use in their instruction from the first day of school each year for those students who had been enrolled in Dogwood. Each summer, the teachers spent time reviewing student data and revising their curriculum maps, as necessary. The biggest revisions occur with the technology, Susan admitted, as the tools and skills students need to master drop to lower grades each year. She wasn't surprised her second grade students were so comfortable going online to conduct research and to create their own concept maps.

Source: John Ross

points throughout the year. Teachers in your school who teach similar subjects or grade levels may engage in this planning together, or you may need to do it on your own. As we've noted throughout this book, often the topics that you teach are mandated by state or district curricula or standards that must be met at a particular grade level. The textbooks and other resources adopted by your school district also may be used for guidance. This annual plan may be driven by a district- or state-developed curriculum plan, scope-and-sequence chart, or pacing guide.

A curriculum plan, or map, can be a valuable source of data for determining the effectiveness of your instruction. It can tell you which content standards you addressed, when, and how often. When combined with student performance data, you can make decisions about how well your plan worked for the students you had. Sometimes you will note consistent problems in student performance that suggest which lessons need to be modified or replaced. If you can create or share school- or district-wide curriculum plans, you and your colleagues can share ideas that lead to master lessons or activities that have the greatest potential for meeting the curricular needs of your students.

Although curriculum maps and content standards may tell you *what* you need to teach, they don't tell you *how* to teach the content, or *how long* to spend on each topic. Pacing guides, scope-and-sequence documents, textbooks, and other teachers' experiences can help you estimate how much time it will take to adequately address the topics you need to teach. It is wise to keep a master calendar of your curriculum plan, but remember that it will need to be adjusted throughout the school year. Some topics may take longer to teach than you estimate, and some may take less time. Analyzing your students' performance data in light of your curriculum plan will help you make better allocations of time in subsequent years.

Unit Plans

The annual curriculum plan is typically divided into unit plans. As you may know, a unit plan covers several days, weeks, or however long it takes to teach a particular topic. Unit plans usually address multiple standards, such as a strand of related content standards, and some may be devoted to concepts referred to as "big ideas." Some examples of big ideas in different domains may be what it means to measure and how to use measurement tools (science), combining information from different resources to communicate to a specific audience (English language arts), or how patterns bring order to seemingly unconnected situations (mathematics).

An interdisciplinary unit addresses a set of standards from several content areas. For example, consider the standards covered in a project in which your students investigate the proposed building of a new school. This project may require them to research the social and legal implications of the site selection (social studies), research and determine the impact on indigenous plants and animals (science), measure landforms and design possible layouts (math), and write a persuasive document that is presented orally with video or other media (English language arts). Unit plans can vary in their format but usually include all the components in the GAME Plan (see Figure A.2).

Daily Lesson Plans

Unit plans are further divided into daily lesson plans. Often, teachers develop draft lesson plans when they develop their unit plans and modify them on a daily or weekly basis depending on how well students mastered previous lessons. Lesson plans include a step-by-step list of activities that

Unit Plans—Common Features

Logistics
- A title
- Grade/level
- Subject
- Duration/time required
- Overview or description or summary

Goals
- Strands, benchmarks, content and technology standards
- Prerequisite skills needed
- Objectives, outcomes, or framing questions

Activities
- Outline of lessons, schedule of events, and procedures
- Materials and resources needed
- Learning environment; physical space arrangements
- Student groupings or interactions

Monitoring
- Assessments
- Adaptations: differentiated instruction for
  - students with special needs
  - gifted students
  - English language learners
- Back-up plans if things do not go as planned

Evaluation
- Place to make notes about modifications needed in the future

Figure A.2
Common features of unit plans.

should take place within the lesson. As you think about your daily lesson plans, identify tasks that you need to do before class, during class, and after class (see Table A.1). We provide a quick overview of these tasks here, but they are addressed in more detail in Chapter 5.

Preparation activities may include arranging the learning environment, preparing handouts and electronic presentations, gathering materials, and assessment technologies. Perhaps you need to remember to check out a particular book from the library or schedule a digital camera. Perhaps your science experiment requires baking soda that you must remember to purchase from the store or digital microscopes you need to reserve. You may need to make sure that software is properly installed and working on the computers in the lab. Or perhaps you need to remember to make copies of your class handout or post it to a file server. List any steps you need to do to get your classroom ready. Include a list of all the materials that need to be created, gathered, or copied before class. Include a list of websites, software, or other media that should be previewed or any demonstrations that should be rehearsed. Make note of the wide variety of things that you need to remember to do *before* class begins.

Your daily lesson plans will also include a list of things that you should remember to do *during* class. Summarize the steps you will take in class and the estimated time for each event. You may want to include personal prompts for things that you must remember to say to the class. Make note of special student groupings and other classroom

management strategies that you want to remember. Include notes on your techniques for monitoring students' progress such as assessments and discussion questions.

After you have conducted the lesson, you'll want to make note of which activities were successful and which need improvement for the next time you teach the lesson. Make note of how long activities really took and what you may want to remember to do the next time. This can include notes on effective strategies as well as less effective ones. You may need to reinforce and extend a lesson that was especially successful. Perhaps you can move more quickly through the materials than you had anticipated. Or perhaps you need to try another way of teaching a concept after an unsuccessful lesson. Although you can, and should, prepare a draft of your daily lesson plans in advance, you will need to fine-tune them on a daily basis. Exactly what will be covered on a given day is usually dependent on what happened previously.

Technology Support for Lesson Planning

Planning lessons, especially for a new teacher, can take some time. However, the digital technologies available to support the lesson-planning process will make it easier for you to develop lessons than the teachers before you. In addition, by supporting collaboration with other teachers across your school or district and allowing you to link to

Table A.1	Common Daily Lesson Plan Activities
Before class	• Arrange the learning environment • Prepare presentations • Prepare paper and electronic handouts and supporting materials • Set up and test technologies
During class	• Gain your students' attention • Tap into your students' prior knowledge • Provide timing prompts to keep lesson on track • Group students • Enforce classroom management procedures • Guide students through activities • Monitor or assess student understanding
After class	• Note successes and items for change • Record timing • Analyze assessment data • Plan for re-teaching, follow-up, or enrichment • Put materials away or organize computer files • Record student progress • Report to other teachers, guidance counselors, or parents, if necessary

APPLY TO PRACTICE

Lesson Plans

1. Find out if you are required to use a particular lesson plan format.
2. Search the web and other sources of lesson plans to locate several plans that you might like to use in your classroom. You can also visit the textbook's companion website for a list of lesson plan websites.
3. Select at least one plan that you might like to use in your classroom. Would you classify it as a unit plan or individual lesson plan?
4. Modify the plan to meet your needs and preferred lesson plan format.

 WEB LINK

For a listing of lesson plan websites and resources, visit the textbook's companion website.

real-time student performance data, these tools support the efficient development of more effective lessons.

You'll find model lesson plans in many places: in books, in magazines, and online. Teachers in some districts and schools also work together to create and store model lesson plans based on relevant content standards. Many times, you can modify one of these lesson plans to meet your needs. Internet resources are also helpful in collecting content information when preparing to teach a new lesson, one on an unfamiliar topic, or in a rapidly changing topic area. You can research background information for your lesson at the click of a button. As you review instructional resources, whether they are

online, in a textbook, on a CD-ROM, or in another form, pay attention to the supporting information for teachers.

There is no standard lesson plan format, but many lesson plans have similar features. Undoubtedly, your school or district will have lesson plan templates you can use. In fact, you may be required to use a specific form. There are also a variety of tools that can support this valuable step in the cycle of instruction. Paper-based lesson-planning books have given way to stand-alone lesson-planning software, which has evolved into networked content management systems that allow teachers to collaborate and tie their lessons to student information systems (see Figure A.3). When used

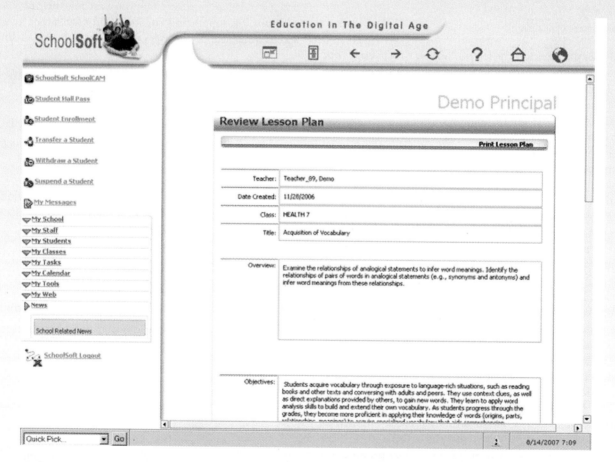

Figure A.3
Screenshot of networked lesson-planning software.

as part of a suite of tools, networked lesson-planning software can be used to post objectives and assignments to a website and may be linked to an electronic gradebook where the student outcomes for those assignments can be viewed in a secure environment by both students and parents. Lesson-planning software may include several templates or may be customized to meet the specific needs of your school or district. All teachers are familiar with a process of developing lesson plans to guide their work, although they may follow different methods to create them.

Since you will develop lesson and unit plans as a result of using this book, we have provided templates for you. These templates are flexible enough to use or adapt in your practice and will also help you demonstrate your understanding of the lesson-planning process to prospective employers. In keeping with the spirit of this textbook, the lesson and unit plans are organized around the GAME Plan process. You can use the unit and lesson plan templates (see the Tools for Use box in this section, at the end of Chapter 5, and on the companion website) or one of your own to complete activities in this book and for your portfolio. In Chapters 13 through 21, you will also find lesson plan examples using the GAME Plan template.

TOOLS FOR USE

Unit Plan Template

TECHNOLOGY INTEGRATION FOR MEANINGFUL CLASSROOM USE

Unit Plan

Unit Title: **Related Lessons:**

Grade: **Subject(s):**

GOALS

Content Standards:

ISTE NETS-S

☐ Creativity and innovation   ☐ Critical thinking, problem solving, and decision making

☐ Communication and collaboration   ☐ Digital citizenship

☐ Research and information fluency   ☐ Technology operations and concepts

Instructional objective(s):

ACTION

Date	Schedule of Lessons	Materials and Resources

MONITOR

Assessment(s):

Accommodations and Extensions:

EVALUATION

Unit Reflections and Notes:

Glossary

acceptable use policy (AUP)   a document that clearly outlines what is and is not acceptable behavior when using technology, in general, and the Internet, specifically, as well as the consequences of unacceptable behaviors

action research   the process of systematically collecting data to investigate some issue in your classroom to determine whether specific techniques work for students and curriculum. Also known as *teacher research* or *teacher inquiry*.

adware   software that incorporates the presentation of advertisements as a condition for operating the software

affective network   processes "the why" of learning that relates to feelings and emotions, and which influences motivation for and engagement with a particular goal, method, medium, or assessment

analytic rubric   a type of assessment rubric in which component categories are broken down

articulation   the ability to describe what you have done and explain what resulted and why, as part of meaningful learning; activity, reflection, and articulation are three components of active learning

assessment portfolios   a collection of artifacts used to assess student learning; an authentic representation of student learning

assistive technology (AT)   any item, piece of equipment, or product system used to increase, maintain, or improve functional capabilities of individuals with disabilities

Assistive Technology Act of 1998   federal act that extends funding for assistive technology to all states and six U.S. territories, supports state-level efforts to establish assistive technology services and resources and encourages services that inform the public about and advocate for assistive technology. Also known as *AT Act*.

authentic assessment   assessment in which students are required to demonstrate understanding of concepts and perform skills within real-world contexts

authentic instruction   the use of real-world issues and problems to facilitate and inspire student learning and creativity

authentic intellectual work   an approach to teaching in which students work within real-world contexts by engaging in tasks that have value beyond school. This approach facilitates the construction of knowledge through disciplined inquiry.

bioelectrical impedance device   tool used to electrically determine one's body composition (the amount of lean cells in body mass versus fat cells)

blog   a journaling and threaded discussion tool for use on the web. An abbreviation for *weblogs*.

carpal tunnel syndrome   a repetitive stress injury commonly associated with keyboard use, in which the median nerve of the hand becomes compressed at about the location of the wrist

Children's Internet Protection Act (CIPA)   federal act requiring schools and libraries receiving funds from the Universal Service Fund to incorporate technology-based solutions that block access to material defined as obscene, pornographic, or harmful to minors. Also known as the *Filtering Mandate*.

Children's Online Privacy Protection Act (COPPA)   federal law that applies to the online collection of personal information by persons or entities under U.S. jurisdiction from children under 13 years of age. It details the responsibilities an operator has to protect children's privacy and safety online including restrictions on the marketing to those under 13.

cognitive feedback   evaluation to help students develop a better understanding of the goals for performance, how their current understanding or skill levels compare to those goals, and how they might improve their performances

collaborative   working in groups in which responsibility is shared with others

collaborative database   a special type of database that supports a shared process of knowledge-building. One example is an online help system in which users can post questions and responses to others' queries.

collectivist   a perspective that promotes situating the individual within a larger community and measures the success of the individual as a factor of the whole

communal   a style of communication in which listening is participatory and listeners provide prompts, feedback, and commentary to the speaker

communication tools   tools that allow person-to-person interactions including e-mail, chat, and discussion boards

compliance   with regard to standards, refers to *who* must meet the standards and what *authority* mandates them

computer-based tutorial   complete lesson on a specific topic offered via computer. Includes 1) the presentation of content, usually with an example or examples, broken up into discrete modules or sections; 2) some method of review that reinforces or tests understanding of the content in the related module or section; and 3) new examples or content that builds on the instructions already provided. Tutorials can be linear or branching.

computer literate   refers to a person who has an understanding of computer history, computer architecture and terminology, basic software applications, and programming

computer vision syndrome   the inability to maintain focus on items displayed on a computer screen causing headaches, loss of focus, blurring, and/or sore neck and shoulders due to extensive, daily computer use

concept maps   graphical tools for organizing and representing knowledge

consequences   in the context of standards, refers to the results of meeting or not meeting standards, including remedial instruction and changes in pay schedules

cookies   temporary computer files that store information during Internet site visits enabling sites to remember who you are and your preferences

critical reflection   to understand different perspectives and use that understanding to set goals for your future behavior or learning

culturally responsive teacher   one who understands and capitalizes on the unique cultural attributes of students, including their experiences, as resources for promoting student achievement

curriculum   a specific learning program, including the educational standards and objectives, that collectively describes the teaching, learning, and assessment materials available for a given course of study.

curriculum alignment   instruction and assessments matched to standards to ensure student mastery of content knowledge and skills

cyberbullying   using information and communications technologies to harass, defame, or intentionally harm another student or group of students

cyberstalking   using electronic means to stalk someone

databases   a type of computer software that organizes information

data projector   presentation device that connects to a computer and projects a computer desktop image onto a blank wall, screen, or whiteboard

descriptive studies   research studies that describe the state of something, often based on surveys or qualitative research methods

didactic   type of conversation, or instruction, in which a single speaker dominates and others listen quietly

digital divide   the disparity between families and students who have access to digital tools and resources and those who do not

Digital Millennium Copyright Act (DMCA)   federal act passed in 1998 that places restrictions on copyrighted materials used for online instruction

directed instruction   a variety of instructional methods that introduce a topic, present the content to be learned, and offer practice to ensure mastery of content

documentation portfolio   a type of assessment portfolio demonstrating growth by incorporating work samples that show a range of student proficiency over time. Also known as *dossier* or *process portfolio*.

Electronic Communications Privacy Act (ECPA)   federal act addressing security and confidentiality issues of electronically disseminated communications

employment portfolios   a presentation of artifacts demonstrating competencies in relation to a desired position or profession

English as a second language (ESL)   programs and instruction designed specifically for people who learn English after learning their native language

ergonomics   the study and development of furniture, tools, and systems that promote productivity in a safe and healthy way

evaluation studies   research that uses quantitative or qualitative methods to determine the effects of an intervention; however, they do not attempt to test a specific hypothesis and do not need a control group

exemplar   a model of acceptable performance, usually given at the same time as the assignment, to help students understand what is expected in a final product

experimental research   a method of investigating an hypothesis about the effects of an intervention by comparing a control group, which receives no intervention, to an experimental group, which is as identical as possible to the control group except that the experimental group receives the intervention

fair use   the portion of U.S. copyright law that allows limited use of copyrighted material without requiring permission from the copyright holder

Family Educational Rights and Privacy Act (FERPA)   federal act stipulating confidentiality of student records and strict guidelines on who can have access to those records

file transfer protocol (FTP)   a way to transfer files from one computer to another using various methods, including transfer of files via a web browser

filtering software   software designed to prevent student contact with inappropriate material when using the Internet

firewall   hardware and/or software that prevents unwanted persons, messages, or software from entering a network or computer

formative assessments   strategies teachers incorporate during instruction to monitor student progress toward mastering learning goals

freeware   no-cost software downloaded from the Internet

geocaching   an activity in which participants use a GPS (global positioning satellite) receiver to hide or locate hidden items

heart-rate monitors   tool that measures heart rate; some can be worn on a wrist like a watch

holistic rubric   assessment in which descriptors touch on each area of instruction/learning without breaking the areas down into separate rating scales per category

hypermedia   hypertext with media elements, including images, sounds, videos, and animation

hypertext   a non-sequential, or non-linear, method for organizing and displaying text

hypertext markup language (HTML)   programming language that provides web browsers with instructions on how to arrange information on a web page

Individual Educational Plan (IEP)   an individualized plan for a student with disabilities that describes the measures teachers must take to accommodate the learning needs of the student

individualist   a perspective that promotes the autonomy of the individual and measures success by individual accomplishments

information and communications technologies (ICT)   an umbrella term that refers to all technology that supports the manipulation and communication of information

information gap   a common language-teaching technique in which each student in a group has a different portion of a set of information

information literacy ability to recognize when information is needed and to locate, evaluate, and use the needed information effectively

integrate combine two or more parts to make a whole

intelligent tutoring system (ITS) a type of educational software that tracks student responses; makes inferences about student strengths and weaknesses; and then tailors feedback, provides additional exercises, or offers hints to students to improve performance. Also known as *integrated learning software (ILS)* and *computer-adapted instruction (CAI)*.

KWHL chart tool that a teacher uses to identify what students know, what they want to know, how they will learn the topic, and what they learned in the lesson

lexile a scale that reports both the difficulty of reading material and student reading ability

link a representation of connection between nodes in a concept map

malware spam containing malicious software

metacognitive learner one who thinks about his/her own thinking and applies strategies to regulate and oversee the learning process

microworld a type of simulation software that allows learners to manipulate, explore, and experiment with specific phenomena in an exploratory learning environment

mindtools computer applications that enable learners to represent, manipulate, or reflect on what they know, rather than to reproduce what someone else knows

multimedia tools instructional tools that contain information in multiple formats, including text, sounds, images, animation, or movies

native language as support to teach students in English with teacher aides translating unfamiliar vocabulary in the student's own language

native-language instruction to teach students academic subjects in their own language

node a representation of concepts in a concept map

objectives statements that describe what the learner will be able to do following the instruction

open-source software free software that allows users to access and modify the underlying code

outcome feedback awareness of whether a response is correct or not

pedometer small device that measures the number of steps an individual takes; can be worn on the wrist or a belt

phishing a type of spam used to steal personal information, identity, and bank account numbers, or even to attempt face-to-face contact. Also known as *carding* or *spoofing*.

podcasts digital audio files downloaded from the Internet and played back on an MP3 player or computer

portable web pages Internet content visited and stored on a local computer for future use

problem-based learning (PBL) student-centered instruction in which students work collaboratively to solve authentic interdisciplinary problems, typically using higher-order thinking skills. PBL is believed to lead to increased 1) content knowledge, 2) problem-solving skills, and 3) self-directed learning abilities.

productivity applications computer programs such as databases, spreadsheets, word-processing and presentation software that allow users to create products more efficiently than is possible without the software, thus, increasing productivity

professional development portfolio a personal tool for individual learning that provides a place for collecting and reflecting on artifacts documenting professional growth over time from a very personal point of view

project-based learning instruction that typically results in some type of product, such as a web page, multimedia presentation, or performance (e.g., an oral report or class presentation using products that students have created)

proxy servers software applications that perform several functions, including filtering and storing Internet content

public domain creative works or information not "owned" by an individual but considered part of the common culture

qualitative data information that converts to words, typically in the form of an interpretive narrative

quantitative data information that converts to numbers, such as test scores or self-report ratings on opinion scales

quasi-experimental studies experimental research in which random assignment to groups is not possible, so statistical techniques are used to determine the extent to which any observed differences between the experimental and control groups may be due to chance alone

real contexts learning environments that allow students to solve actual, complex problems

recognition networks the neural network in the brain that helps to identify patterns

reflection the learner's ability to think over the process of learning and to describe what he/she has done and what he/she needs to do to achieve meaningful learning

render in moviemaking, the process of constructing a single, complete movie file from a collection of clips, stills, transitions, and/or audio input

repetitive strain injuries damage to the soft tissues, tendons, nerves, and muscles of the hand caused by repeated motions, awkward positions, or force occurring during computer use

resolution clarity of an image or letter related to the number of dots per square inch on a computer monitor

resource guide list of material and digital resources applicable to a lesson

rubric checklist or chart that helps students understand what is expected in a final product. Usually is presented in the form of a matrix, with the required components of the performance being listed on one axis and the differentiated levels of performance on the other.

scaffolds external supports for learning or solving problems. Enables learners to perform at a higher level than would be possible without the support.

self-directed learning (SDL) any increase in knowledge, skills, accomplishment, or personal development that an individual selects and brings about by his/her own efforts using any method in any circumstance at any time; ability to set personal learning goals, take action to meet those goals, monitor progress toward reaching those goals, and evaluate the effectiveness of the learning processes and learning outcomes

shareware   software downloaded from the Internet available for free preview for a limited time, after which purchase is required

sheltered instruction   process of teaching academic content in English to English-language learners at a level that they can comprehend while also promoting English-language development. Also known as *content-based instruction* or *Specially Designed Academic Instruction in English (SDAIE)*.

showcase portfolio   a type of assessment portfolio containing samples of exemplary work; often evaluated for entry into a program

simulations   a presentation of simplified versions of phenomena, environments, or processes that allow students to interact with, or manipulate, variables and observe the effects of those manipulations

software evaluation rubrics   forms that provide criteria on which to evaluate educational software, websites, and other digital resources

spam   unwanted messages sent across e-mail technologies

spamdexing   practice of developing websites that purposely deceive the user; also known as *search engine spamming*

sphygmomanometer   device used to measure blood pressure

spyware   software that records usage patterns or collects information from a user unknowingly via computer

standards   content knowledge and skills students should learn or be able to perform after instruction

steganography   process of developing malware that is hidden in text files or pictures

strategic network   the neural network that controls processes for planning, executing, and monitoring your actions

summative assessments   assessments used to evaluate learning after presenting a lesson, unit, or course; examples include end-of-unit tests, state-administered end-of-course, graduation, or college-entrance exams such as the ACT

taxis   a response that a plant makes to different chemical or light stimuli

technical guidelines   step-by-step instructions for using technology

technologically literate   having a general, working understanding of current technologies

Technology, Education, and Copyright Harmonization Act of 2002   a revision of the copyright law which clarifies use of copyright-protected materials for distance education and outlines required actions on the part of schools in order to be compliant. It is commonly called the *TEACH Act*.

technology integration   making technologies an integral part of the teaching and learning process that impacts resources, teacher and student roles, and instructional activities

telementoring   a process for establishing a guided mentoring relationship that incorporates information and communications technologies. Also known as *eMentoring*.

tendonitis   the inflammation, irritation, or swelling of the tendons (which connect muscles to bones) that can be caused by poor ergonomics

think aloud   process in which students verbalize their thoughts as they complete a particular task

topic-centered   a learning environment or a method of teaching students to be direct, precise, and to follow conventions of didactic communication

topic-chaining   learning environment or method of instruction which focuses on strong social context in which time is taken to set the stage for an academic task that is followed through with cyclical and multi-part conversations

transfer   ability to use knowledge or skills in new situations

triangulate   process of using multiple, independent data sources to increase the credibility and validity of research findings

Trojan horse   software program intended to delete all of the data stored on the computer or to cause the computer to turn itself off immediately after booting up

typosquatting   practice of developing websites with URLs slightly different from legitimate website addresses in an attempt to deceive users

universal design for learning (UDL)   approach to instruction in which teachers remove barriers to learning by providing flexibility in materials, methods, and assessments

virtual field trips   use of audio-, video-, or webconferencing tools to tour or interact simultaneously with businesses, museums, galleries using images, animation, videos, and websites

virus   computer software program that attaches itself to another program, replicates itself, and causes damage to software or data on the computer

vision concerns   issues related to how well people can see what is on the computer screen

visualization tool   system that allows learners to picture, or represent, how various phenomena operate within different domains

weblog   a form of journaling and threaded discussion tool for use on the web. Also known as *blog*.

WebQuest   an organized format for presenting lessons that utilize web resources

web server   a computer connected to the Internet running special software that allows it to respond to requests by web browsers

wiki   page or collection of web pages designed to enable anyone who accesses it to contribute or modify content, using a simplified language. Wikis are often used to create collaborative websites and to power community websites.

word-prediction software   tools that suggest words based on common usage patterns, arrangement of letters, or rules of grammar

word-processing software   type of software that allows users to create, edit, and revise written documents

worm   software computer virus that can replicate itself and easily spreads across a network

Index

Italic page numbers indicate material in figures or tables.